Misadventures
of an
American
Abroad

Misadventures of an American Abroad

Big Brother Exposed

Albert E. Tyrrell

Tyrrell

Publisher
Albert E. Terril
12228 Alexander Road
Everett, Washington 98204

Library of Congress Cataloguing-in-Publication Data

Terril, Albert E.
Misadventures of an American Abroad.

ISBN: 0-9626055-0-6

Manufactured in the United States of America
2 3 4 5 6 7 8 9 10
First Edition, September 1990

Book designed by Albert E. Terril

*Dedicated to the thousands of innocent
victims of Big Brother, self-serving news media
and other vicious gossips*

Acknowledgments

A famous Russian author once claimed that writing a book is comparable to crawling on one's hands and knees from Minsk to Valdivostok, so the help of passersby is appreciated more than any nonauthor can comprehend. Consequently, the helping hands of associates, such as those of Skip Corbitt, have been appreciated more than words can describe.

Furthermore, I am greatly indebted to those agencies that so courteously provided the data from which the book's maps were prepared. They include the Hawaii Visitors Bureau, the New Zealand Tourist and Publicity Department, the Australian Tourist Commission, the Information and Cultural Office of Sri Lanka, and the Swiss National Tourist Office.

If I have failed to list some dedicated helpmates, I am very sorry, but space and a deadline have not permitted me to remember all of the contributors and their contributions.

Contents

BOOK 2   Lands above the Equator

BOOK 3   Expo 86

BOOK 4   The Return of Charlie

List of Maps

List of Illustrations

NOTE: Maps and illustrations were prepared by the author.

Prologue:

---◀◉▶---

The Unknown

Unfortunately, I had been introduced to the "Unknown" some fifty years before that day early in 1985 when I applied for an American passport at a post office in Fullerton, California. In fact, the Unknown was one of the basic reasons for the application, since I had finally decided to determine whether it existed beyond the borders and the shorelines of this so-called land of freedom. I was also influenced by another basic reason: a strong impulse to abide by the requirement of practically every country that, before a visiting alien enters it, the alien shall present a legitimate passport to and obtain a stamp of approval from one of its immigration officials. To me that was the most important reason, because my apprehension and deportation for failing to do so would have fractured my sensitive pride.

According to the instructions, a native-born American citizen is required to complete the application and submit it to the Passport Agency along with a previous passport or a certified copy of the applicant's birth certificate. A naturalized American citizen is required to do likewise, but a certified copy of his or her citizenship papers is to be submitted in lieu of the birth certificate. Furthermore, the applicant is required to submit two identical, commercial, 2- x 2-inch photographs, current within six months of the application's date, along with a $42 check or money order payable to the Passport Agency.

After completing the application, I packaged the required copy, the photographs, and the check. Then I returned to the same post office and presented them to the designated postal employee, who identified me from my driver's license and accepted the application package. The passport arrived by mail within the prescribed three weeks, which was surprising in light of the usual responses of American bureaucracies.

New Zealand Consulate General

According to New Zealand's rules, my passport authorized a thirty-day stay. Since I wished to stay longer, a visa was required. Even though the application for a visa could have been made more readily by mail, I chose to apply in person. From previous experiences, I had discovered several inherent advantages in handling some things personally, and this seemed to be one of them. So that was why I drove some forty miles, from my home in Fullerton across Los Angeles, to the offices of the New Zealand Consulate General, which were located in a large building on Wilshire Boulevard.

An elevator silently lifted me to the fifteenth floor, where my objective was located. There the large, glazed door of its entrance provided a clear view of a pair of counter-high, wood-paneled walls, which enclosed the opposite corner of a large room. Through the panels of clear glass atop the walls I saw the head and shoulders of an attractive young woman. As I swung open the door, she glanced toward me through an opening in the glass paneling; then she arose from behind a flat-top desk and approached the opening, so I also approached it.

As I came to a stop in front of it, she asked, "Can I help you?"

"If you can supply me with an application for a visa, you can help me," I replied whimsically.

"Should it cover a business or tourist visit?" she inquired rather formally.

"It should cover a tourist visit," I answered.

"Of course, you realize that you also have to submit a current passport that's valid for six months beyond the intended date of your departure from New Zealand," she added.

"My passport is good for ten years," I said.

"That should be long enough," she conceded with just a trace of a smile while turning to several small stacks of forms located nearby on the same counter that traversed the opening.

Meanwhile, I pondered the possibility that her initial gaze might have been excessively intense and quickly concluded that her behavior warranted further study.

Rotating gracefully from the stacks to the opening, she placed some forms on the counter between us and said, "The application for a visa is to be completed and submitted to this office along with your passport." After another intent inspection of my features, she resumed: "Furthermore, you must hold an open or a confirmed ticket for your departure from New Zealand. In some cases, the applicant may be requested to provide evidence that he has sufficient funds to support himself while in New Zealand."

"That can be arranged," I said. "However, I would like to study this form for a few minutes. If any more questions come to mind, I may want to bug you again."

"That's a wise decision," she said. Then, with a gesture toward the several easy chairs artfully placed about the unoccupied waiting area to my right, she added, "Please make yourself comfortable."

After murmuring, "Thank you," I turned away, strolled into the waiting area, and deliberately selected a chair that provided an unobstructed view of the enclosure.

Meanwhile, the receptionist remained at the opening with her head bowed as if in deep thought. Finally, in response to some inner bidding, she moved to the doorway in the rear wall of the enclosure and disappeared from view. Several minutes later she returned and, with a quick glance at me, seated herself behind the desk.

Shortly thereafter, a mature and rather personable man entered the enclosure through the same doorway, came to a stop beside her desk, turned on one heel, and looked at me. Having deliberately assumed an attitude of deep concentration, I continued my surveillance of the enclosure from the outer limits of my peripheral vision. Since the man had shed his jacket, turned back the cuffs of his white shirt, and planted his hands on his hips, he presented a rather casual appearance for a consul general. He may, however, have been either an assistant to the consul or just a comfortable consul. With a preoccupied air, he turned back to the receptionist and engaged her in a brief discussion, after which he again turned and looked at me. Turning back to the woman, he raised the palms of his hands shoulder high in the universal gesture of c'est la vie and said something that elicited a laugh from her. Then, turning about, he stalked back into his lair.

Since one of the primary purposes of my visit had been served, I collected the forms and moved toward the opening in the glass enclosure, where the alert young woman elected to meet me.

"You have some questions," she guessed.

"Yes," I admitted. "Since I plan to make the trips to and from New Zealand aboard cargo vessels, it's almost impossible for me to hold tickets for departure on such vessels because of their unpredictable schedules. Is there some way that the requirement can be circumvented, say by a bond or by some similar device?"

Shaking her head, she said, "No. New Zealand is very firm on its requirement of a departure ticket."

"I recognize the reason for the requirement," I said, "but are there no alternatives whatsoever?"

Tendering a sympathetic smile, she shook her head.

After pensively studying her for a moment, I murmured, "Thank you," and turned away.

While the door was swinging closed behind me, I quickly looked back through the glass at her and encountered another intent gaze, a gaze that rapidly disintegrated as she hurriedly swung about and returned to the desk.

To me it seemed that I had just been introduced to the Unknown in that consul general's neat offices. However, since I had first been introduced to it many years before, it had to be a reintroduction.

Australian Consulate General

The offices of the Australian Consulate General were also located in a building that stood alongside Wilshire Boulevard but nearer to the central part of the city, so I decided to visit them during the return trip. There a somewhat noisier elevator lifted me to the seventeenth floor of the big office building. Unlike the offices of the New Zealand Consulate General, the entrance consisted of a plain, paneled door, but the larger, less pretentious waiting area was crowded with other applicants. Directly to the right of the doorway was a temporary wall, along which I strolled to the corner of a small hallway, where I paused to study the relatively wide opening. In the structural wall at its far end, a closed doorway was located adjacent to the point where the temporary wall on my right adjoined it. In the temporary wall was an opening in a counter-high glass panel, beyond which the head and shoulders of a relatively young man were visible. Since several people were standing in the line leading to the opening, I decided to seat myself at a vantage point and continue to study the layout of the office.

From the dialects of the applicants surrounding me, I concluded that several of them must be expatriates who were planning to return to the land down under. When the line at the opening had been reduced to one man, I arose and took up a position directly behind him. After he stepped away from the opening, I stepped in front of the sandy-complexioned, red-haired man beyond it. He fixed intent, blue eyes on my features for a moment before cheerfully inquiring, "And how can I help you, sir?"

"I would like to obtain an application for an Australian visa," I replied.

Abruptly, he became extremely preoccupied. Meanwhile, the bony fingers of one of his freckled hands crept to a nearby stack of forms and fiddled with the edges of their sheets while he seemed to ponder what appeared to be an unforeseen problem. After muttering, "Please excuse me for a minute," he disappeared for **several** minutes. Shortly after he returned, a relatively young, dark-haired man brushed past me, opened the nearby door, disappeared through the opening, and reappeared in an adjacent doorway, where he stationed himself and fixed his eyes on my interviewer.

"What do you have on your mind, mate?" he inquired.

"Oh, nothing much," the other man replied. "I just thought we might talk over some things, but we can do it later."

Then they launched an inane discussion while the interloper leaned against the jamb of the interconnecting doorway and the interviewer lounged indolently against the counter that stood between him and me. The conversation seemed to be so contrived, so much like an effort to pass a prescribed interval of time, that I abruptly decided to visually check the entire area for physical evidence of the Unknown. But all that I uncovered were a couple of covert glances from the two men while I was carefully scanning the walls, the ceilings, and even the most remote corners of the partially glazed enclosure without detecting one unjustifiable break in their surfaces. Of course, that search for evidence of a hidden camera was totally illogical, but the many repetitious incidents that had evolved during my past exposures to the Unknown also were illogical, if not abnormal.

As if on schedule, the discussion abruptly broke up, and, after passing through the doorway, the interloper again lightly brushed past me.

Meanwhile, the interviewer laid two forms on the counter between us and pushed them toward me. "This is an application for an Australian visa," he informed me, pointing to the top one, "and the other one contains the instructions for completing the application."

After thanking him, I silently turned away with the forms and continued to ponder a suspicion that I had just been reintroduced to the Unknown for a second time during two potential reintroductions.

By Land, by Sea, or by Air?

Since both New Zealand and Australia are surrounded by water, my method of travel to their shores was limited to vehicles that plied the seas or the airways. A romantic strain in my makeup induced me to venture as far afield as Vancouver, British Columbia, in search of passage on a cargo vessel, and I found it to be available. I had been laboring under the impression that such passage would be less costly than air fare, but such was not the case. The owners of even the rustiest old tubs had discovered that some amateur seafarers would pay exorbitant rates for the questionable privilege of spending a few weeks aboard one of those slow-moving vessels. Apparently, the romantic appeal of the merchant marine had intrigued so many adventurous souls that the owners of such vessels had become equally intrigued with their potential for skimming large quantities of American dollars from some of those weak-minded romantics. I admit to being a romantic, but my practical nature would never permit me to buy so costly a package, and I refused to consider the luxurious passenger liners, for, like the cargo vessels, they were time consuming. Since the remainder of my tenancy on the surface of this earth was becoming more limited with every passing day, I decided to resort to air travel.

As luck would have it, Air Hawaii happened to be promoting its upcoming service between the islands and the mainland. After obtaining a ticket for its inaugural flight from Los Angeles to Honolulu at a cost of $129, I calculated the per-mile cost of the first leg of my journey to New Zealand to be little more than bus fare. The flight was scheduled for the twenty-second day of September, so I waited through a few uneasy weeks for a flight that might never materialize, because maverick airlines were falling like flies in clouds of DDT, and Air Hawaii was a fully qualified maverick airline.

Los Angeles Airport

After making suitable arrangements for a couple of hours away from her place of employment, my fair lady took command of the old Chevy and delivered me from our home in Fullerton to the Disneyland Hotel. From there a shuttle bus conveyed me and my two heavy pieces of luggage to the Los Angeles airport. An isolated section of the airport had been set aside for processing the passengers of the flight, and I found the area to be buzzing with the conversations of excited and exuberant people. Everyone behaved as if he or she knew everyone else, but I deliberately sought out an isolated bench and seated myself at the most remote end of it. I didn't know anyone, and I didn't intend to allow any of those strangers to treat me as an acquaintance.

Meanwhile, the organizers of the extravaganza were erratically scurrying about the area with confused expressions, so I began to suspect that the flight would never take off on schedule, if at all. In fact, the evidence of total confusion induced me to wonder whimsically whether anyone had remembered to order an airplane for the trip. Since no airplane had arrived at the passenger loading dock by one hour after the scheduled boarding time, I began to ponder the possibility that my suspicions might have been more factual than whimsical. About that time an airliner did roll into place, so those particular qualms were allayed.

My constantly roving eyes eventually detected a tall, middle-aged man, who appeared to be systematically circulating among the passengers, so I concluded that he might bear watching. I was inconspicuous about it, so he didn't appear to notice my surveillance when he paused nearby and subjected me to a sharp scrutiny. When my eyes deliberately met his eyes, his eyes quickly veered away, and he hurriedly resumed his tour. Was his behavior more evidence of the presence of an Unknown? I suspected so, but such behavior had occurred so many times before that I had come to look upon it as more of a Known than an Unknown. Nevertheless, as familiar to me as it had become, it remained an Unknown to me, because I was aware of no logical reason for it.

Finally, the first boarding call was announced over the public address system. Simultaneously, the announcer requested that only those passengers holding tickets within a specific block of seat numbers form a line at the boarding gate. Since that block of numbers encompassed seats located in the rear of the craft, I watched alertly for an opportunity to insert myself at the end of the line at a propitious time. When the block incorporating my seat numbers was called, I had already ensured that there would be several other passengers behind me when I arrived at the gate. The passengers moved rapidly past the airline's check-in personnel until I arrived before them; then it stopped. Scarcely two minutes passed before I was motioned onward, but the next passenger also was withheld briefly for some Unknown reason, so I found myself plodding through the tunnel toward the aircraft by myself.

At the entrance of the huge craft, I found two slender stewardesses, who exchanged fleeting glances just before the nearest of them greeted me with the words: "Welcome aboard Air Hawaii." I nodded pensively and continued past them to my seat, which proved to be located near the middle of the wide-body jet.

Left and Right Fields

Meanwhile, José (*ho-say*), the left side of my brain, suggested, "That was a strange routine."

"But it also was a familiar one," insisted Pancho (*paun-cho*) from the right side of my ivory tower. "So it can't really be called strange."

"You guys shouldn't be interjecting your opinions into this prologue," I observed. "What would you suspect, if you were reading an introduction to a book, and two opposing points of view on the same subject were interjected by two idiots in the author's head?"

"In my opinion, that author would be qualified to run for a seat in the Congress," José retorted.

"Naw," insisted Pancho, "since the author is hearing voices, he should not only be barred from running for office but from writing a book."

"That's my point," José insisted. "Most of the candidates for those seats must be hearing voices, or they wouldn't be running for office. Therefore, since the author is hearing voices, he should be elected to one of those offices, because he would fit right into the current Congress."

"I'd rather suspect that the author was deliberately employing silent dialogue as a medium of independently discussing various developments within the framework of his story," Pancho suggested. "Besides, that medium should be much more entertaining and comprehensible to the reader than a long series of boring syllogisms."

"But some stupid psychiatrist is sure to question the author's sanity," objected José.

"Let him," responded Pancho succinctly. "Even a stupid psychiatrist can foresee the advantages of publicity gained by questioning the sanity of a famous author. Meanwhile, the same publicity should sell more of the author's books, so let him."

"But the manuscript has never been professionally edited," José observed, "so it isn't ready for publication."

"We edited it," Pancho countered.

"I know," José responded, "but the author's going to proofread it."

"Aw, he isn't qualified to do that," Pancho protested. "Wye, he doesn't even know how to punctuate properly."

"Even if he did," José resumed, "he would still plug in the punctuation wherever he chose, regardless of where it should be. You know how he is."

"Maybe he'll get the periods in the right places," Pancho suggested hopefully.

"Forget the punctuation!" José silently shouted. "The author has an incredible story to convey to every English-speaking society in the world, and he's gonna do it or be *bleeped*!"

"And he'll probably be *bleeped* too," Pancho somberly predicted. "He doesn't know how to put words together with verve either."

"But he won't lose the reader in his dialogues, like so many authors do," José rejoined loyally. "And he won't wear out the word *said* or use it in conjunction with a question; nor will he use profane or obscene language."

"What about his alias?" Pancho inquired.

"What alias?" José countered.

"He used the name *Albert E. Tyrrell* throughout most of the trip," Pancho responded.

"That was no alias," José retorted. "He was born under that name. Of course, he had to use his legal name when his credit card or passport was involved, so the idea complicated things a bit."

"Yeah, it was a dumb idea," Pancho rejoined. "But he's only half smart."

"Don't be casting any aspersions at me, you idiot," José retorted. "One of the purposes of these words was to explain the unexplainable to the dumb reader, so get on with it."

"Of course the author shouldn't fail to inform the reader that Charlie's opinions were expressed during several different visits prior to his last one," insisted Pancho.

"Naw, they don't appear until the last chapter, 'The Return of Charlie,' so let Charlie do it," retorted José. "Besides, you've already done it."

BOOK 1

HAWAII AND
LANDS DOWN UNDER

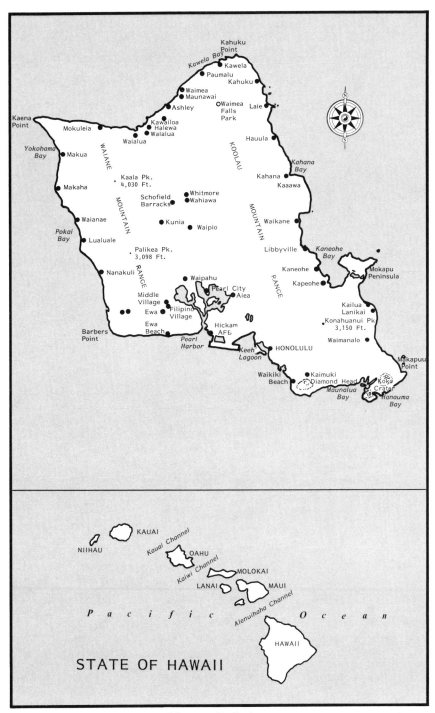

Map of Oahu

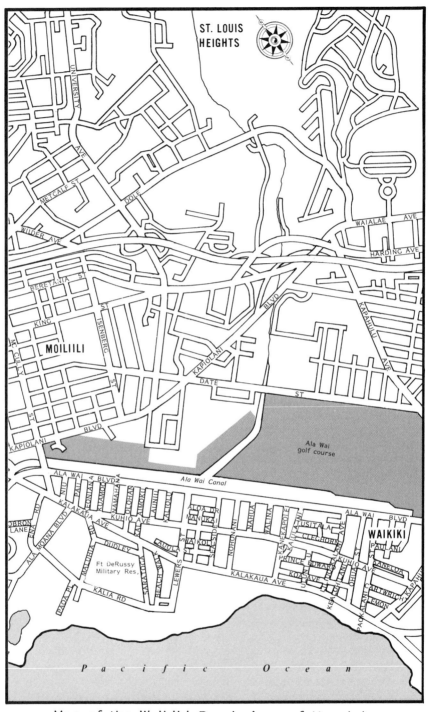

Map of the Waikiki Beach Area of Honolulu

1

Los Angeles to Auckland

Los Angeles to Honolulu

Air Hawaii's inaugural flight from Los Angles to Honolulu could be described as uneventful if one could ignore the drunken party sponsored by the airline's staff. In this case, I chose to ignore it, since a strictly sober condition is no way for any human being to observe his peers when they are behaving like gluttonous animals and childish idiots.

From the instant when the landing gears were fully retracted until the craft reached its cruising altitude of about thirty-five thousand feet, the pressurized air in the cabin became progressively colder. Possibly it was due to the increased demand on the bleed-air system during the climb, which may have consumed twenty minutes, or it may have been due to poor maintenance of the equipment. Nevertheless, a heavy woolen blanket would have been particularly welcome during that interval, but the blankets were not distributed until long after midnight, when several of the drunken passengers had lapsed into sodden stupors. I could have requested a blanket earlier, but the thought hadn't occurred to me. Therefore, it was largely my fault that I had acquired a severe case of the sniffles by the time that the plane was about to settle down onto the runway at Honolulu's airport. There, according to the captain, the ambient temperature was a humid eighty-four degrees Fahrenheit at a quarter past breakfast. After collecting my luggage, I went to the tourist information center, where a cooperative young woman provided me with a list of several economy-class hotels and their locations. Then I moved on to the car rental section and rented a Buick Regal.

Pearl Harbor From the airport, which is located within the general vicinity of Pearl City, I drove north along Pearl Harbor. The western coast of the island was my objective, but I was diverted by an arrow on a small sign, which bore the words "Arizona Memorial." I would have passed by the sign if a reluctant memory had not reminded me that the *Arizona* was one of the warships sunk by the Japanese during their infamous aerial attack on Pearl Harbor.

With the help of similar signs, the Buick and I found the Visitor Center of the memorial to be located alongside Pearl Harbor. There I watched a film of the attack and made a tour of the displays, mostly photographic, which depicted the extent of the damage. From the pier adjoining the Visitor Center I followed a group of other sightseers aboard a launch that was jointly operated by two young naval personnel, one of each sex. After the *sailorette* buttoned up the opening of the railing and cast off the hawser, the sailor slowly maneuvered the small vessel away from the pier and into the harbor, where he gradually advanced the throttle of the diesel engine until it throbbed softly.

The weather was ideal, so the aquamarine water was scarcely disturbed by the balmy ocean breezes. From the craft, the views of the various installations along the sweeping shorelines were magnificent. The clean, clear water contrasted sharply with my memory of the murky stuff that commonly laps the shores of Los Angeles Harbor and some of its adjoining beaches. Suddenly I understood why so many Angelanos return to "Paradise" to spend their brief vacations. Apparently, humans have not yet spoiled the Hawaiian Islands, but they are proceeding apace. Without a doubt, the Japanese attack on the Pearl of the Pacific spoiled some of its luster, but most of the spoilage rests at the bottom of Pearl Harbor.

And that was where we found the *Arizona*. It lay beneath a long, low, swaybacked enclosure, whose wooden wharf rested on the water directly over the steel superstructure of the slain giant. A flag bearing the stars and stripes fluttered proudly above it and its unsung heroes as well as the horror-struck men who had perished with it. After throttling back the engine, the sailor carefully maneuvered the craft alongside the wharf at the seaboard end of the enclosure. In turn, the *sailorette* deftly flipped a hawser around a hawse piece on the wharf. Then she unlocked and slid a section of the railing aside so that the passengers could disembark. And I slowly followed after the other visitors as they surged through the opening onto the wharf's wooden deck.

A casual survey of the interior of the memorial revealed long lists of the names of those who had died during the cruel strike, and there were some pertinent observations concerning the thousands of tons of steel that lie inertly beneath the structure. However, many of the smaller components of that steel behemoth projected above the gentle waves, but they had almost dissolved into rust. In fact, they appeared to have corroded even more rapidly than similar components lying directly beneath the surface of the translucent water. Possibly the lack of sufficient free oxygen had some bearing on the rates at which they had corroded.

Waikiki Beach By the time that the vessel returned to the pier at the Visitor Center, the late morning had become late afternoon, so I decided to find lodging for the coming night. In the process, I found that two of the most economical hotels had let the last of their available rooms, so I settled for one at the Waikiki Surf for $30. It wasn't air-conditioned, but it was well ventilated. Just for the *bleep* of it, I checked the rate at the South Pacific, which was not the most luxurious of Waikiki Beach's hotels, and received a quotation of $120 for a room that was air-conditioned. Obviously, the air-conditioning wasn't worth $90—at least not to a very conservative man—so I complimented myself on my choice and contentedly returned to the Surf.

After removing my travel-soiled clothing, I showered, donned fresh clothing, and ventured forth from the hotel's entrance onto Kuhio Avenue. While strolling deeper into the business district of Waikiki Beach, my anticipations of a modern tourist mecca were rapidly replaced by impressions of a more colonial city. Despite all of the publicity and advertising hype, it seemed to fall far short of other popular vacation spots, such as Miami Beach, Long Beach, and Palm Springs.

After shopping for a place to dine, I settled for a small restaurant in a mall, which appeared to be more of an arcade than a mall. Not only was the food mediocre, but that was where I detected the first firm tokens of the Unknown's presence in Hawaii. True, they were merely tokens, but both the manager and my waitress displayed certain behavioral characteristics that I had come to associate with the Unknown. Consequently, despite the mediocrity of the food, I resolved to return to the place for another meal and attempt to verify my suspicions.

Early in the following morning, I drove the Buick out of the hotel's subterranean parking facility, turned left onto the side street that immediately intersected with Kuhio Avenue, and came afoul of the law. But it wasn't until I had turned right onto the avenue that I detected the blinking lights of the three-wheel scooter directly behind the car. Of course, I had no other recourse (except mad flight) but to obey the signal to stop, so I passively turned the car toward the curb and parked it.

Meanwhile, via the rearview mirror, I ruefully watched while the scooter swung in behind the car and came to a stop. The brown-skinned officer dismounted from it, strolled around the car to the window beside me, and civilly inquired, "Sir, do you know that you drove the wrong way on a one-way street?"

"I do now," I admitted, "but I forgot that it was a one-way street. In fact, I should have remembered it, because I had to drive almost entirely around Waikiki Beach last night to drive correctly into the parking facilities beneath that hotel."

He nodded absently, removed a ballpoint pen from behind the band on his cap with one hand, flipped over a couple of pages of the pad in the other one, and requested, "I would like to see your driver's license please."

After I complied with his request, he noted pertinent data from the license. Then, looking thoughtfully at me, he stated, "You are a senior citizen, aren't you?"

"Yes, I **am** old enough to know better," I responded with an embarrassed chuckle.

"Well, since you didn't appear to deliberately break the law, I'm giving you only a warning," he said. "However, I have to write it up, so it'll go against your license."

"Thank you for being so considerate," I murmured.

While I stared ruefully straight ahead, he scribbled a few notations on the top sheet of the pad. Then he presented it to me with the request: "Please sign here."

After doing so, I looked up at him and said, "Those fifty feet or so of side street between the exit of the hotel and the avenue must be pretty lucrative pickings for you fellows, aren't they?"

With a guilty smile, he accepted the pad and pen, flipped the pad closed, and said, "I hope you enjoy your visit in Hawaii."

"It's off to a better start than it might have been," I conceded while returning his casual salute.

West Coast After driving around the north side of Pearl Harbor, I turned the car onto a meandering two-lane road that eventually traversed the distance between the harbor and the west coast. It may have been the same somewhat primitive road that followed the coast for several miles; however, I could not have traveled as far as Nanakuli along that coastal road because I didn't come upon any sizable settlements throughout the trip.

At one point during the return trip, I noticed a small park located between the road and the adjacent beach, so I turned the car toward its entrance and braked it to a stop in a small parking area. I hadn't noticed the park during the first pass, but I was pleased to have discovered it, since it was a very pretty area with several wooden picnic tables strategically located within the shade cast by several types of exotic trees. The intermittent sounds of waves breaking upon the adjacent beach provided pleasant background music that further induced me to linger awhile, and the fact that I would be the park's only tenant was an additional inducement.

Extracting a mechanical pencil and a pad of notepaper from my briefcase, I left the car and zeroed in on a picnic table. Seating myself on one of its two integral benches, I placed the pad on the rough tabletop and began to inscribe some notes on it regarding my recent activities. Periodically, I paused to savor the balmy breezes and to peer out to sea at the small, scintillating white caps. Born near the horizon, they traveled slowly shoreward until they faded in the shadows cast by high-flying clouds or disappeared below the edge of the large sandbank deposited by previous waves along the shoreline.

It was a quiet, peaceful scene, but the peace was suddenly shattered by the loud sound of a thump, and my startled eyes darted toward its source. A brown-skinned nut assembly had fallen from one of the overhanging branches onto the table, and since it had come to rest within easy reach, I picked it up and carefully inspected it.

It consisted of two ovoid members positioned side by side within a paper-thin shell, which adhered closely to the contours of its contents. After a prolonged study of it, I absently tossed it onto the nearby grass among others of its kind. Then I searched my memory for the identity of a tree that produces a nut assembly which, for some reason, appeared to be so familiar yet so foreign to me. Finally I abandoned the search and returned to my writing.

I was deeply engrossed in it when the sounds of an approaching automobile intruded into my thoughts. Since they were the first of such sounds during the entire session, I used them as an excuse to pause and watch for the vehicle to appear. From beyond a bend in the road, an orange-colored pickup truck eventually appeared and gradually came to a stop alongside the road with its white camper shell gently nudging the luxurious green leaves that hung gracefully from an outspread bough of a tall tree. It was similar to a weeping willow tree but even more exotic than one of those softly draped beauties.

Both doors of the vehicle slowly swung open, and, after stiffly dismounting from it, three brown-skinned young women began gingerly to exercise their travel-cramped muscles. Since they were clad in shorts and colorful Hawaiian blouses, I began to suspect that they were of native Hawaiian stock. After closer inspection of them and the brilliantly colored ties about two of the three sets of jet-black tresses, I became convinced of it. Consequently, I concluded that they must know the names of native trees, so I decided to make some inquiries.

Stiffly disentangling my legs from the wooden members connecting the bench to the table, I arose and approached the women. Meanwhile, they stopped their activities and speculatively fixed three pairs of dark eyes on me.

"Pardon me," I began, "but can you people tell me the names of these trees? That one, for instance?" I added, pointing to the tree limb with the long, shimmering leaves, against which the camper rested.

Intuitively, I had addressed the woman who appeared to be the inherent leader of the trio, and she responded, as if born to the role, by carefully studying the tree's long, gracefully shaped leaves. "No," she finally replied with a shake of her short bob, "I don't know what it's called." Then, directing her attention to her companions, she inquired, "Do either of you know?" And they responded with twin shakes of their black tresses.

"Do you happen to know whether or not those nuts are edible?" I inquired of the leader with a gesture toward the littered grass surrounding my table.

She turned puzzled, dark eyes toward my blue ones and asked, "Do you mean can you eat them?"

That wasn't quite what I had in mind; nevertheless, I nodded, and she shook her head.

"But do you know what they are called?" I inquired hopefully, because I wanted to identify those unique nuts in my notes.

She subjected my features to a long, speculative study while a somewhat cynical expression slowly crept across her rather coarse features. Finally, after peering meaningfully into the watchful, waiting eyes of her friends, she redirected her attention to me and answered, "No, I don't know the name of those nuts, but I know the name of the tree." Pausing as if to build up the drama of the upcoming revelation, she added, "It's called the monkey-pod tree."

The full impact of her statement failed to register on my mind until after I detected the glimmers of amusement in their eyes. Then I began to mentally review my previous inspection of the nut assembly and its apparent familiarity. After comparing their amusement with my review, it suddenly struck me. "Oh!" I exclaimed. Then I belatedly added, "Thank you."

While hastily retreating to the less complicated problems awaiting me at the table, my mind toyed with the possibility that the spokeswoman's expression might have been more *sinical* than cynical. Actually, I had never inspected a monkey in intimate detail; however, from what I remembered of the physical characteristics of those little precursors of the human race, I began to suspect that the name of the tree might have been appropriately selected.

Upon returning to the desk of the Waikiki Surf to register for the second time in as many days, I noticed an attractive young woman, actually a girl, who may not have been more than sixteen. She was perched on a divan, which stood against one wall of the lobby, and it seemed to be no accident that her short skirt had been arranged provocatively above her shapely knees. I surreptitiously studied her with a growing suspicion that the hotel might be operating a lucrative but illegal entertainment business in addition to its legal business. It was a reasonable suspicion, since it is a well-known fact that many such toys of mankind, or of unkind men, begin their so-called careers at such a tender age in the crumbling old hotels on back streets. But the Surf didn't appear to qualify as either a *sin-agog* or a synagogue.

Abruptly, I sensed that I also was being observed, so my eyes quickly swept the lobby and encountered those of a tall, white-haired man. Slowly his eyes veered toward the girl, so he must also have been studying her. Nevertheless, I preferred to believe that his interest was strictly professional, that he was the house detective and much too old and wise for so stupid a game. Furthermore, I preferred to believe that the girl was a silly, venturesome lass who might be deterred from such adventures by the wise advice of such a man.

As the elevator slowly hoisted me upward, I pondered the likelihood that once more the lack of an air conditioner would prove to be no problem. And such was the case, for the temperature of the moist ocean breezes dropped considerably during the night. A light mist was falling when I left the hotel early in the following morning, and it may have been the cause of the drop in temperature.

When I arrived at the same small restaurant, a teenage waitress led me to a table and placed a menu on it. After seating myself, I picked up the menu and carefully studied the other members of the staff across the top of it while she trotted away.

Since I recognized none of them, it was impossible for me to verify my previous suspicions, because none of the previous behavioral patterns were repeated. But I recognized the food: It was still mediocre.

East Coast and Inland   Despite the hovering mist and the roily clouds overhead, I decided to begin a much too casually planned tour of the east coast and the central part of the island. Just minutes after I started it, the wispy clouds parted, and the lush, green slopes of the Kooluapoko Mountains were bathed in golden sunlight, so I complimented myself on the wisdom of my decision. Within a few more minutes, the sun was blotted out, and the windshield wipers were again required. But my refusal to castigate myself for an apparent lack of wisdom was fully justified within the next minute, when the sunlight burst through the feathery mist and dazzled my eyes with the beauty of the mountainous landscape and the adjoining seascape. Meanwhile, the Buick continued to purr contentedly as it sped past the settlements of Kaneohe, Kaaawa, Kahana, and Hauula. Such names! I couldn't begin to pronounce them.

Near the northern end of the island, an attendant demanded $14 for a tour of the Polynesian Culture Center, so I decided that I wasn't that interested in Polynesian culture. From the center, I continued around the northern end of the island to Kawela, a settlement located on the bay of the same name, and continued onward past Waialee and Paumalu. At the turnoff to a secondary road in the general vicinity of a settlement identified as Maunawai, a small roadside sign touted the Waimea Falls, so I turned the car onto the narrow thoroughfare. After several miles of travel through relatively unimpressive scenery, the road ended in a large parking lot, where the Buick and I agreed to stop.

About a hundred yards beyond the parking lot, I came upon a sprawling, single-story building and found that a payment of $6.75 would allow me to pass through the gate in a six-foot chain-link fence and continue to the falls. After a brief conference with the two pursers in my ivory tower, we unanimously agreed that the falls couldn't possibly be worth so large a fee. Neverthelesss, I did cast a speculative glance toward the fence, but one intimate association with such a fence had taught me that the tips of the entwined wires atop such fences are very sharp. I'm quite sure that even a half-smart male monkey would never attempt to scale one of them.

There was a fast-food concession in the building, so I paid an exorbitant sum for a hot dog and a small, ice-clogged Coke. Then, seating myself on a wooden bench beside a rough, wooden table, I slowly consumed the light repast.

En route to the car, the nose of a jeep slowly pulled up beside me and stopped. From its cab a deep voice casually inquired, "Did you see the falls?"

Coming to an abrupt stop, I looked back across my right shoulder at the questioning eyes of a man, who was lazily lounging against the steering wheel of the vehicle.

"No!" I responded almost truculently. "They wanted six seventy-five for a ticket, so I turned around and left. After all, I saw Niagara Falls for nothing, so why should I pay to see a mere trickle of water?"

He leaned back against the thinly padded seat, turned his head, and looked thoughtfully at the well-padded woman beside him. Then he twisted his head and shoulders sharply so that he could view the freckled faces of the three eager, wide-eyed children on the seat behind them. Slowly he turned back to the woman, and their gazes gently melded. Finally he regretfully shook his head, turned a level gaze on me, and banally remarked, "Yeah, I have to agree with you."

Easing up on the brake pedal, he whipped the jeep around in an impossibly tight U-turn and launched it toward the highway. Meanwhile, the disappointed eyes in three small faces peered wistfully back through the rear window of the vehicle toward the general vicinity of the falls.

At the side of the Buick, I paused and pensively thrust the key into the door's lock. "*Bleep* such rip-offs!" I muttered. Savagely turning the key in the lock, I viciously swung the door open.

Meanwhile, I sensed activity in the ivory tower. "But there may have been no charge for the children," José suggested.

"There should be no charge for them," Pancho chimed in.

"Yeah," José agreed. "And that's Al's opinion too."

"For an ultraconservative man, sometimes he can be incredibly liberal where children are concerned," Pancho remarked.

"And at other times he would gladly throttle some of the little demons," José observed.

"But they are the type that never should have been conceived," Pancho rejoined. "Nobody can ever convince me that there's no justification for abortions."

"Unfortunately, it's practically impossible to predict which ones should be aborted," José observed. "However, we can program computers, so why can't we program people to produce desirable future generations? I'll bet that it can be done within reasonable limits by carefully selecting the parents."

"But modern couples will never buy that," Pancho rejoined. "They prefer to play Russian roulette with *luv*, despite the fact that they instantly change sex partners at the slightest whim."

Back at the point where the road intersected with the Kamehameha Highway, the Buick volunteered to turn left, so I allowed it to follow the meandering highway past the old sugar plantation town of Waialua to the point where it merged with the H-2 Freeway. The freeway veered to a southwesterly direction through the central part of the island, which was dominated by enormous fields of sugar canes and pineapples that extended past Wahiawa almost to Waipahu, a town near the north shore of Pearl Harbor.

Pearl City In Pearl City, I wasted some time trying to locate more economical accommodations for the night. Then, even though the hands of a clock pointed to 5:35, I deliberately drove the Buick into a large mall, parked it, wandered into a rather lavish restaurant, and requested that the young hostess seat me at a dinner table. Early as it was, there were six or seven other diners scattered about the large and adroitly divided establishment, but none of them was seated in my immediate vicinity.

A young waitress appeared beside my table and inquired, "Are you ready to order?"

"As ready as I'll ever be," I replied humorously. "Since I had only a small dog for lunch, I'm very hungry."

Cringing, she murmured, "You're kidding," as her eyes doubtfully searched mine.

"Well, it was very small dog," I conceded, "so it might have been just a puppy, but they had scraped all of the hair off of it, so that was difficult to determine."

Being very young, she reacted with a horrified, "Ugh!"

"However, it was enclosed within two halves of a bun," I resumed, "so the dog wasn't all that I had for lunch."

"Oh!" she exclaimed as the light of high noon leaped into her eyes. "Then you had a hot dog for lunch."

"Not really," I responded, "however, it was still warm, but it didn't bleed when I bit into it, so I suppose that some heat must have been applied to it."

"Oh, double ugh!" she exclaimed. Then, after studying my eyes with renewed revulsion, she added, "Give me your order so that I can get away from here." But her sparkling eyes indicated that she didn't really mean to be mean.

After taking my order, she smiled rapturously into my eyes, reached across one corner of the table, and gently patted my right hand. A sharp thrill coursed from the hand through my arm and exploded in my brain. But it wasn't a sexual response. It was produced by the charred top of my hand, which the intense Hawaiian sun had broiled to the color of a rare New York steak. Furthermore, I knew the real reason for that pat, and it certainly wasn't my sex appeal. Intuitively, she knew how to influence the magnitude of a man's tip, irrespective of his age. Unfortunately for the males of the species, women have been programmed that way from time immemorial, so they have cost most of the males their life savings, if not their lives.

As she was about to leave, I asked, "By the way, what kind of plants are those in the hundreds of water-filled little rectangular pools that cover the area just below those windows?" After gesturing toward the heavily glazed wall beyond the line of tables to my right, I added, "Are they some sort of fern?"

"Those are a type of watercress," she answered. "But don't they make a beautiful ground cover?"

"They certainly do," I agreed. "But surely they are used for more than just decoration."

"Some of them are used in salads," she said. Then, tentatively moving away, she added, "But let me place your order."

"Please do," I murmured.

My table stood against a low wall surmounted by sections of hardwood louvers, through which the hostess's tiny podium was dimly visible. Upon approaching the hostess, I had noticed a list of instructions attached to a thin piece of plywood that stood aslant against the base of the podium, so I didn't attach any significance to the actions of the first young waitress who paused beside it, ostensibly to read the instructions. When she continued to stand there and surreptitiously stare between the louvers at me, I began to suspect the presence of the great Unknown, so I deliberately stared back at her. After she fled, two more young waitresses arrived and cast indifferent glances at the list between long stares in my direction. Shortly after my counteroffensive had driven them away, a busboy appeared, but he didn't even attempt to read the list; he just stood there and boldly stared at me. Typically, the recurring acts had built up an intense fury in me, so my angry gaze locked on his for several seconds. When I started to arise and question him, my actions spooked him, and he bolted.

About that time my waitress arrived with the order and silently placed it in front of me. When her eyes furtively evaded my deliberately direct gaze, I concluded that there had been too many coincidences for all of them to be coincidental. To me it was quite obvious that the Unknown was present and still unaccounted for.

Honolulu Airport   After those misadventures, I drove directly to the airport. En route I congratulated myself on my failure to obtain more economical lodging, because I was no longer in a mood to spend another night in either Waikiki Beach or Hawaii. After returning the Buick to the rental agency, I used a courtesy telephone in the terminal to shop for immediate transportation to New Zealand and found that Continental Airlines appeared to be not only the most readily available but the most economical. After locating its ticket counter, I found a surprising lack of activity. In fact, there appeared to be no one on duty.

Eventually I located two native Hawaiian men, a sort of Mutt and Jeff pair, and accosted them with the words: "Can you sell me a ticket to Auckland?"

"We can sell you a ticket to any place in the world," Jeff retorted.

"But I don't want to go to just any place in the world," I protested. "I want to go to Auckland tonight."

"We can meet that requirement too," he cheerfully informed me.

"But we better check before we make any promises," Mutt cautioned him. Then both men converged on a computer that stood on the intervening counter.

"Do you have a passport?" Jeff inquired.

"Yes," I replied and placed the document on the counter between them.

"How are you going to pay for this ticket?" Mutt asked.

"With traveler's checks," I answered, adding a packet of the checks to the passport.

"Do we have to have identification?" Jeff inquired of his partner with a questioning glance.

"I have that too," I interjected, adding my driver's license to the stack.

"I don't think that will be necessary," Mutt murmured. "But let's go through the procedure," Jeff suggested. "We have nothing but time, and you need the practice."

"This could be very interesting," I muttered.

"Why?" Mutt asked warily.

"Let's see what happens," I said. "I've been wanting to get this opportunity for years."

Suddenly both men were alertly watching the screen while the taller one put it through its paces. After one particular series was completed, the shorter one glanced toward the other man and murmured, "Everything seems okay."

The other man nodded and stepped back from the computer.

"But there's one more step," Jeff reminded him.

After pondering briefly, Mutt stepped forward and resumed tapping the keys.

Abruptly, both men peered intently at the screen, and Jeff involuntarily grunted, "Oh-oh!" Then he glanced uneasily at me.

"So you did find something!" I exclaimed triumphantly. "Let me see it," I insisted, thrusting my head and right shoulder across the counter in an attempt to view the screen.

"It was nothing," the short man muttered, placing a restraining hand on my shoulder. "Everything's all right."

"But there must have been something," I protested. "Otherwise, why would you have exclaimed? Tell me what it was, because it's very important that I know so that I can take the necessary steps to counter it."

"Everything's okay," the man insisted.

Meanwhile, Mutt had cleared the screen, so I was unable to see for myself. However, I now sensed in the two agents the same reserve that had always confronted me when I had purchased airline tickets in the past.

Abruptly, a wave of frustration swept through me. "Why won't anybody ever help me?" I complained bitterly. "I can't do it all by myself."

"But everything is okay," Jeff insisted with a pat on my shoulder.

"But it isn't," I protested, "and it hasn't been for the last fifty years."

Honolulu to Auckland

Paradise Lost After suffering indignities at the gate similar to those that I had encountered at the gate in the Los Angeles airport, the aircraft compensated in part by supplying relatively warm cabin air during its midnight climb to the cruising altitude. Meanwhile, I forlornly reviewed the incredible incidents that had evolved from the familiar but still Unknown source, which had destroyed forever my hopes of retiring to a normal life on one of the Hawaiian islands, and I was forced to conclude that it was another case of Paradise Lost.

Shortly after the craft leveled off, woolen blankets were distributed to the passengers. Then the lights were dimmed, so I assumed that we were expected to sleep during the long flight over the deep, dark Pacific. Since I had been assigned an aisle seat with a vacant seat on my left, my sleep was not disturbed. And I did sleep, despite my mind's brief but insistent review of my misadventures in Pearl City.

Auckland Airport As the craft passed through a light overcast during its downward glide toward the Auckland airport, I may have critically strained the components of my seat belt while struggling to catch a few fleeting glimpses of the fabled land of the Kiwis through the nearest of several remote windows. Nevertheless, I did manage one sustained view of several lush, green pastures that extended from one side of the airport to the cloud-strewn horizon. Sleek horses cavorted in one of the adjacent pastures while a herd of Holstein cattle grazed placidly in another one, and thousands of sheep dotted the remaining pasturage as far as the horizon. There were several buildings, but most of them were concentrated near the terminal, and they constituted my last exultant view as the tires of the main landing gears jounced protestingly against the tarmac shortly after eight o'clock.

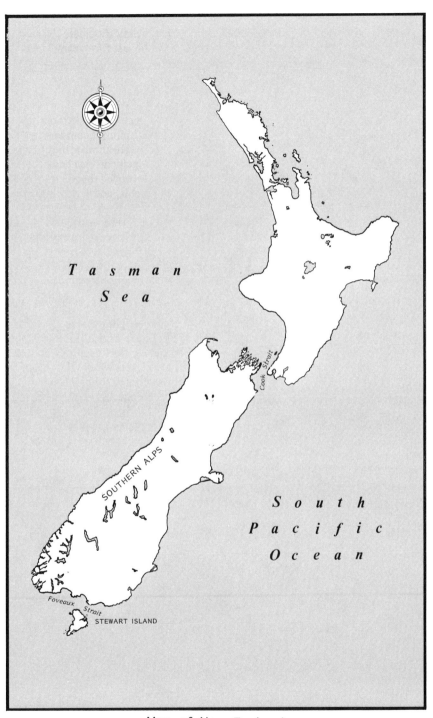

Map of New Zealand

Map of the North Island

2

Auckland

While I was passing through Immigration, a government agent briefly inspected my passport and stamped it: "Temporary Entry (Visitor Permit) from 26 Nov 1985 until 26 Feb 1986, Employment Prohibited." Since no one chose to inspect my luggage, I picked it up and headed in the direction of the main part of the terminal.

At the Tourist Information Centre, an obliging young woman telephoned to several different hotels and finally located economical accommodations for me at the Abby's Hotel. Then she directed me to an in-house branch of the Bank of New Zealand, where I submitted three $100 traveler's checks and received almost twice as many New Zealand dollars.

Auckland Airport to the City

From the bank, I carried my luggage to the front of the terminal and transferred it to the hands of a man who was loading luggage into a compartment at the rear of an airport shuttle bus. I then boarded the bus and seated myself directly behind the driver's unoccupied bucket seat so that he could warn me when my stop was imminent. Shortly before the driver arrived, a chubby matron struggled up the steps and plumped herself onto the aisle seat beside me.

After regaining her breath, she looked at me and announced, "I'm on a tour of New Zealand, but my husband chose to stay in California and play golf every day of the week."

Simultaneously, the bus driver clambered up the steps and slid into the bucket seat in front of us, so I tossed a fugitive smile to her, leaned forward toward him, and said, "I hope that you go as far as the Abby's Hotel."

"Not quoite," he replied, "but Oy kin drop y e off within a couple o' blocks o' it."

"I would greatly appreciate a word of warning from you when we are about to arrive there," I murmured as the man set the vehicle in motion.

"Oy'll wahn ye in toime," he promised, swinging it into the rapidly moving traffic of a main thoroughfare.

As I leaned back against my seat, my traveling companion turned to me and said, "You sound like an American."

"I am," I responded. "I'm from California too."

"What part?" she countered.

"From a small city near L.A.," I replied. "Fullerton, to be more specific."

"Yes, I've heard of Fullerton," she murmured.

Since my eyes were eagerly scanning the luxuriant scenery, I could not have been less interested in continuing the conversation. But she seemed to be a pleasant sort, a lady, even, so I endeavored to keep abreast of her ever-changing subject matter while the bus thundered onward. At one point, it was traveling so rapidly that the woman was thrown sharply against me as it rounded a particularly tight bend in the highway.

"Oh!" she exclaimed with an alarmed expression after regaining her equilibrium. "He almost turned the bus over."

"Not quite," I muttered, ruefully rubbing the spot where my shoulder had struck the window frame, "but he does drive somewhat like an American cowboy." Then, striving to be more diplomatic, I added, "Nevertheless, he probably knows what he's doing, because he must have made this trip hundreds of times."

The man appeared to have overheard our words, because he turned his grizzled head aside and smiled impishly at the woman. The smile was an instant success, even though all that was revealed of it was a ripple of skin at the corner of one gray eye and the fold of flesh that erupted from out of the flat plain of his angular jaw and settled around the corner of his wide mouth. He literally exuded personality, so it was no wonder that the woman's critical mien quickly evaporated.

He must have sensed her reaction, because there was a world of confidence in his voice as he blandly promised, "Oy'll git ye theah sifely, lidey."

After absently studying his square shoulders, I involuntarily burst forth with the words: "You must be from Australia."

"Nah!" he retorted with a baleful glance in my direction.

"Ha!" the woman snorted. "I do believe that you insulted the poor man."

Directing a smile at the back of his head, I insisted: "But you have a similar dialect."

"Weel," he began. Then, glancing quickly aside, he reluctantly added, "Oy geese so."

Turning to the woman, I said, "Apparently, the Kiwis and the Aussies are comparable to the Swedes and the Norwegians in that they derive from similar stocks and cultures, but they pretend to hate each other's...." Stopping short, I cast an appalled glance toward the lady and weakly added, "innards."

She laughed outright, while the driver's shoulders shook convulsively.

My faux pas was followed by a few minutes of silence, but that woman must have been driven by a compulsion to talk, because she suddenly burst forth: "We've lived in California seventeen years, and...."

Then another turn at high speed threatened to throw me against **her**, so I frantically clutched at an ashtray on the wall beside me. Abruptly part of it pulled away in my hand, but the effort did save a collision. Immediately and with a total disregard for my courageous efforts to protect her from harm, that inconsiderate female dramatically thrust a forefinger toward the dangling part and burst into hysterical laughter. No wonder knighthood is dead.

After recovering, she repeated: "We have lived in California seventeen years, and...."

"And before that you lived below the Mason-Dixon line," I interjected.

"Yes, I did," she admitted. "I came from Georgia. How could you tell?"

"I've lived in Georgia, too," I said, "and...."

"Oh, then you could tell," she interposed. Then for several miles she reminisced about her life in Georgia.

She finally paused and inhaled deeply. Meanwhile, I interjected: "I spent three years in Atlanta...."

"This is yoah stop," the driver called back to me across one shoulder as he slowly brought the vehicle to a stop. "I've tiken ye as close to the Abby's as Oy kin."

As the woman arose and stepped into the aisle, I murmured, "I hope that you'll enjoy your tour."

"You, too," she responded as I joined her in the aisle. Then she tentatively thrust forth one soft hand, and I gently squeezed it.

"Actually, her husband should have joined her," José mused as I followed the driver down the steps to the pavement. "But he's probably enjoying this respite from so much chatter. After all, a constant flow of words can drive even the most stable man up a wall."

The City of Auckland

Standing alongside the bus, I watched while the driver unlatched a side door and opened it. Then I pointed out my heavy suitcase to him. Despite the man's rangy, rugged construction, his first tug was ineffective. After carefully setting himself, with a loud grunt he lifted it out and set it onto the pavement beside me. "What do ye have in theah?" he inquired with a gasp. "Gold?"

"Not likely," I responded with a chuckle. But I was to hear that remark again, because some Kiwis love to infer that all Americans are possessors of great wealth.

Inhaling deeply, he said, "To git to the Abby's from heah, go along Queen Strait to Wellesley, which ye'll foind just this soide of that big building." After pausing briefly to point, he resumed: "Cross Wellesley and turn leeft." Pausing again, he glanced down at my suitcase and added: "With that heavy bag, ye'll foind it a bit o' a cloimb, but it's only about a hundred metahs from theah to the hotel, which is located at the cornah of Wellesley and Albert Straits." With that he clapped one large palm against my backbone and added, "Oy 'ope ye enjoy yoah sty in New Zealand."

"Thank you for your help," I responded. "I'm sure to enjoy my stay here if all Kiwis are as cordial and helpful as you have been."

The Abby's Hotel   The two-block walk wasn't too difficult, but I did find the last "hundred metahs" to be "a bit o' a cloimb." I almost failed to make it from the sidewalk up several steps to the landing of what was purported to be the entrance of the hotel. There, behind the glass in one of the double doors, a sign displayed the words *Use the Side Entrance*. Peering through the adjacent glass, I saw that the lobby was in the process of being remodeled, and that deeply discouraged me, because I suspected that the entire hotel might be in a similar condition. Too exhausted to seek another one, I dragged my luggage down the steps, turned the corner, and strode a few steps along Albert Street to the side entrance, which was overhung by the planking of a scaffold. There I found the single doorway to be partially blocked by a pile of bedrolls and duffel bags.

I stared doubtfully at the assortment, but a quick glance through the clear glass of the door at the newly tiled floor and the freshly painted walls of the temporary foyer reassured me. Stepping around the obstructions, I opened the door and entered a small room crowded with youthful backpackers. Some of them were standing, while others sat astride bedrolls, but all of them appeared to be waiting for some form of transportation.

The only other exit incorporated a pair of doors that appeared to be recessed into the far wall, so I picked my way among the backpackers to the doors and found another sign bearing the words *Register on Third Floor*. Obviously, the doors provided access to an elevator, so I finally located the tiny push button and pressed it. After the doors opened, I carried my luggage into the elevator and pressed button three; then it began a slow ascent.

When it stopped, another pair of doors on the opposite side of the elevator unexpectedly opened to the temporary lobby. Picking up my luggage, I advanced about four steps toward the front of a painted, wooden counter, which enclosed a narrow office space that extended the full length of the small room. To my left a small rotary postcard display rack stood atop one end of the counter, and an attractive, dark-haired young woman was seated at a small, flattop desk in the space beyond it. At the far end of the counter a somewhat more mature woman stood stiffly beside an equally mature man.

Nearby stood a rather dapper, gray-haired gentleman, whose steel-gray eyes were shaded from the dim light by the narrow, pulled down brim of a gray, tweed hat. His slender figure was clad in a trim, gray suit whose left lapel bore a small floral boutonniere. Beneath his somewhat aquiline nose, a neat, closely trimmed, gray moustache completed the ensemble. He exuded a very British air, and his erect posture, with one hand held laxly across his flat midriff, accentuated that air.

Immediately sensing tension in the atmosphere, I tentatively came to a stop near the gentleman just as he said, "Furthermore, I had to call and request that someone bring towels to my room." But there was no rancor in the words, which were expressed with a strong British accent, and the tones were carefully modulated.

"We are sorry about that," the other man responded in equally modulated tones, "but the towels were delivered promptly, I believe."

"Then the lift was inoperative for most of one day...," the dapper man countered with a sustained stare.

A long silence greeted the statement, but I noted that the duo's eyes had suddenly become riveted on me, so I concluded that they suspected, as I did, that the statement had been made for my benefit. I also suspected that I had just overheard part of a quarrel, but it was like no quarrel that I had ever overheard in my country. It had been conducted in such good taste that I was still waiting for its climax. But there was to be no climax, because it dissolved into a long silence, during which the dapper man finally tilted his head toward the duo in a stiff bow. Then he did a sharp about face and strode erectly toward the elevator—"the lift," in his words.

Meanwhile, I wondered why he had not characteristically removed his hat in the presence of the ladies. A Canadian gentleman would have done so; at least he would have done so during the forepart of the twentieth century, when I lived in Canada.

Those thoughts were abruptly interrupted by the words: "Can I help you?"

My eyes absently turned toward their source and found that the young woman had risen from behind the desk and now stood on the opposite side of the counter. "Huh?" I grunted. Then I hurriedly added, "Oh, yeah. I suspect that you can. What's your rate for a single?"

"Forty dollahs a dye," she replied.

"What is it on a weekly basis?" I asked.

"Forty dollahs a dye," she responded with a cool, appraising stare.

While I studied her probing eyes, José and Pancho analyzed the woman's attitude and informed me that we were not interested in a weekly basis, so I said, "Then I would like one on a daily basis, please."

She silently placed a pad of registration forms before me, and I registered on the top one. Then, turning the pad around, she marked *26.11* for the time of arrival, *714* for the room number, *1* for the number in the party, and added the rate. Placing the room key on the counter before me, she said, "That will be forty dollahs, please."

I silently extracted my wallet, selected a couple of bills from it, and extended them to her while mentally comparing her cold attitude with the more genial ones that I had encountered at the airport and on the bus. Of course, her attitude may have been influenced by the foregoing altercation, but she had not been directly involved in it, so I concluded that it must have been influenced by some Unknown entity.

While the lift was slowly lifting me and my luggage to the seventh floor, my mind apprehensively toyed with several of the possibilities that might greet me when I opened the door of the room. But my apprehension proved to be unjustified, because the room had been completely renovated, including the fixtures in the tiny bathroom. True, the lavatory was so small that I was forced to wash one hand at a time, but the water closet was of adequate size. Fortunately, the framework of the corner shower was enclosed by shower curtains, because I could never have squeezed into it had solid materials enclosed it. Everything appeared to have been miniaturized. Even the double bed appeared to be smaller than normal, but it consumed most of the space in the room. Scarcely sufficient space remained for a tiny three-drawer chest, a narrow walkway, and a telephone shelf, but the latter had been built across a remote corner of the room to conserve space.

My briefcase fitted nicely beneath the telephone shelf, but stowage of the suitcase proved to be a major problem, since there was no way that I could open it without first opening the door to the hallway. After placing it on the bed and removing all of the articles that I was likely to require, I closed it and futilely endeavored to stow it beneath the bed. Eventually I discovered that it fitted snugly into the space between the far side of the bed and the wall. Truly, that hotel room was the tightest spot in which I had ever found myself, and I've been in some tight spots during my lifetime.

At Large in the City After prying myself out of the tiny room, I boarded the lift, which also could have been called a *lower*, because it did lower me to the temporary foyer. From there I exited onto Albert Street, then turned right on West Wellesley Street, and resumed my previous climb as far as the art gallery. It stood just beyond Kitchener Street in the corner of Albert Park, where I quickly became lost among various meandering footpaths until my arrival at Princes Street, beyond which was Auckland University. Briefly pondering my obvious need of higher education, I concluded that I was too old to enroll. Retracing my steps to Queen Street, I turned north to Galway Street and east to the Downtown Bus Centre. After receiving instructions on how to get to Kelly Tarlton's Underwater World, I boarded the next bus.

From the center, the bus turned east on Quay Street, which paralleled the shoreline of Waitemata Harbor. On my left the intense summer sun generously highlighted the indifferent waves as the vehicle slowly rumbled past the Railway Station and the Sea Bee Air Terminal to Judge's Bay. Beyond that point, it followed Quay Street along a causeway between Hobson Bay and a sheltered marina to Orahei Wharf at Tamaki Drive. There it stopped and disgorged most of its passengers. After crossing the street to the entrance of the Underwater World and parting with a five-dollar bill, I joined a flock of small fry, which was being shepherded through the turnstiles by two women. Meanwhile, I learned that each of the children's tickets cost $2.50.

From the turnstiles, the floor of a concrete tunnel sloped down to a point where sea creatures were displayed in their natural habitat behind the large panels of heavy plate glass that adorned both sides of the tunnel. According to the tout sheet that had been included with my ticket, it was a diver's view of the underwater panorama. Among its 1,000 inhabitants were sharks, snappers, kingfish, and a giant stingray. As usual, the tout sheet overstated the display's qualifications, but it would have been cheap at twice the price (about five dollars in America). Certainly, those rates were a far cry from the rates that my fellow Americans were charging in Hawaii.

Upon returning to the central part of the city, I came upon an open, wooden box alongside a brick office building. As I suspected, it contained a stack of the latest newspapers. Attached to one end of it was a slotted, metal container, which appeared to be a coin box, since three characters denoting thirty cents had been penciled above the slot.

"Apparently, the Kiwis trust their compatriots to pay for their newspapers," Pancho suggested, "but that trust doesn't extend to money."

"But the coin box may have been provided to preclude any pilfering by small children," José suggested.

As I removed a newspaper and placed the required change in the slot, my mind rolled back about fifty years to a similar scene in a much smaller city, which was located in one of the central states of the United States. In it another stack of newspapers rested on a wooden box alongside another brick building. In lieu of the coin box, a small cake pan, containing several coins of different values, sat beside the stack.

A lithe young man swung out of the passing throng and cast a casual glance at the layout. Then he ducked around an adjacent corner into a small alcove, where a black man was preparing to polish a pair of black shoes.

"Hi, Amos," he greeted the man. "Do you have any nickel shoe shines today?"

"No, Al, I don't shoine shoes foah a nickel anymoah," he replied, "but I'll give you the best shoine in town foah a doime."

"I believe you," Al responded as he climbed onto one of the two elevated, wooden chairs. "Every man has to look out for his own interests, so he has to raise his charges to meet the rising costs of living."

Amos left his task and turned toward the other man's scuffed, brown shoes. "Don't stop what you are doing," Al protested.

"Dis man won't be back 'til tomorrow evenin'," Amos retorted. "I'll have plenty o' toime to finish his shoes befoah den." Then he began to industriously brush the dust and grime from the brown shoes.

Meanwhile, Al stared down at his closely cropped, curly, black hair and said, "You really shouldn't leave so much money in that pan, Amos. There must be over a dollar in it, and somebody is sure to clip you for it. That's almost a day's work for you, and the little that you gain from the sale of those newspapers doesn't warrant such a risk."

Amos tilted his head back so that his eyes could look up into those of his client. "Nah, that money is puhfec'ly safe," he insisted. "Everybuddy 'round heah is honest. Besoides, I have to leave enough coins foah my customahs to make change."

"And that's another way that you can be clipped," Al retorted. "Even if the clip is only a dime, it would have bought a hamburger for you."

Amos lowered his head momentarily and concentrated on his task. "Nah," he finally repeated, "Everybuddy 'round heah is honest."

The scene slowly faded away to reveal the stack of New Zealand *Heralds*, and I suddenly felt a kinship with the man or youth who had left them there for his countrymen, confident that they would properly reimburse him. Then the headlines on some of the recent issues of Los Angeles newspapers flashed before my eyes: bureaucratic corruption, burglaries, rapes, and murders. And I wondered if the newspapers were still being marketed the same way in that smaller city. Even though I had not visited the city since that time, I deeply doubted it, because I had ruefully witnessed the rapid decay of the moral structure of the American people during the last twenty years. That had been amply displayed by the types of entertainment that they sanctioned on their television screens and by the various news media's crude and tasteless reports.

Returning to my hotel room, I spread the newspaper across the bed, then turned to the equivalent of an American want ad section, and searched for less costly housing—but without success. Some of the furnished flats were economically priced, but most of the ads were directed to long-term tenants. I particularly noticed that the terms *for hire* had been used in lieu of the American terms *for rent*. After finding the telephone number of a for hire agency, I dialed it, but the agent tactfully expressed the opinion that very few of his clients would be interested in renting to a temporary tenant.

While relaxing on the bed, my mind reviewed several small incidents, which led me to suspect that, even in this remote city, the dark pall of the Unknown was hanging over my head. True, the incidents had been small, and my convictions were not entirely conclusive, but fifty years of exposure to such incidents had caused me to become supersensitive to even the smallest deviations in the behavior of people whom I encountered. Furthermore, a day of exposure to the North Island's hot sun and humid climate had almost convinced me that I should travel to a more comfortable spot on the South Island.

Abruptly, Pancho interjected, "That does it. We're moving on." And since José didn't object, the die was cast.

In response to my signal from the curb in front of the hotel, a driver swung his cab sharply in front of me. "Wheah to, sir?" he inquired, as I slumped onto the seat and pulled the door closed.

"Auckland Station," I replied. Then, turning so that I could study his features, I inquired, "Can you give me the names of a few good restaurants?"

"Weel," he began thoughtfully, "theah's a lot of theem, but it deepends on what koind of food you loik. Foah eexample, you moight loik Rick's Cafe American."

"I might," I conceded with a chuckle. "But when one is in a foreign country, it seems logical to sample the local dishes."

"Theah's all koinds of foreign ristaurants," he muttered. "The Mekong is Vietnamese, the Genghis Khan is Mongolian, you can git Chinese food at the Golden Empire, and Antoines is a French restaurant."

Suspecting that I had confused the man, I countered: "But how about the usual Auckland fare?"

After pondering momentarily, he looked uneasily at me and said, "Oy railly don't know, because Oy don't doine out much, exceptin' an occasional cup o' tay and a bun, but Oy understand that Brandy's is a bit o' all roight."

"That's located in the Old Auckland Custom House, isn't it?" I ventured.

"Yees," he replied. "Have you bin theah?"

"No," I replied, "but I ran across it while wandering through some of the shops in that old building. And I was particularly impressed by the way the building had been remodeled. In America it would have been wasted, and I'm using that word in the underworld sense."

In response to his puzzled expression, I added, "A demolition ball, a bulldozer, and several dump trucks would have disposed of it."

"Oh, that would have been a terrible wiste," he protested.

"Essentially, that's what I was talking about," I muttered.

"Did ye stop by the Woolshid?" he asked.

"Yes," I replied, "but I can buy imported, handmade, pure wool products in America."

"Imported!" he exclaimed with a scandalized expression, which gradually faded away in response to my teasing smile. Nevertheless, he loyally added, "Oy'll hive ye know that New Zealand produces some o' the foinest handmade, pure wool products in the world." And he pronounced the word *product* with a long *o*.

Deciding that I had overstepped, I changed the subject with the question: "Does Auckland have any shopping malls?"

"Weel," he drawled, "theah's Eady's Mall, but theah's moah arcades, such as Canterbury, Century, and Queen's Arcade; furthamoah, theah's shoppin' cintres, such as. . . ."

But I interjected another question: "What about department stores?"

"Farmahs' is the lahgest depahtmint stoah in New Zealand," he responded with an air of pride as he swung the cab alongside a curb in front of the large building that served Auckland as a railway station.

After reimbursing the man, I entered the imposing structure and found myself in a wide hallway. Looking from it through one of the large windows that studded the upper half of the wall on my left, I noted that it enclosed several ticket windows and a large waiting room, in which some hardwood benches were conveniently located. Swinging open the partially glazed hardwood door, I strolled toward the corner ticket window, beyond which a short, broad-shouldered man patiently waited. As I stopped in front of the window, his dark eyes focused on my features and remained fixed on them for several seconds.

Then he absently brushed his dark moustache with a forefinger and, in accent-free words, inquired, "How can I help you?"

"I would like to obtain a ticket for passage to Rotorua," I replied.

"That would be by Road Services Coach," he murmured.

"Oh," I grunted. "Can you direct me to the bus station?"

"I can sell you a bus ticket," he said. "But do you plan to do much traveling in New Zealand?"

"I intend to see as much of the country as possible within the two weeks that I've budgeted for that purpose," I replied.

"Then perhaps you would like to purchase a Travelpass," he suggested. "It will permit you to travel over the entire network serviced by the government's railways, coaches, and ferries for a two-week period at a cost of only one hundred ninety dollars."

I pondered the proposition briefly and nodded.

But he pressed on: "The network covers New Zealand from Kaitaia at the north end of the North Island to Invercargill at the south end of the South Island."

"I'm sold, I'm sold," I responded, forcing a small smile to cover my impatience.

But it wasn't the man's words that had triggered my impatience; it was his sustained stare when I had first stepped in front of the window.

"You'll enjoy Rotorua," he predicted in more formal tones as he prepared the pass. "It's one of the most celebrated health resorts and spas in the world. It's located alongside a beautiful lake bearing the same name. Practically within the city itself, there's a thermal area containing numerous mud pools, hot springs, and geysers."

"According to something that I once read," I said, "it's located within a huge volcanic caldera that covers many square miles."

"That could be," he granted. "There are several widely separated thermal spots around the town, but there are fourteen extinct volcanoes within this area. Of course, the entire New Zealand landmass was created by volcanic action."

"That's what I've been led to believe," I murmured, absently picking up the Travelpass and the seat reservation. "I certainly hope that one of them doesn't suddenly decide to let go in the near future."

As I turned away, he solemnly murmured, "May God forbid."

From Auckland Station, Beach Road and Custom Street East provided a rather lengthy means of access to Queen Street, along which I strolled to Wellesley Street West. There I turned right and climbed the slope to the hotel. During the trip from the hotel's small foyer to my room, the lift voluntarily stopped at the third floor and opened its doors to the temporary lobby. They closed almost immediately, but not before the dark-haired young woman had subjected me to a penetrating stare.

"That gimlet-eyed gal must double as the house detective," José interjected into my thoughts, but I ignored the supposition.

Since I planned to dine in style alongside Kiwis, who are reputed to go formal, I showered and donned my only formal attire: a pair of slacks and a sport coat, plus a white shirt and a necktie. Once more, the lift stopped at the third floor, opened its doors to the temporary lobby, allowed the female house dick to peer into it, and resumed its downward journey to the foyer.

After venturing forth from the foyer, I followed the grooves that my previous trips to the central part of the city had worn into the sidewalks of Wellesley and Queen Streets. Since it was downhill all of the way, it was relatively easy going as long as I stayed in the groove and didn't venture onto the right side of the sidewalk. Not only do New Zealanders refuse to drive on the right sides of their thoroughfares, but their pedestrians tend to avoid the right sides of their sidewalks. At Queen Elizabeth II Square I turned left one block, then right on Albert Street, and continued on to Quay Street, where I paused and looked across the street at the Ferry Berth. After turning left and passing the Travelodge, I stopped at Hobson Street in response to the pedestrian traffic signal.

A step to my left permitted me to press the button on the side of a yellow box, which was attached to the near side of a steel pole that stood beside the curb. Meantime, several other pedestrians collected about me, and a line of cars formed in the adjacent traffic lane of Quay Street. When the motorists' traffic signals finally changed, the pedestrians' signal remained unchanged; nevertheless, the surrounding pedestrians surged across Albert Street while the adjacent line of cars held fast, so I found myself standing alone beside the pole.

That scene appeared to be of particular interest to a tawny-haired young driver seated beside an open window in one of the adjacent cars. In fact, he became so emotionally involved that he called, "Go oan across!"

Looking across my shoulder at him, I refused to heed his advice, because the pedestrians' signal still advised against it.

"Go oan!" he shouted. "Go oan across!"

Momentarily, his equally youthful companion appeared to protest his actions, so he withheld further counsel; however, from the corner of one eye, I could see that he was still staring balefully at me. Apparently, the internal pressure finally overwhelmed him, because he suddenly shouted, "Go oan across! Ye kin mike it!"

To me it wasn't a question of making it; it was a question of abiding by the law, so I smiled pleasantly at him and stubbornly held my ground.

Finally, there was a raucous, ongoing buzz as the signal switched to "walk"; then I deigned to cross the intersection with a couple of other pedestrians whose rate of travel happened to be in synch with the signal.

Meanwhile, my adviser turned disgustedly to his companion and muttered, "'Fride to cross the bloody strait agin the signal."

Again, to me it wasn't a question of fear, because I had come to "fear only fear itself"; it was a question of abiding by the law, of being fully organized, just as every member of society should be.

As I continued along Quay Street, it became part of a wide causeway with Freemans Bay one side and with Hobsons Wharf projecting into Auckland Harbour on the other side. All forms of traffic would have had to stop at the narrow channel connecting the two bodies of water if the Lifting Bridge had not straddled it.

At the near end of the bridge, a small, one-story building stood between Freemans Bay and the street, so I veered purposefully toward an open doorway on the bay side of it. As I drew closer to the opening, the dim outlines of the head and broad shoulders of a middle-aged man became visible. At that moment he appeared to be intently inspecting something on the wide, wooden bench that traversed the far end of the building.

"He's probably calibrating the instrumentation," Pancho suggested confidently.

When my heavily loaded Hush Puppies struck the shack's worn, pine flooring, he whirled about in response to the booming sounds and looked toward me.

"Pardon me for interrupting your work," I said, "but can you tell me if the Floating Restaurant is located in this area?"

He stepped away from the bench, and Pancho's confidence in his own judgment must have been crushed, since the only instruments in the entire shack were some stainless steel cutlery: a knife, a fork, and a spoon. They had been placed rather indifferently beside a large dinner plate, which contained not one but two big steaks plus a huge stack of hash-browned potatoes and onions. Nearby was a large, chipped mug brimful of a dark-brown liquid, from the surface of which a wisp of steam spiraled indolently upward. After a second glance at the large, heavy-set man and his stack of food, I began to consider seriously the possibility that he alone lifted one end of that bridge whenever the need arose.

A bit of ancient courtesy finally surfaced in my mind. "Oh!" I burst forth. "I didn't suspect that you might be having dinner. Don't let me interrupt it, because I can scout around and find the place on my own."

"Don't let my meal stop you," he responded in deep, bass tones. Then he turned and looked through one of the two large windows in the wall above the bench. "Come heah, and Oy'll point it out to ye."

After I stepped forward to his side, he raised one thick arm and pointed toward a small vessel moored alongside a makeshift wharf on the far shoreline of Freemans Bay. "Theah it is," he said. "It's that little, old ferry boat, Oy think it was."

"Yeah, I see it," I muttered. "Thank you much for pointing it out to me. Now

I'll get out of here so that you can resume the meal that I so rudely interrupted."

He turned both palms up in a gesture of c'est la vie and said, "Don't let it bothah ye one minute. It happins all the toime."

Since no sidewalks crossed the channel, I watched for a break in the vehicular traffic before crossing the floor of the bridge. While scurrying across the rectangular openings in its steel grating, my eyes intermittently glimpsed the various components of the steel supporting structure and the choppy water far beneath them. Meanwhile, my Hush Puppies were beating discordant musical notes from the edges of the grating. About midway along the structure, I chanced to see a small vessel approaching the bridge from the vicinity of Auckland Harbor, so I accelerated my pace.

Safely beyond the end of the bridge, I stopped and looked back through one of the shack's windows at the dim outline of the operator's head and shoulders, whose movements seemed to indicate that he was consuming his repast. Unfortunately, the meal was about to be interrupted a second time within scarcely more than two minutes.

"Like the man said," José injected into my thoughts, "'It happins all the toime.'"

Turning away from the view of the window, I looked at the tugboat just as its engine was throttled down. Then a short, deep-toned blast sounded from the end of a slender tube that projected above one corner of its wheelhouse.

My attention returned to the bridge operator, who first peered through the window; then he manipulated some sort of a control.

"Probably a push button," suggested Pancho confidently.

Suddenly, bells clanged and lights flashed at both ends of the bridge, while two pairs of barriers, similar to those at railway crossings, slowly rotated downward and barricaded them. Actually, the whole operation reminded me of the furor that usually erupts around a jackpot in a Las Vegas casino—minus the delighted screams of the winner, of course. However, I've never hit a jackpot, so I've never had that kind of an opportunity to scream, but I've never invested more than a few quarters at any one time either. Furthermore, several years have always elapsed between those quarters.

After the barriers were in place, there was a loud creaking of heavily loaded steel members and the shrill screeching of scraping metal. Then the near end of the bridge slowly began to rise, and it continued to rise in an arc until it stood directly above its opposite end.

Once more, there was a bass-toned blast from the tugboat. Then the deep throbbing of its engine accelerated, and, after a momentary shudder, it moved slowly into the channel and jauntily passed the point where I stood while two lounging crewmen raised their right hands aloft in friendly greetings.

After the tugboat had passed through the channel, I watched the bridge operator during his manipulation of the controls that reversed the huge structure's lifting cycle. When the horizontal barriers had returned to their vertical positions and the warning bells and lights had ceased to clang and flash, several vehicles crossed the bridge, and their headlights rapidly disappeared into the gathering dusk.

Meanwhile, I became cloaked in one of those rare auras of happiness that have touched me so rarely during the last fifty years. I sensed it quickly and just as quickly associated it with the peaceful surroundings—with the waterfront, its denizens, and its characteristic assortment of lounging boats and vessels.

As a boy in Canada, I had loved to prowl about Vancouver's endless waterfront in search of vessels from distant and exotic ports, be they rusty tubs or trim passenger liners. One time, alongside one of the lesser wharves, I found a merchant sailing ship, a big four-master from Bombay, India, and that was one of the high points in my young life. But my finest hour was the time when a tolerant cockney sailor allowed me and a tagalong friend to board a tender that shuttled between one of the piers and the H.M.S. *Repulse*, which was anchored in the middle of Burrard Inlet along with the battleship H.M.S. *Hood* and the cruiser H.M.S. *Adelaide*. Even though the tender was reserved for the friends and relatives of the crew, the cockney sailor agreed to look the other way as we clambered aboard. Consequently, we not only got to board the *Repulse*, but we were given a red-carpet tour of the huge leviathan. With all of the information that I garnered from that tour, I might still be a valuable source of information for the C.I.A., but the *Hood* was sunk in the North Atlantic by the Germans, and very likely the other two ships have been scrapped if they didn't suffer a similar fate.

Apparently that particular section of Auckland's waterfront was not frequented by modern merchant ships, because the only vessel that I found was a small, rusty, old tub with the word *Greenpeace* scrawled across one rust-encrusted wall of its superstructure. Obviously, it hadn't been properly maintained, since its deck was cluttered with equipment, including hydraulic pumps, steel pipes, and pieces of angle iron.

The word *Greenpeace* rang a bell in my ivory tower, and it set my mind to recalling parts of various news reports concerning the international intrigue and manslaughter that had evolved from the Greenpeace movement's plan to lead a protest fleet of ships to France's nuclear test site at Moruroa Atoll. And that action had been planned despite the fact that the atoll was France's private property. During previous protests, French naval personnel were reported to have boarded Greenpeace ships and manhandled some of their crews, but even that had failed to deter the activists.

To forestall Greenpeace's ongoing plans, the French External Security Service was reported to have employed two of its frogmen to plant a bomb on the hull of the movement's flagship, *Rainbow Warrior*, which was moored in Auckland Harbour. Unfortunately, the bomb's explosion not only sank the ship but killed Greenpeace's photographer. With admirable intelligence and efficiency, New Zealand authorities captured the two agents and scooped from Auckland Harbour a French-made rubber dinghy and two diver's air bottles, which proved to be sufficient evidence to convict the agents.

Apparently, the rust bucket that stood before me was the *Rainbow Warrior's* replacement, and I could fully appreciate the reason for the words *Contributions Accepted*, which were scribbled below the vessel's name. That tub was a pile of junk, and an inadvertent sneeze might have sunk it on the spot. Without doubt Greenpeace desperately needed a new flagship, irrespective of whether or not the purposes of the movement warranted it.

The restaurant was still afloat when I arrived there, but the hostess was not at her post, so I slowly climbed a wooden stairway to the upper deck, where I found a lone waitress. Since there was only one other diner, I conned the waitress into seating me at a table beside a window that provided a fine view of the bay and the setting sun.

As she presented the menu to me, I casually inquired, "What happened to the hostess?"

"I suspict she went down to the pub for a beer," she replied.

Looking up unbelievingly from the open menu to her clear eyes, I sputtered, "She did what?"

"I suspect she went down to the pub for a beer," she repeated uneasily.

"Hmm," I mumbled. "That's what I thought you said." Then I tried to place her more at ease by adding, "That throws a lot of responsibility on you, doesn't it?"

"Not too much," she answered. "I haven't been very busy this evening."

"Even if you had been very busy, I'm sure that you would be capable of handling it," I responded with a smile that was intended to be disarming. Apparently it succeeded, because her eyes glowed as she moved slowly toward her post at the top of the stairwell.

Obviously, all of those negative omens should have been viewed as fair warnings by any self-proclaimed gourmet, but I chose to gamble. Besides, I hoped to escape from the usual pall of the Unknown for just the dinner hour, if no longer. So far, it had been a lovely evening, and I had particularly enjoyed my minute with the bridge operator plus the friendly salutes from the men aboard the tugboat. Of course, those small things would have amounted to nothing in the eyes of the average man, but they were more than I usually gained from anybody except chance associates. In fact, that was one of my primary reasons for the trip: more chance associations and a few normal moments.

"Have you decided yet?" inquired the hesitant voice of the waitress at my shoulder.

I glanced up sharply toward her shy, gray eyes and vaguely wondered what it would be like to be that young again. "No," I replied. "What do you recommend?"

"Well, that depinds a lot on what one loikes," she responded with a friendly smile. "I particularly loike the fish and chips."

"At your age I liked them too," I responded with a matching smile.

"People of all ages like them," she countered with an air of growing confidence. "Besides, you can't be very old. You don't act old."

"May Allah bless you, child, for being so sweet," I murmured. "But I am old, at least four times as old as you are."

"Aw, you can't be," she protested.

"If you have been conning me to influence the tip, you have just succeeded," I rejoined with a teasing grin.

Her eyes sobered. "I wasn't even thinking about a tip," she murmured. "In fact, people don't tip very often in New Zealand."

"I was merely jesting," I said. "But since I look so young to you, I'm going to accept your advice and order the fish and chips. Perhaps my old tummy has been conned into believing that it's young again."

"I hope that you won't regret my suggestion," she murmured with a worried frown.

"I'm sure that I won't," I insisted. "Besides, I had already considered the fish and chips, so it wasn't entirely your suggestion that induced me to order them."

"I'm glad," she responded with an air of childish honesty.

While she was slowly trudging toward the galley with her eyes on the order pad, a tall, slender, fortyish woman emerged from the stairwell and cast a casual glance about the room. Then her red-rimmed eyes quickly returned to mine and as quickly flitted away.

"You may have been in the pub a bit too long, old gal," José surmised, "but you could have stayed there for another hour as far as we are concerned."

"Amen!" Pancho erupted.

Meanwhile, the hostess called to the waitress and imperatively motioned to her. After the waitress responded, they stood with their heads together for several seconds, during which the girl cast a quick glance across one shoulder toward me. Some time later she not only delivered my order in silence, as I had expected, but her eyes seemed to avoid my searching eyes.

After she left the table, Pancho observed, "Well, it was a beautiful evening until that gaunt bag spoiled it."

"Um, yeah," José rejoined. "There aughta be a law against the conception of such people."

Actually, the fish and chips served their purpose, and the tab of slightly more than eight dollars didn't upset my stomach. Therefore, those factors, plus the fact that the teenage waitress had brightened my drab existence for a few short minutes, induced me to leave a dollar tip.

As José suggested, "Without doubt she started out right, but she was led astray by a wayward associate of the Unknown."

When I began the long return trek, the hands of my wristwatch pointed to 9:30, and the fish had already begun to chase the chips in tight circles about the inner walls of my stomach, but I had come to expect such reactions whenever the Unknown was introduced to someone who had been nice to me. Furthermore, for several years I had been convinced that the constant recurrence of such stress-filled incidents would eventually cause me to become the third victim of cancer within my immediate family.

Upon approaching the vicinity of the *Greenpeace*, I veered toward it and found that the unglazed openings were unlighted, so it was logical to conclude that no one was aboard the dirty, cluttered, and ugly old scow. A brief pause and a closer inspection of the barnacle-covered waterline of the steel hull revealed that, since its exposed areas had become deeply eroded, it was either dissolving into red rust or the barnacles were consuming it. Consequently, it might end up—down, that is—on the bottom of Auckland Harbour along with the *Rainbow Warrior*.

Resuming my stroll alongside the hundred-foot length of the decrepit peace-maker, I pondered the illogical reasoning of its small crew, which appeared to be bent on employing slingshots and stones to confront a nuclear giant while the giant was endeavoring to ensure peace and freedom for its citizens by being prepared to defend itself from a much greater giant. After all, how much faith should France invest in its allies, especially the United States, which forsook its ally, little South Vietnam, when the going got tough?

As luck would have it, another tugboat signaled to the bridge operator shortly before I arrived at the edge of the channel, so I patiently waited and watched while the lifting and lowering cycles were repeated. After they were completed, I inspected the mechanism at the far end of the bridge and mentally marveled at its simplicity.

Meantime, the shadows had darkened, so I turned away and began to stride toward the bright lights of the inner city at an accelerated pace. The hands of my watch stood at 10:10, and the sun had just disappeared into the western horizon, somewhere beyond the distant, invisible shoreline of Australia. Since that southern sun was an extremely unfamiliar quantity to me, I began to ponder some of its idiosyncrasies, such as its tardy settings and its intense ultraviolet rays.

"Without doubt it's very different from the northern sun," José suddenly interjected.

"Why so?" Pancho asked.

"Why shouldn't it be different?" José countered. "After all, this sun is in the Southern Hemisphere, so it should be different from the sun in the Northern Hemisphere."

"Hmm," mumbled Pancho, "I never viewed it from that angle before, but you have a point. Why shouldn't two suns be different—unless they are twins?"

Upon arriving at the corner of Wellesley and Albert Streets, I was breathing deeply, so I climbed the steep grade slowly. But my pleasure in arriving at the hotel was dissipated by a pair of prying eyes when the lift paused at the third floor. After showering and brushing my teeth, I crawled into the sack and began to ruminate on the strange behavior of the hostess. Meanwhile, the fish continued to frantically pursue the chips in my churning stomach, and they persisted in the activity far into the night, while my mind insisted on reviewing my puzzling misadventure over and over.

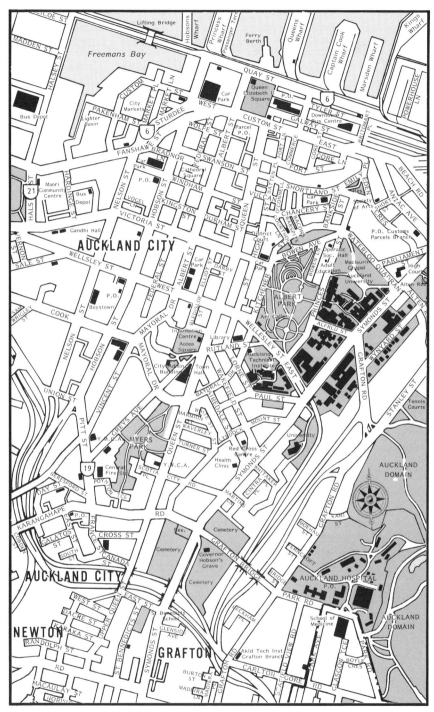

MAP OF AUCKLAND

3

Auckland to Rotorua

After a light breakfast at the hotel's coffee shop, I taxied to the Downtown Bus Station and joined a group of passengers beside the Rotorua bus. Shortly before its scheduled departure, the bus driver posted himself at its front entrance with a pencil in one hand and a clipboard in the other one. A passenger immediately stepped toward him, and, like New Zealand sheep, the other passengers formed a line behind him with me near the rear of it. When I stepped in front of the driver and confidently extended my Travelpass to him, he glanced at it and extended an open palm toward me.

In response to my puzzled expression, he said, "You should also have a seat reservation slip."

"I don't remember receiving one," I muttered. "But I'll step aside and search for it."

"Hmm," he mumbled, peering through the thin pocket of my shirt. "That may not be necessary." Then, thrusting two fingers into it, he removed a folded slip of paper, unfolded it, glanced at it, and said, "Everything's in order, but you really should have read the pamphlet that the agent gave you. It would have saved this delay."

"I'll read it," I promised.

After checking a square in the chart on the clipboard, he waved me on. Turning away, I stumbled up the steps and trudged toward my seat with the guilty realization that I must have absently folded that slip of paper and slipped it into the pocket of my shirt after the ticket agent had placed it on top of my Travelpass. Very likely it had spent the night on the tiny chest where I had deposited the articles from my pockets before removing my clothing for the night. Nevertheless, when I found that I had been assigned a window seat, the momentary embarrassment was replaced by the pleasurable anticipation of viewing the upcoming panoramas of picturesque New Zealand countryside.

Shortly after leaving the city, the bus traveled through some of the most beautiful pastoral scenes that I have ever viewed. Interspersed between the sheep ranches, which are called stations in the lands down under, were several dairy farms, mostly stocked with holstein cattle but with an occasional herd of jerseys or guernseys. It is unlikely that even the finest color photographs could have surpassed those scenes. Since spring arrives during November in the Southern Hemisphere, it definitely was the best time of the year to be touring one of the most beautiful countries in the world.

At the first stop, a dignified lady paused just beyond the open entrance, thrust a small travel case onto the topmost step, grasped a handrail, and laboriously hoisted herself up the steps to the side of the case. After picking it up, she plodded along the aisle while her faded, blue-gray eyes alertly darted from one seat number to the next. Upon arriving beside my seat, she stopped, rested the case on one corner of it, and looked up at the flanged shelf.

"I'll put it up for you," I volunteered, sliding along the seat toward the aisle.

"No, Oy kin do it," she insisted. Then, raising the case over her head, she slid it into place.

"Very good, and very independent," I remarked, sliding back to my end of the seat.

"But don't lit me forgit to tike it with me when Oy git off," she commanded, settling heavily onto the other end of the seat.

Responding with a quick smile, I turned to the window and watched while the driver delivered a mailbag to the small post office before which the vehicle stood. From there he strode to the open doorway of an adjoining grocery store and called through it to someone. Within seconds, the slender, apron-clad figure of a middle-aged man appeared with a two-wheel dolly, and the driver swung alongside him while the merchant rapidly trundled the dolly to the rear of the bus. Minutes later, they reappeared with the merchant still controlling the handles of the dolly while the driver trotted alongside it, steadying several cases of fully charged glass milk bottles that rocked precariously about as the dolly's small, rubber tires bounced over the uneven surface of the asphalt pavement.

"Does this bus carry milk?" I burst forth incredulously.

"Yis," the woman replied, "and it hauls lots of other things, too, such as mile and frite."

I studied her features from the corner of one eye and quickly arrived at two conclusions: First, her slightly florid complexion seemed to support my suspicion that a faint Scottish burr attended the otherwise typical Kiwi dialect; furthermore, the fine lines about her eyes indicated that she must be about sixty-five years old.

"Those services must slow down the passenger service tremendously," I observed.

"But they make the passingah rites much lowah," she deftly rebutted. "Shuahly, you wouldn't want thim to be any hyah than they ah, would you?"

"Very likely they are high enough," I conceded. Since economics seemed to be a matter of paramount importance to the woman, I chose to avoid antagonizing her on some similar issue by changing the subject, so I asked, "Is the countryside as pretty as this all of the way to Rotorua?"

"Somewhat," she answered, "but it gits much roughah and prettier just befoah we git into Rotorua." After a momentary silence, she added, "So you ah going to Rotorua.... You'll like it.... It's a beautiful town.... Lots to do around Rotorua."

"Thank you for the information," I said. "It's nice to know that I've had the good fortune to select the right town for a side trip."

"Ah you on a touah?" she inquired, leaning her well padded-body forward and peering up into my eyes.

"Well, yes and no," I answered. "Since I have a three-month visa, I intend to use all of it to see this country and to get to know some of its people, so I **am** on a tour, but it **isn't** a formal one in that I'll decide **what** I see and **when** I see it. That's one reason why I purchased a fifteen-day Travelpass. On it I plan to make a tour of the North and the South Islands; then I plan to locate in the city or the area that most impresses me and study the people and their living patterns.

"Oh, that Travelpass **was** wise," she remarked. "It will prove to be very economical if you don't sty too long in one plice." After a brief pause, she asked, "Where ah you from? The Stites?"

"Mostly," I replied. "But I spent my boyhood in Canada."

"What paht of the Stites ah you from?" she asked.

"That's a difficult question to answer," I responded with a chuckle. "Actually, I've lived in many of the states, but I came here from Los Angeles, California, with a brief stop on the island of Oahu in Hawaii."

"Oh, Los Angeles is a very big city, isn't it?" she inquired.

"Yes, very big and very dirty," I replied. "Quite often the air becomes so polluted that the authorities invoke critical smog alerts." In response to her puzzled expression, I attempted to explain: "During those alerts, the use of automobiles is limited to trips that are absolutely necessary, and people are advised to exercise very sparingly, especially those who are very old or very young. Furthermore, people with certain allergies and breathing problems are advised to remain indoors."

She sat back against the seat with a pleased expression, clasped her hands on her ample lap, and said, "Well, that's one thing we do have: lots of clean, frish ayah."

"Yes, the winds from the Tasman Sea change it every minute on the minute," I retorted impulsively.

"That isn't strictly so!" she protested. "True, the wind is very strong in some areas, but the mountains shield many other areas from it."

"I'm sure that such is the case," I hurriedly interposed. "Too impulsively, I allowed those words to erupt in response to my experiences with the wind in Auckland."

"Aye, it acts up a bit theah at times," she conceded, "but it's much strongah in Willington. It's right on the strait, so the wind buzzes through it much of the time."

After a short silence, she inquired, "Are cahs very costly in the Stites?"

Following a brief study of the question, I drawled, "Well, a new Chevy costs between sixteen and eighteen thousand dollars, depending on the extras the buyer orders."

"That's a lot of money," she murmured, "but cahs are terribly costly in New Zealand. We bought one recently, and it cost us over thirty-eight thousand dollahs."

"That's terribly costly," I agreed, but my mind had already applied the exchange rate to the New Zealand sum and found that it was not far out of line with the cost of a Chevy Caprice in Los Angeles. But their car may have been smaller than the Caprice, since New Zealanders tend to buy smaller cars because of the high cost of "petrol."

"Do your homes cost a lot too?" she persisted.

"Some do," I replied. "For example, I recently sold a small, two-bedroom home for one hundred twenty thousand dollars, even though it's located in a rather remote area of Los Angeles County."

"Aye, that's a lot of money!" she exclaimed. "Recently, we bought a three-bedroom home for our daughter and her family. We paid fifty-three thousand dollahs for it, but we got a very good proice on it."

"It surely sounds like you did," I said. "Some of our homes are selling at such prices too, but they are located in small towns far from large cities. Most of the properties within the environs of Los Angeles are greatly overpriced, often selling for more than twice the price of equivalent properties in remote, small towns."

Meanwhile, my mind had converted the cost of the woman's three-bedroom home into an amazingly small 27,000 U.S. dollars. Then I glanced at the somewhat dowdy woman and began to reassess my initial opinion of her. Apparently she had to be classified among those ultraconservative souls who appear to predominate in New Zealand, and the reassessment seemed to be verified by her next statement.

"Things have become so costly," she complained. "Of course, Oy could have taken a pline from Gisborne to Auckland, but the fayah would have been noinety dollahs each wye, so Oy'm roidin' the boos. Such things become moah and moah costly while the fahmahs' products bring liss and liss," she continued mournfully. "Wye, the farmah is lucky to git twelve dollahs for a lamb, and it costs much moah than that to produce it." After pausing to inhale, she resumed: "That's why we sold owah fahm, but we wuh lucky, because we sold it when the proices wuh hoy. Most of the fahmahs hild on in hope that things would git bittah, but they got worse. Now many of them will lose their fahms—what with high interest rites and low proices foah theyah products."

Silence prevailed for several minutes until, to keep the conversation going, I volunteered: "So you invested that money in city property and a new car."

"Moy man saw what was happinin' to the sheep," she responded, "so he bought goats."

"Goats!" I exclaimed incredulously. "Are they a good investment?"

"They ah," she insisted, "oah they wuh, at least. He got in when the proice was low, and he sold out when the proice was hoy. He shuah mide a lot of money on goats."

"But who would ever buy goats at a high price?" I countered.

"Othah fahmahs," she answered.

"For what purpose?" I persisted.

"For breedin' stock," she replied.

"And to whom would those farmers sell the kids?" I countered. And there was a growing suspicion in both sides of my ivory tower that I was being conned, that a simple Kiwi babe was getting my goat.

"To othah fahmahs for breedin' stock," she responded with a trace of a smile.

"This has to be a takeoff of the old pyramid scam," I muttered. "At the end of the line, some of those farmers are going to get stuck with an awful lot of goats." Then I glanced speculatively at her and suggested, "In fact, those farmers may be eager for somebody to get **their** goats." But the awkward pun sped across her stringy, gray hair without touching one strand of it.

"The Ayrabs will buy them," she responded smugly.

"The Ayrabs?" I repeated involuntarily. "What will they do with them? Breed them?"

"Maybe," she responded with a doubtful expression. "But moah than loikely they'll eat thim."

"Eat them!" I exclaimed. Convinced that I had misinterpreted her words, I requested, "Will you please run that by me one more time?"

With a tolerant smile she repeated: "Moah than loikely they'll eat thim."

"That's what I thought you said," I muttered. "But why don't they eat mutton? It's less costly, isn't it?"

"But they prefuh goat meat," she answered, "and they ah willing to pie hoy proices to git it."

"Ohhhh," I exhaled thoughtfully.

Once more, silence prevailed for several minutes. Then she took off on another tack: "American politics appeah to be a bit differint from owahs, but some of the sime problems seem to aroise."

"True," I agreed, "but the people in power influence the difference, and the voters influence the problems by influencing the people in power."

"Reagan is gitting pritty old to run America," she stated firmly. Then, less positively, she archly inquired, "Isn't he?"

"Well," I began pensively, "there are some sound reasons to doubt that. I, for one, doubt that the age of his mind has been detrimental to the welfare of the nation. After all, most of the members of the Russian Politburo are old men. Furthermore, practically every society throughout the history of mankind has chosen its oldest and most experienced men to guide and govern it; meanwhile, the greater strength of its younger men has been employed in its defense. Besides, what politician ever needed brute strength to win a debate?"

"But Russia's new leadah is a much younger man," she countered with a sharp glance.

"True," I granted, "but the Politburo may have wearied of burying prime ministers."

"Maybe," she responded in skeptical tones.

"Gorbachev may be smarter than the others," I admitted. "At least, I surely hope so." Then I looked expectantly at her, but she didn't take the floor, so I resumed: "However, Reagan appears to have done much better than any of our recent presidents, so I can't believe that he's too old to run the country, not as long as he retains his health, and that appears to be under control." Then, feeling the presence of a whimsical smile, I was morally obligated to substantiate it. "Actually, he and I were born during the same year," I informed her, "so we are almost the same age, seventy-four, and I still intend to run for the presidency."

She turned startled eyes toward me and wonderingly exclaimed, "You are that old and still bummin' 'round the world!"

"But Reagan is still bumming around the world and running the country to boot," I retorted with a chuckle.

After a tolerant smile, she inquired, "What do you plan to do in Rotorua?"

"First, I'll attempt to find an economical place to spend the night," I answered.

"How much do you usually pay for lodging?" she asked.

"Forty dollars in Auckland," I replied, "but I hope to do better in Rotorua because it's much smaller. It also is a popular tourist spot, though, so I may have to pay even more."

"Oh!" she exclaimed. "That's an awful lot for just a plice to sleep." Then, fixing an appalled stare on my features, she suggested: "Why don't you go to a hostel? They charge only a few dollahs."

"Well," I began cautiously, "I prefer a room with all the amenities, including a bathroom; besides, I treasure my privacy."

"You don't have to sleep in a dormitory in a hostel," she protested. "You can get a private room, but you have to share the shower and . . . and things."

"Well, I'll look into it," I promised, but two of my fingers were crossed.

"It could save you twenty or thirty dollars," she persisted. "That's the same as money earned."

"True," I agreed. But the philosophy really didn't apply to the problem at hand, since it involved certain sacrifices that I was not prepared to make.

For a few minutes I silently watched the prevailing bush lands fade into an occasional pasture and wondered if the trip was winding down. Then she shattered the silence: "Theah's a lot going on in Rotorua. You'll find it to be an interisting plice to visit. In fact, you can spind two whole dyes just visiting the geysahs and the thermal powah installation."

"I surely intend to see all of those things," I said.

"We left the Hamilton and Cambridge areas long ago," she volunteered, "so we should be arroiving theah in a wee bit."

"There have been lots of trees along this end of the trip," I observed, "but I strongly suspect that most of the native timber has been logged off, because I've seen several clumps of much larger trees in particularly inaccessible spots."

"Practically all of the trees in New Zealand have been removed to make way foah pastures," she remarked, "but most of this particulah land is too rough foah sheep, so the trees must have been removed for their lumbah."

"Isn't that a golf course?" I burst forth, pointing to the scene beyond an opposite window.

She looked toward the distant greensward and answered, "Yis, that's the Lakeview Golf Course, so we should be entering Rotorua very soon."

"According to a map that I happened to see, the city is located at the end of a lake with the same name," I said.

"It is," she granted, "and Taniwha Springs is also located on it about six kilometers off in the distance." Gesturing to our left, she added, "You should see its foine natural springs and watahfowls. On a nearby hilltop theah also is an example of an ancient fortified Maori Pa site, which you moight foind interisting."

A few minutes passed in silence; then the bus followed the highway around a sharp right turn. "That must be the lake," I ventured, pointing to the scene beyond the opposite window.

Nodding, she said, "Soon we'll be coming to Fairy Springs, which is the home of the Patupaiarehe, the Maori fairy folk, wheah two million litahs of crystal cleah watah well up iviry owah of the dye through black obsidian and whoite pumice sands."

"Just beyond it is Rainbow Springs," she resumed. "Theah several huge pools have been stocked with rainbow and brown trout."

"How do they manage to keep them stocked?" I countered. "Those fish are cannibalistic."

"They keep the viry young fish in nursery pools," she answered. "Alongside the pools are native ferns, aviaries containing various species of native birds, some deer, and even a few woild pigs. It's a viry colorful and interisting plice to visit."

"The highway has become Fairy Springs Road," I announced abruptly.

"Yis, but the highwye will tuhn off of it shortly," she predicted.

In fact, the bus traveled over streets bearing several different names during the time that it followed the highway's meandering route past Kuirau Park and the Rotorua Public Hospital to the point where it turned from Ranolf Street onto Amo Hau Street. Then it swung from the highway and stopped beside the station that adjoined the New Zealand Railroad System, but the bus driver didn't announce the name of the stop. Eventually, I was to learn that New Zealand's bus drivers rarely announced the names of stops.

Rotorua

Meanwhile, milady had become involved in a study of the passengers waiting to board the bus. To gain her attention, I purposefully grasped the handle of my briefcase and mumbled, "Well, nobody said so, but this must be Rotorua."

Finally noticing my ready attitude, she exclaimed, "Oy'm sorry! Oy forgot that you git off here." Then she jumped to her feet and stepped into the aisle.

"Thank you," I murmured, moving into the aisle. "I hope that you enjoy the remainder of your trip."

"I hope that you enjoy your visit to New Zealand," she called after me.

I stopped, turned toward her with a teasing smile, and warned: "Don't forget your carryon."

"No, Oy won't foahgit it," she promised; then, as an afterthought, she added, "Thyank ye jist the sime."

An inquiry directed to a man at the bus station elicited the information: "There's a travel office just a short hike up Fenton Street."

Even though the short hike proved to be a mere four blocks, my heavy luggage made it seem twice as far. Just beyond the intersection of Haupapa and Fenton Streets, I came upon the small, single-story structure, and, as the man had also stated, it was located directly across the street from the Civic Theatre. Through one of the large, plate-glass windows of the travel office, I saw a young man in a neat business suit standing behind a counter at the far end of the room.

After a short struggle at the glazed entry door, I managed to insert my luggage and myself into the room. "Good day," the man cordially called to me.

"True," I agreed. "Is it also true that you can help me find economical lodging for the coming night?"

"I suspect that I can be of help," he answered. "What kind of lodging do you have in mind?"

"Something clean and comfortable," I replied.

"Well, the Princes Gate meets those requirements," he said, "and it isn't too costly."

"What is your definition of 'too costly'?" I countered with a faint smile.

"Well, uhm," he mumbled. "Are you by yourself?"

"Yes," I answered.

"Then you can get into the Princes Gate for thirty-seven dollars," he said. "Furthermore, it's located just around the corner, so there'll be no cab fare."

"How far around the corner?" I asked.

"It's directly behind the Civic Theatre on Arawa Street," he responded with a gesture toward the huge building across the street. "It's just a short walk."

"That's less than a short hike, isn't it?" I asked. Then, in response to his puzzled expression, I explained: "The last man to give me directions told me that it was just a short hike to this office, and it seemed more like a long journey to me."

He glanced down at my luggage, nodded sympathetically, and added: "It can't be more than a couple of blocks."

"That's half as far as the short hike," I observed, "so I suspect that I can make it."

"Then you'll take the room?" he inquired with his head cocked to one side like an owl.

"Yes," I replied. "It's unlikely that anything can be gained by shopping around for a better rate."

"It's a good rate," he insisted. "If you like, I can take the payment." Then, in response to my startled expression, he added, "I'll give you a receipt, of course."

After submitting the money and stowing the receipt, I asked, "Is there a public telephone in the vicinity?"

"No," he replied, "but this one is available for local calls."

"Despite the close proximity of the hotel," I said, "I still would like to call a taxicab, because I'll want to convey some soiled clothing from the hotel to the coin-operated laundry that I passed during the trip from the station."

"I'll call one for you, if you like," he offered.

"I'll gladly reimburse you for the call and your time," I murmured while withdrawing a handful of change from one pocket.

Thrusting both palms toward me in a pushing motion, he commanded, "Put your money away. A local call will cost this office nothing, and there certainly will be no charge for a simple courtesy."

"I was afraid of that," I responded with a smile, "but I would never take advantage of your kindness if a public telephone were accessible."

"Think nothing of it," he said. Then, picking up the instrument, he dialed a number and requested a cab for me.

The cab delivered me to the hotel, which proved to be an old, two-story, wooden structure conforming closely to the designs of the Victorian era. After instructing the driver to wait, I passed through its wide entrance, turned left to the desk, and was greeted by a cordial, "Good day, sir," by the middle-aged man behind it. Responding in kind, I submitted the receipt to him.

Glancing perfunctorily at it, he genially said, "We are glad to have you as a guest, Mr. Tyrrell."

After I had registered, the man placed a key on the counter before me and said, "To get to your room, go through that double doorway and cross the lounge. In its far wall you'll find a smaller doorway letting into a hallway that will lead you directly to it. Please let me know if you need anything."

After placing my luggage in my room, I returned to the cab with a bag of laundry and said, "Please drive to the coin-operated laundry located about three blocks beyond the intersection of this street with Fenton Street. It'll be on our right." He nodded amiably, set the vehicle in motion, and delivered me and my burden to the curb in front of the laundry within three minutes.

The female attendant at the laundry, a slender, dark-haired veteran of some forty-five Austral summers, obligingly instructed me in the finer points of operating the equipment. Even though she pointed out that some of her customers dropped off their laundry, which she ran through the system, I chose to launder my own soiled raiment. From casual observations, I found her to be a self-driving and diligent worker, but that seemed to be characteristic of most New Zealanders.

Since my New Zealand currency was at a critical ebb, I decided to more effectively employ the time that normally would be wasted in waiting for the wash cycle to be completed, so I quickly traversed the few blocks to the railroad station and reserved a seat on the bus that was scheduled to depart for Wellington at 8:30 the following morning. At that point, seeing that insufficient time remained for me to find a bank, exchange my traveler's checks, and return to the laundry in time to transfer my wet wash to a dryer, I crawled into one of the cabs that stood beside the station. As Lady Fortune chose to dictate, I not only visited a bank but disposed of the cab driver and strode triumphantly into the laundry just as the wash cycle ended.

The energetic attendant insisted on helping me transfer the damp clothing to a dryer. Consequently, since it became apparent that there was no way I could stop her, I surrendered to her. Such is the generous nature of many New Zealanders. After the dryer completed its assignment, I sorted and folded the items of clothing; then I tucked them into a plastic bag that the attendant insisted on providing for no charge beyond the nominal $6.75 for the use of the equipment.

After a brief wait at the curb in front of the laundry, I hailed the driver of a passing cab. "Where to, sir?" he inquired as I crawled into it.

"The Princes Gate, please," I answered with a smile.

After a quick double take, he pensively set the vehicle in motion, while I deliberately refrained from explaining my reason for the short cab ride.

When the vehicle stopped in front of the hotel, I requested, "Please wait for me, because I'll return as soon as I can stow this bag." And he nodded with the air of one who finally saw reason in my madness.

Upon returning, I said, "Please drop me off in the vicinity of the thermal area."

He stared ahead toward the end of the block where Arawa Street narrowed and asked, "Do yuh mane the gahdens?"

Later I learned that he must have been referring to the Government Gardens directly ahead of us. At the time I wasn't aware of that, so the question puzzled me. Nevertheless, I philosophically nodded. Then, more definitively, I added: "Please take me to the place where the geysers and mud pots are located."

Turning thoughtful eyes toward me, he then slowly swung the cab about in a U-turn. At Fenton Street he turned left and continued past the railroad station and the diagonal Te Ngae Road intersection, which formed the far boundary of the Arawa Park Race Course. There I began to detect a change in the atmosphere.

Looking across at the driver, I asked, "What is that strange odor?"

"What odah?" he countered.

"Am I smelling sulfur?" I rejoined.

He looked toward me with a whimsical expression and replied, "It could be, but Oy don't riley know, because Oy can't smill it."

"That cinches it," I responded with a chuckle. "It is sulfur, and you've become so used to the odor that you can no longer detect it."

"Aye, that could be," he granted. "By the wye, Oy'll tike ye up to the top gite; that wye ye kin walk downhill through the displyes." Pausing briefly, he looked at me and continued: "Ye will come out at the point wheah this strait beends."

Momentarily "wheah this strait beends" puzzled me, because I had been taught that a straight has no bends, but Pancho quickly set me straight without throwing one curve.

"From theah," the man resumed, "ye kin eithah walk back oah call a cab. The attendant at the gite will be glad to call one foah ye."

From the bend, the highway was called Hemo Road. Midway along it, the cab veered into a driveway, where we parted company after a mutually satisfactory exchange of currency.

It was already mid-afternoon when I stepped in front of the window of the small box office that housed the brown-skinned ticket vendor, so she informed me, "Since the Maori Arts and Crafts are unattended at this time of day, you have to pay only the four-dollar fee for entry into the thermal area."

I submitted the sum, and she presented a ticket to me. "Thank you," I murmured. "But where do I go from here?" And she pointed toward the nearest of two gateways.

En route to the thermal area, small signs designated byways that led to several small wooden structures, one of which was identified as "Model Pa." Another sign bore the words *Mauri Arts and Crafts*, and still another was identified as the Kiwi House. There, I found a lone kiwi in what a pamphlet called "its simulated nocturnal environment, which the shy, flightless bird prefers." Sometime later I learned that the Model Pa was a replica of a pre-European fortified Maori Pa (village).

A winding, asphalt pathway led down to the bubbling mud pools, boiling springs, silica terraces, and geysers. At frequent intervals, small signs warned pedestrians not to stray from the beaten path. The famous Pohuto Geyser wasn't doing its thing, but I saw the site, whatever that may mean. Meanwhile, the atmosphere continued to carry a strong stench of gaseous sulfur, which must have been escaping into it from the clouds of vapor billowing up from several widely separated fumaroles.

Drops of rain were falling in a widely scattered pattern by the time I arrived at the "Little Village," where a brown-skinned woman was stationed at the window of another small box office. Some of the raindrops were leaving wet spots the size of quarters on my blue windbreaker, so I dashed from the thermal area into the nearby shack of an ice-cream vendor. While purchasing an ice-cream cone to justify my presence there, I speculatively scanned the adjoining small park through a large, plate-glass window. As if in response to a silent prayer, the sun's rays burst through a crevice in the feathery clouds and lit up the area like a heavenly spotlight, so I carried my purchase out to a picnic table that stood under a huge tree. Seating myself, I began to consume the delicacy while watching the playful antics of half a dozen small children. Meanwhile, the sun and the clouds became engaged in an infinitely old conflict, so I wiped my lips and their surrounding beard with a paper napkin and hurriedly arose. A quick glance detected a metal waste container that stood against the trunk of the tree, so I tossed the crushed napkin into it in passing and pushed on toward the business district with several wary glances across my right shoulder at the threatening overcast.

From force of habit, I turned right from Froude Street onto the near side of Fenton Street and successively noted several approaching cabs, but all of them were engaged, probably by passengers who had walked to work in the morning. Nonetheless, I continued to stride along the right side of the street and anxiously watched for an available cab while the oncoming clouds began to shed a few tears. Abruptly, a bright light flashed on in the murky interior of my cranium, and, in response to it, I stopped, watched for a break in the traffic, and dashed across the street to the opposite sidewalk. Scarcely a minute passed before an available cab approached from behind me, and I immediately flagged the driver.

"Hello, neighbor," the man greeted me. "It appeahs that Oy arroived in jist the nick o' toime, because that cloud looks like it means business."

"You are the proverbial Good Samaritan," I responded with a laugh. "But I could have done this earlier, if I had not forgotten that you New Zealanders drive on the wrong side of the road."

"The wrong soide of the road...," he began; then his eyes settled on my teasing grin. "Oh, yees," he rumbled in chorus with a roll of thunder, "so you were walking on the othah soide of the road, the wrong soide of the road." And he laughed heartily.

"The right side," I insisted with a chuckle.

Suddenly the windshield was awash in a virtual downpour. "This is not a rine!" he exclaimed, cautiously applying the brakes. "This is a bloody rivah!" Almost instantly it subsided, but it renewed the assault within another block. "Jist a bunch o' bloody showahs," he muttered with an air of finality.

Fortune dictated that I was to be spattered by only a few drops of the warm liquid as I dashed from the cab to the cover of the hotel's entrance. As the man said, "Jist a bunch o' bloody showahs."

The hands of the lobby's clock were approaching the hour of seven when I strolled from the building into the sparkling rays of the slowly declining sun. Since the laundry's attendant had told me that the Lewisham Restaurant served the best dinners in town, I headed in that direction. At least, I headed in the direction that she had told me to take from the hotel. Apparently New Zealanders direct visitors much more effectively than the average American does, because her instructions guided me directly to it.

Like most New Zealand restaurants, it was small with no more than a dozen tables, of which, only one was occupied. I stopped at the small podium and patiently waited, but no maitre d' appeared.

Finally, the middle-aged man at the occupied table caught my eye and said, "He's in the kitchen, but he shouldn't be long, because he's about to bring us owah suppahs."

"Thank you," I responded.

Then my eyes searched the dimly lighted room for the most likely location of the kitchen and found that it appeared to be hidden behind two of the room's walls. They not only enclosed its far right-hand corner but formed an opposing cul-de-sac, which accommodated three small dining tables. Shortly the door in one wall of the kitchen swung open, and a relatively young man emerged into the cul-de-sac, turned sharply toward the dining room, trotted down two steps, and approached the couple.

"Your meals will be ready in a few minutes," he informed them. "Meanwhile, is there anything that I can get for you? Some hot tea, perhaps?"

The man turned questioning eyes to his pretty and somewhat buxom companion. Then, as if in response to a telepathic communication from her, he answered, "No, thank you."

The waiter bowed almost imperceptibly, turned away, and strode purposefully toward me. Since he seemed to be the only member of the service staff, he appeared to be functioning not only as a waiter but as the head waiter and host. En route, he automatically swept a menu from the stack on the nearby cashier's counter, where, I later discovered, he also served as the cashier. Meanwhile, the man's dark-eyed gaze acquired an all-too-familiar intensity until my equally intense gaze forced it to turn evasively to the menu just before he came to a stop before me.

"One for dinner?" he inquired with a slightly foreign accent.

Even though his dark suit needed pressing and his black shoes lacked a recent shine, I glanced down uneasily at my dusty Hush Puppies. Self-consciously, I ran one hand along one thigh of my worn blue jeans while the fingers of the other one probed tentatively at the open collar of my blue shirt. In fact, my only gesture toward formality had been to belatedly don my travel-stained, blue windbreaker.

"Do you serve dinners to transients?" I asked.

"We serve people as they come," he responded with a thin smile. Turning about, he led me along the only aisle past the nicely attired couple and up the two steps onto the elevated cul-de-sac. After placing the menu on the nearest table, he inquired, "Will this be satisfactory?"

I took stock of the tables with their arrays of matching white tablecloths, white cloth napkins, gleaming silverware, and sparkling wine glasses. "This is great," I murmured. Meanwhile, he silently stood by while I seated myself and opened the menu. "Is this a German restaurant?" I inquired.

"Well, sort of," he replied. "It's Austro-Hungarian. The cheef is from Austria, and I'm from Hungary."

"Then you are partners," I ventured.

"Well, sort of," he replied. "Would you like some of our good German beer?"

"I don't usually drink alcoholic beverages," I answered, "but let's make this a special occasion."

Returning shortly with a stein full of beer, he asked, "Are you prepared to order now?"

"Yes," I replied, "I would like the Wiener schnitzel dinner."

After delivering the order to the kitchen, he returned to my table and prepared to light the candle in the tall, pot-metal candlestick that stood to one side of it.

"That's not necessary," I protested. "Besides, I am much less conspicuous in the twilight."

Nevertheless, he silently completed the task; then he stood back and watched the flickering flame until it burned steadily. Turning a whimsical smile on me, he whispered, "Actually, I'm trying to tease a few more customers into the house."

The dinner proved to be excellent; furthermore, the tab for it, a fine chocolate mousse, a beer, and the tip amounted to less than twenty-five dollars, about thirteen U.S. dollars.

It was early in the following morning when, with my luggage in hand, I lumbered into the hotel's lounge in search of a telephone and encountered three elderly Maori men engaged in a slowly progressing series of conversations on the only public telephone. In other words, they were conducting them in relays, and the instrument must have already changed hands many times, because each member of the trio was constantly responding to his afterthoughts. When they finally ran out of words, mostly Maori, the last speaker placed the phone on its hanger. Meantime, another member pushed one of the two ornate swinging doors open into the lobby, and the trio straggled in an erratic single file through the opening.

As I hurried toward the telephone, I happened to notice a pair of black oxford shoes standing on the carpet in front of what might have passed for a Louis XIV chair. I swung about to call to the men, but the thought occurred to me that one of them might decide to start another series of endless telephone conversations, so I turned about and approached the instrument. Unfortunately, there were no instructions on how to operate the *bleeped* thing, so I regretfully followed them into the lobby. After immediately locating the shoeless culprit, I concluded that I must be a good detective. (Well, okay, so it wasn't that big a deal, since he was the only shoeless one.)

Looking from the small senior citizen's sock-clad feet to his amiable features, I teasingly informed him: "There's a pair of black shoes standing on the carpet in front of a chair in the lounge with nobody in them."

He cast a guilty glance at the toes of his socks, which immediately turned up. "Oh, yees," he muttered, "they ah moine. Oy foahgot to put theem on."

My Hush Puppies were close behind the socks when they arrived at the shoes, because José and Pancho had advised me to make a victim of the obligated little reprobate, so I asked, "Will you please explain to me how this telephone works?"

"Oy'll be glad to," he responded with an eager smile.

"Wheah do you want to call? Long distance?"

"No, not long distance," I responded with what seemed to be a guilty expression. "I want to call a cab."

"Weel, theah's nuthin' to it, thin," he insisted with an obvious air of disappointment. "Jist pick it up and dial the numbah."

"But how much money do I have to insert?" I countered. "And where is the *bleeped* coin slot?"

"Don't need no money," he answered patiently. "Heah, Oy'll call it foah ye, if ye loik." And he did.

"Thank you very much," I mumbled somewhat abjectly. How else does a big city Caucasian react after he has been outsmarted by a Melanesian from the New Zealand sticks?

Meanwhile, the other two brown-skinned characters had joined us, and we absently watched while my benefactor pulled on his shoes. Then, without an invitation, the trio followed me through the swinging doors into the lobby, on through the entrance, and all of the way out to the sidewalk that adjoined the curb. There I lowered my luggage while they clustered congenially about me. Apparently, they had committed themselves to seeing that I got safely aboard the cab. After all, they may have had a point, because even a Caucasian of average intelligence might wonder what a Caucasian dummy might do when he tried to climb into a cab, especially a Caucasian who had proved to be incapable of calling a cab on the simplest of foreign telephones.

Since the Maoris seemed to be a sociable lot, I endeavored to be sociable, and I found it to be a bit of a chore, since I had rarely engaged in social repartee since the advent of the Unknown. It proved to be an exhilarating experience even though I played the role of a listener throughout most of the time while we waited for the cab. From their comments, I gathered that they were retired ex-residents of Rotorua who were visiting the area and renewing old friendships. They seemed to delight particularly in pointing out to each other the changes that had occurred in the town since they had resided in it.

When the conversation began to lag, I looked at my benefactor and asked, "What kind of business were you engaged in?"

"Business," he muttered uneasily. "Oy've neevah bin in a business. Oy was a butchah."

Sensing that I had unintentionally downgraded the man in his own eyes, I cast about for a way to alleviate the situation, and it proved to be easier than I expected.

"But that's a business," I insisted, "a very skilled one, in fact."

The words must have had the desired effect, because he began to describe enthusiastically some of his adventures as a butcher in Gisborne. I particularly wanted to ask him if he knew the lady who had been my companion throughout most of the trip to Rotorua, but we had not introduced ourselves, so I lacked her name. At that point the taxicab arrived, so the chatter terminated briefly.

Glancing down with the intention of picking up my luggage, I found that it was being conveyed to the rear of the cab by two of my associates, while the third one stood by to raise the trunk's lid as soon as the driver unlocked it. After the driver quickly accomplished that task, he stood by and amiably directed the trio's combined efforts in stowing the heavy luggage. When it was in place, he slammed home the lid and proceeded to exchange a barrage of friendly words with them. To me it was obvious that they viewed themselves as equal countrymen who spoke a common language and fully understood each other despite their racial heritages.

Upon arriving at the station, I found the hour to be much too early to board the bus. In fact, it had not even arrived yet, so I went in search of someone who would check my luggage.

"It's too early to accept any of the luggage that goes on that bus," insisted the man in the warehouse.

"But isn't there some place where it can be checked temporarily?" I asked. "I want to get some breakfast, and I don't want to lug these heavy bags with me."

"Slip theem onto that sheelf," he suggested, pointing to an open bin with several other bags in it.

"But couldn't they be included with those other bags by mischance and shipped out on the wrong bus?" I countered.

"Naw, I'll keep an eye on them," he promised.

"That's above and beyond the call of your duty," I rejoined, "so please accept this as a token of my appreciation." And I pressed a dollar bill into his reluctant palm. He followed me through the wide doorway of the warehouse with his hand still extended, but I ignored it. "By the way," I said, "do you happen to know if there is a good restaurant in the immediate vicinity?"

"At this toime o' dye," he muttered with a doubtful expression. After thoughtfully scratching his tawny topknot, he added, "Oy doubt if theah's any koind of a restaurant open yeet. But these boys moight know o' one." Then he pointed to four brown-skinned boys who were sprawled in various relaxed attitudes on a long bench that stood against one wall of the station.

"Do ye know wheah this man can git a bite to eat?" he called to them.

Their responses were simultaneous and very clamorous, so I threw up my hands in despair, but my companion readily interpreted their inputs.

"They sye theah's a bikery open at this toime o' dye," he informed me, "but it doesn't serve hot meals, jist rolls and coffee owah tay."

"Well, that's better than nothing," I observed. "Where is it located?"

Since the boys had been listening, another barrage of conflicting instructions erupted from them, so I looked appealingly at my interpreter.

"Come with me," he commanded. Then, leading me around one corner of the station, he pointed east along Amo Hau Street. "See that big rid soign?" he asked.

"Yes," I replied.

"Weel, the bikery is located jist beyond it," he said.

"Thank you," I murmured gratefully and struck out toward the red sign.

While I was striding rapidly along the sidewalk, José and Pancho ruminated about how generous and cooperative many New Zealanders had been. "The biggest problem is to avoid being swamped by courtesy and kindnesses," Pancho observed.

Upon approaching my objective, I observed a sign bearing the words *American Doughnuts*, and my pace quickly accelerated. Meanwhile, José exultantly exclaimed, "That's for us!"

Swinging open the glazed door, I beheld a large, well-lighted room with several pieces of baking equipment located about the rear of it and a small cashier's counter near the middle of it. As I approached the counter, a young woman swung from the rear area toward it, and we arrived on opposite sides of it simultaneously.

"Can Oy heelp you?" she inquired.

"I would like about a hundred American doughnuts and a glass of milk," I responded with teasing eyes.

"We haven't biked any doughnuts yeet," she murmured, "and we have only coffee owah tay."

My enthusiasm collapsed, but it was due more to the girl's intent stare and her cold, distant attitude than to the lack of doughnuts. "Okay," I muttered, "then make it a sweet roll and a cup of coffee."

After placing my purchases atop the bare, plastic surface of a small table, I seated myself on the chair that stood beside it, while Pancho and José mulled over the apparent presence of the Unknown. "But that was not the first of such observations in Rotorua," insisted Pancho.

"Right," José agreed. "In fact, similar responses were the main reasons for Al's quick decision to reserve a seat on the morning bus."

During the ensuing discussion, the roll and the coffee disappeared without my knowledge. While I was collecting the debris from the quick repast, José philosophically suggested, "So let's add this misadventure to our growing collection of misadventures."

Back at the station, I sought out the friendly warehouseman, but before I could utter a word, he called: "Yoah luggage is on the Weelington bus, suh!"

"Thank you!" I called back. "You've been very helpful."

"Have a noice roide," he responded with a smile and a friendly salute.

"It's amazing how much the normal behavior of people can influence one's spirits," Pancho observed as I strolled toward the area where the bus stood.

"How would you know anything about normal behavior?" José countered caustically.

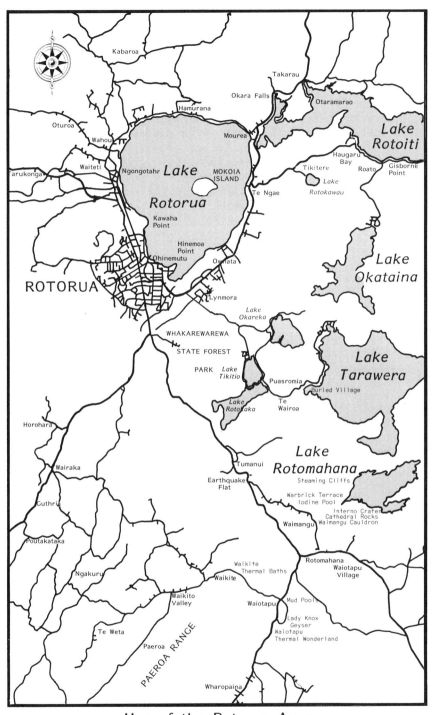

Map of the Rotorua Area

4

Rotorua to Wellington

While impatiently pacing the pavement beside the bus, I noticed a young man sitting on one of the wooden benches that stood against the brick wall of the station. He was clad in the usual suntan shorts, short-sleeve sport shirt, a pair of three-quarter-length wool socks, and a pair of highly polished brown, oxford sport shoes. Since the socks had been drawn up to exactly the same point below each knee and folded down identical distances, he appeared to be a particularly fastidious individual. That observation seemed to be borne out to some extent by the precise manner in which he had positioned the duffel bag beside him, its lines conforming strictly to those of the bench. My observations induced José and Pancho to assure me that he must be a particularly neat and organized young man.

But those observations were not what first attracted my attention to him; it was the extremely deep indentation at the center line of his lower lip. Some romantic young women might view those lips in the light of an inverted heart and be intrigued by them. But what man knows how any young woman will react to a young man? Certainly not this one, because women of all ages have always been enigmas to him.

The bus driver eventually appeared beside the bus with a clipboard clasped between his left forearm and his chest and purposefully positioned himself beside the open doorway of the vehicle. Quickly grasping the handle of the duffel bag, the young man arose and advanced toward him, and I swung in behind the youth. After accepting the young man's seat reservation, the driver glanced speculatively at the seating chart on the clipboard, marked it, and said, "Take seat four dee."

As the young man moved toward the doorway of the bus, I stepped forward and presented my travel authorizations to the driver. After inspecting them, he returned them, marked the seating chart, and said, "You may take seat four cee."

And that was how a man of some twenty-five years and a septuagenarian became seatmates during a day-long bus ride from Rotorua to Wellington. Since there was a large gap in our ages, I assumed that the bus trip would be a quiet one. Furthermore, I rarely initiate a conversation with a stranger, so I prepared to monitor the ongoing discussion (argument) between José and Pancho regarding our misadventures in Rotorua.

"Are you going to Weellington?" a nicely modulated voice inquired from beside me.

Turning toward its source and ignoring the combined claims of Pancho and José that he must be a local lad, I answered, "Yes. Is that also your destination?"

"Yees," he replied, "and I surely hope that we get going, because the bus is already late getting started, and it's sheduled to arrive in Weellington at eight-thirty this evening."

"Twelve hours is a long time to spend on a bus," I muttered dispassionately.

Agreeing with a nod, he offered his right hand and added, "My name is Jan Hoffman."

After I reciprocated in a like manner, he turned away and directed his attention through the window at the activities alongside the bus while I absently studied my clasped hands. In the interim, despite the man's uncharacteristic name, José and Pancho concluded that, because of his intermittent pronunciations of the letter *e*, he must be a New Zealander.

"After all, the Dutch featured in the history of the country, too," Pancho reasoned.

"But not within the last two hundred years," José contended.

Propitiously, Jan turned away from the window and said, "No doubt you are visiting New Zealand."

"Yes," I replied.

"Did you visit the Whakarewarewa Thermal Area?" he asked.

"If that's the name of the local thermal area, then I visited it," I answered, "but the geyser wasn't in a mood to erupt at the time."

"It's called the Pohutu Geyser," he informed me unnecessarily, "and you would have been amazed to see it shoot thirty-two meters into the air."

"During a visit to Yellowstone National Park, I saw Old Faithful perform," I said, "and it reputedly reached a height of one hundred eighty feet."

"How often does it erupt?" he inquired.

"In nineteen eighty-three it was reported to be erupting at approximately one and one-quarter hour intervals," I replied.

"Hmm," he mumbled thoughtfully. "That's quite often." Following a momentary pause, he asked, "Have you seen the Wairakei Thermal Station yet?"

"No," I ruefully admitted. "From what I saw around Rotorua, I concluded that the entire thermal area had been oversold, so that was one reason why I advanced my scheduled departure by a day."

"I doubt that any of the thermal sites have been oversold," he opined. "However, about eighty kilometers from Rotorua, the highway passes right by the Wairakei Thermal Station, so you'll be able to see it from the bus."

"Hmm," I exhaled. "That's about fifty miles, so the thermal activity must be distributed over a rather large area."

With an affirmative nod, he said, "In fact, this town practically sits on a volcanic fault extending from Mount Ruapehu in the south to White Island, which is located fifty kilometers off the north coast. Along it are several other active thermal areas, such as Waimangu, Waiotapu, Orakei Korako, and Hell's Gate-Tikitere, some of which produce spectacular geysers, violently boiling springs, bubbling pools of mud, and varicolored silica terraces."

"Nature is surely wasting an awful lot of energy in this area," I observed with a smile.

"Not all of it is wasted," he rejoined. "For example, some of the energy beneath Rotorua has been tapped by bore holes to provide hot water and central heating systems for most of the hotels and many of the larger homes. And a large paper mill at Kawerau is powered by energy derived from thermal bore holes."

Since Jan's revelations were so interesting, I had failed to notice that the driver had finally assumed his post until the engine violently protested against being wakened.

"Finally we are getting under way," Jan muttered.

"Will there be any points of interest along the way other than the thermal station?" I inquired.

"The Whakarewarewa State Forest Park will appear to the left of the highway immediately after we pass the thermal area," he predicted.

"No doubt that will consist of native trees," I suggested.

"Very few native trees remain in New Zealand," he said. "Unfortunately, most of them have been harvested for their timber and to clear the land for pasturage. At the beginning of this century, many varieties of imported trees were planted in the park to determine the most suitable substitutes for the rapidly disappearing native trees. The beauty of the Redwood Grove particularly attracts the local hikers.

"And those trees were imported from Northern California," I speculated.

"Yees," he said. "Within one hundred kilometers of Rotorua, there are one hundred sixty thousand hectares of government-controlled plantations and two hundred twenty thousand hectares of privately controlled plantations. So far, the soil and climatic conditions produce mature Radiata pine trees within twenty-five to thirty years, and they can be used commercially from the time they are ten years old. It takes sixty years, however, to produce mature Douglas fir trees."

"Surely the timber is not exported," I ventured.

"No," he said, "the Waipa State Sawmill is New Zealand's largest sawn timber mill, and it's located just off this highway in the State Forest Park. The Kinleith Mill produces plywood, pulp, paper, and sawn timber. At Kawerau, the Tasman Mill produces pulp, paper, and sawn timber, while the Wakatane Board Mills specialize in cardboard, heavy paper production, and paper recycling. But I suspect that some sawn timber is exported."

"You appear to know a lot about the New Zealand timber industry," I observed.

"It has been my business for the last four months," he responded with a shy smile.

Despite my glance of increased interest, he failed to expand on the statement. Instead, he said, "There still are a few native forests. For example, Lake Okataina is almost surrounded by native bush, extending from its shoreline to the skyline. That is only part of a large scenic reserve, which extends across adjacent Lake Tarawera and all of the way up Mount Tarawera to the edge of the volcano."

"Where is all of this fantastic landscape located?" I wistfully inquired. "More specifically, that is."

"Most of it is about ten kilometers to the left of the highway," he replied, "but it is accessible from Rotorua only by means of the Lake Tarawera Road. You should have traveled along that road; it's very scenic."

"How did so much native forest escape the sawyers?" I inquired.

"The Lake Okataina Scenic Reserve was ceded to the government by the Ngati Tarawhai in 1931," he answered. "It contains large areas of virgin forest, consisting almost entirely of the podocarp-hardwood type of trees, such as the Rimu, Totara, Tawa, Kahikatea, Rewa Rewa, and Konini." Pausing, he cast a quizzical glance toward me and added, "The lake's shores also support some Pohutukawa." Apparently he relished the locutions of the exotic names.

"Huh," I grunted. "I strongly suspect that the novice tree student finds the native names of those trees even more difficult to spell and pronounce than their Latin equivalents." With a gratified smile, he then turned toward the window while I passed the time by speculating on the names of the few native trees that we passed from time to time.

After several minutes he turned to me and said, "You really should have seen the Buried Village. To get to it, you would've traveled along the road that I mentioned. It passes through a particularly scenic area with the park on one side and fine farms on the other. Then it skirts the beautiful Blue and Green Lakes just before entering the Te Wairoa Valley."

"Are those lakes very large?" I asked.

"Green Lake is about one kilometer wide and four kilometers long," he replied. "And Blue Lake is about a third as large, but it is four hundred seventeen meters deep."

"Jumping jelly beans!" I exclaimed. "That's a depth of over twelve hundred feet."

With a faint smile he added, "The road passes the village just before it terminates at a boat ramp on Lake Tarawera."

"And the village?" I reminded him with questioning eyes.

"It was buried when Mount Tarawera suddenly erupted in eighteen eighty-six," he responded. "One hundred fifty-three people perished, and the sites of the famous Pink and White Terraces were destroyed."

"The terraces were nearby?" I asked.

"No," he answered, "their sites are located on the north shore of Lake Rotomahana, which is accessible only by boarding a launch that makes a round trip from the ramp on Lake Tarawera to the Waimangu Thermal Valley."

"There appear to be a number of lakes in this area," I remarked.

"There are eleven," he said. "And they range from two hundred seventy-nine to four hundred thirty-seven meters in depth." Then, with his fair features registering a wry grimace, he added: "Not the place to be if one can't swim, eh?"

"Some people have drowned in their ten-foot swimming pools," I countered with a smile.

After a nod he pensively returned to the passing scenery, while I mentally reviewed his information. Meanwhile, the forest on the left side of the highway stopped, but a stand of geometrically spaced trees was visible on a distant slope.

"Very soon we should pass Tumunui Station," Jan interjected into my thoughts. "It's a multimillion-dollar mixed farming enterprise where deer, cattle, sheep, and goats graze on pastures scattered over three thousand hectares of beautiful bush land."

"Probably a government operation," I suggested.

"I don't know," he admitted. "But only the government has that much money in this country's cramped economy." Then he redirected his attention to the changing scenery. But within minutes he turned toward me as if about to make a statement.

"We are approaching another point of interest," I ventured.

"We are approaching the Waimangu Road turnoff, which leads into the Waimangu Thermal Valley," he said. "You really should have seen the Southern Crater as well as Waimangu Caldron, Cathedral Rocks, and the Inferno Crater. Beyond those exotic thermal phenomena are the Iodine Pools, Warbrick Terrace, Steaming Cliffs, and the sites of the Pink and White Terraces."

"I admit to having left too soon," I said, "but do those names truly represent thermal phenomena?"

"Well," he began, "the Waimangu Caldron is the world's largest boiling lake, and the water in the Inferno Crater's lake rises and falls about ten meters every month. Furthermore, there are huge steaming cliffs, plus many boiling springs and fumaroles just beyond them."

Looking thoughtfully at him, I admitted, "Maybe I did leave too precipitously."

He nodded decisively, and we lapsed into another period of silence.

"Waiotapu," I later read aloud from a road sign.

"Besides some mud pools," he responded, "there are the Champagne Pool, the Bridal Veil Falls, and the Lady Knox Geyser, which erupts daily at ten-fifteen in the morning."

"Yeah, I surely left too soon," I ruefully admitted.

He nodded emphatically, and we mentally withdrew to separate worlds for some time. I was roused from mine by the reduced thunder of the engine as the driver swung the vehicle onto the shoulder of the highway and gradually braked it to a stop.

There was a protesting squawk from the public-address system just before the expanded tones of the driver's voice announced: "On the right side of the bus is the Wairakei Power Station, which was constructed to utilize some of New Zealand's natural thermal energy. Bore holes were drilled deep into the earth to tap a four-hundred-fifty-degree Fahrenheit volcanic steam field. This, however, is only one of the geothermal sources utilized to produce four percent of the nation's electric power."

There wasn't a lot to see, just a number of interconnecting, large-diameter pipes and valves from which a few wisps of steam spiraled slowly upward. And there were some minor supporting structures. What particularly impressed me was its cleanliness. There were no columns of jet-black smoke billowing up from towering masonry stacks into the pristine upper atmosphere to create acid rain and other corrosive polluters of the earth and its atmosphere.

"No huge piles of coal with their clouds of dust to leave drab imprints on surrounding structures," Jan interposed as if reading my mind.

"Uh-huh," I grunted. "That must have been a very interesting project. At one time I was a fluid systems specialist in the aerospace industry, but we were confronted with design problems that involved cryogenic fluids as well as extremely hot ones."

"That was in America, wasn't it?" he inquired.

"Yes," I answered, "but I was also a landing gear specialist at one time. Consequently, I was merely a mechanical engineer in a field that doesn't begin to possess as much potential as the burgeoning electronics field does."

"I'm glad that I chose it," he murmured. "In fact, I've found it very interesting."

"In what phase of it are you involved?" I inquired with increased interest.

"I came to New Zealand on a scholastic assignment," he replied. "During the last four months I've been working as a computer programmer for a timber company to gain experience in the application of what I have learned in the university. Now that I've finished that assignment, I'm on my way back to Holland for six more months of academic work, after which I hope to receive a master's degree."

"Hmm," I remarked. "That sounds like a lot of scholastic work."

"Yes, I've been very busy for a long time," he muttered, "not only during my advanced education but before it. In Holland the universities accept only those students whose lower-school scholastic ratings are in the upper ten to fifteen percent, so I had to work very hard to qualify."

"Apparently you've succeeded," I remarked. "Not only do you speak English very well, but what you say implies that your mind is effectively organized."

"Thank you," he responded, inclining his head forward in a small bow. "Of course, I studied German too, so I also speak it fluently."

I glanced sharply at his bowed, blond head and almost asked if both Dutch and Frisian are spoken in the Netherlands, but Pancho wouldn't allow me to reveal our ignorance. "At one time I could read and interpret both French and Spanish," I said, "but I've never been able to speak either of them fluently."

We mentally shifted gears for several minutes; then he fixed speculative eyes on my eyes and asked, "Is it true that some American athletes are granted scholarships to attend American universities? And do they study only physical education?" he added with a pained expression. Sensing it, he endeavored to hide it behind the palm of one hand while adding, "Another American told me that, but it seemed so incredible that I'm afraid I doubted him."

"Apparently it's true," I admitted reluctantly. "At least it's reported to be true of those large universities that strongly promote basketball and American football. Furthermore, some alumni associations have been accused of illegally showering star high school athletes with lavish gifts and promises of big salaries to induce them to enroll in their respective universities."

"But what can those athletes do after they graduate from a university with a degree in physical education?" he countered with doubt-filled eyes.

"They can teach physical education," I retorted with a laugh. "That is, if they can speak coherent English."

"That seems to be such a terrible waste," he protested.

Peering cautiously at me, he added, "That money would serve much better if it were used to improve good minds."

I pondered the suggestion for several seconds while absently running my fingers through my beard. "True," I finally conceded, "but different societies often have very different standards. For example, some of those star athletes leave their big universities and go directly into professional basketball or football, where they become instant millionaires. Obviously, American standards have slipped out of synch with those of many other countries. And the erotic mini-movies exhibited by several of America's television channels bear that out."

"Yees, indeed," he interjected. "There's one in particular. . . ." Then, after mentioning the name of a popular American soap opera, he added, "That's a very good example."

"That's a very bad example," I retorted with apologetic eyes.

"Actually, it is," he quickly agreed, "and that's not just my opinion—and yours. A Filipino man, who was an associate, told me that he and his countrymen watch that show just so they can say, 'Thank God, we are not like those people!' "

Fixing an analytical gaze on the man, I was amazed by his apparent emotional involvement with the issue. Obviously he wanted to expand on the statement, and my embarrassed silence provided the opportunity.

"Those Filipino people actually exult in being superior to the characters in that television show," he insisted. "That Filipino man also said, 'As a people, we don't behave that way.' " Then, squaring around and looking directly into my eyes, he added, "To them and to us Hollanders, the welfare of the family is everything, and the efforts of every member of the family are directed toward supporting every other member of the family. In that show everything is done to destroy the family. It's. . . it's unnatural. It's inhuman!" he ended on a strained, high note.

"True," I agreed, "but don't judge all Americans by that stupid TV show. It's designed to display the decadence that is presumed to exist within the ranks of extremely rich Americans. It doesn't represent the behavior of the average American. Very likely many of the average Americans who watch that show have also said, 'Thank God we don't behave that way!' Actually, very few Americans are that decadent."

"We hope," José silently interposed.

"However," I resumed, "I'm convinced that the people who produce such shows are decadent."

With a more relaxed expression and in less strident tones, he resumed: "I've known several Americans besides you, and none of them impressed me as being decadent."

"Thank you from me and all of the other good Americans," I muttered. "Unfortunately, that stupid TV show presents Americans to foreigners in a very unfavorable light, so it should be canceled. As far as I'm concerned, I've already done that because I always turn to another channel whenever my search happens to turn it on. I consider it to be the lowest of lewd trash; furthermore, like liquor and drugs, a constant diet of it is not only addictive, but it can warp the mind."

"Sometimes we have no other choice," he rebounded defensively. "Very often that is the only entertainment being displayed on the two or three available channels."

Mentally chastising myself for an unintentional lack of tact, I said, "It's doubtful that such shows harm stable adults, but I deeply resent the fact that no real effort is being made to protect highly impressionable children from their evil influences."

Nodding absently, he turned away and gazed thoughtfully through the window.

"Are any of those trees native to this country?" I inquired with a gesture toward the passing landscape.

"Yes," he replied. "One was left in that swail. See?" And he pointed to the large, towering trunk of a tree from which a few thick, stubby branches projected from its mid-section upward.

"That looks a lot like a Douglas fir," I observed, "but its pine needles are collected in tighter clumps, and it doesn't have as many clumps as the fir trees have."

"Thousands of imported seedlings have been planted in this area," he said. "In fact, there is one of the projects. See!" Pointing to a grove of relatively young trees, he added, "See how the lower branches have been trimmed away from the trunk for the first ten feet? That's done not only to accelerate the tree's growth but to free the trunk of limbs that could grow to large sizes and create equally large knots in the lumber. Consequently, with fewer and smaller knotholes in the lumber, it should be stronger."

Obediently, I studied the luxuriant evergreen trees, which conformed closely to those among which I used to romp during my trips over Little Mountain to caddy at the Shaughnesy Heights Golf Course in Vancouver, British Columbia.

"Those trees grow much more rapidly here than in their native land," he resumed, "but I don't know how much that affects the strength of the lumber."

"It seems that trees should grow very rapidly in this warm, moist climate," I suggested.

"Some do," he granted, "but there is one native tree that grows very slowly." Holding up his right hand with its thumb and forefinger scarcely parted, he added, "Like that much in one year."

I glanced from the digits to his eyes and said, "That's radially, of course." And he nodded.

"But the wood is hard," I surmised.

"Yes, very hard and very old," he replied. "In fact, some New Zealand trees continue to grow for up to fifteen hundred years."

"That's a long life span," I conceded, "but some of California's redwoods are believed to be twice that old, and another conifer, which grows in the wastelands of another western state, is still older. However, it is small and gnarled, whereas the redwood is tall and straight. And the conifer's habitat is hot and arid, while the redwood favors a mild, moist environment." Fixing my eyes on his, I concluded: "Therefore, many variables appear to affect the growth rates of different trees." And he nodded.

"Many of the New Zealand hardwoods finish beautifully," he resumed. "In fact, some of them are used in the manufacture of fine furniture."

"That surprises me," I admitted. Meanwhile, my mind had been toying with still another function of trees, so I added, "Some of those older trees must have provided shelter for many generations of native mammals. In fact, several changes in the physical characteristics of those mammals must have evolved during fifteen hundred years."

"But there were no native mammals except two species of bats," he protested. "Of course, many species of birds inhabited the trees, but the bats probably lived in caves. With no predator mammals on the ground, several flightless birds evolved, including the ten-foot-high moa, which man hunted to extinction. Also, there were the weta and the long-beaked kiwi, which the people have adopted as the country's emblem."

"Yeah," I interjected. "I saw one of them in the Kiwi House at the thermal area."

"But I doubt that you'll ever see one in the woods," he said. "They are extremely shy creatures, so shy that they feed at night."

At that instant, the public-address system emitted some static and coughed deprecatingly; then the driver's voice announced, "We ah coming to a reest stop, wheah we'll remine foah thirty minits." After braking the big vehicle to a slow stop in front of a tiny post office, he resumed: "You'll foind refreshmints in the building directly ahead and to the leeft o' the bus. The toilets (an archaic word to my American ears) ah located about fifty metahs beyond the cafe. Be shuah to be back in the bus by teen-fifteen, because at teen-sixteen this bus will no longah be heah."

There were amused titters from some of the passengers, and the man responded by turning his angular features toward them and beaming back at them.

"Most of New Zealand's bus drivers seem to have lean, angular features," Pancho observed.

"They may have evolved from a Nordic heritage," José suggested.

"Very likely many of those Nordic ancestors also controlled steering wheels," Pancho speculated, "the helms of Viking vessels.

Jan inserted his right hand into the envelope in the cloth back of the seat in front of him and removed one of two bananas that he had placed there. Then, as an afterthought, he removed the second one and offered it to me.

"No, thank you, Jan," I murmured. "Bananas tend to counterattack my stomach when it attacks them."

Upon descending from the bus, I decided to give my seat partner a break from my society, so I strolled alongside the main street of the small town and took stock of it. Since it consisted of one each of the usual small town's businesses, my mission was quickly accomplished. Turning back, I wandered off in the direction of the rest facilities. There I found the word LADIES painted above the first doorway, so I didn't tarry. Above the next one was painted the word GENTS, and, since I was aware that it was a contraction of the word *gentlemen*, that gave me pause, but I entered it anyway.

The essential equipment proved to be serviceable but not too clean. After washing my hands under the cold water from the lavatory's single faucet, I scanned the barren walls for a paper towel dispenser and discovered an electric blow-dry unit. After staring indecisively at it for a moment, I disgustedly dried my hands along the sides of my blue jeans.

Meanwhile, another male passenger stepped back from the latrine, completed a vital reclamation procedure, then nonchalantly sauntered through the doorway despite the sign on the wall that clearly advised him to wash his hands. I can't make a positive statement, of course, but he must have been familiar with the short-comings of such facilities.

Several minutes later I paused in front of the small cafe and studied the neatly lettered sign on the near side of an A-frame that stood on the sidewalk near the curb. At its top in large letters was the coined word TAKEWAYS, and below it in smaller letters were the words *Hot Meat Pies*, *Mince Pies* (also of meat), and *Hot Cross Buns*." Cold ham and cheese sandwiches, sweet rolls, and freshly brewed coffee or tea were also available.

From the doorway of the establishment, I saw that a glazed showcase domi-nated the far side of the room. Several tables with plastic tops were attended by chrome-plated, stainless steel chairs with plastic seat covers, all of which were indiscriminately distributed about a lineoleum floor. Picking my way between the other passengers to the showcase, I came to a stop beside an urn containing clear, hot water. After a brief study, I determined that the tea customer was expected to select one or more bags of tea from an adjacent tray and place it or them in one of the nearby porcelain cups; then he was to pour some of the hot water from the urn into it. The coffee customer was expected to perform a similar function on the spoonfuls of coffee, which he was expected to deposit in a cup from the open container that stood on the tray beside the tea bags. So much for beverage research in a foreign land down under, but I was seeking a glass of milk.

There must have been few requests for it, because the middle-aged frump who took my order snatched a glass from the back bar and disappeared into a storage room at the rear of the establishment. Eventually she returned with what had been a full glass of milk, a fact attested to by the number of driblets that coursed along the side of the glass.

Meantime, I had been inspecting the cold sandwiches stacked atop the large, glazed display case that stood beside a small, glass-enclosed display case containing hot meat pies. Torn by indecision, I finally tossed discretion to the winds, selected one of the plastic-wrapped cheese sandwiches, and approached the cash register. For slightly less than one New Zealand dollar, about fifty cents (U.S.), the combined purchases proved to be surprisingly economical. In my country just a glass of milk would have cost half a buck, and the cheese sandwich might have cost a buck or more, depending on what the establishment stacked on the plate with it.

Several of the tables were still available, so I systematically placed a paper napkin on the top of one of them, laid the sandwich on it, pulled out an adjacent chair, and seated myself for a peaceful snack. But that was not to be, because the Dutchman suddenly appeared at the opposite side of the table.

"May I share this table with you?" he asked.

"Of course you may," I answered. "Why don't you take that chair in front of you."

He had scarcely seated himself before a senior citizen with clean-shaven but somewhat florid features appeared at the far end of the table and genially inquired, "May Oy join you gintlemin?"

Jan cast a glance toward the man's enviable thatch of snow-white hair; then he looked at me, so I accepted the unspoken invitation to act as the host.

"In light of that unctuous request," I replied, "I don't see how we can refuse, so you may join us if you promise to behave like a gentleman." I was as startled as the Dutchman was by my impulsive impudence, but my teasing smile was intended to belie any malicious intent.

The tall newcomer's hand paused on the back of the chair that he had so confidently withdrawn from the table. After his eyes did a quick double, he appeared to analyze the smile. Then an invisible but inscrutable curtain dropped over them.

"Oy'll behive," he promised like a small boy while settling onto the chair. "Moy nime is Jimes Smith, but moy friends call me Jim."

"You may call us Al and Jan, respectively," I responded with appropriate gestures, "but we'll continue to call you James."

After another double take, he inquired, "What paht of America ah you from?"

Since my caps had just sheared off a large segment of the sandwich, my tongue thrust it into the northwest corner of my mouth so that I could answer the question. "How did you arrive at the conclusion that I'm from America?" I asked.

"Boy certain behavioral characteristics," he retorted obscurely. After responding to my impudent grin with a trace of a smile, he cheerfully inquired, "You ahn't on a touah, ah yuh, Al?"

"I'm not on a professionally organized tour," I answered. "However, I hope to see more of this country than I would see on one of them."

"That's smaht," he observed, biting deeply into his sandwich. "Too often touahs ah nothin' moah than big rip-offs." Nodding his heavy crop of hair as if seconding his own opinion, he then inquired, "Wheah you goin' now?"

"Wellington," I answered.

"Did you know that Weellington is the capital of New Zealand?" Jan interjected to me.

"No," I replied. "So far I've had no reason to wonder about which of the major cities is the capital. If I had, I suspect that I would have selected Auckland as the most likely candidate."

"That's typical," Jim interposed. "Most visitors assume that Auckland is the capital."

"Weellington is more centrally located than Auckland," Jan volunteered, "so it was the best choice."

"Some New Zealanders would question that," Jim countered. But the reason that he didn't pursue the subject may have been linked to New Zealanders' inherent tactfulness. And.that may have been why he changed the subject. "How long do you plan to sty in Weellington?" he asked.

Typically, the persistent questioning aroused suspicions of the Unknown in my mind; however, after a brief inspection of the man's guileless, gray eyes, I replied, "A couple of days maybe."

"That should be enough," he judged. "Then Oy suppose you'll go across to the South Island." And I nodded.

Staring thoughtfully across the top of my head while masticating a large bite from his sandwich, he gulped audibly and stated, "Oy used to live in Queenstown, which is located in the southern paht of the South Island.

"Oh, you should go to Queenstown, Al!" Jan burst forth. "And don't pass up the nearby fjords. They are absolutely fantastic. In fact, they rival the beauty of the Norwegian fjords." I accepted the young man's opinion with respect because I suspected that it was derived from personal experience.

The shy young man may have felt that he was being excluded from the conversation with the advent of Jim, because he persisted in taking part in it. "Were you in business during the time that you lived in Queenstown?" he inquired.

"He was a used-car salesman," I rudely interjected.

The older man directed amazed eyes toward me and sputtered, "How did you know that?"

His response was so unexpected that I was forced to stall for time while pondering a suitable answer. First, I considered admitting that he had the engaging personality of a fine salesman; then I toyed with confessing that I had played a long shot. Instead of either, I said, "I'm psychic—spelled *s-i-c-k-i-c*."

After carefully studying me for several seconds, he confidently muttered, "You plied a long shot."

My expression was intended to be noncommittal, but my smile of approval must have confirmed his suspicion, because a triumphant gleam leaped into his eyes and a smile tugged at one corner of his mouth.

An inspection of my wristwatch induced me to say, "We better move out, men, because the bus driver threatened to leave on schedule regardless of whether all of the passengers are aboard."

Shoving back our chairs, we arose in unison and straggled toward the small doorway, but Jim veered toward me and grasped my left arm. "Most o' those people down theah in Queenstown ah honest," he murmured confidentially, "but Oy hive to wahn you to watch out, because some o' theem moight troy to take advantage of a pahticulahly naive American."

After my eyes warily probed his mischievous orbs, I reluctantly surrendered without a struggle. "According to the good book, the dictionary, that is," I muttered, "the word *naive* is generally defined as dumb."

"Roight on!" he responded with a laugh and a heavy slap on my shoulder before amiably turning away. But he returned immediately, clutched my left arm, and resumed in the same confidential tones, "Howevah, if you should hive any dealin's with those people down theah, tell theem that you know me, and they'll tyke good cayah o' you."

"I'll bet they will," I retorted, "especially when they recall that you were a used-car salesman."

He didn't even wince, so he must have been an excellent used-car salesman. He even responded with a friendly smile when I stopped and allowed him to precede me into the bus. However, he paused long enough to say, "Oy shuahly hope you enjoy yoah visit to New Zealand." Then, with another heavy slap on my shoulder, he agilely climbed into the vehicle.

"Even though Al and that guy are from different hemispheres," José began, "they seem to understand each other."

"That's because both of them have a sense of humor." Pancho remarked.

"You call that nonsense a sense of humor?" José countered. "It's no wonder that I'm the only one of this conclave with a sense of humor."

After restoring a semblance of order in my ivory tower, I found Jan seated beside the window, watching various members of the local gentry as they strolled to and fro, collected in groups, or dashed frantically across the street in pursuit of one or more fleeing brats. Silence endured while practically all of the passengers and a very frustrated bus driver waited for one delinquent passenger. When he finally emerged from a nearby place of business, the driver deliberately gunned the motor to speed him on his way, but the self-centered character glanced calmly toward the pulsating vehicle and continued his slow gait.

"Oy don't know whoy it is," the driver muttered to no one in particular, "but theah's always one o' theem on iviry bus."

Jan and I exchanged smiles, but neither of us chose to mention the driver's earlier dictum, because it obviously had been an empty threat; however, his tolerance proved to be limited. While the latecomer was strolling nonchalantly along the aisle toward his seat, the driver simultaneously raced the motor and released the clutch. As the vehicle lunged forward, the man was thrown headfirst toward the rear of it, but he saved himself by frantically grasping the upper corner of his seat while lurching past it. Turning about and pulling himself forward to the seat, he stared darkly at the rear of the driver's head before collapsing onto the seat. But there was no sympathy on any of the grimly smiling faces that leered back at him.

Looking at Jan, I murmured, "That sudden acceleration was against the system's rules."

After an emphatic nod, he whispered, "I won't tell anybody if you won't."

I registered a small smile but deigned not to respond, because no response was required.

The bus had traveled some distance before more words were exchanged, and the first of them was induced by a novel scene; at least it was novel to me.

"Look at the large herd of red deer!" Jan exclaimed. Then he leaned back to permit an unobstructed view of the animals. They were grazing peacefully within a compound, which was enclosed by a high, woven, wire fence whose posts extended about ten feet above the ground.

"Beautiful animals!" I exclaimed. "Probably imported from England or Scotland."

"More than likely they were netted in the South Island's bush by men in helicopters," he said.

Looking doubtfully at him, I muttered, "That seems too costly to be practical."

"But the deer run wild," he objected, "so the only costs are those of the men's time, the helicopters, and some special netting equipment. Furthermore, a good hind used to bring about thirty-five hundred dollars as breeding stock, but the price has dropped lately because of adjustments in the government's taxing practices.

"And the bucks?" I posited.

"In the wilds they used to be shot from the air," he responded with a pained expression, "and the carcasses were sold to packing houses. The best bucks are currently used for breeding purposes, and the others are converted into venison."

"Is there that much demand for venison?" I probed.

"Apparently there is," he replied. "And foreign demand is growing very rapidly, because calorie-conscious people have discovered that venison is about half as fat as the meat of domestic animals. However, its current cost is about four times that of beef." Pausing, he looked at me and added, "But there are other valuable by-products of the bucks, such as the antlers, which are shipped to Korea, Taiwan, and Hong Kong."

After pensively studying him, I asked, "For use in the manufacture of an aphrodisiac?"

Frowning doubtfully, he answered, "It's supposed to be for medicinal purposes. Furthermore, the tails, penises, and leg sinews are shipped frozen to ports such as Hong Kong."

"For medicinal purposes," I ventured with a small smile.

Without changing expression, he added, "When the value of the skin is included with the values of those other inedible parts, the value of the stag's carcass must amount to a sizable sum."

I nodded, and we lapsed into a period of reverie. Eventually I broke the silence with the statement: "Since this fair land was inhabited by only winged creatures before its invasion by modern man, it could not have been the site of the Garden of Eden despite its great beauty."

"Why?" he countered with a curious expression.

"There are no snakes," I answered. "In fact, that's the nicest thing about it."

Smiling tolerantly, he said, "I doubt that snakes are a real threat to people. In the tropics I found that they usually escape into the jungle whenever they encounter people."

"I suspect that to be true of most wildlife," I surmised. "However, some American snakes can become extremely obstinate. For example, I've seen a diamondback rattlesnake curl up on a footpath and literally defy anybody to pass. And I've never argued with any of them about their right of way."

"Are they very poisonous?" he inquired.

"They are classified as pit vipers," I replied, "so the bite of one of them can make its victim very ill, and it can kill the victim when its strike is directed at a particularly vulnerable part of the body, such as the throat."

He turned thoughtfully toward the window, and I lapsed into a mental study of various other subjects. After a lengthy interval, I broached one of them: "What do you know about that big land reclamation project in Holland?"

After some thought, he suggested, "You must be referring to the Oosterschelde Barrier, but it isn't a land reclamation project; it's a land protection project."

"But you are referring to the project that involves a huge adjustable barrier, aren't you?" I asked.

Following a nod, he answered, "For one thing, I know that it has cost billions of guilders and thirty years of effort. But it's sheduled to be completed in nineteen eighty-six."

"Why was such a costly project ever started?" I asked.

"Because there was a great need for it," he replied. "In nineteen fifty-three a violent storm created a huge tide that breached most of the dikes in the delta region, and eighteen hundred people drowned. As a consequence of that disaster, the government built several new dams, thereby reducing the shoreline by seven hundred eighty kilometers. But by the time the dam was to be started at the mouth of the Oosterschelde, certain political pressure groups had persuaded the government to substitute an open surge barrier, which would preserve the estuary as an important source of mussels and oysters."

"A barrier that can be closed when the need arises," I speculated.

To a nod and an "uh-huh," he added, "Only once or twice a year and during the monthly tests."

"That must have been a very involved engineering problem," I suggested.

"Some of the finest engineers in the world have called Dutch engineers 'Masters of the Sea,' " he responded with a pardonable air of pride.

"How did they gain the experience necessary to solve so tremendous a problem?" I asked.

"Dutchmen have been pushing the sea back since the eleventh century," he responded with a smile still tinged with pride, "and Dutch windmills have been pumping water back into the sea since the early fifteenth century. God created the world, but we Dutch made Holland."

I glanced toward the young man's pride-filled eyes and felt a surge of pleasure in his open expression of nationalism. Unfortunately, it has been lacking much too long in the makeup of my countrymen.

"Just how was this sea monster put together?" I inquired.

"The engineers had to start from scratch," he began. "Not only did they have to develop a radically new design concept for the barrier, but they had to design and build a fleet of enormous construction vessels. They also had to prepare the sandy bottom of the Oosterschelde for the structures by compacting it with giant vibrating needles. Then, to prevent its erosion, massive sand and gravel mattresses were laid down on it from a huge vessel. On each of the foundations, an eighteen-thousand-metric-ton reinforced concrete pier was carefully lowered by another enormous vessel. Then one of the world's largest floating cranes was used to hoist the traffic beams into place, and...."

"The barrier supports a roadway too?" I interjected.

"Yes," he answered, "and its structural duct contains the electrical and hydraulic systems that control the gates. Then the crane set a concrete cap unit on each of the piers and hoisted the steel gates into position. Finally, the hydraulic gate lifts were placed on the caps, and two huge concrete beams were positioned between each sequential pair of piers."

"How high does the finished structure stand above sea level?" I asked.

"I don't know," he replied, "but the piers are twelve stories high."

"That would be one hundred twenty feet above the foundation," I muttered. "Add about ten feet for the roadway, and the cars should be traveling over one hundred and thirty feet above the seabed. But most of that structure would be subjected to terrific pressure from the waves."

"So the core of each pier was filled with sand," he said. "Then five million tons of rocks were placed around the bases of those piers."

"Hmm," I mumbled. "That must have been an awful lot of work."

"The Dutch people are hard workers," he said. "In fact, our shirts are sold with their sleeves already rolled up."

After tossing a startled glance toward him, I smiled appreciatively; meanwhile Pancho observed, "So our shy seatmate appears to have a sense of humor after all."

Digressing from the subject, I said, "Somewhere I read that Holland was about to launch a big land reclamation project."

"The only proposed polder is the one planned for the IJsselmeer, which was formerly called the Zuider Zee," he said. "But many of our people contend that we don't need more agricultural land, even though Holland is one of the most densely populated countries in the world."

"If the land is reclaimed, how will it be done?" I asked.

"Dams and levees will first be constructed; then the water will be pumped out into the sea," he replied.

"What about the salt-saturated seabed?" I inquired.

"Rainwater will leach out the salt," he said. "Then it'll be drained away by canals and pumped into the sea. Within twenty years the soil will be usable; within another twenty years it'll be good agricultural land."

"Perhaps some of your Dutch hydraulic engineers ought to be assigned to the salt problem that exists in the central part of California," I suggested.

Since we had beaten the subject to death, we were content to watch the ever-changing landscape for some time.

I next inquired, "By the way, does Holland have any nuclear power generators?"

After pondering the question for several seconds, he shook his head and answered, "I don't know of any, but I can't say for sure."

"I doubt that it has any, because there would be no place to dispose of the nuclear waste," I stated. "In fact, we haven't solved that problem either."

"There's always the sea," he suggested with a smile. "We pump most of our runoff fertilizers and insecticides into the sea."

"I don't condone that at all," I retorted. "However, nuclear waste is a far different problem, because its radioactivity continues for thousands of years. During that time not only will it destroy sea life but it will get into other parts of the food chain and poison them. Furthermore, there's no suitable place on this earth where such waste should be stored, and the cost of placing millions of tons of it into rockets and propelling it into the sun is prohibitive."

"The scientists will come up with a new solution to the energy problem," he insisted confidently.

"I think that I know what you are referring to," I said, "but I doubt that they'll ever get more energy out of any of those costly systems than they put into them."

"I was referring to the very latest developments," he responded with a prolonged stare. "Of course, you know the difference between fission and fusion?"

"I'm aware of the difference," I replied. "However, to most of us old-timers fission and fusion are confusin'."

Turning alert eyes toward me, he burst forth: "Yees, yees, yees!" Then he swept one palm across the other one and chuckled delightedly.

After a quick double take, I checked a gnawing suspicion that he was just being courteous, but he actually appeared to enjoy what could be mistaken for a pun.

Meanwhile, Pancho observed, "No wonder Al has never been able to score with his humor in our country; it has European overtones."

So far the bus had passed several tiny settlements, the largest of which were Taupo and Turangi, and it stopped briefly at each of them to discharge passengers, freight, and mail. To my knowledge, it didn't handle any live freight, but I strongly suspected that one shallow, cardboard crate with small holes punched through its upper surface may have contained baby chickens. At each stop the vehicle acquired as big a load as it discharged.

While the bus was following the two-lane highway around the base of a high, snow-capped mountain and over the foothills that adjoined it, I turned to Jan and said, "This terrain looks disturbingly like the high wastelands of Northern California."

"It is drier," he granted. "In fact, it is too dry to support enough forage for cattle and sheep."

"That high mountain may be causing the rain-laden clouds from the Tasman Sea to rise and drop most of their loads onto its snow fields," I speculated.

"Yees," he agreed. "That must be Mount Raupehu—it's about twenty-eight hundred meters high."

"Hmm," I exhaled. "Nine thousand feet is a fairly high mountain, even in California."

Momentarily, my view was completely obscured by Jan's head as he peered intently toward the vast snowfields that spilled about halfway down the mountain's tortuous slopes. Then his attention was directed to the smaller, symmetrical cone that stood some distance beyond the end of it.

"That cone looks like it may have been thrust up from the plateau by a volcano," I suggested.

"Yes, it certainly does," he agreed. "In fact, both mountains may have been created by volcanic action."

"During the summer all of that snow on top of Mount Raupehu will probably melt," I speculated.

"It may not," he said, "because all of the snow in the glaciers on the Southern Alps never melts." Then, looking at me with an embarrassed smile, he added, "Of course, all of the snow in the glaciers never melts; otherwise they wouldn't be glaciers."

Within minutes after the bus passed beyond the mountains, the rough terrain turned into green, rolling hills with sheep on them.

"This is beginning to look like we may be approaching a plain," I remarked.

"We won't cross any plains between here and Weellington," he rejoined. "In fact, the city itself is built on bluffs overshadowed by relatively high mountains on three sides and by the sea on the other one. But it's amazing how rapidly the terrain can change. For example, just a few minutes ago we were traveling through dry, brush- and rock-strewn wastelands; now we're cruising over rolling hills covered with green grass."

Then, looking pensively at me, he resumed: "When we flew over the Himalayas during the flight to New Zealand, those high mountains—the highest in the world— stopped very abruptly somewhere in India. It's amazing how rapidly the terrain can change. That terrain, however, is partly explained by tectonics: The plate on which India rests is being thrust under an adjoining plate."

"I'm not one to readily accept the theories espoused by the scientific community," I said, "but that particular philosophy could explain the presence of that range of massive mountains."

"But there are no volcanoes among them," he said. "At least, to my knowledge, there are no volcanoes among them."

"That may be due to the massive nature of the upthrust material," I suggested.

"Are you implying that the material overlying the line of contact between the two plates is so thick that it fully contains all of the heat generated by the friction?" he asked.

"Something like that," I answered. "Perhaps it's so thick that the heat is forced to take other avenues of escape, such as into the subterranean rocks and magma."

"Well, that sounds reasonable," he murmured.

"It may be reasonable," I concurred, "but it probably isn't the total reason. Old Mother Earth is very adept at concealing her secrets from us and from our so-called scientists. Too often they are dead wrong, but they'll never admit it, of course."

"Uh-huh," he grunted.

I suspected, however, that his heart was not entirely in the effort, because youths are so susceptible to the words of those who set themselves up as authorities on certain subjects—sometimes all subjects. Fortunately, youths do possess that characteristic; otherwise college students would throw their textbooks through the nearest of their classrooms' windows and depart from the halls of learning.

He turned abruptly from the window to me with gleaming eyes and said, "I suspect that I recognized a landmark just now, so we must be nearing our destination. Very soon we'll be there, and tomorrow morning I'll be winging my way to Holland and home."

"Then you'll be a bona fide 'Flying Dutchman' without sails," I suggested and immediately regretted it.

"A bona fide Flying Dutchman without sails," he murmured with questioning eyes.

Smiling self-consciously, I explained: "That was something that I read about many years ago. It concerned a legendary Dutch sailing ship that some sailors claimed to have seen off the Cape of Good Hope. According the legend, the captain of the ship had been condemned to sail his ship against the wind until Judgment Day."

He turned delighted eyes toward me, and in his excitement he literally sputtered the words: "Then you were implying that I may be dumped out of the aircraft over the Himalayas and become a legendary Flying Dutchman who has to fight the forces of gravity until Judgment Day."

"That's pretty *bleeped* good for a Dutchman!" I exclaimed with a laugh. "Many years ago," I resumed, "a fabulous gold mine, called the Dutchman, was reported to have been found in one of the western states. However, after returning to the nearest western bar, the man who found the mine was never able to relocate it, so it became known as the "Lost Dutchman Mine." I don't know why they first called it the Dutchman Mine, unless the finder was a Dutchman, but no Dutchman that I've known would ever lose so valuable an asset."

"Yees, yees, yees!" he exclaimed delightedly, swinging one palm across the other.

"Nevertheless, you'll be a Flying Dutchman come tomorrow morning," I reminded him.

Nodding happily, he turned to the window; then he immediately turned back to me, and announced, "Finally we are in Weellington. We'll arrive at the station within minutes. I promise it."

Having been a bit youthful myself one time many years ago, I could appreciate how much the boring trip must have weighed on him. When we arrived at the station, I bestowed a tolerant smile on him and wished him a pleasant flight, while he hurriedly expressed similar sentiments and scrambled to escape from the bus as soon as the flow of exiting passengers permitted.

5

Wellington

Contrary to everyone's expectations, the bus had terminated its trip at the New Zealand Railroad Station instead of at the nearby bus terminal. After pausing at the front of the huge structure, I set my luggage on the concrete slab and proceeded to study the vicinity and the environmental conditions. A light, misty rain was falling, so I was introduced to New Zealand's capital city under rather unfavorable circumstances. In several respects, the city reminded me of San Francisco, what with the rain, the steep hills, and the wind. Since I have never agreed with the many San Franciscans who boast of that city's beauty, Wellington was obviously off to a slow start as far as I was concerned. Nevertheless, I will give the city this much: Not only was it more beautiful than San Francisco during that cloudy, rainy evening, but during that same evening it was more beautiful than San Francisco during a sunny day.

Slowly my gaze wandered toward two of the bus's passengers, who were deeply engaged in a conference with the driver of the first of several taxicabs that stood along the curb. The three slender, attractive people would have made a picture postcard, even in the misty rain, so I immediately decided to return to my diet.

One of the two passengers, a man of about sixty-five, swung away from the driver, picked up two pieces of luggage, and called back, "Oy don't know how fah it is, but we want to go to Brooklyn."

"That's about eight thousand miles northeast of here," I interjected facetiously from above him.

Stopping abruptly, he swung about and looked up at me. "Not yoah Brooklyn," he called with a chuckle. Then, as if it constituted a mutual bond, he proudly announced, "Oy've been theah, too."

The driver looked up at me and courteously gestured to the cab behind his vehicle, but the world traveler was not content with that. "Can't we drop you off somewheah?" he called to me.

"No, thank you," I called back with a smile. "You appear to know where you are going, but you don't know how far it is or in what direction to go. Besides, I don't see any wings or pontoons on that cab."

Responding with a hearty laugh, he went to help the driver stow the luggage, and he was still laughing while he and his mate crawled into the vehicle. From the open window he genially called, "You Americans!" And as the cab moved away, he raised one hand in a friendly parting gesture.

After it left, I continued to stand and survey the surroundings beyond the small park in front of the terminal. Across the park and to my left, I detected a tall, relatively old building, along the far corner of which the words *Waterloo Hotel* were displayed on a vertical sign with the letters stacked in sequential progression from top to bottom. Meanwhile, the next cab moved up into the vacated space, and its driver turned questioning eyes toward me. On impulse, I descended the steps, strolled around to the right side of the vehicle, and peered through the open window at him.

"Can I be of service?" he inquired.

"I've been considering the Waterloo Hotel," I replied. "Do you happen to know whether its rates are reasonable?"

He looked sardonically at me, and I suspected that he was about to tell me to get lost, since no cab fare would be involved. Instead, he muttered, "Oy don't know about the rites, but it has been sittin' theah since Adam was a boy, so it's a bit out o' dite. Theah ah much noicer hotels fathah out."

Of course, I could see the logic behind his reply, because it involved a large cab fare, so I stubbornly persisted, "But is it clean, and are the rates high?"

"Aye, it is clean," he granted grudgingly.

"Thank you," I murmured. Then, after pondering whether a tip was in order, I vetoed it, because many New Zealanders are somewhat sensitive about accepting a tip for a simple courtesy. But I really should have engaged his cab for the two-block trip to the Waterloo, because my heavy luggage exhausted me long before I arrived in the ornate lobby.

During my approach to its long, hardwood desk, a relatively mature woman appeared from behind an artistic screen consisting largely of obscured glass. Assuming the conventional position behind the desk, she posed the usual question: "Can I help you?"

"Yes," I replied. "I would like to know the rate for a single."

"Foahty-foah dollahs," she answered.

Turning about, I studied the brightly patterned carpet and the cherubic statues of wood nymphs that served as the basic structures of the electric lamps. In the light of those lamps and previous experiences, it seemed to be a fair rate, but I was deeply concerned about the room. Would it prove to be like the one in the Abby's Hotel?

Turning back to the woman with an apologetic smile, I said, "Thank you, but I would like to see if I can beat that rate." And she nodded indifferently.

Picking up my luggage, I trudged wearily across the exotic carpet to the entrance. At the curb, I gratefully set the luggage on the sidewalk and waited for a cab to cruise by, but Bunny Street must have been reserved for rabbits, if not for the birds, because every cab that zeroed in on the station invariably used Featherston Street, so I was forced to cross the park again.

While the driver and I were stowing my luggage in the boot, I inquired, "Do you know of an economical hotel or motel?"

"Yees," he replied. "Theah's lots o' theem."

From the station, he turned onto Waterloo Quay, which soon became Custom House Quay. "Lambton Harbour is just beyond these warehouses," he informed me. "Would you loik to see a bit o' the city while we search foah lodgings?"

"That seems like a sound investment," I replied.

"The Parliament buildings are located just above the station on Brown and the Terrace," he volunteered with a questioning glance.

"No, let's not go back," I responded to the unspoken suggestion. "If there's something to be seen during our search, fine, but I don't want to go out of our way to see anything."

Nevertheless, I saw the Queens Wharf, the public library, and the town hall before seeing any hotels. Two of the hotels proved to be booked up, three had rooms but no attached baths, and I turned down three others. In the process, we traveled over most of the central part of the city, including such streets as Mercer, Victoria, Willis, and Lambton Quay.

After finding that the last hotel involved rooms with a remote bath, I returned to the driver and said, "Take me to the Waterloo Hotel."

"But it's roight at the station," he protested.

"I know that," I retorted. "I was there just before we began this tour of the city, but I foolishly believed that I could beat the rate."

"But you did see the city," he pointed out, "so the tour wasn't a total loss."

When he dropped me off on the Waterloo Quay side of the hotel, I regretfully gave him a ten-dollar bill and told him to keep the difference. Meanwhile, I automatically added it to the forty-four-dollar rate of the hotel room, because I've always followed a policy of penalizing myself for conspicuous errors in judgment, irrespective of any associated benefits.

Once more I dragged my luggage through the doorway of the Waterloo and across its seething carpet to the massive hardwood desk, beyond which the desk clerk stood with her head bowed over some paperwork. "Well, I was unable to beat your price," I announced. "Therefore, like MacArthur, I have returned."

Raising her head, the clerk revealed a much younger, prettier set of features than the previous clerk possessed. "Can I help you?" she inquired.

"Uhm, uh, yeah," I finally expelled. "I would like a single room."

"Please sign the register," she requested, placing a pen before me.

I picked it up and peered at the topmost of the registration forms. Then I deliberately glanced up and intercepted the expected stare. Even though she quickly averted her eyes, the intentness of the stare had already revealed the presence of the Unknown. I frowned grimly at the form, indicated my home address, and affixed my signature to it.

"That will be sixty dollars," she informed me.

Standing transfixed with my mouth agape, I sensed that my features bore what some authors love to describe as an appalled expression. "But, but . . . ," I stammered, "I was told that the rate would be forty-four dollars." And she frowned.

After silently exchanging sharp stares with her, I pointed toward the outline of the woman behind the obscure glass and insisted, "Ask the lady in that office."

"No, that won't be necessary," she replied, changing the receipt with a couple of vicious swipes of the pen.

"The fact that it wasn't necessary indicates that there may be various ways whereby an unscrupulous desk clerk can cheat the guests, the management, or both," Pancho speculated.

"That proves that you have a very suspicious mind," José rejoined.

"That comes from many exposures to the moral debauchery and chicanery of human beings. . . including my closest associate," Pancho retorted belatedly.

After counting out the money, I laid it on the desk, picked up the receipt and the key, and stuffed them into a jacket pocket. Then I hoisted the luggage and strode across the lobby to the elevator—the lift, that is.

Several minutes later I inserted the key into the latch of a door bearing the number *505*, unlocked it, opened it, and confidently flipped the adjacent light switch. Then I nearly dropped dead in my tracks, because there wasn't a stick of furniture in the small, narrow room.

"Hey!" Pancho silently exclaimed. "What gives?"

"Yeah," José alertly rejoined. "Where do we spend the night? On the floor?"

"Either that or in an open suitcase," Pancho remarked. "That would be too small, you idiot," countered José. Fortunately, I forestalled a mental riot by noticing two other doors: one at the far end of the elongated room and the other in a side wall, so I concluded that it must be a hallway providing access to two rooms that could be used either separately or as a suite. Of course, the presence of number *504* on the far door helped to justify that conclusion.

When I opened the door in the side wall and flipped the adjacent light switch, my conscience was immediately assailed by pangs of guilt, since a quick glance revealed that the room contained not just one but two double beds plus a so-called sit bed. The huge, plate glass mirrors in the pair of hardwood frames beyond the light switch rolled smoothly away to reveal two large wardrobes. In addition to those luxuries, two tall chests of drawers stood along one wall, and a combination telephone and lamp table occupied the space between the double beds. Not until I had traversed the entire length of the large room did I discover that I was still carrying my heavy suitcase; the briefcase was standing against the wall near the doorway. Slowly my eyes swept the room in search of luggage racks, and my mesmerized mind first refused to recognize the two big, hardwood luggage racks standing against the opposite wall. After lowering my suitcase onto one of them, I recovered the briefcase and placed it in the middle of the other rack, where it looked very small and forlorn, despite the fact that it contained a load that had almost hyperextended one of my arms.

In the large bathroom, I found the usual fixtures along with both a tub and a shower. True, the fixtures and their fittings were old fashioned, but they functioned perfectly. Everything was in its place, and it had been meticulously maintained. Every inch of that bathroom's surfaces was covered by a fine grade of porcelain tile.

A second inspection of the bedroom revealed that each of the windows had been fitted with an exterior window somewhat like a storm window, but all of the windows were unique in that they had been permanently closed. I looked expectantly toward the ceiling and immediately detected the cleverly camouflaged vents of the central air-conditioning system. Turning about, I ruefully looked down through a window at the pavement some fifty feet below.

"What do we do in case of fire?" Pancho wondered.

"I certainly hope that there's more than one fire exit," José chimed in.

"Let's cast those qualms aside," Pancho proposed. "For once, fortune has really smiled on us, so let's live it up a bit."

"Uh-huh," I grunted. And that turned out to be the case—almost.

After luxuriating in the beautiful shower, I donned my essentials and added my only slacks and sport coat. Following a ride on the lift down to the lobby, my peripheral vision easily detected the protracted stare of the pretty desk clerk. From the entrance of the hotel, I strolled along Bunny Street and turned left on Featherston Street, which eventually intersected with Lambton Quay and, in turn, intersected with Willis Street. The hands of my watch pointed to several minutes past the hour of nine, so most of the businesses were closed, but the pubs and restaurants were still open. And since it was a Saturday night, they were flourishing. One of them was Cobb and Company, which I assumed to be part of a chain of pubs and kitchens, since the name had been emblazoned on the exterior of a restaurant in Auckland. I found that the establishment was housed in the Saint George Hotel, which stood at the corner of Willis and Boulcott Streets.

Just beyond the wide doorway, a glance to my right, through the openings in an artfully devised screen wall, revealed that the bar was buzzing. Even though the hands of my watch were nearing the hour of ten, the place was crowded with Saturday night revelers. Despite the noise, I approached the perky hostess in the tiny cubicle on my left, casually placed my left hand on its small counter, and asked, "How long will I have to wait for a single?"

Her baby blue eyes didn't even waiver as she smilingly replied, "About twenty minits."

"More like double that," José silently speculated. But I nodded.

With a pencil poised over the pad before her, she requested, "Please give me yoah nime."

"Are you proposing to me?" I countered.

Her eyes came to parade rest while she pondered the question; then they smiled delightedly. "Oh, you Americans!" she exclaimed with a flip of one supple hand, but it didn't quite touch my hand.

Under similar conditions in Los Angeles or New York the hostess would have grasped my hand and tenderly squeezed it. Such are the differences in the social graces of different societies.

After I responded properly to her request, she suggested, "You can wite in the bah if you loik."

I looked doubtfully past the end of the screen wall into the bar and nodded. Then I wandered toward the opening at one end of it in spite of the fact that I had previously quenched my thirst with a glass of clear, sparkling fresh water from the springs and snowfields of the North Island.

"We'll call you whin yoah table is ready," she called after me. And I nodded again.

First, I decided to buy a beer to justify my presence there; then my eyes searched for a place to put that presence. Along the wall to my left were three tables: The first two would accommodate couples, and the third, which was nearest to the bar, would accommodate a foursome. It was occupied by a young couple and an attractive, gray-haired woman who must have been between fifty-five and sixty years old. Obviously, the table would accommodate still another person, and I immediately sensed that the older woman was staring speculatively at me. Since the first of the other two tables was occupied by an attractive couple in the thirty- to thirty-five-year range, I had only two choices: respond to the older woman's bold stare or take the second table. So I seated myself at the latter on the upholstered bench that traversed the length of the wall. Then, clasping my hands atop the table, I waited patiently for someone to take my order.

After several minutes, the total absence of service in the immediate area finally percolated through my preoccupied mind and dripped down into my consciousness. A short study of the activities around me revealed that some of the patrons were making round trips to the bar for beers or ales. Others must have brought their own (B.Y.O.), since the bartenders were mixing and serving the liquor to them. During the study, my peripheral vision informed me that the gray-haired woman was studying me, but I attributed it to an interest in my unkempt beard; possibly she was wondering what kind of man would wear such an unsightly thing. At times I had wondered about it too, but never for long, because it served an obscure purpose in my attempts to uncover the Unknown.

While passing the trio on my way to the bar, I surreptitiously detected another of the woman's protracted stares. During my negotiation of the two steps down to the lushly carpeted floor of the bar, I noticed that one of the bartenders had also fixed a protracted stare on me, but I had expected that. In the process of renegotiating the two steps, I was so preoccupied with stabilizing the liquid in the beer stein that the woman's deliberate stare unexpectedly struck my eyes head on, but I tactfully diverted my gaze toward the steps.

Just after I seated myself on the bench with the beer stein positioned authoritatively in front of me on the small table, a relatively tall, shapely blonde swung past it on her way to the unoccupied booth that stood opposite the table of the trio. After sliding onto the upholstered bench that faced in my direction, she generously crossed her knees, opened her evening bag, and began one of the endless searches that is so characteristic of the females of our species.

I really shouldn't have allowed my eyes to wander in her direction, because I could have stared at the opposite wall, toward the dining room, or at the bar. But she was seated in front of the bar, so my eyes involuntarily returned from their other excursions to those self-confident features. They weren't particularly pretty features, but they were handsome—even after some thirty years of life's uncertain vicissitudes. Putting it bluntly, the woman had an enormous amount of sex appeal.

She finally found the package of cigarettes and inserted one of them between her carefully marked red lips. She seemed to be aware of the stir that her presence had created, because every action seemed to be staged. Even the simple act of inserting the long, white cylinder between sexily pouting lips seemed to be contrived. But she didn't light the weed; instead, she pulled her skirt a bit higher, which not only relieved some stress on the fabric but revealed more thigh. Her beige-colored evening gown continued to drape lovingly across one smooth, white shoulder, but it totally avoided the other one, where, without support, the action had caused it to slip still lower and reveal even more curvilinear white flesh.

"Humph, a pro," I muttered to my untouched beer.

About the same time, a murmur from the couple to my right, followed by a derisive chuckle and a titter, induced a cautious glance in that direction, which revealed that they also were watching the woman.

During that performance the gray-haired woman finished the dark-colored concoction that she had been drinking. Then, opening her handbag, she extracted a roll of bills and placed them on the table in front of the young man, who may have been her son-in-law, since the younger woman exhibited some of the woman's physical characteristics. Replacing the handbag on the upholstered seat, the woman then leaned back and draped her left arm along the top of the seat. Apparently she was promoting a twofold purpose, because the forefinger of the heavily jeweled hand, which was draped along the back of the seat. twitched convulsively in my direction as she leaned toward the man and whispered a request. Picking up the bills, he arose, turned, and stared doubtfully in my direction. After thoughtfully juggling the bills for a moment, he turned back to her and expressed an opinion that left her staring wistfully at me while he took off toward the bar.

I instantly approved of his decision. Many years before, I had been involved in a similar situation wherein my ravishing, red-headed girlfriend had requested that

I invite an unknown older man to join our party of three, and I had responded in a like manner. But I'm sure that my redhead's white-haired mother put her up to it, because the redhead wasn't given to making such requests.

Suddenly a somewhat disheveled, dark-complexioned man with a dark moustache and bleary, dark eyes strode purposefully past my table and slumped onto the bench opposite the blonde. "Uh-huh, a customer," I promptly surmised. And a quick glance toward the couple on my right found them in the midst of exchanging leering smiles.

But my convictions were sharply shaken when I overheard the blonde say, "I wondered if you would be on time, and you weren't—not quite."

The man mumbled a somewhat befuddled response, so I was unable to interpret what he said—not that I was eavesdropping! After all, he was speaking in low tones and his back was to me, so my straining ears couldn't hear what he said.

Even with the impromptu floor show, the twenty minutes passed slowly, but when the last second ticked off, I turned and looked toward the cubicle that housed the hostess and intercepted two intent stares: hers and that of a tall, bony waitress. Characteristically, they hurriedly turned away.

Throughout all of those activities, I continued to detect an occasional stare from the gray-haired woman, but I carefully avoided meeting another one head on. During a life span of seventy-some years, I had learned to spot a predatory woman, and that one was no New Zealand lamb.

The carefully modulated tones at the blonde's table suddenly stopped; then the man abruptly arose and lurched away from it with a belligerent expression on his liquor-inflamed features. The blonde watched indifferently while he bolted unsteadily along the aisle past my table, but she must have realized what the onlookers must be thinking, because she shrugged her shapely shoulders and raised both hands with their palms up in the familiar gesture of c'est la vie. Meanwhile, the gown slipped dangerously lower, but she didn't heed it.

"No sale," I muttered to my pint of warm beer. Then, along with the adjacent couple, I watched the man's erratic departure. However, just minutes after he left the area, his rangy figure reappeared from the general direction of the entrance, and it was borne unsurely onward by the same long, wavering strides. At the side of the blonde's booth he came to a stop, briefly teetered back and forth, and collapsed onto the bench opposite her triumphant eyes.

"Her eyes certainly are expressive," I wistfully mumbled to my slowly evaporating beer.

"She's fully aware that she has hooked him," it responded, or so it seemed.

I did a startled double take, but the beer, with scarcely a bubble of foam on it, appeared to be so innocent that I was forced to conclude that my mind was playing tricks on me. I suppose that such things are possible at my age.

Since the man's angular body was hunched over the table with his head close to the blonde's, I was unable to hear the ensuing conversation. Of course, I wasn't deliberately eavesdropping! However, the product of the conversation must have been mutually satisfactory, because they arose and left the lounge.

"Sale," I muttered to my flat beer, but its only response erupted from one last bubble as it burst with a burp. A beer burping? That's unusual. Then I remembered that it was New Zealand beer and nodded my head knowingly.

"But Al's conclusion regarding the couple may have been totally in error," José suggested.

"True," Pancho agreed. "And he's the one who always claims to give everyone the benefit of the doubt. Actually, he's no better than the average human being."

"Oh, I wouldn't go that far down the scale," José protested. "But the incident could have derived from a lovers' quarrel, or it could have evolved from any one of several other reasons. Furthermore, it wasn't any of Al's *bleeped* business."

"Right!" Pancho concurred. "But it did provide entertainment during the hour that we waited for Al's name to be called."

Eventually the young hostess led me from the bar, along an aisle, and through the dining room to an alcove; then she gestured summarily toward the smaller of the two available tables, laid a menu on the corner of it, and departed.

After I seated myself on the upholstered seat that extended the full length of the far wall of the alcove, Pancho exclaimed, "What a change in attitude!"

As I reached across the table for the menu, carefully modulated tones inquired, "Can Oy git something foah you from the bah?"

Looking up from the menu, I silently shook my head, and the barmaid hauled her scantily clad hips away while I continued to resent the behavior of a very misinformed hostess. A tall, awkward waitress replaced the barmaid. Her inherent awkwardness appeared to evolve from slightly deformed wrists and ankles, so I resolved to be particularly kind to her despite my treatment by a mentally handicapped member of the staff. Besides, she appeared to be very young and inexperienced, and I am inclined to tolerate such shortcomings. Youth a shortcoming?

"Kin Oy hilp you," she inquired eagerly.

"Yes, thank you," I replied. "Can you tell me how the lamb is prepared?" Instantly sensing that I had confused her, I attempted to clarify the question. "I'm familiar with leg of lamb and rack of lamb, but the menu doesn't describe its lamb," I explained. "What kind of lamb is it and how is it prepared?"

For several seconds her eyes expressed the tortures of thought. Then she admitted, "Oy'm sorry, but I really don't know. Howevah, Oy kin ask the cheef."

"No, don't bother the chef with such minor details," I said. "Since lamb is a popular local entrée, it should be good in any form, so I'll have it." And I threw in a warm smile for good measure.

She heaved a sigh of relief, murmured, "Thank you, sir," and made the necessary notations on the order pad.

"Oy'll plice yoah ordah roight awye," she promised with an equally warm smile. Then she lumbered away.

It's amazing how kindness begets kindness. In fact, the innocent child-woman's sanguine reactions had momentarily erased my unhappy thoughts regarding the behavior of the hostess, so I leaned back against the bench's plastic upholstery and happily anticipated a fine meal in the relative peace and quiet of the isolated alcove.

Then Miss Fortune struck in the form of the hostess, who suddenly appeared in the aisle with her eyes fixed purposefully on the alcove. And she was leading the trio from the bar directly toward it. After the briefest of discussions, the younger of the two women acceded to the older woman's suggestion by seating herself on the bench near me and sliding along it to its far end; then the young man seated himself beside her. Meanwhile, the older woman seated herself on the nearest of the two chairs opposite them. Then, looking diagonally across the two tables into my distraught eyes, she smiled sweetly. Since the party had carried their partially consumed drinks with them, they declined the immediate services of the supple barmaid, who apparently took her cues from the hostess.

While waiting for my dinner to arrive, I absently listened to the young man's description of the deplorable condition of the sheep market. When the party's glasses were drained, the young man signaled to the barmaid. Meanwhile, la mère dug out her roll of bills.

Abruptly, she paused in the act, stared speculatively across the two tables toward me, and asked, "Would you like a drink?"

I was so startled by the unexpected invitation that I tactlessly replied, "No, thank you," without considering how the rejection might strike the ears of more tactful people.

Obviously she hadn't expected a rejection, because a pained expression flitted across her even features. I cringed internally, for no gentleman would have responded so crassly to such a question. Meanwhile, the sexy barmaid, who had been hovering in the background, moved forward—ostensibly to take the order. In the process, she murmured to the woman some words that escaped me, but I strongly suspected that they were intended to escape me. In any event, shortly after she left to pick up the orders, la mère excused herself and departed in the same general direction.

Upon her return, the young man began what proved to be a somewhat desultory conversation, while I resolved to wait for a likely spot to break into it and attempt to correct my faux pas.

Finally, turning to the man, I said, "Please pardon me. Since I'm obviously from another country, I have good reason not to know very much about your country's agricultural and economic problems. Can you tell me how much the average sheep brings on the open market?"

"Will, that depinds on several differint factors," he replied. "Foah ixample, one must considah the toipe of sheep as well as its age and condition." Then he looked coldly at me and added, "But America has created an impossible situation for New Zealand's farmahs."

Beneath his superficial courtesy, I sensed strong resentment, but I wasn't prepared to criticize him for that, since I had unintentionally treated a member of his family rather shabbily. Clearly, the situation didn't call for the usual New Zealand friendliness. Possibly he had denigrated my country deliberately to strike back at me, so I decided to escape from the awkward situation as quickly as possible.

"I suspect that American sheep ranchers are being subsidized by the government," I admitted, "so American consumers have to be paying exorbitant prices for sheep products; however, for comparison, about how much does a New Zealand lamb cost on the hoof?"

"As Oy said, that depinds on many differint factors," he retorted, "but a farmah is lucky if he gits twelve dollahs foah a good lamb."

My mind quickly exchanged those dollars for six U.S. dollars; then I incredulously shook my head and muttered, "No wonder Americans aren't buying rack of lamb; they are paying five or six prices for it."

"That's what Oy mean," he protested. "The American governmint is penalizing New Zealand farmahs for operating their businesses skillfully and efficiently."

"Meanwhile, the American Congress is cutting the throats of both the New Zealand farmers and the American consumers to buy the votes of a few Idaho sheep ranchers," I gently corrected him. Then, looking diagonally across the tables at the older woman, I murmured, "By the way, I wish to apologize to you for an unintentional rudeness. My health doesn't permit me to indulge in certain caustic substances, such as hard liquors, and that's why I declined your generous invitation."

"I'm sorry that you aren't in good health," she responded courteously but in a distant manner.

"To me her attitude seems to imply that Al can drop dead as far as she's concerned," José observed.

"But we should not reject a suspicion that her attitude has been strongly influenced by something other than just his rejection of her invitation," Pancho rejoined.

"True," José responded. "There's a strong likelihood that a minion of the vast Unknown conferred with her during that brief period while she was away from the table." And I absently nodded agreement.

Turning back to the young man, I said, "Thank you for the information. It proved to be most enlightening."

He inclined his head slightly, and I suspected that he had taken a cue from the older woman, since his manner exhibited the same distant attitude.

Fortunately, my unfortunate waitress chose to deliver my mutton at that point, but her attitude also had become remote and distant during the interim. In fact, just before leaving, she fixed a strange stare on my features, almost as if viewing a creature from outer space. "Can I get anything else for you?" she asked, but the previous impersonal friendliness had escaped from her expression.

"No, thank you," I responded with a thought-filled stare. Then I sensed that the previous impersonal friendliness had also escaped from my expression.

But friendly smiles had not escaped from all of the dining room's personnel, because a slightly older waitress, who exhibited no physical handicaps whatsoever, deliberately veered from the normal route between the dining room and the service bar to cast a flirtatious smile toward me. I stared incredulously at her until she disappeared behind a projecting corner. Then, with a dark scowl, I mused, "Despite the Unknown's claims to the contrary, I'm not your kind of man, foolish woman."

In spite of my waitress's change in attitude, I left a generous tip for her, not because of her misfortune but because she had given me a few minutes of friendliness unaffected by the Unknown. But I was so dispirited by the developments that I chose to ride from my Waterloo back to the Waterloo.

Early in the following morning I was the first guest to venture into the hotel's Baronial Falstaff for breakfast. If its heraldic decor was a measure of its dinner cuisine, I might have done better there than at the Cobb and Company. That is not intended to imply that the food was as good as home cooked. It was the usual New Zealand fare, which I had found to be consistently clean and wholesome but nothing to write home about.

In this case, it was served in the continental style, which meant that each diner served himself somewhat like one does at a smorgasbord. Therefore, I was not confronted by any of the staff until I appeared at the cashier's counter. But even that proved to be too much exposure, because the chubby, middle-aged woman who accepted my payment responded with a strange stare, which corresponded so closely to that of the Cobb and Company waitress that they could have passed as sisters or as mother and daughter.

Map of the South Island

Ferry en Route from Wellington to Picton

6

Wellington to Fox Glacier

Wellington to Picton

Shortly before seven o'clock the following morning I entered the waiting room of the railway terminal, placed my luggage alongside one of the oaken benches, seated myself on it, and absently scanned the empty waiting room. Since my wristwatch indicated that there was time to burn before the shuttle bus was to leave for the ferry terminal at Aotea Quay, I extracted some notepaper and a pencil from the briefcase and became absorbed in a rambling account of my previous experiences in Kiwi land.

Later, when the shuttle bus swung alongside the ramp of the massive terminal and discharged me, along with some twenty other passengers, I carried my briefcase to a vantage point, set it on the concrete, and stared up in awe at the huge ferry. And the awe was justified, because it appeared to be as large as some transoceanic passenger liners. It had to be, since it was capable of transporting not only hundreds of passengers but hundreds of automobiles and a surprising number of the New Zealand Railroad System's little red freight cars.

Since my luggage was checked to Christchurch, I checked myself through the gate and followed a line of passengers along a series of huge ramps onto the vessel. Several internal stairways later, I found myself atop the vessel in a passenger lounge that lay between a large dining area and a more heavily populated forward lounge. Pausing at the connecting doorway, I saw that the forward lounge's multimullioned windows provided a fine view of the wave-strewn harbor, so I pushed onward. Since a moving picture screen was displaying a silent flick that I vaguely remembered from my childhood, I seated myself in the first row among several other children. But I quickly forsook it for the forward rail immediately after the atmosphere was literally rent by the deep tones of the ferry's foghorn.

The sky was heavily overcast, and a light mist was falling when the behemoth moved slowly away from the dock. As it moved more purposefully from the harbor into the strait, a bevy of fast-moving, low-hanging clouds began to obscure the shoreline. Despite the thin haze that hung over the water forward of the bow, distant whitecaps were visible, but I was unable to see the north end of the South Island. After the vessel cleared the dim, hulking mass of the North Island, cold, gusty winds swept its decks, and I quickly sought refuge from them behind the glass in the forward lounge. The strait's favorable latitude must have had no bearing on the ambient temperature, because the fingers of those gusts felt like they had just been dipped into the frigid waters of the Antarctic Ocean.

While many of the other passengers watched the antics of the figures on the movie screen, I chose to watch the ever-changing, wind-tossed sea and the scudding clouds that so teasingly caressed its whitecaps. When the sun finally pierced the wispy clouds, I returned to the rail and watched the play of its rays on the luxurious, green slopes of the last of the North Island's string of small, offshore islands.

Almost three hours later, some of the islands that surround the north end of the South Island came into view under a china-blue sky, whose few fleecy, white clouds cast soft, undulating shadows that picturesquely mottled the scene. When the details of those islands became more sharply visible to me, I was enthralled by their lush, exotic beauty. Most of them were uninhabited, so growth of the native bush had never been marked or marred by mankind; consequently, it completely covered the islands' steep slopes from their rolling ridges to their rockbound shores. A few small trees were scattered about the slopes, but the growth consisted almost entirely of dense brush and bushes that tended to group in families. Many of them were in full bloom with each family exhibiting a particular color. The softly blended patches of beige, white, gray, and lavender were intermixed and draped so gracefully across the gently rolling slopes that each island presented a truly awe-inspiring vista. It was the type of scene that transfixes great artists and reduces wordsmiths, such as I, to inarticulate wonder.

For some time the vessel followed a relatively deep channel, which snaked its way through the aquamarine waters that lay between the mainland of the South Island and several small islands. The islands appeared to be components of a mountain chain whose peaks intermittently projected up through the waves from the ocean's floor before the chain finally became a major part of the mainland. In addition to their inherent beauty, those mountaintops served the more practical function of shielding passing vessels and parts of Marlborough Sound from the winds of the Tasman Sea. Behind some of the larger islands the surface of the sound subsided to almost mirrorlike smoothness, so I was permitted to view inverted reflections of the South Island's tree-clad slopes.

I had deliberately selected the larboard rail, because the vessel's superstructure provided considerable protection from the wind during those intervals when there was no island on the starboard side. During one of those intervals my gaze involuntarily turned to a point about one hundred yards forward of the vessel, and it remained riveted to it while I alertly waited to see if the suspected action would be repeated. Shortly it **was** repeated. Then another dark, finlike object pierced the sound's choppy surface, surged ahead parallel to the vessel's course, and disappeared into a wave. Suddenly I was startled to see a sleek, gray body break clear of the waves in a long, parabolic curve and plunge gracefully back beneath them. Abruptly, a similar body duplicated the maneuver; then, in patterns somewhat like sine waves, several of the beautiful creatures arose from the deep in unison and began to undulate through the waves. My incredulous eyes turned toward a middle-aged man, who was hunched over the rail at the point where it terminated at a steel bulkhead some six feet forward of me.

Then I moved tentatively toward him and said, "Pardon me, sir. Very likely this is a familiar sight to you, but have you seen those big fish out there?" And I pointed toward the area of activity at the very instant that two of the streamlined bodies catapulted out of the briny depths and slipped smoothly beneath the surface.

After observing the performance, his eyes turned back to mine with just a hint of a smile. "Ye main those dolphins at ply?" he asked.

My eyes made one more trip to the playground just as another so-called big fish exhibited his skill; then I whipped around to the man and ruefully exclaimed, "Wye shore, they **are** dolphins!" And even I could detect the embarrassment in my words: "I really should have recognized them, because I've seen them at Marine Land, and I've seen them in TV shorts many times..., but they look so different out here in their natural habitat."

He smiled tolerantly, and I hurriedly retreated to my post beside the rail; however, minutes later, he left the protection of the bulkhead and joined me.

"Do ye see that flat at the base o' those two slopes?" he inquired, pointing toward a particularly beautiful setting just above the shoreline.

"I assume that you are pointing to the flat covered by that small grove of trees," I answered.

"Yis," he replied, "but theah's moah than jist trays theah. Theah's siviral cabins tucked awye among those trays, and Oy'm going to spind the nixt two wakes in one o' thim; that is, Oy'll be stytioned theah, but Oy'll be fishin' iviry dye." Then he made as if to return to the shelter of the bulkhead.

"What a wonderful spot to spend a vacation," I murmured dreamily.

Looking back across one shoulder with glowing eyes, he nodded. Then, turning about, he settled against the rail beside me, and we silently watched the idyllic fishing camp slowly disappear behind one of the encroaching slopes that seemed to plunge directly into the sound. Without doubt our dreams differed, but they could not have differed much, despite the fact that I have never been one to seek out and destroy wildlife for sport. But there are many different things for which that particularly beautiful cul-de-sac could be used: Aside from just living in it, one could emerge from it at will, stroll about, breathe deeply, and savor the wild beauty of raw nature.

Picton From the top deck of the ferry I could easily see why Picton had become one of the principal gateways to the South Island: Not only was it ideally located to communicate with the principal cities of the North Island, but its beautiful surroundings provided an irresistible appeal to vacationers and tourists like myself. It was snuggled so picturesquely among the low foothills of the surrounding mountains that I had a momentary impulse to cancel my reservation on the train and linger awhile.

Another massive structure, similar to the one at Aotea Quay, greeted the ferry when it docked. In fact, it was so massive that it dwarfed the largest structures in the surrounding town. From it I followed another line of the craft's passengers through several ramps and tunnels to the terminal, from which I strolled to the adjacent train station.

Picton to Christchurch

A train was standing alongside the station platform, so I approached the conductor and presented my seat reservation to him. After glancing at it, he directed me to board Car R, the first of four coaches connected in line to the diesel-powered electric locomotive. Since Christchurch was to be the last stop on the day's run, I assumed that more than one of the other coaches might be disconnected from the train en route. Unfortunately, I forgot to verify that assumption.

While the train was moving through Picton's railroad yard, the view from the window beside me included several small, red freight cars, each of which was equipped with just two pairs of small, flanged, steel wheels that fitted nicely on the narrow-gage rails. To the eyes of an old railroad man, they seemed to be more like components of a toy train or a Toonerville Trolley than like those of a full-fledged train.

After the train cleared the city limits, the view gradually unfolded into ongoing panoramas of beautiful mountains buttressed by gracefully undulating foothills and the lush, green floors of connecting valleys. The weather could not have been more serene, but it must have been preceded by heavy rains, because the landscape gleamed like highly polished jade. However, the steepest rock-clad slopes didn't shine like jade, nor did the wool of the sheep that grazed on the jade slopes, but their innards must have been as green as grass, because they certainly were consuming a lot of it.

Usually the sheep's woolly coats were light-gray in color, but some of them were a pristine white, and still others were jet-black. However, I saw no polka-dot coats. Since there were some brown-coated sheep, the colors of most of the human races were represented, but I saw no sheep with yellow or red coats. Perhaps they are found only in China and on American Indian reservations.

Nevertheless, the sheep along those miles and miles of green slopes must have numbered up into the millions. Their woolly bodies dotted the countryside wherever blades of grass grew, and they grazed on it peacefully until some member of the flock was spooked by the rumble of the approaching train and responded to it by bolting. Then the members of the flock would surge en masse away from the fenced right of way and scamper wildly up the slopes like so many bouncing balls of woolen yarn. Obviously, sheep are dumb, almost as dumb as some people that it has been my misfortune to know.

In line with that train of thought (I was on a train, so what else?), I recalled that artists always depict sheep as clean animals "with fleece as white as snow," and I have foolishly believed those depictions, but that long train trip completely disillusioned me. During it I found them to be particularly dirty animals, some of them with shoulder-high, earth-colored high-water marks. Of course, those marks indicated that they had attempted to bathe, but their choice of bathtubs verified oft-repeated claims that they are insufferably stupid. After all, even half-smart animals would never use a mud hole for a bathtub—excepting pigs. Furthermore, not one of those sheep appeared to know what toilet paper is manufactured for. In my opinion, those artists should be hauled into court and charged with misrepresentation, at least the artists that wouldn't have to be dug up. But they probably wouldn't be convicted, because I later learned that when sheep are first introduced to fresh spring pastures they often scour until they adapt to the new forage. The austral spring arrives in November, and it was November.

The train passed through Koromiko, a small farming community, and touched base at Taumarina, which overlooks the Wairau Valley. There, according to history, several early settlers were massacred by Maori warriors as late as 1843.

Blenheim, the capital of Marlborough Province, with a population of about fourteen thousand, was the largest town through which the train passed. After leaving it, the terrain slowly changed to rolling hills against a distant background of high mountains. And the vegetation gradually deteriorated to dry native growths that reminded me of the sparse vegetation on some of Southern California's high deserts. Eventually, the rolling hills gave way to a low-lying plain largely occupied by Lake Grassmere, parts of which had been divided into shallow, rectangular ponds. Such ponds have been employed along with solar evaporation to produce all of New Zealand's salt since 1952.

From Lake Grassmere the rails followed an inland course as far as the Ure Bridge area, where they swung east along the often precipitous coastal mountains through such settlements as Wharamui, Kerkerengu, Parikawa, Clarence, Rakautara, Kincaid, and on into Kaikoura. En route, the train passed through several tunnels in the steep slopes of the Kaikoura Mountain Range, whose roots are buried deep in the bottom of the adjoining Pacific Ocean. It sped through some of the tunnels within seconds, but others consumed up to several minutes. From a railroad man I learned that some of those periods of darkness were spent in snowsheds, which function primarily as means of deflecting snow and debris into the ocean as they slide down the steep mountain slopes from much higher elevations. At that latitude snow rarely falls on terrain that is less than several hundred feet above sea level, so it has some distance to slide before arriving at the snowsheds.

Like most travelers, I was relieved as the train sped past the smaller settlements, but I was particularly relieved when it sped past Half Moon Bay, which lies just a few miles northeast of Kaikoura. The natives used to call it Uumutaoroa, which translates into the long cooking oven. That name was reported to have been bestowed on it by some Maoris who participated in a notable "cookout" many years ago. Since no one told me exactly how long ago, I feared that some of those innovative "chefs" might still be around! At the time, I could think of nothing worse than to have my bare bones displayed beside a Maori Uumutaoroa with the native words *yum-yum* inscribed on them.

The train had been billed as an express, but it must have stopped five times before it completed its journey. At Kaikoura it stopped for all of thirty minutes to permit the passengers to take on food and beverages and to visit the facilities located at each end of the small depot. It was while I was seated on the train waiting for it to resume its journey that I began to wonder if there were any justification for my far-out suspicion that the word *depot* might have derived from a very early but still familiar piece of sanitary equipment.

Shortly after leaving Kaikoura, the train swung inland, so there were no more beautiful seascapes. The surrounding terrain turned into a gently rolling plateau, but it continued to be green and picturesque. Meanwhile, the engineer ignored small settlements, such as Hundalee, Parnassus, Onuhi, and Bokairn, but he brought the train to a stop at Kaiapoi. A few minutes later the whistle sounded, and the train resumed its pace across several miles of farmland. Finally it came to a stop at the railway station in Christchurch.

Christchurch   After reclaiming my luggage, I went to the ticket counter and attempted to reserve a seat on the next train to Greymouth, but all of them had been booked, so I settled for a seat on the early morning bus.

A cab stood at the curb in front of the station, so I approached the driver and asked, "Do you know where the Best Western Motel is located?"

"Yis," he answered. "It's on Papanui Road."

"Okay, let's give it a try," I suggested, and we turned toward the boot to load my luggage.

From the station the cab followed Moorhouse Avenue to Montreal Street, where it turned north.

"Hive ye been in the city befoah?" the man asked.

"No," I replied as my suspicious eyes probed his guileless ones.

"Thin would ye loik foah me to droive by Cathedral Square?" he inquired. "It's a rathah imprissive soight. In fact, it's about all that the city has to offah the tourists. No foin harbor; the estuary is about tin moiles east o' heah."

"But I caught a glimpse of a large park to our left," I remarked.

"That would be Noath Hagley Pahk and the Botanical Gahdens," he informed me. "Would ye loik foah me to droive by thim?"

"No," I responded. "We'd best find a motel for me before all of them are booked for the night."

Nodding equably, he then directed his attention to the task. After a casual left turn onto Victoria, which immediately became Papanui Road, he turned sharply across the street onto the driveway of the Colonial Inn and stopped the vehicle in front of its small office.

"All booked up," I announced when I returned to the cab.

"That's surproisin'," he muttered while starting the motor.

"However, the manager suggested that we go back and try the next one," I said. "He suspects that it may have available accommodations."

"That would be the Ashford Village," he mumbled and almost immediately proved the statement by turning the cab onto the motel's driveway.

A slender, attractive young woman greeted me and performed the usual functions that provide one with such accommodations. After dispensing with the cab driver, I repaired to my temporary abode and washed away the grime that had accumulated during the day-long journey. Then, leaving the Ashford, I crossed Papanui Road in the twilight and strolled south past several other lodges, such as the Altair, the Town House, and Camelot Court. Actually, I was seeking a fast-food restaurant, but I finally settled for a nice dinner in the small restaurant at the Camelot Court. During the short walk back to the Ashford, Pancho and José finally agreed that we had detected none of the usual indications of the Unknown's presence. That observation deeply puzzled me, and it filled me with buoyant hopes that finally we had shaken the scurrilous scourge.

Christchurch to Fox Glacier

As usual, I arose early, so it was not yet seven o'clock when I finished repacking my luggage and fully organizing myself to greet the coming day and its unpredictable misadventures. Minutes later, from the window of a taxicab, I gazed out on the clean, orderly streets of the relatively prosperous central city which, at its conception, had been laid out in a rectangular pattern. However, the beautiful cathedral, which dominated the very center of the central city, appeared to be totally out of synch with it and with the buildings housing businesses that largely catered to the surrounding agricultural community.

Fortunately, the bus wasn't loaded to its fullest capacity, so I had an entire seat to myself. From the station it followed Highway 1 to its intersection with Highway 73, which, according to a small road map, pursued a relatively straight, westerly course across the Canterbury Plains.

Shortly after the bus got under way, the driver began to display considerable ability as a tourist guide. In fact, I began to suspect that he might have functioned as one before his last reincarnation, because he possessed an inherent talent for exposition in words that were practically free of the characteristic New Zealand dialect, and I had several reasons for doubting that the public-address system was translating them.

"Christchurch is reputed to be the most English city outside of England," he stated while maneuvering the vehicle into the scattered traffic on Highway 73, "but its people are the finest to be found in these beautiful islands or within the British Empire."

"Hmm," José observed. "If I know one whit about human psychology, that man has to be from Christchurch."

Some distance beyond the city limits, hedgerows began to dominate the flat landscape, and the man responded to their appearance: "As you can readily see, the farmers are removing many of those smaller hedgerows, because they have found that particular type of gorse to be nothing more than an obnoxious weed. Consequently, the farmers are replacing it with various types of evergreen trees, such as spruce or fir. Not only are they much more controllable, but they grow to greater heights." After pausing to maneuver the cumbersome vehicle around a truck, he resumed: "However, those taller hedgerows serve a much more important function than to add beauty to the landscape and to define different pieces of property. They are used primarily to break the forces of the winds from the Tasman Sea. After those winds find their way around the mountains, over them, and through their passes, they literally sweep across the Canterbury Plains. You'll notice that most of the farm buildings are protected by groves of trees, some of them quite large. But many of the largest trees also are being removed because their limbs can break off under the force of the wind and drop off onto the roofs of the buildings and damage them."

After a brief pause, he resumed: "Often, during the winter, those winds are bitterly cold, so cold that the farmers must shield their livestock from them, and that's why you see rows of trees along the sides of the collection pens (corrals). Of course, the sheep could be sheltered in barns, but those barns would have to be extremely large to house a thousand sheep, so only the newborn and sickly animals are housed in them. Besides, the other sheep have their sheepskin coats to keep them warm," he added in philosophical tones.

Meanwhile, the bus passed through Toldhurst, West Molton, and Aylesbury, where the highway turned in a northwesterly direction. Fields of small grains, such as wheat, oats, and barley, prevailed throughout the area, but there were several large herds of dairy cattle, and sheep were always in attendance regardless of the crops that the land produced. In one equipment yard I saw an old threshing machine, so I assumed that some of the grain must still be threshed, despite the fact that combines have been employed in America since the 1920s. Soon the bus passed a field where the bundles of grain had been shocked ("stooked" in Canada), so it must have been harvested by a binder. Eventually my assumption was supported by glimpses of several of those ancient harvesting machines in the equipment yards of two other farms. The equipment must have been drawn by tractors, since there were few draft animals in any of the pastures. Such harvesting techniques are archaic, but most of the fields contained no more than forty acres, so the use of huge combines may have been impractical. Furthermore, New Zealanders are extremely conservative people, so some of that equipment may have been fifty years old.

The prevailing colors of the sheep were off-white to gray, intermingled with a few shades of brown or black. So-called black sheep appear in all species of the animal kingdom; however, in proportion to the total numbers, there appeared to be fewer of them among those flocks than there are within the human race.

The bus paused at each of three towns: Sheffield, Annot, and Springfield. Beyond them the terrain not only became much rougher, but the vegetation deteriorated into relatively dry grass and weeds plus some scattered growths of brush. Eventually the appearance of increasingly rough and rocky highlands began to remind me somewhat of Northern California's desolate highlands, but none of California's scenery can compare with even the scrubbiest of New Zealand's fabulous scenery.

The engine labored a bit during the climb to Porter's Pass, which, at 929 meters (3,050 feet), is no towering height, but that was the first one. To the south of it nearby Lake Lyndon rested serenely in a small depression at the end of the Craigieburn Range, and the Torlesse Range extended north from it. The Craigieburn Forest also extended north from it, but its trees must not have impressed me, since I failed to notice them.

Even though settlements were small and far apart in those mountains, the bus passed right through Castle Hill and Cass before stopping at Bealey, which scarcely warranted the stop. There the driver volunteered to telephone lunch orders ahead to Kumara Junction, where the journey would be interrupted by a thirty-minute break. He even read a brief menu to the passengers via the P.A. system. Meanwhile, I pondered the possibility that he might be serving two masters. In fact, that was the main reason why I failed to place an order—that and the belief that I would be able to obtain a sandwich at another source. But my logic turned out to be in error on both counts.

The elevation of Arthur's Pass proved to be about nine meters less than that of the first one, but it was much more impressive, because the highway had now penetrated the Southern Alps. First off, I was inclined to suspect that the name was a misnomer, since the mountains possessed neither the rugged, rocky characteristics of the Swiss Alps, which I had viewed only in photographs, nor the towering, sheer rock walls of British Columbia's Rocky Mountain Range, which I had viewed in the flesh. There were numerous huge boulders and tremendous slides consisting of decomposed black rock, but they had evolved on the slopes of mountains whose maximum elevations rarely exceed seven thousand feet. Nevertheless, a few splashes of white began to appear on some of the peaks, and my respect for them grew with each additional splash. Some stretches of the highway had been hewn from solid rock; consequently, a cross section through it would have revealed a vertical rock wall on one side, a horizontal rock roadbed, and in some places a sheer drop of thousands of feet on the other side.

In the general vicinity of Arthur's Pass, the driver noisily switched on the P.A. system and announced: "On your left you'll see a small lake that's about the size of a municipal swimming pool. If you have a pickax and a shovel with you, and if you don't mind getting wet, you can go to the center of that lake and dig straight down through solid rock into the center of the five-mile railroad tunnel."

Of course, the statement lacked the intended humor, but it displayed a certain amount of imagination, and it did convey the information that the courses of the highway and the railroad intersected at that point but at vastly different elevations.

Shortly thereafter, the bus entered a particularly tortuous stretch of highway where each turn was so sharp that the driver was forced to bring the vehicle to a stop until oncoming traffic had cleared the turn before squeezing the bus around it. During one of those maneuvers, chancing to glance down through the window, I hurriedly closed my eyes because there was nothing between that side of the bus and the bounding spray of the Otira Rapids two thousand feet below. That glance would have terrified even the average victim of acrophobia, and I'm not an average victim of it. Fortunately, the voice of the driver distracted me, because we victims of acrophobia are reputed to behave irrationally at times.

"Caravans and trailers are banned in this particular area because of the high winds that often blast through the Otira Gorge," he asserted.

"Humph!" José grunted. "Probably it's because those vehicles could never safely negotiate the sharp turns."

Then Pancho chimed in: "If there had been a guardrail along the gorge side of this road, the bus would never have made it between the rail and the opposite sheared-rock wall."

Just beyond that point the driver braked the vehicle to a stop beside a relatively large stream of water that poured down the face of the rock wall into a large catch basin, from which it cascaded through a concrete flume under the roadway and into the gorge. Arising from my seat, I peered through the opposite window at the other end of the flume, from which the stream of water burst forth high above the gorge. There vicious updrafts whipped it into fine spray as it fell toward the tortuous course of the Otira River far below.

"Let us also spray," José suggested, as I clasped my hands and closed my eyes against the familiar tug of the phobia on my innards.

Meanwhile, that stupid driver continued to allow the bus to perch precariously on the edge of the world while he harangued the passengers about the beauty of the view and the characteristics of the waterfall. "Sometimes it rains so hard up here that the culvert can't dispose of the water fast enough," the man said, "so it gushes across the road."

Suddenly, my hands involuntarily clasped each other so tightly that my knuckles cracked loudly as I visualized how much that stream of water could have eroded and weakened the roadway's substructure on the gorge side. Then, realizing that the substructure had to be solid rock, I relaxed with a sigh. Sometimes I worry too much, and that time may have been one of them. Meanwhile, the driver released the brakes, and the bus rolled slowly toward the next sharp curve.

"In fact, it rains a lot up here," the driver resumed. "That is, if you consider one hundred eighty inches per year a lot of rain. I repeat, one-eight-o inches, which translates into a very wet depth of fifteen feet." Pausing, he glanced across his left shoulder at the nearest passenger and added: "Rains of up to twenty-five inches have been reported here." But he failed to include the durations of such rains, an important factor in such statistics.

From Otira, just a wide spot in the highway, the bus continued down the steep grade into the depths of the gorge. Meanwhile, the driver returned to discussing the rainfall: "All of that rain helps to maintain a thick cover of beech trees on the slopes of the surrounding mountains."

No doubt the statement was true, but I couldn't see any mountain slopes, hence no beech trees, because they were obscured by the sheer rock walls of the gorge.

En route, the bus passed Aichens, Jacksons, Wainhinhi, Turiwhote, Dillmanstown and Kumara, but few of the settlements could qualify as even wide spots in the road. Finally it arrived at Kumara Junction, the long-awaited rest stop, where the passengers were forced to disembark into a light rain.

Kumara Junction consisted of one long, two-story, wood-frame building whose drab, gray siding and shingled gable roof had become mottled by patches of gray-green moss. The structure loomed starkly against the lush background of freshly washed trees, bushes and ferns, which covered that part of the narrow coastal plain on which they stood. And the building's grimy colonial-style windows glared uninvitingly at the oncoming throng of passengers, who were scurrying toward the small stoop that led up to the unsheltered door.

Meanwhile, I continued to sit in the bus and mentally castigate myself for being such a smart donkey. Obviously, there was no other source of food and beverages in the area, and I had refused to place an order when the opportunity was offered. Finally I arose and went to see what was behind that drab, weather-beaten, wood-paneled door.

It screeched protestingly while swinging open into a narrow entry hall. To the right of the door was an open doorway letting into a small bar. Directly beyond the entry hall, an even narrower hallway extended into dim depths that appeared to merge with total darkness. Strolling into it, I found its only sources of light to be the randomly open doorways, which were located equidistantly along both walls. A glance through one open doorway revealed a small room in which a sway-backed bed was positioned along the opposite wall near a narrow, colonial-style window. Dim, gray light flowed reluctantly through the window into the room and spilled through the doorway into the hall.

Near the middle of the hall, a door on my right suddenly opened, and one of the male passengers shouldered through the opening and squeezed past me, so I caught the edge of the door with one hand and stepped through the opening to see what, if anything, was beyond it.

A number of tables and chairs were distributed about the relatively small room, and all of them were occupied by passengers who had been smart enough to place orders with the driver. While my eyes were searching futilely for a vacant chair, the eyes of a middle-aged woman speculatively studied me from an open doorway in the far wall.

Finally she slowly strolled toward me and inquired, "Kin Oy hilp you?"

After another frustrated survey of the crowded room, I redirected my attention to her and answered, "I don't see how you can. There's no place for me to sit, even if these ravenous creatures haven't disposed of the last crumb of food."

"Theyah's nuthin' moah," she murmured. "In fact, Oy jist served the last of the ordahs."

"I suspected that," I responded with a rueful grin. "It never occurred to me that this would be the only place where food could be obtained during this stop."

"Yis, this is the only plice," she granted. "Furthahmoah, it's the only plice of any koind in Kumara Junction. Howevah, Oy may be able to foind a plice foah you to sit," she added with a beckoning forefinger while turning about.

I followed her into the adjoining room, which proved to be a relatively large kitchen. A wooden table and four wooden chairs stood in the far left-hand corner, and the bus driver was seated uncomfortably in the nearest of the chairs. She slowed to a stop beside him and placed the knuckles of her right hand beneath her right jaw with her forefinger projecting upward along her slightly flushed cheek.

"This man would loik a plice to sit...," she began tentatively.

Apparently she followed a policy of treating the man with special deference, hence the private table. Perhaps it was a wise policy, because he obviously could take his busload of paying guests to another such place, if one existed in that sparsely populated land. Consequently, the man probably packed a lot of clout in Kumara Junction's only place of business.

After glancing toward her, he looked up at me and genially said, "Sure, mite. Pull up a chair."

His substitute for the word *mate* was the first dialectical word that I had heard him utter, so I assumed that it was a deliberate attempt to present himself in the typical Kiwi manner.

While I was adjusting myself to the unique characteristics of the old wooden chair that stood on the other side of the table from the man, the woman turned toward the far corner of the room. "Oh!" she exclaimed as if suddenly discovering gold. "Oy've some soup! Would you loik a bowl of soup?"

Since she had graciously sought to place me at ease, I couldn't reject the offer, so I answered, "Yes, soup will be fine."

"No, Al! No!" José warned me. "You particularly detest thin, watery soups. Remember?"

"And this one probably has been thinned with rainwater," Pancho somberly predicted.

Selecting a large, shallow bowl from a stack of crockery, she trotted across the worn linoleum flooring to the far corner of the kitchen, where a battered, aluminum kettle stood on an ancient range. Grasping the handle of the ladle projecting up from within the kettle, she began to scoop some of its thin, watery contents into the bowl while I peered across my right shoulder at the operation and cringed.

"It's vegitabull soup," she belatedly informed me from across the room.

"Great!" I exclaimed dishonorably. "I haven't had my quota of vegetables today. But make it small, because I'm on a diet."

Before delivering the bowl of soup, she paused and peered through the steam-clouded panes of the window in the wall beyond the end of the range and woefully exclaimed, "Oh! It's beginnin' to rine very hahd agin."

The driver glanced toward the window with a displeased expression and growled, "It's always raining when I come here! In fact, I've never been here when it hasn't been raining!"

"Oh, he's jist teasin'," she protested to me as she carefully set the bowl of hot soup before me. "It doesn't always rine heah."

"Yes, it does," he insisted with a mischievous gleam in his eyes. "This is absolutely the wettest place in the entire world."

They continued to disagree about the weather while I set to my task, and a task it proved to be because I had to literally force the bland, tasteless stuff down my gullet.

"It's truly amazing what people will do under the influence of a strong sense of obligation," José observed.

"Yeah, but Al brung it on himself," Pancho rejoined, "so he's suffering the consequences of his stupidity."

As I shoveled the last spoonful past my rebellious lips, the woman switched her gaze from the driver to me and archly inquired, "How was the soup?"

"Great!" I lied cheerfully. "It really hit the spot." Then I tenderly touched the spot under my diaphragm where the stuff had collected into a burning ball.

"And it's amazing how often an essentially honest person will lie to protect the emotional sensitivities of someone who has been kind to him or her," Pancho added belatedly.

"Possibly it's a product of our modern culture." José rejoined. "In this case, it may have been just a strong sense of fair play."

Apparently the driver had been waiting for me to finish my task, since he had been shifting uneasily on his chair. Leaning forward, he suggested, "Well, it's about time for us to push on."

"Oh, yes," I responded. "I hope that you haven't been waiting for me." And we arose in unison.

"No," he said. "There's really no pressing hurry, but I have to remove some cargo from the bus and stow some more in it before we resume our journey."

"The soup will be sivinty cints," the woman interjected.

"Oh, yes," I repeated with a sense of guilt. "I almost forgot to pay for it."

Then, digging two identical coins from a pocket in my jeans, I dropped them into her outstretched palm. After absently glancing down at them, her eyes immediately returned to them while her expression slowly changed to one of deep thought.

"What did I give you?" I asked, thrusting forth a horizontal palm. "I often mistake your twenty-cent pieces for fifty-cent pieces."

"They ah about the sime soize," she granted, dropping them into my palm with a bemused stare.

But the bemused stare continued even after I dug out a dollar bill and submitted it to her with the words: "Let's call it a deal."

"That stare is too familiar for comfort," José suggested.

"But we habitually refrain from condemning anyone on insufficient evidence," Pancho rejoined. "After all, the woman may have been fascinated by this outlander's 'stringe accint.' "

"Or she may have suspected him of trying to con her out of some small change," José retorted.

"Honest people rarely suspect others of dishonesty," Pancho observed, "and we have already been deeply impressed by the inherent honesty of New Zealanders."

Nevertheless, after joining some of the stragglers in the narrow hallway, I resolved to investigate the matter further, so I diverged from the entry hall into the bar (pub), where a tall, middle-aged man presided. A lone customer stood before the small, hardwood bar with one hand clutching the handle of a stein, so I stepped around him and selected a candy bar from a rack at the far end of the bar. After retracing my steps, I submitted a bill to the barman and encountered a duplicate of the stare that the woman had conferred on me.

While I strolled pensively through the doorway into the entry hall, Pancho volunteered, "So we are forced to conclude that the Unknown is present even in this wet, remote outpost halfway around the world from our homeland."

Since my seat reservation indicated Christchurch to Fox Glacier via Greymouth, I was deeply puzzled when, shortly after the bus pulled away from the old hotel, it turned south and traveled alongside the cloud-shrouded, wind-tossed Tasman Sea.

"Possibly the bus travels via Greymouth only when it contains Greymouth passengers," Pancho surmised. And I nodded.

According to a travel brochure, Greymouth is located at the mouth of the Grey River, which is about twenty-five miles northwest of Kumara Junction. The brochure also claimed that Greymouth is the principal town in Westland and that its present population doesn't begin to approximate its population of fifty thousand in 1866, which was generated by the frantic rush for business sites along the river's frontage and by the scramble for gold in the adjoining valley. At that time there were fifty-seven hotels in the city, but they served a very transient lot, some of whom were the miners who boozed their way to the diggings. One year later an official census set the static population at 28,400. During the period between 1865 and 1873, 2,951,399 ounces of gold were extracted from the rocks and streambeds of the area. At its current value, that much gold would fetch more than one billion relatively valueless U.S. dollars.

According to another source, Westland is bounded on the west by the Tasman

Sea and on the east by the Southern Alps. Generally speaking—writing, that is—the west coast's terrain consists principally of alluvium and glacial deposits from rivers and streams originating among the mountains and glaciers of the Southern Alps, which constitute New Zealand's greatest geologic fault and one of the major faults in the earth's surface.

Westland National Park covers some 88,605 hectares, which are the habitat of numerous varieties of vegetation and animals. Paramount among the various varieties of native trees and other vegetation are the Rimu and Rata trees, which are supplemented by numerous types of ferns and clinging vines at the lower elevations and several varieties of Alpine grasses and plants at higher elevations. The park is populated almost exclusively by birds.

From Kumara Junction the bus passed through the tiny settlements of Awatuna, Kaihinu, Houhou, and several more showers before stopping in Hokitika, which contained all of the advantages that Kumara Junction lacked.

"Since no more than fifteen miles of lush rain forest separate Kumara Junction from Hokitika," José began, "it appears that politics and personal economics must have dictated the premature rest stop at the old hotel."

"But the biological needs of the passengers may have been a deciding factor," Pancho observed.

The name *Hokitika* is said to derive from Polynesian navigational terms: *hoki*, to return, and *tika*, in a straight line. But the navigational skills of those early Polynesian navigators should never be denigrated, because they successfully traveled thousands of miles through becalmed and often stormy seas first to reach those beautiful islands and then to colonize them.

Beyond Hokitika we were blessed by occasional breaks in the cloud layer. At one particularly scenic vista the sun shone so brilliantly that the driver swung the vehicle onto a turnout and stopped it so that passengers bearing cameras could photograph the wave-sculpted shoreline and the intermittent lines of whitecaps as they broke on the sandy beach and on two tiny islands, whose pointed peaks projected sharply upward from the rock-strewn floor of the sea. One minute the still atmosphere was gentle and soothing like that of a warm summer day; the next minute the winds thrust dark clouds across the face of the sun and drove heavy drops of rain against the lightly clad bodies of the farthest ranging photographers while they scurried to regain the protection of the bus.

"A perverse monster must control the reins on the winds that charge across the Tasman Sea," Pancho mused smugly from his dry enclosure in the bus.

"Certainly no man can predict which route they will pursue next," José rejoined.

That proved to be the last seascape for some distance, because the highway veered inland, where its few wide spots became even fewer and narrower; some of them were identified by only a mailbox alongside the pavement. If one's eyes were quick enough, they might detect a small dwelling and some sheds lurking among the trees beyond it.

"In midwinter—about the fourth of July—I'll bet that this stretch of highway becomes very desolate, indeed," José speculated as the bus charged onward.

"Very likely it becomes especially desolate when the winds from out of the northwest drive roiling, dark clouds across the turbulent Tasman Sea and slam them against the rocky crags of the Southern Alps," Pancho chimed in. "No wonder they drop their cargoes of moisture; the impact must be cloud shattering. And no wonder there's a verdant rain forest on the western slopes of the Southern Alps."

From Hokitika the small settlements and the mailboxes of the tiny dwellings bore such names as Rimu, Ross, Fergusons, Evans Creek, Harihari (not to be confused with Hairy Harry), Te Taho, and Whataroa. Abruptly the bus swung from the roadway onto a wide, paved turnoff and continued along its sweeping arc to a stop beneath an ornate porte cochere.

"This is the Franz Josef Hotel, where we'll remain for thirty minutes," the driver announced. "Food and refreshments are available in the restaurant to your left, and the hotel's facilities are appropriately identified. Please return to the bus within thirty minutes."

I joined the line of passengers as they stiffly stepped from the vehicle and slowly filed into the attractive restaurant, which proved to be operated somewhat like an American cafeteria. Directly ahead of me was a plump woman of about forty-five, whose buxom superstructure was shrouded in what some Americans crudely call a sweatshirt. Across the back of it the word BELIZE was stenciled in black letters. Momentarily, the line slowed while a woman stalled at the sandwich counter while she tried to make up her mind; meanwhile, the word BELIZE continued to confront me and continued to remind me that I had considered visiting the tiny Central American country at one time.

"Pardon me," I murmured across one of the woman's round shoulders, "but does this word imply that you have visited Belize?"

She rotated about a quarter turn and eyed me with the female's usual suspicion; then, misreading the true character of her questioner, she cast caution to the winds and replied, "Yes, I was there about three years ago."

"Did you find it interesting?" I persisted.

"Well," she began slowly and stopped. Then, with a thoughtful expression, she added, "It's a very small place, you know."

"I suspected that," I said.

"I mean the capital of Belize," she murmured as if trying to correct a misconstruction.

"I assumed as much," I responded with a smile. "In fact, it would almost have to be the capital, because I understand that there are few urban areas in the country."

"There's an interesting barrier reef with lots of marine life just off the coast," she tossed across the round shoulder while moving forward to a stack of trays. Then, with a tray clutched in her hands, she turned and smiled apologetically back at me. Responding with an understanding smile, I also selected a tray and followed her to the glass-enclosed cabinets containing the prepared foods.

The prepared foods were limited to hot meat pies and cold sandwiches; therefore, since I had not yet sampled one of New Zealand's hot meat pies, I grasped a pair of tongs and transferred one of them from a small, glazed oven onto my tray. At the cashier's counter I requested a glass of milk and found that apparently the approval of Parliament was required, because a brief discussion erupted among the personnel before a special courier was dispatched to a remote storage room for it. Consequently, since I had previously suffered similar experiences, I concluded that milk is not a popular beverage among New Zealanders.

With the lightly loaded tray in hand, I stepped away from the cashier's counter and paused to study the layout of the room. Once more, the sun was in full bloom, and it literally poured through one of the large, well-equipped room's two walls of multimullioned windows. My eyes finally found an unoccupied table, so I carried the tray to it and unloaded its contents onto the Formica surface. While seating myself on one of the four chairs, I noticed that the relatively young oriental woman who had held up the departure of the bus at the last rest stop had also chosen an unoccupied table that stood on the slightly elevated floor to my right. Therefore, I resolved to keep her under my personal surveillance, because the bus driver was not the only one who had been irked by her tardiness.

After finishing my repast, I looked across one shoulder toward the oriental woman's table and found that she had already escaped my surveillance, so I decided to search for her. From the restaurant I strolled into the lobby and paused to study some posters lauding the advantages of viewing the glaciers from the cabin of a cruising aircraft. Then I went to locate the "appropriately identified facilities." After that detour I wandered through the hotel's entrance, where I came to an abrupt stop and stared disbelievingly at the oil-stained area of the pavement where the bus had discharged its passengers not more than twenty minutes before. Only a few drops of fresh crankcase oil marked the spot where it had stood. While I pondered the possibilities that I had misjudged the hour and that the bus had departed without me, the Belize woman rounded one corner of the hotel with two other women, with whom she apparently had formed a travelers' alliance. They also paused and stared fearfully toward the spot where the bus had stood.

"The bus driver left without us," I called to them. "Not more than seconds have passed since I saw him dustin' down the highway toward Fox Glacier."

They exchanged uneasy glances; then, after a brief conference, I heard relieved titters, which compelled me to wonder why, of all the sexes, members of the female sex are the only ones who titter. At that point Belize left the other women and advanced toward me.

"You were inquiring about Belize," she said, fixing her brown eyes on my watery, blue ones. "In the restaurant I didn't have an opportunity to properly answer your question."

"But the answer is obvious," I interjected with characteristic wariness. "Snorkeling is about all there is to do in Belize. Right?"

"Right," she replied. "Of course, there's the jungle," she added with an appraising stare.

It was the stare that convinced me, because there was that all-too-familiar air of the Unknown in it.

"Very likely I would dislike the jungle," I rejoined. "Jungles consist of dank undergrowths overshadowed by towering trees, where I might be captured by savages and served up as the entrée at one of their famous communal dinners. If not that, then I might meet up with a hungry python or a boa constrictor, and I've never been formally introduced to such reptiles; besides, I am subject to attacks of claustrophobia, and the boa isn't called a constrictor by chance."

Her expression clearly indicated an awareness of my struggle to be whimsical, but I was saved from further embarrassment by the arrival of the bus. While I lingered at the open doorway of the vehicle, my eyes futilely searched the lush lawns and shrubberies for the short figure of the oriental woman. Finally, giving up the quest, I climbed aboard the bus and strolled along the aisle toward my seat. While approaching the Belize woman's seat, I was startled by the effusively friendly gleam in her soft, brown eyes. They literally invited me to take the aisle seat beside her. Responding with just a trace of a smile, I continued onward to the seat that had been assigned to me. She even turned about and cast a beckoning glance in my direction, but I refused to respond to that baited hook.

"After all, why should he?" José inquired. "He merely asked if she had been to Belize, and she answered the question."

"Besides, we detected tokens of the Unknown in her stare," Pancho added.

After seating myself, I saw that the other two women had chosen unoccupied seats in her immediate area even though prior to our arrival at the hotel they had opted to cluster closer together in two adjacent seats. In fact, one of them had occupied the aisle seat beside Belize. It was obvious to me that, for some Unknown reason, they had separated, because they had been as thick as thieves. Apparently they had concluded that my innocent inquiry had been an attempt to strike up an acquaintance with Belize. Nevertheless, they continued to bat remarks back and forth like Ping-Pong balls. From the corner of one eye, I watched while the tall, slender member of the trio turned about and studied me through her dark-rimmed spectacles. Then, incredibly, she looked across the aisle and smiled approvingly at Belize, who had been surreptitiously watching her. At one point numerous comments were being exchanged in low tones between the trio, but I refused to eavesdrop. However, I did select a very appropriate time to do so inadvertently, because the slender woman suddenly leaned across the aisle toward Belize and murmured, "I wonder if he'll be able to stand it." Then the other two women responded by placing their hands over their mouths, but their actions failed to subdue their hilarious titters.

Of course, I recognized the crude old cliché, and I felt a deep surge of revulsion.

Even Pancho was moved to remark, "Humph! Who brought up the subject of sex anyway? Particularly abnormal sex?"

"Certainly not any of us," José interjected. "Heretofore, I've been favorably impressed with the ladylike behavior of New Zealand women, but that was anything but ladylike. In fact, those gals must be perverted; otherwise they would never have responded so favorably to the smoke screen laid down by the Unknown."

The speculations were interrupted by the roar of the motor, and the sound surged again as if the driver were about to engage the clutch. Impulsively, I called: "Driver! I believe that one passenger is not yet aboard."

He nodded absently and continued to gun the motor while staring grimly into space. Meanwhile, the slender brunette looked back at me and murmured, "Oy suspict he knows."

After allowing the motor to subside to idle, the driver set the hand brake and went to confer with a male member of the hotel's staff, who was standing in the entrance. The driver then returned to his post, and the other man disappeared into the building. Shortly thereafter the hotel man reappeared at a side doorway and raised one arm as an apparent signal, to which the driver responded by releasing the brakes and gunning the motor.

Simultaneously, the slender woman turned back to me with a very agitated expression and exclaimed, "Oh, Oy do believe he's goin' to leave huh behoind."

But that proved not to be the man's intention, because he drove the bus completely around the large hotel and braked it to a stop on the same spot. Then, relaxing against the back of the seat, he waited expectantly. Once more, the hotel man appeared, but at another side doorway, and signaled as before.

The driver nodded, grimly gunned the motor, and engaged the clutch. As the heavy vehicle charged up the long ramp toward the highway, the slender brunette lowered her head in despair and slowly shook it from side to side. Fortunately for the miscreant, the driver responded to the stop sign at the highway. Simultaneously, the slender woman shouted, "There she is!"

But the driver's eyes were already fixed piercingly on a small target moving rapidly along the curve of the downward-sloping highway toward the bus.

"I suspect he knows," I called maliciously to her, but her eyes were intently watching the little Oriental's sturdy legs, which were pumping like pistons as she raced along the shoulder of the highway as if pursued by a clutch of demons and dragons. Clad in a dark denim jacket and pants, she appeared to be as wide as she was high. In fact, a slightly conical reed hat would have completed the picture of a typical oriental peasant woman in one *bleep* of a hurry.

Meanwhile, the doors of the bus swung invitingly open, but she paused before the opening and cast a wary glance toward the driver. Then, matching each step with a gasp for a breath of air, she clambered quickly up the stairs.

"So you've been making friends again," the man remarked mildly.

"Hmm," José mumbled. "I'm always surprised by the subtleness of criticism, if any, from the ever-courteous New Zealanders."

"Yeah, me too," Pancho agreed. "An American bus driver would have exploded like a skyrocket and just as loudly."

The Oriental didn't respond to the driver's remark; she just lowered her black bangs and minced slowly along the aisle toward the rear of the bus.

"I wonder if she understands English," José wondered.

"To my knowledge she hasn't said a word to anyone during the entire trip," Pancho responded. "Surely she wouldn't be traveling so far in a foreign land without some knowledge of its language."

There was an inexplicable gleam of triumph in her black eyes as she slowly clumped past my seat in a pair of crude, square-toed shoes that had to be intended solely for service, since they had no aesthetic value whatsoever. Her dark-rimmed spectacles had slipped slightly askew on her pug nose, and she was just setting them straight when the bus lunged forward. She gasped, grabbed a hand grip, and dived onto the seat behind me.

"No doubt the bus's sudden surge was a product of the driver's pent-up fury," José observed.

"But the act was justified," Pancho claimed, "because she could have hurried along that aisle."

Later, after extracting a brochure from my briefcase, I discovered that, shortly before arriving at the hotel, the bus had passed the Okarito State Forest, within which the Okarito Lagoon is located. At the point where the lagoon joins the sea, the old mining town of Okarito still stands. But I had seen neither the lagoon nor the town from the highway, because the roadway veered inland through that area.

According to the brochure, during the early mining era three to four thousand ounces of gold were transported from Okarito to Hokitika during each of the steamer's trips, but no mention was made of the time that transpired between those trips. But it must have been substantial, since the the engines of such steamers were stoked with coal or wood at that time, so they were constrained to move very slowly.

North of Okarito, along the Waitangirota River, is a small colony of Kotuko (white heron), which is one of New Zealand's most protected species of wild fowl. In fact, it is so carefully protected that an act of Parliament, more or less, is required for even a certified ornithologist to gain access to the colony.

According to the same brochure, Franz Josef Glacier was named after the emperor of Austria in 1862 by its discoverer, Julius Haast. It begins along the main divide of the Southern Alps and drops about seventy-five hundred feet throughout its nine-mile course before terminating in a half-mile-wide glacial wall that stands some eight hundred feet above its base, which is about seven hundred feet above sea level. Because of its steep descent, the glacier flows at rates varying from three to fifteen feet per day, depending on the season.

Besides the Franz Josef and Fox glaciers, there are more than sixty identified glaciers within the Westland National Park, but only Franz Josef and Fox are readily accessible to the public. Approaches to them are through typical Westland bush and fern, which subsist on ancient moraines deposited in the valleys by the glaciers of the last Ice Age.

In the midst of this glacial wonderland stands Mount Cook, which is surrounded by a national park bearing the same name. Its peak extends more than 11,600 feet above the nearby Tasman Sea, and it is New Zealand's highest mountain.

Looking up from the brochure toward the sparkling white fields of Franz Josef Glacier, I watched them slowly disappear behind other less imposing mountain slopes. Then those slopes were replaced by a train of slopes that limited the view of an ever-changing panorama of tall, vine-encumbered native trees, tree ferns, their smaller cousins, and numerous lush, flat-leaf plants and trees. Some of the flat-leaf plants reminded me of the skunk cabbages of southwestern British Columbia and the cabbage palms of Southern California and Florida. I observed a greater variety of plants, bushes, and trees along that section of the western coast than in any of the areas that I had visited on the North American continent.

Meanwhile, Highway 6 crossed many streams and several rivers by means of bridges, which were designed to permit only one vehicle to cross them at a time. Consequently, when two vehicles approached a bridge from opposite directions, the last one to appear was required to park on the wide ramp alongside the bridge approach until the first one passed it. To an old bridge builder, such as I, it was a practical design for that remote area of New Zealand, since there was little traffic over those rain-slogged roads. Besides, it fitted well to the conservative Kiwis' purses.

Like so many glacier-fed streams the world over, the water flowing beneath most of those bridges was so crystal clear that the underlying gravel and stones could be viewed in the most minute details. But the water flowing over one of those streambeds was rendered practically obscure by a milky-gray substance that probably evolved from the terrain through which the water had flowed.

"A particularly light volcanic ash may be suspended in it," José authoritatively opined.

"Naw," Pancho disagreed as authoritatively. "That milky cast is created by a trace of platinum."

"Aw, that's stupid," José retorted. "Even molecular platinum would be much too heavy to remain suspended in water."

"I know that," Pancho retorted. "However, in this land where so much precious metal has abounded, platinum seems to be so much more romantic and exciting than prosaic volcanic ash, so it's more fun to view it as a trace of platinum."

Fox Glacier Hotel   I could have spent the night at the Franz Josef Hotel. However, before leaving Christchurch, I had cornered the bus driver and asked, "On which of the glaciers is it most economical to spend the night: Franz Josef or Fox?"

After submitting a thin smile, he had answered, "It's best to go on to Fox Glacier. Franz Josef will cost you sixty to seventy dollars, whereas Fox will amount to about half that."

So that was why I ended up in the hotel at Fox Glacier. Even though it was an old, two-story, wooden structure, it had been carefully maintained. The tariff on my comfortable room was only thirty-four dollars, but a tasty lamb dinner and the subsequent breakfast of fat bacon, eggs, and toast boosted that sum to fifty-four dollars.

The dinner hour proved to be a large experience, since in that ornate, old dining room I was the only diner who had made no major concessions to formality. Of course, there were no dinner gowns or tuxedos, but all of the men wore jackets and the women appeared to have donned their most complimentary raiment. But I also wore a jacket, my old blue blazer, which was in perfect harmony with my old blue jeans. Consequently, I didn't wonder when, with a particularly austere air, the thin and somewhat ancient hostess very deliberately led me to a remote table that stood against an equally remote wall.

"How were we to know?" Pancho burst forth. "After all, this is one of the most remote spots on the most remote coast of one of the most remote islands on the face of one of the most remote planets in the solar system."

Following a study of the situation, José answered: "There are some oft-repeated stories of Englishmen who habitually dressed for dinner in the depths of the Amazon jungle."

"After this experience," Pancho resumed, "I've decided that those stories aren't so far-fetched."

Following a quiet night in the sack, I returned to the dining room and broke my fast. Then I strolled into the lobby and carefully compared the hands on the face of its big wall clock with those of my watch. I didn't intend to chance missing the 8:45 bus to Queenstown. If I did, there would be a whole day to invest in such activities as casing the tiny village, exploring the rain forest, and trekking to the glacier, none of which particularly intrigued me. Besides, there was an overwhelming possibility that most of the day would be dominated by the Storm King, thereby restricting my activities to the hotel's lobby, its lounge, the dining room, and my room.

During an inspection of the lobby's posters, I discovered that if the Storm King decided to take the day off, I could join one of the local bus tours or indulge in a flight over the glaciers in an airplane, but I have never been given to such extravagant indulgences. In fact, I suspect that I am just as conservative as the New Zealanders.

"A hike to the glacier would be very cost effective," suggested Pancho. "There you could clamber over the pinnacles of ice and explore the crevasses." And I shuddered uncontrollably for an instant.

"What's the matter, Al?" José inquired. "Are you afraid of the cold?"

"Naw, he isn't afraid of the cold," Pancho answered for me. "He has endured some of the lowest temperatures that Saskatchewan has offered. He's afraid of falling into one of those crevasses." Momentarily I visualized myself in the cold, crushing clutch of one of those critters, and I shuddered again.

"Let's drop the subject before Al starts climbing a wall," José suggested.

"Yeah, let's drop it before his imagination brings on an overwhelming surge of claustrophobia," Pancho responded. "His phobias are very painful problems at times."

After silently shaking my head to clear the ivory deck, I checked my watch for the umpteenth time, because I had acquired a phobia about missing that bus.

Turning away from the poster, I looked through one of the lobby's windows at the paved area beneath the porte cochere, where the driver had stopped the bus during the previous evening, and I burst into an involuntary chuckle. A sextet of backpackers was milling about it without any apparent rhyme or reason. Since backpacking is a national pastime in New Zealand, backpackers had been strung along the route from Auckland to the rain forest, but there had been no septuagenarian backpackers among them. Actually, one of the elderly gentlemen in the sextet may have been eighty years old. Watching them move about singly, in pairs, and eventually in a happily chatting group, I could see that they were having a ball, and I envied them.

7

Fox Glacier to Queenstown

When the bus arrived, I was among the first of the dozen or so passengers to board it. My seat proved to be located in the central part of the vehicle, which was eminently satisfactory since shocks from impacts with imperfections in the surface of the highway would be most effectively dissipated at that point. Shortly after settling onto the seat, Pancho reminded me that I had failed to check the destination of the bus, which was usually displayed above a side window if not over the windshield. I almost fainted from fright until José pointed out that the seat reservation indicated my destination, and, since the driver had accepted it, I must be on the correct bus. It's extremely wearing to be such a worrier; fortunately, however, a reasonably logical mind has been my salvation—okay, call it an occasionally logical mind. Nevertheless, that momentary weakness led to the conclusion that guided tours are so popular because many other "nervous Nellies" prefer to pay professional guides to push them around during their trips abroad.

The elderly backpackers were the last passengers to board the bus, and the first six seats had been reserved for them.

"Hmm," Pancho mused. "So they aren't going on a hiking trip after all."

"Then why are they wearing their gear?" countered José.

"How the *bleep* could I know?" retorted Pancho. "They just now showed up in the garb."

"Oh, I get it," José responded confidently to his own question. "They are returning from a hiking trip."

But that logic also proved to be faulty, because the vehicle hadn't traveled more than four miles when it slowed to a stop on the right side of an approach to a single-lane bridge that spanned the Fox River. As the folding doors swung open, the backpackers struggled to their feet and noisily exited. By that time my confidence in my buddies' logic had reached an all-time low.

The backpackers seemed to sense the curiosity of the other passengers, because they displayed a certain cocky air that appeared to shout, "We're going to climb Fox Glacier despite what you skeptics think!" As the bus pulled away, they waved wildly to its passengers. Most of the remaining passengers waved back, and several of them enthusiastically clapped their hands.

My eyes continued to follow the warped and bent figures of those ancient backpackers as they formed a single line and began to climb the steep, grass-grown, gravel trail that followed the course of the wide, cascading stream to the glacier.

"I surely hope that they have enough insect repellent," Pancho remarked. "That environment consists of a stream, dewy grasses, and rain-drenched thickets, plus the moist winds of the Tasman Sea to keep them that way, so it should provide an ideal breeding habitat for sand flies."

"Yeah," José agreed, "those little 'bug-gers' should be out in full force today." Meanwhile, I involuntarily scratched an imaginary bite on my ankle."

They are said to infest this entire coast," added Pancho. "Consequently, many uninitiated tourists will be initiated to them, and they will be doing what uninitiated tourists as far back as Julius Von Haast have done: scratch sand fly bites for no less than two days."

"Since moss is usually moist, it may be a breeding bed for sand flies," José observed.

But that observation was a product of his logic, so it may not have been supported by scientific fact. He mentioned moss only as a possible source of sand flies, because it covered practically everything, even the top branches of the tallest trees. Furthermore, it clung to and hung from rusty, barbed-wire fences, so it encountered no problems in forming velvety, green coats on the shaded sides of wooden fence posts. Even the sheared faces of roadside rocks were embossed by it. However, moss didn't appear to adhere to tree ferns, possibly because their surfaces were too smooth and dense.

Tree ferns were the most unique plants I observed in the lush valleys and on the mountain slopes that face the wet winds of the Tasman Sea. They consisted of relatively slender trunks, composed somewhat like those of palm trees, topped by arrays of flat ferns, which also were similar in shape to the tops of palm trees. They often extended to heights of thirty feet, while their lesser but more gregarious cousins clustered about their trunks and about the trunks of the Rimu and Rata trees. Clustered with them were some plants that looked very much like the cabbage palms of Florida.

Vines grew promiscuously, often hanging from the highest branches of towering trees. There were all kinds of vines: coarse ones with large, glossy leaves, several other types with delicately shaped leaves, and filamentlike vines with tiny, fragile leaves. The latter often displaced the moss on the faces of the sheared rocks, as did another growth similar to watercress. That rain forest exhibited more varieties of plants and more of the typical characteristics of a real rain forest than do any of the rain forests on Washington State's Olympic Peninsula.

After crossing the Fox River, the highway veered inland through the one-horse settlements of Karangarua, Manakaiaua, and Jacobs River. At Bruce Bay the sea was briefly visible as far as Mahitahi; then the highway strayed away from it to Lake Paringo and on to Lake Moeroki, where it swung southwest and followed the coast as far as the Haast River Bridge.

The bridge, completed in 1964, was slightly less than twelve feet wide and slightly more than half of a mile long, and it was equipped with two twelve-foot by one-hundred-foot passing bays; consequently, it qualified as a single-lane bridge. Nevertheless, it provided relatively uninterrupted traffic flow over a river that carries the second largest volume of water in New Zealand.

From the bridge the highway followed the south bank of the river inland for some thirty miles, during which it climbed steadily into the upper reaches of the valley. The mountainous background remained, but the rain forest rapidly faded away. Abruptly, the highway forsook the river valley and rapidly ascended to the

Haast Pass, which lies within the Mount Aspiring National Park. The pass is only about 1,750 feet above sea level, not much of a pass according to North American standards, but the surrounding Southern Alps are still quite rugged by any standards.

After the highway left the rain forest, the terrain became much rougher, even a wasteland. Only dry grass and equally dry brush were sustained by the small amounts of rain that fell from the eastbound clouds, most of whose moisture had been drained from them as they ascended to pass over the ridges and peaks of the Southern Alps.

Soon the wasteland gave way to green, rolling hills with a backdrop of hazy, purple mountains. Many different spring flowers were blooming over large areas, but deep-yellow blooms dominated the scene. In fact, they literally obscured their relatively large, light-green bushes, which covered the floors of some of the nonarable canyons and valleys. In one instance, an entire mountainside had been painted yellow by those beauties, but they always stopped at the fences that outlined fields and pastures. Therefore, I suspected that the farmers probably cultivated their pastures to eradicate all of the plants that didn't produce wool or lamb chops.

But sheep were not the only ranch animals along that particular stretch of highway; there were several large herds of deer and goats. For a country that once harbored only birds, with the advent of human beings it appeared to have become a veritable menagerie what with its domestic livestock and animals of the hunt, such as red deer, chamois, and thar. Of course, glowworms don't really qualify.

Some New Zealanders are particularly proud of their native glowworm population, which inhabits parts of the Westland National Park and some caves in a few other parts of the islands. But I wonder if those people are fully aware of a problem that may prevail among those little beasties.

For example, one summer while I was still a mere lad—about a hundred years ago—my family visited my grandparents' farm in Nebraska. During our stay I was exposed to and often fascinated by the flashing lights of the fireflies as they cruised through the still, warm air past the gently swaying lawn swing, where the family commonly congregated in the deep dusk. I particularly remember one little firefly who carried a tiny, red lantern, which must have been connected to her electric generator, because it flashed on and off like a neon sign. Of course, I knew nothing of such things then; however, now that I do, I wonder if those strict, Presbyterian New Zealanders should not be warned about the probable morals of their glowworms.

Shortly after the Makarora River appeared along the right side of the highway, the roadway widened just a smidgen to squeeze in the settlement of Makarora. And that was the first evidence of human habitation during the long trip from the Haast Bridge.

The river soon terminated in Lake Wanaka, a virtual scenic gem set among high mountain peaks. Discounting the wide mouth of the river, the lake is about thirty miles long and somewhat less than two miles wide. Its surface is about 875 feet above sea level, and in places it is more than 930 feet deep, so those places are below sea level. The lake's Maori name, Te Waihakaata, translates into "Mirror Waters," which proved to be appropriate, because we were rewarded by an inverted view of a nearby mountain scene.

After the bus had traversed about half the length of the lake, we were treated to a view of a few relatively imposing buildings clustered picturesquely about a cove along the far shore. Suddenly the P.A. system sputtered, and the driver's voice boomed forth: "Those buildings that you see on the far side of the lake belong to a very wealthy man of these parts who operates a large sheep station covering several thousand hectares of prime grazing land plus two or three mountains. As you can see, no roads lead to those buildings; therefore the only way that anyone can get to them is by boat or helicopter. How is that for complete isolation?"

"Man, oh man!" exclaimed José. "That's for us. I wonder how much cash we'll have to put together to buy that guy out."

"Plus some pier-launched torpedoes... and an anti-aircraft gun," interjected Pancho. "Of course, we would have to guard against the persistent encroachments of the Unknown."

Just beyond that point, the highway turned northeast around a long neck of water projecting from the near side of Lake Hawea, whose surface area approximated that of Lake Wanaka. But its surface had been raised from its normal level to 1,175 feet above sea level by a dam that had been constructed to serve the Roxburgh Hydroelectric Station.

I really hate to admit this, but I became lost in that part of New Zealand, even aboard a partially loaded bus; consequently, I cannot truthfully name the town where the bus stopped for the rest break, but it may have been Wanaka, which is located at the south end of Lake Wanaka. I realize that no one should ever get lost in a country as small as New Zealand, but the South Island **is** the largest of its two major islands, so I sincerely hope that that's sufficient justification. However, I've even become lost in the relatively small city of Santa Monica; so some of my associates have unkindly contended that I could get lost in a three-by-three-foot closet in broad daylight, but no one has ever listened when I pointed out that such closets rarely have windows. Invariably, they have countered that I am always floundering around in the dark anyway. Nevertheless, I got lost, but three of the other passengers also got lost: the little oriental woman and the two allies of Belize. When they failed to return to the bus, the driver didn't see fit to wait for them, so I suspected that they were supposed to get lost there.

Shortly thereafter, our bus lost its driver, but another one lost its driver simultaneously. The bus was tearing down the slope of one of the metal-surfaced stretches of the highway, where the gravel had been pounded into a veritable silicon powder, and I was fearfully staring through the window into the bottomless chasm on my left. After I reluctantly tore my terror-stricken eyes from the chasm, they involuntarily fixed on another bus just as it rounded a curve, partially obscured by a sheared rock wall, and charged up the grade toward our bus. Momentarily, both drivers appeared to become confused, because they simultaneously turned their charges onto one of the rare shoulders of the highway and brought them to a stop. Meanwhile, their individual clouds of silicon dust melded into one massive cloud comparable to that of a nuclear blast. Worst of all, my bus had stopped on the very edge of that deep chasm, so I quickly turned my head away from the window and watched while the drivers left their respective charges and disappeared into the center of the cloud. Apparently the drivers either got lost or became even more confused, because the driver who emerged from the cloud and assumed control of our bus wasn't the one who had been·driving it. But the confusion was cleared up somewhat when the new driver laconically announced, "Driver change."

The new driver pushed the vehicle rapidly along the highway, which continued to descend along a sinuous course carved from the rock wall of the chasm. The chasm gradually became a gorge with a burgeoning river on the bottom of it. As the bus rounded one of the many curves, it began to slow, so I curiously looked ahead and beheld an incredibly long line of motionless vehicles. When the bus came to a stop behind the last of them, the driver opened a small window on his right and silently listened to the words of a burly, middle-aged man clad in workman's attire and a hard hat. After conveying his message, the workman raised the base of the stop sign, which he was stabilizing in one hand, and transported it to the rear of the bus.

Meanwhile, the driver turned about, faced the questioning eyes of the passengers, and said, "There'll be a forty-five-minute wait to allow construction to proceed, so you might as well get out and stretch your legs a bit, but don't wander too far from the bus because there won't be another one along here until this time tomorrow."

Some of the passengers snickered at the implication, but he hadn't frightened me, because I had seen one of his kind literally running around in circles to save a certain little oriental woman from just such a fate. Even though the passengers had forty minutes to leave and return to the bus, there was some unnecessary jostling at its open doorway as they stepped down onto the loose rock granules that covered the shoulder of the highway.

"There must be some Americans among those passengers," Pancho softly suggested, but I was absently stepping into the aisle behind the last passenger. After stepping down onto the shoulder, I found that two young men were exhibiting their manly prowess by hurling several small pieces of rock toward the far side of the river, but their missiles dropped ignobly into the water along its near bank. The distance also deceived me when I picked up a flat rock about the size of a discus and stared speculatively toward the river. Awkwardly rotating myself through the gyrations of a discus thrower, I dramatically released it, but the *bleeped* thing dropped like a rock onto the near bank of the river.

"Evidently sixty years of a relatively sedentary life-style have taken their toll," José gently consoled me.

"I suspect that it's the fat that has replaced his muscles," Pancho brutally rejoined.

"It could be too much *pauncho*," his partner snidely observed. And the observation launched one of their long wrangles.

Meanwhile, I stood and stared morosely at the spot where the rock had struck while Belize and several other health bugs walked briskly along the shoulder of the highway to the point where it curved. Several minutes later I was still staring morosely at the same spot when Belize returned.

"Hi," she murmured, slowing to a stop before me.

"Hi," I responded none too genially.

An awkward silence ensued; then I inquired, "Did you happen to notice the mountainside that was covered with yellow flowers back there a ways?"

"Do you mean the lupines?" she inquired.

"Lupines?" I countered with a stare. "In my country lupines are blue."

"Those are lupines," she insisted.

"So one learns something new every day," I responded doubtfully but with uncharacteristic tact.

Then I recalled that white, pink, and blue lupines are native to several of the eastern states, so there was no reason why they could not be yellow in New Zealand. After all, many of the country's other plants are similar to but uniquely different from the plants of the Northern Hemisphere.

"If you go to Belize, you should continue on into Yucatan," she volunteered. Then peering intently at me, she asked, "Or have you been there already?"

"No," I replied, "but it's practically next door to Belize, and since both countries are so close to my country, there's no logical reason why I shouldn't see them."

"You'll like Yucatan," she murmured, staring off into space. "It's the most beautiful country that I've ever seen."

"Even more beautiful than this one?" I countered incredulously.

Having already rendered the answer, she ignored the question. "Many of the old Mayan ruins have been uncovered, and they're very interesting," she said. "That area once supported an advanced form of civilization, you know. Besides those ruins, there are so many other unusual things to see, such as the tropical jungle with its wide variety of plant life, strange mammals, and exotic birds."

"You must be a member of Yucatan's Chamber of Commerce," I suggested with a smile.

She fixed a pair of puzzled eyes on mine, so I began to suspect that she must be from Europe, because Europeans rarely understand so-called American humor. And the suspicion induced me to inquire, "Where are you from? Europe?"

"Germany," she replied. "I'm from Hamburg."

"You certainly have covered a large part of the world," I remarked. "What do you do for a living?"

"I work for the health department," she answered.

"A nurse, probably," José speculated.

"Yeah," Pancho agreed, "she even looks like a nurse."

"That explains your aggressive attack on this steep slope," I responded, gesturing toward the highway.

Responding with a smile, she murmured, "I like to walk."

After glancing toward the open doorway of the vehicle, I exclaimed, "Oops! The other passengers are beginning to board the bus, so I suppose that we should do likewise."

Of course, I allowed her to precede me up the steps and to her seat. And there may have been another invitation in her eyes for me to join her as she stepped aside and settled onto it. I can't say for sure, because I wasn't looking into her eyes. My mind was preoccupied with other thoughts.

"After so many years in voluntary social exile, Al has come to prefer his own company," Pancho observed.

"That's especially true when he suspects potential company of having succumbed to the weird incantations of the Unknown," José rejoined.

After all of the passengers had returned to the bus, the driver climbed aboard and seated himself behind the wheel; then he stared thoughtfully ahead at the long line of vehicles, which was beginning to move slowly onward.

Finally he turned abruptly toward the assemblage and said, "Someone has asked about the apparent inefficiency of these often hour-long waits to accommodate construction. Of course, there is one obvious alternative: The workmen can always close the highway." Then he faced forward and started the motor.

"Possibly a passenger spoke disparagingly to the man about the policy of detaining the vehicles," Pancho speculated.

"And possibly that passenger was a tactless 'furriner' like Al," José injected, "so the criticism may have rankled in the man's bosom, if men possess such things."

"Consequently, since most New Zealanders are fiercely nationalistic," Pancho resumed smoothly, "he may have countered with the most absurd alternative that he could conceive, even though he had several more logical ones from which to select."

After leaving the gorge, the highway passed through several settlements, and the paramount ones were Lugate, Queensbury, Lowburn, Roaring Meg, Gibbston, Arrow Junction, and Lower Shotover. Most of them were located in the valley of the Clutha River, New Zealand's largest river. Just before arriving at Roaring Meg, the highway turned west into the Kawarau Gorge; then it crossed and recrossed the Kawarau River before finally entering Queenstown.

Queenstown

The town is located midway along the north shore of Lake Wakatipu, which is shaped somewhat like a partially collapsed letter *z* with its top and bottom elements pointed almost north and south. If that doesn't adequately describe its location, look at the map of New Zealand, because I may have still been lost somewhere on the southern end of the South Island.

Since the town had been so highly recommended, I greeted what appeared to be its outskirts with high expectations, but they were completely dashed by the time the bus arrived at the station, because those so-called outskirts proved to be the town itself. In fact, what I initially assumed to be a shopping mall proved to be the main business district. Meanwhile, I had been taking stock of some of the motels and hotels and found the largest one to be located opposite the station on the far side of Beach Street. The station clock indicated a few minutes before six when I collected my luggage and headed across Beach Street toward the towering hotel bearing the familiar name of Travelodge. But this Travelodge appeared to be much more sumptuous than those that I had seen on the North American continent. Nevertheless, I lugged my luggage through the garishly orange and purple lobby to the front desk, where one of the two attractive young women archly inquired, "Can I help you?"

After tendering a skeptical smile, I replied, "I doubt that you can, but you really should tell me what this hotel charges for a single so I can record the rate for posterity."

"One hundred forty dollars," the vixen responded with scarcely any accent but with apparent relish.

"That's even more than I expected," I responded with a shocked grimace. Meantime my hands were groping for the handles of my luggage.

Upon returning to the station, I found the perky little road services clerk in the act of closing shop at exactly six o'clock. Hurriedly thrusting one Hush Puppy between the door and its jamb, I pleadingly inquired, "Can you direct me to a public telephone?"

"Yis," she replied, "theyah's one in the wee, rid building at the idge of the pahk. If you'll go around that building ovah theyah," she added with an out-thrust forefinger, "you'll foind it aboot fifty metahs along the soidewalk." I found it in spite of the fact that she had described it as a "wee, rid building."

"Oh, a little, red telephone booth," José and Pancho chorused when I finally spied it. Then, fishing through my pockets for some change, I hooked a lone fifty-cent piece.

"It has to be too big," Pancho insisted as I entered the booth and searched for instructions on how to use the instrument. As usual, there were none.

"Someday," I growled, "I'm going to learn how to operate a New Zealand telephone."

Meanwhile a ruggedly constructed man of about fifty came to a stop outside the booth and assumed a waiting attitude. Immediately stepping from the booth, I said,

"Please make your call, because it's going to take me some time to determine how this *bleeped* thing works."

"Ohhh?" he exhaled with a puzzled expression. "Can I help you?"

"No, but thank you very much," I replied. Admittedly, the memory of that embarrassing experience in the lobby of the Princes Gate Hotel still rankled, so I was determined to make the call myself. "Please make your call," I insisted.

"Thank you," he murmured, sidling into the tiny booth.

When he left it, I approached him and asked, "Can you change this for me. It's the smallest coin I have."

After staring at the coin with a puzzled air, he inquired, "Do you want to make a long-distance call?"

"No," I replied ruefully, "I only want to call a cab, but I've never used this type of telephone, and there are no instructions on how to use it."

"Ohhh," he exhaled again. "I can do that for you." Then he turned about and reentered the booth.

I immediately appeared at his shoulder with the coin in my outstretched hand, but he vehemently shook his head, so I slipped it into the nearest of his hip pockets and retreated to the adjacent sidewalk.

A few seconds later he thrust his head from the booth and asked, "Where do you want to go?"

"I don't know," I admitted, "but a cab seems to be the best way for me to shop for an economical hotel or motel."

Momentarily, the lines of his features jiggled like those on an emotionally disturbed computer screen until they finally registered comprehension; then he nodded and returned to the instrument. After completing the call, he stepped from the booth and attempted to return the coin to me.

"No," I responded with a stubborn shake of my head. "Your time was worth much more than that, especially to me."

But the equally stubborn good Samaritan tossed the coin at my feet, so I had no choice but to pick it up, because all of my ancestors would have erupted from their graves if I hadn't.

"A cab will be here within five minutes," he informed me with a gesture toward the narrow street.

"I surely appreciate your help," I said.

"I'm glad to have been of service," he responded.

"I don't see why they don't place some instructions in those *bleeped* phone booths," I grumbled.

He chuckled; then, with a light, left-handed slap on my right shoulder, he said, "Enjoy your stay in New Zealand." With that, he turned about and strode along the sidewalk.

Meanwhile, I skeptically studied the heavy traffic and the automobiles parked along one curb of the narrow street. Nodding in response to the lads' suggestions, I picked up my luggage and retraced some twenty steps to an intersecting driveway. Upon lowering the luggage to the sidewalk, I turned about and found a taxicab to be standing in the street opposite the booth. Not only had my good Samaritan returned to it, but he was directing the driver to the spot where I stood. Needlessly, I motioned to the driver. While the cab rolled slowly toward me, I marveled at the kindness and the consideration of New Zealand's Good Samaritans. They reminded me so much of the Good Samaritans who still populated parts of my country some sixty years ago. Unfortunately they are no more.

"I moved to this driveway because the street was so congested at that point," I explained to the driver as we carried the luggage to the rear of the cab.

"Yis, a man could get killed theah," he admitted. Then, with a loud "Uhhh!" he hoisted the suitcase and stowed it in the trunk. Then, turning to me, he asked, "Whut ye got in theah? Gold?"

And I laughed as boisterously as when I first heard the cliché. New Zealanders aren't the only ones who can be Good Samaritans.

After we had assumed our respective positions on the front seat, he asked, "Wheah do ye want to go?"

"That's a good question," I replied pensively. "But I'm not going to spend any time in that towering pile of steel, concrete aggregates, and cement." Then I pointed through the windshield toward the nearest wall of the Travelodge.

"Oy don't blime ye one bit," he muttered. "Mybe a motel would do."

"Yes, a motel would do," I agreed, "as long as it isn't too far out of town."

"Will, Oy just happen to have a frind who runs one," he muttered, thrusting the nose of the cab into the traffic, "and his proices ah the lowest in town. Moight Oy give him a buzz?"

"Please do," I replied.

"He usually fills up early," the man resumed, "but he should still have some spice at this toime. It's only six-thuty."

Unfortunately, his "buzz" netted a negative response. "That's surproisin'," he muttered. "Usually he isn't full up so early in the evenin'. Howevah, the Poines will loikely have a plice foah ye."

On the way to it, I noted that the cab traveled along Shotover Street, Marine Parade, and Man Street. Then I lost track, but it hadn't traveled far before veering onto a street that terminated at the entrance of a motel. The unimpressive wooden structures appeared to be about forty years old, but I allowed the cab to roll to a stop on its asphalt driveway.

Turning to the driver, I commanded, "Don't remove the luggage, because I may be right back."

At the entrance to the office, the glazed sliding door chose to defy me, but it finally yielded. From the opening two strides carried me to a long, wooden counter, where a small sign instructed me to press the buzzer on the adjacent wall, so I pressed it. While I was impatiently waiting for a response, my eyes studied the half-dozen mattresses that had been stacked somewhat indifferently in an adjoining cubicle.

According to my standards the management was definitely disorganized, if not disorderly, but my study was interrupted by the sounds of footfalls rapidly descending several remote, wooden steps. The narrow door in the wall to my left suddenly burst open, and a tall, comely woman hurried breathlessly through the opening and came to an abrupt stop on the opposite side of the counter.

After a couple of deep inhalations, she posed the usual question, "Kin Oy hilp you?" Meanwhile, her brown eyes carefully studied my features.

"Possibly," I granted. "How much do you charge a single guest for one night?" A troubled veil crossed her eyes as they fixed thoughtfully on the large window behind me.

"Oh-oh!" chorused José and Pancho. "She's about to come up with a reason for rejecting us."

Assuming a resolute expression, she turned her eyes to mine and answered, "Oy have only one lift, but the showah doesn't work."

"Well, that sort of scotches the deal," I said, "because I have to have a shower."

"Oh, it works," she insisted, "but...."

"It works, but it doesn't work," I suggested with a teasing smile.

From her skeptical glance, I gathered that she didn't cotton to the suggestion, but she responded favorably to the smile. "Will, it doesn't drine propahly, but...."

"But if I don't mind standing knee deep in soapy water, it works, hey?" I countered with another teasing smile.

"Yis," she answered. "If you don't moind that, you can have it for thuty-foive dollahs instead of foahty."

"Well, a shower is intended to make one wet," I reasoned, "and that one certainly should do it in spades."

"If you could wite to tike yoah showah," she ventured, "theah won't be a problim, because Oy've called a plummah, and he should be heah any minute now."

"That can be arranged," I granted, "but won't those accommodations be worth forty dollars after he fixes the shower?"

"But you will be subjicted to an inconvenience in the meantoime," she murmured, "so the proice is still thuty-foive dollahs."

"It's a deal," I said and reached for my wallet.

When I returned to the cab, the driver greeted me with the words, "Did you talk her into it?"

"No," I responded with a chuckle. "She talked me into it." But I didn't attempt to explain. In fact, no one would have believed the explanation; at least, no American would have believed it.

After we unloaded the luggage, I paid the fare. Then, while adding a substantial tip to it, I said, "This is for your assistance in locating economical lodging for me."

"Thank ye," he responded with a pleased expression.

"You earned it," I murmured.

"Yis, we must've sived about nointy dollahs on whut ye would've had to pie at the Travelodge," he suggested.

"One hundred and five," I rejoined.

"Theah can't be that much difference between thim," he protested. Then, while sliding behind the wheel, he added, "But Oy'm glad to've been of some assistance."

"You cheapskate, Al," Pancho tauntingly informed me as I picked up the luggage and moved toward the motel unit.

"But I would never have paid that much for a place to sleep," I countered. "I would have spent the night on a park bench first."

"And he ain't kiddin'," José interjected.

"Heah is yoah milk!" soprano tones shrilled from some distance behind me.

Glancing across one shoulder toward the office, I found the woman poised on the edge of the concrete stoop like a bird about to launch itself into the air with a pint of milk under one wing.

After assessing my fully loaded status, she called, "Nevah moind, Oy'll bring it to you."

"No, save it," I called back to her.

"But you'll need it foah yoah coffee oah tay," she insisted while hurrying toward me.

"But I don't drink coffee or tea," I retorted.

"Will, Oy'll bring it anywye," she said. "Besoides, you ah intoitled to it."

Dashing past me, she hurriedly opened the door so that I could stride directly into the unit—or into the part of it that proved to be either a large dinette or a small living room. In either case, an oval table with four chairs stood against one wall, and a sitbed stood against the opposite wall. Several easy chairs were distributed about the remainder of the room. The woman turned toward the far end of the small kitchen on our left and stowed the pint of milk in the tiny, deck-high refrigerator at the end of it. Then she joined me in an unscheduled tour of the place.

"Hmm," I mumbled approvingly, "a sitbed in the living room and a double bed plus a sitbed in the master bedroom." After leaving the luggage in the doorway, I peeked into the second bedroom and exclaimed, "Two more double beds in here! Wye, I could entertain a whole line of chorus girls in this place."

"You shuahly could," she said. But there was a world of skepticism in her eyes as they wandered from my gray beard to my bald head. "This is yoah home to do with whatevah you want."

"Of course, I was kidding," I insisted hurriedly.

"Of coahse," she responded with a smile as we came to a stop at the entrance. Glancing toward the kitchen, she added, "It's a shime that you don't drink coffee oah tay, because theah ah plinty of both. That milk will be wisted."

"No, it won't," I retorted. "I'll drink it."

She stared at me as if I were a creature from outer space but tactfully refrained from expressing her thoughts. Instead she began: "If you want to purchase some groceries...."

"I won't," I interjected. "I'll go out for a bite."

"Then you should follow this strait to where it intersicts with the nixt one," she suggested. "Theah you should turn roight and follow the curve toward the cintral paht of town." After a short pause, she added, "Oy shuahly hope you injoy yoah suppah and a noice noight's sleep."

"Thank you," I responded thoughtfully. "But I still have one small problem and that is a wake-up call. Do you rise early?"

"Whut toime do you want to git up?" she countered.

"I don't know," I admitted. "The road services office closed before I could reserve a seat on the bus to Invercargill; however, I'm sure that it won't leave before eight o'clock."

"Oy suspect that that bus leaves aboot tin o'clock," she murmured, "but Oy'm not shuah of it."

"Then there's no reason for me to create a problem," I said.

"Theah's no problim," she insisted. "In fact, Oy'll tike you to the station in toime to catch the bus."

"No!" I retorted. "I'll call a cab."

"Oy'll tike you in the cah," she insisted. "It's jist a shoaht run."

"Let's wait and see what the morning brings," I suggested evasively.

"Oy'll tike you to the bus," she said stubbornly.

There comes a point when no gentleman resists a lady's wishes, so I threw up my hands in defeat. Besides, I had begun to suspect that she was secretly expecting that I would lay the equivalent of the cab fare in her hand, and that was a *fair* deal.

After removing some of the accumulated grime, I followed the woman's directions, which took me alongside a small park to a busier thoroughfare that curved through a pleasant neighborhood. From there I found my way to the small business district near the lake. Pausing briefly at the recessed entrance of a Chinese restaurant, I studied the menu posted high on one of its plate glass windows. Since it appeared to be designed to serve two or more patrons, I continued on to the Pizza Hut, which stood nearby on the same side of the street.

A chubby young woman, who couldn't have been more than eighteen, led me to a table that stood against the far wall, where I selected the nearest of three chairs. Meanwhile, I turned curious eyes toward the sharply inclined back of a young woman who was the sole occupant of the table for two tucked into the adjacent corner. She was notable in that her flaxen locks were draped picturesquely forward over a paper napkin on the otherwise bare table as the cramped fingers of her right hand laboriously guided a ballpoint pen across the napkin while the splayed fingers of her left hand strained to hold the napkin in place.

While seating myself, I accepted the menu that the waitress thrust before me. "Thank you," I murmured. Then, after quickly inspecting it, I looked up at her, pointed to an item on the menu, and asked, "Is this the smallest pizza that you serve?" And she nodded amiably. "I'll never be able to pack in that much pizza," I protested. "Don't you serve partials?"

Shaking her head, she cheerfully suggested, "You kin tike wots lift with you."

"That isn't practical for me," I rejoined, searching the menu for my favorite combination. "I'm traveling across country in public conveyances, so I *can't take it with me*. Besides, the smell of a decaying pizza might start a riot on a bus full of hungry passengers."

From the confusion in her eyes, I concluded that my attempted humor had misfired, so I said, "One of the small pizzas smothered with mushrooms and *red-hots* should be more than sufficient."

Since the confusion in her eyes deepened, I reviewed my words and added, "On second thought, please change those red-hots to pepperoni chips." And the confusion disappeared. After marking the order pad, she turned away to place the order.

"Please add a glass of milk to that order," I called to her belatedly.

Fortunately she didn't add the milk to the pizza, but she acted almost as foolishly. She immediately placed the glass of milk on the table in front of me, where it became progressively warmer with the passing of each of the twenty minutes that I waited for the pizza to be baked and delivered to me. After delivering it, she strolled to the side of the deeply engrossed writer and inquired, "Would you loike something moah?" Goldilocks mutely responded with a shake of her flaxen curls.

In the interim, a woman and two small children left the table located diagonally across the corner from mine. After it was cleared and readied for the next diners, a tall, ruggedly constructed man and a somewhat buxom woman, both of whom looked to be in their middle thirties, replaced them. After placing their orders, they participated in a desultory conversation interspersed by long silences, which are so typical of two people who spend much of their lives together.

Meanwhile, a search of my pockets uncovered a pamphlet that I had reserved for just such an occasion as this, so I unfolded it and began to read it. According to that supposedly infallible source, Queenstown evolved from a gold rush to the banks of the Shotover River, which in the early 1860s was known as the richest river in the world. Consequently, the town abruptly acquired a relatively large population, which, because of the rapid decline of gold mining, dropped to about 190 in 1900. At that time most of the local transportation was confined to lake steamers, one of which, the *Ernslaw*, is still in service. Subsequent to its fabrication in Dunedin, in 1912 it was transported over land in sections and assembled in Kingston, which is located at the southern end of the lake. Presently the town has a permanent population of about 3,000, but it is seasonally expanded by several thousand visitors, many of them from abroad.

After the waitress had delivered my pizza and departed, we stared warily at each other for an instant; then my eyes flicked toward the writer's inclined back. "Miss,"

I called tentatively. But she was deeply engrossed in her efforts, so I called out, "Miss!" Turning her head, she peered across one canted shoulder toward me. "Would you like to split this pizza with me?" I asked. "It's far too much for me to consume."

"Splitz?" she responded with a puzzled expression. Then it was my turn to be confused, but I quickly recovered. "Yes, split it," I responded, "divide it. In other words, you take half of it, and I'll take the other half."

"No, thank you," she responded pleasantly in somewhat throaty tones with a shake of her curls, "I've already hadt vun."

"Too bad," I muttered with a baleful glare at the steaming heartburn. "I hate to waste food."

After repeating the smile, she returned to her task.

Isolating one of the six pie-shaped pieces of pizza, I cut off a large piece and thrust it into my salivating mouth. Then I hurriedly grasped the glass and ingested a large mouthful of its contents, but the warm milk failed to cool my mouth's seared surfaces. Of course, pizza is most tasteful when it is hot, but that pizza had to be hotter than Hades, because almost every bite was followed by an ingestion of warm milk. And I have hated warm milk with a deep and abiding passion ever since the times when I probably gorged myself on it during the initial months of my life.

Suddenly, the writer turned about on her chair and asked, "I vonder if you vill help me."

I shifted a bite of milk-saturated pizza to one side of my mouth and cautiously replied, "Wye, yes, I suppose so." Meanwhile, dollar signs began to spin on my mind's computer screen, as José urgently warned, "Watchit, Al! Whenever a woman has solicited help from us in the past, it has invariably involved money."

"Yeah," Pancho interposed, "and usually it has been our money."

So there was a world of caution in my words when I asked, "What kind of help?"

"I'm planning to take a valk through a particularly beautiful area," she explained, "undt to do dot, I haf to cross a farmer's property." After pausing and pondering momentarily as if searching for the correct words, she continued, "I vunt to talk to him on der telephone undt explain vot I vunt to do, but I can't find der proper vords. Vill you help me vid dis?"

After releasing a pent-up sigh of relief, I replied, "I'll be glad to help you." Then I turned thought-filled eyes toward the pizza.

Seeming to read my mind, she immediately protested, "Oh, I don't mean right avay. I vill continue to write vot I vish to say until you are finished, den idt vill help if you vill read vot I haf written. All right?" And her eager smile was so contagious that I felt my lips follow suit.

"All right!" I responded. Then she smiled delightedly and returned to whatever she was doing to that poor, defenseless paper napkin.

I had judged my capacity accurately, because my hunger was completely satiated after the third piece of pizza had joined two of its companions. Following a regretful inspection of the remaining three pieces, I thoughtfully fixed my eyes on the couple. Never would I have done such a thing in my country, but this was not my country, so I struggled to my feet and stepped across the corner of the room to the side of the man.

"Pardon me, sir," I began. "Please don't take offense at what I am about to suggest, but will you accept the remainder of my pizza? I haven't touched a hair of it, and I particularly hate to waste food."

Of course, he stared curiously at me for an instant; then the weathered wrinkles about his blue eyes deepened into a smile. "Shuah, we'll tike it," he responded genially.

"Great!" I exclaimed as I swung around and swept up the pizza pan in one smooth motion and presented it to him. "There you go. Enjoy it."

Of course, it was an illusion, but the pan seemed to diminish in size when the man's huge palm engulfed one side of it. "Thank you," he said. "We won't wiste any of it."

"That responsibility is yours, now," I responded with a grin, "so my conscience is clear." Then, crisply dusting both palms together, I turned away as if something of real importance had been accomplished.

But that was not to be my last task, because a slightly guttural voice called, "Can you help me now?"

"Of course, I can," I responded to the blonde in the corner. Returning to my table, I slumped onto the chair and asked, "What was that problem again?"

She swung around and leaned over the back of her chair. "I'm planning. . . ," she began.

"Why don't you bring your notes to the table and take that chair opposite me?" I interjected.

She eagerly made the adjustments, repeated her previous words of explanation, and thrust the paper napkin before me, but it was no help whatsoever. Not only had many of the words been crossed out and crossed out again, but the ink had so saturated the soft paper that the words were scarcely legible.

After futilely attempting to decipher them, I looked across the table at her and suggested, "Will you please go through that explanation one sentence at a time, and I'll try to reconstruct each one on paper as you do."

"Yah, I vill gladly do dat," she said.

Meanwhile, I gave up a futile search of my pockets and muttered, "But I'll have to find something to write on. Let me see if the cashier has some paper."

"Vait!" she commanded. "I tink dot I haf someting here in my bag."

I watched skeptically while she rummaged through the trash trap, but she actually found a piece of blue-lined notepaper of sufficient size for a few sentences.

While she was extending it and the pen to me, her pale blue eyes peered deeply into mine. "It's zo kind of you to help me wid dis problem," she murmured.

It was strictly overkill, because she had already won me over as easily as my lovely granddaughter could have. But I had never come to really know that young lady, because I have always refused to expose her to potential harm at the hands of the Unknown.

"These will do nicely," I said, accepting them.

"Dot pen is nodt too goot, but idt vurks," she observed.

Placing the paper on the table before me, I crouched over it with the pen poised while pondering the problem. Finally I stated, "Basically, you want permission from the farmer to cross his property. Right?"

"Yah, dot's vot I vunt!" she exclaimed, punctuating the statement with a sharp clap of her slender hands. "Dot vord *permission* I could nodt remember."

Then I lapsed into a brown study while she peered up at my face like an anxious child. When I began to write, she released a deep sigh of relief, and I could not restrain the smile that surged to my lips.

After completing the tiny paragraph, I carefully edited it while she intently studied my expression. Then, after clearing my throat, I said, "This isn't much, but it may be enough. In any event, this is what I've written." Aloud, I then read, "Please pardon my speech. I am German, and I often have difficulty in expressing myself in coherent English. To be brief, I wish to take a long walk through some of New Zealand's most beautiful terrain. To do this, I must cross your farm, so I am requesting your permission to do so." Then I glanced at her beaming features and asked, "Is that what you wanted? Is it enough?"

"Oh, yah! It is vunderful!" she exclaimed ecstatically. "Especially der last pardt. But vot does der vord *coherent* mean?"

"Actually, it derives from the verb *cohere*, which means to stick together," I replied. "In this case, it means that certain words fit together properly and express a logical thought."

She looked doubtfully at me for a moment but made no further reference to the sentence containing the word *cohere*. Therefore, I suspected that she would use only "der last pardt," because pride would compel her to excise that second sentence.

"Thank you wery much," she murmured as we arose in unison. "I could never haf done it by myself."

"But you had already solved the problem," I protested. "All that I did was to rearrange some of the words."

"No, I tried undt tried," she insisted, "but I could nodt get the vords right."

"Do you need any help with the telephone call?" I inquired. Then I hurriedly added, "Unfortunately, I can't help you with that, because I have yet to learn how to operate these crazy New Zealand telephones."

"No, I haf everyting dot I need now," she responded with a triumphant wave of the paper.

"I surely hope that I find an editor who is as easy to please as you are," I muttered.

There were question marks in her eyes, but she didn't request an explanation. And I didn't offer one.

About halfway to the cashier's counter, my memory prompted me to return to the table and deposit a tip for the waitress. There I found the German girl struggling to insert her arm into the second sleeve of her sweater-jacket, so I paused to assist her, but she independently shook her curls and insisted, "I can do it."

On arriving at the cashier's counter, I was greeted with a smile by the young woman who may have been the "frau" of the tall, handsome young man who stood in the background and glowered at me.

"Did you enjoy your pizza?" she inquired.

"I certainly did," I replied. After placing the check face up on the counter along with two bills, I added, "However, it proved to be twice too big for me, so I gave half of it to one of your hungry patrons."

Smiling tolerantly, she picked up the bills: first the drab, gray-colored one, then the orange-colored one. After casually inspecting them, she looked askance at me.

Following a thoughtful study of the brightly colored bill, I extended my right hand palm uppermost and mumbled, "Yes, I can do much better by myself than that. I mistakenly assumed that the orange bill was a fiver."

"Yis, the foives and the fifties ah easily confused," she conceded. "Oy always look twoice at those bills."

"A wise precaution," I murmured, stowing the two bills in my wallet. Then I extracted a single bill, which had been printed in green ink on an off-white background, and I looked twice at it despite the fact that it was not orange colored. On one side the numerals *20* were printed in diagonally opposite corners, and the words *TWENTY DOLLARS*, undersigned by the nation's chief cashier, were located alongside a picture of the queen in all of her glory, crown, and queenly raiment. On the other side the words were located somewhat higher to accommodate a picture of a native pigeon perched on a branch.

"Yep, I'm pretty sure that this is a twenty-dollar bill," I stated, placing it on the counter.

Smiling faintly, she picked it up and placed it alongside the cash register. Then she removed a bill from the machine and handed it to me. An inspection of one side of it revealed that, excepting the numerals and the words, its printing practically duplicated that of the twenty-dollar bill. But its characters, which had been printed in blue ink, claimed that it was of the ten-dollar denomination. On the opposite side a picture of the kea, a native parrotlike hawk, had been substituted for the native pigeon.

After completing my inspection of it, I looked at her and said, "Yep, that's a ten-dollar bill."

Like a child playing an entertaining game, she placed the last bill on the counter. It was printed in a drab, gray ink and bore a picture of the tiny New Zealand fantail. Then she stacked some coins atop it.

"During these times that stuff is just peanuts," I muttered, picking up the debris, "so it really isn't worthy of an inspection."

Following a burst of laughter, she said, "Don't foahgit the old adage, 'Tike cayah of the pinnies, and the dollahs will tike cayah of thimsilves.'"

Nodding sagely, I turned away with my eyes fixed intently on the currency. While carefully arranging it in my open wallet, I bumped solidly into the German girl.

"Oh, hi!" I exclaimed inanely. "Fancy bumping into you here." And she stared at me with such a puzzled expression that I resolved to forsake such nonsense forevermore. After stepping aside so she could advance to the counter, I added, "I hope that your telephone call proves to be successful."

Actually, the remark was directed toward the glowering man in the background. In the past I've always followed the policy of allowing the chips to fall where they would. But in this case I intended to leave no false impressions on the minds of nice Kiwis, even on the minds of those who may have been exposed to the Unknown.

"I'm sure dot idt vill be a success," she confidently responded across one shoulder in passing. With an absent nod, I tipped a mythical hat and pushed the door open.

During my stroll along the deserted street toward the motel, Pancho opened up: "My thoughts keep returning to that glowering man, the one who acted as if he was the manager."

"And mine, too," José rejoined. "Did he observe Al in the act of transferring the remnants of his pizza to his neighbors?"

"I wondered about that, too," Pancho responded. "I particularly wondered if he was irritated by the act. If so, there was no justification for it, because Al had paid for the pizza, so he could dispose of it in whatever manner he wished, even feed it to a stray dog—if the dog would eat the bleeped thing."

"Or did he suspect Al of attempting to pick up a very young woman who could be less than one-third his age?" José wondered. "If so, the manager had to be very stupid, indeed. But one has to be as old as Al to fully understand why such a suspicion has to be so stupid."

"However, there also was the possibility that he had been exposed to the

Unknown," Pancho suggested, "so he may not have been completely at fault.".

At the motel's driveway I paused briefly to mull over still another problem. Finally, swinging toward the doorway of the office, I struggled with the balky sliding door until it reluctantly opened. Then I strode to the counter and pressed the button that previously had summoned the manager. Almost immediately there were sounds of softly scampering footfalls on the remote steps, followed by two or three solid thumps, which I instantly interpreted as the sounds of a falling body.

"Allah take heed!" I exclaimed. "She has fallen down the stairs."

I looked frantically about the room for an access to the door that opened to the stairwell, but there was only one means of access: the one over the four-foot-high counter in front of me. I had just resigned myself to the ordeal of crawling over the counter when the door burst open, and a small demon exploded through the opening, followed closely by a somewhat larger demon.

The smaller boy burned rubber as he came to an abrupt stop on the opposite side of the counter. Meanwhile, the larger boy reached forward and grasped the seat of the smaller boy's short pants, so he pulled up directly behind him.

"No!" he shouted. "Let me ask him. Oy'm the oldest!"

Staring solemnly down at them, I inquired, "Ask me what?"

"Whatchya want?" they chorused.

"I would like to speak to the lady who I strongly suspect is your regretful mother," I responded with a smile.

"Okye, Oy'll git her," the smaller boy volunteered.

"No, Oy'll git her!" the other one screamed. "Oy'm the oldest." Then he pushed the smaller boy headfirst against the counter and bolted through the still open doorway. Then there were the rapidly receding sounds of sneakers solidly thumping against every other wooden step. Obviously, the boy was scrambling to maintain his advantage.

Meanwhile, the junior member of the family ruefully rubbed his forehead and muttered, "He won't foind her up theah. Oy'm gonta git her." Then, grasping the near edge of the counter, he swung one battle-scarred knee over it and swarmed across it like a monkey. Suspecting that Junior knew what he was doing, I gave him a three-minute start; then I strolled through the open entrance and met the trio at the corner of the building.

"Hi," I greeted the woman. "I'm sorry to bother you again, but we set no time for you to take me to the bus station—that is, if it won't be too big a problem for you to do so."

"It won't be a problem," she insisted. "Moy husband leaves foah work at sivin, so Oy kin tike you as soon as he leaves."

While I was mentally reviewing the ambiguous statement, Pancho nudged José and exclaimed, "Man! I sure hope her husband isn't standing in the background listening to this conversation."

Then I looked warily across one shoulder as José responded, "Yeah, he might not be the understanding type."

In response to her questioning gaze, I said, "That will be great. I'll get to the reservation counter before eight o'clock, and if you are right about the time, I'll have time for a bite of breakfast before the bus leaves."

"Okye, thin you'll buzz me sometoime aftah sivin?" she inquired.

"I will," I promised. "Thank you again and good night to y'all."

"Good noight," they chorused. "By the wye," she called after me, "the plummah has been heah, and the showah works."

"Then I owe you another five dollars," I rejoined.

"No," she retorted, "the deal still stands."

Obviously she was one very stubborn woman, so I waved to the trio and strolled down the slope toward my home for the night.

Early the following morning the shower worked beautifully. I was dried, clad in a set of clean clothing, and ready to leave by seven o'clock. Nevertheless, some twenty minutes had passed before I ventured tentatively into the office. It seemed wisest to be *bleeped* sure that the woman's husband was long gone, because I was wary about how he would react to my date with his wife.

"Good morning," she greeted me. "Did you sleep well?"

"Like a lamb," I responded.

"Will, Oy suppose that's tops foah anybody in New Zealand," she responded whimsically. "Ah you riddy to leave?"

"Yes," I replied. "Is it too early for you to leave?"

"Now is as good a toime as any," she answered. "Oy'll back the cah down to yoah unit so that you won't have to carry those heavy bags so fah."

"That's mighty 'thoughty' of you," I said.

She turned her head and stared thoughtfully toward me. "You ah a bit of a kiddah," she suggested, "ahn't you?"

Since the suggestion was at least partially accurate, I sensed an enigmatic smile. "Well, I'll go and get my luggage," I volunteered in lieu of an adequate response.

The automobile was one of those compact models that are so popular among New Zealanders, but it provided ample space for my luggage. As usual, I sat to the left of the driver. After she parked the vehicle at the bus station, I promptly reached for my wallet, but she immediately interpreted the action.

"Oy don't want nuthin' foah bringin' you heah," she insisted, placing a restraining hand over the wallet. "Oy'm glad to be able to hilp you."

I gently pushed her hand away from the wallet and extracted an orange-colored bill from it. Then I stared intently into her eyes and said, "You've already had your way about the rate, so you can't expect to have your way about this."

"But Oy merely wanted to hilp," she protested.

"You have two options," I growled. "The first one is to take this bill, and the second one is to cower in a corner tonight and listen to your husband rant and rave about your riding around town with a traveling salesman."

"What traveling salesman?" she countered.

"The one that I'm going to describe to your husband over the telephone if you don't take this bill," I responded with a sharp stare.

Her smooth features broke into a number of smile marks as she looked searchingly into my eyes. "Oh, all roight, Oy'll tike it," she conceded, "but Oy only wanted to hilp."

While submitting the bill to her, I said, "Actually, I'm still ahead in the game, because this bill only brings the cost of the unit up to the standard rate, so thank you for the free ride to the bus station."

Then, peering intently at me, she said, "But you wouldn't have really called moy husband, would you? You were kiddin', weren't you?" But her tones lacked real conviction.

"Return the bill to me and see," I challenged her.

She thrust the bill toward me, but I ignored it. Then, with an expression full of conviction, she murmured, "You ah sweet."

"Thank you from the bottom of my heart," I responded. "That really makes my day." With that, I opened the door, crawled out of the vehicle, and resumed my trip around the world.

Three other potential passengers preceded me to the reservation counter, so I stood on my heels and patiently waited. Meanwhile, I studied a bus driver who appeared to have some reason, probably an ancient one, to confer with a particularly attractive young woman who presided over one end of the reservation counter.

For a man of about twenty-eight, he was exceptionally slender and well built. Typically, he wore tan shorts; a neatly pressed, short-sleeved, tan shirt; a pair of three-quarter-length, tan socks; and a pair of brown, oxford shoes that reflected errant light rays like mirrors. His light-brown hair was neatly combed, and it had been trimmed to an inverted peak at the point where the back of his head joined his muscular neck. His serene, brown eyes and lightly tanned, angular features matched his attire perfectly. Even I could see that he could very well be the answer to any maiden's prayer, that is, if such a creature still exists. When he moved athletically away from the counter, I could see that his height topped six feet by about four inches.

After the lead passenger was tendered a seat reservation, the line moved up one space, so I followed suit. Then my admiring eyes returned to the "hunk"; at the same instant the wide door beyond him swung open to admit another tall hunk. The two men greeted each other by their given names as the newcomer's long strides carried him toward the other man's outstretched right hand. After they had casually completed the ancient ritual, the new arrival stepped back half a step and looked across the other man's head toward the sunlit entrance behind the incoming passengers.

"Wow!" I exclaimed softly. "Some of these New Zealanders are veritable giants. That guy must be close to seven feet tall."

Then the young man ahead of me turned questioning eyes toward me, so I resolved to keep my thoughts to myself. Meanwhile, the reservation clerk was beckoning for him to advance, so I pointed a forefinger toward her, and the man hurriedly moved forward while I returned to my study of the tall bus drivers. Their conversation had been conducted in the carefully modulated tones that New Zealanders commonly employ, so I had overheard few of their words, but their voices became more audible when they were about to part. The shorter of the duo accepted the other man's extended right hand, reached forth with the other one, and genially slapped his friend's sizable upper arm.

"Okay, I'll be seeing you on the road then," he said. Relaxing his handclasp, he stepped back.

The taller man stared malevolently down at him for an instant and growled almost belligerently, "Yis, but you bittah be on the roight soide o' the road."

The other man stopped still, shot a startled glance toward him, and grinned widely. Silently shaking his handsome head, he turned away with the grin still intact and made his exit through the same door through which the taller man had entered.

"No doubt he had the same mental picture that I had," Pancho ventured. "A picture of two buses thundering along the left lane of a two-lane highway toward a head-on collision."

"No wonder that giant insisted that his friend be on the 'roight soide o' the road,' " José interjected. "However, for the same reason, it would have to be the left side of the road in our country."

The reservation clerk imperiously beckoned, but this time it was to me, so I hurriedly emerged from my reverie and advanced toward the counter, but she was not quite finished with the preceding passenger, so I came to an abrupt stop.

"Of course, you could have taken the bus to Milford Sound," she called to him. "However, without a reservation at the hotel, theah would be no place foah you to spind the noight, so you ah better off to proceed as we've planned."

She turned apologetic eyes toward me, so I imperiously greeted her majesty with the words: "I would like to reserve a seat on the next bus to Invercargill." Then I planted my Travelpass on the counter.

She glanced at it and quickly jotted some characters on the top sheet of a form pad, which she tore free and presented to me along with the crisp words: "The bus to Invercargo will leave promptly at tin-fifteen. Oy advise you to be heah early." There was no reason for me to quibble with her about my destination, because I was already aware that the natives commonly converted the last three letters of the word *Invercargill* into an *o*.

With my luggage checked and a seat on the bus assured, I decided to see the town, so I struck out along the sidewalk that had taken me past the "wee, rid building" during the previous evening.

I rarely use the word *lovely* in any form, because I've always believed that it's one of those words that only women and sissies can successfully employ. Nevertheless, on that particular morning the gentle sunlight transformed the small lakeside park into an entity of incredible loveliness. I grant, however, that my mood may have been responsible for the light in which I viewed it. I had been luxuriating for several hours in a tiny world where the inhabitants had treated me normally and very kindly. Apparently they had not yet been unfavorably influenced by the Unknown. Consequently, one of those rare waves of happiness surged through my being from my bald pate to the scuffed toes of my Hush Puppies, so that may have been why that park down under the equator appeared to be so lovely during that particular spring morning in the middle of November.

From the park, I wandered among some of the adjacent streets along which several small business buildings were clustered. Rising above the business district and away from the lake were a number of foothills, on which most of the housing, much of it luxurious, was perched on ascending terraces. The town and the adjacent lake were surrounded by the Remarkables, a series of serrated mountain peaks, whose green slopes were cluttered with the off-white forms of peacefully grazing sheep. That Queenstown setting was so uniquely beautiful that my *sole*, both of them, in fact, responded by returning me to the park for a closer inspection of it.

After strolling through the small park, I ventured out onto the weathered, wooden planks of a relatively narrow pier that extended some fifty feet from the shoreline and about six feet above the surface of the water. While slowly moving toward its far end, I peered down through the clear water at the points where the pier's round, wooden piles emerged from the lake's bed, which rapidly descended from a depth of just a few feet to a dimmer depth of some twenty-five feet. Then, raising my eyes, I looked toward the middle of the lake and wondered if that happened to be one of the spots where it is a thousand feet deep.

About six feet from me, a gray-and-white gull stood dreamily sunning himself atop one of the projecting wooden piles with one of his horny feet withdrawn into the white feathers of his lower fuselage. Meanwhile, he totally ignored me. Occasionally, he would deign to reply to a cruising member of his own kind, but he refused to say a word to me, even though I greeted him with some perfectly intelligible, if not intelligently arranged, English words. Perhaps my accent confused him; after all, he must have been a New Zealand gull.

In the shallows along the shore several ducks vied for bonanzas, such as the bugs and insects that darted through the water from one clump of light-green weeds to the next or to the green moss that so indiscriminately clung to the weeds and stones. Whenever one of the ducks ventured farther out onto the deeper water, I made a game of predicting its target at the very instant that it stretched forth its long neck and, with its webbed feet churning, shot like an arrow toward the bottom. Those varicolored birds must have been inflated with air, because they would make those deep dives; then they would bob to the surface like corks. Often they disagreed among themselves about one thing or another, possibly politics or religion; then one would take off after another one with its webbed feet madly kicking at the surface of the water and with its wings beating the water into a froth. I never determined the real reasons for those attacks or the intentions of the attackers; however, one particularly aggressive little character usually took off with its neck stretched tautly forward and with its bill wide open as if about to bite the tail feathers of its frantic foe. I saw no teeth, but Donald Duck has exposed his buck teeth to me on TV from time to time, so I suppose that New Zealand ducks are equipped with similar teeth.

Despite the squabbling ducks and the screeching gulls, the environment was so soothingly peaceful that I lazily leaned back against the weathered,wooden rail. Fortunately, a sharp, cracking sound from it warned me in time, so I hurriedly withdrew from it and thoughtfully studied the likely temperature of the water.

"Hmm," Pancho mumbled. "After coming directly off of those glaciers, that water could be very refreshing, to say the least."

Then I absently backed against the opposite rail and allowed my avid eyes to sweep the gently undulating, green horizon overhung by a pale-blue sky, across which fleecy, white clouds roamed so slowly that one could imagine that they were grazing. On what? On the sun's rays, perhaps?

"Fleecy, white clouds grazing on a pale-blue sky!" José exclaimed. "Man, you are losing your cotton pickin' marbles." Then I shifted my weight, and that rail also protested, but I merely cast an uneasy glance toward the surface of the water.

"So you can still swim... I hope," Pancho nervously propounded.

"He feels too lackadaisical to give a *bleep*," José observed. Once more my eyes turned toward the lush mountain slopes and their broods of softly rolling foothills. "So this is why so many people travel from the four rounded corners of the earth to this small town," José mused.

"It's set in one of the world's few remaining beauty spots," Pancho contributed, "but it's so fragile and vulnerable, and people are so thoughtless and destructive. Inevitably they will destroy it, because people always foul their nests."

"Since we've been a small part of it," José resumed, "we have reason to know the procedure. First, the bulldozers will come along with the carryalls and the compacters to prepare the sites and construct the streets. After the materials are deposited on the sites, cranes will be moved into position, and workmen will swarm over the mushrooming structures like ants on a pot of honey."

"Finally hordes of human beings and their pets will flood the new homes, the multiple housing units, the shopping malls, and the commercial buildings," Pancho injected. "Suddenly the intrinsic beauty of the land will have been replaced by the geometric monstrosities that commonly dominate human campsites, such as Rome, London, New York, and Tokyo."

"But the worst is yet to come," José insisted. "Those thousands of people must have places for their games and off-road toys. Landfills must be provided for materials that they will promiscuously cast away and for toxic wastes from factories."

Not to be outdone, Pancho inserted: "What with contamination of the ground water and the lake's water by those toxic materials, plus the pesticides that will be applied to plants and trees to control unwanted insect life, the fish, the squabbling ducks, and the lazy gulls will be no more.

"Our species will have completed its usual cycle," Pancho resumed. "It will have fully controlled its environment, and...."

"But will it?" José countered. "Will clean, acid-free rain continue to fall as often? Will the sun and the moon continue to shine as brilliantly?"

A ray of sunlight bounced from a ripple into one of my eyes, so my gaze automatically returned to the surface of the lake. Then my mind began to review a Maori legend of the demon that is said to dwell beneath its surface. The ancient Maoris claimed that the mysterious variations of several inches in the depth of the lake are caused by the breathing of the demon. As further justification for the legend, they claimed that the intervals of time between the depth variations closely correspond to the normal breathing cycle of a human being.

"We haven't detected any perceptible rise and fall of the surface," José observed. "Nevertheless, the Maoris could have something; if so, I suspect that there's a perfectly logical physical reason for the variations in depth."

"If that legend is based on fact," Pancho began, "I strongly suspect that the demon will turn out to be a monstrous human being with gills and shoulder-high fins."

"Like the only demon that we've ever encountered," José interposed, "namely, the Unknown."

After glancing toward the Ernslaw Wharf, against which the seventy-five-year-old, coal-fired steamer lounged, I reluctantly pushed myself away from the rail and slowly strolled shoreward. From the end of the pier, I spied a park bench and turned toward it; however, upon arriving in front of it, I was aghast at what I saw. Then I glanced fearfully aloft as a gull wheeled directly over my head, lowered his flaps, and experimentally manipulated his rear stabilizer controls. Meanwhile, his beady eyes stared speculatively down at my bald head. Even though he left without creating a problem, there was an evil look in his eyes, so I may have glanced up at the most propitious instant.

After a careful inspection of the bench, I selected an uncontaminated spot and gratefully relaxed onto it. It seems to me that idle philosophizing shouldn't require a great expenditure of physical energy, but mine does. However, idleness isn't one of my characteristics, so I opened my briefcase and removed a small map and some literature from it. Then I began to compare the advantages of a trip to Te Anau and Milford Sound with those of the upcoming trip to Invercargill.

After considerable study, I slapped my forehead while José and Pancho chorused, "You goofed, Al!" Then, placing a forefinger on the point where Queenstown was indicated on the map, I traced Highway 6 about halfway to Invercargill, where the forefinger chose to follow the sinuous route of Highway 94 through the Oren River Valley, with the Eyre Mountains to the north and the Takitimu Mountains to the south.

"You could have taken that route," Pancho grumbled, "or you could have gone to Manapouri instead. It's located on the southeast corner of Lake Manapouri, which is touted to be New Zealand's loveliest lake."

"Its surface is some five hundred fifty feet above sea level," José added, "and its bottom plunges to a depth of thirteen hundred seventy-five feet, so it has to be about eight hundred seventy-five feet below sea level."

"But let no geologist try to convince me that it was gouged out of solid rock by a gigantic glacier about twelve thousand years ago," I mumbled. "That's the way that it was laid down during its volcanic creation many thousands of years before the Ice Age."

My eyes darted guiltily about to see if my mumblings had been audible to anyone, but there was no one within the immediate vicinity. Then I began to read softly aloud: "At West Arm, site of New Zealand's largest hydro-electric project, water is taken from the head of the lake to a powerhouse six hundred sixty feet underground and conducted through generators ten feet below sea level, where it is discharged through a twenty-eight-foot-diameter tunnel into Deep Cove on Doubtful Sound."

"Man!" exclaimed José. "What you caused us to miss."

Nodding dolefully, I continued on to the next paragraph, which dealt with the town of Te Anau, and my spirits really bottomed out. "Of course, it would be located on a lake with the same name," I mumbled. "With an area of more than two hundred square miles distributed over a length of about thirty-two miles and a width of six miles, it is the largest of the southern lakes," I read. "Its surface is about six hundred twenty-five feet above sea level, and, since some of it is in excess of eight hundred fifty feet deep, part of it is more than two hundred feet below sea level. Not only does it contain trout and salmon, but along its shores are the Te Anau Caves (the Caves of Swirling Waters), which are accessible only by boat. These caves contain whirlpools, underground waterfalls, and at least one beautiful glowworm grotto."

Then, in response to whisper-soft sounds, I paused and looked up toward the lower surfaces of the white fuselage and beautifully tapered wings that hovered motionlessly if not unstably about twenty feet overhead while one cocked, beady eye stared curiously down at me. Apparently my warning glare dissuaded him from making a bombing run, because he dipped one wing and darted away.

"Man, did you ever miss the boat this time!" exclaimed José. "But I wonder if that description may not be a bit overhyped like it was for that Marine Garden in Auckland."

"The best way to determine that is to see those areas," Pancho remarked, "and we should see them sometime."

"Oh-oh," I grunted. "So the fjords are located along Milford Sound. That Dutchman led me to believe that they were located on Lake Wakatipu. However, since he was so ecstatic about them, he must have visited them, so I must have misinterpreted something he said. Nevertheless, this brochure claims that Fiordland National Park, at a bit more than one million hectares (about three million acres), is not only the largest national park in New Zealand but one of the largest in the world. And it is the only known habitat of two rare birds: the Takahe or Nortornis and the Kakapo."

Then I stopped and protested, "All of that and nothing about the fjords! But the Eglinton and Hollyford Valleys are mentioned plus beech forests; high, rugged, snow-capped peaks; and several mountain lakes. And there are an awful lot of camping accommodations all of the way to Cascade Creek, so it must have something going for it. Mount Christine is shown to be almost eight thousand feet above sea level, so the country must be pretty rough. Oh-oh! This proves it: Homer Tunnel, with its raw rock walls and a ten percent grade, accommodates only one lane of traffic, so the traffic is forced to stop and wait for thirty minutes out of each hour to allow the oncoming traffic to pass."

My eyes quickly scanned the upcoming lines of words. "So now they tell me that Milford Sound is the best known and the finest of the fjords in South Westland," I muttered. "Its notable features are Mitre Peak, with an elevation of five thousand feet, and the Bowen Falls, which cascade about five hundred feet into the sound."

Silently folding the map, I placed it and the brochure in my briefcase. "I'm not about to cancel my reservation to Invercargill," I mumbled, "but I really should."

After removing a mechanical pencil and a notebook from the briefcase, I placed the case across my knees and utilized it as a desk while recording some of the incidents of the last few days. Meanwhile, ever-increasing numbers of pedestrians were strolling past the area along the sidewalk that paralleled the nearby lakeshore. But my penetrating stare passed harmlessly through their bodies and continued onward to the far shore of the lake while I painfully attempted to recall the exact details of each incident. And that may have been why I failed to clearly hear the first greeting. In fact, I didn't even see the young woman until she repeated, "Goot morning," and waved to me.

But the slanting rays of the morning sun were partly at fault, because her slender figure stood directly in front of the slowly rising ball of fire. From force of habit, I turned my head and peered across one shoulder, since, almost invariably, the Unknown has been crouching in the background whenever a pretty young thing has waved to me. But there wasn't even a bodacious gull in the area.

My puzzled eyes turned back toward the blurred figure while José bluntly stated, "She must have confused you with somebody else. Besides, you're on the other side of the world, so who would wave at you?"

"Yeah," Pancho interjected. "When was the last time some sweet young thing waved at you?"

I was about to admit that I couldn't remember the last time, but the slowly advancing figure completely blocked out the sun, so I could distinguish more than just the outlines of a slender body and pretty blond hair.

"Goot morning," she repeated. "How are you feeling dis glorious spring morning in Nowember?" And her whimsical smile seemed to imply that she had fully anticipated the likely impact of "spring morning in Nowember" on my mind.

"Oh!" I blurted inanely. "I'm sorry, but I didn't recognize you because of your clothing." Then I frowned deeply, since, even to me, the words seemed to infer that she had not been clothed during the previous meeting, so I quickly added, "I meant to say that you are clothed differently today . . . but just as attractively."

Her pleased smile more than justified the many hours that my boyish eyes had pored over words describing the courageous exploits and the gallantry of the knights of King Arthur's court and other heroic members of that golden era. Of course, no knight would remain seated in the presence of a fair damsel, so I began to dispose of my burden, but she intuitively sensed my intention and reacted to it by thrusting her arms stiffly along her thighs with both palms horizontal to the grass.

"Please don't rise," she implored. "I happened to see you sitting here, undt I stopped by merely to inform you dot der telephone call vorked beautifully." And her clear, blue eyes glowed with happiness.

"I'm very pleased," I responded. "I know how important it was to you."

"Again, I vunt to tank you for your help," she said. "I could not have succeeded widout it."

"Oh, yes, you could," I insisted. Then, with another surge of gallantry, I added, "All that you would have had to do was to go out to the man's farm and make your request in person."

She peered pensively into my eyes while her agile mind processed the words. Then a soft glow of pleasure slowly suffused her fair features. "You are zo zweet," she murmured.

"That's one of the two nicest things that have been said to me today," I responded.

"Vot vas der udder vun?" she inquired.

"The very same words were used but with a different accent," I responded, and a touch of pride crept into my suddenly gruff tones.

"Ah-ha!" she exclaimed. "Den dot proves dot I'm right."

Bowing my head to hide the mist in my eyes, I asked, "In what part of Germany do you live?"

"I'm from Munich," she answered.

"Oh!" I exclaimed, "That's a nice city!"

"It is der capital of Bavaria, vich is der most beautiful part of Germany," she informed me with evident pride.

"That's what a friend told me last spring after he returned from a tour of West Germany," I said. "He also visited Hamburg."

With a perky nod, she murmured, "Yes, dose are der usual cities dat der tourists wisit."

"Oh, but he was born in Germany," I rejoined. "Furthermore, he had visited the country several times, so he knew where he wanted to go."

"Is he now an American?" she inquired.

"Yes, I'm afraid so," I answered somewhat puckishly.

"Den he vas an immigrant," she persisted.

I sensed that there was a hidden purpose behind her words, but, choosing not to question her regarding it, I answered, "In a sense, I suppose that he was, but he was only six years old when his parents migrated to the United States. However, he may have been processed, too, because he was born in Germany, so he was a German in the eyes of the U.S. bureaucrats; consequently, he wouldn't become a German citizen until he reached the prescribed age. You know how confusing government bureaucrats can make the simplest problem."

After a preoccupied nod, she murmured, "Vell, I must go now, because I haf to prepare for my beautiful valk." And once more her contagious enthusiasm reached out to me.

"I hope that it meets the heights of your expectations," I submitted in cautionary tones.

"I'm sure dot it vill," she said softly. "Goodbye."

"Vaya con dios," I responded.

"Muchas gracias," she responded with a wave of one slender arm. Then she moved gracefully away with quick, sure steps that quickly accelerated to smoothly metered strides.

"It's amazing to what extent some Europeans have been educated," José mused. "She spoke those Spanish words like a Castilian."

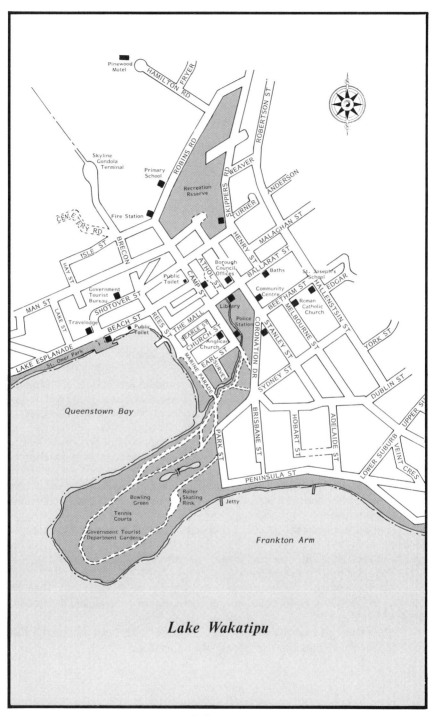

Map of Queenstown

8

Queenstown to Dunedin

Queenstown to Invercargill

I had deliberately planned the trip to Dunedin with a stopover at Invercargill but arbitrarily deleted it en route. The bus to that southernmost of the South Island's largest towns was indifferently patronized. Nevertheless, it stopped to deliver and pick up freight at many of the villages and way stations, but it delivered and picked up few passengers. Within the first twenty-five miles beyond Queenstown there weren't even any wide spots in the road, so the lack of patronage was due in part to the unpopulated countryside. After leaving the southern leg of Lake Wakatipu, the highway clung closely to the Oreti River, which meanders between the Eyre Mountains on the west and the Garvie Mountains—that is, if the latter can be called mountains. The wider spots along the road consisted of Garston, Nokomai, Athol, Parawa, Eyre Creek, Five Rivers, and Lowther. In the vicinity of Lumsden, the rest stop, a red fescue grew in large quantities. Chewing fescue, it was called, and much of it was exported to the United States and Great Britain.

In Lumsden the bus rolled to a stop beside a small, wooden structure that appeared to be more of a warehouse than a bus station. Nearby was a small take-away restaurant. After engoring one of its sandwiches, I tightly zipped up the front of my jacket and set out for the rest facilities. They proved to be located some fifty paces from the restaurant but in line with the path of a strong westerly wind that must have come directly off of the Antarctic ice pack by way of the Tasman Sea.

From the facilities I continued across the adjacent street to the Old Lumsden Hotel, which appeared to have survived for no less than a century. Nevertheless, it was still in business; at least its pub was. I yearned to inspect the interior of the weather-beaten, two-story, wooden structure, but a peek through one of the pub's grimy windows revealed several denizens who appeared to be equally ancient and weatherbeaten, so I turned back and crossed to the far side of the railroad.

A quick guesstimate of the town's population put it at about fifteen hundred, depending largely on how many of the dogs and cats one counted. My unplanned tour carried me along the far side of the street that paralleled the railroad, and it terminated at a relatively modern motel. After inspecting one of the units through an open doorway, I sought out the office and rapped on its closed door. An attractive woman of about fifty opened it, peered through her spectacles at me, and reacted in a familiar manner. Nevertheless, I decided to follow my original intention.

"What do you charge for a single?" I asked.

"Twenty-foive dollahs per dye," she answered.

"And what would it be by the week or month?" I persisted.

"Twenty-foive dollahs per dye," she retorted.

"Thank you," I murmured and turned away.

At the intersection of the sidewalks I quickly glanced across one shoulder and found her to be still standing there staring after me. And our interlocked stares remained locked until my strides carried me beyond the corner of the building.

"Hmm," José mumbled. "Incredible as it seems, the Unknown appears to have preceded us to this remote town."

"That is, if our intuitions are to be relied on," Pancho injected, "and we've found them to be reliable."

A gust of wind rattled the boards of a nearby wooden fence, and I glanced thoughtfully toward it as José observed, "Oh, well, we have no overwhelming compulsions to make this town our home anyway."

"But it would be emotionally rewarding to find a nice, small town to hole up in for the next few months," Pancho remarked. "One that's untainted by the Unknown."

The terrain south of Lumsden gradually became rougher, but there were no mountains; in fact, my map identified the area as the Hokonui Hills. There were several farm buildings and small settlements scattered among them. In the vicinity of Winton the farm buildings were spaced more closely. Beyond it, the farms and dwellings began to crowd each other a bit, and the farms lost out completely by the time that the bus followed Highway 6 to Clyde Street. There it finally stopped beside the large masonry structure that housed Invercargill's combination railroad and bus station.

Invercargill   The city's name was created from *inver*, Gaelic for the mouth of a river, and *Cargill*, after Captain William Cargill, the first superintendent of Otago. The urban area appeared to be more highly industrialized than the nearby agricultural area warranted, but the several stock-show banners stretched across some of the city's street intersections seemed to deny that there was insuffient economic support from the agricultural area.

After checking my luggage at the station, I ventured forth from the impressive old landmark. Directly across the street, my eyes settled on another impressive old landmark, the Railway Hotel, which dated back to the 1890s.

"That may be a place to spend the night," Pancho mused. "That is, if it's still habitable, and it appears to be."

"We aren't likely to need a place to stay," José rejoined. "I sense that Al isn't too enamored with this town."

From there I struck out for the business district, propelled along by the force of the cold wind. It may have been the wind that turned me against the town, but I suspect that it was the austere simplicity of its business blocks and the unimaginative layout of its streets that did it. Since Invercargill was located on a flat, coastal plain, its streets had been laid out in precise rectangles. Therefore, to some extent, the city reminded me of some of the cities located on the central plains of North America.

After braving one sustained blast of that cold wind, I returned to the station, approached the pretty young woman who presided over the ticket counter, and announced, "I would like to reserve a seat on the next bus to Dunedin."

Following a thoughtful inspection of my features, she said, "That bus doesn't leave until late this afternoon."

"It's much too far to walk, so I'll wait for the bus," I volunteered whimsically.

"What's wrong with Invercargo?" she countered. "Why leave after so short a stay?"

The question caused me to wonder why she had so readily recognized me. She must have particularly noticed me among the small group of passengers that had straggled from the Queenstown bus into the station. Nevertheless, I set aside a festering suspicion involving the presence of the ever-lurking Unknown.

"Brrr," I rumbled. "Invercargill is much too cold and windy for me."

"But the weather gets cold and windy in Dunedin too," she said. "Just ask Teresa if that isn't so. She used to live there."

At the sound of her name, the other young woman looked up at me from her task, so I asked, "Is that so, Teresa?"

Following an emphatic nod, she added, "But it doesn't get as cold or as windy there as it does here."

"But you still prefer to live here," I persisted.

"No!" the first girl interjected. "She would like to return to Dunedin."

My eyes remained fixed thoughtfully on Teresa's pretty brown ones, and those thoughts moved me to inquire, "Why?"

"Dunedin is much prittier than Invercargo," she replied. "Besoides...."

"Besides, many of your friends live there," I added for her.

"But she has friends here too," the other girl again interjected.

"Teresa will always have friends," I volunteered. And the girl's sunny smile fully justified the effort.

With the reservation stowed safely in my wallet, I braved those frigid gusts once more during a two-mile trek along the main thoroughfares in futile search of a barber pole.

Eventually José suggested, "Maybe New Zealanders don't display poles with red and white spiral stripes in front of their barbershops."

"Of course, they don't," Pancho chimed in. "Nobody but an idiot would expect to find barber poles in New Zealand—or in any other foreign country, for that matter. They are an American innovation."

I could have pointed out that they had silently joined in the search but I didn't. During another, more objective search, practically every barbershop that we found consisted of a single, small room tucked behind another small business, such as a tobacco shop or a shoe repair shop. But all of them were closed, so I had to agree with some of the local yokels who suggested that the barbers had gone either to the stock show or to the nearest pub. Bowing my head to the cruel blast, I fought my way back to the station, which proved to be practically deserted, and it remained that way until shortly before the bus was scheduled to depart. Meantime I whiled away the hours catching up on my notes.

Invercargill to Dunedin

While waiting in line to board the bus, I happened to overhear a conversation between two bus drivers. In part, one of them said, "I didn't have enough passengers on my bus during the last trip to pay my salary."

"You shouldn't worry about a little thing like that," the other one retorted. "Your salary will be paid even if there are no passengers on your bus."

"Such is the lot of most government-operated services," Pancho observed. "No government has ever operated public services efficiently, and none of them ever will."

Scarcely one-third of the seats were occupied when the Dunedin bus pulled away from the station; therefore, the government must also have been deeply in the red for that trip. In spite of the several small settlements along Highway 1, the number of passengers decreased at each stop.

About thirty miles beyond Invercargill the bus stopped at Mataura, which is nationally renowned for its freezing works and its large dairy products processing plant. It also is the home of the New Zealand Paper Mills.

Some eight miles farther north the bus entered the town of Gore, which is situated on the banks of the Mataura River at the junction of the Southland Plains and the southern end of the Waimea Plains. Large lignite coal fields lie near the town, and it also is host to the largest cereal mill in the Southern Hemisphere. Gore is the second largest town in the Southland and the commercial hub of one of the wealthiest agricultural areas in the country. To the average American, it is inconceivable that so large an urban area should still be called a town, but the population of a New Zealand city must exceed twenty-two thousand, where five thousand usually does the trick in the U.S. of A.

The next town, Balclutha, is located about the point where the highway crosses the Clutha River, the largest of New Zealand's rivers and the source of large quantities of white bait (smelt).

Beyond Balclutha is Milton with about three thousand inhabitants. Like most of the towns along that part of Highway 1, it sits in a relatively flat area, enhanced by green, rolling hills, with a backdrop of somewhat rougher terrain to the west. Most of the surrounding area is devoted to the cultivation of small grain crops, such as wheat, oats, barley, and rye.

Dunedin The terrain became more rolling and picturesque as the bus neared its destination. Even the roadway improved when it became the Dunedin Waitati Motorway, and the beautiful underpass at Maxwelton Street contributed to a growing impression of an up-and-coming, modern city. But that impression faded somewhat after the bus rolled deeper into the city. From the motorway it lumbered along Pine Hill Road, crossed to Cumberland via North Road and Duke, and veered along Gowland to Castle Street. There a quick glance through the adjacent window revealed several red, tile roofs overhanging the ornate, Oumaru and bluestone facade of the Dunedin Railway Station highlighted by the red rays from the dying embers of the southern sun. Meanwhile the bus rumbled onto Anzac, which merged with High Street. Then the driver swung the vehicle into the Railway Bus Terminus, which fronts on both High and Cumberland.

After recovering my luggage, I carried it through the entrance of the station to the first of two cabs and willingly surrendered it to the driver, who stowed it in the boot of his vehicle.

When we had assumed our respective positions in the vehicle, he posed the typical question: "Wheah do ye want to go?"

"That question calls for a conference," I confessed. Despite his perplexed expression, I resumed: "First off, I suspect that a motel will cost less than a hotel. Which would you recommend for the greatest economy?"

"Will," he began slowly, "Oy suspect that a motil will cost liss." And with that profound conclusion, he stopped, looked blankly at me for several seconds, and

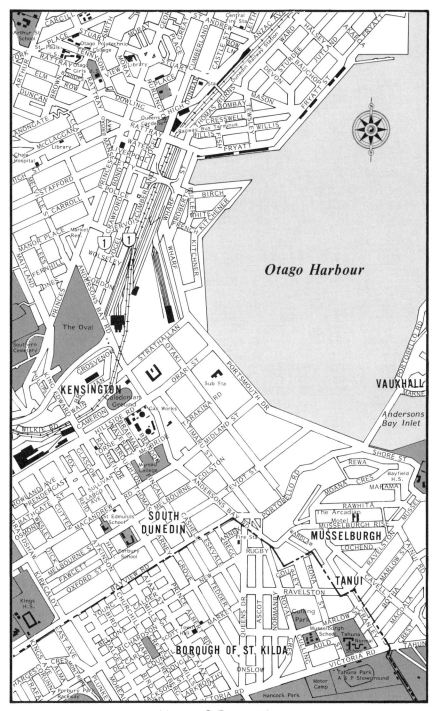

Map of Dunedin

WHITE HERON *(Egretta Alba)*

A water fowl, often called Kotuka by the Maoris, is found in scattered numbers throughout New Zealand. However, during the austral spring, they collect in South Westland, their only known nesting site. Mature birds stand approximately 3 feet high.

ROYAL ALBATROSS
(Diomedea epomophora sanfordi)

Taiaroa Head, Dunedin, New Zealand is claimed to be the only site in the world where a breeding colony of the Great Albatross nests within close proximity to human beings.

KIWI *(Apterix)*

One of New Zealand's several flightless, ratite birds that are related to the extinct moa.

Some of New Zealand's Unique Birds

finally drawled, "Which one do ye want to go to?"

After turning a startled expression toward him, I hesitantly answered, "Since I've never been in this city before, I don't have the foggiest idea. Can't you suggest one?"

He frowned and shifted his hands uneasily on the steering wheel. "Will," he finally murmured, "theah's one up on the bluff, and theah rites ah firely low."

"Is it close to a restaurant?" I countered.

"No, it isn't," he admitted. "In fac', yuh probably would have to tike a cab to a ristaurant, because the plice is practically inaccessible foah anybuddy without a cah."

"Hmm, let's scratch that one," I mumbled while carefully studying the man's features. "What other possibility can you suggest?"

Apparently thinking was an excruciatingly painful process for him, because he frowned deeply and finally suggested, "Let me ask Angus. He probably knows o' one."

I nodded absently, so he opened the door and ambled back to another driver, who stood beside the second cab.

"Huh," grunted Pancho. "That guy must have come directly to the big city from a sheep station. I wonder if he has a license to drive this crate."

The driver finally returned to the open doorway and placed one forearm above it. Then, lowering his head, he peered at me and said, "Angus climes the Cherry Court is a pritty good bet. Besoides, it has a doinin' room, so yuh won't have to go out to eat."

"Okay," I muttered. "Let's try it."

I will say this for the man: He drove well for a man who prefers the left side of the street. Of course, it wasn't the *right* side of the street, but most of the other drivers favored it, too, so we didn't meet any vehicles head on. After making a fairly adept U-turn on George Street, he stopped the cab beside the trunk of a large tree that stood near the curb in front of the Cherry Court Motel.

"Oy pahked heah so yuh won't have to drag yoah luggage across the strait," he informed me.

I finally managed to squeeze through the opening afforded by the door after it had been pushed against the tree trunk. Slamming the door closed, I placed one forearm above the open window; then, after leaning down, I grimly commanded, "Wait while I inquire regarding the availability of a unit."

Logically, the command was obviously unnecessary, because I had neither paid the fare nor collected my luggage. But the mind of that creature was something other than logical, so it was logical for me to suspect that he might take off with my luggage and forget where he had delivered me.

While striding toward the office, I quickly analyzed the layout of the imposing, two-story, wood-and-stucco structure and arrived at the conclusion that it was not actually as imposing as it appeared to be. After the glazed entry door responded to my push, I glanced through an open doorway in the far wall of the lobby, and my conclusion was confirmed by the large, central courtyard beyond it.

Of course, the middle-aged woman at the desk greeted me with the usual question: "Can I hilp you?"

"What is your rate for a single?" I countered.

"Fifty dollars," she replied. Meanwhile, her cold eyes carefully inspected my features.

"Thank you," I responded grimly and turned away. Then, abruptly rotating about on one heel, I added, "On second thought, I'll take one for tonight only."

Following completion of the transaction, I moved toward the entry door. Meantime, José suggested: "You could have continued the search if you'd had even a half-smart cab jockey." Then I swung the door wide to allow a young couple to enter before I exited. "As it is," he resumed, "that harridan's mind has obviously been corrupted by the Unknown."

"But we have encountered that problem wherever we've gone," Pancho interjected. "Furthermore, the problem appears to have been spread over the entire face of the earth, so we might as well treat this trip as a research program and uncover as much information on it as we can."

When I returned to the cab, the driver continued to sit stolidly behind the wheel until I leaned down and called, "I would like to pick up my luggage, please."

After crawling slowly from the vehicle, he raised the lid of the boot and absently watched while I wrestled the heavy suitcase free from its grasp. He even had to return to the meter and read it before he could inform me of the bad news. Truly that character had to be a prime case of non compos mentis. After paying the fare, I silently picked up my luggage, trudged through the lobby to the courtyard, and followed a sidewalk along one side of the central court to a stairway that led up to Unit 233 via a narrow balcony.

According to a notice beside the telephone, the charges for breakfast ranged from $7.50 for a light meal to $10.00 for a heavy one. Apparently there was an open season on all dinner guests.

Nevertheless, I returned to the cold-eyed vixen at the desk and inquired, "Where is the dining room located?"

"The dining room is closed, but it will be open for breakfast," she replied.

"Thank you," I murmured.

At the small, brightly painted grocery store diagonally across the street from the motel, I purchased some rolls and a pint of milk for $1.20. Then I dined in my room.

When the light of day awakened me, I arose and subjected my reluctant body to the usual morning ablutions, donned fresh raiment, and reviewed the notice beside the telephone. Past experience compelled me to suspect that the light breakfast would be a choice of dry cereals plus fruit juice, toast, and a beverage; the heavier one would include eggs, fat bacon, and one of the local specialties, such as unbrowned hash-browned potatoes. A mental picture of the greasy bacon immediately induced me to pick up the telephone and call a cab.

The cab driver proved to be a genial sort who was obviously in full possession of his faculties. After we were under way, I asked, "Do you happen to know where I can get a good breakfast for a reasonable price?"

"Will, Woolworths have a pritty good breakfast of iggs, bacon, toast, and coffee foah about foive dollahs," he replied. "Ye can't do much bettah than that anywheah."

"That's for me," I responded. "Where's Woolworths located?"

"It ain't fah," he answered. "Its up neah the Octagon. In fact, theah it is roight theah. See?" And he pointed toward the heavily glazed front of a large masonry building. "Oy'll drop yuh off jist around the nixt cornah, and yuh won't have moah than twenty metahs to walk."

"Thank you for making my day," I said, placing the fare along with a lavish tip in his extended palm.

"It's amazing how widely the services of cab drivers vary throughout the world," Pancho remarked.

"They probably vary in direct proportion to the drivers' intelligences and in accordance with local demands," José added superciliously.

At the point where the sidewalk intersected with that of the main thoroughfare, I paused, turned to my right, and looked toward the Octagon. Then, turning about, I strode to the nearby entrance of the Woolworth store. Despite numerous signs that boasted of discount rates, it appeared to be more of an arcade than either a discount or variety store.

Pausing before a glazed showcase where large quantities of fresh meats were exhibited, I was confronted by a friendly butcher, who asked, "Kin Oy hilp you?"

"No, thank you," I replied. "I'm an outlander who is merely satisfying an insatiable curiosity."

"Theah can't be much food value in that," the man responded with sparkling eyes and a lurking smile.

Following a startled glance and an appreciative grin, I said, "Actually, I'm extremely interested in food value. In fact, I'm looking for the restaurant."

"Oh, that's located roight along this aisle and to yoah lift," he responded with an appropriate gesture.

"Thank you," I murmured and took off as directed.

Beyond the meat department, I passed several unlikely associates, including a display of electronics equipment alongside a garden center. The ladies' and men's ready-to-wear were needlessly segregated from each other not only by electric washers and dryers but by plumbing fittings and other items of hardware. I began to suspect that there might be stocks of bulldozers and draglines in that store, but my arrival at the restaurant terminated the tour.

I must have been too early to encounter the morning breakfast rush. In fact, no one preceded me along the well-defined walk leading to an outpost where a young woman sat at a small table.

"Kin Oy hilp you?" she inquired.

"Do you have fresh orange juice?" I countered.

She ruefully shook her head.

"Then can you fix me up with one egg, a piece of ham, and some toast?" I inquired.

She nodded, punched the items into a computer, and asked, "How do you want yoah igg?"

"Over easy," I replied.

"Tea oah coffee?" she persisted.

"A glass of milk, please," I responded with a trace of a smile.

After a brief session with the electronic gear, she murmured, "That will be two dollahs and eighty-six cints, please."

While she was selecting the change from my five-dollar bill, my eyes casually studied the unoccupied dining area. As she placed the change in my palm, I asked, "Am I supposed to sit in any specific area?"

"No," she replied, adding to the collection an angular piece of plastic on which a numeral was embossed. "But please place this on the table that you silict, and yoah ordah will be delivered to you within a few minits."

The egg turned out to be poached, 40 percent of the ham was fat, and the toast was cold, but I had found such orders to be par in New Zealand, so I was not particularly shook up about it. Besides, I could not have obtained a similar breakfast in my country for twice the price in U.S. dollars, so a little tolerance was in order.

My next most urgent mission involved cashing some traveler's checks;

however, since the banks were not yet open, I returned to the corner where the cabby had dropped me. While waiting for the pedestrian-crossing light to change, I peered speculatively toward the Octagon, which at one time may have enclosed a small, picturesque park, but the ravages of progress had reduced it to a monstrous traffic barrier. Eight short streets form the Octagon, and the traffic from each of the external streets that intersect with them is circulated about the Octagon to whatever exit the driver chooses, be it another short street, another external one, or one of the two thoroughfares that pass through the center of it. It is a veritable maze. To complicate the situation further, each segment of the Octagon bears a different street name. Stuart Street, one of the two thoroughfares, passes indirectly through the obstacle course, but the other one, George Street, becomes Princes Street beyond the Octagon. Since I had purchased and carefully studied a street map of Dunedin, I was relatively familiar with its layout, so I obviously didn't intend to get lost in that part of the city. From the map I had already concluded that the Octagon and the city's several other mazes contributed greatly to the likelihood of a visitor, such as I, getting lost.

At the center of the Octagon I found a tiny, parklike area where a statue of a seated Robert Burns was enclosed within a rectangular space by forty-two-inch-high iron rails. The right forearm and hand of the Scottish poet's statue were extended horizontally with a quill pen between its fingers, and the other hand hung laxly alongside its left thigh.

"I wonder if the sculptor determined whether the man was, indeed, right handed," mused Pancho.

"That's a ridiculous thought!" José retorted. "But what else can be expected from that side of an engineer's brain?"

Then my mind flashed back to the time when my immediate supervisor discovered that he had designed an aircraft's aileron flight control system so that the left- and right-hand ailerons moved simultaneously in the same direction. Of course, he had hurriedly and shamefacedly revised the design, because it would have caused the craft to climb or descend instead of bank right or left as required.

"If that sculptor erred in a similar fashion," Pancho resumed, "then not only should he be dug up, but he should be forced to revise the statue. He probably would have to reconstruct it in its entirety, however, because I'm reasonably sure that exchanging the arms would never work."

"What an idiotic thought!" exclaimed José. And that initiated another brawl, which I wisely chose to ignore.

There also was the Star Fountain, a complex hydraulic system, which was reputed to produce various fine sprays of water in conjunction with the exotic effects of slowly changing colored lights and soft music. But I didn't wait until nine o'clock for the first scheduled exhibition.

Fixing my eyes on St. Paul's Cathedral, which overlooks the park, I recalled that a would-be authority had claimed Dunedin to be the most perfectly preserved Victorian city on the earth. I grant that much of the hundred-year-old Victorian architecture remains in superb condition, but I lack sufficient knowledge about the designs of cathedrals to state positively that St. Paul's Cathedral exhibits any influences of the Victorian era. I prefer to suggest that its designer may have "ripped off" portions of several fine European cathedral designs, since the cathedral's facade incorporates a couple of well-done Gothic arches and a pair of beautiful steeples. Furthermore, its external side walls are reinforced by heavy buttresses similar to those employed on some architecturally renowned European cathedrals.

Scarcely more than a block distant from the cathedral, I found the First Church of Otago, which was constructed of white Oamaru limestone and completed in 1873. It is reputed to be one of the finest churches in the nation, so St. Paul's Cathedral may have to take a back seat.

After the Bank of New Zealand opened, an exchange of three $100 traveler's checks netted me about $580 in coin of the realm. Even the pudgy, little male clerk seemed to be suffering from shock when he counted out the currency—at least, that was how I interpreted his odd expression and intent stare.

With sufficient funds in hand, I set out to find a barber pole, but not one of those striped symbols of the trade was to be found along the entire lengths of either George or Princes Street. I did locate a unisex shop and one hair stylist's shop, both of which were operated by women. But I chose to surrender my beard to a male barber, since I suspected that a female barber might comb my curly whiskers into ringlets and tie brightly colored hair ribbons on them. Retracing my steps and checking all of the shoe cobbler and tobacco shops, I found that none of them concealed a barbershop.

Finally resolving to seek assistance, I entered a liquor store, and the proprietor greeted me with the words: "Good morning. Can Oy be of service?"

"You can be, if you don't object to a nonprofit transaction," I conceded with a smile.

After staring thoughtfully at me for a moment, he cheerfully volunteered, "You ah from New York, and you've become lost in owah small city."

"Not bad," I conceded, "but I'm from Los Angeles, and I've been unable to find even one barbershop along the entire main stem of this city."

"You ah moah loikely to foind thim along the soide straits," he muttered. "In fact, theah's one behind a cleaning establishment located just around that cornah." And he pointed out the corner for me.

"Thank you," I said. "I'm sorry that I can't do some business with you, but my doctor has advised me to avoid liquor."

With a judicious nod, he said, "A woise man, that doctah. Oy nivah touch the stuff moysilf." After turning a startled expression to him, I executed a casual salute and exited.

While I veered toward the corner, José suggested, "That case is similar to the one concerning the shoe cobbler's children in that...."

"True," Pancho interjected. "They never have any shoes to wear, but that doesn't apply to this case."

And that precipitated an argument that was still in progress when I strolled into the cleaning establishment.

The tall, middle-aged male proprietor looked expectantly at me, so I pointed to my beard and said, "I've already had it cleaned. Now I want to get it trimmed."

Following a stolid stare, he courteously gestured toward the open doorway in a pony wall that separated his domain from the adjoining barbershop. Continuing on into the rear of the establishment, I came upon a man of some forty-five summers who was industriously honing a straight-edge razor.

As he looked up from the gleaming blade, I teasingly inquired, "Do you perform beard surgeries here?"

After studying my quizzical eyes for a moment, he countered, "Do you want yoah beahd removed?"

Once more, my so-called humor had obviously backfired on me, so I meekly answered, "No, but a trim is long overdue."

With a quick gesture toward the first of the two barber chairs, he requested, "Please be seated."

Before I could move off of my heels, he whirled about, placed the razor and stone on the backbar, swept up an apron, and with one fluid motion hurriedly dusted the seat and arms of the chair with it. Then he stood rigidly at attention beside the chair while I climbed aboard it.

After placing the apron across my bay window, he pulled the top of it tightly against my neck and tied the strings with a flip of the wrist that reminded me of a rodeo cowboy hog-tying a calf. Then, thrusting his left arm around my shoulders, he leaned forward, placed his lips opposite my right ear, and shouted, "Do yuh want a close oah medium trim?"

Cringing from the thunderous sound waves, I cautiously began, "Well . . . ," because I was unsure of what those terms might mean in the Southern Hemisphere. Then, casting caution to the winds, I boldly added, "Leave well-defined outlines of my beard and of what little hair remains on my head."

My words set a virtual dynamo in motion. After swinging around to the backbar, he rebounded from it with a comb in one hand and a buzzing electric clipper assembly in the other one. Believe me, that man wasted no motions as he swept the clippers expertly around my head and ears. Since a few stray strands of gray hair already defined my bald spot, he wasted no time on that.

With the last swipe at my curls he swerved toward the backbar and smoothly exchanged the comb and clippers for an adjustable clipper assembly. Adjusting it en route, he turned purposefully to me. Unfortunately, I had become so mesmerized by all of the activity that I had failed to take the opportunity to escape. First, he grasped the top of my head with the widely splayed fingers of his left hand; then he ran the clippers from the front of my left ear to my chin and impatiently flipped the clump of severed whiskers onto the apron directly in front of my horror-stricken eyes.

It was so macabre that I was reminded of the time when, as a teenager, my tonsils were removed in the doctor's office. And it was almost as painful, but the doctor didn't impatiently flip the severed tonsils onto the apron directly in front of me. He carefully saved them, because fresh meat was hard to come by during the Great Depression.

Actually, I wasn't particularly fond of that beard; in fact, I detested it, but it provided some advantages. Foremost among them was the likelihood that it slightly hampered the activities of the Unknown. And it freed me from the odious task of shaving, of course. Despite my dislike of the beard, we had become closely attached, and this total stranger was rapidly separating us the hard way. But it was too late to do anything about it, because he had already finished the sides of my face and was concentrating on the areas along the sides of my neck and under my chin. There, even more than before, the rapidly moving clippers dragged whole clumps of un-severed whiskers from their moorings. At one point I was just about to scream when he stopped, took a quick swipe at an untouched clump on one side of my face, then stepped back and laid the tool on the backbar.

Meanwhile, I exhaled a long, quivering sigh of relief, but the vapor from it immediately fogged the mirror that the barber had thrust before my eyes. He really hustled, that barber did, but he didn't bustle, not once. He was much too efficient for that. When the fog cleared, I stared aghast at the image that confronted me. Suddenly I felt an enduring empathy for the poor, newly shorn sheep.

I must have been in deep shock; otherwise I would never have numbly nodded and mumbled, "Yeah, a vast improvement." In fact, that must have been the case, because my limbs shook so much that I staggered in a circle after dismounting from the chair. "Hmm," I mumbled. "I must have been sitting too long." But that could not have been the reason. According to the clock over the backbar, only eight minutes had passed since I entered the shop.

"Compare that time with the forty-five minutes that your old barber in Fullerton spent on your last trim," José propounded, "and it becomes crystal clear why the U.S. can no longer compete on the open market."

"But Bill doesn't leave any divots when he does his bit," Pancho objected. "In fact, he's a perfectionist, and that's the main reason why he can't compete on the open market."

"Furthermore, it isn't feasible to ship a beard or a head of hair to another nation for a trim job," José resumed, "but that doesn't apply to hairpieces, of course."

"The hair in a hairpiece doesn't grow, you idiot," Pancho protested so loudly my ears rang.

Ignoring the ensuing riot, I started toward the cash register, where the barber stood waiting. Then I remembered my jacket, so that shock treatment must have worked, because I usually forget it. When I arrived at the cash register, the barber's predatory eyes were fixed on his next victim as the fingers of one hand impatiently tapped the top of the register.

"That will be eight sivinty-foive," he informed me.

By the time that I regained the relative safety of the street with its speeding autos, backing trucks, muggers, and such, the lads had calmed down and developed a philosophy regarding New Zealand's barbers.

"The government really shouldn't permit them to serve their apprenticeships as sheep shearers," Pancho stated, as I pensively ran my right forefinger through the stubble on my chin.

"Now you can fully understand how a newly shorn lamb must feel when it gets up on shaky legs and slowly totters away from the shearer," José claimed. "Naked, that's how it must feel. Naked."

"But you got even with that son of a sheepherder, Al," Pancho injected. "You were so unstrung after the ordeal that you forgot to tip the *bastid*."

Later, about seven o'clock in the evening, I finally found the small sign that I had noticed earlier in the day. It hung beneath one of the marquees that projected out from one of the masonry buildings, which dominated the eastern side of George Street near the Octagon. And it bore the tantalizing word STEAKS. In fact, that was my paramount objective when I entered the doorway of the restaurant. Beyond the doorway was a tiny foyer, where I paused to study the layout.

A dozen wooden booths were equally distributed along the walls of the narrow room with a narrow aisle between them. At the rear of the room, a counter separated the dining area from a small kitchen, in the middle of which a tall, middle-aged man industriously stirred pots and shook pans with both hands while his towering, white chapeau bobbed and teetered precariously with every motion.

Standing beside one of the two most remote booths was a middle-aged woman who appeared to serve in all capacities, so I assumed that she was the chef's mate; therefore, she must have been not only the general overseer but the one in charge. Nevertheless, it was the teenaged waitress who escorted me to the last available table, which must have been an afterthought, because it had been squeezed against one wall of the foyer. Two straight-back chairs had been placed at the ends of it, but I doubt that the table could have accommodated two standard-size dinner plates.

The steak wasn't bad, but I usually do much better. However, it could have been the fault of the meat. After all, the sign bore only the word STEAKS, so the meat could have come from the rump of a tough, old bull.

When I arrived at the cashier's tiny counter, I found that the middle-aged woman also served as the cashier. She directed only one cautious glance toward my bearded features at close range, but I had detected a couple of distant ones during the meal. Of course, it could have been the beard that had attracted her attention, but beards aren't that uncommon these days, even in New Zealand.

Back at the Cherry Court, I forked up another fifty bucks for a second night, but I set out early in the following morning to find more economical lodging. My first try involved a large, colonial house that was located on the opposite side of the street from the Cherry Court but some two blocks closer to the central part of the city. Its small, wooden nameplate seemed to imply that rooms might be for hire there, so I decided to investigate. As I approached the entry door, a young woman bustled through it, smiled pleasantly, and courteously held it open for me. After thanking her, I strolled through the opening into a dimly lighted hallway and passed by several closed doors before coming to the open doorway of a dining room.

There I encountered a well-knit young woman, who stared suspiciously at me and inquired, "Whom do you wish to see?"

"The manager, I suppose," I answered. "But can you tell me if a room might be available?"

After subjecting me to another suspicious inspection, she shook her head and added, "Not presently. But how did you get in here?"

I returned the inspection and answered, "The door was open, so I walked in."

Following a quick glance in the direction of the entrance, she started toward it, so I fell into step behind her. While reaching for the doorknob, she turned her head and angrily stated, "This door is supposed to be locked at all times!" Then, after jerking the door open, she tried the latch. Turning a pair of ultrasuspicious eyes on me, she growled, "This latch is locked, so how did you get in here?"

Visions of being incarcerated in a Dunedin dungeon for breaking and entering erupted on my mental screen, and I didn't like the picture at all. "Well," I murmured tentatively, "when I arrived at the door, a young lady was just leaving, and she graciously held it open for me, so I came on in."

After studying my eyes for a moment, she seemed to conclude that they were honest eyes and that my story made sense. "Well, she shouldn't have done that!" she bit off and swung the door wide open.

I was so glad to escape that I eagerly accepted her open invitation to leave. Later, while mentally reviewing the incident, I was unable to shake the impression that the trim little gal had actually tossed the hip pockets of my blue jeans out of her normally locked Victorian doorway onto the concrete sidewalk. In fact, I even caught myself in the act of inspecting those pockets when I was about to hang the jeans in the closet that evening, but there were no marks or abrasions on them.

That misadventure may have been the primary reason why I crossed the street and strode so purposefully past the Cherry Court to the Garden Motels, which I had noticed during my previous trek to the flamboyantly painted grocery store.

"Good morning," the young manager pleasantly greeted me with a protracted stare.

"Good morning," I responded. "What is your daily rate for a single guest?"

"Thirty-foive dollahs," he answered.

"And what is it by the week or month?" I persisted.

After frowning briefly at the countertop, he turned apologetic eyes to me and answered, "Since we usually fill up the units at the daily rite, we don't discount it for long-term guests." Then, thrusting one hand below the level of the counter, he transferred a small, folded map to the top of it and resumed, "Howevah, theah ah some cheapah motils awye from the city." Unfolding the map, he circled three small, black rectangles scattered along Musselburgh Rise, which appeared to be a prominent thoroughfare in the southernmost part of the city. "If you'll call one oah moah of thim, Oy suspect you moight foind what you want. Theah nimes ah shown in the indix." And he pointed to the index located in one corner of the map.

After briefly studying the map, I concluded that the area was too remote for access afoot, so I said, "Since I like to see what I'm buying, I'll call a cab and make a tour of that area. But please let me jot down the names of those motels."

"No, take the map with you," he insisted, pushing it toward me.

After thoughtfully accepting it, I protested, "But that thing has to cost something," and reached for my wallet.

"No, take it," he persisted. "It's all yoahs."

From the look in his eyes, I suspected that he might be offended if I continued to press the matter, so I folded the map and tucked it into my shirt pocket. "Thank you very much," I muttered gruffly.

"Such acts of generosity never cease to emotionally confuse Al after having spent a lifetime in a particularly greedy society," Pancho observed.

"Where can one find any other type of society?" José countered.

From the Garden Motels I returned to Cherry Court's Unit 233 and used its telephone to call a cab.

"Wheah do you want to go?" the cab driver asked as soon as I settled onto the seat.

Leaning toward him, I thrust the open map before him and said, "Let's first go to the motel in that circle at the end of Musselburgh Rise. From there we can stop at any other motels that we come upon during the return trip."

Following a brief study of the map, he nodded and returned it to me. Easing the cab into gear, he took off in a southerly direction along George Street to Albany Street, where he first turned left, then right onto Castle Street. From there he maneuvered it around the railway station via Anzac and High, which I readily recognized as the same route that the bus had followed. After a relatively short run along Cumberland, the driver turned the cab left onto Andersons Bay Road and continued along that thoroughfare until some time after it became Musselburgh Rise.

At a daily rate of thirty dollars, the Bayfield Motel proved to be a possible prospect. And I told the manager, Tim, as much. However, I also warned him that I was shopping and that he would receive a call from me if I found a better deal.

Neither the Adrian nor the Chequers proved to be prospects, so only one more possibility remained on Musselburgh Rise. Eventually a large sign bearing the words *The Arcadian Motel* came into view, and it seemed that the cab voluntarily turned to the right onto the motel's wide driveway. Then, almost as if it had been there many times before, it came to a stop directly in front of the open doorway of the office. Stepping down from the cab, I strolled through the open doorway into a relatively large office, but no one was minding the store. I was about to leave when my roving eyes spotted a note prominently displayed atop the big, oak desk, so I moved to it and read, "I am working in Unit 6 or 7." Retracing some steps, I continued on and finally found the moon-faced manager of the motel in Unit 6.

"Good mornin'," he greeted me with a wide, infectious grin, which stretched the pink flesh around his merry, green eyes so tightly they became mere slits. Simultaneously, he removed a large handkerchief from a hip pocket and mopped away several beads of perspiration from his smooth brow.

"And good morning to you," I responded cheerfully. "Somebody suggested that I contact you regarding a relatively long-term rental."

"How many people will theah be?" he countered.

"Just me," I replied, pointing my right forefinger to the middle of my chest.

"How long?" he persisted.

"Well," I began cautiously, "I prefer to rent by the week; however, if things go well for me, I may stay for the duration of my visa. It limits me to three months, and I have used two weeks of it."

"Let's go to the office, where I kin review our shedules," he suggested.

After entering the office, I came to a stop before the near side of the desk while the big man settled ponderously into the swivel chair in front of it and began to study the large paper pad bearing the numbers of the motel units along with their scheduled dates of occupancy.

"Hmm," he finally mumbled. "Unfortunately, we can't take you right away."

"How soon will one be available?" I asked.

His green eyes returned to the schedule briefly; then they fixed on my blue ones. "Three, maybe two days," he replied.

"And what would the rate be?" I asked.

"The rate," he mumbled thoughtfully. "Oh, yes, the rate!" he suddenly exploded with a chuckle. "That's the most important factor of all... to both of us."

I didn't even try to restrain the smile that erupted in response to the man's effervescent outburst. Without doubt he possessed a very engaging personality.

"Well," he began. After pursing his lips and pondering the problem for a while, he finally added, "We could let you have a unit like the one you found me in for twenty-five dollars per day on a weekly basis."

Following a vigorous nod, I said, "That's the best deal that I've been offered so far."

"It's nice of you to tell me that," he murmured.

"When can you book me?" I asked.

"Well," he muttered, "that'll take a wee bit o' homework, and I can't do it immediately because we have to finish readying the units. If you'll leave your name and telephone number, I'll reorganize our schedule to suit the new situation and call you some time after one o'clock."

"Fine," I responded. "My name is Tyrrell, which is spelled *t-y-r-r-e-l-l*, and I'm in Room 233 at the Cherry Court Motel. Unfortunately, I don't remember the telephone number."

"I have that," he rejoined, "and I promise to call you shortly after one o'clock." Then he bounded out of the swivel chair as if his 230 pounds were no weight at all.

"I'll be waiting for your call," I responded, turning toward the open doorway.

"Oh, I should have hurried!" he shouted from directly behind me. "It costs money to keep a cab waiting."

"Yeah," I rumbled, "the cab driver may withhold my luggage when I'm unable to pay the tab for this trip."

The green eyes peered at me uncertainly from between their narrow slits while their owner chuckled, but even I comprehended the true reason for the chuckle: It was tendered more in sympathy for than in appreciation of the attempted humor.

We stepped from the edge of the stoop simultaneously, but I moved toward the cab while he turned toward the open doorway of Unit 6. When he was about to pass the driver's open window, he paused while the two men exchanged long stares—too long, in fact. Then he nodded to the driver in a friendly manner and continued toward his objective.

"Wot luck?" the driver inquired after I was seated.

"The best yet," I replied. "It's five dollars per day less than Bayfield, and I'm not likely to beat that."

Back at the Cherry Court, I waited impatiently for the telephone call. Shortly after one o'clock the telephone clamored stridently, so I raised the instrument and said, "This is Al Tyrrell."

"This is Wilfred at The Arcadian Motel," a gruff voice informed me.

"I've been waiting for your call," I responded.

"Well, it appears that we can take you Sunday afternoon," resumed the gruff voice.

"Fine," I responded. "When do I put down the money?"

"You can pay when you come in or you can pay at the end of the week," was the reply.

"I'll pay when I assume residence," I said. "Thank you for the call. It has established some roots in this city for me, so to speak."

"Then we'll see you Sunday afternoon," the voice responded in tones of finality.

After spending that night at the Cherry Court, early in the following morning I appeared in the office of the Garden Motels, where a sixty-some-year-old woman presided.

"Good morning," she greeted me. "How kin Oy hilp you?"

"Well," I began, "yesterday a pleasant and very cooperative young man assisted me in finding long-term lodging, but it won't be available for a couple of days, so I intend to throw some of my current business his way to compensate him in part for his time."

"Oy'm that young man's mothah," the woman responded with a pardonable gleam of pride shining through her efforts to appear professional. "He has been working much too hahd, so moy husband and Oy have come heah to hilp out foah a few dyes."

"Then all of us are trying to help him," I ventured.

Following a brief study of my eyes, she said, "It's noice of you to try to repay him foah what is really just a business courtesy."

"Unfortunately, many of the business people from my part of the world have forgotten the importance of business courtesy," I murmured.

"But you don't appeah to be that type," she countered. "Ah you in business?"

"I was once," I answered, "but time has pigeonholed me, so I've retired."

"That's the fate of all of us, Oy feah," she murmured, as her eyes studied a chart lying on the desk. "How many will theah be in yoah pahty?"

"Just one," I replied. "But I would like to retain the unit for two days."

"Do you intend to pay by cridit cahd?" she persisted.

"No," I answered, "I prefer to pay cash, and I would like to pay in advance."

"That's the bist way," she said. "So many of the newah generations have taken to spinding thimsilves into bankruptcy by promiscuous use of cridit cahds."

"That's a surprising remark from a member of a socialistic society," I remarked with a teasing smile.

"Owahs is a socialistic governmint," she conceded, "but most of us New Zealandahs ah very conservative people."

"I have noticed that," I said, "and I highly respect your people for it."

"That will be sivinty dollahs," she finally decided.

Silently exchanging the money for a receipt and a key, I then turned away and grasped the doorknob.

"If you should requiah anything, please infoahm us," she called to me. With a nod, I pushed the door open and departed.

I spent much of the two-day wait seeing the sights. Despite the fact that I had viewed the Dunedin Railway Station from various points of vantage, I returned to it for a more thorough inspection, during which I studied not only its exterior in more detail but its highly decorated interior.

In its time that exotic landmark must have cost a mint of money, since all of its basic structures, consisting of the long, two-story building, its gables, the huge, stone portico with adjoining covered walks, a clock tower surmounted by a cupola, and one larger cupola atop the highest gable, were minutely detailed in Oumaru limestone. Not only were the arches and rails intricately decorated with the white stone, but every Gothic window and dormer bore its share of the burden. Despite my suspicion that it was a bit overdone, I considered it to be a fine example of early art and craftsmanship. Inside the eighty-year-old structure the excesses continued into the mosaics of the floor, which were dominated by the railway motif, and into the iron scrollwork that surrounded the ticket windows as well as the stained-glass windows that featured the steam engine and its contemporaries.

A short distance from the station I came upon the Early Settler's Museum, which displayed hundreds of photographs and many tintypes of the early settlers dating back as far as the 1860s. In particular, there were photographs of groups of farmers and their threshing equipment, circa 1915, which reminded me of the pictures of my father's threshing equipment and the farmhands standing on the plains of Saskatchewan, Canada, early in the twentieth century. At that time it was the most modern equipment that money could buy, but seventy years of progress would qualify it for a museum, too, if it still exists.

Some of the early steam engines particularly interested me. Included among them were several small, narrow-gage railway steam engines and a few steam-powered farm tractors. Among the various displays were several old electric trolley cars whose designs could have vied with the Toonerville Trolley.

In general, the museum helped to piece together the city's early history, which began with its founding in 1848 by a group of Presbyterian Scots. However, the populace of Dunedin (the ancient Gaelic name for Edinburgh) swung sharply away from its early religious principles with the discovery of gold in Otago. Gold was a major contributing factor in the growth of its population and its per capita wealth. But I had found that those early religious principles still survived among many of the people that I met.

9

The Arcadian Motel

Shortly after ten o'clock Sunday morning a cab delivered me to the door of The Arcadian Motel's office, and after opening it, I struggled through the opening and set both pieces of luggage on the floor. Within seconds the heavyset manager strode into the room through a wider opening that communicated with the adjoining living quarters.

"Good morning, Mr. Tyrrell!" he boomed.

"Good morning," I responded. "I'm a little early, but I didn't want to exceed the Cherry Court's checkout limit."

"We don't have your unit quite ready," he rumbled apologetically. "We found it in worse shape than what we usually do. Some people are not as careful as others."

"I know what you mean," I responded with a chuckle. "I rented apartments to people for a few years. Sometimes I had to use a shovel to clean up after the tenants left.

"Well, give us half an hour, and we'll have it ready for you," he promised. "Meanwhile, you can leave your luggage in the office and go take your morning constitutional . . . or you can wait here, if you prefer. In that case, I'll place an electric heater in here, because it's a wee bit cold this morning."

"No, don't do that!" I insisted. "It isn't that cold. Besides, I would like to walk about and see some of the neighborhood. What would be the best direction for me to take?"

"You might like the view from up on the rise," he suggested. "From there you can look down on many of the homes, or you can look out toward Saint Kilda Beach, which is only a wee distance away."

"Sounds like a good suggestion," I granted. A couple of strides carried me to the doorway, where I paused and added, "I'll make sure that my trek lasts through the next hour." Then I resumed walking.

"We'll have your unit ready in half an hour," he called after me. Extending one arm in a casual wave, I continued to stride rapidly along the driveway.

The sky was heavily overcast, and a light mist was falling on the municipality of Musselburgh, but I was prepared for the worst, so I buttoned my topcoat tightly around my Adam's apple to exclude the mist borne on the gusts of a cold wind. At the point where the sidewalk intersected with the driveway, I turned east along Musselburgh Rise, which soon veered in a northeasterly direction, and slowly climbed to the top of the rise. From there, despite the inclement weather, I could see the not-too-distant Pacific Ocean, but the view of Andersons Bay Inlet to the north was obstructed by a higher element of the rise. Following a casual study of the architectural designs embodied in the surrounding homes, I concluded that they were well constructed, well maintained, and from fifty to one hundred years old.

During the return trip I chanced to look down on a lawn-bowling match in what may have been Culling Park, which I later found to be located some three or four hundred meters south of the thoroughfare. Despite the weather, all of the bowlers were uniformly and meticulously clad in white from head to toe, including caps, sweaters, trousers, and shoes; furthermore, I'll bet that the underpants of those old-timers were also white. That mist-laden scene strongly reminded me of similar ones that I had come upon as a boy in Vancouver, British Columbia.

Upon returning to the driveway of the motel, I stopped and studied the complex for several minutes. To my left was a long, two-story, wood-frame structure with a newly painted, corrugated sheet-metal roof, and I found it to be rather attractive despite its severe lines. The roofs of the office and the units also were of corrugated sheet metal, but they retained their original galvanized surfaces. The rear of the office was attached to and extended slightly beyond the far corner of the two-story structure's near wall. Directly beyond the far wall of the office was a four-inch diameter steel pole surmounted by a steel crossbar, which supported the ends of four clotheslines that extended some twenty-five feet alongside a wood paling fence to a similar supporting crossbar and pole. In addition to its glazed door, the external walls of the office were dominated by large windows that provided unobstructed views of the complex, including the three combined units that stood beyond the end of the clothesline.

To my right, four combined units extended from the setback line to a point opposite the far wall of the office, where a ten-foot access alley had been provided between that combination and the laundry, which was combined with three more units. The asphalt pavement between the two lines of structures provided more than adequate parking space for a dozen automobiles.

Abruptly, my study was interrupted by the manager, who burst through the open doorway of the laundry. With the top of his bare head turned toward the wind, he hurried across the paved parking area toward the office. Bounding up onto the concrete stoop like an overweight gazelle, he thrust aside the sliding door; then, noticing me, he gestured violently for me to join him.

When I strode through the open doorway, he practically shouted, "There's no reason for you to stand out there in the cold and rain when we have a clean, dry unit all ready for you."

"I was just casing the joint," I responded with a smile.

"Casing the joint?" he murmured perplexedly.

"Those words evolved from the American underworld," I explained, "so don't pay any attention to them. In fact, never pay any attention to much of what I say, because I have a bad habit of trying to be funny, but most often I'm the only one who is amused by my humor."

"But if you would explain . . . ," he began tentatively.

"If you have the time, I would like to register and pay for the coming week," I interjected.

"Of course, I have the time," he said, "but you can pay at the end of the week if you like."

"No, I prefer to pay in advance," I said.

"Just as you like," he responded cheerfully, withdrawing a large receipt book from a desk drawer. "I already have your name, of course, but I failed to introduce myself when you were here before. My name is Wilfred Radford." After extending a plump right hand, whose softness hid sinews of steel, he formally added, "I'm an equal partner with my cousin, Isibelle Jerkens, in the ownership of this motel."

"I'm glad to know you, Mr. Radford," I mumbled, carefully separating the fingers of my numbed right hand.

"Let's see," he muttered, scribbling some calculations on a piece of scrap paper. "That will be one hundred seventy-five dollars for the coming week, I believe."

"Amazing!" I exclaimed. "You New Zealanders get the same answers as we Americans get from the same multiplicands. How do you do it?"

His eyes registered confusion for an instant; then, with a wide grin, he said, "I suspect that you are what you Americans call a 'kidder,' eh?"

"But this is no kidding matter," I protested, placing the money on the desk. "It always pains me greatly to part with so much money."

The grin remained in place until the receipt was completed; then, slowly rising, he submitted it to me and said, "Now I'll show you to your new home away from home."

We came to a stop at the small stoop in front of the entrance of Unit 3, where Wilfred dug a key from a capacious trousers pocket. Meanwhile, lowering my luggage onto the asphalt pavement, I pointed to the two-story structure and said, "No doubt that was a home at one time."

"Yes," he said, "and it's about ninety years old; however, it has been remodeled, of course, and the unit directly opposite this one was incorporated at the time."

"How old are the newer units?" I asked.

"They were built fourteen years ago," he replied. "Unfortunately, the previous owner got into a financial bind, so I took it over for Isibelle and me at a very good price."

Nodding sagely, I said, "That's the way most good deals are won."

"I really hated to take advantage of the poor blighter," Wilfred protested, "but he was about to lose the motel."

"I wasn't criticizing you," I insisted. "After all, he created his own problem, and somebody would have gained at his expense, so why shouldn't you and Isibelle be the fortunate ones?"

"Running a motel has been no great sport," he mumbled thoughtfully, "for either Isibelle or me. In fact, we've been thinking about selling it."

"But you have an advantage that the previous owner didn't have," I suggested. "You can sell it on your terms."

With an emphatic nod, he opened the door and escorted me through the unit. Back at the doorway, he handed the key to me and said, "I hope you enjoy your stay with us. If you should need anything, please call us."

"Thank you," I said as a loud buzz sounded from the front eaves of Unit 3.

"Oh, that's the telephone again," he muttered with a groan. Then, with apologetic eyes, he turned away and dashed through the open doorway toward the office. Meanwhile, I strolled to the opening and peered up at the buzzer.

"In terms of noise, it looks like we've been assigned the most undesirable unit of the lot," José mused.

"However, those raucous summons probably will be limited to only the morning hours while the owners and their staff are engaged in readying the units," Pancho suggested.

Since Unit 3 didn't have a stairway, it couldn't be compared with our town house in Fullerton, but there were several other reasons. Nevertheless, it was as close to being my Dunedin town house as my penny-pinching nature would permit. The only access to the unit was via the front entrance, whose door opened into what was to serve me as a fifteen-foot-square combination living room, bedroom, studio, and office. In the wall directly opposite the entrance was a door that opened to a small walk-in closet. Alongside that closet was another door that opened to a closet, within which the water heater was concealed. Both of those doors were cleverly constructed of vertical, shiplap boards that blended nicely into the vertical, shiplap boards of the wall. And that particular wall extended some eleven feet from the floor to and around the exposed, four- by six-inch wooden beams that supported the slightly pitched ceiling's two-inch-thick planks of compressed insulation material. The beams, shiplap boards, and other wooden components of the room were stained a dark mahogany color.

About halfway from the cream-colored, concrete block wall that also served the adjoining unit, the shiplap wall projected one foot into the room. From that projection a seven-foot-high wooden framework extended to the opposite cream-colored, concrete block wall, which also served an adjoining unit. Not only did the wooden framework enclose an open doorway that provided access to the small kitchen and dinette, but it supported several panels of obscured glass. Short pieces of vertical shiplap extended from the top of the framework to the beams and the ceiling.

Actually, the obscured glass effectively concealed a small table and two straight-back chairs, but the open doorway revealed several components of the kitchen mounted along the far wall of the eight- by ten-foot area. Most conspicuous of them was the Shacklock Orion 21 electric range, which was fitted between the end of the stainless steel sink and the Formica-like surface of the gray wall. A small, cream-colored wooden cabinet was mounted in the far corner over the tiny kitchen pullman.

Slightly beyond the open doorway, a door in the Formica-like gray wall opened directly to a curtain draped across the shower door in the adjoining bathroom. To the right of the three- by nine-foot space was a narrow, three-foot-long lavatory pullman, and a two- by three-foot window consumed much of the far wall. Just beyond the shower door was a narrow doorway with a sliding door, which provided access to the three- by five-foot area housing the water closet located below a small window in the wall at the far end of the area. Typically, the water closet assembly consisted of a white, plastic water tank and a white, ceramic toilet bowl. The tank was mounted as high on the wall as the lower edge of the window trim would permit, and a one-half-inch-diameter, chrome-plated pipe extended from the bottom of it down into the upper rear end of the bowl. A three-inch-diameter discharge line projected from the lower rear end of the bowl into the wall, and a plastic seat and thin, plastic lid covered the top of the bowl. A plastic toggle button was inconveniently located on the center line of the tank directly below its plastic cover. Its operation was typical of other water closets that I had encountered throughout New Zealand in that when the plastic button was pressed, the water in the tank was released with a force and a roar which compared favorably with that of Niagara Falls at flood level. Dual water faucets (no cold- and hot-water mixing valves) had been provided in both the bathroom and the kitchen.

Distributed about the living area were two small stools, which probably had been provided for the unlikely possibility that more than two people could be squeezed into the dinette (or into the unit itself, for that matter). Viewed from the entrance, the head of a double bed stood against the far cream-colored, concrete block wall with just enough space between the edge of the bed and the large, front windows to permit maintenance operations. A tiny, three-drawer nightstand stood between the bed and the end of the adjacent sitbed, which was nicely camouflaged by a slipcover and two upholstered pillows to simulate a sofa. An ancient colored television set stood midway along the near concrete wall with an upholstered armchair positioned symmetrically on each side of it. On the wall above the set, one of the motel's calendars displayed the current month. In the space above the month were two pictures of the scarlet-breasted parakeet (*neophrema splendida*). A mobile electric heater stood before the door of the closet that housed the water heater. In the space between the entrance and the windows stood a small telephone stand surmounted by a cream-colored telephone and its cradle. On the cradle were two buttons: one for outside lines and one for communicating with either of the two telephones in the office.

Not only do the above details reveal some of the life-style and culture of our southern cousins, but they set the scene for what transpires in some of the following chapters.

After hanging my limited wardrobe in the closet, I picked up the briefcase, seated myself in an armchair, and began to sort the various bits of literature that I had collected. I quickly came upon a brochure covering Dunedin's points of interest. Of course, it was deliberately couched in terms intended to create a burning desire in the heart of every literate tourist to view the city's natural and historical treasures, but I rarely yield to such a desire, totally, that is.

According to the pamphlet, Dunedin's Scottish founders chose for their settlement one of the most magnificent harbor settings in all of New Zealand. Uncrowded and spacious, the city is richly endowed with beaches, parks, gardens, and a fine cultural heritage that is reflected in its architecture, universities, and museums.

Among the most impressive of the city's attractions is Glenfalloch Woodland Gardens, which is nestled into a beautiful twenty-seven-acre valley. It offers a view of a pioneer homestead, a stream, and a beautiful woodland garden that includes renowned rhododendrons and azaleas. Despite the intoxicating words, according to an adjacent picture the pioneer homestead looked more like a small, wood-frame hotel than like a homestead.

The Otago Peninsula offers one of the world's most fascinating glimpses of marine wildlife in its natural setting. At Penguin Bay and Seal Island one can watch the yellow-eyed penguins march up from the surf and climb into their nests while sleek seals bask in the warming rays of the sun on a rocky islet, which is scarcely more than thirty feet from the shore.

Larnach Castle harks back some one hundred years to its origin and design, which includes fabulous carved ceilings, Venetian glass, and many antiques from that early era. From a prominence of some one thousand feet above the sea, the tower affords an unobstructed view of the surrounding seascape and landscapes.

Nowhere else in the world do the albatross nest as close to civilization as they do at Taioroa Head; in fact, this is the only colony found on an inhabited mainland. The albatross is the largest of sea-oriented birds, and, with a wingspan of up to eleven feet, it falls in the classification of soaring birds. Consequently, it nests only in those areas where high winds prevail concurrent with favorable updrafts. The birds mate in October and hatch their young during the following January.

Olveston is Dunedin's most unique and stately home, a veritable treasure house of antique furniture, paintings, priceless silverware, rare porcelains, and ornaments collected from all over the world. It exemplifies the age of gracious living. Among its thirty-five rooms, the most impressive are considered to be the drawing room, the billiard room, the great hall (dining room), and the kitchen. From an inspection of an accompanying picture I decided that the building looked more like a hotel than a home.

After replacing the material in the briefcase, I ventured into the small kitchen and began taking stock of what the cabinet drawers and shelves contained. While inspecting the stainless steel cutlery, I heard the entrance door slam against its stop, followed by the sounds of rapid footfalls crossing the thin carpet that covered the concrete slab. As I turned about, a heavyset woman with several towels clasped in her arms bustled through the opening and disappeared through the bathroom doorway. Seconds later she reappeared in it, stepped to the countertop, deposited two dish towels on it, silently turned about, and retraced her steps.

"No doubt that's Isibelle." Pancho mused. "But why didn't she introduce herself?"

Obviously, there was no immediate answer to the question, but one was quickly forthcoming. Several minutes later, as I stepped through the office doorway, Wilfred shouted, "Mr. Tyrrell! Did we fail to provide something?"

"No, not to my knowledge at least," I replied. "I merely stopped in to ask where I can get a container of milk."

"We can give you a bottle of milk," he answered. "In fact, we always provide a pint of milk for our overnight guests; however, we don't commonly extend that courtesy to permanent guests, who receive the benefit of a discount."

"That's logical," I responded. "It's nice of you to offer the courtesy this time, but I prefer to pay my way."

With an approving nod, he said, "You can purchase almost anything you might require from the Dairy." After pausing and correctly interpreting my confused expression, he added, "That's a store that's located about two blocks west along this side of the street. It carries not only dairy products but small stocks of various other packaged or canned foods."

"Thank you," I murmured and turned to leave.

"By the way," he called. As I turned toward him with questioning eyes, he added, "You must have wondered when Isibelle barged in on you a while ago. She didn't know that you had arrived. She won't do that again."

"That was no problem," I rejoined, "and you can tell her that I suspected the reason."

"Of course, she should have introduced herself," he resumed, "but she's a country girl, so she doesn't know what to do under unusual circumstances."

"Apparently, she's smart enough to know what she should have done under the circumstances," I murmured. "Please tell her to forget the matter." Turning about, I exited.

From the driveway I strode past the fronts of several residences before coming upon a commercial area consisting of a butcher shop, a produce store, a tiny fast-food shop, and several similar establishments.

After ascending the wooden steps that led up to the glazed door of the Dairy, I opened it and stepped forward onto the worn linoleum that covered most of the wooden floor, which yielded slightly under my weight. Directly ahead of me and dominating the center of the floor was a stack of shelves stocked with loaves of bread, cakes, and cardboard boxes containing various dry foodstuffs, such as breakfast cereals, cookies, and wafers. To my right was a checkout counter, beyond which a middle-aged brunette sat on an upholstered, metal stool. We exchanged calculating gazes; then my eyes turned to the large, glazed refrigerator door on my left and fixed on the pint bottles of milk stored behind it. After extracting one of them, I wandered along the U-shaped aisle that provided access to both the wall shelves and the central stacks, from which I selected appropriate items for my upcoming meals. When I arrived at the checkout counter, the brunette silently rose and methodically rang up the prices of the items as I placed them on the counter.

After packaging them, she said, "That'll be foive dollahs and sivinty-six cints. You'll receive a thirty-cint refund whin you return the bottle."

With a nod, I silently picked up the package and strode toward the door. While swinging it open, I turned so that my eyes would sweep the area in which she stood, and they encountered another calculating gaze.

"It's a bit too early to draw any conclusions," José mused while I was cautiously descending the weathered, wooden steps, "but it appears that both Wilfred and that gal have been in contact with the Unknown."

After stowing my purchases in the kitchen of Unit 3, I returned to the office.

"Did you get some milk?" Wilfred greeted me.

"Yes," I replied, "but I should wash some of my clothing. What's the best time of day for me to do that?"

"We follow a policy of washing the motel's linen during the morning," he replied, "so the most convenient time for the tenants is during the afternoon. But it might be better to wait until tomorrow afternoon on the chance that the sun will be on hand to dry your clothes."

"But he could use the electric dryer, Wilfred," a voice interjected.

My eyes swung toward its source and encountered the blue eyes of the heavyset woman, who had silently appeared in the communicating opening. Wilfred's green orbs swung toward the woman; then they returned to me, and he announced, "This is Isibelle." Then they turned back to the woman, and he added, "This is Mr. Tyrrell."

"I'm sorry I burst in on you a while ago," she apologized. "I supposed the unit was still vacant."

"No apology is necessary," I responded. "The sequence of such events is easily comprehended."

Since the ensuing silence threatened to become awkward, I murmured the name, "Isibelle.... Does that name derive from the name Isabella, who was a member of Spain's royalty?"

"Oh, no!" she protested. "My ancestors migrated to New Zealand from Scotland, and I'm as proud of having descended from them as if I had descended from royalty."

"Then you are a pure Scottish lass," I slyly ventured.

Her eyes wavered, veered toward Wilfred's intent gaze until it sought refuge in the desktop, and flicked back to my eyes. "Well," she began cautiously, "I am one hundred percent Scotch."

"Not even one drop of bourbon in your veins?" I pursued relentlessly.

"I'm beginning to suspect that Mr. Tyrrell has some Irish in his makeup," Wilfred interjected with a chuckle.

"Some," I conceded. "But Tyrrell is an English name, so I should have stopped in the much more Anglican Christchurch instead of Dunedin, since there's not a drop of Scotch in my veins . . . , not to my knowledge anyway."

Meanwhile, Wilfred had volunteered no information regarding his ancestry; in fact, he appeared to be particularly reticent about it, so I began to suspect that there might be a Polynesian in his ancestral woodpile. Physically that suspicion appeared to be extremely unjustified, because the man had not only golden-blond hair but the peaches-and-cream complexion that young women the world over attempt to duplicate from jars of creams and tubes of pastes.

"Wilfred," I resumed, "the name Radford would seem to indicate an English origin."

He pondered the statement for several seconds as if it involved a monumental decision; then, in his inimitable fashion, he exploded, "That would seem to be right!"

During the ensuing period of silence, the lads mulled over the man's apparent reluctance to discuss his ancestry. "Possibly there was a Maori in his family tree," Pancho suggested.

"Naw, the evidence doesn't support it," José insisted. "Besides, that doesn't have to be the case for him to have evolved from a poly-something-or-other, because he and Isibelle are cousins. Therefore, half of his genes must have been derived from a Scottish parent."

"And the other half could have been derived from an English parent," Pancho injected.

"Yeah," José conceded. "No wonder he has refused to discuss his ancestry."

With that problem solved to my satisfaction, I decided that the ongoing period of silence warranted my departure, so I turned to the woman and said, "I'm glad to know you, Isibelle." Then, raising a vertical palm to the man, I added, "Thank you, Wilfred, for your suggestion regarding the laundry." With that, I turned about and stepped through the doorway onto the stoop.

"Be sure to call us if you require anything or any additional information," the man called after me. And I again raised the palm to him.

About six o'clock in the following morning, I clearly heard the doorknob rattle, so I strode from the kitchen to the door and pulled it open. Simultaneously, a copy of the *Otago Times* flopped onto the carpet.

"Good morning, Mr. Tyrrell!" Wilfred shouted from the door of Unit 4 in tones that were supposed to represent a whisper. Then, removing a rolled copy of the newspaper from the bundle clasped under one arm, he slipped it between the doorknob and the doorjamb. After turning back and ambling toward me, he added, "Apparently I didn't waken you."

"No," I replied, "I usually get out of bed before this time of day."

"Why?" he countered.

"I have an important mission in life, so I can't waste my remaining time by lying in bed," I responded with a small smile. "By the way, is there a stationery store in this area?"

"What do you want?" he inquired. "Some paper? The grocery store probably has some of that."

"Yes, it has," I said. "Two lined tablets and five lead pencils. But I want a special type of notepaper."

"Wilcouls probably has it," he said.

"Where are they located?" I asked. "I'll board a bus and go see what they stock."

"But the buses aren't in service," he objected. "They are on strike; that is, the drivers are."

"Oh, you're right," I responded. "It was in the headlines of the last newspaper, so I should have remembered it."

Momentarily, his eyes assumed a thoughtful mien. "I tell you what," he began. "I'm going into Dunedin after one o'clock, so you can ride with me if you don't mind waiting."

"That'll be great," I rejoined. "I'm in no hurry; besides, I still have enough sheets left to keep me going during the morning."

"I'll call you when I'm ready," he promised, turning away.

At one o'clock the bell of my telephone sounded off, so I dropped the mechanical lead pencil and went to subdue the bell.

"Hello, Albert!" Wilfred's full-bodied voice boomed into my ears in tandem. Stepping to my right, I peered through the open doorway toward the office, where Wilfred sat at the desk with the receiver pressed to one ear.

"Humph!" José erupted. "It's a tossup which is the loudest: the sound of his voice over the wire or its sound across the intervening space."

"Obviously, the use of the instrument is redundant," Pancho remarked phlegmatically.

Seeing me in the doorway, Wilfred raised one hand and shouted, "I'm ready to make the run into Dunedin. Can you break away from what you're doing?"

"I can leave any time," I replied.

"All right," he said, "then I'll get my wee Ford and be out front in just a minute."

"I'll be there," I promised.

Meanwhile, Pancho literally screamed, "That wee stuff confirms our suspicions that Wilfred must be partly Scotch, so he must be a poly-something-or-other."

"Of course, he could have acquired the usage from Isibelle," José suggested.

"Aw shut up!" I interjected, hurriedly exchanging house slippers for Hush Puppies. "I can think for myself."

"What with?" they chorused.

While hurrying from Unit 3 toward the car, I decided that its size compared favorably with the size of the average American compact. "Nice car," I murmured after opening the door and slumping onto the bench seat beside Wilfred. "Engine sounds good, too. An import, no doubt."

"Well," he drawled, "not entirely. Very few New Zealand cars are imported. In fact, ninety percent of them are assembled in New Zealand from imported parts, and that may be why they cost so much."

"How much do they cost?" I asked.

"It varies according to the car, of course," he replied. "However, I bought this one second hand at a pretty good price, and I intend to sell it to somebody for a better price. I buy and sell cars quite a bit. Nevertheless, a new car like this would cost a bit more than thirty thousand."

"Wow!" I exclaimed. "Even considering the difference in the exchange rate and transportation of the parts, that's very high."

"Taxes make up the difference," he said laconically.

After parking the car against the curb in front of Wilcouls' Crawford branch, Wilfred suggested, "Let's see what they have in here." Then he opened the door and moved quickly toward the heavily glazed brick front of the store.

I was hard pressed to keep up with his short, quick steps; in fact, it was he who opened the door. The showroom was not large, but the ceiling was high, which was typical of Dunedin's architectural designs, especially those of the latter part of the last century.

While I was being served by a tall, relatively young salesman, I noticed that Wilfred was closely inspecting the pens displayed in a small, plastic Pantel showcase. After I had selected some notepaper and a ream of typing paper, he appeared alongside me with the few items he had selected.

"Here, put these with mine," I instructed the salesman, reaching for them.

"No!" Wilfred shouted, withdrawing the items from my grasp. "You're not going to pay for mine."

"Let me pay for them," I pleaded. "After all, you saved me a cab fare—or a long walk at the least."

"But I was coming here anyway," he protested. "I'll pay for them."

Since I had learned not to oppose any New Zealander who was intent on rendering a kindness or a service to his fellow man, I paid for my purchases, and we departed.

Apparently Wilfred had deliberately scheduled his trip to the city to conform to my pressing requirements, because he turned the nose of the wee Ford toward the motel after we left the stationery store.

"Don't you have any more errands in the city, Wilfred?" I inquired as he swung the car onto Cumberland Street.

"No," he replied. "All that I really had to get was a pen. One of our guests preempted the last one from the office." Then, after turning the car left onto Strathallan and right onto Portsmouth Drive, he resumed: "The blighter probably knew that it was a new one, so he intentionally stuck it in his bloody pocket."

"Oh!" I exclaimed. "Isn't that beautiful?"

"What?" he countered, as his eyes swung in the direction of my enraptured gaze. "Oh, the harbor," he mumbled.

"And that rich, green, sloping plateau above the clay-colored cliff," I added.

"It **is** rather nice, isn't it," he granted, fixing his gaze on Otago Harbor to our left. Meanwhile, my eyes fondled the sun-drenched slope dotted with trees and attractive homes that overlooked the water wonderland.

"By the way, from what source did the word *Otago* derive?" I asked.

After removing one hand from the steering wheel and thoughtfully scratching the blond bristles behind one ear, he muttered, "I don't recall hearing where that name came from."

"I've wondered about it several times," I confessed, "but I finally discarded the suspicion that it derived from an Irish name."

After directing his puzzled eyes to mine, he exclaimed, "Oh! Like O'Reilly?"

"Yes," I answered. "But I've never heard of an Irishman named O'Tago. In fact, it sounds more like a name from Madrid or Rome than from County Cork."

"I doubt that it's an Eyetalian name," he observed. And that was where we left it.

During the morning following our trip to Wilcouls, Wilfred stopped by to exchange a few words. Just as he was about to leave, I said, "I'll buy you that drink whenever you say so."

"What drink?" he inquired with a puzzled frown.

"The one I owe you for taking me to Wilcouls yesterday," I replied.

"You don't owe me anything for that," he insisted. "I was going there anyway."

"But you saved me some cab fare," I persisted.

"I was going there anyway," he repeated. "Besides, I don't drink."

"Neither do I," I rejoined, "but I would gladly watch while you break your resolution at my cost."

"Oy don't drink," he repeated in the vernacular, "but Oy'll till you wot: You can buy me one of those big bott uhls o' limonide."

I had been quietly complimenting myself on how quickly I had picked up a completely foreign language after having spoken a *bastid virgin* of it throughout most of my life, but, for some unknown reason, those words stopped me cold.

And the man's eyes indicated that he sensed it. "You know," he began to explain, "one o' those big bott uhls o' bubbly." Then he thrust forth both big palms with one positioned about fifteen inches above the lower one. I still didn't know what he meant, but my nod lied for me.

During my next trip to the tiny grocery store, I fixed speculative eyes on the middle-aged grocer and asked, "What is Wilfred's favorite drink?"

Following a thought-filled moment the man emerged from behind the counter and led me to a large, refrigerated storage cabinet. From it he removed a bottle whose base must have measured about four inches in diameter. And it must have measured some fifteen inches in height. Extending it to me, he said, "Oy suspect this is what you ah askin' about."

Cradling it in the crook of one arm, I turned the label up and read: "One quarter litre of carbonated water, sugar, food acid, and flavour." It also indicated that the source was Oasis Industries, Ltd., Auckland. Dominating the yellow label was the word LEMON with the word BUBBLY superimposed in slightly smaller letters.

I looked incredulously up at the tall, slender grocer and asked, "Do you mean to tell me that Wilfred is addicted to this stuff?"

His eyes wavered under my direct gaze, "Will," he began uneasily, "it **is** whut he loiks."

"Thank you for tipping me off," I murmured. "I'll take this one with me, but please be sure to keep a supply on hand, because I already owe the man much more than the cost of this one, and this may be the only way that I'll be able to repay him for his kindnesses."

There was no one in the office when I arrived with my purchase enclosed within a brown paper bag, but Wilfred apparently heard me enter, since he immediately ventured forth through the connecting opening.

"Albert!" he exploded. "So you've been shopping for your evening meal."

"No, for some bubbly," I responded, presenting the bag to him.

Accepting it with befuddled eyes, he pulled forth the bottle, and the confusion fled from them. "Aw, you shouldn't have done that," he protested. "I was going to Wilcouls anyway."

"But reciprocation was in order," I murmured, exiting toward Unit 3.

"Thank you, Albert!" he called after me.

While I was waving away the man's gratitude with one hand, my mind was carefully monitoring an ongoing argument between the lads about how badly the poor man was addicted to the liquid.

"Al's contributing to the delinquency of a major," José insisted with an air of finality.

"You brats shut up!" I commanded, unlocking the door of Unit 3.

About three days before Christmas I appeared in the office with a brown paper bag in one hand and a bottle of bubbly in the other one.

"Good morning, Albert!" Wilfred boomed. Then, detecting the bottle, he protested, "Albert, you should stop doing that." But he gratefully, even eagerly, accepted the heavy bottle while suspiciously eyeing the paper bag.

"Yes, I have something for Isibelle, too," I responded to his gaze.

"Isibelle!" he shouted across one big shoulder. "Albert is here, and he would like a word with you."

When the woman appeared in the opening, I said, "Good morning, Isibelle. How is your battle with the migraines progressing?"

"Good morning," she responded. "My head feels pretty sore this morning, but I had to ignore it until we finished readying the units."

Meanwhile, her eyes strayed toward the paper bag, and I began to suspect that Wilfred had revealed to her my intentions despite my request that she be kept in the dark.

"As you probably know," I began, "occasionally I've brought Wilfred a bottle of carbonated lemonade as a token of my appreciation for the use of his typewriter. Meanwhile, it appears that I've ignored your many kindnesses, but such is not the case. In fact, some time ago I checked with Wilfred about your preferences, so here is something that may please you." Then, removing a one-pound box of Continental Milk Tray chocolates from the bag, I presented it to her.

"Oh, you shouldn't have done that!" she protested with an air of poorly contrived surprise.

"Oh, yes, I should have," I retorted. "However, I have one question." Then, in response to her patiently waiting gaze, I asked, "Has Wilfred shared his bubbly with you?"

"Yes," she replied.

"I suspected that he would," I said, "so this is intended to compensate for his inroads on your goodies." And I presented a second box of chocolates to her.

"Aw, what are we going to do to this man to stop him?" she protested to Wilfred.

"What can we do?" he countered with a shrug and a wide grin.

Then, fixing a cool, blue gaze on me, she exclaimed, "This is just like Christmas day!"

"But these insignificant items are not intended to be Christmas presents," I insisted. "Several days ago, when Wilfred informed me that you preferred milk chocolates, I went directly to the store to buy some, but only assorted chocolates were in stock. Consequently, these were obtained by a special order, so considerable time elapsed before they were delivered. I would have done the same thing even if it had been the Fourth of July."

Looking toward her, Wilfred volunteered, "That's America's Independence Day." Then he looked interrogatively at me, and I nodded.

"Furthermore, no special overtures are intended," I resumed with my eyes fixed intently on those of the woman. "I'm probably twenty years older than you children, so such overtures would not only be out of bounds but ridiculous for one of such advanced age."

"I doubt that you are twenty years older than I am," Isibelle murmured.

I chose not to pursue the subject further, so a momentary silence evolved.

Meanwhile, Wilfred had withdrawn into the background of the conversation, but he leaped into the ensuing breach with the words: "Albert, Isibelle and I have conferred, and we agree that we would like for you to share our Christmas dinner."

I stared absently at the top of the desk and uneasily pondered the situation. Apparently reading my mind, he quickly added, "There'll be only the three of us, excepting Isibelle's son, who will come to tea later in the day, so it will be just a friendly little party. And your gifts have nothing to do with our invitation," he insisted. "We've invited other motel guests to join us at the dinner table when they, like you, were isolated from their families and friends during the holidays."

"Yes," Pancho silently interjected. "You are the kind of people who would do something like that."

Meanwhile, I looked at Wilfred and said, "You people are getting so far ahead of me that I'll never catch up; however, my heart and my mind refuse to permit me to decline so generous an offer."

Like so many residents of midcontinent North America, many New Zealanders partake of their principal meal at midday, and they call it dinner; consequently, that Christmas dinner was scheduled for midday.

Even though I had not donned a suit or tied a necktie in many moons, upon appearing in the large opening that connected the office to the adjoining living room, I was carefully clad in slacks and sport jacket, plus a white dress shirt, a necktie, and a pair of socks, whose color almost matched that of my gray Hush Puppies.

Wilfred laid a magazine aside, arose from the sofa that stood against the mullioned windows to my right, and advanced toward me with an outstretched right hand. "Merry Christmas, Albert!" he boomed. "You shouldn't have dressed for this simple occasion. You should have dressed casual like Isibelle and me."

"Merry Christmas to you, Wilfred," I responded along with my right hand. "Actually, that's not the case, because I can't remember one occasion when you and Isibelle have been dressed casually."

"Well," he drawled, "we do have to present a businesslike air to our clientele, but we don't consider you to be one of those transients."

"Then you won't object if I remove my jacket," I suggested.

"Do so, by all means," he loudly insisted.

Glancing toward the open neck of his dress shirt, I said, "If it hadn't taken an hour for me to tie my necktie, I would have arrived a little earlier. I haven't worn one of the stupid, archaic things for years."

A skeptical smile hovered about his lips as he said, "You are on time, so there's no problem; besides, Isibelle has just finished putting the dinner together."

Simultaneously, the woman cruised through the doorway in the far corner of the room with a large, glass bowl carefully supported by both hands, and she placed it lovingly in the center of the large dining table, which was set slightly apart from the far wall. Then she stepped back and admired the setting. Apparently the bowl contained various fresh fruits entrapped within the soft mass of a rich, red Jello.

"Merry Christmas, Isibelle," I greeted her. "How is your health today?"

Turning toward me, she paused momentarily and typically pondered her response before responding, "Merry Christmas, Albert. As you know, my health is governed by my head, and it never has been too good."

"Nevertheless, she has prepared a fine feast for us," Wilfred interjected loyally.

"I hope that there's enough for all of us," I responded loudly, because the woman had a slight hearing impairment. From her startled expression and Wilfred's incredulous eyes, the timing appeared to be right, so I smiled inanely and added, "I haven't eaten a thing since I received your kind invitation."

Isibelle's work-flushed features relaxed into one of her rare smiles, but I strongly suspected that Wilfred's loud laugh was expelled more in relief than in actual amusement.

Meanwhile, the woman's eyes carefully checked the heavily laden table. "Well," she murmured, "everything will be ready as soon as the hot food is served."

"Albert, why don't you take that chair at the end of the table," Wilfred suggested, "and I'll take this one on this side between you and Isibelle. That way we can all share in the conversation as well as the dinner."

"Okay," I responded equably, "as long as you don't place me too far from the food."

Since the other man was closer to the woman than I, I made no move to seat her, but neither did he; therefore, with an absent-minded air of independence, she seated herself. And her air of independence seemed to imply that she had been seating herself throughout most of her lifetime. There was a brief pause in the conversation while she murmured a few words of thanks for the repast; then both of my hosts began passing bowls of hot food to me faster than I could dispose of them.

While desperately juggling a bowl in each hand, I shouted, "Just wait a cotton pickin' minute!" at Wilfred, who was trying to pass a third bowl to me. "I'm hungry, but please give me an opportunity to stack some of this delicious food on my plate."

In the characteristic vernacular, the man retorted, "Will, Oy was troyin' to buzz it past you so there would be enough lift foah Isibelle and me."

After a startled inspection of the man's smiling eyes, I said, "Wilfred, that remark indicates that you do have a certain sly sense of humor after all. At least I hope that it was intended to be humorous."

"Oh, I ashuah you that it was," he earnestly insisted.

"But you don't have the heart of a humorist," I muttered, "because those characters rarely extend any mercy to their victims."

"Then you aren't really a humorist at heart, Albert, despite your teasing remarks," he countered.

Looking pensively into his practically concealed eyes, I murmured, "Thank you, Wilfred." With that, the conversation subsided in favor of mastication.

It was a fine farm-style meal; consequently, the duck and the mutton had been carved in the kitchen and placed on large, porcelain trays along with some dressing. Then they were delivered to the table. The bowls, which were being passed so frequently, contained nicely broasted potatoes, stewed carrots, stewed peas, and other vegetables. Certainly there was enough food for a group of ten normal diners. But Wilfred was no normal diner; in fact, he returned to the kitchen for another large helping of duck, mutton, and dressing, so he qualified as a veritable trencherman. Meanwhile, Isibelle and I marked time by picking at our food so that he wouldn't be dining alone.

Among the several different types of dessert was a dish that Isibelle vaguely identified as truffles. I remembered that truffles consist of fungi that French farmers often find in forests with the help of swine, which love the delicacy. When the swine's sensitive olfactory nerves detect it among the roots of the trees, they eagerly root about and uncover it. Of course, the farmers immediately steal the product of the piggies' efforts. Such is the nature of mankind.

After tasting all of the desserts, I came to the conclusion that Isibelle must have confused the word *truffles* with some other exotic French word or that she had confused me, which is no great accomplishment. Nevertheless, I found no truffles in the dessert, but there may have been some in the dressing.

"Those desserts are wonderful," I complimented her.

Immediately picking up the nearest bowl, she thrust it toward me and insisted, "Here, have some more. You've scarcely eaten any of it."

"No," I responded with outstretched palms. "I've packed in all that I can hold. But let me pass it to Wilfred." And I did.

After briefly studying the contents, he shook his head and rumbled, "I've had some of that, but I could use a wee bit of that." And he pointed toward another dish to my right, which I passed to him. Then I fastened fascinated eyes on him as he scooped a massive serving from the bowl and stacked more atop it.

The sometimes desultory conversation touched on various subjects. Among them, Isibelle recalled some of her experiences during a trip to Scotland and the Orkney Islands.

At one point she wistfully said, "Despite the mist and the rain, I loved Scotland. Even though there were so few sunny days, I thought that it was beautiful. Of course, all of my ancestors came from there, so I may be a bit biased."

"I don't doubt that," I responded. "But you wear it very well."

"Perhaps you'd like the Old Settlers Museum," Wilfred mumbled around a mouthful of food. "It displays many pictures of the bonny Scotch settlers."

"I've already been there," I said, "and I did like it, especially the pictures of the old binders that I so fondly remember from my boyhood on the plains of Saskatchewan. In fact, I suspect that some of them must still be in use here, because I saw some shocked grain during my tour of the islands. By the way, we called the stacked bundles of grain 'stooks' in Canada. What do you people call them?"

"I don't really know what they are called," Wilfred murmured, turning inquiring eyes to Isibelle.

"I don't know either," she admitted. "We always had our grain combined."

"What does your son do for a living? Farm?" I inquired.

A pained expression flitted across her features. "He's a truck driver," she answered. "I tried to get him to take to farming, but he didn't want to become a farmer. I even offered to help him get started. And I could have done it too, couldn't I, Wilfred?" she inquired with a glance. And the man nodded.

Silence settled upon the small assemblage while Wilfred returned to a duck bone and began to polish it with his greasy lips. Finally, raising his eyes to mine, he asked, "Did you happen to read the article in the paper about that boy whiz from China?"

"Yes," I replied. "Some of those Orientals are very smart."

"Lots of them came here during the gold rush," he murmured absently. "Some of them might not have been too smart, but all of them worked very hard."

"I've always found the latter to be the case," I said. "For example, I vividly remember a boy who migrated from China to Vancouver, British Coloumbia. And I particularly remember the time when my eighth grade teacher, who was a Scotchman named Baines, stood before us with one arm around the lad's shoulders and introduced him to us."

Pausing, I looked at Isibelle, who smiled as if the man's name struck a familiar chord in her memory. Then I resumed: "Since the class consisted of only boys, eighteen of us, Mr. Baines addressed it, 'Gentlemen.'" Then, looking sharply at the other man, I interjected, "Of course, that was a misnomer, but he mistakenly used it from time to time." And Wilfred responded with a delighted chortle. "Nevertheless," I resumed, "to 'gentlemen' Mr. Baines added, 'you have a brrand new classmate from China. Howevah, since I can't prronounce his firrst name, I've called him Angus, so this is Angus Lee Young. Trreat him like the gentleman that he obviously is.'"

It seemed to me that Isibelle's cool, blue eyes softened and misted a bit in response to the thought that one of her ancestors' countrymen had elected to assign a popular Scottish surname to an oriental waif with a Chinese surname that Occidentals found to be unpronounceable.

"At the time," I resumed, "we were seated according to our monthly scholastic standings: The top scholar was precariously perched on the edge of the first seat on the left side of the room, and I occupied the second seat. Within three months, to my great chagrin, Angus had gained possession of that coveted first seat, but I still occupied the second seat. Nevertheless, I didn't resent his precedence or him, because we had become close friends. Of course, Mr. Baines didn't help the situation one bit by pointedly observing that a member of the class with a language barrier had gained the prestigious position by hard work. However, since I was closer to the boy, I knew something that Mr. Baines may not have known: Angus had gained that goal while working in his older brother's produce market during most of his spare time. Consequently, he must have burned a lot of midnight oil to accomplish all of that in such a short time. In my opinion, Wilfred, oriental people are very dedicated workers," I concluded.

There was a brief silence while the minds of my listeners were shifting gears; then Wilfred suggested, "The Japs have proved that. They have beaten the Americans at every point on the compass."

"A lot of their successes are due to the rapid growth of socialism in America," I protested before recalling that New Zealand is a hotbed of socialism. But I defiantly continued, "No system of government can operate efficiently without the incentive of individual gain."

"But socialism is not all bad," the man objected. "The poor people should not be permitted to starve."

"In my opinion, no real democracy would ever permit any of its constituents to starve," I observed, "but no politician should ever be allowed to buy the votes of any pressure group by generously diverting the wealth of producers into the laps of nonproducers through the medium of socialism."

"But the government should act with compassion," he persisted.

"I agree, and that's the favorite plaint of the liberal politicians in our country," I retorted. "But they never define the word; nor do they limit the use of it. Unfortunately, the not-so-poor people in large pressure groups are treated compassionately to the point of luxury while individuals and smaller groups are allowed to suffer. In America, compassion is used as a political tool at enormous cost to the economy. If the practice continues, the nation's economy will collapse to the level of a Third World nation's economy. Consequently, from being the wealthiest nation on the surface of the world America will be struggling for economic survival. Not only will there be skyrocketing inflation and universal poverty, but the many different ethnic groups will rebel."

The words were greeted with reluctant nods followed by silence. Meanwhile, we gazed regretfully at the dishes.

"Well," I began tentatively, "paraphrasing some ancient words, 'all good things must come to an end so that one good thing shall not corrupt the earth.'" Then, glancing whimsically toward each of my hosts, I added: "Consequently, we are confronted by the dishes, and, since Isibelle created this fine repast, it seems only fair that Wilfred and I should wash them."

"Well," the woman murmured pensively, "that would be nice; first, however, I'll wash the pots and pans."

While she did so, Wilfred and I cleared the table; then she took off to do some of the endless chores that normally burden those who operate motels.

Wilfred elected to wash the dishes while I wiped them. However, since I stood by and patiently waited for him to rinse the soapy dishes stacked high on the rinse board of the sink, I got off to an extremely slow start.

Finally I cautiously inquired, "Can't I be rinsing those dishes, Wilfred?"

"We usually wipe them as they are," he responded across one shoulder.

"Oh!" I exclaimed. "Then I better get going."

"We kin rinse them if you prefer," he suggested tentatively.

"No, let's do them your way," I hurriedly rejoined.

While I set to the task, Pancho observed, "After a lifetime among American dish washers, we've never before encountered one who didn't rinse his or her dishes."

"But we've observed some American dish washers, usually bachelors, who washed their dishes in only tap water," José rejoined, "even cold tap water sometimes."

"Apparently the world is full of dish washers who employ dissimilar practices," Pancho concluded philosophically.

Several days later, while placing an empty milk bottle and forty cents on the slab to one side of the office doorway, I spotted a middle-aged man standing in front of the desk. Meanwhile, he was supporting one end of an animated conversation with Wilfred, who was lounging in the swivel chair.

Immediately after Wilfred responded to the clamoring telephone, from above my bowed head I heard his visitor say, "Good morning."

Looking up, I found his dark eyes staring down at me from the doorway, so I returned the greeting. Recalling that he had been residing in an adjacent unit for almost a week, I assumed that, like many of the other guests, he was spending his "holiday" in the area, so I added: "Finally you are having some nice weather for your holiday."

"Well, it really hasn't been a holiday, as such," he rejoined. "We came down here to attend our son's wedding. Actually, we haven't minded the rains, because the weather has been cool. In Auckland it gets pretty hot and sticky during this season."

"That's what I didn't like about Auckland," I muttered, standing upright, "the high humidity combined with the intense heat."

Through the nearby full-length window, I absently watched Wilfred replace the telephone, approach us, and come to a stop behind the other man. "Yes," he interjected, "about ninety-seven percent humidity." Nothing, and I mean absolutely nothing, ever escaped the man.

"That statement reminds me of an incident that I really should never relate," I said, "but I am going to do so, despite the likelihood that you fellows will probably never believe another word that passes my lips."

After glancing at each man to ensure that I had his undivided attention, I resumed: "Some thirty-five years ago I was employed by a consulting engineering company, which had assigned me to the Goodyear Aircraft Company in Akron, Ohio." Looking toward each man to determine if he was aware that Akron is an American city, each of them urged me on with a nod, so I continued: "Akron is located about thirty miles from Cleveland, which sprawls along the south shore of Lake Erie. Since Lake Erie is one of the five Great Lakes, the surrounding area possesses a rather humid climate. One particularly wet day it was raining cats and dogs, and all of them splashed gobs of water when they hit the earth running." After pausing to savor the tolerant smiles of my listeners, I continued, "Suddenly, a door of the engineering office was opened by one of my associates, who paused in the doorway and dramatically announced, 'I've just come from calling the weather station at the airport. After I facetiously asked the guy on the other end of the line if it was going to rain, he swore that their instruments were registering one hundred five percent humidity.' Once more he paused, and after swinging an interrogative gaze about the room, he asked, 'Is that possible? Could those instruments actually register one hundred five percent humidity?' Then another engineer glanced up from his work and answered, 'Perhaps he also was being facetious.' Following a careful check of each pair of eyes, I added, "We never did agree that a humidity of one hundred five percent was possible."

I grant that those men behaved like true New Zealand gentlemen in that they chuckled and exchanged skeptical glances, but neither of them questioned the veracity of the story.

"A number of years ago we had an American photographer from Phoenix working with us on a special commercial job," the dark-eyed man began. After visually inspecting each pair of eyes to determine if we knew where Phoenix was located, he resumed: "In spite of the fact that he was a good photographer, he encountered problems in handling and drying film in Auckland's high humidity. Furthermore, he ran into problems with colors fading from the film." Pausing, he fixed his eyes on mine and said, "You may not know this, but there are more ultraviolet rays in New Zealand's sunlight than in that of any other country. Of course, we New Zealanders were aware of that; in fact, we fully understood both problems, so we were able to solve them for him."

Pausing again, he cast a glance toward Wilfred, then fixed his eyes on mine, and added, "As you probably know, Phoenix has one of the driest climates in the United States." In response to an interrogative gleam in his eyes, I nodded, so he resumed, "According to that photographer, the reason that Phoenix is so dry is this: Once every year a small cloud appears on the horizon, floats over the city, and drops a small shower of rain."

"That's pretty close to the facts," I conceded, "but the man failed to add that not one drop of the rain in that cloud ever falls on the city."

"It doesn't?" he countered with a curious expression.

"That's right," I retorted dryly (pun intended). "The atmosphere over Phoenix is so hot and dry that the rain from that tiny cloud immediately vaporizes into a wisp of steam and escapes into outer space."

Since New Zealanders are very generous people, my listeners anointed my eager ears with the balm of laughter.

10

Life in a Motel

I had been scratching for almost a week—not just once in a while but quite often, and not in just one spot but in many spots. Consequently, I began to suspect that the cause was an animate one. To my knowledge, I had never been exposed to such things before, but I had heard some pretty lurid stories about them from characters who had. Since there were claims that they could be acquired from certain plumbing fixtures and even from comforters and upholstered furniture, I began to worry.

I literally spent hours before the mirror waiting and watching for one of the critters to bite some spot on my face, where I could see it; however, when I did acquire an urge to scratch a spot on a bare arm, I was never able to verify my suspicions. Nevertheless, some of those little guys are said to be very small, so I was not completely satisfied that there wasn't something there.

One day, while sitting in my combined studio–living room–office, typing up a storm (maybe twenty words per minute), I chanced to glance through the front window just as two of the motel's new guests carried some of their belongings from a dusty and battered pickup truck into the unit opposite mine. It was an unusual combination for the Arcadian Motel in that one of them was a very disheveled white man, and the other one was a slatternly black woman. That set the cogs in my ivory tower to really spinning; consequently, my mind's eye could virtually see a similar assortment of unclean people carrying some of their belongings into Unit 3 some time before my occupancy. After all, Wilfred had stated that the previous tenants had left it in worse condition than usual, so I could have inherited some very undesirable by-products of their stay.

Bugs Bunny or Bunny Bugs?

It was not entirely by chance that I happened to meet Wilfred between the office and the laundry about ten o'clock the next morning. Following his cordial greeting, I said, "Wilfred, obviously, a public place like this is frequented by various types of people, some clean and some dirty; consequently, after some of the dirty guests depart, you must encounter occasional problems with some of their small and undesirable associates."

He fixed thoughtful eyes on me. Meanwhile, from his expression, I gained the impression that his agile mind was attempting to interpret what I had said. Abruptly, his green eyes assumed that cautious, hooded look, which has so often accompanied my other ventures into uncharted waters. Since he remained silent and appeared to be warily waiting for me to enlarge on the subject, I recklessly forged ahead.

"I'm not claiming to have acquired such a problem from any of those people," I said, while José screamed that I was making a *bleeped* fool of myself. "But I've suddenly become afflicted with an abnormal compulsion to scratch, and there's no apparent justification for it."

"Probably nerves," Wilfred finally volunteered. But his eyes refused to meet mine squarely, so I suspected that he also lacked faith in the theory.

But the man's words provided something more for me to worry about, because it actually could have been nerves, that is, if I have any, and I must have them, since physiologists claim that all human beings have them. However, since I've never seen any of them, I've never been fully convinced of that. But the man's suggestion set me to worrying again, and, as I've previously noted, I can really worry! Consequently, I began to visualize all sorts of possibilities, including a visit to a psychiatrist, who would be likely to recommend shock treatments irrespective of whether I was actually a Bugs Bunny or merely a bunny with bugs.

The thought terrorized me, because I happen to be one of those individuals who advocate the elimination of such archaic tortures on the grounds that they are merely modern substitutes for jungle witch doctors' spear thrusts, which were supposed to release the evil spirits believed to be imprisoned in their victims' bodies. According to the historical calendar, that was only yesterday, so medical science really hasn't progressed very far during the last one hundred years, has it?

Actually, I might have ended up in a psychiatric ward, but the whims of fate intervened. Since I was aware of the management's penchant for saving the cost of operating the clothes dryer, I followed the prevailing policy of hanging my wet wash on the clothesline. But the weather had been inclement for several days; therefore, by the time that a sunny day arrived, my laundry had grown to such a size that it filled the tub of the Champion, Series 2000A, automatic washer. Nevertheless, I scooped a cupful of laundry detergent from a large, cardboard box garishly identified as "Drive," dumped it onto the clothing, lowered the lid, and actuated the starting switch. As usual, I stood by to ensure that the machine didn't walk out of the building with practically all of my clothes during its spin-dry cycle. Meanwhile, my eyes followed the advertising hype on the detergent box: "Powered with hungry ENZYMES which eat dirt and stains. Marketed by Levers New Zealand Limited, Petone."

After the machine did its thing and finally came to a stop, I removed the wet clothes from it, loaded them onto a cart, and wheeled them out to the clothesline. From the pockets of a tent-cloth apron, which Isibelle commonly hung on the cart, I extracted several plastic clothespins and carefully pinned the garments to the clothesline to keep the gusty wind from sweeping them away. Then I stepped back to admire the artistic effect of my random selection of red and yellow pins.

Some hours later, when I returned to determine if the pins had held and if the clothes were dry, my eyes were attracted to a narrow, white streak along one of the seams of my blue jeans, so I scraped some of it off with the end of a fingernail, and I was amazed by how nice that nail looked with an undercoating of white instead of its usual black. After carefully inspecting the white, powdery material, I went in search of Wilfred and found him in the laundry.

"Wilfred, I've discovered what makes me itch," I announced abruptly.

After casting a startled glance in my direction, the man's wary eyes hurriedly searched for some avenue of escape besides the open doorway where I stood. Finally he inquired, "And what could that be?" in the first unaccented words that I had ever heard him use.

"Just now I inspected some of my freshly laundered clothing," I answered, "and I found gobs of undissolved laundry detergent imbedded in various parts of the fabric, such as the seams. Very likely my body has been reacting to concentrations of that caustic detergent, and that's why I've been scratching."

The big man heaved a man-sized sigh of relief. "We may have been unusually fortunate," he boomed with renewed confidence, "but we've never had any of the problems that you suspected."

"May good fortune continue to smile on you," I murmured fervently. "Meanwhile, I am going to run all of my clothing through the washer without any detergent whatsoever . . . and in smaller batches."

Like many people, I operate on the principle of "as a last resort, read the instructions," so I dug out the lurid, yellow-and-green detergent container and immediately found what I sought: "Always ensure that powder is thoroughly dissolved. Rinse articles thoroughly in clean water."

The Birds and Bees

By the early teens, most youngsters have heard about the birds and the bees, and many of them have been exposed to the subject several times, often reluctantly. Apparently, some pixilated adults just can't wait to tell teenagers about the birds and bees, but normal adults know that many of them would be better off if they were never told about them.

Nevertheless, I picked up this story about the birds and the bees from one of Wilfred's pamphlets, and an evil genie compels me to include it. Therefore, if this episode is being read to a child, such as a sixteen-year-old boy with a history of gangsterism, perhaps the reader should turn to the next episode. Perhaps the reader should do it anyway.

First off, these particular New Zealand bees are not like any of the North American varieties—not that they are weird or something; at least I don't think so. These particular bees frequent the forests, where a very prolific little critter bores into the bark of beech trees. Or is it beach trees? No, it has to be beech trees, because the trees are found only in the forests, not along the beaches.

The tiny borer loves to dine on the sap that flows between the bark and the inner trunk of the beech tree to its limbs, twigs, and leaves. Like all of nature's creatures, there is waste from this metabolic process, and the borer excretes it through a tiny tube. Consequently, while the waste from multitudes of these tiny critters is sliding slowly and insidiously down the trunk to the base of the beech tree, it turns the bark almost black. Likewise, some of the limbs are attacked by these wee beasties, and most of that waste is excreted directly onto the forest's floor. Now, unless someone or something intervenes, all of that waste builds up an impervious layer over the roots of the trees, shielding them from falling rain and eventually causing them to die.

Fortunately, Mother Nature has intervened in favor of the trees—she has alerted all of the forest's bee colonies regarding the incredible sweetness of the dark waste, so the bees literally swarm among those beech trees, avidly collecting the dark, viscous liquid. Therefore, very little of it reaches the forest's floor, so practically every beech tree survives, despite the hordes of tiny marauders biting its bark. And that's one case of where there's a bark there's a bite, eh wot?

Of course, the bees not only dine on that sweet nectar, but they make honey from it. At first, the picky New Zealanders reprocessed the honey, or they fed it to the hogs, which are connoisseurs of excreted matter. Then the New Zealanders discovered a great demand for the dark, super-sweet delicacy in Europe, so they took it away from the hogs and shipped it to the less picky Europeans. But the New Zealanders never revealed the source of the honey to the Europeans, so they treat it as gourmet food.

Since this anecdote concerns the birds and the bees, I can't ignore the birds. But my source didn't reveal whether the birds were as picky as the New Zealanders, so I can only assume that some of the less picky and more pecky birds may have dined on bees that had become pickled from consuming too much of that intoxicating nectar.

Assault, Murder, or Rape?

Whichever it was, the crime must have been committed some time between the hours of two and three o'clock Saturday morning, and the strange drama was played directly beyond the concrete block wall against which the headboard of my bed rested. I may have slept through some of the initial rounds, but the sounds of loud voices had finally wakened me. Actually, I wasn't annoyed at the time, because I had to get up anyway.

While I was in the tiny bathroom washing my hands, I recalled that the likely cast must consist of two young people. While I was returning to Unit 3 from the laundry late in the previous afternoon, I had found them leaving the rusty, old car that had been newly parked in front of Unit 2. The man was a nice, clean-cut young fellow with dark, wavy hair, and the woman was a living doll with clear, blue eyes and curly, light-brown hair.

Apparently they were spending the weekend at the beach, because I later noticed that some bathing attire had been placed on the pavement to dry in front of Unit 2. At the time I wondered why they had not first washed the sand out of them and then hung them on the clothesline to dry, but some people aren't that concerned about sand, dirt, and oil stains. Nevertheless, that was the last evidence of activity in Unit 2 until I was wakened by the loud tones.

Actually, it must have been the girl's loud protests that had wakened me. They seemed to be building up into a massive fury, because the tones rapidly increased in volume like the crescendos of some Italian operas, and they rhythmically flowed and ebbed as if she were pacing to and from the intervening wall or an open window. Occasionally, they would stop entirely as if she had granted the other listener a brief audience. If that was the case, then his emotions and tones must have been masterfully controlled, because I heard his voice raised only once, and that was in a short burst that sounded as if it had been rendered in a mood of frustrated anger.

Whatever those pauses involved, such as pleadings or petitions, she wasn't buying any of them. In fact, her strident tones eventually took over entirely, that is, until she viciously pulled the front window closed, but that was only an instant, because she resumed the loud onslaught all of the way to the rear of the unit, where she slammed closed two more windows.

"Great! Now I can get some sleep," I mumbled into my pillow.

But that was not to be the case, because she really cut loose then, and few of her words were derived from the English dictionary. In fact, most of them must have been handed down to her from several generations of Celts and Saxons, because they were so salty that they would have brought tears of admiration to the eyes of even the toughest old stevedore, so salty that they even pierced that six-inch concrete block wall.

"It's amazing that so beautiful a creature should possess such a crude and ugly mind," José volunteered, but neither Pancho nor I saw fit to pursue the matter further.

Meanwhile, the man must have been sacked out on the bed while the girl continued her interminable pacing. Occasionally it must have carried her too close to the bed, because a brief struggle would ensue, punctuated by a resounding slap. Then the pacing and the harangue resumed.

That routine must have continued for about fifteen minutes, but the last, brief struggle terminated in a slap and an instant of intense silence; then a solid object struck the opposite side of the wall just above my head, and there were several tinkling sounds as its various parts fell away.

"Wow!" Pancho exclaimed. "This's becoming serious. Maybe we should call the police before that vixen ruins that poor boy for life."

At that point the tide of battle seemed to turn in his favor, because the sounds of their voices began to emanate from the same general area: hers, loud and protesting; his, soft and coaxing. Then there were the sounds of an intense struggle punctuated by grunts, groans, and the muffled tones of the man's voice.

And the girl's strained voice stridently responded, "No you won't. If you do, it will be over my dead body!" Suddenly there was a blood-curdling scream, followed by complete silence. Well, almost complete silence.

"Oh!" exclaimed José. "That vicious brute has stabbed her. We should have called the police while there was still time to save her . . . him . . . uhm, them."

Despite our obvious guilt, I immediately fell asleep, but my slumbers were disturbed by a surreal scenario in which a tall, dark, young villain lurked purposefully behind a tree in a dark and forbidding forest, through which a footpath meandered. Meanwhile, the light-brown, curly locks of Little Red Riding Hood bounced jauntily about her shoulders as she skipped happily and unsuspectingly along the path and merrily chanted an obscene waterfront ditty.

After about the third rerun, I awoke and rolled over just as Pancho sleepily mumbled, "It's incredible that a woman with such a foul mouth should 'protest so loudly.'" After briefly reviewing the episode, I rolled back into the previous position and buried my head in the pillow. Then José added, "So the moon must have been tilted in an unfavorable attitude."

The Cleaners

Shortly before midday there was a tentative knock on the door, so I strode from the kitchen across the living room to it. As I swung the door open, Wilfred greeted me: "Good morning, Albert. May I enter and exchange these fresh towels for your used ones?"

"Of course, Wilfred," I replied. After brushing past me, he scurried through the living room and the kitchen into the bathroom.

Upon returning to the living room, he said, "While I'm here, I might as well tidy the place a bit." Then, after looking about the unit, he added, "Not that it ever needs much, because you keep your digs much neater than most women keep theirs."

"In my opinion, the state of one's surroundings indicates the state of one's mind," I rejoined. "Filthy surroundings, filthy mind."

"You may have a point there," he granted, stepping through the open doorway to the maintenance cart. Returning with fresh bed linen, he added, "At least, I usually find that the guests who are untidy about their units also are untidy about themselves."

Meanwhile, I had stripped the used linen from the bed and assumed a waiting attitude on the opposite side of the bed. "Aw, you don't have to help me with this, Albert," he protested.

"Two of us can do the job in one-fourth the time," I insisted. "Besides, I would be ill at ease standing around watching you work."

"I understand," he said. Then, after flipping the far side of the bottom sheet toward me, he quickly stuffed its near side between the mattress and the box spring. From previous observations, I had noticed that the man always worked very intently at whatever he was doing. In fact, beads of perspiration were already trickling down his ruddy features as he stepped back from drawing down the top sheet and tucking in its bottom corner. "You make a neat military corner," he remarked. "Where did you learn that?"

"In the military," I replied with a vague smile.

"You never mentioned being in the service before," he countered with a narrow stare.

"World War One was a long time ago," I rejoined blandly.

After stopping to stare up at me for an instant, he slowly stood upright and said, "That's a deliberate prevarication."

"No, it isn't," I insisted. Meanwhile, I mentally observed that it was characteristic of the man to avoid use of the word *lie*. "I merely stated that World War One was a long time ago, and it was. Actually, I learned how to make those corners about nineteen thirty-two while I was a member of the Nebraska National Guard's Hospital Corps."

Smiling ruefully, he shook his head and muttered, "Always kidding."

After transferring the vacuum cleaner from the stoop into the unit, he inserted its plug into a wall receptacle, actuated the starting switch, and began to vacuum the carpet industriously. Actually, those were not the proper words, because the man was moving the suction head about so rapidly that the vacuum's groaning electromechanical system was incapable of performing its designed function. Consequently, he stirred up more dust than he trapped in the vacuum cleaner's bag.

Meanwhile, he glanced at my mesmerized eyes and repeated a familiar question, "Have you been sleeping well, Albert?"

Since I couldn't hear the words because of the roar of the unit, I read his lips. For the same reason, I nodded instead of shouting the answer. In the silence that ensued after the equipment was switched off, my tones sounded overly loud as I said, "I've been sleeping well every night until about two o'clock this morning, when a minor riot broke out next door, so I did miss some much-needed beauty rest."

Typically, he either ignored or missed the weak attempt at humor. After pointing toward Unit 4, he asked, "Do you mean this 'next door'?"

"No, this 'next door,'" I responded facetiously with a gesture toward the opposite wall.

"Oh," he grunted, scratching the back of his head. "I had some doubts when they registered as man and wife, but if they had a fight, they must be married."

"But they may not have been," I muttered. "From the racket, it sounded like the gal was being deflow...."

"Huh-uh!" he interjected positively. "There ain't any of those things any more.

In fact, they are as extinct as the auk. But I wonder what the fuss was about."

Typical of the usual amateur psychologist, I eagerly volunteered, "There could have been several reasons. For example, she may have been masochistic, in which case she yearned to be mauled before submitting. Of course, she could be frigid, too. After all, forty percent of the women are either partly or wholly unresponsive."

"That's not what the sex therapists claim," he countered. "They claim that most of those problems can be overcome."

Vigorously shaking my head, I said, "Sex therapists are usually psychologists or psychiatrists bent on selling their services, irrespective of whether they are effective or not."

At that instant Wilfred's middle-aged helper cautiously peeked around the door frame and inquired, "Anything foah the trash lyedy todye?" So the subject was dropped, but it may have been too late to avoid an impropriety, because her expression seemed to indicate that she had overheard part of the dialogue.

Along with a shake of my head, I replied, "No. I've disposed of the trash already."

"Okye," she responded, tilting the small dust cap from one side of her head to the other. "Now, I'm the cleanin' lyedy." Then she marched past us toward the bathroom with a brush in one hand and a container of bowl cleaner in the other.

"By the way," I called to her, "I forgot to wish you a good morning, so good morning."

Stopping in her tracks, she glanced quickly at her wristwatch, shook her head, and said, "It's lightah than you think. It should be good afternoon now." Then she smiled like a pixy.

Actually, it was an old game: One day, several weeks before, I had greeted her with a good morning shortly after the noon hour, and she had responded in a like manner, so it had become a game for a couple of simple-minded people.

"You go ahead and do the bathroom, Zita," Wilfred called to her, "and I'll take care of the rest."

"Zeta," I immediately interposed. "That's the name of a letter in the Greek alphabet. Are you a Greek, Zeta?"

"It's Zeeta," Wilfred interjected. "I'm sorry that I failed to introduce you to her. Albert, this is Zita."

Favoring her with what I fondly assumed was my most whimsical smile, I murmured, "After six weeks of daily nonsense, we are finally introduced. If you aren't Greek, what is your ancestry?"

After carefully considering the question, she proudly announced, "Oy'm a New Zealandah."

"But from what country did your ancestors come?" I asked while Wilfred looked on with a bemused expression.

"New Zealand," she replied with a puzzled frown. "Moy mothah was boahn and rised in Milton, and moy fathah kime from Goah."

Wilfred surrendered a sympathetic glance to me and then began to collect his equipment.

With a tolerant smile, I said, "Yes, Zita. You are a bona fide New Zealander. In fact, since your parents were New Zealanders, you have to be a native."

"Oy'm no nitive," she protested with flashing eyes.

"He doesn't mean that you're a Maori," Wilfred interposed.

"That's right," I stated, "but since you were born here, you have to be a native New Zealander."

Following a thoughtful review of the statement, she cheerfully said, "Okye, if you sye so."

While Wilfred was removing the vacuum cleaner, Zita quickly dusted the few items of wooden furniture, made a few passes at the door ledges, and announced, "Will, Wilfred, that's anothah one done."

"Yes," the man responded from the vicinity of the doorway with a weary sigh. "There's only one more to do."

"Let's go do it," she proposed. "Meanwhoile, Albert kin return to pace and quiet."

"That proves it!" I exclaimed. "Wilfred, did you notice how she pronounced the word *p-e-a-c-e*? It sounded like *p-a-c-e*, so the Oxford dictionary must use different pronunciation symbols for the pronunciation of its words than the Webster dictionary uses."

"She may be right," he protested. "The word could have evolved from the Latin word *pac*, which translates as peace."

"I believe that the Latin word for peace is *p-a-x*," I suggested. "For example, *pax vobiscum* translates as peace be with you."

For the first time, Wilfred appeared to be about to differ with me on an opinion. "However, the *p-a-c* in Pacific Ocean does translate from Spanish into peaceful ocean," I hurriedly interjected. "Of course," I added more tactfully, "the Spanish language was derived almost entirely from Latin."

He pondered the argument briefly, nodded, and stepped aside to allow Zita to exit.

"In my opinion," Panco injected, "that man is an educated man despite his eighth-grade education, which he constantly denigrates."

"Furthermore," José added, "during our many conversations with Wilfred, we've discovered that the man is a library addict, that he has read most of the classics several times, and that he lacks only a bachelor's degree to be recognized as an educated man."

"But that's merely an academic measure of one field of learning," Pancho objected. "It doesn't indicate that the holder is educated. Like many so-called educated people, he lacks the ability to distinguish between fact and fiction."

"In other words, he lacks sound judgment," José suggested.

Wilfred in an Expansive Mood

Initially, my adventures in Musselburgh had been confined almost exclusively to the Arcadian Motel and its immediate surroundings, so most of my social life was limited to infrequent associations with Wilfred and Isibelle.

One pleasant evening, after a light dinner, I strolled aimlessly from the kitchen toward the open doorway of Unit 3 and casually looked toward the slab in front of the motel's office, where a solitary milk bottle gleamed whitely beside the open doorway. After briefly pondering its likely ownership, I continued on across the driveway, stopped beside it, and leaned forward. Just as I stood upright with the top of the bottle clutched in one hand, Wilfred's voice boomed, "Albert! You forgot your milk again."

"Uh-huh," I grunted, rotating about one heel so that I could look through the window toward the swivel chair where the man was wont to loll. And there he lolled behind the cluttered desktop, grinning like a Cheshire cat. After strolling into the office, I stopped short of the desk, stooped, and set the bottle on the floor alongside one Hush Puppy. Then, standing upright, I placed both hands on my hips and looked down at him.

From between the folds of flesh that completely hid his eyelids, he looked up at me and, in an uncharacteristically heavy Scotch brogue, genially inquired, "How be ye this evenin', Albert?"

"I'm well, thank you, Wilfred," I replied. "And you? You also must be well, since you appear to be in exceptionally high spirits."

"I feel great!" he exclaimed. "Just great!" Then, placing both hands atop the chair's armrests, he tilted it sharply back and exposed even more of his protruding paunch. "I had pork bones and beans for supper," he murmured, gently patting the paunch with an air of supreme carnal contentment. Then, as an afterthought, he added, "And they feel great too."

Obviously the man was in a very expansive mood; therefore, to launch him on his favorite subject, I suggested, "Then you really don't have a thing to complain about."

As I had expected, a frown creased his otherwise smooth forehead. "Well," he muttered, "I'm fortunate to have relatively good health, but my back bothers me a lot while I'm making the beds. When I fell off of that thirty-foot pole. . . ."

"And crushed two vertebrae," I interjected.

"Yes, I've told you the story before," he responded with apologetic eyes. "Nevertheless, those vertebrae do bother me quite a bit."

"The crew must have taken to calling you 'Cat Bradford' after that accident," I suggested with a chuckle.

"No, but you probably remember that I did land on my feet like a cat," he responded with a pleased laugh. "However, they continued to call me 'Wilf,' 'Brad,' or 'Snow,' . . ." Then he paused and studied my expression as if trying to determine my reaction to the last nickname, but my features must have been as deadpan as I had intended them to be, because he trailed off: "depending on what each man was used to calling me."

"Then none of them called you 'Ralph,' " I countered.

"No," he responded with a frown. "Why would I be called that?"

Smiling wryly, I confessed, "That has to be my private joke, because it involves a long-enduring American commercial that must not have reached these shores; otherwise you would have recognized it. It's too complex to explain readily."

After a dutiful chuckle, he ruined my whole evening by saying: "I don't care what they call me as long as they don't call me too late for a meal."

Of course, I had to chuckle—albeit grimly.

"I don't want to bore you with the subject," he resumed, "but the pains in my back do bother me a lot, maybe even more than Isibelle's migraines bother her. But she can't stand pain, so she fusses about it while I just go on making the beds."

I stared through the window toward a distant street lamp while my mind considered the likelihood that the element of pain had become a bone of contention between the two partners. "But you do receive disability compensations, don't you?" I inquired, even though, through the man's piecemeal accounts, I had become familiar with practically every aspect of the accident and its aftermath.

"Yes," he replied. "I got a fifty percent disability allowance from the railroad, but some of the wheels are trying to beat me out of my just dues. Nevertheless, I expect to win in the end."

"You must have had many interesting experiences during thirty years of service," I suggested.

"Twenty-nine years," he rejoined. "Of course, my accident interfered with my receiving full retirement benefits, and now they are trying to beat me out of my fifty percent disability."

"That's a massive injustice," I muttered. "In fact, the railroad should cancel the fifty percent disability and grant you full retirement, since you were involuntarily retired because of the accident."

"I have initiated a claim for it," he said.

"After you recovered, you could have been assigned to a desk job or some sort of a traveling job until you had earned full retirement rights," I ventured.

"I didn't want a desk job," he retorted. "I prefer to work out in the clean, fresh air. As for a traveling assignment, each crew took care of its own problems."

He paused and stared through the window at the gathering dusk for a moment. "However," he then resumed, "there were some interesting experiences, and one comes to mind, but I wasn't involved. It involved two other members of my crew who were sheduled to travel to the north end of the islands. Of course, they were assigned to the same stateroom on the sleeper, and that was where the problem arose."

Pausing once more, he looked at me and explained: "Actually, I got the story from another crew member, who got it from Joe, who was one of the travelers, so I really don't know anything about Herman's side of the story." Then, as an afterthought, he added, "Herman was the other traveler."

"That was apparent, so get on with the story," I urged. "Suddenly I am all ears."

After critically inspecting my ears and tactfully refraining from comment, he resumed, "Joe had the lower berth, and, of course, Herman had the upper one. According to Joe's report, shortly after they retired, Herman allowed one arm to dangle over the edge of his berth. Meanwhile, his fingers began to fiddle with Joe's comforter." There he stopped and stared searchingly into my eyes as if trying to determine whether I had arrived at the same conclusion that he apparently had.

Sensing that more words of encouragement were expected, I chose to be negative. "Perhaps there was a logical reason for Herman's strange behavior," I countered. "Perhaps he had inadvertently dropped a package of cigarettes onto Joe's comforter and was merely trying to retrieve it."

"That's a possibility," he conceded, "but no one ever suggested that or any other likely possibilities before."

"That's human nature," I retorted caustically. "Unfortunately, I'm just as human as the next man; therefore, even though I was twenty-three years old before I learned that there actually are such strange creatures, I would be inclined to go along with Joe's suspicions. After all, Herman might not have been a smoker; furthermore, the average smoker probably would have called out, 'Hey, Joe, I accidentally dropped my cigarettes into your berth. Please take one and return them to me.'"

"Well, there had been some rumors about the man," he tentatively murmured. "So what else was Joe to suspect?"

He allowed reasonable time for a rebuttal, but I merely made the universal palms-up gesture of what else?

"Joe was a pretty hard-headed character," he resumed, "so he may have thrown a punch at Herman. But no one ever told me that he did. Nevertheless, Herman always gave Joe plenty of clearance on the job from that time on."

"Management should have canned the guy," I growled. "A character like that can ruin the efficiency of any work force. Very likely it's as disruptive as inserting a woman into a gang of men, but that's disruptive for a different reason, of course. Without doubt a smart manager would have canned the guy."

"I question whether he was that much of a problem," he said. "I'm inclined to be rather tolerant of such people and for a good reason: If all of those weirdos were discharged, they would end up on the dole. Then the taxpayers would have to support them. As it is, they support themselves."

"Then society has to endure their stupid behavior," I protested. "I say that they should be isolated from society, because they not only infringe on the rights of normal people, but they pose a threat to upcoming generations. Theirs is an addictive disease—almost an infectious one.

"Then society would have to support them," he stubbornly insisted. "Besides, they can't control their behavior, and society shouldn't penalize them for that."

"That's a lot of *bleep bleep* spread by some psychologists and psychiatrists," I retorted, "but I happen to be one of the many independent thinkers who don't believe it. In my opinion, anybody can control his impulses if he really wants to, and it's up to society to make such people want to control their filthy impulses. Very likely those impulses were introduced to them by other weirdos; therefore, society has only to break the line of communication to stop the production of new generations of queers. Obviously, the best way to accomplish that is to isolate the current stock from society."

"By putting them in prisons?" he countered caustically.

"Yes, if that's the only way to accomplish the desired end," I retorted. "Actually, tolerance is the main reason that the problem has grown so rapidly during the last three decades. In fact, such behavior is most prevalent in those societies where tolerance of it is viewed as a virtue. In more disciplined societies it is practically nonexistent, as are some of the other no-no's, such as adultery. For example, not long ago a couple of young, high-cast Arabians were convicted of adultery by one of the particular nation's highest courts, and they were beheaded."

Wilfred's green eyes suddenly exhibited explosive levels of both shock and horror. "That's not an example of social discipline!" he shouted. "That's the lowest form of barbarism!"

"It does seem to be a bit extreme," I admitted with a smile, "but you have to grant that such discipline must be a great determent. In any event, that young couple will never commit adultery again."

"I seriously doubt that it's a determent," he said. "For instance, the beatings that some of your young goons inflict on homosexual men in cities, such as San Francisco, don't appear to deter them."

"That's merely a class war," I muttered. "Weirdo against weirdo. According to some psychologists, queerdom consists of masochists, sadists, and perverts. Therefore, those so-called goons are really queers who have lost control of their sadistic impulses. Malicious gossips possess some of the same characteristics but to a lesser degree. Nevertheless, the effects of their words on the mentalities of their victims can wound, torture, and even kill just as effectively as physical violence. Therefore, some of those people should be isolated from society too, because they are just as sick as their more physical counterparts. The only difference is their modus operandi. Unfortunately, some of the worst offenders are firmly established in the various news media."

"According to your precepts, most of our society should be behind bars," Wilfred stated mildly.

I possess a particularly devilish smile, which I reserve for special occasions, and, since this obviously was a special occasion, I turned it on full bore. Apparently, Wilfred recognized his danger, because he abruptly tilted his chair forward and stared watchfully at me.

"There's an old Quaker quotation that aptly covers that statement," I muttered.

"Maybe I should withdraw the statement," he suggested uneasily.

"But I don't remember exactly how it goes," I added.

"Then I won't withdraw it," he responded with a sigh of relief.

"But I can paraphrase it," I rejoined.

"On second thought...," he began, but the tones of my voice drowned out the remainder of the intended statement.

"It seems that everybody in the world is a bit daft," I chanted while the man continued to eye me warily. "Excepting me and thee," I added, and he relaxed perceptibly. "But I have come to doubt even thee," I finished with a flourish, and he sagged like a punctured balloon.

But he immediately returned to the fray. "Society should never infringe on anybody's civil rights," he insisted. "No truly democratic government should ever permit that."

"But weirdos have no civil rights!" I flashed. "They sacrificed those rights when they took up their unnatural sexual practices. I'm convinced that if society will take a firm stand on this issue now, the current growth of homosexuality can be terminated immediately, and the present stock of queers can be reduced to zero within two or three generations."

"How?" he countered.

"I've already described the method," I observed impatiently, "but I'll summarize it: First off, the hard-core element must be isolated from society so that it cannot contaminate upcoming generations."

"I'm obviously much more tolerant than you are," he interjected, "so we'll never see eye to eye on some issues."

"And as long as people continue to tolerate such behavior, it will continue to ruin the lives of countless young victims," I growled. "The least that society should do is to demand that every mentally warped adult who molests a minor be immediately removed from society for the remainder of his unnatural life."

"You've covered part of one of the three classes," he observed, "but what about the other two?"

After pondering the question for a moment, I answered, "In my opinion, much of the sadism practiced by various societies has evolved from mental conditioning. Take the Irish people, for example: Most of them appear to be morally disciplined, but some of them seem to delight in murdering innocent civilians, including women and children. Obviously, no intelligent human being would ever condone such undisciplined behavior for any reason whatsoever, especially political ones, so something must be very awry in the minds of those people."

"Over several generations those minds may have adapted to that kind of behavior," he volunteered.

"You probably hit the center of the bull's eye," I responded with approving eyes. "In other words, you suspect that those minds have become conditioned to barbaric acts by years of exposure to similar acts by predecessors, who have been mistakenly canonized by followers whose values had been similarly warped."

"It makes sense to me," he muttered.

"That philosophy may apply to some of the Arab societies too," I ventured.

"Like the one that beheads adulterers," he suggested.

"That's a different case," I insisted. Then, after briefly reconsidering it, I added, "But not entirely. Basically, Arab societies are extremely disciplined because of very strict religious beliefs, such as those incorporated in the Islamic faith."

"Somewhat like the faith of the Irish," Wilfred suggested.

"Yeah," I agreed. "So the minds of many Arabs have been so conditioned to mayhem and murder in the name of their religion that they honor those fanatics who deliberately sacrifice their lives to bomb certain objectives, such as crowded business centers and public buses. Objectives that possess no military values whatsoever. Apparently they are bent on the indiscriminate murder of people, guilty or innocent. Unfortunately, most of those sacrificial lambs have been conned into believing that they'll be rewarded for their services by a ticket on an equivalent of the Orient Express to their particular Valhalla. But I doubt that any oriental god or prophet, be he Mohammed, Buddha, or Allah, would ever grant even a steerage class ticket on a sampan to a vicious barbarian or murderer."

Following an approving nod, Wilfred murmured, "That's one issue that we do agree on, and you covered it very nicely, so we can put it to bed."

"From the nature of your statement, I gather that I'm being dismissed for the evening," I suggested, "so let me pick up my bottle and my opinions and repair to Unit 3."

"I didn't intend to imply that you should leave," he protested apologetically. "I don't have anything to do, and you are through with your work for the day, so there's no reason for you to hurry off. Besides, Isibelle is away for the evening, so we can continue to discuss these offbeat subjects, and there are lots of them." Then, smiling drolly, he suggested, "How about making the next one women?"

"Yeah, the average male conversation invariably gets around to the subject of the female race," I said. "However, at my age, I suspect that most men finally concur with George Bernard Shaw's opinion that the average man wastes far too many of his most productive years chasing women when that time could be used for much more constructive activities."

"But New Zealand women chase the men," he countered with a lewd smile.

"Actually, that's the case the world over," I rejoined, "but the women consistently con men into believing that men are the aggressors."

"Maybe Isibelle can fix you up with one of her lady friends," he suggested. "Some of them are in your age bracket."

"Maybe, but no thanks," I retorted. "I've reached that point in my life where I can't endure women in my age bracket. In fact, I'm filled with revulsion by the thought of just touching one of those old biddies." As an afterthought, I whimsically added: "However, I might respond to the allure of a svelte sixteen-year-old, but we would be totally out of synch from a social standpoint, of course."

Wilfred tried to hide his expression of disapproval, but without success. "I would surely suspect so!" burst involuntarily from his lips. Suddenly I realized that my whimsical word picture had exceeded my usual farcical proclivities, but I refused to attempt to repair the damage.

"Let the man believe whatever he will," Pancho recommended. "As one unusually astute man once said, 'People will believe whatever they want to believe, regardless of the facts.' "

After gazing pensively into the man's cold eyes until they veered away, I said, "It appears that we've exhausted the subject matter, so I'll leave you to your thoughts for the nonce." Pausing at the open doorway, I looked back at him and added, "Sweet dreams, my prince, or whatever the quotation. . . ."

"Shakespeare, wasn't it?" he eagerly interjected.

Following a brief study of the question, I confessed, "I really don't know." Then, for want of a logical answer, I added, "Maybe it was Henry Ford."

While he was rupturing from uproarious laughter, I hurriedly escaped before he insisted that I accompany him to the library to unearth the actual quotation and its author. If Shakespeare, then the unearthing after four hundred years could be an extremely upsetting experience.

"Good night, Albert!" he called after me. And I raised my right arm in a parting salute.

"I wish he had accepted Al's suggestions of 'Al' or 'Bert,' instead of 'Albert,' " José mused, as I strolled toward my cubicle. "Only the women in his family have ever called him Albert."

"But Al has reciprocated by calling him Wilfred," Pancho rejoined, "so I suppose they are even. But I wonder how he would respond to 'Snow.' "

Isibelle in an Explosive Mood

Actually, those parting formalities proved to be premature, because I returned to the vacant office about an hour later to borrow one of the various travel brochures that were displayed on the low table, which stood against the wall opposite the desk. While I was crouched over the table studying one of the brochures, Isibelle, still clad in her evening finery, entered the office from the living room with a spray can in one hand.

"I came to borrow one of your travel pamphlets," I attempted to explain.

Usually the words would have elicited an immediate reply followed by a lengthy conversation, but the woman appeared to be in no mood for words of any kind. In fact, she seemed to be deliberately ignoring me during the time that she was silently moving along the periphery of the room, diligently spraying the house flies that had unwisely elected to roost on the walls near the ceiling. Actually, *roost* is the appropriate term, because some New Zealand house flies grow to the size of small eagles, and those flies were no exceptions. She must have been in a particularly vicious mood, because she deliberately held the nozzle of the spray can against the noses of those poor critters and executed them with neither a blindfold nor a last cigarette. When she pulled the trigger, they instantly dropped from the wall and plopped onto the floor as inertly as if they had been blasted by a twelve-gage shotgun.

Apparently responding to the sound of my voice, Wilfred also entered the office from the living room, and, with a wary glance toward his partner, he cordially shouted, "Albert, can I help you?"

"No, thank you," I replied. "I've found what I wanted to borrow from you."

"Are you sure?" he countered, placing one solid arm about my shoulders.

"Yes, this should do it," I answered impatiently.

"Why don't you take one of each," he suggested, extending his other hand toward the pamphlets. "That way you'll be doubly sure."

"No, this is all I need," I insisted, pushing his groping fingers away from the other pamphlets.

"Remember, I've told you several times that you may have whatever travel pamphlets you might need to describe your travels through New Zealand," he reminded me.

"Yes, I remember," I replied, wondering why that heavy arm about my shoulders was propelling me so indomitably through the open doorway onto the concrete slab.

Sensing that he had manipulated me from the office for some reason, I shot an accusing stare into the man's guileful eyes, which wavered guiltily. Simultaneously, we turned and looked toward the office at the same instant that Isibelle flounced out of it into the living room. Meanwhile, I was startled to see a wisp of what seemed to be smoke curling upward from the woman's neat coiffure, but it had to be contrails of stray fly spray.

Exhaling what seemed to be a deep sigh of relief, the other man effusively suggested, "Come to me any time, and I'll be glad to help you with your research in any way that I can."

"Thank you, Wilfred," I murmured. "Have a restful night."

"Likewise," he responded.

As I pensively strolled toward Unit 3, José remarked, "I wonder what could have caused such a dramatic change in Wilfred's attitude. Certainly, it was very unlike that of the man who, not two hours before, was locked with Al in a life-and-death debate over the relative merits of tolerant and intolerant human behavior."

"It has to be associated with Isibelle in some way," Pancho insisted. "What kind of a sin have you committed, Al, that might have offended her?"

I silently shook my head; then José suggested, "Surely, Wilfred wouldn't tell her about Al's aversion to touching those old biddies."

"Oh, yes, he would," Pancho retorted. "And to somebody like her, who is almost over the hill, that would be particularly infuriating, especially when the source is a man who is skidding down the far side of that hill."

"That has to be it," José concluded. "That was why Wilfred practically pushed Al out of the office. He was afraid that she would jump onto Al and claw out his eyes, so he pushed him out of her way to avoid an insurance claim. Without a doubt, that man talks too much."

"He's not the only one," Pancho countered. "If a certain party had not imparted a rude opinion to a second party, who was in a particularly expansive mood, the second party would not have conveyed that opinion to a third party, who was plunged into an explosive mood by the revelation."

"You are out of order, Pancho," I mumbled, unlocking the door of Unit 3 with a vicious twist of my wrist.

"What are you going to do about it, judge?" José countered. "Throw him into a jail cell?"

Of course, I could do nothing about it, so I decided to pull on my pajamas and retire for the night.

"Take off your clothes, first!" Pancho silently shouted.

"Oh, yeah," I muttered. Then, after removing my pajama trousers, I removed my jeans. Sometimes those two guys can be a real burden to me, but I don't know what I would do without them.

11

A Touch of This and That

Touch and Go

If it hadn't been for Wilfred's good intentions, I would never have touched the woman, so he was the one who was really responsible for that intimate little interlude with Isibelle. Certain situations turn up some strange bedfellows, and this one was no exception, because Isibelle and I had never appeared to be particularly attracted to each other.

Actually, the incident evolved from a relatively unimportant coincidence wherein Wilfred happened to be standing by in Unit 3 at the instant when I thrust the clip of my mechanical lead pencil against the flap of my shirt pocket and broke the last thread that retained one corner of it. Of course, neither of us made a big issue of it, but the stupid pencil did. Artfully evading my frantic clutch, it dived over the flapping flap, performed an exhibitionistic triple somersault, and crashed tail first onto the thinly carpeted floor. After flipping the flap disgustedly, I recovered the pencil and shook it experimentally, but there were only the discouraging sounds of many tiny particles striking the inner wall of the barrel. Meanwhile, the other man looked on dispassionately.

Later Isibelle made a special trip from the office to the laundry, where I was doing my *weakly* wash. After her usual stereotypical greeting in the dialect, she said, "Wilfred mintioned that a pocket has been toahn from one of yoah shirts. Since Oy happen to have moy sewing machine set up foah some of moy work, why don't you bring it to me, and Oy'll stitch it back into plice foah ye."

"Aw, I won't have you wasting any time on that old shirt," I insisted. "I'll just throw it away. But thank you for the generous offer."

"It won't be a wiste o' moy toime if the shirt lasts another yeah," she protested.

A thoughtful look into the woman's intent blue eyes led me to conclude that a lot of time might be saved by yielding to her request, so I muttered, "Okay, but I refuse to bring the shirt to you until it has been laundered."

Conceding a nod and a tolerant smile, she turned about and trudged back to the office.

About two days later I stepped into the office to exchange a few words with Wilfred just as Isibelle entered it from the living room. She appeared to have just returned from a lost weekend, so I asked, "How are you, Isibelle?" But she only groaned and made a wry grimace.

"Isibelle is having one of her migraines," Wilfred volunteered.

"Ohhh, too bad!" I exclaimed in commiserating tones. "I had an ex once who suffered from those things pretty often. We found that the pain seemed to be relieved somewhat when I massaged the muscles of her neck and shoulders; consequently, I eventually became a fairly proficient masseuse." In response to the woman's startled expression, I mentally reviewed the statement and hurriedly added, "Obviously, I should have used the word *masseur*."

She tried to smile, but the attendant pain proved to be too much for her. "Moy daughter used to massage moy nick and shouldah muscles," she murmured, "and it did seem to hilp a lot."

I looked speculatively at her for an instant, but my mind immediately rejected the proposal that was on the tip of my tongue, because neither of those characters would have viewed it in its true light.

"Well, I'll leave you people to your problems and return to mine," I finally muttered for want of anything more constructive to say. Sidling through the partially open doorway, I strolled thoughtfully toward Unit 3.

"Hmm," José mumbled en route. "It's unlikely that Wilfred knows anything about the art, so it appears that Al is morally obligated to offer his services, regardless of how the offer is received."

When I returned to the office, my prospective patient was no longer in evidence, so I peered cautiously at Wilfred and said, "If Isibelle would like to try one of my massages, I would be glad to give her one. After all, I owe her that much for repairing my shirt."

"I'll ask her," he said. After disappearing into the living room, he quickly reappeared with the woman at his heels. Since there was an air of awareness in her attitude, I assumed that she had overheard my proposal, so I said, "I won't guarantee to do any good, but I'll gladly try to alleviate some of that pain with a massage."

She and her cousin exchanged significant glances; then, turning her eyes to me, she said, "That's very thoughtful of ye, but Oy have an appointment with my hayahdrissah in about an owah, so if ye'll give me a wee bit o' toime to git ready foah that, I'll call ye whin Oy'm foinally ready. Okye?"

"Okay," I agreed.

Then I retreated to Unit 3 and to my lazy typewriter, which obviously hadn't done a thing since I had left. Meanwhile, my two lieutenants pondered the advisability of my patient's appointment with the hairdresser. "Like Wilfred has inferred," Pancho finally concluded, "she may not be in as much pain as she claims to be."

Some thirty minutes later the bell of the telephone clamored, and when I lifted the instrument, a woman's voice murmured, "It's me . . . Isibelle. Oy'm riddy whinivah you ah."

"Okay," I responded. "I'll be there in a matter of seconds."

In the office I was met by both members of the clan, but the woman assumed the lead role, which was a switch because the man had always dominated previous conversations. Now he hovered thoughtfully in the background.

"Oy have only fifteen minutes befoah Oy have to leave foah the hayahdrissah's," she advised me.

"Okay, then this will have to be a 'quickie,' " I rejoined with a sly glance at the man. Then I followed her into the living room, and he silently fell in behind me.

"A straight-back chair is probably in order," I suggested.

After he silently produced one from a corner of the room, the woman seated herself somewhat self-consciously on it while I moved into position behind it. Then the other man reluctantly moved slowly in the direction of the kitchen.

"Wilfred has koindly volunteered to do the dinnah dishes," she explained with a pleased chuckle.

I stepped slightly to one side of her and carefully inspected her flushed features, but they failed to corroborate a momentary suspicion that she might be putting on an act to gain some attention. Then I moved back behind her.

As I tentatively placed one hand on one of her solid shoulders, she pleaded, "Please be gentle."

"Hmm," José mused. "I wonder where we've heard those words before."

Meanwhile, there was a loud crash in the kitchen, which sounded as if a very large dish had fallen into a sink full of dishes.

"Oh!" the woman exclaimed with a start. "It sounds loik **that man** is bryekin' iviry dish we have."

"Maybe he should pay more attention to what he's doing," I muttered.

"And less attention to what's transpiring in the living room," Pancho silently added.

"Of course, you'll tell me when I strike a particularly sensitive spot," I suggested.

"Yis," she promised, "but the back o' moy nick and the spice between moy shouldah blides ah wheah Oy usually hurt most."

"Okay," I murmured. "But suppose that I start here." Then I began to work the muscles across the tops of her shoulders between my thumbs and the tips of my gently flexing fingers."

"Oh!" she exclaimed. "That feels so good!"

Immediately, there was the sound of another crash; then the clatter of dishes ceased entirely for some inexplicable reason. "Apparently, **that man** has broken your last dish," I ventured. And she simpered. It is difficult for one to visualize a 160-pound woman simpering, but that one simpered.

"I wonder what is going on in that man's mind," José interjected. "Whatever it is, it has to be pretty weird."

"But both of these characters have reacted very strangely to a perfectly normal offer to repay a kindness in kind," Pancho volunteered.

The task turned out to be much more difficult than I anticipated, because the woman's muscles were so solid that my fingers could scarcely penetrate them to the knotted nerves that I suspected of being the source of her problem. But I must not have failed entirely, because the fifteen minutes became twenty minutes before Isibelle suddenly exclaimed, "Oh! Oy'm runnin' lite foah moy appointmint. Thank ye so much."

"You certainly are welcome," I mumbled, massaging each of my weary hands. "I hope that my efforts relieved some of the tension. If you can relax during the remainder of the day, the attack may disappear by nightfall. According to some authorities, migraine headaches usually subside then, but that may be an old wives' tale."

By that time she was standing with her hands pressed tightly against the sides of her head. "Oy shuahly hope Oy mike it to the hayahdrissah's," she mumbled distractedly.

About one minute later Wilfred joined me on the slab in front of the office as she slowly drove her small auto past it and mimed the words, "Oy'll be all roight."

"Sometimes she gets double vision so bad she can't drive," he explained to me.

Midway of the following morning I encountered Wilfred during our coinciden-tal journeys across the pavement. After an exchange of the usual amenities, I asked, "How is Isibelle's head this morning?"

"Her headache is gone," he replied, "but she was violently ill just after she left the hairdresser. In fact, she almost called me to come and pick her up, because she had a very bad attack of double vision, but she made it back on her own."

"Oh, what an unhappy development!" I exclaimed. "I must have done more damage than good."

"She claimed that she hasn't had so severe an attack for years," he added almost acrimoniously.

I glanced sharply at him, but the malice, if any, wasn't big enough to ruin my day, so I whimsically exclaimed, "Oh-oh! She may even sue me for malpractice or something."

Apparently my tactic worked or he had a change of heart, because he immediately insisted, "Naw, she would never do anything like that. She has one of those very severe attacks once in a great while, and you just happened to strike one of them. However, she could sue you for practicing medicine without a license."

"But I didn't prescribe any medicine," I protested. "Besides, I have a license."

He looked sharply at me; then a knowing grin lit up his ruddy features. "I don't know about America," he muttered, "but you can't practice medicine in New Zealand under a builder's license."

A Bird Falls from the Sky

Action photographs of the fiery blast that tore the space shuttle *Challenger* from the sky had been featured in the previous evening's newscast, so there really was no reason for Wilfred to be discussing the catastrophe with me shortly after eleven o'clock the following morning. Nevertheless, there he was: lounging comfortably in the easy chair, while my tailbone pressed painfully against the unyielding seat of the straight-back chair. Meanwhile, the old typewriter stood stolidly on the small chest of drawers and overlooked the scene with an air of bored rejection.

"Say, that was some explosion!" he exclaimed after the usual greetings had been exchanged.

"Yeah, NASA put on quite a blast for that schoolteacher," I responded callously. "No other American astronaut has ever been given such an initiation."

Following a critical glance, he muttered, "It was unfortunate that a woman, who probably was a mother, should be aboard the shuttle during that particular flight."

"I have no sympathy for either the woman or the men who accompanied her," I growled. "My sympathies are for their families, who are truly the unfortunate ones. They are the heirs of foolish family heads whose overwhelming yens for fame and fortune drove them to accept the blandishments of equally foolish bureaucrats and politicians; otherwise they might never have boarded that ill-fated vehicle."

"Why were they so foolish?" he countered. "Up to now the shuttle has made many successful flights."

"It was common knowledge that the fuels in the shuttle's propulsion system were violently explosive," I retorted, "so the bureaucrats who sanctioned the use of such fuels had to be either foolish or totally inconsiderate of the safety of their astronauts. Wye, I bet that even the Russians wouldn't have taken such a gamble."

"The Russians have made some mistakes, too," he rebutted.

"But this was an obvious mistake from the first," I countered. "How will

America look in the eyes of the world if the next shuttle blows up on the pad? And it could happen. Furthermore, each of those birds and their nest cost over one billion dollars. It's no wonder that America has a massive federal deficit when the representatives of the taxpayers spend tax money so promiscuously on programs that serve no earthly purpose whatsoever."

"One more blast like that one would probably terminate the program," he murmured.

"You know it would!" I retorted.

After absently studying the carpet for a moment, he said, "But many more people die in the crash of a big commercial airliner, and they are forgotten overnight. I don't see why the news media made such a fuss over the deaths of a mere seven astronauts when hundreds of people die in one of those crashes."

"There are many cogent reasons for that," I responded, "and one of them has to be the news media, which made those astronauts famous. Furthermore, billions of dollars in damages resulted from the destruction of the shuttle, and only millions are involved in the crash of a large airliner. Foremost among the reasons is the design and construction of the shuttles, which have constituted an ongoing media story, so it has received an enormous amount of publicity."

"But what could have caused such a massive explosion?" he murmured with an air of recurring amazement. "It practically filled the sky with streamers of white smoke."

"Part of that so-called smoke was water vapor," I said. "It was produced by the combustion of thousands of pounds of liquid hydrogen in conjunction with more thousands of pounds of liquid oxygen, both of which were separately contained by the booster package. However, the two small boosters contained solid fuel, which burned at a controlled rate, so it's unlikely that they were the source of the explosion." (Later I regretted that rash opinion, but who's perfect?)

After considering my speculative answer for a moment, he asked, "But if the solid fuel was more controllable, why wasn't it used exclusively?"

"That's a good question," I answered. "Very likely the designers would answer that since solid fuel is heavier than liquid fuel, some liquid fuel was used to keep the booster package from becoming so cumbersome that it would be unable to propel the shuttle into orbit about the earth."

Following a brief study, he countered, "If liquid fuel is so much lighter, then why was it not used exclusively? After all, during an explosion like the last one, it doesn't much matter how big it becomes, because the astronauts can't be any deader than dead."

"That's also a good question," I responded with an approving nod, "and the best answer that I can generate on such short notice is this: Some of the booster's components were designed to be recoverable for obvious economic reasons. In fact, that's an advantage which none of the current breed of missiles enjoy, but the tremendous cost of the shuttle and its launching system has transcended that advantage; however, there are some others that may help to make it reasonably practical. If not, then American taxpayers have been saddled with still another tremendously costly white elephant through the generosity of their inept scientists, engineers, and spendthrift politicians.

"But the shuttle program is supposed to be one of the greatest engineering feats of this century," he protested. "Some of the smartest engineers and scientists in the world were involved in its design and development."

"And some of the dumbest ones were involved in it," I retorted. "I worked on that program. Since I was so closely associated with it, I know what I'm talking about."

From the abrupt change in the man's expression, I realized that I had blundered badly. Furthermore, I could see that he literally yearned to respond to the stupid statement with both barrels, but he allowed it to pass unchallenged.

Fortunately, he did so, because my sense of honor might have compelled me to defend it on the field of battle. Consequently, a lot of blood would have been spilled, and it would have been my blood, because the man was as strong as a red bull. Besides, my nose bleeds automatically at the mere thought of physical violence. In fact, that's why I never watch boxing matches on TV.

A Busted Gut

For a moment it seemed that Wilfred's sharp gaze would surely pierce my left earlobe while he was pondering what I suspected would be another mind-boggling question, but he merely stated: "It seems to me that engineers are a lot like doctors."

"Why?" I countered.

"After that shuttle disaster, one has to conclude that some of them are not very good diagnosticians," he answered. "And that's why I don't trust doctors at all."

"Then you don't trust engineers either," I rejoined.

"Why?" he asked.

"Because you just concluded that some of them are not very good diagnosticians," I retorted.

Following a long, thoughtful stare, he tactfully inquired, "What's your opinion?"

"Don't trust engineers either," I responded emphatically. "They are mere human beings, too."

Nodding absently, he said, "But I have a personal reason for distrusting doctors, and it's related to something that happened to me a few years ago when I got a pain in my...." After stopping and gesturing toward his paunch, he added, "I thought it was a temporary thing, but it continued to pain me so much that I finally went to a doctor, who diagnosed it as a case of acute indigestion. He prescribed something for me to take to alleviate the pain, but it got worse. During my next visit the doctor prescribed something that was supposed to act on my gall bladder, and that didn't help any either. By that time I couldn't hold down any food, so he didn't attach any importance to the information that I hadn't gone to the toilet for days." Then he fixed his eyes on mine as if trying to determine whether I had perceived the implication of the problem. I nodded knowingly, so he resumed: "Finally, the doctor admitted that he didn't know what was wrong with me, so he called in an accessory."

"An associate?" I interjected as tactfully as possible.

"I meant what I said," he retorted stubbornly. "Nevertheless, the other doctor was also a surgeon. After a conference they decided that my gall bladder wasn't functioning properly, so they put me in a hospital, and the surgeon took it out. However, in the process, he discovered that I was full of . . . ," and his tones trailed away while he peered at me as if trying to determine whether I was familiar with the highly technical four-letter term.

Of course, I was familiar with it, since I had first heard it at the tender age of four from the lips of one of my father's Canadian farmhands. However, when I strode into the big farm kitchen and confidently demonstrated my ability to use it, my Aunt Onie firmly instructed me never to use it again, or she would wash out my mouth with soap. Consequently, that word has remained emblazoned in my brain ever since, but I've never used it. Well, almost never, because every time that I've unintentionally disobeyed her edict, I have involuntarily glanced across my shoulder to see if Aunt Onie was standing there with a bar of soap in her hand, even though she has been sitting just to the right of Allah some eleven years now.

I had suspected Wilfred of having such a problem from the first, but I was amazed that the surgeon had not corrected it while he had the man's paunch open. Meanwhile, the impatience in Wilfred's probing gaze alerted me to the fact that I had been woolgathering again, so I blurted, "Obviously, you had a ruptured appendix."

"From just my description of the symptoms, even you were able to correctly diagnose the problem!" he shouted. Then, leaping to his feet, he literally screamed, "But neither one of those idiots could diagnose peritonitis!"

For an instant the man appeared about to blow his top, so I seriously considered the desirability of getting something, such as a pacifier, to quiet him a bit, but I had waited too long to act.

"Look at what they did to me!" he shouted, jerking the front of his shirt open and ripping off two buttons in the process. The action effectively revealed a livid scar that extended from just below his rib cage, down his big belly, and into his trousers. "Not only that," he added, "but they took out a perfectly good gall bladder. Another doctor, who was there at the time, informed me of that after I was released from the hospital." Pausing, he inhaled deeply and resumed: "I should have sued them for malpractice, but we don't have the kind of laws here that you have in America."

"Thank your maker for that!" I exclaimed with heartfelt fervor.

"I could've got a couple million dollars for that gall bladder in America," he said regretfully. I don't recall another time when he indicated any American advantage, whatsoever, over New Zealand.

Psittaciformes Unfortunately, I was attacked by another of my irrational afterthoughts. "By the way," I began, "isn't *parrotonitis* a disease that commonly attacks domestic fowls? In fact, I'm sure that it must be the same disease that Ameri can poultrymen have been fighting ever since some bird fanciers illegally imported a few parrots from South America."

From the man's cold expression, I realized that I should never have mentioned the matter, but I had done so only in the interest of science. Nevertheless, I had to respond to that cold expression, so I protested, "But you have to admit that I did correctly diagnose your problem as *parrotonitis*."

"That disease never attacks human beings," he retorted contemptuously. "It afflicts an order of birds known as *psittaciformes*, and it's called *psittacosis*."

I have to admit that, since the man was already standing over me, I really looked up to him after he laid those scientific terms on me. That is, I did until later, when I happened to find the term *psittaciformes* beneath the picture of a New Zealand parrot printed on one of the motel's calendars. Obviously, it was a dirty, low-down (down under) trick. And that is particularly so, since I was unable to find the word in my *American College Dictionary*. Eventually, in sheer desperation, I looked up the word *parrot*, and there it was: "any of numerous hook-billed, fleshy-tongued, often gaily colored birds which constitute the order *psittaciformes*."

The Psycho Logists

Meanwhile, Wilfred buttoned his shirt's remaining buttons, tucked it into his trousers, and returned to the easy chair with the air of a conquering hero, which I found a bit hard to take.

"No doubt your experience with those medical practitioners proved to be very unfortunate," I said, "but you could have fared much worse in the health care field.

"I don't see how," he retorted. "Those doctors almost killed me."

"You could have been a victim of a psychiatrist," I suggested.

"Hmm," he mumbled. "I've heard of them, but I don't know much about them."

"Neither do I," I admitted, "but I know how they operate."

"But they don't operate," he objected. "In fact, they treat mental illnesses."

"Aw, you know what I meant," I protested.

"I know only what you said," he retorted. And I glared stonily into his triumphant eyes until they forced mine to take refuge in the carpet. Finally, I looked up and resentfully muttered, "One thing I do know is that some of them are one hundred percent phonies."

"Those are rather pointed words from one who has just claimed that he doesn't know anything about psychiatrists," he said.

"I've read quite a bit about them," I rejoined, "so I'm merely repeating what someone else professed to know."

"So you have no proof that they are phonies," he persisted.

Deliberately ignoring the sally, I resumed: "One particular writer claimed that many psychiatrists use their psychology degrees and a benign couch-side manner to con susceptible dupes into believing that they, the psychiatrists, are endowed with certain supernatural powers that enable them to cure the dupes' mental disorders when the dupes are the only ones capable of controlling their emotions."

"But the psychiatrists probably know how to guide the dupes to cures," he suggested. "Besides, that's only one writer's opinion."

"Yes, that's only one writer's opinion," I growled through clenched teeth. Meanwhile, José and Pancho were hurriedly estimating the number of days that it would take for that man to finally drive me into some psychiatrist's sanctuary unless I quickly escaped from his corrosive influence.

"On what source was that writer's opinion based?" he inquired in rather conciliatory tones.

"A research team's report," I growled. "According to it, the percentage of cures claimed by a specific group of psychiatrists was practically identical with the percentage of cures accruing from a program wherein the patients relaxed in an environment of peace and quiet without any costly counseling by psychiatrists."

"Very likely those were only mildly disturbed patients," he suggested. "But what would the comparison have been for patients who had lost touch with reality?"

"For now, let's not discuss patients who have lost touch with reality," I proposed through tight lips.

"Okay," he responded equably, but his piercing gaze induced me to wonder if his sharp logic had finally pierced my overstressed steam boiler and caused it to blow a hole through the top of my head. Finally he added, "If psychiatrists and psychologists serve no practical purpose in the scheme of things, then they are an economic drag on society."

"That's why I refused to serve as a sponsor for my daughter when she opted to become a psychologist," I said.

"So what did she become?" he inquired.

"She's a practicing psychologist," I replied.

"Oh-ho!" he shouted. "So you used the wrong psychology on her."

"Apparently so," I muttered morosely. "But she got her master's degree strictly on her own efforts, so I doubt that she'll ever be an economic drag on society." Then, after a thought-filled minute, I added, "She's a stubborn little pixy."

"Maybe we should take another look at psychology," he suggested.

"I would particularly like to return to psychiatrists for a moment," I requested. "It's surprising how much their so-called talents are being misused."

"Wye shore," he responded genially. "But I hope that you are not going to tell me about some more diagnostic errors."

"This one concerns what I suspect are deliberate diagnostic errors," I muttered, "and they took place during a murder trial in the eastern part of the United States. Not only did five psychiatrists testify for the defense on the question of the defendant's sanity, but five more psychiatrists testified for the prosecution against him." After pausing to peer at Wilfred, I added, "Consequently, five of those psychiatrists must have perjured themselves.

"Not necessarily," he rejoined. "In fact, all of them may have testified honestly."

"If so, then fifty percent of them had to be in error," I retorted, "and that's a pretty poor performance ratio in any profession. In fact, one gets the same odds for heads and tails by tossing a coin an infinite number of times."

"Hmm," he mumbled pensively. "I see what you mean. But that defendant may have been one of those in-between cases, so neither group of psychiatrists was one hundred percent right or wrong."

"I don't buy the currently popular philosophy that nothing is ever one hundred percent of anything," I growled. "To me, black is black and white is white, and never the twain shall meet—or meld into gray."

After an indifferent shrug, the man mildly remonstrated, "What! No polka dots?"

Ignoring the remark, I resumed: "There also was a psychologist in the southwestern part of the country who had established himself in the minds of local prosecutors as an authority on criminal behavior; consequently, they used him almost exclusively to psychoanalyze alleged murderers. Unfortunately for some of the alleged murderers, that psychiatrist invariably classified every defendant as of the criminal type and claimed that he was capable of murder. Therefore, practically all of the defendants were convicted.

"In some of the histories of your Southwest, I've read of a hanging judge," he said, "but I've never read of a hanging psychiatrist."

"Like Judge Roy Bean, he may have had a psychological problem," I rejoined. "Since he hasn't made the headlines lately, the courts may have finally concluded that he was a bit too consistent in his analyses. If so, then some innocent victims of the system may have escaped."

"What about the previous defendants?" he asked. "Were all of them guilty, or were some of them victims of the system?"

"Who knows?" I countered. "I doubt that the psychiatrist did, and he probably could not have cared less. After all, he was getting an enormous amount of invaluable publicity."

"Apparently you don't trust psychiatrists any more than I trust doctors," he suggested.

"I don't trust either brand," I muttered, "but I trust psychiatrists and psychologists least of all, largely because I can't see how anyone can logically expect to come up with an accurate diagnosis when he doesn't even have the equivalent of a ruptured appendix to guide him to the correct conclusion."

"That appears to indicate that you still don't approve of your daughter's choice of a career," he murmured.

"My daughter's choice of a career is her business," I retorted. "I only hope that she realizes sufficient personal satisfaction from it to justify all the time that she has spent qualifying herself to practice a nonscience (nonsense), which the average adult human being automatically and effectively practices without recourse to its nomenclature and cult beliefs."

"Are you implying that we are practical psychologists?" he inquired.

"Can't you readily determine and evaluate the behavior patterns of your associates and clients after almost sixty years of exposure to the behavior patterns of thousands of human beings?" I countered.

"Yes," he responded slowly and thoughtfully. "I seem to know how to get along with people, so I suppose that I'm something of a psychologist."

"You are an excellent psychologist," I said, "and I'm not trying to butter you up. I've watched you operate this motel, and that opinion is based on those observations."

A pleased smile rippled across his full features. "But we can't place a degree in psychology after our names," he burst forth, "so how do we identify ourselves?"

Subsequent to a brief interval of thought, I plucked a sheet of scrap typewriter paper from a nearby stack and removed the mechanical lead pencil from my shirt pocket. Turning aside on the chair, I placed the sheet of paper on one corner of the chest of drawers and hastily scribbled a notation.

"What are you doing?" he inquired, as his curiosity drew him from the easy chair to my shoulder. From there he peered at the paper and read aloud, "Tyrrell and Radford, Psycho Logists."

A weak smile tugged ineffectively at his lips as he looked down into my eyes and muttered, "I might buy it if you change it to read 'Radford and Tyrrell, Psycho Logists.'"

Weather Vanes

It was about eleven o'clock in the morning, and the ambient temperature stood at 21 degrees C (70 degrees F), from which it had not varied by more than three degrees throughout the entire summer. Strolling to the open doorway of Unit 3, I turned west and scanned the sky over a distant bluff for tokens of what the prevailing elements of the atmosphere might portend during the following fifteen minutes. Except for the fleecy, white clouds that rode the west-to-east airstream, the sun-splashed sky appeared to pulse with softly diffused solar energy. Therefore, I decided to gamble on my ability to make the roundtrip from the motel to the nearest small market before one of those oncoming containers of swirling white vapor inadvertently bumped against an updraft and spilled some of its precipitates onto Musselburgh.

After arriving at the far side of the wide thoroughfare, I looked back across the rooftops of the motel and was dismayed to discover that many of the fluffy, white nimbi appeared to be converging on a not-too-distant mountaintop. Furthermore, an errant member of that sea of far-flung platinum blonde beauties had wantonly descended on a downdraft to caress the gently contoured, bald head of a mountain, and her filmy white raiment had been torn into shreds by the rapacious air currents that inhabited the adjoining canyons. At the moment only a few misty remnants of her attire clung to the proud beauty as she futilely struggled to escape from the slashing air currents.

Meanwhile, more oncoming beauties deployed about the mountaintop and extended their streamerlike arms as if beseeching the canyons' air currents to release their victim. Obviously, her sisters of mercy would fail in their mission; therefore, fearful of being inundated by the flood of tears that were sure to accompany the ensuing wake, I jogged the remaining distance to the market.

Likewise, I jogged throughout the return trip. Since I was looking directly at those suddenly dark and sullen clouds, I noted how rapidly the scouts of the angry army ascended when they struck the updrafts from the mountaintops that overlook Otago Harbor. Very likely that rapid ascent, in conjunction with the cooler air over Otago Harbor, would produce precipitation, so I increased the rate of my pace. I almost made it to the office with the bottle of "bubbly" before the first drops fell. After dashing through the open doorway, I turned about and watched intently as a veritable deluge began. Apparently those platinum blonde beauties must have been heartbroken over the demise of their errant companion, since, after donning conventional mourning attire, they shed tons of big, fat, warm tears during the ensuing shower.

The tears were still falling when the sounds of sandals softly scuffing the carpet reached my ears from the direction of the living room, so I turned around just as Wilfred's wide form filled the opening between the two rooms.

"Good morning!" he shouted, continuing into the office.

"Not really," I disagreed. "It's raining cats and dogs out there. But a good morning to you anyway."

"Typical Dunedin weather," he responded with a tolerant chuckle that seemed to condone it. "If you don't like the way it is, just wait a minute."

"Yeah," I drawled. "Just a few minutes ago I looked up toward the sunny western sky from my doorway and concluded that I could make it to the market and back with ease; however, after getting to the other side of the road, I looked back and discovered that I was being pursued by the meanest pack of clouds ever to escape from the Tasman Sea. In fact, I had to really scamper to avoid being saturated."

"Typical Dunedin weather," he repeated, as his eyes focused on the bottle in the grasp of my right hand. "You didn't go and buy another bottle for me!" he protested loudly. "I told you not to do that anymore."

"What's the problem?" I countered. "Can't you and Isibelle consume it as rapidly as I deliver it?"

"Yes," he said, "but the use of that old typewriter isn't sufficient reason for you to buy so much of it."

"You know very well what I would have to pay to rent a typewriter," I retorted, "so allow me to continue to do my thing."

"But," he began, as I placed the bottle on the desk.

"Butt me no buts," I interjected. "This is only a small token of my appreciation, and I intend to express more of it before I leave here."

"Thank you very much," he murmured, reaching forth and patting the big bottle. "I assure you that both of us enjoy these tokens very much."

The Best Cafe

The best it wasn't, but the fish and chips were good. It was located in a relatively old business block on the north side of Stuart Street between Cumberland and Castle Streets. Alongside it was a couple of other small businesses, including a purveyor of baked goods and a Chinese restaurant. From the sidewalk, a recessed doorway gave access to the cafe through a small, austere foyer, which provided the options of mounting an open stairway on the far wall or of passing into the small dining room through a narrow doorway in the wall on the right.

It was my fourth trip to the cafe, so I confidently pushed open the recessed door, passed through the foyer, came to a stop, and cased the joint. To my left, an old-fashioned cash register stood atop a wooden counter whose enamel paint matched the clinically clean, off-white, flat paint on the walls, but no one was standing behind it. And no one volunteered to escort me to a table, so I threaded my way between the dozen or so tables to one located alongside and about midway of the wall on my left. As usual, I selected the chair with its back to the wall for the same reason that I always selected that particular chair. From it I had an unobstructed view of the small dining room, and much of the kitchen could be viewed from it through the six-by-three-foot opening above the service counter in the opposite wall.

After covertly studying the half-dozen other early diners, I seated myself at the linen-covered table, removed the paper napkin from beneath the stainless steel cutlery, and tucked one corner of it just above the third button of my shirt. Then I sat back while my eyes searched for the chubby, blonde teenager, usually the only waitress on duty at that hour, and they found her seated at a table in the far corner of the room, avidly perusing an open paperback book. She must have finally come to the end of the page, because she raised her eyes and guiltily scanned the room. When her eyes met mine, she reluctantly turned the book face down on the table, placed both plump hands along the edges of the table, hoisted herself awkwardly from the chair, squeezed between it and the edge of the table, and picked up a menu. While she was approaching my table, I quickly concluded that the undulations of her substantial undercarriage must not be contrived, because they were too obviously built into it.

"Good evening," she murmured, placing the menu on the table.

"Good evening to you," I responded with folded arms. "How is the blue bass this evening?"

"Oy'm sorry," she replied, "but we haven't been able to git any blue bass litely. Howivah, we have some noice bream and sole."

"I prefer the sole," I said. "The main reason why I asked about the blue bass is that I've never sampled either that kind of bass or the orange roughy, both of which are supposed to be New Zealand delicacies."

"The bass is very good," she insisted.

"Very likely," I responded with a chuckle, "but your sales pitch is wasted this evening."

"Oh yis, that's roight," she murmured absently. "We don't have any."

After marking my order on the top sheet of a small pad, she retrieved the menu, turned about, rhythmically wended her way between the tables to the service counter, removed the sheet from the pad, and deposited it on a service tray. Then she eagerly hurried back to the table in the corner, slumped onto the chair, and buried her nose in the paperback.

Meanwhile, my mind pursued a likely parody of the plot within its lurid cover.

From the reader's intense interest, I concluded that she must have arrived at that very critical point in the novel where she was quaking with fear that Robert's entomological research assignment in the most remote reaches of the upper Congo might preclude his being apprised of Gail's condition in time to return and do whatever had to be done to insure that the baby would not be born out of wedlock.

My eyes returned to the service counter just as the slender, gray-haired chef picked up my order and glanced toward the buxom, gray-haired woman who had paused in the doorway of the dining room just long enough to exchange glances with him. Then she strolled directly to a table near the end of the cashier's counter, where a couple in about the same fiftyish age bracket was seated. After the greetings, she seated herself in one of the two remaining chairs, and the trio entered into a desultory conversation. Since the table was also located near the wall, it was relatively convenient for me to maintain an inconspicuous surveillance of its occupants.

However, it wasn't until I was finishing my fish and chips that it paid off. After a glance in my direction, the buxom lady must have dropped a comment onto the table between her two companions, since they immediately looked toward me. Of course, they could have been looking to one side of or beyond me, but I had thoroughly checked out the area, so I could be the only likely target of that pair of sharp stares.

My observations were interrupted by the waitress, who appeared beside my table and submitted the check. As usual, her attitude was impersonal, which was one of my reasons for returning to the place. Apparently the elderly, American gentleman with the gray beard had never been pointed out to her. It pleased me that she treated me as one of the many nonentities who frequented the place. But I was reasonably sure that the buxom woman had been aware of my presence from my first visit, and that didn't please me. Another reason for returning to the place was to verify that suspicion, and I was firmly convinced that my mission had been accomplished.

Nevertheless, after leaving a small tip on the table, I resumed my observations during the process of arising and strolling past the trio toward the cashier's counter. No one looked up as I passed, but a pall of silence seemed to hang over the table. Meantime, the buxom cashier's eyes appeared to be fixed on some point in outer space. Furthermore, when she arose and moved behind the counter, her eyes never met my probing gaze throughout the transaction. After I received the change, my eyes carefully followed the movements of my fingers as they thrust several small bills into my wallet. Suddenly, with practiced timing, I turned my head, and my sweeping gaze encountered the combined stares of the couple at the table.

Meanwhile, the cashier coolly murmured, "Thank you," without looking at me.

"Hmm," Pancho mumbled, as I thoughtfully turned about and exited through the foyer. "People's reactions are so predictable."

A Business Venture

Since Wilfred had so eagerly volunteered to communicate with a member of the Motel Association regarding a particularly economical source of photocopies, the reproductions of my rough draft had been delayed three whole days while I waited for him to report his findings. Finally, I selected three potential sources from the telephone directory's yellow pages and communicated with them. In response to my request, each of the sources submitted its quotation to me via the telephone line.

Of course, propriety dictated that I confer with Wilfred before I committed myself to a contract, so I went in search of him and found his maintenance cart parked before the open doorway of Unit 9. I peered into the unit, but no human being was visible; however, certain remote sounds indicated the presence of a very active one.

"Good morning, Wilfred!" I called.

A pink head was thrust around the jamb of an open doorway, and Wilfred's voice boomed, "Good morning, Albert. Can I be of some help to you?"

"Of course, you can," I responded with a chuckle to hide my sense of guilt. "It seems that I always interrupt your work when I want the answer to a question. This time it concerns that member of your association. Did you contact him?"

He bowed his head and lowered his eyes, so I immediately suspected that he had forgotten to call the man. "No," he drawled. "However," he quickly added, "I tried several times, but the man was never there."

"It's regrettable that you've had to waste so much of your valuable time," I murmured. "Meanwhile, I've done some research and found that some of Dunedin's businessmen must be either crazy or very greedy, because three of them have submitted quotations that vary by as much as one hundred percent."

His eyes wavered momentarily. "That could be," he granted, "but there are greedy people all over the world, even in America."

"Especially in America," I responded amiably. "The only thing that keeps American businessmen honest is competition, and some of them evade that by getting together and fixing prices. However, even though I've sampled only a few of the services, I am inclined to go along with the lowest bidder."

"You may not be able to do any better," he granted.

"Agreed," I retorted. "But thank you for trying to help. Fortunately for you, I'm going to be too busy to bother you any more today." Then, pivoting on one heel, I strode to Unit 3 and called a taxicab.

Some ten minutes later I had just climbed into the cab when Wilfred dashed madly from the open doorway of Unit 9 and shouted, "Hey, Albert!"

The driver glanced toward me, and, in response to the bidding in my eyes, he reined in the horses.

When Wilfred appeared beyond the open window beside me, he breathlessly gasped, "Which of the companies did you decide to use?"

Such intense interest in the finer details of my personal business struck me as being very unusual, so I reacted with a speculative stare, to which he responded by self-consciously lowering his gaze.

"Well, I was just wondering if it is a reputable concern," he murmured defensively.

Inherent caution urged me to name one of my other two possible sources, but I ignored it and brusquely answered, "Cannon."

After pondering briefly, he nodded sagely and murmured, "Yes, I suppose that Cannon's all right."

The company proved to be located on Filleul Street near the Octagon, but we almost missed the small sign, because the word *Cannon* was overshadowed by the somewhat larger words *Office Machine Services*. When I strolled into what appeared to be a rather large showroom, I found no one in attendance; however, after a brief wait a tall, dark-haired young man stepped through an open doorway in the far wall and approached me.

"Good morning," he greeted me with scarcely any dialect and a somewhat probing stare.

I returned the greeting; then, with a teasing smile, I added, "You were about to be minus one new typewriter, but your entry forestalled the act."

"We have some very fine ones," was his unsmiling rejoinder. "May I show them to you?"

"No, that's not the purpose of this visit," I replied, skeptically studying the new equipment, which was artfully distributed about the showroom floor. "In fact, I may be in the wrong department. Earlier I called this company regarding some photo-copying work, and I talked to a man who submitted a price on it. Is that work done here?"

"You must be Mr. Tyrrell," he suggested.

"And you must be the man with whom I discussed the work," I countered. And he nodded.

"Is that the material that's to be copied?" he then asked.

Glancing down at the battered cardboard box that rested on my left forearm, I nodded and added, "As I stated during our telephone conversation, four collated sets of these two hundred twenty-three sheets are to be copied." Then, after my eyes had futilely searched the room for the area where such work was likely be done, I asked, "Will it be convenient for the work to be done while I wait?"

"Yes," he responded with a faint smile and a gesture toward the roomful of gleaming equipment. "As you can see, there's no one ahead of you."

"Is it to be done on one of these beautiful display models?" I asked incredulously.

"Actually, they are demonstration models," he replied, "but we use them for customer service, too. Meanwhile, let me get someone to set up this piece of equipment," he suggested, tapping the glossy top of a machine that dominated the foreground of the showroom. Then he turned away and disappeared through the doorway in the far wall.

After a moment's thoughtful study, I moved alongside the machine. But my preoccupation with its various gimmicks failed to obscure the fact that the man was absent for an unreasonably long time.

Finally he returned with a very attractive young blonde. "This young lady will copy your work," he murmured. Then he silently faded away. But he must have traveled no farther than just beyond the far wall, because I glimpsed some desks through the doorway before the door closed behind him. Meanwhile, I tendered the box to the woman, who extracted about two dozen of the sheets and absently riffled them.

Then, looking at me, she asked, "Do you want to use both sides of the copy paper?"

"Can you do that and still collate the sheets?" I countered.

"Yes," she answered.

Suddenly I recognized an all-too-familiar air of reserve in her attitude. Simultaneously, José suggested, "Wilfred must have communicated with some-body in this store after we left; otherwise, why the strange attitudes of the personnel?"

"No, that's illogical," protested Pancho.

"Illogical as it is," José retorted, "somebody must have communicated with them, because...."

"Pardon me," the woman interjected, "but did you say yes or no to using both sides of the copy paper?"

Peering at her through a mental fog, I answered, "I'm very sorry, but I fear that

I've been woolgathering." Then, after a momentary pause, I countered, "The use of both sides should be less costly, shouldn't it?"

"Yes," she granted with a guarded glance, "there'll be some cost savings."

"Okay," I muttered, "then let's use both sides."

With an approving nod, she then placed the sheets in a hopper that stood atop the copier. After carefully adjusting some controls, she pressed a button, and the machine sprung into action. Automatically, it made four copies of the first sheet and progressively thrust each of them into one of four separate compartments in a mobile collector, which moved discriminately up or down to distribute them in a collating rack. Then the first original was flicked away, and the second was processed in a similar manner. The uncanny performance was fascinating.

The woman monitored the operations for a few minutes; then she also disappeared through the far doorway. Periodically she returned to insert more originals into the hopper. About twenty minutes later, I was still standing by, when I chanced to notice a bearded man who was veering from the rain-spattered sidewalk toward the entrance of the showroom. Within a few feet of me he slowed to a stop and directed his attention toward the busy copier. Momentarily I suspected that he might be another client, but there was a certain air about him, which seemed to indicate that he was a member of the establishment. Furthermore, he seemed to be particularly aware of me.

Eventually the man directed an intent stare toward me, but it quickly skittered away when I matched it. Then he strolled to the side of the machine and carefully inspected its operations. Apparently satisfied with them, he turned away from it and moved toward a narrow doorway in the wall against which I stood. From the ensuing sounds, I suspected that he made a short telephone call, perhaps to the office beyond the far wall, because the tall man soon emerged from it, cruised across the showroom to the narrow doorway, and pulled the door closed behind him. They remained closeted in the small office for about ten minutes; then the younger man left, and the bearded one sauntered from the office. As he came to a stop beside me, my thoughts were becoming murkier by the minute, because the pattern of behavior was so familiar.

After watching the gyrations of the machine for several minutes, he said, "It looks like you've been pretty busy."

I deliberately feigned an air of puzzlement on the chance that he might drop some clue regarding his strange behavior, but he merely gestured toward the stack of remaining typewritten sheets and added, "You've done a lot of typing. What is it? A report of some kind?"

"Well, sort of," I granted with a forced air of geniality. "However, it's a very rough draft that most people would ridicule, but it could be grist for a book."

While my right forefinger and its opposing thumb involuntarily toyed with the fringes of my beard, I wondered why a relatively handsome younger man would grow a beard unless it was a very unusual one: blue, for example. Obviously, it added many years to his apparent age. Meanwhile, despite my assumed preoccupation with the operations of the machine, I easily detected another probing stare, but I chose not to intercept it. Finally he turned about and sauntered back into the office.

"Obviously, that man has something on his mind," José mused, "but far be it for us to try to straighten him out. From bitter experience, we've learned that it can't be done."

"But I wonder who served as the source of his confusion," Pancho added. "Wilfred? Or was it the Unknown?"

Later the tall man returned to the small office and immediately emerged from it with a large, corrugated-paper box, which he placed on the floor. Then he kneeled awkwardly beside it and removed two quart-size, clear plastic bottles that contained an ominous-appearing, dark liquid.

"Do you have a license to sell that stuff?" I inquired garrulously.

"Sure," he replied. "Why do you ask?"

"Well, it is intoxicating, isn't it?" I countered.

"Yeah," he exhaled, rising with a bottle in each hand. "And it's bad for the blood, too."

After shooting a glance loaded with respect at him, I impulsively exclaimed, "Good shot!"

He accepted the accolade with a pleased smile and turned toward the far doorway.

"You really earned that wicket!" I called after him as he loped away with a smug expression on his clean-cut features.

When the work was completed, the blonde placed a cardboard box on a nearby work table and stowed the four sets of copies in it. Then she turned about and presented the statement to me.

Following a quick glance at its bottom line, I slowly shook my head.

"What's the problem?" she inquired with a defensive air. "It's accurate, because I checked it very carefully."

"I'm not questioning its accuracy," I replied. "I'm questioning the accuracies of the other quotations."

"Why?" she asked. "How much was quoted for the job?"

From a pocket I fished the slip of paper, on which the names of the potential suppliers had been listed along with their quotations. Then, folding it back so that only the quotations were visible, I revealed them to her.

"One hundred and eighty dollars!" she exclaimed. "Wye, we did it for almost half of the middle one, the one hundred thirty-four-dollar quotation. We really didn't do badly, did we?"

"Thanks to you and your suggestion, the job cost about one hundred and fourteen dollars less than the highest quotation," I replied, extending the payment to her.

For just an instant her eyes glowed as if they were about to participate in a smile, but her lips refused to cooperate.

"Such is the power of the enemy," Pancho murmured. Cradling the box on one forearm, I moved toward the doorway into the lightly falling rain.

"That young woman appears to be such a pleasant person," José suggested. "In fact, she seemed to be the type that smiles a lot, but she never smiled throughout our stay, not once."

12

━━━━━━━━━━━━━◄❂►━━━━━━━━━━━━━

Musselburgh

Butcher, Baker, and Candlestick Maker

There were two butcher shops in the tiny Musselburgh shopping area, but I confined my purchases to the neatest and cleanest of them, which was located across the main thoroughfare from its competitor and diagonally across from the motel.

The butcher was a short, sandy-haired man who may have been forty-eight. He was a good butcher; in fact, he appeared to be a much better butcher than most of the union butchers who dominate the Los Angeles scene. His talents may have been somewhat limited, however, since his showcase never displayed filet mignons, Spencer steaks, or New York strip steaks. Of course, it was a bit much to expect to find New York strip steaks in New Zealand. His sirloin cuts were superb, and his T-bone steaks were nice, too, but I never found a porterhouse steak in his or any other showcase during my stay in that island nation.

The man was a specialist at preparing ground and minced meats and at dismembering the carcasses of fowls; however, aside from the entrails, the greasy mutton birds were left intact. Mutton birds? Yes, they were a novelty to me, too. Eventually, I learned that they are not related to sheep in any respect. Actually, they are small ducks, which frequent the backwaters of the South Island's endless shoreline. He must have been a full-fledged butcher, because I observed more than one carcass of a whole sheep, sans its sheepskin coat, hanging on the steel rack that stood in one corner of the shop. He also disassembled the carcasses of hogs, made sausage, and prepared hams, which were cooked in the basement of the shop. The man was something of a character in that he was always cutting up, but it was characteristic of him to be something of a cutup, of course. After all, he was a butcher.

Not only was Wilfred one of the butcher's best customers, but they were close friends. One time, shortly after I discovered the shop, Wilfred and I were discussing the relative merits of the local butcher shops, and he said, "If you want a really good ham, get one of Graham's cooked hams. In my opinion they are even better than packaged hams."

"I was going to buy a piece of ham from him once," I responded, "but when he displayed the cut end of the ham to me, it appeared to be forty percent fat, so I decided against it."

"Oh, that's what I like about them," the big man retorted with what could have passed for a lecherous leer. "That's what makes them so sweet and juicy."

I almost cringed in response to the involuntary mental picture of Wilfred in the process of consuming one of the butcher's cooked hams while a stream of fat-laden juice trickled from one corner of his full, sensuous lips. Obviously, there were several reasons for much of the man's 230 pounds, and all of them must have been related to food.

Late one morning I strolled into the butcher shop, and a buxom, middle-aged woman greeted me with, "Good dye. Whut kin Oy hilp ye with?"

"I suspect that some ground meat might fill the bill," I replied, absently studying her softly waved, brown hair.

"How mooch would ye loik?" she asked, withdrawing a small metal scoop from a bin beneath the counter.

"Hmm," I mumbled, as the cogs in my ivory tower meshed and began to grind furiously. "How about a kilo?"

"We ah mykin' some frish," she murmured. "Would ye moind wytin'?"

"Not at all," I answered. "In fact, I have lots of time but very little money."

To which she smilingly inquired, "Ah ye enjoyin' a noice holidye?" and returned the scoop to the bin. Without waiting for my answer, she slowly moved to the open doorway in the wall between the shop and the back room, where she murmured something to the butcher, who was feeding a meat grinder.

After she returned, I answered, "I'm enjoying the day in spite of the rain, but this is no holiday for me, because I work eight hours every day of the week."

She expelled a long, "Ohhh." Then, pausing as if mentally groping for an appropriate rejoinder, she added, "Will, that keeps ye out o' mischief, doesn't it?"

"At my age it is easy to stay out of mis . . . chief," I responded with an anemic smile.

Emerging with a bulging plastic bag of ground meat, the butcher stated, "This is a kilo." Then he stopped and rested it on one apron-covered knee while his doubt-filled eyes studied mine.

"That's a kilo!" I exclaimed incredulously. "Apparently I should have stuck to pounds, because I know something about them." Then I stepped back and hoisted my belt a bit higher on my paunch.

"Yis," he responded with his ever-ready smile. "How aboot half of it?"

"That's more like it," I answered. "I would never be able to use a full kilo before it began to crawl."

Nodding emphatically, he then placed half of the bag's contents in a metal tray and set it behind the shop's plate glass window. After weighing the remainder, he said, "That will be two-eighty, please." Then, when I submitted the exact change to him, he added, "Thank ye koindly."

After studying his features for several seconds, I asked, "By the way, what's your ancestral background?"

"Huh!" the woman interjected. "Now ye've struck on sumpthin' to talk aboot!" And she began to move toward the doorway of the back room. Meanwhile, both sides of my brain began to squabble over the extent of my faux pas.

While interlocking his hairy arms across the bib of his apron, the little man's eyes absently followed the broad beam of the escapee. Then, turning his merry orbs on me, he loudly answered, "Scotch and West Indian."

Early on, the man had quickly become my favorite Musselburgh character, so I would never have intentionally embarrassed him—or any of the other characters for that matter. Nevertheless, my incredulous "No!" didn't help the situation one bit, nor did the words, "I suspected that you might have evolved from Welch stock, but it never occurred to me that you might be Scotch." Too obviously, I had ignored the West Indian element; consequently, I would have fared better by remaining silent— or in bed.

"Yip," he responded cheerfully. "Moy fathah was Scotch, and moy mothah was West Indian." Then, thrusting forth both arms for my inspection, he added, "But Oy'm pritty whoite, wouldn't ye sye?"

"You certainly are," I replied. But my inner self was being consumed by the flames of a very deep and private hell, so I made a desperate attempt to alleviate the pain by saying, "I'm writing a travelogue on New Zealand, so that's why I ask such questions. The answers help to establish an overview of the nation's society and its culture." But my troubled mind refused to accept those words as justification for the question, so my soul continued to writhe in pain. Fortunately another customer swept aside the one-inch-wide strips of plastic fly guards that hung from the header of the doorway and entered the shop, so I resorted to flight.

After pushing aside the same alternately blue and white strips on my way out, I turned right and traveled about fifty paces to a point where another four paces through the doorway to my right placed me in close proximity to some luscious bakery products, mostly cakes. Actually, the store was not a bakery in the true sense, because the baked goods were baked elsewhere and delivered to it. Furthermore, like the Dairy, it stocked bottles of fresh milk, packaged cereals, frozen foods, canned foods, overripe bananas, and green tomatoes (*tomahtos*). It also stocked a supply of hot meat pies, hot minced pies, and a few hot pastries, which I had found soothed my sweet tooth, so it could be called a bakery.

Normally the store was operated by a man, his wife, and a teenaged daughter. But that family was enjoying a three-week holiday in Cornwall (New Zealand, not England), so grandpa and grandma were substituting for them.

"Good moahnin'," the seventy-year-old man greeted me. "Ah ye managin' to sty out of the rine?"

"No," I replied, "but the rain doesn't bother me, because the drops are so far apart that I can walk between them. This climate reminds me of Vancouver's— Vancouver, British Columbia, that is. There most of the rain falls in the form of a light mist, but it falls all winter long—or so it seems."

"Dunedin could use a lot moah rine this yeah," he muttered. "This is the sicond droyest season on ricord."

Meanwhile, my eyes had been scanning the shelves without success. "I know that they must be here," I mumbled, "but I haven't been able to locate them."

"Locate what?" he inquired, moving from behind the checkout counter toward me.

"Sugar and salt," I replied.

"Heah's some salt," he said, lifting a large, cylindrical container from a nearby shelf and offering it to me.

"Oh, yes," I murmured. "I must have walked right by it. But don't you stock smaller quantities? That would be a year's supply for me."

Replacing the salt container alongside three bottles of Watties Tomato Sauce (ketchup), he scanned the adjoining shelves and said, "No, theah doesn't appeah to be anything smallah, but heah is the shugah." And he plucked a two-pound paper bag of the sweetener from a shelf and offered it to me.

"I'm sorry, but that also is too large," I said. "The quantities must be very small, because my visa limits my stay in New Zealand to just three months."

Looking speculatively toward the elderly lady at the cash register, he called, "Do you know whethah we have any smallah quantities of shugah and salt?"

"Yis," she replied, "some of each ah theah. They ah located...." Then, from a lifetime of experience with the man's shortcomings, she reconsidered the situation, hurried to his side, and quickly removed a small plastic bag of sugar and a tiny cardboard cylinder of salt from the sundries shelf. Then, turning to me, she said, "These ah what you wanted, ahn't they?" I nodded, and she turned on her heels to serve another customer who had appeared at the cash register.

To the man I said, "That has solved my immediate problems, so why don't you assist this lady." And I gestured toward the plump, middle-aged woman who was patiently waiting at the man's shoulder.

"Thank you," she murmured to me. Then, fixing her eyes on the other man, she softly inquired, "Do you have any Hahpic Perfumed Toilet Cleanah?" And the distracted man turned tortured eyes on me for just an instant before leaving to search for it.

After collecting a few other items, I carried them to the checkout counter, stacked them near the cash register, and carefully placed the package of meat alongside them. The old man must have readily located the cleaner, because he quickly returned to the counter and began to plug the costs of my purchases into an ancient mechanical calculator. From afar, his frau cast several doubtful glances in his direction, and their intensity wasn't alleviated when he tore off the tape, placed it on the counter, and began to check it manually against the items.

Looking up at me from his crouched position, he said, "Oy haven't used one of these things litely, so Oy'm chicking the total." And I nodded approvingly. However, after looking toward the growing line of impatient customers, he cast a confused glance toward the two sets of equally confused numerals, straightened up, and arbitrarily stated, "That will be foah dollahs and sivinty-two cints, please."

Since I wished to avoid embarrassing him before the other customers, I silently extended a five-dollar bill and two pennies. The two pennies caused him to pause, but he came up with the proper change. Reaching beneath the counter, he produced a small, corrugated paper box and hurriedly thrust my purchases into it.

Upon my arrival in the kitchen of Unit 3, I removed the items from the box and placed them on the deck of the cabinet. Then, with a stubby lead pencil, I noted their approximate costs on a scrap of notepaper and obtained a total that exceeded seven dollars. While replacing them in the box, I heard the sounds of hurried footsteps from just beyond the open doorway, and my eyes involuntarily swung toward it just as the slender figure of the elderly grocer loomed in it.

"You foahgot yoah meat!" he called to me.

"Oh, yeah, that I did," I responded, absently scratching my head and trying to determine why he considered me to be the culprit when he had packed the box. "Meanwhile, I've discovered that I owe you some more money," I called to him. "If you'll come here, I'll show you why." After he arrived beside me, I resumed: "According to these rough values, I owe you much more than you charged me. Why don't you see what you make of it using the actual costs."

After peering intently at my calculations for several seconds, he murmured, "Wye yis, it does appeah that Oy mide an erroah." Then, one by one, he removed the items from the box and carefully listed their costs in progression. Finally he said, "Oy mike it to be eight dollahs and twenty-foah cints. Do you agree?"

"Yes," I replied, "and that makes a lot more *cents* than before, doesn't it?"

He nodded absently, so the pun apparently swept by him undetected. "Thank you for bringing the erroah to my attention," he murmured.

"And thank you for bringing my meat to me," I said. "Actually, your trip proved to be advantageous to both of us. But let's take this empty box back to the store, where you can give me some change for the large bill that I'm forced to give you in supplemental payment."

While I was returning from the store along the driveway to Unit 3, one of the motel's new guests, a short, broad, and somewhat beefy man, slowly brought his car to a stop beside me and called, "Theah was a tall, elderly man lookin' foah yuh. Did he foind yuh?"

Since he was staring curiously at me, I responded in kind. "Apparently he did," I finally answered, "and thank you for directing him to me." He smiled amiably, waved nonchalantly, released the brakes, and the vehicle rolled away.

"These people never cease to amaze me," Pancho mused as I unlocked the door of Unit 3. "To my knowledge, we've never seen that man before, yet he knew not only to whom he should direct that old man but where our unit is located. I wonder if Wilfred has been bird-dogging us for the entertainment of his transient countrymen."

Later, while I was in the office regaling Wilfred with my account of the man's error, he interrupted, "Oh, so that's what he wanted to see you about. He came in here in a dither and wanted to know where the man with the American accent was located. And I replied, 'Oh, that must be Mr. Tyrrell,' so I showed him where to find you."

"Actually, he wanted to deliver a package of meat that he had failed to pack with my groceries," I explained pensively.

On my way back to Unit 3, José suggested, "That heavyset man must have been in the office during Wilfred's directions to the elderly gentleman. Apparently he couldn't resist an opportunity to listen to the liquid tones of an American accent, so he used our chance meeting on the driveway as an excuse to do so."

"I suspect that I've been unduly suspicious of Wilfred," Pancho concluded uneasily.

Eventually the hamburger was consumed; therefore, returning to the butcher shop, I found the butcher and his youthful helper cutting up, as usual.

"Good morning, Scotty," I greeted him.

"Good dye," he jovially responded. "How is the wroightin' comin'?"

"It's coming as well as can be expected considering the source," I responded with a wry smile.

"Yuh wuh askin' me aboot moy ancistry," he reminded me.

Following an internal wince, I responded with a subdued, "Yes?" and reluctantly allowed my eyes to urge him on.

"Will, one of moy foahbeahs lift Scotland for New Zealand in eighteen foahty-three," he resumed, "and he brought a rose with him."

"A young woman, no doubt," I interjected.

"Yis, he did bring his woife," he granted with a tolerant smile, "but Oy should've made it cleah that it was a rosebush that he brought with him, and he planted it on the fahm he wristed from the wilderness and tinded foah so many yeahs. Howevah, Oy won't go into the details of how it came to pass, but that rosebush is now planted in front of the Old Settlahs Museum."

"That rosebush has to be pretty old by now," I said. "I've been to that museum and found it to be extremely interesting, but I didn't see that specific rosebush, so

I'll have to go back not only to see a hundred-and-forty-year-old rosebush but to make another tour of the museum."

"If yuh do, yuh'll see pictuahs of some of those old Reids on the walls," he said. "They were among the first fahmahs in this area, so they were practically isolated from civilization. They were also confronted by many problims. Foah ixample, in nointeen yeahs, the woife of that fahmah boah nointeen childrin."

"Really!" I exclaimed with a chuckle.

"Will, theah wasn't mooch but fahm work to do in those dyes," he protested defensively. "No towns, no autos, no pived roads—and no tellies."

"I suppose that menopause finally terminated the mass production," I ventured.

"She doyed at foahty-two," he responded with a shake of his sandy hair.

"No towns, no autos, no paved roads, no television, and no hospitals," I muttered.

"And no hospitals," he concurred with a nod.

A thought-filled silence settled on us until I said, "That's an interesting sketch of some of your family's history, and it's something that I can use, but I should pick up a pound of ground meat and let you go back to earning a living."

"Cahn't Oy sill yuh a kilo todye?" he inquired with a light laugh, quickly setting about to assemble my order.

"A pound will do," I responded ruefully.

After placing the package on the counter and cheerfully accepting the payment, he murmured, "Thank yuh koindly and have a noice dye." My right hand grasped the package, transferred it to my left hand, and automatically waved a parting salute just before it swept aside the blue-and-white plastic fly guards.

Later in the day I returned to the shop and found only the butcher's helper. "Oh," I mumbled, "has the butcher left for the day?"

"No," he responded with a shake of his sandy hair. "He's below, but Oy'll call him if you wish."

"No, I don't wish to interrupt his work," I answered. "But you may be able to fill in some of his vital statistics for me."

"Oy'll be glad to hilp, if Oy kin," he responded.

Nodding absently, I said, "Unfortunately, he and I have never formally introduced ourselves, so I don't know his full name."

"Grime Reid," he retorted.

"Grime," I mumbled. "How is it spelled?"

"*G-r-a-h-a-m*," he responded.

"Oh, of course," I rejoined, casting an embarrassed glance at the young man's light-blue eyes. "And I suppose the last name is spelled with two *e*s."

"No, it's spelled *r-e-i-d*," he carefully enunciated.

"Of course," I murmured with another embarrassed glance, "it would have to be spelled that way to be Scotch."

He nodded absently, but it is probable that neither of us was sure of the accuracy of my statement.

"How long has Graham been a butcher?" I asked.

"Twinty-eight yeahs," he replied. "Howevah, he's a boilahmykah boy tride."

"He is!" I exclaimed. Then I suspiciously studied the young man's fair features and interjected, "By the way, I've been remiss in that I first should have requested your name.

"The sime," he replied laconically. "Grime Reid. Oy'm his son."

"That's nice," I remarked, noting the statistic. "A father-and-son business is particularly nice relationship. I assume that you are an apprentice butcher."

"No, Oy completed moy apprenticeship last yeah," he replied. Then, squaring his shoulders, he added, "Oy'm a butchah now."

"Congratulations," I said. "What constitutes a tour of apprenticeship in New Zealand?"

"One thousand owahs," he replied. "But oy got through in a bit liss, because they allow toime off foah good grides. Howevah, an apprentice also has to serve foive yeahs in one plice."

"Who are 'they'?" I countered.

"The Laboah Depahtmint," he replied. "They conduct the classes and give the ixaminations."

"What do they teach?" I persisted.

"The theory of butchery," he answered. "How to break down a beef, the physiology of various animals, knowledge of bacteria, and how to combat thim.... Usually theah's about thirty in each class." And I understood that he meant students, not bacteria.

A small, age-bent man pushed aside the strips of fly guard and entered the shop, so I glanced up from my notes to the young butcher and said, "You've been very helpful, but I won't interrupt your business any longer. Thank you for the information."

"Oy'll be glad to hilp you any toime," he said. "Have a noice dye."

After stepping aside to allow the newcomer access to the showcase, I thrust myself between the swaying plastic strips.

The Mussels of Musselburgh

According to one authority, a mussel is defined as a bivalve mollusk, especially an edible bivalve of the family *Mytilidae* and a freshwater clam of the family *Unionidae*. Furthermore, the word *mussel* is a variation of the Latin word *musculus*, from which the English word *muscle* was derived. Therefore, since no brains or bones were mentioned, a mussel must be just a muscle unless the shell can be considered to be bone. If so, then a mussel must have a lot of backbone, which is one creditable feature at least.

Almost any day in fair weather or foul, mussels were to be found strolling along Musselburgh Rise. Like many of the life forms that inhabit the seashore, they came in various types, shapes, sizes, and colors. The dominant type was Caucasian, which usually exhibited the physical characteristics of the male or female sex; however, there may have been some nonconformists among them. The males tended to be taller and more rugged than the females, but I invariably found the female shapes to be much more attractive than those of the males. The exposed parts of their anatomies, such as the heads, the arms, and the lower limbs, were inclined to be of a pinkish, off-white material, often spattered with tiny, brown spots. In most cases they displayed a blond or auburn topknot, some of which may have been phony, but various shades of brown, black, and gray were also displayed. And others bore white topknots, which contrasted sharply with still others who bore no topknots at all.

About nine o'clock in the morning, following my trip to Office Machine Services, I stacked the initial rough draft of *Misadventures* on a set of its copies, tucked them under one arm, and struck out for the main thoroughfare. After traveling about fifty paces alongside it in a westerly direction, I looked up from my oscillating Hush Puppies and beheld the figure of a tall, elderly man approaching me. Since I didn't recognize him, I assumed that he was a stranger, so I prepared to respond to the customary genial greeting. But when the man was about to pass me, he looked not only at me but directly through me without changing his set expression.

"Hmm," José mused. "Despite the fact that we've never seen that man before, he must be a mussel from this *burgh*."

"Otherwise he would have greeted us as cordially as his neighbors did when we were strangers to them," Pancho chimed in.

Continuing on to the Cavell intersection, I crossed Musselburgh Rise, and another fifty paces took me to the entrance of the branch post office, whose door was obviously locked. I did a few turns around the patio until the relatively young postmaster unlocked the door and pushed it open. Then, seeing that I was reaching for it, instead of holding it open for me, he deliberately allowed it to swing closed before I could catch it.

"That guy has to be far too crusty to be a normal mussel," Pancho muttered as I savagely pulled the door open. "So he has to be some sort of a crustacean—a wood louse, for example."

Meanwhile, I intentionally overshot the attractive young blonde who stood at the first station, but she proved to be the only clerk in attendance at that early hour. Retracing my steps, I caught the postmaster in the act of whispering sweet nothings into her shell-like ear. Suddenly her features were convulsed by hysterical laughter, and they were still distorted by it when I stepped before her. Meantime, she intently inspected my features.

"I would like to purchase one of those heavy manila envelopes for the purpose of mailing these documents to the United States," I stated coldly, pointing toward one of the items displayed high on the wall behind her.

She absently reached into the counter in front of her and withdrew a similar envelope.

"That's too small," I objected.

"No, it is lahge enough," she insisted.

Angrily, I squeezed the documents into the envelope to prove her error.

"See!" she exclaimed triumphantly. "It is lahge enough."

"It's large enough to accept the documents," I conceded. "But how do you propose that I seal it?"

After studying the envelope for a moment, she admitted, "Mybe it is a wee bit too small aftah all." Then, reaching below the counter, she withdrew and submitted a much larger envelope to me.

"But that one is too large," I objected. "Don't you have an intermediate size like the one on the wall?"

She shook her curls.

Removing the documents from the smaller envelope, I then inserted them into the larger one, folded the excess length back over the package, held it up for her inspection, and asked, "Will your people accept this package if I tape it in place?"

She nodded her curls vigorously.

"Okay," I muttered. "Then I'll take this envelope and four of the smaller ones."

"But I have only three smallah ones," she objected.

Fortunately, the wood louse happened to be passing, and he must have overheard the exchange, because he stopped at the next station, fished a fourth envelope from beneath the counter, and rudely flipped it onto the counter in front of me. Lowering my eyes to keep my bitter glare from ravaging the blonde's fatuous features, I paid for the envelopes and left.

"No doubt," José began, "she also could have found an envelope of the intermediate size at that adjoining station if she had not been so inefficient."

"As it is, we must buy more stamps to mail that additional dead weight all of the way to the U.S.A.," Pancho added.

Of course, it wasn't that big an issue, but it served to release the fury that had erupted in me in response to the woman's reaction to the whispered words.

"That blonde is a cute little clam," Pancho observed, as the big door yielded to me. "But she has to be a strange one, because nice female clams don't respond favorably to a male crustacean's salacious remarks, assuming that that was the nature of his remarks. Of course, that conclusion has been drawn from a multitude of similar behavioral patterns observed throughout most of the states within the United States."

From the post office I returned to the main thoroughfare, turned east, and continued to the entryway of the tiny market, where I stopped and tried to recall the two items required to complement my upcoming lunch. My distracted mind finally succeeded, so I stepped into the unusually crowded market and paused to drool over the cakes in the bakery display. After I reluctantly withdrew my eyes from the cakes, they encountered the intent gaze of a more than voluptuous woman who stood some fifteen feet from me. Even though I had never seen her before, she acted as if she knew me. In fact, a smile began to form on her full lips, so I quickly averted my eyes, which automatically returned to the cakes.

Only seconds elapsed before I sensed that the worn, wooden flooring was yielding ominously beneath the soles of my Hush Puppies. My eyes commonly work in close coordination with my feet, so they darted toward the source of the additional strain and detected a pair of large, serviceable shoes. Since the feet of an equally large woman were fitted into them, my eyes involuntarily turned upward and encountered the same intent gaze. Simultaneously, the woman's substantial superstructure was about to ravage my right shoulder as she ostensibly pressed closer to view the cakes. I recoiled as if bitten by an adder—or by an electronic calculator maybe. My effort to escape by stepping around her was foiled by her bulk, because she blocked the entire aisle.

As I turned toward an intersecting aisle, she moved into an adjoining aisle and said, "Pahdon me." By that time I was long gone. In fact, I had snatched up one of the required items on the way, and, after a sharp turn, I picked off the second one.

Meanwhile, she looked wistfully after me and plaintively called, "Ye didn't railly have to go aroun'." But she must not have realized how "railly" big she was.

I had just escaped from that woman to the sidewalk and resumed my homeward journey when an attractive, well-stacked young woman approached me from the opposite direction. After a quick appraisal, I confidently assured myself that this particular mussel would be no problem to me because of her apparent youth. Nevertheless, when she was about to come abreast of me (hers, of course), she suddenly raised one shapely arm and coyly fluffed the curls at the back of her head; meanwhile, her smoldering eyes boldly challenged mine. I was so startled that I almost walked headfirst into a power pole.

After recovering my equilibrium, I tottered to the window of the nearest storefront and peered intently at my reflection. With a baffled shake of my head, I muttered, "This has never happened to me before, so it has to be the beard; it's driving these women crazy. If that little mermaid with the seaweed brains intended to insult me, she certainly succeeded. But if she was challenging me to engage in what is strictly a young man's game, she also insulted me. After all, dignity is very important to us senior citizens. In fact, that's about all we have left, so I won't voluntarily sacrifice mine for anything in this world."

After a thought-filled pause, I added, "And if that chubby abalone thought that she could pick me up in that crowded store without shedding copious quantities of her blood, she had to be insane, because the witches of Musselburgh would have quickly organized a clambake and served her as the entrée. Furthermore, every son of a witch in the community would have eagerly joined in the orgy."

Turning away from the window, I resumed my trek to the motel while absently noticing that a relatively young woman, clad in a rather abbreviated sundress, was slowly moving in the opposite direction along the far side of the thoroughfare. But it wasn't the attractive figure that drew my attention to her; it was the woman's guarded gaze, which was immediately averted when it met my cold eyes.

After some thirty paces I paused at the residential driveway where I habitually stopped before crossing the busy thoroughfare. After checking the roadway on my right for oncoming vehicles, I looked in the opposite direction, and my eyes clashed with still another guarded gaze from the sun-loving mussel, who had paused beside the far curb. Once more, she averted her gaze and turned away.

Yes, it has to be the beard, I mused. It's a ready means of identification, and I really should shave it off, but I'll be *bleeped* if I will. I'll do that when I get to Sydney.

After a simple lunch, I removed a bottle of Wilfred's favorite beverage from the tiny refrigerator, escorted it across the pavement into the office, and set it in a conspicuous spot on the desk. It may have been the soft shuffle of my house slippers, the thump of the bottle on the top of the desk, or Wilfred's constant alertness that drew him to the interconnecting doorway. Of course, his quick glance at the bottle identified the reason for my presence.

"Albert!" he protested, "I told you to stop doing that. My old typewriter isn't worth all of the goodies that you've been bringing in here."

"Yes, it is," I retorted. "You know very well how much it would cost me to rent one, that is, to hire one."

"Well, thank you, anyway," he murmured, hoisting the bottle in one big hand. "But you must promise never to do it again."

"I don't make promises that I don't intend to keep," I stated implacably and eased myself through the partly open doorway onto the concrete slab.

"Albert," he called, "you are a terrible man!"

I immediately sensed that he was deliberately using the ambiguous charge to cover more than just my gift, and the injustice of the act infuriated me. "I am not!" I shouted. "In fact, I am an exceptionally fine man, and I intend to prove it."

"Yeah?" He countered.

"Yeah!" I fired back at him. "Read *Saga of Defiance* after it's published. It will present all of the facets of my life in detail. And any intelligent person who reads it will realize what a fine person I really am." Whirling about, I charged blindly toward my current refuge.

Misadventures at the Dairy

During the remainder of the day I pounded so constantly on the keys of the ancient typewriter that I forgot to insert the usual forty cents in a clean milk bottle and to set it on the concrete slab beside the office. Since the milkman had no reason to leave milk for me, I was forced to carry the empty milk bottle some two blocks along Musselburgh Rise to the intersection of Moana Cres, where the Dairy stood.

As usual, the short, middle-aged brunette was posted behind the checkout counter. Meanwhile, a skinny, teenaged girl stood on the near side of it while the brunette punched the costs of the girl's purchases into the calculator. My tour took me to the opposite side of the store, where I came to a stop in front of the refrigerated cabinet that stood against the wall. Stooping low, I slid aside one of the cabinet's glazed doors and removed a bottle of milk. As I stood erect, the girl took off rapidly from the counter toward the doorway and struck a flimsy, metal display rack, leaving it and its packaged stock on the floor. The little mussel immediately came to a stop and turned horrified eyes toward the brunette, who waved her on toward the doorway. After the girl had gratefully escaped, the woman hurriedly erected the rack and replaced the stock. Since a considerable amount of debris remained on the worn linoleum floor, she removed a battered broom from its nearby hiding place and prepared to clear it away. Meanwhile, I had moved to the side of the checkout counter and deposited the two bottles on it. Pausing in her task, she looked toward me and called, "Please excuse me foah a minute."

"Take your time," I advised her. "I'm in no hurry."

After quickly sweeping the debris into a small pile, she pushed it under the display rack while I restrained a smile. Then she rested the broom against the counter, returned to her post, and said, "That will be foahty cints, please."

I presented a dollar bill to her, and she responded with a handful of small change. "Whoosht!" she exclaimed, running one hand across her brow. "It's hot in heah. Oy'm goin' to tyke this off."

"Go ahead," I impulsively retorted. "I'll let you."

She thoughtfully fixed her dark eyes on me as I moved away toward the doorway; then a muffled giggle drifted down to me on the third of the three rickety, wooden steps.

"What struck her funny bone?" Pancho inquired, as I stepped down onto the sidewalk.

"Ha!" exclaimed José silently. "Al's going to have to be more careful about how he phrases those quick retorts. That gal is no freshwater clam. In fact, I suspect that she is a pretty salty one, so she must have misinterpreted his response to her statement to mean the proverbial G-string instead of that heavy, denim apron."

Such seemed to be the case, because she behaved very coyly when I returned on a similar mission during the following evening. When I placed the succeeding pair of bottles on the counter, I inanely murmured, "Obviously, I forgot to put out my milk bottle again."

"Aw, you ah jist using that as an excuse to come up heah to see me," she retorted flirtatiously. Then she placed the change in my hand with a cloying touch.

"That's the truth," I responded, nonchalantly moving toward the doorway. "But don't tell your husband, because he's much too big for me to tackle."

"The biggah they ah, the hahdah they fall," she countered.

"But I fall pretty hard too," I tossed back to her, skeptically eyeing the three rickety steps.

"Oh, yeah?" her muffled voice drifted down to me as I successfully stepped from the last step onto the sidewalk.

"Now you've gone and done it again," José berated me. "She misinterpreted that stupid remark to mean that you are a pushover. If you aren't more careful, you're going to become an innocent victim of the hands—and maybe of the feet—of that big husband of hers. Wye, he towers over you by six inches; besides, that particular mussel has muscles on his muscles."

Since I failed to set out the milk bottle on schedule during the second day after my trip to the Dairy, I found myself en route to the Dairy again. When I entered the store, the brunette's husband was standing on the far side of the checkout counter serving a team of two customers, who were standing on the near side of it. Meanwhile, three middle-aged women, including the brunette, were slowly approaching along the same aisle in which I was moving. As they were about to pass me, two of them looked directly through me while the brunette cautiously smiled, but her usual coy "Hi!" was conspicuously missing.

When they passed me, an impish impulse compelled me to greet her with a friendly "Hi!"

After a short silence, a firm "Hi!" drifted back to me.

"She has guts," Pancho grudgingly admitted.

"Yeah," José agreed, "but it was very unwise of her to dare the wrath of those two witches."

All of the other customers had left by the time that I arrived at the checkout counter, so I placed the two milk bottles on it directly in front of the tall man and said, "Please wait one minute."

"Of course," he murmured, stowing the empty bottle in a crate. "I wasn't planning to leave."

Turning toward the candy display, I added, "I have only one major vice, and my sweet tooth is clamoring madly for me to cater to it."

After I placed a large, segmented chocolate bar alongside the bottle of milk, the man peered down at it. "Let's see," he began without a perceptible dialect. "You owed me forty cents for the milk, and that will be another two seventy-five." After punching the values into the calculator, he added, "so the total is three dollars and fifteen cents."

"Two dollars and seventy-five cents for a twenty-five cent candy bar!" I exclaimed without apparent malice. "Hmm, it appears that I should have my sweet tooth extracted."

"Surely you can afford one small vice," he protested, while his eyes carefully studied my features. "If it were not for my vices, I would be a wealthy man."

"At least you'll have some great memories," I responded with a tolerant smile. Then, picking up my purchases, I moved slowly toward the open doorway.

"But I can't retire on memories," he called after me.

"But you can retire with memories," I reminded him from the doorway.

A few days later I again failed to set out the milk bottle on schedule; however, when I entered the Dairy, a much younger brunette was seated behind the checkout counter. And I did a quick double take, because she was almost an exact duplicate of the older woman. Meanwhile, a middle-aged man with long, stringy, straw-colored hair was speaking into a wall telephone, which was housed in the small, dark alcove directly opposite her. From the corner of one eye, I watched him. First he paused and stared at me; then he futilely attempted to attract the young woman's attention.

After withdrawing a bottle of milk from the refrigerated cabinet, I strolled into the more remote reaches of the store in search of other purchases. By chance, I glanced up from an inspection of some colorfully packaged chocolate wafers at the instant that the woman's attention was attracted to the alcove. After a prolonged stare, she turned abruptly and looked toward me. However, when her dark eyes met my intent gaze, she immediately lowered them and turned her back to me.

When I approached the counter and placed the bottle of milk and a box of the wafers on it, she coldly accepted payment for them without looking at me.

"Is that man really deaf and dumb?" I brusquely inquired.

"What man?" she countered.

"The one at the telephone," I retorted.

After turning a piercing gaze on me, she tossed the change onto the counter and turned her back to me.

While picking up the change and pensively moving toward the doorway, I was unable to shake an insistent impression that a grim smile was endeavoring to fracture the harsh planes of my rigid features. After descending the three rickety steps, I picked up my pace.

Meanwhile, Pancho inquired, "How can a deaf and dumb man use a telephone? To do so, he would have to be able to both hear and speak."

"Of course, he would," José responded, "but I suspect Al was implying that a normal man doesn't usually employ gestures to communicate with a pretty young woman."

There was a long silence while Pancho digested the statement. Finally, he exclaimed, "Ohhh!" Then there was an enduring silence.

Some time later I was forced to make another trip to the Dairy. When I entered it, the middle-aged brunette greeted me with the usual "Hi," but it lacked the warmth of previous greetings.

"So mother and daughter have been comparing notes," Pancho remarked.

After responding with a friendly "Hi!" I asked, "Is your husband on the premises?"

Her eyes brightened at the prospect of another word game. "Oy've told you to always wite until he leaves befoah you come up heah," she retorted.

"And how am I to know when he leaves?" I countered. "The least you can do is to place a lighted candle in the window to indicate when the coast is clear."

"Will, you didn't see any loighted candle in the window this evenin', did you?" she retorted just as the man strolled into the store from a small, adjoining room.

I grinned fatuously at him. After all, what else could I do? Not only did he have six inches of additional reach on me, but he was thirty pounds heavier and thirty years younger than I.

"Well, how do you like our small, underpopulated country by now?" he inquired informally.

"Fine," I replied. "It's a great country, despite its size, and most of the people are great, too. But the government should ensure that it remains underpopulated by closing its gates to all immigrants." After pausing to construct my thoughts, I resumed: "Furthermore, growth of the population would be stabilized tremendously if the government would subsidize both the purchase of TV sets and the production of public TV programs."

"Why?" he countered with a puzzled expression. Then he fixed his eyes on mine; meanwhile, I silently restrained the enigmatic smile that tugged at my lips. Finally, his eyes lit up like a neon sign, and he exhaled a long, "Ohhh!" Then, turning to his wife, he grinned idiotically.

"You shuah ah slow this evenin'," she murmured tolerantly to him.

After selecting a bottle of vintage milk from the refrigerated cabinet, I moved across the store and placed the two bottles and a one-dollar bill on the counter. While the tall man leaned down and stowed the empty bottle, his wife reached for the bill.

"Wait a minute!" he commanded, rising. Then his eyes slowly swiveled from hers to mine. "Aren't you going to feed that sweet tooth this evening?" he asked.

"Nope," I retorted.

"Why not?" he countered. "You surely didn't have it extracted, did you?"

"Nope," I repeated. "I found that dentistry is too costly, so I decided to starve the *bastid* to death."

He smiled faintly and nodded understandingly. Then, turning toward the woman, he said, "Okay, give the man his change. Apparently one bottle of milk is all that we can squeeze out of him this evening."

She deftly transferred the bill to the till and handed the change to me along with some gibberish.

"I'm sorry," I murmured, "but I didn't get that last part."

To a clearly enunciated "Oy said," she again added the gibberish.

"I'm very sorry," I murmured contritely, "but I still failed to get that last part. In fact, it didn't even sound like English. Are you teasing me?"

"She probably wasn't speaking English," the man interjected. "After all, she never went to school."

She tossed an exasperated glance toward me, then murmured, "Oy meahly said that foahty cints from one dollah leaves sixty cints."

"Aw, I should have understood that," I muttered. "I'm sorry about that stab at your English. Actually, I'm the one who doesn't speak English. I speak 'Americanese.'"

"You speak English with an American accint," she responded with a forgiving smile.

The simple statement startled me, because I had been blissfully laboring under the impression that everybody in New Zealand but me was speaking with an accent.

"Naw, it wasn't your fault," the man belatedly interposed. "Actually, she isn't very smart."

"She is smart!" I retorted with a glance at the lowering storm in the woman's dark eyes. "In fact, she's a very smart kid."

The clouds immediately gave way to a sunny smile, and I breathed a sigh of relief. Of course, I may have erred, but it seemed that the man treated me much more genially after that mild exchange. Apparently he was very fond of his mate, but he certainly had a strange way of expressing it.

"By the way," he resumed, "don't you ever get lonely in that motel all by yourself?"

"No," I replied thoughtfully, "not really. After all, I'm in the best of company."

"But doesn't that get boring?" he persisted with a vague smile.

"No," I answered. "My mind is fully occupied by my work."

"But don't you get tired of work?" he asked. "I do."

"I'm very tired this evening," I admitted, "but there's a good reason for it: I worked from seven to seven. That's why I missed the milkman, and that's why I arrived here so late in the evening."

He shook his head incredulously. "I couldn't stand that," he muttered. "It would drive me up a wall."

"It doesn't bother me in the slightest," I rejoined. "I enjoy work that challenges me. In fact, that may be why I remained in engineering so long. It involved some very complex problems, such as shooting for the moon and propelling the shuttle into orbit about the earth. However, I wasn't involved in the most exotic of those problems, but I solved some very complex ones that were associated with them."

"Surely you have one little vice," he protested.

I sensed that, for some Unknown reason, the man was deliberately prying; nevertheless, I controlled my rancor and admitted, "I have a few little vices, such as a very active sweet tooth, but I have no major ones. Besides, I'm too old to be influenced by the silly impulses that control the behavior of you younger people."

After treating me to a wide grin, he looked quizzically at his wife and muttered, "I hope I never get that old."

"You may be surprised by how rich life can be after the body's chemistry has slowed down to a more tenable rate," I said. Then, picking up the bottle of milk, I sauntered slowly toward the door. After opening it, I glanced back to find the man's head bowed as if in deep thought.

"Apparently you gave him something to wonder about," Pancho remarked, "but what I wonder about is why anybody should suspect another of nonexisting vices."

Then I accelerated my steps, because, among other things, I still had to take a shower.

A Troublesome Guest?

When I swung onto the driveway, a quick glance through the office windows revealed that Wilfred was seated at the desk, so I continued to the open doorway.

"Good evening, Albert!" he exploded with even more ebullience than usual.

"And a good evening to you," I responded with uncharacteristic formality.

"How can I help you this evening?" he inquired with wary eyes.

"You can answer one simple question," I answered.

"And what is that?" he countered.

My eyes locked intently onto his as I asked, "Is my presence here creating too much of a problem for you and Isibelle?"

A startled expression crossed his full features. "Wye, no," he muttered, "of course not. In fact, Isibelle specifically instructed me to be sure to take good care of your unit while she's away on a wee holiday."

"Okay," I drawled, thoughtfully studying the man's evasive eyes, "but if I do become too much of a problem to you people, be sure to let me know, because I refuse to be a source of trouble to anyone."

"Aw, you aren't any trouble at all," he protested uneasily. "Wye, your unit is always as clean when we do it as it was the day that we last did it. You are no trouble whatsoever."

"As you well know," I growled, "I mean real trouble." Then I turned about and strode toward Unit 3.

Sans crainte

Tyrrell

The Only Smudges on My Escutcheon

13

Thumbnail Sketches

The Public Relations Man

After analyzing my question of the previous evening, Wilfred must have mistakenly assumed that some of the fences at Unit 3 required mending, because his characteristic knock resounded from the door shortly before eleven o'clock of the following morning. It sounded so imperative that I impatiently pushed my chair back from the typewriter and approached the door belligerently.

"Good morning, Wilfred," I greeted him almost antagonistically. "What takes you from your work so early in the day?"

"Good morning, Albert!" he shouted in particularly jovial tones. Then he glanced across one shoulder toward Zita, who was wheeling the maintenance cart toward its storage area. "We had only three units to make up this morning," he answered, "so we finished a bit early."

"Then you probably have some time to burn," I surmised.

"Yes," he replied, "so it would seem. Therefore, I decided to come over here and take you away from your work for a while, because you've been working much too hard lately.

"I never work that hard," I said. "True, I do put in a lot of hours, but I use most of them just thinking."

"That's work!" he retorted. "At least it is for me."

Apparently the man had come to visit, so I reluctantly suggested, "Come in and set a spell."

With one wide sandal already poised to step across the threshold, he said, "I will if it won't interrupt something important."

"I never work on anything that important," I blandly informed him, "so why don't you take that chair by the TV set, and I'll continue to use this one." Then, reversing the straight-back chair, I seated myself on it with my back to the typewriter.

"With Isibelle away, it's fortunate that we had so many stay over," he said, settling into the other chair.

Following a shake of my head, I muttered, "It never ceases to amaze me how consistently you keep this place full."

"Well, this is our best season," he observed. "Besides, we have a great many repeats, and they help a lot. But we don't have as many scheduled after the holidays, so we may not be as fortunate then. People are not spending like they have been. They don't have the money after they pay much higher rents and buy groceries at inflated prices."

While my mind cast about aimlessly for a subject to keep the conversation going, a deep silence ensued. "By the way," I finally began, "how well did the auto sale go last week?"

"There wasn't much action," he answered. "In fact, only three cars were sold." Then he looked apologetically at me and added, "I would have invited you to accompany me, but you appeared to be rather busy at the time."

"I would have enjoyed a change of pace," I admitted, "but I was particularly busy at the time."

Meanwhile, a smile tugged insistently at one corner of my mouth in response to a mental picture of Wilfred's appearance during the morning after his return. He always claimed that he didn't consume alcoholic beverages, and, since there was no evidence to the contrary, I believed him. But he appeared to be so beat during that particular morning that José demanded an explanation for it. Consequently, Pancho immediately suggested: "He might have deliberately left Al in Unit 3 so that he, Wilfred, could have an illicit fling far from the prying eyes of his fellow mussels."

"But we shouldn't condemn ourselves for such suspicions," José responded, "because they serve to support still another suspicion that, despite a lifetime of bachelorhood, he possesses normal impulses."

"Did you read that bit in the morning paper about the policeman?" Wilfred injected into my thoughts.

"Yes," I replied, "but such illegal antics don't surprise me one bit. In fact, they don't begin to compare with some of the incidents in the Los Angeles area. For example, shortly before I left the city of the angels, five police officers in the Hollywood precinct were indicted on charges of functioning as a burglary ring while they were off duty."

The man's only responses were a scowl and a shake of his head, so I added, "In another outlying area, some police officers were not only suspected of complicity in manslaughter but of trying to cover it up. Allegedly, one of them tried to subdue a young, black prisoner with a choke hold, and it killed him. It was claimed that other officers collaborated with the killer in an attempt to simulate a suicide by stringing up the body in the dead man's cell."

Wilfred's pink features blanched and expressed appropriate horror, but, dissatisfied with those effects, I resumed: "According to one macabre report, two San Fernando police officers were charged with having accepted a contract from a woman to murder her husband."

"Absolutely incredible!" he exclaimed.

"True," I agreed, with some satisfaction, "but something like that is always going on there. If some cop hasn't shot a child or an unarmed suspect on schedule, then another one compensates by committing a crime of equal magnitude, such as throttling a prostitute because she refuses to submit to him without an advance payment."

"Why is there so much crime there?" he asked. "Here the police are supposed to protect the citizens, not rob and murder them."

"It may not be quite as bad as it seems," I suggested. "In fact, there are some obvious reasons why there appear to be more police crimes in that area than there are here. And one of them has to be the relative sizes of the police forces. The size of the Los Angeles police force probably exceeds that of the combined law enforcement agencies of New Zealand by a factor of two. It has to be that much larger, because it serves a city with a population that's more than two times the population of this entire country. But I suspect that New Zealanders have much higher moral standards than those of the Angelanos; consequently, New Zealand's police officers probably have higher moral standards than those of the L.A. police officers, because the members of both forces are selected from their respective societies."

A particularly irritating expression of egotistical satisfaction spread across the man's broad features. But he didn't accept the opportunity I allowed him to expand on the subject, which was uncharacteristic of him.

"Unfortunately, too many wrong numbers are attracted to law enforcement careers," I resumed. "No doubt the lavish retirement benefits awarded by the Los Angeles City Council entice many recruits, but the opportunities for graft probably appeal to some, and others are attracted by the personal power derived from a policeman's badge."

"That's it!" Wilfred interjected.

"That's what?" I countered.

"The personal power!" he retorted. "That attracts many of them, especially the young recruits. They seem to be particularly addicted to the use of their power."

After turning a thoughtful gaze on him, I took off on another tack: "In my country politicians are even more addicted to applying power. Obviously, public offices also offer many opportunities for unscrupulous officials to squeeze graft from equally unethical government contractors. Consequently, the poor taxpayers get stuck for the cost of some stupid project, such as a dead-end tunnel. That has to be the prize political white elephant of the century. It's incredible that the voters continue to permit such political chicanery. Furthermore, it's incredible that they vote the same crooks back into offices, where they can repeat such devious acts."

"I don't know anything about that tunnel," he muttered, "but we have our share of graft, too."

"According to news reports, that tunnel is in Los Angeles," I said, "and it's supposed to be one of the pet projects of the mayor and certain members of the city council. They have others, such as the Rapid Transit System, which is projected to cost billions of dollars. Cost records compiled on similar projects, which have been completed and are operating in San Francisco and Washington, D.C., reveal that the initial costs will never be recovered. Furthermore, the system's maintenance costs will exceed its revenues, so the taxpayers will have to subsidize its operation."

"But the taxpayers surely must support such projects," Wilfred protested. "Otherwise, how could the politicians obtain the money for them?"

"They pay some engineering firm a fancy sum to conduct a study," I replied. "The firm's glowing report cons the taxpayers into subscribing to the project. After all of the chips are down, the taxpayers discover that the project doesn't do all that it was projected to do; furthermore, they discover that it has cost twice as much as the study predicted. I know about those things, because I worked for the U.S. Army Corps of Engineers during the time it was constructing the dams for the Los Angeles Flood Control District, and those dams always cost twice as much as predicted. It was a case of deliberate deception. After all, who's going to stop building a dam after it is half completed? It just doesn't make sense—or dollars—to stop."

"Why do the politicians generate such deals?" Wilfred asked. "Surely the voters rebel against such tactics."

"Huh-uh," I grunted. "Obviously, such projects provide a tremendous opportunity for political graft, so the politicians smoothly con the voters into believing that someone else is responsible for the problems, probably some politician in the opposing party. With such rich plums for the picking, it's no wonder that some wealthy politicians gamble their own funds, along with millions more in campaign funds, to win public offices."

"But they claim that they wish to serve society," Wilfred interjected with a wry smile.

"They intend to serve only their own selfish interests," I muttered disdainfully. "In fact, I strongly suspect that American politics is one of the most rewarding financial careers in the entire world."

"Our politicians appear to do pretty well for themselves, too," Wilfred insisted. The man appeared not to particularly relish having his small country's status subordinated to that of any other country, even to the extent of its political chicanery. "But our traffic officers surely do love to exercise their power," he added.

I carefully restrained an insistent smile that kept responding to a nagging suspicion of the reason behind the man's repeated references to the subject.

"In fact, I was exposed to some of it very recently," he growled.

And the impulsive smile suddenly burst it bonds. To cover it, I placed one palm over my mouth and said, "Fortunately, traffic officers who have stopped me in the States have always been reasonably courteous. Since they hold relatively low positions on the police power pole, few motorists try to bribe them, because those who do can end up in jail, so potential graft isn't likely to appeal to recruits who expect to become traffic cops."

"Maybe that's what makes some of our officers so obnoxious," he suggested. "No graft."

The involuntary smile returned. After firmly subduing it, I resumed, "My few traffic tickets covered all of my direct brushes with the law, because I've always tried to be a law-abiding citizen. Not one of those tickets was earned by a deliberate infraction of a law." Then, fixing my eyes firmly on his, I added, "But that doesn't preclude the possibility that I might have unintentionally stepped on some autocratic little bureaucrat's toes, does it, Wilfred? A bureaucrat who might have vengefully and illegally employed his power to initiate a fiery hell on earth for me, a fire he well knew that other little bureaucrats would habitually feed as long as I live."

His eyes wavered uneasily and turned toward the open doorway. Meanwhile, the ensuing silence seemed to echo and reecho through the room.

Counterattack

I hadn't intended to drive the man away with a discussion of my lifelong problem; I had merely used some hard-nosed words to rebut his unforgotten attack of the previous evening. Nevertheless, I resolved to employ some of my own brand of public relations pap, but none of it immediately came to mind. However, from the most remote reaches of outer space, an orbiting inspiration suddenly swung earthward and plunged into my brain. Since such extraterrestrial visitors rarely invade software dominated by voids, only a couple of curious brain cells inspected it. Concluding that it was, indeed, a sound immigrant, they decided to give the motel's P.R. man a taste of his own medicine, so his almost sullen silence was ignored, and the program was launched.

"Wilfred," I began with overdone ebullience, "would you be interested in some thumbnail sketches of a few of the more salient features of my upcoming autobiography? Or do you have that much time to waste?"

"Well," he began tentatively, "I really don't know, because I've never viewed a thumbnail sketch of a regurgitated autobi. . . ."

"Far enough!" I shouted. "That's my routine." Then, in lower tones, I asked, "Would you or wouldn't you?"

"I have the rest of the day," he responded with an air of overt eagerness.

After gazing pensively at him for a moment, I sternly warned, "This is to be no soap opera, I'll have you know."

"All right, all right!" he retorted. "I just wanted you to know that, since Isibelle is away, I've got lots of time."

A smile pried at my lips, because it was so typical of him to lounge about and seek opportunities to chat with the tenants while his partner was away. Then my errant thoughts were blasted far out into Otago Bay by the strident clamor of the telephone's buzzer.

While lugubriously extracting himself from the depths of the easy chair, Wilfred looked at me with a frustrated expression and obediently moved to the open doorway. Pausing there, he looked back and promised, "I'll be right back." Then he dashed toward the office.

Meantime, my mind began to search through a clutter of historical records for a logical point from which to launch the first of the proposed minisagas. Eventually, it turned up the semester when I enrolled in a psychology class at the university for the primary purpose of learning some of the whys and wherefores of human behavior. I quickly discovered that the class dealt almost exclusively with very elementary psychology, such as the human nervous system and its responses to external stimuli, so my purposes were stalled.

About midway of the term, the professor gave the class a university-level intelligence test, and my Intelligence Quotient (IQ) shocked both of us: the professor, because it vastly exceeded the caliber of my classwork; and me, because it didn't exceed the highest attainable level. Consequently, I shrugged it off as being a lot of nonsense.

Impatient with the slow, progressive nature of formal education, I impulsively decided to do some research on the more advanced aspects of psychology in my own inimitable style. The decision was more typical of a naive freshman than of a sophisticated sophomore such as I, but I made the decision anyway.

As a high school athlete, I had been liberally exposed to both the psychology and the physiology of other male athletes during the heat of competition, as well as in the heat of subsequent hot showers, so I quickly concluded that more male psychology would bore me to death. But I had been exposed to very little female psychology, and female physiology was still an intriguing mystery to me. If, however, I had been exposed to female athletes under the same disillusioning conditions—during the heat of competition and in the heat of the subsequent hot showers—no doubt I would have discarded the entire project for the same reason.

As it was, I had never been exposed to females under any conditions until my last three semesters in high school. Furthermore, the few girls to whom I was exposed remained just as chaste after those exposures as they were before I chased them; therefore, they must have been very fast women, indeed, because I was the school's star sprinter. Consequently, my curiosity regarding the psychology and physiology of females hadn't abated one whit by the time I entered that university classroom. In fact, it may have grown apace under the influence of my speculative fantasies, so curiosity could have been the actual reason for my proposed research.

Considering that background, it isn't surprising that my first extracurricular research was to be devoted exclusively to the psyche of the female university student. But I soon dropped that particular aspect of the project, mainly because I lacked the courage to get that close to a female university student; besides, I wasn't fully convinced that they possessed psyches. I was about to drop the entire project, because part-time employment, study time, and tightly scheduled classes consumed practically all of my available time. But a few coy glances and some flirtatious flips of this and that drew me into closer associations with some of my subjects: a classmate or two and one flirtatious number that I encountered in the university's library.

Strictly from observation, my research turned out to be very enlightening, but it also disturbed me, because I quickly discovered that few of those young women appeared to be the angels they were cracked up to be. For example, they invariably ignored the age-old practice of being introduced to a strange man by a mutual acquaintance. In fact, many of them made bold and obtrusive overtures to young men whom they wanted to meet. Then, after succeeding, they flirted outrageously with them.

I was unable to determine what the little darlings hoped to gain by such behavior, except a husband perhaps. But that had to be a long shot during those economically troubled times, since few of the young men were employed. Unemployment stood at an all-time high of 25 percent, and young people occupied the bottom notch on the employment totem pole, so an employed young husband was hard to come by, even by theft. Consequently, many of their parents had mortgaged the family homestead to send them to the university, where they could obtain a sheepskin that might serve them a better purpose than the one on the barn door.

Curiosity induced me to venture into that maelstrom, even though I didn't intend to be trapped into matrimony until I graduated from the university. Of course, the normal yen for a mate may have drawn me into it, too, but I may have been influenced by some of my peers' boasts of sexual conquests. But when I managed to maneuver a subject to the point where such a conquest seemed imminent, I could never pursue the objective further, because I had been saving myself for a particularly wonderful dream girl: a girl the likes of whom had never been created and whom, I now realize, could never be conceived by any pair of mortal human beings.

Furthermore, I had been strongly influenced by the advice of my grandfather during one of his periodic visits to our home. I always suspected that my mother induced him to substitute for my father, whom I, at seventeen, had not seen in seven years. Whatever the driving force, my grandfather appeared near the spot where I was weeding the garden and eyed me uneasily. Finally he muttered, "Very likely you are interested in girls by now."

After a momentary stiffening, I resumed the task, but my eyes refused to meet his, because he was invading my privacy. Since I respected him too much to point it out to him, I maintained a stolid silence.

Apparently he viewed the matter in the same light. Nevertheless, he cleared his throat and said, "When you finally get around to going with a girl, be sure to pick one that you would be proud to marry."

With that sound advice and my own dreams, I found it impossible to pick a girl, even for experimental purposes. While I was saving myself for that wondrous creature of my dreams, I assumed that she would be saving herself for me like any honest dream girl would.

The First Installment

I was trying to assemble those thoughts into a logical order when I heard the slap-slap-slap of Wilfred's flat sandals against the pavement as his quick steps brought him closer to my doorway. Then my mind slipped some cogs and whirred futilely in a frantic effort to organize those memories into an acceptable presentation before he arrived.

"Okay," the big man thundered as he stepped across the threshold, "I'm ready for the first installment."

"I intend to start with the time when I was still attending the university," I began thoughtfully and came to an abrupt stop. Obviously, no public relations man was I, because I was floundering like a ship with a broken rudder in turbulent, storm-tossed seas. But there was a reason for that: Suddenly I had arbitrarily decided to drop the bit about the research program, because I was sure that my audience of one would never understand it.

"Start wherever you want," he said with an airy wave of his hands. "It's your story."

After a brief session with the lads, I recklessly began: "At twenty-two I was still a virgin." Then I stopped, glanced speculatively at him, and added, "Not many men can honestly claim that."

"Oh, I don't know about that," he protested. "I. . . ." Then he stopped as if suddenly reluctant to reveal his thoughts.

I surreptitiously studied his features as my mind reevaluated a recurring suspicion that he might be impotent. Of course, such a man could maintain total celibacy throughout his lifetime with ease, so he might view a period of twenty-two years as an insignificant sacrifice to the altar of virtue, especially when it was measured from birth.

Finally, in response to his impatient stare, I said, "Of course, I intended to terminate that state with my virgin bride." Then I paused and slowly added: "But that woman turned out to be no virgin."

He submitted a wry expression but no condolences. Then, as I was about to continue, the buzzer summoned him again. Once more, he extracted himself from the grasp of the chair and hurried toward the open doorway, where he paused, turned toward me, and drolly said, "I'll be right back, so don't go on without me."

I raised both hands and thrust their palms toward him in a pushing motion, so he took off at a gallop, and his thundering footfalls literally drowned out the strident tones of the buzzer.

My mind returned to the philosophies of yesteryears, one of which gave it pause: the oft-debated philosophy that it may be better for a young man to sow a few wild oats before he marries, provided, of course, that none of them germinate. Even a lifetime of jarring experiences had not yet convinced me of the soundness of that liberal psychological opinion, despite the fact that shortly after marriage I began to wonder if other women were different from my new bride.

I had good reason to wonder, because something seemed to be missing from the physical relationship. Finally, the young woman volunteered the information that she wasn't properly adapted physically for mutually satisfactory conjugal relations.

At the time the problem appeared to be insurmountable, but she had obtained a book on the subject, a thin, blue book, which I eventually came to detest. According to its author, a psychiatrist, about 40 percent of American women possess similar problems, ranging in severity from limited sensitivity to total frigidity. Where limited sensitivity was the problem, he recommended stimulating foreplay, but he warned that it should not be continued to the point of culmination. Even though the recommended solution contributed to several successes, I wasn't convinced that a normal relationship had been experienced, so I resumed my research on a minor scale.

Subconsciously I probably intended to experience the reactions of a properly constructed partner, even at the cost of all-important loyalty to my legal partner. However, when a likely opportunity finally presented itself, I found that I was unable to cheat on her. Of course, I expected total loyalty from my mate, and since my code of ethics didn't include a double standard, my conscience must have foreclosed on my selfish intentions. Therefore, I forsook such activities and concentrated on the most effective forms of foreplay, but I adhered strictly to the author's mandate.

Those thoughts were so engrossing that I failed to hear Wilfred's noisy approach until he stepped across the threshold.

"Okay!" he shouted, bearing down on the easy chair, "Let's get on with that installment."

I looked absently at him while my mind was summarizing those thoughts, and it immediately discarded them, because Wilfred was not the type of man who could possibly understand either the problem or its recommended solution.

Emergence of the Unknown

Then my mind suggested an account which I was sure that he wouldn't understand, because I didn't fully understand it myself. Nevertheless, I began with: "It started some time during the second year of our marriage."

"What started?" he countered immediately.

"Something that seemed to be detrimentally affecting our many friendships," I pensively answered. "And some of those friendships extended all of the way back to the time when we were classmates in high school. In fact, the influence became so intense that I finally accepted employment in the highway department of another state. There, relations with our new neighbors and my professional associates returned to normal for a while, but they gradually deteriorated into similar attitudes."

"What attitudes?" he interjected.

"Attitudes of reserve and even avoidance," I muttered.

The man suddenly found something of great interest in the pattern of the carpet to study, and he continued to study it in a deep silence. Meanwhile, I resumed: "Once more, I sought and found employment in the highway department of an even more remote state, where I became the chief draftsman of the Highway Planning Division. There our daughter was born alongside more evidence of that devastating influence."

I paused and glanced toward my listener, who was perched precariously on the edge of his chair with his eyes fixed on me, but they quickly returned to their study of the carpet. Turning to the big window, I absently stared through it at the sun-drenched pavement. Then, with a deep sigh, I said, "During the next four years I changed employment several times but always to no avail, because that ugly influence always sought us out, and we inevitably ended up with no friends. Finally I became so concerned about the future of my small family, especially the future of my daughter, that I journeyed from Seattle along the entire West Coast in search of a different type of employment. The reason: again to escape from that indomitable influence, which I suspected was being transmitted by people whom I listed as references on my applications for employment. Even during that trip I invariably detected its onerous presence whenever I was about to accept one of those different types of employment. Finally, in sheer desperation, I appealed to the Los Angeles office of a highly publicized bureau of the federal government."

"But what was . . . ," Wilfred began; then he subsided into silence.

"What was the reason for all of that?" I substituted. "That's what I asked the government agent to investigate. Later he claimed that he had investigated it and was unable to find any reason for it. Furthermore, he claimed that my name was not to be found in any of the police files."

"How about the files of that agency?" Wilfred asked. "It sounds to me as if you might have suspected the agency of being the source of your problem."

"That thought had occurred to me," I admitted. "After all, the Unknown influence had to cross many state lines to reach those remote states. When I insisted to him that there actually was such an influence, he claimed that it was a figment of my imagination. Eventually I arrived at the conclusion that the agent was the one who was suffering from delusions, because he proposed a weird and absolutely illogical program."

"What was the nature of it?" he asked.

"That's a long story," I replied, "and it will be described in concise detail in my upcoming autobiography."

"There's that regurgitated autobiography again," he muttered.

Bestowing on him what might be called a jaundiced look, I resumed: "At first I flatly rejected the program, but the man threatened to close the door on any further appeals to that agency, so I reconsidered it."

"That sounds like blackmail," he interjected.

"It was blackmail, bureaucratic blackmail!" I retorted angrily. "But I had no recourse but to accept it; besides, he did promise that I would never regret accepting it."

"It sounds like you couldn't lose," Wilfred ventured.

"That's what I thought," I said, "but it turned out to be the biggest mistake of my entire life."

"Why?" he asked.

I paused while briefly considering what would have to be a long, detailed explanation and immediately tossed it aside. "It's too long a story," I answered, "but I advise you never to trust a bureaucrat."

"Why?" he repeated.

"For the same reason that I just stated," was my impatient reply. "But I can tell you this: About two years later someone, a total stranger, tipped me off that I had been royally double-crossed."

"How?" the man inquired.

"It would take too long to explain," I responded tolerantly, "but it'll be fully explained in my. . . ."

"In your regurgitated autobiography," he interjected.

Ignoring him, I resumed: "According to my code of ethics, a promise is an ironbound pact, as sound as a legal contract, on which I will never renege. Consequently, when I discovered that the agent had defaulted on his promise, I was justifiably furious, and, in a mood of particularly high dudgeon, I made a solemn promise to myself that I would employ every legitimate tactic available to me in an all-out war on the furtive forces behind that obscure and destructive influence."

"Including that bureau?" he inquired.

"Definitely!" I retorted. "It was with that in mind that I belatedly began my autobiography about four years ago."

Frowning deeply, he murmured, "It doesn't seem right for anybody to defy law and order."

"What law and order?" I countered. "This is a case wherein those who are supposed to support the law are out of order. Persecution isn't sanctioned by the laws of either of our countries; yet that's what I've been subjected to in this country as well as in mine."

His eyes slithered away from my stabbing stare and again sought refuge in the carpet's pattern; then he lowered his head as if in deep thought. Finally, raising it, he said, "I'm still not sure that you took the right course." But his eyes refused to meet mine.

"How else does one combat such high-handed tactics?" I countered. "Mahatma Gandhi did it with passive resistance, and my campaign has not differed substantially from his. Actually, I patterned mine from his. Of course, I haven't gone on a hunger strike," I resumed more mildly. "I like gourmet food too much to do that. And I've never resorted to a breechcloth, because a diaper probably would never fit my fat fanny."

The tactic worked as I had intended that it should, because Wilfred responded with a relieved chortle. Then his eyes resumed studying the carpet.

"Actually, there are few differences between the ways in which my civil rights have been breached and the ways in which the civil rights of Andrey Sakharov and Anatoly Scharansky have been treated by the Russian KGB." I said. "Of course, I'm still free to travel around the world at will, but those same Unknown influences appear to have been extended to cover me while I am abroad, so freedom to travel doesn't represent real freedom in any sense of the word. Furthermore, I haven't been imprisoned, as they were, but that can be done on a minute's notice. Other law-abiding American citizens have been thrown into prison on the flimsiest of charges, so it could happen to me, too, especially if I were to irritate some stupid bureaucrat too much. Don't ever discount the power of any government bureau over the individual. There are plenty of instances wherein petty little bureaucrats of the Internal Revenue Service have. . . ." But my harangue was interrupted by an automobile, which swung past the window and stopped in front of the office.

Glancing apologetically toward me, Wilfred said, "I'm sorry, but I'll have to leave for a while, because that probably is the party who made the last call."

I nodded, but my mind was already retrieving more bits and pieces of the past from its ancient files. Once more, it suffered through the throes of arriving at a vital conclusion that appeared to be the inevitable solution: that a divorce could salvage my daughter's future. Fortunately, fate intervened in a very devious way, so a divorce was finally granted despite my mate's bitter opposition. But I was bitter about it, too, because my code dictated that that marriage should have been a lifetime commitment. Nevertheless, the fact that my daughter would no longer be threatened by the far-reaching evil influence was a great relief to me. Like most divorces of that era, large alimony and child support payments consumed most of my income, so the lack of sufficient funds reduced my social life from practically zero to zero.

Eventually I succeeded in increasing my income to the point where it would support a limited social life; actually, let's call it a limited psychological research program. But the program assumed a very different pattern from the original one in that the physical aspects of my subjects also were included in it. Under its new guise, I soon discovered that, physically, women are very similar, but their sexual reactions vary delightfully. Consequently, the fantasies that I may have entertained regarding physical differences were completely dissolved. Furthermore, I found that physical involvement with a subject without emotional involvement served to dilute and degrade the relationship; therefore, I was given to long periods of total abstinence. In fact, there were times during which I had to force myself to continue my campaign against those furtive Unknown forces.

Pausing, I peered through the big window at Wilfred, who was articulately introducing a pair of new tenants into the unit directly across the driveway from mine. Mentally I complimented him on being a particularly good public relations man. Then my mind returned to its self-appointed task.

The Smudges

To my knowledge, despite the large number and variety of my concubines, only two of them ever left even a smudge on either my escutcheon or my shining, stainless steel armor. Furthermore, the responsibility for one of those smudges appeared to rest on the shoulders of what must have been a particularly despicable and loathsome type of interloper. The other may have derived from just the association if, indeed, a smudge actually was deposited.

I happen to be one of many conservative Americans who believe that the First Amendment to the Constitution has been grossly misinterpreted by the courts. Since the authors of that amendment were very moral men who exercised considerable self-discipline, it seems unlikely that they intended to grant to anyone the right to publish and distribute salacious reading materials in this country. In fact, the sparsely worded amendment doesn't specifically permit that right, but our highest legal authorities have arbitrarily concluded that it doesn't deny it either, so the morals of our adolescents are being corrupted by a flood of such material.

Likewise, many of the judges in our highest courts have claimed that they don't know the difference between right and wrong. But I do. Consequently, if this page and any of its directly associated pages are likely to come to the attention of juveniles or to be distributed in public places, such as libraries, they shall be removed from the document.

Since I am a very private person, it wracks my inner being to reveal such personal experiences. In fact, my inner being has been subjected to constant tortures during the preparation of this book, but I have endured them because someone has to counterattack Big Brother. Otherwise the people of this nation and their posterity will never enjoy the blessings of liberty and justice that the Preamble to the Constitution so profoundly subscribes.

Of course, this question may come to some minds: Are such inputs really necessary to achieve the objectives of this document? The answer is yes, they are essential to it, but an attempt has been made to present them in a reasonably cultured yet informative manner without titillating the mind of the reader; therefore, the material is not intended to be pornographic. In fact, it is presented in the same formal manner that prevailed during the era of Sir Francis Bacon and William Shakespeare.

Smudge One The first of the episodes involved an attractive blonde waitress who was about fifteen years younger than I. She was a vivacious little pixy with clear, blue eyes and a peaches-and-cream complexion. And she quickly inserted herself into my affections even though she proved to be one of the unfortunate 40 percent. Nevertheless, I employed the same manual technique that I had developed for a similar problem, and I succeeded where others must have failed; consequently, she clung tenaciously to me.

This was unfortunate, since it conflicted with my policy of forming no alliance that would interfere with my ongoing practice of constantly changing female associates in open defiance of the Unknown. But I didn't permit it to interfere entirely with that practice. Despite the fact that she apparently knew of the other associates, she still clung to me.

However, I was finally forced to conclude that she must have formed an alliance with the Machiavellian Unknown, because she began to buzz my telephone after each of my other liaisons and subtly refer to it. Obviously, she could not have acquired the knowledge from local gossips or from her own observations, since she lived on the opposite side of the city, so she must have acquired it from some Unknown source that had to be closely monitoring my activities. It was during one of those telephone conversations that she finally laid down the ultimatum: "You must stop these activities, or I won't be seeing you anymore."

"Okay," I immediately retorted, "then we won't be seeing each other anymore," and gently replaced the instrument.

I suspect that I was wise to accept the ultimatum, because she was very easily influenced; consequently, she could have been deliberately manipulated by the Unknown to serve its nefarious purposes.

Some time later I received a note from her bearing the words: "I enjoy being with you so much that I have changed my mind. However, another very good reason is that you are a king in bed. Please call me."

Of course, my heart was touched, but I didn't call her. If she expected that statement to tease my ego, she had used the wrong tactic, because I didn't consider any man to be a king in bed when his success was based on years of experience in employing a particularly deft middle finger whose tip probably possessed more sensitivity than her clitoris. But that technique may have been instrumental in creating one of the smudges on my escutcheon.

Since the minds of particularly moral readers may be unfavorably impressed by certain details of the upcoming episode, they are presented as discreetly as possible in the following one-act play. The primary purpose of the play is to describe a true-to-life relationship between normal human beings in which the potentials for misinterpretation by the warped mind of an interloper become readily apparent. The visible cast is strictly nonunion, but it becomes fully unionized before the curtain falls. Of course, the interloper is nonunion and remains so. To protect the guilty, the names of the actors have been changed.

* * * * * * * * * * * * *

THE TRAGEDY OF THE UPSIDE-DOWN BED

[DRAMATIS PERSONAE]

ROMEO, King of Hearts.
JULIET (Honey), beautiful, blonde courtesan.
INTERLOPER, Phantom of the Night.

[SCENE: Inglewood, California, U.S.A.]

ACT I

SCENE I. [*Corner of bedroom with headboard of bed against wall on viewer's
left. On viewer's right, narrow passageway separates far side of bed from wall in
which window overlooks foot of bed. Two obscure draperies are drawn across
window, but sliver of dim light passes between them and illuminates toes of bare
foot, which connects to vaguely outlined male figure reclining along far side of bed.
Head of figure is supported on palm of hand, whose arm is buried in pillow. Figure
appears to be watchfully waiting for somebody to appear from beyond closed door
near headboard on viewer's left. Finally, door swings slowly open, and gradually
expanding band of light casts blue-gray path across otherwise colorless carpet.*]
    Romeo. [*From bed.*] You certainly took your sweet time.
    Juliet. [*From doorway.*] But you would want me to brush my teeth thoroughly,
wouldn't you?
    Romeo. Why didn't you just put them in a glass of water. That would have been
a lot quicker.
    Juliet. Wye, you insufferable boor, you!
    [*Winsomely curved outline of small female figure blots out most of light, which
turns curly topknot into crown of spun gold. Meanwhile, figure on bed is too
occupied pulling bedspread over nudity to notice picturesque tableau.*]
    Romeo. Turn off the *bleeped* light! [*In more polite tones.*] Please, Honey.
    [*Derisive giggle from doorway. Then light flicks off, and female figure charges
blindly through dimness and catapults onto male figure.*]
    Honey. Ouch! [*Splat!*] Don't pinch so hard, Romeo. That really hurt.
    Romeo. I'm sorry, Honey. Here, let me kiss it well.
    Honey. No! I know you much too well to fall for that. You'd bite it.
    Romeo. That's what they are made for. After all, almost every man has been
sustained by similar ones during his early life.
    Honey. Yeah, but he didn't have teeth then.
    [*Sounds of cuddling and fondling ensue.*]
    Honey. Whew! It's hot in here! Let's open the window.
    Romeo. The window is open. We're just too close together.
    [*Sounds of much tossing and turning.*]
    Romeo. [*From bottom of bed.*] Whoops! Wrong side. I forgot that I'm a rightie.
[*Slowly and suggestively slides across partner's supine figure and assumes similar
position on her right. Stretches both arms over head, interlocks fingers, and rolls
palms outward with loud popping sounds.*]

Honey. [*As right palm strikes Romeo's right thigh with loud splat.*] Stop cracking your knuckles and get cracking.

Romeo. You've just blundered into a pun. [*Snickers lewdly; then he lowers left arm onto bed while right arm comes to rest between Honey's limbs. Apparently, fingers fall short of their goal, so he inches along until relationship is satisfactory. Meanwhile, he notes that a sliver of faint light flows through slightly parted draperies across Honey's feet into corner of his right eye, so he inches a bit farther. Figures remain side by side while Romeo's deft fingers trace partner's various erogenous zones. Action continues for considerable time, during which Honey appears to fall asleep, but occasional tremors of various muscles activated by highly titillated nerve ends belie fact. Erotic movements approach personal area; then evasively withdraw. Honey sighs impatiently, but teasing tactics continue. Finally, hand hovers over personal area, and partner's body stiffens briefly; then it relaxes as hand begins to undulate and rotate about one finger in gentle, massaging motions, which continue for a long time. Suddenly Honey arches back and stiffens muscles as if she would if she could, but she can't. Immediately, all motion ceases, and small body relaxes.*

Meanwhile, Romeo peers about as if sensing that something is missing from scene. Finally notices absence of faint light across Honey's feet and his tousled hair. Quickly raising head, peers toward its source, and light makes belated return, so head drops back onto bed. But it abruptly jerks upward in response to faint sounds emanating from beyond open window: crunching sounds, such as those produced by leather soles on a gravel-covered surface. But light continues to greet his eyes, so head drops back onto bed.

Then task is resumed with much lighter touch, but it grows progressively firmer. Once more small body arches upward and quivers slightly while its right hand reaches toward Romeo's groin. Meanwhile, Romeo's motions slow to a crawl, and touch becomes as light as a feather. Honey's hips roll ecstatically from side to side. Then her head lunges toward area of groin and passionately showers kisses on it while Romeo's manual motions intensify. Suddenly Honey tugs imperatively at rigid lever in her grasp, and Romeo immediately reverses field and enfolds her in bare hug.]

Honey. [*In muffled tones.*] Ow!

Romeo. Sorry, Honey, but you had that coming.

Honey. [*In muffled tones.*] You just stumbled into a pun. [*Chortles inanely; meanwhile, bedspring pops loudly, and she lapses into hysterical laughter, which gradually subsides into a few strained gasps.*]

Romeo. Hmm, that was quite a caper.

Honey. [*In muffled tones.*] Get off of me, you big ape! You weigh a ton. Besides, it's too hot with you on top. [*Erupts like tiny volcano and rolls Romeo off onto floor; then sits up and giggles delightedly while watching him struggle back onto edge of bed.*]

Romeo. [*Moving toward her with both pairs of thumbs and forefingers extended.*] Vengeance is mine.

Honey. Don't you dare! That can hurt. [*Snatches up pillow and buries most vulnerable parts in it.*]

Romeo. [*Returns to bedside and ponders, but cautiously glances around at her from time to time. Finally lunges toward open doorway and closes the door behind him. Sounds of running water are heard. Soon he emerges in pair of white shorts that loom out in dim light.*]

Honey. [Wriggles to side of bed, hops onto carpet, and scampers hurriedly past him, but not rapidly enough. Pop!] Ouch!

Romeo. [Pursues, but not rapidly enough; door slams in face. Stands thoughtfully by it; then calls out.] There's a new tube of toothpaste in the left-hand drawer. [*As if in response to afterthought.*] But don't use my toothbrush!

Honey. [Giggles derisively.]

Romeo. [Slowly approaches window and pulls one drape aside, revealing narrow, dimly lit courtyard. Loose gravel lies on bone-dry earth below window. Remains at window long time. Finally, shaking head, allows drape to fall back into place; then carefully pulls its edge across edge of other drape, thereby closing aperture.

[*House curtain falls.*]

* * * * * * * * * * * * * * *

Smudge Two   The second episode also involved an attractive blonde, but she was employed as a secretary. She possessed one of those size-six figures that defies any attempt to determine its age. Since I had learned from experience never to expect a woman to reveal her true age, I didn't ask, but she must have been between five and ten years younger than I.

Unlike the previous blonde, she was a quiet person with shy, light-blue eyes and ash-blonde hair. Furthermore, she not only proved to be among the fortunate 60 percent, but she was one of the most fortunate of those fortunate women. Consequently, I voluntarily reserved all of my playtime for her. It was well invested, because she could match me ten to one and win nine times out of ten; furthermore, she apparently had no maximum limit. The fantastic relationship continued for about five months; then a devil crept into my bed, and what happened is best described in the following play.

* * * * * * * * * * * * * * *

THE TRAGEDY OF A DEVIL IN BED

[DRAMATIS PERSONAE]

SIR LANCELOT (Lance), adventurous knight.
GUINEVERE (Guin), adventuress, day or night.

[SCENE: Downey, California, U.S.A.]

ACT I

SCENE I: [*Curtain rises to reveal bedroom with headboard of double bed centered below wide window in far wall. Pair of draperies are drawn so tightly across window that no light penetrates. On viewer's left, dresser stands against adjoining wall, in which nearby doorway is closed. In dim light, outlines of two figures are clasped together in age-old battle of sexes. Lower figure places one slim hand along shoulder of upper figure and pats it imperatively. Uppermost figure withdraws slightly from lower figure.*]

Lance. Guin, you are really something. I've been keeping track of your trips to the top of the hill, and that one makes thirty in less than three hours. I wonder what the score was last week when we were together for almost five hours.

Guin. [*Chuckles softly.*] But I haven't done that all by myself, Lance.

Lance. Yeah, but I just came along for the ride, and it has been great.

Guin. [*Chuckles softly; then pats partner's shoulder absently.*]

Lance. Ready, huh?

Guin. No, that pat was a mistake.

Lance. I don't think it was a mistake. Maybe we should continue to keep track and go for five hours again tonight.

Guin. No! Let's not. Last week was too much for me. In fact, after you took me home, I stayed in bed until noon. Then I got up and prepared a light lunch, but I was still tired, so I went back to bed.

Lance. And I was just beginning to look up to you as a superwoman.

Guin. [*Gently pats partner's head.*]

Lance. In fact, I've been planning a weekend in San Diego. After the he-man detective in the whodunit solves his case, he usually spends a whole weekend in a hotel room with a beautiful broad. Since you are a beautiful broad, I'm planning to treat you right for once. However, I am no he-man detective.

Guin. [*Pats partner's cheek; then murmurs.*] But you are a real he-man.

Lance. T'anks gobs, little moll. You just made my day—night, that is.

Guin. [*Chuckles; then murmurs.*] There's no reason for us to spend a whole weekend in San Diego doing what we normally do in one evening. Besides, I have my weekend homework to do, and I can't do it if we are in San Diego.

Lance. But we really should get together for one weekend and see what we can do with it.

Guin. I suspect that any man who spends a whole weekend in a hotel room with a woman spends ninety percent of the time drinking and sleeping.

Lance. Hmm, that sounds as if you are speaking from experience. [*Long silence.*] Sorry, little moll. [*Then rolls sideways onto bed and pulls her to him.*]

[*Size-six figure cuddles closer as house lights dim to total darkness for several minutes. When house lights restore dim scene, Guin is crouched midway over Lance, who wakens; then rises onto one elbow and blearily studies his partner's activities while she looks impishly at him from beneath lowered brows.*]

Guin. You didn't really intend to sleep all night, did you?

Lance. No, but that's not necessary, you know. If you don't believe me, come here. [*Extends arms toward her.*]

Guin. [*Ignores him while continuing caressing and fondling activities.*]

Lance. That's enough of that nonsense!

Guin. [*Lowers head and adds lips to activities.*]

Lance. [*Watches curiously as if from another planet.*] Come here, you little devil! [*Grasps one of her arms.*]

Guin. [*Shakes off grasp and continues activities momentarily, then suddenly slides off bed with one palm over mouth and dashes toward doorway beside dresser.*]

Lance. [*Sits up in middle of bed with arms clasped about knees and absently listens to the sounds of flowing water from beyond closed door. Finally, door opens, and a slender wraith emerges, pauses, then glides to bed, crawls to position beside him, and assumes similar attitude.]*

Lance. *[Stares at lowered head for a moment; then mutters.]* You did that on purpose, didn't you?

Guin. *[Remains stolidly silent.]*

Lance. *[Continues to stare at lowered head.]* Why? Surely you gained no pleasure from it.

Guin. *[Whispers.]* I got some kicks.

[Figures sit in silence for several minutes.]

Lance. I better take you home so that you can get some sleep. I'm very sorry that I kept you here so long last weekend. You really should have told me that you were tired and wanted to go home.

Guin. *[Whispers.]* I wasn't tired at the time. In fact, I didn't want to go home, but Sunday was pretty rough.

Lance. That does it. Off to home with you. *[Slides off far side of bed and slowly feels way around end of it to near side. Pauses and stares down at forlorn little figure. Finally seats himself beside her and places one arm around her shoulders. Meanwhile, house lights dim.]*

[House curtain falls.]

* * * * * * * * * * * * * *

The Exorcist Sunday followed that eventful night, so I had plenty of time to review and study the problem that had evolved from it. Since I had become rather fond of the shy, size-six devil, I spent most of the day trying to convince myself that I really didn't have to do what I had already decided to do. Subconsciously I was trying to forestall what amounted to an execution. In my mind's eye, I stood somberly beside the guillotine with my head shrouded in a black headdress while the ash-blonde curls of my paramour spilled forlornly about the hole in the guillotine's block. And it was I who was about to release the cord that retained the glistening blade at the top of the guillotine's tower. What a switch!

I actually had to force myself to sit down to a table and draft the letter. Of course, its sole purpose was to dissolve the relationship, and it did that, but doing it gently was the biggest problem. In fact, far into the night, I struggled through several approaches to it, but none of them accomplished the purpose as kindly as the case warranted. I certainly hope that the clumsy letter didn't make that likable little devil hate me forevermore, because we may end up having to stoke the same furnace after the Battle of Armageddon.

Of course, I should have done it in person, but I knew that I could never compel myself to look into those shy, pale-blue eyes and say what had to be said. Furthermore, I strongly suspect that, given a choice, she would have chosen the crude manner in which it was done.

But there's one aspect of the problem that has always bugged me: Why should such a wonderfully endowed woman ever want more, especially that? My typically inept psychological speculations have included several plausible answers, but I've favored a plot in which the woman's GI ex-husband must have spent most of his leaves in Asian brothels. Then, after returning home to his faithful frau, he demanded the same weird practices employed by the oriental prostitutes. In my opinion, it must have been a conditioned pattern of behavior, because, of all women, she had no logical reason to deviate from the norm.

There were other aspects of the problem, too, such as the likelihood that she may have practiced her expertise on other men. If so, then she must have acquired a lurid reputation, because many men gossip about their sex partners. Consequently, somebody would normally have warned me about her strange proclivities. However, thanks to the Unknown, my case was not a normal one, so I would be the last to hear about it. But it's unlikely that I would have believed such a warning, because I've learned to doubt all gossip, including that peddled by the news media and the Unknown.

The Many Capers

My mind was still groping for the next acceptable subject when Wilfred returned to the easy chair. "Now how about one of those stories from your autobiography," he suggested.

I silently shook my head, so he coyly inquired, "But you didn't go on without me, did you?"

After a momentary pause to gain his undivided attention, I replied, "Yes, I did." Then, after savoring his startled expression, I added, "But the subject wouldn't have interested you, I suspect, because it concerned several of the many women that I seduced to spite the furtive force that seems so determined to bar me from the entire female race. You wouldn't be interested in anything like that, would you?"

He courageously shook his head, but his expression screamed, "Oh, but Oy would! Oy would!" in dialect, yet. Then he asked, "How many women?"

"I don't know," I admitted. "I've always been more interested in quality than quantity, but the number must extend into three digits. However, that number is probably considered to be small potatoes by some of the notorious celebrities of the stage, screen, and sports worlds. According to several self-proclaimed authorities on the subject, some of those totals are closer to four digits than to three."

My eyes caught the man's widened, green orbs at the exact instant when they appeared to be calling me a *bleeped* liar, but I ignored them, because I had merely repeated what I had read, which was media gossip, of course.

"But those characters were not hampered by an all-powerful and unscrupulous enemy," I resumed. "Nevertheless, I finally came to the conclusion that my enemy might be a questionable blessing in disguise, because it's amazing how many women flock to and around any man who is reputed to be particularly susceptible to their charms. Consequently, instead of driving women away from me by denigrating me, the Unknown was pimping for me. When I finally arrived at that far-out conclusion, I immediately backed off from my campaign, because it obviously wasn't serving the purpose for which it was intended. Besides, I've always been a one-woman man, and I was engulfed in a wave of shame for the promiscuous life that I had been so ineffectively leading; consequently, I welcomed the excuse to withdraw from it."

Meanwhile, Wilfred's eyes had assumed a glazed appearance, which may have indicated that he was suffering from traumatic shock. Finally he shook it off and impatiently prompted me: "So you backed off."

"Yeah," I responded absently. "I didn't entertain another member of the female race for a long time."

"How long?" he countered.

"Oh, maybe a week or even ten days," I answered. Then, in response to his scandalized stare, I added, "Actually, it was some five or six months."

"That's still not very long," he muttered thoughtfully.

"Not extremely long," I conceded, "but it might have continued much longer if I hadn't met and become infatuated with a slender brunette who had migrated from Seattle to Los Angeles to attend school."

"To attend school!" he shouted incredulously, arising from his chair.

"Not kindergarten," I protested. "Don't be so shocked. She was within the legal limit. In fact, she was about forty years old, but she looked much younger."

After the man slumped back into his chair, I resumed: "We had a lot in common. For instance, both of us had spent our childhoods on the central plains of Canada, and we had lived in Seattle at almost the same time."

The First Tryst

I paused while my mind wandered back to our first tryst. We had driven to San Diego for the weekend, where we visited the zoo and exchanged insults with the monkeys. After cocktails and steak dinners at the Cotton Patch, we had repaired to a motel room, even though no plans for the night had been discussed and no questions had been asked regarding them.

After we were ready to retire, *ma intrigue amoureuse* wandered thoughtfully toward one corner of the bed, where she seated herself, raised both knees, and wrapped her arms around them. After staring off into space for several minutes, she directed her dark-brown eyes toward me and softly said, "You realize that marriage usually precedes this sort of thing."

Of course, I didn't respond in words—no reasonably smart man would—but I did respond. After "this sort of thing" had run its course, she whispered, "That's what I expected," almost as if I were not there with her.

Momentarily, I was unable to fit the words to any logical pattern; then they slowly slipped into a familiar slot. Very likely she had been exposed to the Unknown's denigrating guile shortly after we first met, but she had not entirely bought the package. Of course, I would never know whether that logic was actually on target, but I chose to assume that it was. Her involuntary revelation of faith in me touched my heart. In fact, that may have been the point when infatuation turned into love, "whatever that may be," as a charming prince so aptly put it.

"Ahem!" Wilfred loudly reminded me.

"Oh, yes," I muttered. "Where was I?"

"You had a lot in common," he answered.

"Yes, we did," I murmured, "but sex was not part of it." After casually noting the impact of that bombshell, I continued: "From the first, I suspected that she was frigid." Then I paused and mentally recalled how artificial and staged her reactions had seemed during the heat of that first tryst.

"Then what?" he urged me on.

"No change," I replied. "I continued to see her because we did have a lot in common. After all, sex is a very small part of the human equation. In fact, if all other things had been normal, I would have asked her to marry me. But I don't have to tell you that all other things were not normal, do I, Wilfred?"

I paused to watch his reactions to the blunt question, but his eyes carefully avoided mine under the pretext of having to shift his weight on the chair into a more comfortable position. So I shook my head for him and continued: "I have been faithful to that woman for seventeen years . . . even during the eight months when I was in St. Louis on a consulting engineering assignment. During that time I suspected several female associates and chance acquaintances of not-so-subtlely volunteering to engage in liaisons with me. Since such activities would serve no apparent purpose in my incessant war with the Unknown, I passed them up, but the real reason for doing so was my penchant for being a one-woman man.

"I invited her to join me in St. Louis for a four-day weekend, which she accepted, but it was not so much for sex as for companionship. We had a ball traveling all over the southwestern section of Missouri and part of Arkansas. Likewise, I returned to our home in Topanga for a visit with her on the same basis. However, just after I returned to Topanga from St. Louis for the last time, I decided that, since sex was not really her forte, I would relieve her of the task of faking any more responses, so I've abstained for all of six years now."

Wilfred turned a dubious expression toward me, but I ignored it. "She probably suspects that my advanced age is the reason, but the real reason is longevity," I said. "Many old-timers have failed to outlive their spouses because they've tried to match their bedroom performances of fifty years before. Even though their hearts have been willing, their hearts have been unable to withstand the strain."

Man with a Mission

Pausing, I stared absently at the pattern of the carpet for a moment. "I have an important mission to perform before I go," I finally added. "At least it's important to me. In fact, it's so important that I don't intend to permit anything to interfere with its completion, least of all sex."

"And what might that mission be?" Wilfred asked.

"I must complete and publish my autobiography," I replied. "It will serve my purposes even better than the day in court that I was never granted. It's obvious, however, that I've already been tried and convicted of some Unknown crime by some unseen and Unknown entity that continues to impose its sentence on me. And even though my autobiography may substitute for my day in court, nothing can compensate me for the cruel character assassination to which I have been subjected; nor will it compensate me, my family, and my few loyal friends for the embarrassment and emotional anguish to which we have been subjected."

"Ahem!" Wilfred injected. "According to some American newscasts, many people are suing offenders for damages and winning big awards."

"Shyster lawyers are largely responsible for that wave of injustice," I retorted, "and they ought to be stopped before all of the liability insurance companies are forced to close shop. To me, money has come to mean very little, because I'm close to the end of the trail, and I can't take it with me. Besides, nobody ever fights 'city hall' and wins, because city hall houses the courts, and the courts follow a policy of protecting their own."

"And let's not forget that city hall has its own public relations department," Wilfred volunteered, "and it always paints city hall in such rosy hues that no plaintiff can win."

"That's so true!" I exclaimed. "But that policy can also be applied against my autobiography. Its beneficial effects are bound to be undermined by PR releases that smirch it and bolster city hall."

"Yeah," the other man agreed. "Nobody can win against such consummate liars."

After exchanging rueful glances with him, I insisted, "But I have to try, even though I know that the public relations departments of several large government agencies will spare no cost and bend many laws in their efforts to save face."

"I strongly suspect that we may have the same problem." he said. "Every time somebody uncovers a bit of political dirt, every party member gets out his shovel and bucket of sand and tries to cover it up."

"There's a perfect parallel to that simile in the House of Representatives," I rejoined. "Every time that Tip O'Neill makes a particularly stupid political faux pas, a veritable deluge of favorable propaganda about him floods the news media during the following day, so his stuff must be prepared in advance and held in abeyance until a dire need for it arises. Wye, those guys must spend millions of the taxpayers' dollars on public relations alone."

Wilfred must not have been particularly interested in the new subject, because he struggled out of the chair and said, "Well, I really should be shovin' off."

"I hope that my minisagas haven't bored you," I rejoined.

"No, not at all," he insisted with thoughtful, downcast eyes. Then he looked up, grinned infectiously, raised his right hand, and shouted, "See you later!" Then he boisterously stormed through the doorway.

14

Big Brother Emerges

Politics and Ecocomics

During my next session with Wilfred in the motel's office, we became embroiled in a mild discussion of politics. Suspecting that it was time to change the subject to something else, such as economics, I asked, "Did you read that article in yesterday's newspaper about the government's decision to grant amnesty to the sheep men for the money that they owe it?"

"Yes," he responded with a wary glance in my direction.

"Do you remember my prediction that, despite Lange's claims to the contrary, their political pressure would eventually force him to capitulate to their demands?" I persisted.

"Yes," he repeated, "but Lange's strongly worded statements to the effect that he intended to restore some semblance of order to this nation's economy regardless of what political pressures were brought to bear on him were what got him into office." Obviously the man was in no mood to expand on the subject.

Socialism on the Rack

Nevertheless, I continued to badger him: "Doesn't it bother you when the government arbitrarily decides that you must pay some sheep man's debt?"

"Well, the farmers have had a pretty rough time of it since Lange became prime minister," he replied, "and it all stems from his efforts to employ Reagan's capitalistic policies. When Muldune was prime minister, he had too big a heart for such policies, so he took care of the farmers."

"It certainly was bighearted of him to use your tax dollars to buy their votes," I retorted.

"But somebody had to take care of them," he insisted, "and the government is the logical one to do it."

"Apparently you have lost sight of the fact that you are the government," I countered. "The farmers should be required to take care of themselves, like everybody else does."

"Obviously you have no sympathy for the farmers," he observed. "Furthermore, you don't know about the countless problems that confront them. If you did, you wouldn't talk the way you do."

"Like you, I grew up on a farm," I rejoined, "so I do know something about those problems. In fact, one summer, when I was only fifteen years old, I operated a two-hundred-twelve-acre ranch-style farm with only an occasional inspection by my uncle to insure that I was properly cultivating the crops and feeding the four carloads of steers that were being fattened for market. I'm sure that sixty years haven't totally obliterated what I knew about farming at that time."

"You were very young to be running a farm all by yourself," he murmured doubtfully, but a glimmer of reluctant respect had crept into his eyes.

"Actually I managed it for my uncle," I admitted. "Usually he stopped by Saturday afternoons on his way to the stock auction to insure that I had everything under control. But he never had much to say about how I was doing the work, because I had worked for him several summers, so I knew how he wanted things done."

"There's so much to know about farming," he insisted. "It takes years to learn all about it."

"I didn't say that I knew all about it," I protested, "but I knew enough about it to successfully operate what passed for a small cattle ranch. And I still know enough about farming to realize that no one ever learns all there is to know about it. New farming knowledge and techniques are being developed every day. I don't know the first thing about how to operate a sheep ranch or what to do at lambing time. From what you've told me about it, I seriously doubt that I would ever be interested in serving as a midwife to a flock of pregnant ewes."

"Well, Muldune knows something about the farmer's problems," he muttered, "and he had their interests at heart, but he was voted out of power, probably by the people in the urban communities. After all, most of New Zealand's population is concentrated in four cities."

"Very likely he was voted out of office by those people because they resented having to support the farmers and sheep men in addition to their own families," I suggested. "It was the logical thing for them to do. In the U.S., unfortunately, many pressure groups, such as the farmers, have grown too large to be overcome at the polls, so the economy is being strained to the breaking point. Even so, none of those selfish political pressure groups will relent."

"As a result, the price of lambs has dropped to thirteen dollars," he resumed as if he hadn't heard a word of my harangue. "Meanwhile, the farmers in England are being guaranteed seventy dollars by the government. In my opinion, our government should do as much for our farmers. It's only fair."

"I don't agree," I retorted. "It has been socialistic policies, such as that, which have drastically lowered England's overall standard of living; furthermore, they have practically destroyed the nation's economy. In fact, those policies have plunged England so deeply into debt that, if Margaret Thatcher had not come along and imposed some austerity on the government, England probably would have defaulted on her debts to foreign lenders by now."

"But some of the English people are suffering under her tight policies," he protested. "In fact, I doubt that she will remain in power much longer."

"I suspect that you may be right about that," I conceded. "But the reason for the people's so-called suffering lies not so much in Thatcher's policies as in previous policies: giveaway policies that created a great national debt. Now the nation's tax revenues are being consumed by the interest on it. Even so, the nonsuffering beneficiaries of those previous policies are demanding that the government continue them irrespective of the fact that they'll catapult the government into a bankruptcy that will cause all of the English people to suffer. Manifestly, Thatcher has foreseen that catastrophe, but too many of the English voters can't see beyond their selfish noses."

"According to some of your American newscasts, your country has accumulated a debt of almost two trillion dollars," he rejoined, "so capitalism doesn't appear to have done any better."

"Most of that debt has evolved from the socialistic chicanery of some of our congressmen during the past fifty years," I countered. "But a large part of it has come about during the last twenty years because of other factors, such as a costly war, rearmament for World War Three, and support of the so-called entitlements, which are not so much entitlements as they are ongoing grants from our weak-willed congressmen to strong pressure groups. Even though the politicians created the monster, it can't be blamed entirely on them, since the voters willingly collaborated with the villains."

"How?" he countered.

"By permitting the self-serving politicians to con them into selling their votes for subsidies and entitlements," I replied.

"Isn't that like selling your own body for thirty pieces of silver?" he inquired.

"Very good!" I exclaimed with an approving nod.

"By the way," he added, "what does the word *entitlements* mean?"

"In the early thirties our first socialistic president and his Congress introduced social security to the American people," I answered. "At the time it was considered to be a form of government insurance that was to be paid jointly by the insured and their employers. At retirement age each insured was to receive monthly payments, based on those insurance payments plus the accrued interest, which were to be distributed over the average remaining life span of the insured."

"But how does the word *entitlement* derive from that?" he asked.

"I really don't know how the term was derived," I confessed, "but I assume that since the insured paid for the insurance, they were entitled to some returns from it."

"Surely there was nothing wrong with that plan," he protested.

"It was introduced when I was in my early twenties," I said. "Even then I was acute enough to foresee some of its shortcomings. At the time I insisted to some of my contemporaries that it was wrong of the government to force its citizens to embrace a system from which many of them feared they would never realize any return. Most of my contemporaries agreed with me, because we could foresee that our wasteful government would spend all of the funds before we reached retirement age."

After studing my passive features for a moment, he asked, "And how did you fare?"

"Great!" I retorted. "I've received more than one thousand percent profit on my investment, and, if I'm lucky, I could receive another thousand percent before I cash in my chips."

He turned mesmerized eyes on me and said, "I don't see how you can possibly complain about that."

"Oh, but I can," I said, "and I will, because somebody will have to pay the difference between what my employers and I paid into the system and what I'm receiving from it. Very likely that somebody will be my daughter and possibly her children—my grandchildren. No matter how one looks at it, that's unfair."

"Actually the government will make up the difference," he informed me condescendingly.

"There you go again!" I shouted in frustration. "You've forgotten who the government really is, at least who actually pays the bills. But I have yet to reveal the bad news: My wasteful government has spent all of the Social Security program's funds; therefore, it has been forced to borrow heavily from the Medicare program to keep things going. Nobody knows who will pay that loan, but I'm betting that the coming generations will have to pay it; that is, if anybody does."

"What do you mean by that?" he asked.

"Some economists suspect that, relative to other currencies, the value of the dollar will be forced to very low levels either by the government's deliberate manipulations to maintain a competitive edge in the world's market or by inflation; consequently, the debt can be paid off by dollars worth only ten percent of their present value."

"That would be terrible!" he exclaimed. "Wye, everybody would lose."

Government Intrigues

"It's akin to national bankruptcy," I claimed. "Actually one of the worst of the current forms of governmental intrigues is the constant manipulation of the rates of exchange between the world's currencies."

"That's no problem in New Zealand," he interjected confidently. "The rate of exchange between New Zealand and America hasn't changed appreciably for some time."

"I've been watching those rates very closely," I said, "and what you claim is true, but that's really bad news for you New Zealanders."

"Why?" he asked.

"The value of the U.S. dollar has dropped about thirty percent relative to currencies such as the deutsche mark, the Swiss franc, and the Japanese yen; therefore, New Zealand's dollar has dropped in the same relationship to them. Consequently, those Japanese cars that you New Zealanders like so much will cost you thirty percent more, and your lumber, wool, and other products will fetch thirty percent less from the Japanese. What's more, if you New Zealanders were to deal exclusively with Germany, Switzerland, and Japan, your standard of living would be sixty percent less than that of the people in those three countries."

"But the same applies to America," he protested.

"True," I granted, "but neither one of us is likely to feel much of that drop for a long time."

"Why?" he inquired.

"Because it usually takes a long time for such changes to affect the countries in which they occur," I replied. "But we'll feel it immediately when we travel in the countries I mentioned. That's one of the penalties that governments under financial stress involuntarily impose on their nationals to keep them from spending their money abroad."

"But that won't affect you here," he insisted.

"Of course not!" I retorted. "But it will affect me when I return to the States and try to buy a Japanese car."

"But you shouldn't buy a Japanese car," he countered. "You should buy an American car."

"That would be my inclination," I admitted. "However, according to our news media, I would be buying an inferior product," I added with a chuckle. "Consequently, my standard of living would be affected. Any way that we look at my government's decision to devalue the dollar, it was a bad one for both of us."

"According to what I've read," he began, "it was intended to stabilize the balance of trade."

"I've read that, too," I said, "but I'm sure there are much better ways of doing that: ways that won't lower the standard of living for millions of retired people. Many of those people practically subsist on the interest from a few liquid assets whose value has been deliberately reduced thirty percent by a profligate government. I'm sure there are ways that won't permit wealthy people from other nations, like Japan, to buy up our real estate and industries at discounts of thirty percent or more. I'll bet that such losses offset many times over the gains in the balance of trade."

"I wonder why governments do such stupid things," Wilfred murmured absently.

"Because governments are controlled by politicians who consider only those options that will detrimentally affect them and their careers the least," I growled savagely.

"Oh, it can't be all that bad," he protested with a chuckle.

Restore the Gold Standard?

"Oh, but it can be," I retorted. "Despite politicians' claims to the contrary, eventually both of us will suffer from the devaluations. Let me give you an example of one politician's trickery or stupidity. During the early seventies, our president was Richard Nixon, who voluntarily shook the U.S. off of the gold standard. At the time he claimed that his action wouldn't affect our standard of living in any way. Meanwhile, I screamed to the high heavens that such would not be the case, but my cries were drowned out by the silence of my countrymen."

"You spoke to an audience about it?" Wilfred countered sharply.

"No, of course not," I admitted with a rueful grin. "My scream was but the cry of a voice in the wilderness."

"Apparently discarding the gold standard caused no great problem," he demurred. "In fact, you probably have just as much and even more money now than you had then."

"True," I admitted, "but that money buys only one-tenth as much real value now as it did then."

"Aw, that can't be so," he protested. "Sure, it may buy a little less than it did then, but not one-tenth as much."

"Suppose that you were to buy one troy ounce of gold today," I suggested. "About how much would you have to pay for it?"

Following a momentary pause, he replied, "About seven hundred dollars."

"Yeah, but those are New Zealand dollars," I rejoined. "In U.S. dollars, it would amount to about three hundred and fifty dollars, wouldn't it?" And he nodded, so I went on, "When Nixon canceled the gold standard, one troy ounce of gold was worth slightly less than thirty-five U.S. dollars."

"Hmm," he mumbled. "That is approximately one-tenth of what it is worth now, all right." Then, after a moment's consideration, he added, "But the price of gold has varied radically since that time. In fact, it has been more than twice as high as it is now, so it isn't right to use gold as a standard for control of the world's currencies."

"Shortly after Nixon's action, gold did surge to very high dollar levels because of the rabid activities of speculators," I admitted. "And its U.S. dollar values gyrated between two hundred and ninety and three hundred and thirty in nineteen eighty-four. In nineteen eighty-five it varied between three hundred and three hundred twenty-nine U.S. dollars. At its present rate of increase, I predict that it will be at three hundred forty-two U.S. dollars on April Fool's Day nineteen eighty-six."

With doubt-filled eyes, he stated, "That's just a wild guess."

"I've been studying the effects of the dollar's devaluation on the price of gold for several weeks," I said, "and I'll bet that my prediction doesn't miss by more than a tenth of a percent."

"Humph!" he grunted. "The price of gold does appear to be reasonably stable. True, its increase in value relative to U.S. dollars from the midpoint of nineteen eighty-five through March of nineteen eighty-six may be attributable to the decline in the dollar's value."

"If so, it amounts to only ten percent of the dollar's decline relative to the mark, franc, and yen," I pointed out, "so Germany, Switzerland, and Japan must have increased the value of their currencies relative to gold by the remaining twenty percent."

"Since the values of most of the major currencies relative to the value of gold have stabilized somewhat," he began, "it appears that they could be returned to the gold standard."

"Possibly," I granted, "but U.S. politicians will never consider that option as a means of stabilizing the world's currency, even if the other major nations would collaborate."

"Why not?" he asked.

"Because they have become so accustomed to printing useless money to cover shortfalls accumulating from their promiscuous spending that, like you and your socialism, they have become hooked on it," I answered. "In fact, there may not be enough gold in the world to stabilize all of the dollars floating over it. Furthermore, the nation may no longer have sufficient collateral to warrant such a massive purchase of the metal. After all, we've been rapidly selling off large hunks of our most valuable real estate and natural resources to the financial giants of other nations."

"But I'm not hooked on socialism," Wilfred protested peevishly. "In fact, I'm very conservative. Most of us New Zealanders are conservative."

"I agree, but most of you New Zealanders have become hooked on socialism," I insisted. "It's such an insidious disease that you haven't recognized the fact. It's a lot like cancer in that one doesn't recognize it until the pains of having to pay the piper strike home. By that time it's too late, because, once infected, any attempt to remove the carcinogens of socialism usually proves to be fatal to the patient. Invariably, the people rebel."

"But I can give up socialism," he protested. "I can do anything that I set my mind to."

"Yeah," I responded derisively, "just like the average chain-smoker can give up smoking."

Capitalism at Risk

"But some aspects of socialism are desirable," he insisted. "For example, no society should ever allow any of its members to starve to death."

"I don't know of any capitalistic societies that do," I retorted. "Actually, there is one primary difference between capitalistic and socialistic societies, but that difference is vital to the existence of the society, whichever it is. In my opinion, a capitalistic society stops short of supporting its indigents, whereas a socialistic society tries to support the entire society; consequently, no one is left to pay all of those massive bills, so the society goes bankrupt. It's as simple as that."

"But what other forms of government can we turn to?" he protested. "We have already agreed that communism is no good."

"Communism is merely socialism with some tricky political overtones," I growled. "So there's no way that it can qualify as an alternative. But capitalism can be made to work successfully."

"How?" he inquired skeptically.

"Before I get into the solution of the problem, I would like to relate a bit of history," I proposed. Since he nodded, I resumed: "During the forepart of the eighteenth century a French statesman and author, Alexis de Tocqueville, made a yearlong tour of the United States for the purpose of determining how the American economic and political systems functioned, and he was favorably impressed by what he found."

"That doesn't make sense," he protested, "because capitalism obviously isn't all that great."

"But that was a much purer form of capitalism," I countered. "Democracy had not yet been infiltrated by so much socialism. Nevertheless, de Tocqueville came up with one very astute criticism of what then was a relatively pure form of a capitalistic democracy."

"He claimed that it wouldn't work," Wilfred interjected with hopeful eyes.

The man's eagerness to prove that capitalism was a failure tickled my funny bone, so I allowed a chuckle to escape and said, "Actually, he implied as much."

"I knew it!" he exclaimed with the air of a small boy who wanted to clap his hands in church but didn't dare.

"According to that so-called French philosopher," I resumed, "the primary weakness of a capitalistic democracy is the inherent tyranny of the masses."

"Tyranny of the masses," he repeated with a puzzled expression.

"Yeah," I drawled. "I interpreted the words to mean that in a democratic form of government a large mass of people possesses the inherent capability of imposing its will on a smaller mass of people through the peoples' mutual right to vote on certain issues, including issues that can detrimentally affect the finances of the smaller mass."

"Humph!" he grunted disparagingly. "That's a very obscure explanation, but I suspect that I know what you are trying to say. If so, then democracy does permit a certain amount of tyranny on the part of the largest group or party."

"And that's what the sheep men have done to you and some of the other urban voters," I observed. "But they only threatened the incumbent politicians with their voting power in combination with that of their urban families and friends."

"That's not fair," he protested. "We should have had the right to vote on that issue."

"And that's what I've been trying to tell you," I said, "but you've been insisting that somebody has to take care of the farmers. Obviously, that's another weakness of the system."

"But how should the system be changed?" he inquired somewhat sullenly.

No Quick Fix "First of all," I began, "the representatives of our people, your Parliament and our Congress, must prepare legislation that outlaws the transfer of any individual's wealth to another individual through the medium of the government. For example, every taxpayer should be taxed at the same rate—everyone should have equal rights. Of course, our governments also must eliminate the existing products of mass tyranny, such as the subsidies and the entitlements."

"But all of that can't be done overnight," he objected.

"Right," I agreed, "but the entire mess can be phased out at a rate of five or ten percent per year."

"That sounds fine, but who'll take care of the farmers when the price of lambs is too low for them to make a profit?"

"The farmers will," I retorted. "Let them form combines that control the number of lambs to match the demand. The same combines might even include banks to finance the less successful farmers during economically trying times. There are many things that the farmers can do for themselves when they can no longer turn to the government for an automatic handout from the taxpayers."

"That sounds fine, but the farmers aren't the only ones affected, because all of us would have to give up our security."

"Who has any security when the country is forced into bankruptcy?" I countered. "And New Zealand is threatened by it."

"It would never work!" he exploded incongruously.

"I'm sure that you are right," I rejoined.

"Why?" he countered. Then, sensing my startled reaction to the question, he ruefully added, "Yes, I'm asking you to tell me why I said it would never work?"

"People," I murmured with an amiable grin. Then, in response to his puzzled frown, I added, "People would keep it from working because, once they have savored the easy fruits of a socialistic society, they no longer have the yen to make it on their own. In other words, they are hooked on socialism."

Minority Rule

Apparently Wilfred chose to counter a stab with an indirect stab. "According to some newscasts," he began, "there's a lot of racial conflict in America."

"I've heard similar newscasts," I admitted.

"Well, isn't that an example of mass tyranny?" he asked. "After all, blacks are in the minority, aren't they?"

"Not necessarily," I retorted. "Most of those conflicts erupt between racial groups of relatively equal sizes, such as blacks versus Mexicans. According to some reports, there are fewer whites than colored peoples in Los Angeles. If so, then the whites have become a minority group."

"But the whites still dominate the political scene, don't they?" he asked. "If so, then that would be an example of minority tyranny, and that doesn't make sense."

"Well," I drawled, "that's a difficult question, because the mayor of Los Angeles is black, so one can't honestly say that the whites dominate the political scene."

"According to some of your news analysts," he resumed the attack on another tack, "Los Angeles has become the pot capital of the continent."

"Yeah," I growled. Then, choosing a devious avenue of escape, I added, "Apparently it's rapidly deteriorating from a melting pot into a slum pot, and nobody in a position of authority is doing anything about it. In fact, illegal aliens are reported to be flooding Los Angeles at an incredible rate. Soon the Mexican population will exceed the combined populations of all other ethnic groups."

"Couldn't they be a threat to the nation's security?" he inquired.

"Our highly vaunted national security is a farce," I said contemptuously. "Any nation that can't guard its borders against the influx of hungry neighbors can't possibly protect them from the movements of highly trained enemy spies."

"Fortunately, New Zealand doesn't have that kind of a problem," he rejoined. "We don't have any international boundary lines."

Racism

"That's a definite advantage," I granted, "but you do have a problem with the Maoris."

"We have no problem with the Marys," he insisted. "Neither the Marys nor we newcomers are racists."

I stared curiously at him while my mind slowly digested the statement and converted the dialectical word *Mary* into *Maori.*

"In fact, we and the Marys get along very well together," he added.

"Apparently the country's National Council of Churches doesn't entirely agree with that philosophy," I said. "It has recommended that the nation be renamed Aotearoa, which is an Austronesian name, of course. Furthermore, some Maori activists are currently trekking from this country to Castro's Cuba for the avowed purpose of learning all there is to know about advanced liberation techniques. That, in particular, does nothing to confirm your claim of racial compatibility."

The man appeared to be thunderstruck. "I didn't know that," he murmured distractedly. "It doesn't seem possible."

"Almost everyone protests to high heaven that he's not a racist," I said, "but everyone is a racist to some degree. It's human nature to favor one's own kind."

"But the South African whites are the worst racists," he insisted.

"I doubt that they are more inclined to be racists than the South African blacks," I retorted. "Presently, many public figures, such as our politicians and the news media, have found it politically expedient to attack the South African government for its current policies, but the blacks have been deliberately creating trouble and unrest."

"That's no reason for the whites to murder them," he protested. "Besides, they only want their freedom."

"I support appropriate punishment for the murderers," I said, "but that includes the black murderers, too. As far as their freedom is concerned, I suspect that they are much better off with the status quo than with their freedom."

"Everybody should be free," he insisted firmly.

"But look at what has happened to all of the other African countries where blacks have obtained their freedom," I protested. "Every one of them is deep in debt, and most of them are at war with one or more of their neighboring countries. Even in the most stable countries many of the urban blacks have returned to their tribes, where they gang up on neighboring tribes to take their land or steal their livestock. From what I've read about black Africans, I have to conclude that they are their own worst enemies. Furthermore, as slave masters, they are crueler than white slave masters. In my opinion, the blacks who have been granted their freedom have found that they were much better off under the guidance of white people. The African black people are neither ready for nor capable of governing themselves."

Threat of the CIA

He stared sullenly through the open doorway for a moment; then, placing one hand on the big bottle that I had delivered to him, he insisted, "Don't bring any more bottles of bubbly to me. Promise me that."

"I'll promise nothing of the kind," I said. "As long as I'm using your typewriter, I'll be owing you; therefore, since you refuse to accept direct payment for its use, I'll repay you in my own way. I refuse to be obligated to you or anybody else. I particularly pride myself on always paying my own way."

Suddenly, he turned his sullen gaze fully on me and burst forth, "Albert! You are a terrible man."

Of course, the statement was supposedly intended to imply that I was terrible in the sense that I had refused his request, but it was obvious that chance had not entered into his use of the same ambiguous words that had created such a violent reaction from me several days before.

"I am not!" I shouted. "In fact, I'm a very honorable man, and eventually I intend to prove as much."

Obviously he was both surprised and startled by the force of my response. "Oh, yeah!" he shouted. "How?"

"Yeah!" I countered heatedly. "As for how, I haven't written two thousand two hundred and seventy-six rough draft pages of an autobiography on a mere whim. Those pages, plus about one thousand more, will provide a very detailed exposition of my entire life to anyone who is fair minded enough to read them. Furthermore, any such reader with any sense at all will readily realize that I have been terribly maligned."

"Yeah?" he responded with considerably less conviction.

"Yeah," I repeated. "Of course, I can only guess at the source of the information from which you apparently have formed your opinion, but anybody who has had as many opportunities to observe my behavior at close range as you have within the last two months should exhibit better judgment than to attach any credence to it."

I paused to permit a rebuttal, but he chose sullen silence, so I resumed: "In fact, I challenge you and your source to prove that that opinion is justified."

"You better watch out!" he shouted malevolently. "They might set the CIA onto you."

The warning so startled me that my reply followed my slowly evolving thoughts too closely. "I don't see how the CIA could have become involved in my adventures abroad," I mumbled. "But even if the Unknown does include that gang of alleged international cutthroats, I'm not frightened in the least, because they have no license to badger me. Besides, my life has almost run its course, so I have little to lose should some 'regrettable accident' strike me down in remote New Zealand. But I deeply doubt that the CIA is even aware of my existence, much less waiting to pounce onto me, because it has no legitimate reason to do so. If there were such a reason, I would have been clapped into a jail cell at the time. Certainly I would never have been granted a passport. As it is, my open defiance of some Unknown agency has merely incited vengeful innuendos under the cloak of anonymity."

"If I were you, I would be very careful," he muttered. "It doesn't pay to defy people in high places."

"Whoever they are, they have earned that defiance and even my contempt," I retorted.

"Those people are appointed to protect law-abiding citizens," he persisted, "so they should be treated with respect, and no one should ever defy them."

"When they properly conform to that function, then I'll respect them," I countered. "As it is, members of the FBI have been publicly accused of murders for which no agent has ever been tried, and the CIA has a number of black marks against it for alleged involvement in foreign murders, such as that of the Chilean leader. Don't try to frighten me with any more of those acronyms, because I don't scare worth a *bleep*! Nevertheless, I'm pleased to finally discover that the Unknown actually is Big Brother." Then I fixed my cold eyes on his, but they refused to meet mine, so I turned away and angrily barged through the doorway toward my domain.

Meanwhile, Pancho insisted, "I'll bet that that compulsive gossip opened up with his ambiguous attack for the sole purpose of being able to report to his buddy mussels that he really told Albert off."

As I fumbled with the latchkey, José chimed in, "And I'll bet that he loses no time in reporting appropriate bits and pieces of that altercation to one or more of them."

The key finally turned, and the knob followed suit. Then I savagely pushed the door open, stepped through the opening, and slammed the door closed so violently that the calendar on the adjacent wall nervously jumped from its plastic hanger and collapsed in total disarray onto the TV set.

15

Beginning of the End

A Reconciliation?

About nine o'clock of the next morning the sounds of a motor caused me to look up from the keyboard of the typewriter toward the big window and watch dourly while Wilfred parked the oldest of his two "wee" Fords in front of it. My eyes continued to follow his blocky form as he thrust open the car door, stepped quickly through the opening, closed the door, and jogged heavily toward my open doorway.

"Good morning, Albert!" he called to me in a particularly cordial manner, as I responded to his knock. "I'm taking a load of trash to the disposal yard," he hurriedly added. "Would you like to ride along?"

"No, Wilfred," I responded very formally, "but thank you for the invitation. If I leave this typewriter for one minute, not only will it immediately go to sleep, but I'll probably spend the remainder of the day formulating excuses for staying away from it."

"Aw, come on, Bert," he coaxed in his most ingratiating manner. "You spend too much time at that thing. You really should get away from it for a while. The disposal yard is located on the other side of the city, so we won't be gone long. Besides, the trip will provide you with an opportunity to see more of our fair city."

From his rare use of the nickname, I immediately suspected that he was indirectly pressing more for a reconciliation than for companionship during a relatively short auto trip, and that suspicion may have been what induced me to say, "I would like very much to see some of the outlying areas of the city before I leave."

"Well, get your jacket and come along, then," he urged. "That's where we're going."

Truckin' When we approached the small, four-door car, I found the space behind the front seat to be crammed with bundles of old newspapers, collapsed cardboard boxes, and several paper bags stuffed with grass and hedge clippings. After tortuously crawling through the left front doorway and onto the seat, I discovered that I couldn't sit back against the seat without being stabbed in my right ear by one of several sharply sheared rosebush stems. But I stubbornly refused to point out the problem to Wilfred; instead, I leaned diagonally against the door and thrust my left arm across the ledge of its open window.

Meanwhile, he cautiously crawled behind the steering wheel, started the motor, and amiably ventured, "It's a nice morning for a ride."

"Yes, it is," I responded with a reserved air, but it immediately melted when the many other "noice moahnin's" flooded my memory, so I impulsively added, "In fact, this has been the most pleasant of my seventy-four summers."

"Or is it your seventy-fifth summer?" he countered.

Casting a questioning glance toward him, I belatedly remembered that this summer had been spent "down under" during the Northern Hemisphere's winter. "You are right!" I exclaimed. "Actually, I've lost one winter and gained one summer during my stay in New Zealand, so I can no longer employ the early American Indian's practice of referring to my age as so many summers. Furthermore, I have now lived through seventy-three winters and seventy-five summers, which would very likely have confused not only the early American Indians but some of the present generation."

His laugh was much more exuberant than the remark warranted; in fact, it was wasted, because his first friendly overture had won me over—we were reconciled. But I sternly reminded myself to keep him on probation, because my previous experience with such people had taught me that he would likely repeat the crime.

Meanwhile, a repetitive slapping sound induced me to inspect the tires of a nearby vehicle for evidence of a loosened retread, but I found none. Then, looking toward Wilfred, I discovered the source of the sounds: The strong breeze from the open window was continuously riffling the pages of some old newspapers, which were slapping smartly against the man's rugged right shoulder. Suddenly the problem of the rosebush stems seemed to deteriorate to level zero, so I relaxed against the back of the seat until one of the stems pressed sharply against the lobe of my left ear. I wasn't about to allow Wilfred to present a more rugged and masculine appearance than I despite the twelve-year difference in our ages.

Musselburgh Rise had become Andersons Bay Road, and the vehicles were moving rapidly along it when we approached the Hillside Road intersection, where a small, red car swung around the corner and darted in front of the Ford. Wilfred quickly slapped one flat foot against the brake pedal and skillfully avoided a collision, but there were some ephemeral damages: Wilfred's nerves were frayed, and the sharp stem almost fractured my earlobe.

Of course, the other driver was a total stranger to both of us, but Wilfred proceeded to picturesquely and profusely describe the man's family tree in the most finite details. From that outburst alone, I concluded that Celtic words uttered in furious dialect possess some distinct advantages over even the most abbreviated of Americanized English words.

Vehicular traffic gradually diminished as we traveled beyond the central part of the city, so I redirected my attention from the traffic to the immediate surroundings while Wilfred began a running account that incuded some pertinent data and local history.

When my attention was attracted to an upcoming concrete structure, he immediately volunteered, "That's where some of our fresh fruit is processed and stored."

"That's very interesting," I said, "because we have some similar structures in the Chelan-Wenatchee area of Washington State, but they are devoted almost exclusively to the storage of fresh apples under carefully controlled atmospheric conditions."

"Apparently we employ the same technology," he remarked.

"The user's biggest problem is to be on hand when the fruit is first placed on the produce counters in the supermarkets," I said. "If the consumer waits too long, the fruit will have mellowed so much that it's no longer juicy and tasty."

"Of course, we don't have any supermarkets in Musselburgh," he admitted, "but we are coming to a big one right now. See?" And he proudly pointed to a relatively small, wooden structure that stood on a small knoll about one hundred yards from the roadway.

My first impulse was to say that that supermarket would not fill one corner of the average American supermarket, that American supermarkets often cover whole city blocks, but I subdued the tactless impulse in time.

Shortly thereafter, we came upon the trash disposal area, which proved to be similar to some of its American counterparts, even to the methods of operation. After beckoning to us, a workman directed us to an area where Wilfred backed the Ford alongside a pickup truck, whose cargo of cut or broken plasterboard and other scrap building materials was being unloaded along a line of previously deposited waste materials. Meanwhile, a big bulldozer moved slowly along the line and systematically worked the waste materials into the loosened soil. We unloaded the Ford to the point where only several protective sheets of plastic remained; then Wilfred dug out the stubby end of an aged broom and carefully swept out the debris. When that task was completed, we removed the sheets of plastic and neatly folded them; then Wilfred stowed them in the boot. Obviously he was not only a conservative man but a precise and organized one.

An Unexpected Tour

After we left the trash and waste to the disposal of the bulldozer and a large flock of scavenging gulls, it became apparent that Wilfred had never intended to return directly to the motel. If traversing main thoroughfares, such as Kaikorai Valley, Brockville, Taieri, Pine Hill, North, and Opoho Roads, could be considered to be a tour of the city, then we toured Dunedin. En route, we viewed the fertilizer works, the Roslyn Woolen Mills, the Waikari Hospital, and numerous schools, parks, and golf courses. From one high hill we even enjoyed a clear view of the Borough of Mosgiel, which lies some fourteen miles from the center of Dunedin.

To any inhabitant of the Los Angeles area, such a claim probably raises doubts, but there isn't one particle of smog per billion parts of that rain-washed atmosphere. To ensure that, Mother Nature always provides no less than a gentle breeze to sweep the air clean of all contaminants as it shepherds large flocks of cumulus clouds across the sun-splashed, light-aquamarine sky. At least that's what we saw. Even though the weather was typical of the latter part of the austral summer, most of the gently rolling hills were still green, as were the parks, golf courses, and those parts of the flower gardens that weren't ablaze with color. I was particularly impressed by the greenbelt that traverses the central part of the city. In addition to a golf course, a civic garden, a cemetery, and some parklike expanses identified as town belts, it contains a pool and some schools. Many small parks and recreational reserves are also scattered about the city, so few Dunedin residents are located more than a five-minute walk from a greensward.

From some of the hilltops the light aquamarine of the sky was matched by the deeper aquamarine waters of Otago Harbor and the Pacific Ocean, whose whitecaps brilliantly reflected the softly filtered sunlight between the shadows cast by the high-flying sky trains. At one of the scenic reserves we looked across the tips of tall beech trees toward more rolling hills. Dunedin is a pretty city, but a few more groves of mature trees would establish it among the world's most beautiful small cities.

While the Ford was parked at the curb in front of the Waikari Hospital, Wilfred abruptly volunteered, "As you can see, this complex is no longer in use." After pausing and meeting my curious gaze with a faint smile, he added: "It cost the city millions of dollars to build it; then the city fathers discovered that nobody would use it because it's located too far from the city's center." Following another pause and a wry expression, he resumed: "I suppose that that is one point in favor of capitalism, because no big corporation would ever make a mistake like that."

"They make mistakes, too," I said. "In fact, they make many mistakes; however, if they can't correct those mistakes economically, they disappear from the commercial scene entirely. Unfortunately, when a government makes a mistake in either a capitalistic or a socialistic venture, it is permitted to repeat that mistake. That's why governments should never be permitted to delve into what is normally considered to be a private enterprise."

Several times during the tour Wilfred swung the car onto side streets, along which we invariably found one of the houses that he had built. Without exception, they were attractive, well-built, wood-frame structures, and my opinion of his capabilities rose progressively with each viewing.

At one point I asked, "Did you prepare all of the plans for those houses?"

"Well," he began somewhat undecidedly, "yes, I made up the floor plan in each case. Then I turned it over to a carpenter who built it."

"Then the details of the elevations and the roof were actually his creations," I suggested.

"Yes," he reluctantly admitted, "but I pointed out other houses to him from which he copied some of those details." Then, with a thoughtful mien, he asked, "How did you build your houses?"

"I used a slightly different approach," I answered cautiously.

"How different?" he persisted.

Since he had deliberately attacked me so recently, I decided that there really was no good reason why I should treat him so tactfully, so I answered, "Of course, I prepared a floor plan, like you did; however, in each case I included the elevations, the roof, and the details of their construction. Furthermore, I provided details of internal items, such as cabinets, closets, and fireplaces, if there were to be any. In some cases I even provided details of the plumbing and the electrical systems."

"That must have been an awful lot of work," he muttered. "The carpenter did all of those things for me."

"He must have been a very talented carpenter," I said. "In fact, every one of those houses looks great."

Of course, Wilfred may have justifiably accepted the statement as an indirect compliment for selecting such a fine carpenter, whereas I had intended it only to be a compliment to the carpenter. In any event, I swear to Allah that the man's chest suddenly expanded to the point where his entire facade took on the appearance of one massive paunch.

"I was building speculatively," he said, "so I always built what would sell."

"I had a general contractor's license," I said, "so I built houses according to the whims of my clients, but I designed every house that I built, and I did all of that design work between seven in the evening and midnight. From the hours of seven in the morning until five in the afternoon I supervised the construction of up to ten houses at one time. I assure you that I was a very busy man."

"I would certainly think so," he responded with a skeptical expression.

Then José began to berate me for revealing so much of my building career and for expecting the man to believe it. "From bitter experience," he reminded me, "we've learned that many people readily accept the most illogical of falsehoods and just as readily refuse to accept the most logical facts."

Raceways? As we approached the central part of the city from the Woodhaugh area, every driver seemed to be accelerating his vehicle instead of reducing its speed as is normally required by law. Just after another near miss at an intersection, I said, "According to a recent article in the newspaper, the government intends to do something about the number of fatalities from auto accidents in this country."

"It's about time," Wilfred retorted. "But they don't have to make any more laws. All they have to do is require that the police enforce the ones we have. Everybody is driving too fast and taking too many chances in heavy traffic like this. Something has to be done about it, and it should be done immediately."

At that instant his point seemed to be particularly well taken, because we and the motorists around us were exceeding the forty-kilometer-per-hour speed limit by no less than fifteen kilometers. Suddenly I involuntarily clenched my hands into fists and forcefully thrust my right foot against the floorboard as the front bumper of the Ford almost merged with the rear bumper of a Simca, whose driver was desperately braking it to avoid striking the car directly ahead of him.

"That's true," I growled through clenched teeth, "but the problem seems to be one of too much conformity, because everybody is driving like a complete idiot."

"Yeah," he agreed absently. "Everybody is driving too fast and taking too many chances."

With that statement still fluttering on the air waves, he adroitly swung *à droite* to pass the slower moving Simca and missed removing its right rear fender by no more than two inches. The man's skill or luck could not be denied, because he didn't even have the advantage of my unobstructed view.

Meanwhile, I fervently hoped that the Ford would never be involved in any homicides of any kind, because my right footprints were permanently imprinted all over that sheet metal floor panel. After carefully reconsidering the problem, I decided that those prints could never be traced through the records to me, because it seemed unlikely that Doc Doty took my footprints after he slapped my fanny in that small hospital in Seward, Nebraska, some seventy-four years ago.

But Wilfred's wild maneuver proved to be wasted, because the lines of traffic were halted by the next stoplight, so the Ford ended up in the same position relative to the Simca: directly behind the car that stood beside the Simca.

As the vehicles surged ahead in response to the green light, Wilfred suddenly pointed to a pedestrian who was being chased to the curb by the Simca. "See that!" he exclaimed as he narrowly missed the neatly crafted *posterieur* of a comely lass. "The drivers extend no courtesy whatsoever to the pedestrians."

"Yes, I saw **that**!" I exclaimed and turned my head to hide an insistent smile. "Last week, after a dinner at the Best Cafe," I resumed, "I boarded a bus at the point where Princes Street intersects with the Octagon, and when the driver released the brakes, I'm sure that he deliberately swung the vehicle as close to a young woman as he could without actually striking her. She was so frightened that she stumbled and almost fell in her frenzy to escape from that big juggernaut."

"If she had fallen, the bus probably would have run right over her," he volunteered.

"Probably," I granted without real conviction.

"There's no justification for that kind of driving," he muttered. "No wonder we have so many fatalities on our streets."

"In California the pedestrian always has the right of way," I remarked.

"They have it here, too," he rejoined. "Haven't you noticed how all of the cars come to a stop when you walk across our street at the Cavel intersection?"

"Yes," I replied, "but it is equipped with a special pedestrian crosswalk prominently marked with big, fat, white lines so that no driver can fail to see it. The next such crosswalk may be six or eight blocks away; consequently, any pedestrian who tries to save steps by crossing the street between them has to run for his life, because all of the drivers appear to consider him to be fair game. In California pedestrians always have the right of way regardless of where they walk."

From the man's expression, I gathered that he was mentally inviting me to return to California if I didn't like the way that pedestrians were being treated in New Zealand, so I wisely dropped the subject.

A Pound of Flesh

About ten o'clock during a Friday morning I pushed aside the blue-and-white plastic streamers guarding the doorway of the butcher shop and sauntered into its dimly lit interior. Meanwhile, the junior "Grime" broke away from the small group of townspeople that had collected in the rear room and advanced toward the counter.

"Good moahnin'," he said. "How kin Oy hilp ye?"

"Well," I began contemplatively, "I really came to do some negotiating, so I suppose that I really should be conferring with 'Grime' senior."

After an amiable nod, he turned away and moved toward the rear room. Pausing en route, he turned and called back, "If ye want to boy the shop, he moight sill it pritty chaip this moahnin'." And I responded with a smile.

He huddled briefly with the older man, who ducked his head in agreement and turned toward the doorway. Jauntily approaching the counter, he cordially called, "Good dye. How be ye?"

"Fine, thank you," I replied. "And you must be enjoying good health, because you appear to be in a cheerful mood."

"Moy hilth is foine," he granted, "but Oy have to stye hilthy, because this plice demands moy constant attintion."

"According to your son, you might be induced to sell out for a pretty cheap price this morning," I ventured with a smile.

"Wot!" he exclaimed incredulously. "Me sill this shop? Not on yoah loife. It's all that stands between me and stahvation. In fact, Oy'm practically stahvin' as it is."

"You starve!" I retorted derisively. "You'll never starve with all of this luscious meat to eat."

"Oy don't dayah eat any of this mate, because Oy have to sill iviry kilo of it to pie moy criditoahs," he claimed. "Othahwoise they'll close me up."

I fixed a skeptical gaze on the man's cheerful countenance and said, "No doubt you are anxious to get back to work, so I'll get to the reason for this visit." His eyes assumed an expectant expression, so I resumed: "Both Wilfred and Isibelle have been very helpful during my stay at the motel; therefore, now that I'm about to leave, I would like to tender a token of my appreciation to them."

"They won't accipt direct piemint," he guessed. And I nodded.

"I tried to get Wilfred to set a rental rate on that old typewriter of his, but he refused," I added. "Furthermore, not only has Isibelle sent Wilfred over to my digs several times with plates full of goodies, but she has done some sewing for me, so I owe both of them."

"That's jist loik thim," he murmured with a nod. "They ah viry koind people."

With several mental reservations, I finally seconded the nod, because kind people are reputed to give vent to their baser impulses. Even so, I still intended to repay them for their kindnesses and let their unkindnesses shift for themselves.

"A rental typewriter would have been relatively costly," I resumed, "but Wilfred's machine didn't warrant equal consideration, because it incorporated several obsolete symbols, such as the pound in lieu of the dollar. Furthermore, a few of the hammers continued to stick even after it was cleaned, so they were a terrible nuisance."

"Oy kin see whoy he refused piemint," the little man remarked with several affirmative nods.

"Nevertheless, I feel that I owe him much more than the few bottles of bubbly that I've delivered to his office at regular intervals," I added. Then my mind wandered off into the wild blue yonder until I sensed that Graham was impatiently waiting for me to state my intentions, so I said, "Even though Wilfred hasn't demanded the usual pound of flesh for the use of his typewriter, I've decided to give him and Isibelle at least one, if not more of them, depending on your avaricious nature."

The butcher's eyes gleamed impishly. "So ye want me to cut that pound of flish off of you, eh?" he inquired.

My puzzled eyes studied the man's smiling features until José and Pancho finally interpreted the teasing intention behind the words. "No, you crazy comedian!" I blurted. "I want you to give me a receipt for the fifty dollars that I'm about to give you, but it should reflect that much credit for Wilfred and Isibelle."

"That wye they kin have a pound of whativah koind of flish they want," he suggested, "be it beef, poahk, chicken, oah mutton buahds even."

"Right on," I said. "Including the mutton birds, because that incredible man claims to like those greasy little beasties. However, I suspect that even they would be more palatable than that pound of flesh that you are so eager to carve from me."

"Please foahgive moy bluntness," he slyly requested, "but Oy'm compilled to agree with that palatable bit; furthahmoah, theah's the mattah of tindahness to be considahed."

"Watch your words, young fellow!" I warned him. "Don't forget that I'm bigger than you are."

"But don't foahgit that Oy'm the one with the cleavah," he retorted with a wide grin, plucking one of the grisly tools from a chopping block.

After silently exchanging smiles with him, I suggested, "Why don't you put that thing back on the chopping block and write a receipt before I lose my head in more ways than one."

Silently returning the cleaver to the block, he removed a pad and pencil from different repositories in his blood-stained apron and scribbled a brief notation. Meanwhile, I dug a colorful fifty-dollar bill from my wallet and flipped it onto the counter.

Extending the pad to me, he inquired, "Will that do it?" And I nodded, so he recovered the pad, tore the top sheet from it, placed it before me, and asked, "Whin do ye pline to leave?"

"Sunday morning," I replied.

"And wheah do ye pline to go from heah?" he persisted. "Bike to America?"

"Not directly," I answered. "I intend to continue on around the world via Australia."

"Oh!" he exclaimed. "That should be a wondahful trip."

"It should be," I granted. "However, for several very cogent reasons, I suspect that it will prove to be otherwise." After pausing and carefully studying the man's expression, I added, "No doubt it'll prove to be as interesting as my trip to New Zealand, but I don't expect the scenery to equal that of New Zealand."

"You loiked owah scenery?" he inquired with a gleam of pleasure peeking from his eyes.

"Yes, very much," I replied, "and I like the people, too." Then I stopped, and our gazes collided as if drawn by strong magnets. "That is," I added, "I like the New Zealanders whose minds haven't been perverted by false propaganda. Unfortunately, I've encountered some very strange behavior patterns among some of the residents of Musselburgh; consequently, my opinions of some New Zealanders are not very complimentary."

Frowning deeply, he murmured, "New Zealand is rathah remotely located, and it has a rilatively small population, consisting lahgely of the discindants of immigrants from the British Isles. Consequently, they still ritine many of the beliefs of theah ancistahs, so they ah a wee bit set in theah wyes."

"I have no quarrel with either their ways or their beliefs," I muttered. "In fact, I've retained many of the beliefs of my ancestors, who migrated to America from Great Britain, and I'm somewhat set in my ways, too. Therefore, I tend to be rather critical of people who are prone to judge a person on the basis of unsubstantiated rumors instead of by his behavior."

His eyes sharply inspected mine; then he asked, "Has somebody said something?"

"No," I responded with a pensive glance, "but I read people very readily, so no words were required to alert me to the fact that, incredible as it seems, a certain dark cloud has followed me all of the way from America. Why do you ask? Were people warned not to say something?"

"We have truly enjoyed yoah visit heah," he insisted. And his attitude seemed to imply that, aside from evading the question, he was trying to convince me that no dark cloud had influenced his opinion of me.

"And I've enjoyed my visits to your shop," I responded with a feeling of deep regret, stretching forth my right hand.

He grasped it strongly and warmly, like every steady, level-headed man does. "Ye'll come bike to see us?" he inquired in commanding tones.

"I'm afraid not," I muttered. "After my travelogue is published, I may not be welcome in New Zealand."

"Oy don't see whoy not," he protested.

"Nobody likes to have his errors paraded before his eyes and the eyes of other people," I murmured, "and stupid bureaucrats like that least of all."

Nodding sagely, he suggested, "Will, come and see us anywye."

After staring thoughtfully at the countertop for a moment, I gruffly muttered, "I might just do that, but it may have to be as an illegal alien."

"That'll be all right, too," he responded with a chuckle. "Do that, and we'll tyke cayah of ye whoile you ah heah."

"Thanks for the invitation, Graham," I responded, again grasping the hand that he had extended to seal the bargain. "You've been one of the good guys, and they have become such a rare species that I never use the term loosely."

Meanwhile, the small, elderly man who had just entered the shop stopped in his tracks and stared at me with an air of avid curiosity. Characteristically, I stared coldly into his eyes and rudely brushed past him on my way to the doorway.

"That's one thing that we particularly despise," José mused. "Somebody who subjects us to a fish-eyed stare."

"Yeah," Pancho agreed. "Especially when it's somebody whom we've never seen before."

The Exodus

At six o'clock Sunday morning the elements were still undecided about how to treat my departure from Dunedin. Nevertheless, by the time that I had showered, broken my fast, and laundered the last of my soiled clothing, the sun had penetrated the hazy overcast. So I placed the damp shirts in the electric dryer and hung the other items—a pair of jeans, a pair of pajamas, some socks, and two pairs of shorts—on the clothesline. While they were drying, I removed the few remaining items of food from the refrigerator and deposited them, along with some other waste, in one of the four-gallon metal containers that stood along the base of the wooden fence, which was located just beyond the clotheslines.

At ten o'clock I strode to the doorway and found that a cleaning cart was parked in front of Unit 4, so I continued to the unit's open doorway.

"Wilfred!" I called.

Isibelle emerged from an inner doorway and coldly said, "He's nixt doah." Then she gestured toward Unit 5.

I wondered why the sudden frigid air, but I understood why when she stepped aside and the figure of her new cleaning woman was revealed. Apparently she was trying to prove to the woman that she, like her neighbors, completely disapproved of this ancient outlander.

"Thank you," I responded with even greater courtesy than usual. Then I turned about and departed. I was determined not to become involved in an exchange of rudenesses, especially since the woman was old enough to know better.

At the doorway of Unit 5 I repeated my previous call, and the man's head and shoulders popped through the upper part of an inner doorway.

"Albert!" he shouted in his usual ebullient manner. "What can I do for you?"

"This time it's a question of what I'm going to do for you," I retorted.

"Albert, what are you up to?" he inquired with a ridiculous giggle.

Suddenly I was convinced that the butcher had briefed him regarding my intentions, despite my request that he not do so. Nevertheless, I continued on with the charade as if such were not the case.

"Why don't you take a brief break," I suggested. "What I'm about to do concerns both you and Isibelle."

"Now you haven't gone and got some more goodies, have you?" he rejoined in an apparent attempt to cover his guilty knowledge.

"No, this is a much more practical gift," I replied, turning toward Unit 4.

From close behind me he called, "Isibelle! Albert has something that he wants to give us."

The woman's cold features slowly preceded her bulky body through the kitchen doorway, beyond which her new menial labored over the sink. Since Wilfred had usually benefited directly from my largess in the past, I had intended to present the gift certificate to her, but her irrational change of attitude so irritated me that I turned about and presented it to him.

"Oh, it's a certificate of fifty dollars credit at the butcher shop!" he exclaimed coyly. "Just for the use of that old typewriter."

"Plus some baking treats and repairs to some of my clothing," I reminded him. But I was already on my way out of the unit, because the illogical behavior of people has always turned me off, and Isibelle's cold response was a prime example of such behavior.

Wilfred followed me through the front doorway, where we stopped and he uneasily asked, "Albert, you won't forget your promise not to apply that stupid British dialect in the dialogues that involve me, will you?"

A picture of a previous scene flashed onto my mental TV screen, where, in response to one of the episodes that I had allowed him to read, he had childishly protested, "But Oy don't loik the wye you've indicated my dialict. It makes me sound too much loik a bloody Englishman."

"But very likely those crudely crafted scenes involving you will never get beyond my friends and family," I had observed. "Besides, they are much too rough for publication."

"No. Oy think that they are very good," he had insisted. "In fact, Oy think that they could be published as they are."

As the picture faded, I looked directly into his eyes and promised, "I assure you that if any of this material ever gets into print, the bulk of your dialogue won't be in dialect."

After an absent nod, he glanced down at the hand containing the certificate and insisted, "You shouldn't have done this." Then, after a long pause, he loudly added, "Albert, you are a terrible man."

"You've said that before just as deliberately," I retorted icily, "and my answer is much the same: I'm one of the good guys. Furthermore, very soon I'm going to tell my side of the story to the public, and I promise you that it will point up how very sick some of you people are."

Then the injustice of the man's response to my generous overture finally struck my mind like a bludgeon, and I was filled with disgust. Such examples of the shallowness of human nature have always disgusted me; nevertheless, I was determined to treat him courteously.

"It's very easy for someone to make false claims," I muttered. "And in most cases I've found that it doesn't appear to bother the individual's conscience one bit. Unfortunately, there's no possible defense against some claims. For example, suppose that someone claimed you to be infected by AIDS. How could you successfully refute such a claim? You can't entirely. Even if you obtained a medical certificate disproving the claim, only some of those who had heard the claim would learn of the error; consequently, the rumor would continue to grow and eventually destroy you. Big Brother can do that to you if he chooses to do so, and there's nothing that you can do about it." The man's features bore a very thoughtful expression as he turned about and trudged back to his task.

Meanwhile, I strolled to the clothesline and inspected my laundry, and since it proved to be unexpectedly damp, I moved it into the electric dryer. While I was returning to Unit 3 from that task, the large, middle-aged blonde who appeared to be spending most of her "holiday" in the opposite unit suddenly barged through its doorway.

"Whoy ah you mykin' so miney trips back and foahth?" she called. "You ah goin' to weah out the pivemint at this rite."

I paused in the middle of the "pivemint" and pensively studied her. Apparently she was still trying to strike up an acquaintance, but I had looked into a mirror recently, so I was firmly convinced that the man in front of the image was a most unlikely prospect for her "holiday" fling.

"I'm planning to leave here shortly," I explained, "so I've been doing some last-minute laundry."

"You ah goin' to continue yoah world touah," she responded more informatively than interrogatively.

"Yes," I replied.

Meantime, José egotistically reminded me, "I warned you that Wilfred or Isibelle, and probably both of them, have been informing her and the other tenants of your historical background."

"And your future plans, too," Pancho inserted.

"Yes, he's leaving today," Wilfred interjected from directly behind me.

"Have you noticed how often that man appears on the scene whenever one of the tenants engages Al in a conversation?" Pancho inquired.

"Of course, I have," José retorted. "After all, it was I who first pointed it out to you. Furthermore, I also pointed out that Wilfred probably shows up to forestall his chance exposure as Al's advance agent, so to speak."

"If so, the man's efforts have been totally wasted," Pancho rejoined, "because that woman practically exposed him by trying to flirt with Al immediately after her arrival."

"Yeah, but Al refused to waste his valuable time," José observed, "even though she paraded before her open doorway in what would have been a sexy, new sunsuit if she had possessed the wherewithal to make it sexy."

"It's unlikely that her fat-mottled thighs would have tantalized even a much younger man than Al," Pancho chimed in.

"Yes," José resumed, "everything that the woman has done and said indicates that Wilfred must have repeated Al's oft-told history to her."

"Over the years we've become much too aware of the compulsions of some people to be the bearers of startling news regardless of whether it's fact or fiction," Pancho responded, "and Wilfred fits the mold to perfection."

Since I had nothing to contribute to the lopsided conversation, I abruptly broke away from the group with the words, "Please excuse me, because I must prepare for my upcoming departure."

By eleven o'clock I was at loose ends: My luggage had been carefully packed, the bus schedule had been checked several times, and I had become bored with waiting for time to pass. Even though it was still much too early to leave, I finally decided that it wouldn't be any more tiring to wait at the bus terminal. Besides, I wanted to arrive there with sufficient time to study the surroundings and determine whether my departure was being officially monitored, so I called a cab.

Since there was no immediate need for a taxicab, one appeared before the doorway almost before I had replaced the telephone on its cradle. After carrying the heavy suitcase and the almost equally heavy briefcase to the rear of the vehicle, I helped the driver stow them in the boot. Then he strode back toward the open car door while I trudged toward the opposite door.

I had just placed my hand on the handle when, in somewhat strangled tones, a voice shouted, "Albert!"

I turned toward the source, which proved to be Wilfred, of course. Like a big, disheveled eagle, he stood as if poised for flight from the edge of the stoop of Unit 5. Then he took off toward me with his flat sandals slapping against the pavement so hard that each sharp report sounded like a shot from a pistol. His thick legs moved with surprising rapidity for a man with so much bulk, but the brief dash must have been taxing, because he was breathing heavily when he pulled up in front of me and stretched forth his right hand.

"You weren't going to leave without saying goodbye, were you?" he inquired anxiously.

Momentarily I pondered ignoring the eager hand, and such a rejection would have been fully justified after the man's vicious attack of less than an hour before. Unfortunately, I've always been afflicted with a kind heart, so I reluctantly extended my right hand.

He grasped it almost convulsively. "Have a nice trip," he rumbled.

"I'll try," I muttered, "but I suspect that it will not turn out that way. By the way, Wilfred," I added in louder tones, "be very careful in selecting the next man that you back up to, because he may have AIDS."

He turned startled eyes toward mine; then they veered anxiously toward those of the driver, who was staring curiously at him, almost as curiously as some of the mussels of Musselburgh had stared at me during the past few weeks. After turning away and opening the door, I glanced back at Wilfred and found that he was still standing there with his right hand slackly outstretched and his mouth hanging agape. Possibly, for the first time in his life, the man had become inarticulate.

"Maybe that'll teach you not to spread false rumors, Wilfred," Pancho mused as I pulled the door closed after me.

"Now you can better understand how impossible it is to defend yourself against such claims," José added.

Many times since that bitter warning, I've deeply regretted the quick, impulsive act. If the cab driver has used those few ill-advised words to start a rumor about Wilfred, I have laid a terrible penalty upon him for his attacks on me. However, if these words are ever published, they may let him off the hook; consequently, he should pray that this book is a best-seller—especially in New Zealand.

Just Waiting There was no one in the large waiting room when I arrived at the bus station, so I stacked my luggage at one end of an oaken bench. Then, slumping onto it, I began to mark time. Some time later two young Maori women entered the room through the ornate front entrance and took possession of another oaken bench, which stood against the same wall that housed the entrance.

Finally, bored with sitting and staring at the elaborately decorated high ceiling, I arose and strolled to one of the two travel posters that dominated the wall opposite the entrance. After studying it for some time, I turned about and slowly moved back toward my bench.

Meanwhile, one of the voluptuous Maori women had assumed a supine position face down on the bench with the upper parts of her tan bosom revealingly supported upon her tan forearms. As my eyes absently swept across her figure, her dark orbs boldly clung to mine until my gaze swept onward in the direction of my destination.

As I settled against the high back of my oaken bench, José volunteered, "I wonder what can be going on in the young woman's mind. Aside from sex, she surely recognizes other differences, such as race and age."

"If she has a mind," Pancho began, "she must have been bored to death to try to tantalize an old man."

"If she has a mind," José repeated, "she would have shown Al the respect that's due a senior citizen."

The number of passengers steadily grew until more than thirty of them were strung about the room. Meanwhile, a slender, dark-complexioned man entered the room and inconspicuously scanned the throng. Momentarily, his eyes rested on my two pieces of luggage, but he never looked directly at me. Some minutes later he strolled across one corner of the room to a public telephone and remained there long enough to speak briefly into the instrument. Then he replaced it on its cradle, strolled out of the room, and did not reappear. Minutes later most of the passengers boarded the express to Christchurch while somewhat more than a dozen of them remained to join me on what turned out to be a milk run.

16

Dunedin to Christchurch

The one o'clock bus from Dunedin to Christchurch was supposed to be an express, but it made a number of stops during its trip through the several small settlements tucked among the rolling hills. Some of the towns supported substantial businesses, larger than a general store, that is. For example, many of the principal buildings in Oamaru were constructed of a white stone that had been cut from a quarry within the immediate area, so it was no whistle-stop.

Some fifty miles north of Oamaru, the bus made a rest stop at Timaru, whose large businesses must have been partially supported by the adjacent fruit-bearing area. It also served as a shipping point for most of the grain and mutton from the province, and it was the home port for a small fishing fleet, so it definitely warranted more than a general store. Like Oamaru, many of its principal buildings were constructed of a local stone, bluestone in this case. Since Timaru overlooked Caroline Bay, it also was a popular seaside resort; consequently, with such a diverse economy it appeared to be more progressive and thriving than the average New Zealand town.

After the bus pulled to a stop, I trailed the other passengers out of it and followed the bus driver's directions to the rest facilities. From there I strolled into the nearby cafeteria and selected a sandwich, a glass of milk, and a small cupcake. After making the stop at the cash register, I turned away from it and visually searched the small dining area for an available table, but all of them were occupied.

While I was pondering the possibility of sharing a table with someone, a young woman with two boys detected my dilemma and beckoned for me to join them at their large table. I hurriedly scanned the area for alternatives, but there were none, so my eyes returned to the trio. Since the woman again beckoned to me, I slowly approached the table while my eyes still sought for an alternative.

"Come on," she called. "There's plenty of room for all of us."

"There doesn't appear to be any other available space," I rejoined apologetically.

"I know, so come on and join us," she insisted.

I studied the situation briefly and decided that surely I couldn't get into any trouble with a much younger woman in the company of her two small sons. Nevertheless, while I was awkwardly squirming onto the remaining straight-back chair, my mind was carefully reviewing a childhood warning never to accept gifts or offers of transportation from strangers, but an offer of space at the table of an exotic young beauty had never been mentioned, so I unwisely relaxed my vigilance.

Meanwhile, the dark-haired woman was indifferently disciplining the dark-skinned urchins, who appeared to be between seven and nine years old. Obviously, her efforts were wasted, for as soon as she diverted her attention from them to me, the older boy immediately poked the younger one in the ribs.

After I had become uncomfortably ensconced on the chair at my corner of the table, she looked across at me and asked, "Have you traveled far?"

"About halfway around the world," I responded lightly.

"From America," she guessed.

I nodded.

"Are you on your way back to America now?" she asked.

"Not directly," I replied. "From here I'm going to Australia. From there I plan to continue on around the world; that is, if it actually is round. If it should prove to be flat, as I have always suspected, then I'll probably travel in a circle."

Peering sharply at my eyes and apparently detecting the teasing gleam in them, she smiled, absently broke off a piece from her sandwich, and said, "We are from Brisbane."

"Oh!" I exclaimed for no apparent reason. "I've been led to believe that it's one of Australia's larger cities. Is your family in business there?"

Following a probing gaze she gestured toward the boys and answered, "This is the family. I'm single."

The manner in which she made the statement induced me to wonder if she had ever been married. "Then you are probably employed," I ventured. "Or do you just maintain the family?" And I also gestured toward the two lads, who were obviously listening intently to the exchanges.

"I work in a market near where we live," she murmured with a guilty glance toward her offspring.

"Then you are a checker," I speculated.

"Yes," she answered.

The older and darker boy looked across his shoulder toward her and caustically remarked, "But you don't work there all of the time, mum."

"Well, I'm working there part-time now," she admitted to me, "but I hope to get on permanently."

"That seems like a nice place for you to work," I said. "Is it close to your home?"

"Yes, it's very convenient," she answered. "I can walk to work."

Apparently the smaller boy had either pushed or pinched his sibling, because the bigger boy suddenly turned and leveled a blow at his shoulder.

"Hey!" the woman shouted. "You fellows behave. You're not in the outback now." Then, turning back to me, she mildly inquired, "Where do you plan to go in Australia?"

"I have an open flight to Sydney," I replied, "but I have no further plans."

"Then you aren't on a tour," she said.

"I'm not on a tour," I admitted. "I'm just groping my way around the world." Fixing my eyes on hers, I asked, "If you were to plan a trip through Australia for a touring outlander, where would you suggest that he go?"

Her eyes pensively studied the top of the table for a moment; then she looked up at me and asked, "Why don't you come to Brisbane? In fact, I'll give you my name and address, and you can come and see me while you are there. Wouldn't you like that?"

My eyes must have revealed my amazement, because she lowered hers with an uneasy air.

"What's to be seen up there other than the Great Barrier Reef?" I finally inquired.

"Brisbane," she answered. "Of course, you could go from Sydney to Melbourne. It's a pretty big city."

"I'm not interested in seeing big cities," I said. "They are very much alike."

"Well, you could come to Brisbane and go snorkeling along the reef," she persisted with a calculating glance.

Actually, I had been considering a trip north from Sydney to Brisbane, but I suddenly decided that Brisbane was off limits to me, and one of the reasons was sitting directly across the table from me.

Finally, I looked at her and pointedly observed, "That might be a bit much for an old man."

Apparently I had failed to get the message across to her, because she then suggested, "You could ride out to the reef in a glass-bottom boat and view it and its underwater gardens through the bottom of the boat. I think you would like that. In fact, you might like Brisbane and want to stay awhile."

"What other points of interest are located on this side of Australia?" I asked.

Once more she studied the top of the table; finally, looking up from it, she replied, "There's Alice Springs; however, it's located in the middle of the continent."

"What's so spectacular about Alice Springs?" I countered.

"Well, it's reported to have some nice vacation spots," she answered. "And it's the jumping off spot for the trip to the Uluru National Park, which includes Ayers Rock and the Olgas."

"And what's so spectacular about Ayers Rock?" I persisted.

"It's a massive, red rock," she answered. "The biggest solid rock in the world, in fact."

"I suspect that some of the people in Georgia will take exception to that statement," I responded with a light laugh. "They claim to have the biggest solid rock in the world, but it may be just the biggest solid rock of a specific composition, such as granite or limestone."

"Ayers Rock is more than eleven hundred feet high," she resumed, "and the distance along its base exceeds five miles, so it has to be the largest monolith in the world. Besides, much more of it extends beneath the surrounding desert."

"Stop! Stop!" I exclaimed lightly. "You have convinced me. But since thoughts of a journey into the desert of central Australia are repulsive to me, I'll probably never be able to check those dimensions."

"There are lots of beautiful scenery and beaches along the eastern and northern coasts," she murmured, "and Brisbane provides the best access to them." Then she smiled coyly at me.

There was no way that I could miss her message, but I chose to ask, "Why don't you have an Australian accent?"

A pleased smile lit her features; then she replied, "I lived in Canada for a while."

"Oh, so did I," I rebounded. "In what part of Canada did you live?"

"In Ontario," she replied.

With a shake of my head, I said, "Some of my boyhood was spent on the plains of Saskatchewan and a bit more of it on the west coast of British Columbia, but I've never lived in any of the eastern provinces. Since that time I've been in parts of

Ontario: principally Windsor, Toronto, Hamilton, and some of the towns along the north shore of Lake Ontario."

Since she didn't pick up the conversational ball, I assumed that she had lived in none of those urban areas. Meanwhile, Pancho suggested, "She may have been married to a French Canadian, since that could account for the dark features of her offspring."

"Naw," José retorted. "The boys' features are darker than a mixture of Anglo and Gallic bloods would warrant. In fact, their features are dark enough to have been produced by a union with a Malaysian or even an aborigine."

During the ensuing silence the subjects of our study suddenly erupted into a flurry of fisticuffs, and the woman absently intervened. However, as she withdrew from them, the older one made a belated pass at the other one, who responded with a couple of solid punches to the attacker's shoulder.

"Hey, you guys!" she exclaimed. After separating them, she warned, "Behave or I'll leave you here and go back without you." Apparently they considered it to be a bona fide threat, because they created no new disturbances.

Meantime José and Pancho were sorting through several different possibilities. "She might be an international tramp who depends for survival on the largess of male associates, on the handouts of a socialistic government, or on both," José proposed.

"Perhaps she's hoping to expand that income from the pockets of an old man whom she may have deliberately contacted at a rest stop en route to her base of operations," Pancho suggested.

"If so," José resumed, "she's working on the wrong prospect, because that man has never knowingly associated with any kind of a tramp. In fact, he's so cautious about and suspicious of chance female acquaintances that she could be the Mona Lisa in disguise."

"In this case don't bank on that," Pancho advised.

"Then we'll continue to be ultracautious," José responded virtuously.

After a brief lapse in our conversation, the woman turned to me from a surveillance of the boys and resumed her attack: "I think you should come to Brisbane, because you'll find more natural beauty there than in most of the other parts of the eastern shoreline."

"The suggestion does appeal to me," I responded with deliberate obscurity to avoid a suspicion that I was either accepting or rejecting her invitation. "However, I particularly dislike very hot climates, so I suspect that Brisbane would probably be much too hot for me."

My eyes studied hers during my brief attempt to determine if she had fielded the deliberate innuendo, but they detected no evidence of it. Nevertheless, to cover my tracks, I added, "In fact, I've been planning to spend some time in Tasmania for that very reason."

"Tasmania is nice," she granted grudgingly, "but there's nothing to do there. Hobart's not large, and it's the island's only city. It's a nice place to visit, but I suspect that a long stay might be very boring."

"And she's implying that Brisbane won't be boring," José interjected wistfully.

"But Al is not about to find out for himself," Pancho insisted firmly.

With those opinions in mind, I slowly arose and said, "It was very kind of you to share your table with me, and I thoroughly enjoyed our conversation. It has been especially nice to talk to someone who has lived in my part of the Northern Hemisphere. We have a long way to travel, so we'll probably bump into each other again." Since she smiled pleasantly, I assumed that she didn't resent my failure to request her name and address.

"I'm sure that wherever you travel in Australia, you'll enjoy it," she called after me.

In passing the cashier's counter, I glanced beyond it, and my eyes intercepted the same cold stare from the same plump, middle-aged woman who had so aloofly accepted my payment thirty minutes before. Two paces later, I glanced across the same shoulder toward her and found that she was exchanging very knowing glances with an equally plump, middle-aged woman.

"So they've been fully briefed," José injected into my thoughts. "Apparently Big Brother has removed his wraps, so our outgoing trip is to be much different from the incoming one."

"But we expected as much and even predicted it," Pancho remarked. "After fifty years of dealing with that monster, we've acquired the equivalent of a doctoral degree in his type of abnormal psychology, so it's easy to predict how he will react under any given set of circumstances."

Beyond Timaru the highway veered inland from the Canterbury Bight and passed through Ashburton, which was about half of the distance between Timaru and Christchurch. Finally the bus pulled into Christchurch's New Zealand Railroad Services depot, which stands within a triangle created by the intersection of Victoria and Durham Streets.

After recovering my luggage, I lugged it to a public telephone and tried to call one of the local motels, but I soon gave up in despair. Apparently every New Zealand telephone had my number, so it was futile for me to try to get one of theirs.

Upon turning away from the instrument, I almost bumped into the woman from Brisbane, who was replacing the adjoining instrument, but she didn't see me for looking right through me. Of course, that didn't surprise me, since so many similar incidents had occurred in the past, both deliberately and absentmindedly.

Meanwhile, the older of her sons was bearing down on her. "Are we gonta have a place to stay?" he inquired anxiously, pulling up beside her.

The woman placed one arm across the backpack on his shoulders, pulled him against her thigh, and murmured, "I don't know yet, because no one answers the telephone."

"But they know we're coming, don't they?" he inquired protestingly.

"Yes," she continued to murmur, "I sent them a card, so they must know that we're here. Maybe they're out shopping or something."

"Maybe they've gone outa town or they didn't get the card," he suggested with a worried expression.

Despite the woman's apparent snub, my heart reached out to the waifs. Meanwhile, my mind tried to explain away the apparent snub as the product of a preoccupied or overwrought mind.

"What will we do if you can't get them on the telephone?" the boy asked, as the second one rounded a corner and hurtled toward them at breakneck speed.

"Don't worry," she murmured, absently reaching out and corralling the backpack of the newcomer. Then, pulling it and the boy against her other thigh, she added, "I'll call again in a few minutes. Maybe they'll answer then."

Sanity must have fled my mind, because I continued to hover in the background until she finally returned from the telephone to the eternally squabbling brats with an extremely discouraged air. Obviously, sanity **had** fled my mind, because I was about to suggest to the woman that, since I sensed their problem, I would foot the motel bill for her and her brood.

Fortunately, Pancho intervened in the nick of time. "Don't be a sympathetic fool, Al," he warned. "Neither she nor Big Brother will believe that your motive is strictly altruistic. Despite the fact that her actions seem to indicate that she has been briefed, she might eagerly accept the offer, especially if she is, as we have so readily suspected, a woman whose primary medium of exchange is her body."

"Yeah, listen to reason, Al," José injected. "Of course, we've come to recognize the character of Big Brother only by the products of his surreptitious behavior. Nevertheless, with that knowledge to go on, we know that he would place another black mark opposite your name if you do this insane thing, so listen to reason."

"Yeah," Pancho chimed in. "Since all bureaucrats are drawn from society, Big Brother's minions can't be expected to reason logically, so the dark cloud that has hovered over us so long will only become darker, even though your gift to that family would terminate the misadventure."

"From Big Brother's past performances, we know that his mind must have evolved from a cesspool," José interceded, "so its reasoning is sure to be contaminated. Listen to reason, Al."

Reluctantly picking up my luggage, I turned about for one last look at the unhappy trio, and my eyes involuntarily settled on the eyes of the older boy. They bore the same concerned expression that mine must have borne when, at the same age, I stood alongside my mother and two sisters in front of the Regina railroad depot with three heavy pieces of luggage.

"Why is there no one here to meet us?" my younger sister piped.

"Mostly because no one knows that we're coming," my mother replied.

"Can't we pay someone to take us there?" my older sister inquired.

"Yes, but we can't afford that luxury," my mother murmured brokenly.

That forlorn cry on the desolate plains of Saskatchewan tore my heart to shreds. At that instant I became a man. I had to become one because the self-centered head of our family had forsaken his responsibilities.

"Then we'll walk," I muttered gruffly, reaching down and picking up the two heaviest suitcases.

"How far is it?" my older sister asked.

"About seven miles," my mother replied, as she glanced down uneasily at the smaller girl.

Manlike, I sensed her concern and responded, "We'll stop and rest for a while when she gets tired."

"But you can't carry both of those heavy suitcases," she protested.

Manlike, I insisted, "Yes, I can." Later I breathed a sigh of relief when she insisted on lending a helping hand to the handle of one of them while the two girls shared the handle of the much smaller one.

Fortunately, after about two miles of bone-tearing travel along the unpaved road, a kind-hearted Canadian by the name of McCracken stopped his touring car alongside us and genially invited us aboard. But he refused to drop us off at the driveway alongside his farmhouse, which happened to be located about one mile nearer the city than our destination. As they say in Dixie, he "carried us all the way." Consequently, one day when the man's son, Archie, was attacked by our school's bully I was morally obligated to step into the fray and subdue the aggressor. But the act also served to cement a growing friendship with Archie, who shared the two-mile trek to and from the one-room, country schoolhouse.

Christchurch Revisited

With that memory in mind, I felt like a traitor as I reluctantly turned my back on the lad and carried my luggage through the station to the rear of a taxicab that stood at the curb.

After stowing the luggage in the boot, the driver peered intently at me and asked, "Wheah would you loik to go?"

"To a nice, economical motel," I replied.

"Theah's a numbah of thim on Papanui Road," he suggested somewhat tentatively.

"That sounds familiar," I responded, "so let's see what we can find on Papanui Road."

When I settled back against the seat, Pancho sounded off: "Al's all guts. He has no heart whatsoever."

"If you are referring to the previous problem, that's not strictly so," José insisted. "He has lots of heart, but he doesn't have the guts to defy the mores of a pixilated society."

"The *bleep* you say!" Pancho shouted silently. "Why do you suppose Big Brother has been hounding him all of these years?"

"Theah ah some motels," the driver interjected into the melee and nodded toward our left, "and theah ah moah of thim on this soide of the road." Then he gestured to our right.

After peering at some of the structures, I suggested, "Let's go to the end of the line and then come back."

"Okye," he responded with a disapproving glance in my direction. "You must be from America."

Peering pensively through the gathering gloom at him, I pondered the likelihood that his conclusion derived more from my decision to waste more coins on the meter than from my accent. Certainly no New Zealander would be so wasteful. "Yes," I finally admitted.

"Theah ah only a few moah motils in this area," he said. "Then we'll have to travel some distance to. . . ."

"I suspect that we've gone far enough," I interjected. "In fact, that one looks like the one where I stayed last time," I added while pointing across my shoulder to our left.

"The Ashford Village?" he muttered.

"Uh-huh," I grunted. "I'm sure that's the one. Let's go back and see if they have available accommodations."

Looking back, he braked the cab sharply, made a U-turn, and drove onto the driveway of the motel.

"Please wait while I determine if there's a vacancy," I requested, swinging open the door.

Upon returning I muttered, "Nope. No vacancy," in response to the question in his eyes.

"That's surproisin'," he muttered. "Shuahly they still have a vikency." And he repeated the intent stare that he had bestowed on me at the bus station.

"But the manager was very courteous," I protested almost defensively. "In fact, she telephoned the adjacent Colonial Inn and found that they have a vacancy."

Long ago I had discovered that certain service people, such as cab drivers and waitresses, often display evidence of the Unknown's blight, so I had sufficient reasons to be extremely suspicious of the man's curious illogical behavior.

At the Colonial Inn I stared searchingly into the eyes of the personable young man at the desk, but his reactions to my presence seemed to be quite normal. Nevertheless, I pursued the matter further by saying: "I'm following up on a recent inquiry from the Ashford Arms." Then, after looking sharply into his eyes and still perceiving no token of the unusual, I added, "From the inquiry I gather that you have a vacancy."

"Yes," he replied, "we have several of them. What kind of a unit do you wish?"

"An economical single," I replied. "But I'll gladly pay a small premium for the use of an alarm clock if you have one. I have to catch the seven-thirty train to Picton in the morning."

"We have lots of requests for alarm clocks," he replied. Then, reaching beneath the countertop, he withdrew a large, old-fashioned alarm clock and placed it on the counter in front of me.

I watched as he scribbled my name and several numerals on a registration form bearing the familiar symbol of the Best Western motels. Meanwhile, I slowly extracted forty-eight dollars in bills from my wallet and placed them on the counter. Then he stamped the form paid.

Picking up a copy of the form, I accepted the key and turned toward the doorway. Abruptly I came to a grinding stop and returned to the alarm clock. "How much for the use of this?" I asked, reaching for my wallet.

Thrusting both palms toward me, he vigorously shook his head and said, "That's part of our service."

"Thank you very much," I muttered. "You New Zealanders never cease to amaze me. In my country I would have had to pay practically a new price for the use of that clock for just one night."

After smiling pleasantly, he tactfully added, "I'm sure that many such things are handled differently all over the world."

Following a nod, I asked, "Is there a good restaurant close by?"

"There aren't any really close by," he drawled, "but we have an excellent coffee shop. Would you like for me to warn the hostess that you are planning to patronize it?" In response to my puzzled expression, he added, "Otherwise they might close the kitchen a bit early this evening."

"It won't be necessary for you to warn her," I said. "I'll quickly stow my luggage, wash up, and go directly to the coffee shop."

While trudging from the small office, I continued to ponder the nature of the motel manager's proposed warning. "Probably the usual," I muttered, pulling up sharply in front of the driver, who was waiting uncertainly at the rear of the cab.

"Pahdon me," he responded with a questioning glance at me from beneath lowered brows.

"No pardon required," I retorted. "At my age some people take to talking to themselves, and all of us are old enough to know better."

"Oh," he grunted. Then, noting the receipt in my hand, he began to undo the baling wire that cinched down the boot's handle against its damaged latch.

After stowing my gear in my second-floor unit, which was located in one of the motel's rear structures, I freshened up a bit and sought out the coffee shop.

A relatively short, dark-complexioned, black-haired woman of about forty approached me with a menu pressed gracefully against her bosom by the splayed thumbs and fingers of both brown hands. "Are you still serving dinner?" I inquired.

"Yes," she responded with a friendly smile. "Apparently you are the man whom our friendly manager requested that we be on our toes and watch out for."

Following a quick double take, I announced: "Never before has anybody with such a friendly smile ever admitted to me that she had been requested to watch out for me."

"Oh, you deliberately twisted my words," she protested, playfully tapping my chest with one corner of the menu. "Nobody would ever have to watch out for a nice man like you."

"That's what a lot of girls have thought and lived to regret," I retorted, twirling a nonexistent tip of my nonblack moustache.

"Oh, you're a kidder," she responded with a chuckle, repeating the playful tap on my chest. "Where would you like to be seated?"

I looked about the somewhat crowded dining room and saw that, with the exception of one elderly gentlemen, the diners consisted entirely of women, and all of them were attractively clad in much better than the equivalent of worn blue jeans and a wilted, blue shirt with short sleeves.

"Isn't there a more remote place where you can seat me?" I inquired wistfully.

Smiling understandingly, she said, "Obviously we don't have many gentlemen diners this evening, but these women are all ladies. They won't bite you."

"I certainly hope not," I muttered darkly, as she turned about and led me into another equally small dining room, where only two other diners were seated.

"Would you like this table?" she inquired, gently tapping its top with the menu.

"Well," I began with a wary glance toward the two women at the adjoining table.

"Or would you like that one?" she asked, after interpreting my glance. Then she pointed toward a larger, more remote table that stood in almost total darkness.

"If you don't mind, that one is more to my liking," I admitted. "I'm not attired to dine out this evening."

"We are not that formal," she disclaimed. "But please excuse me for a few minutes, while I get a candle for this table. Then I'll take your order."

"True, the women are not attired in evening dresses," José mused, "but they obviously have gone to great lengths to present themselves to their best advantages."

"So most women don't really dress to attract the eyes of men," Pancho observed.

"According to the attire of these women," José rejoined, "they actually dress to impress their own kind with their fineries and their artistic abilities."

A more detailed inspection of the diners in those parts of the two rooms that were still visible to me from my isolated table induced Pancho to opine, "They actually appear to be more British than the British themselves."

"But I certainly approve," José injected, "because they look so much more organized and cultured than the slobs in the Los Angeles area."

Following my guilty glance at my own attire, Pancho concluded: "And Al is an outstanding example of those slobs."

Shortly after the dusky hostess had installed a lighted candle at my table, she returned with a pad and pencil to take my order.

"So you function as a waitress, too," I remarked.

"Yes, I sort of fit in wherever there's some work to be done," she responded with a light-hearted chuckle.

Meanwhile, I pointed a forefinger toward an item on the open menu. With a shake of her head, she said, "Unfortunately, there are not many options left, because we have been very busy this evening, but there is some lamb and. . . ."

"That suits me," I interjected.

"Fine," she murmured, noting it on the pad. "And would you like some tea while you wait?" Then, as if on second thought, she added, "Or some coffee perhaps? We do have coffee for those who prefer it."

"Neither," I responded with a smile. "But I would like a glass of milk with the meal, if you please."

After she left to place the order, my gaze absently strayed toward the two women at the other occupied table. Then, much less absently, it was strongly attracted to the dark-haired woman who was seated facing me. Apparently sensing my probing gaze, her eyes veered from those of her companion to mine, which guiltily fled the scene. It may have been the lighting, the setting, or both, but she appeared to be exquisitely attractive. Several minutes later my eyes involuntarily betrayed me again, and the woman's eyes immediately intercepted their wayward gaze. Her eyes bore the confidence of a woman who was accustomed to attracting the eyes of men—or the eyes of women, for that matter—because she was a beautiful creature, a creature whom everyone would view with open admiration. But her eyes were not flirtatious eyes.

During my meal I tried to avoid looking toward that table, but I succumbed several times, and invariably the woman sensed my gaze and met it. One time she smiled, so she must not have been annoyed by those occasional invasions of her privacy. In fact, she seemed to treat them as just tributes of a lowly subject to a member of the royalty. In still another instance she smiled, looked toward her friend, and murmured something, but I was unable to read her lips. Seconds later that friend cautiously looked across her left shoulder at me; then she quickly turned away after our gazes collided.

The women then inclined their heads to each other, and this time I easily read the beauty's lips as she whispered, "He's cute, isn't he?"

I doubt that her friend fully agreed with her. In fact, I was very thankful that the candlelight at my table was dim enough to confuse such a beautiful creature. Of course, my beard hid many imperfections, but I knew from experience that women are very inclined to forgive the shortcomings of men who admire them. Since that woman could not have been half my age, I'm sure that neither of us had any stupid ideas regarding a closer relationship. Furthermore, I had arrived at that enviable point in my life when a man can admire a woman's beauty without being expected to make the usual male overtures—passes, that is.

After finishing the repast, I patiently waited for the hostess to appear with the check and absently wondered what could be keeping her. Apparently she was in the part of the other dining room that was not visible to me, because I could hear the low tones of her voice interspersed with other feminine exclamations and comments. Finally she came into view with a baby in her arms, and I saw that she was slowly moving from table to table so that each group of diners could admire the child, who was decked out in all of the finery that its proud mother could affix to its tiny body. The parade continued up to and including the dark beauty and her lady friend, who clucked and cooed over the infant like two doves.

"Would you like to hold her?" the hostess inquired of the beauty.

"Oh, yes, please allow me," she begged, extending her arms.

With the baby tucked safely in them, she peered down into the child's bemused eyes and spoke endearingly to it, and it responded with a fatuous smile. Obviously, it loved the attention. Then she looked across the top of the tiny head toward me.

I was unable to restrain an admiring smile. Even José was moved to remark, "No artist has painted or ever will paint as beautiful a version of the Madonna and Child."

"Don't surrender to your emotions, Al," Pancho warned. "Don't express your admiration or make any innocent overture that can be misinterpreted by anyone, least of all, the beauty and her friend."

"Yeah, we haven't enjoyed so much social acceptance within the last fifty years," José injected. "Ain't it great?" And I gloried in it just as much as the child, who was drooling over its sudden acclaim.

"Surely," Pancho interposed, "Big Brother must have dropped a loop while he was knitting his deadly web for our entrapment in Christchurch."

When the child was returned to the arms of the hostess, she looked speculatively at me. After briefly studying my mesmerized eyes, she must have decided that I shouldn't be passed up, so she moved slowly toward me.

"So you are a baby sitter, too," I ventured, as she stopped beside my table.

"Yes, at the moment, I am," she granted. "Her mother is in the other room with some friends. She used to work here, so she brought this little doll in to show her off."

"And justly so," I murmured while the child and I exchanged curious stares.

"Would you like to hold her?" she inquired. Apparently she considered the act to be a great privilege.

"Oh, no!" I immediately protested. "I'm much too old for her."

Momentarily a puzzled frown hovered over her eyes; then it disappeared. After a low-keyed laugh, she murmured, "You must be from America, because Americans are the world's greatest kidders."

"Yes, I'm an American," I admitted. "However, I have the same attitude toward children that one of my countrymen, W. C. Fields, had. He professed to hate them."

"Oh, but he only professed to hate them," she protested. Then, peering down into the baby's eyes, she puckered her lips at it and softly asked, "How could anybody hate this little angel?"

At that instant the "little angel" looked at me, expelled a throaty chuckle, and drew a deep, ecstatic breath.

"See, she likes you," the woman insisted, "so how could you possibly hate her?"

"She's a living doll," I conceded. "Furthermore, she is a very astute judge of gentlemen."

The dark eyes crinkled in a pleased smile as she hoisted the child from one arm to the other one and murmured, "I've had her for quite a while now, so I better take her back to her mother and get your check."

"Take your time," I said. "There's no hurry for that check, because I could remain here in this congenial atmosphere for the remainder of my life." And I meant it.

"How nice of you," she murmured. Then, hoisting her burden up against one shoulder, she turned about and slowly moved away while the baby's bright eyes peered back across the shoulder at me.

After receiving the check, I arose and retraced my steps to the table where the two women still sat with the contents of partly depleted teacups before them. In passing, I could not restrain an impulse to inspect the features of the proud beauty more closely. The effort was well invested, because, incredible as it still seems, she looked up and smiled at me. Fortunately, I still remembered how to bow my head ever so slightly just as I had been taught during my boyhood in British Columbia.

As I pushed the door open, the hostess called, "Be sure to return for breakfast."

"Unfortunately, I'll be on the way to Auckland by that time," I said. "By the way, where were you born?"

"In Malaysia," she replied.

"Amazing!" I exclaimed. "You speak so much like an American."

Chuckling delightedly, she murmured, "So many people have told me that."

Releasing the spontaneous smile that surged to my lips, I pushed open the door.

"Have a nice journey!" she called after me.

"Thank you," I called back. "I'll try."

"So that's how people behave toward us when Big Brother hasn't maliciously influenced them," José remarked, as I strode around the near corner of the coffee shop.

While I was veering toward the wooden stairway that led to my abode for the night, Pancho belatedly added, "How sweet it is!"

Typically, I awoke long before the alarm was set to sound off, so I pushed the toggle back to "silent," tossed the bedcovers back, and arose to greet the new day. After the usual morning ablutions, I pulled on clean clothing. Then, assuming a comfortable position on a straight-back chair beside the small breakfast table, I proceeded to describe roughly the adventures of the previous day on the pages of a notebook. At six o'clock, after stowing the notebook in the briefcase and calling a cab, I carried my luggage out to the curb and waited for the cab to arrive.

"Good moahnin'," the cab driver greeted me, as he came around the rear of the vehicle to help me load the luggage. "Wheah ah we bound?"

"To the railroad station," I answered. "That's on Moorhouse Avenue, isn't it?"

"Aye," he replied, so I assumed that he must be a Scottish outcast among the largely English populace.

"There's some time to burn before the train is scheduled to depart," I muttered, "so we don't have to go directly to the station."

"So ye would loik to see some of owah fayah city," he surmised.

"Yeah," I responded. "Why don't you make a brief tour of the the high points in the central part of the city?"

After pondering the suggestion briefly, he said, "Will, Oy could tyke ye pahst Hagely Pahk and on into the city propah. Would ye loik that?"

"Sounds okay to me," I answered.

"Oy big yoah pahdon," he rejoined.

Once more I was forced to realize that my dialect and rapid speech confused some New Zealanders as much as theirs confused me. "I'm sorry," I responded slowly. "I meant to say that your suggestion sounds like an acceptable one."

"Thin ye would loik to see the pahk?" he countered.

For want of better communication, I silently nodded.

Minutes later the cab turned onto Holleston Park Terrace, and I immediately exclaimed, "Oh, there's a pretty stream winding through the park!"

"That's the Avon Rivah," he informed me. "It loops around the Botanical Gahdins and loops again whin it leaves the pahk."

"It certainly adds a lot of color to the park's other natural scenery," I observed appreciatively.

"We have many pritty pahks and ricriational facilities in the city," he stated proudly.

"What is the population of this city?" I inquired.

"About three hundred thou," he replied. Again there was that tone of pride in the words, almost as if he was responsible for part of that population. Maybe he was.

"Then it's a relatively large city," I ventured.

"It isn't lahge loik London oah Tokyo," he said, "but it's one of the foah lahgist cities in New Zealand."

I carefully repressed an impulse to point out that there were only four cities in New Zealand. However, that was not strictly so either, at least not in the terms of the New World, where many New Zealand towns would be identified as cities.

"Would ye loik to see the cathedral?" he asked.

"Yes, I would," was my reply. Then, stooping very low, indeed, I paraphrased a popular American TV commercial: "In fact, I shouldn't leave here without it."

He tossed a questioning glance in my direction, but no words followed it.

From Holleston we traveled east on Cashell Street and north on Montreal Street to Worcester (*Wooster*) Street. A right turn soon brought us into close proximity with Cathedral Square, where I received the full impact of the century-old Gothic structure. For a man who greatly appreciates the arts and craftsmanship of mankind, it was a treat.

"This is a very pretty city," I observed.

"Christchurch is called the Gahdin City of New Zealand," he reported proudly.

"That may be partly due to the English people's love of gardens and flowers," I suggested.

"Ivirybody vies foah proizes foah the foinist flowah gahdins," he said, "and not just those of English ancistry. Even the businesspeople stroive to suhpass each othah."

"My country could do with a little of that spirit," I muttered, as the man slowed the vehicle to a stop in front of the elaborately decorated railway station. A brief study of its architecture led me to conclude that New Zealanders also pride themselves on the ornateness of their public buildings.

After the driver extracted my luggage and set it on the adjacent curb, I paid the fare. Then I added a substantial tip for services rendered beyond the call of duty. Like so many of the service people in that country, he seemed to be somewhat embarrassed by the tip, but he courteously thanked me for it.

17

Christchurch to Wellington

Christchurch to Picton

Of course, I was retracing my previous passage over the rails that connect Christchurch to Picton, but almost three months had elapsed since that passage, so I was interested in the effects of the austral summer on the vegetation. There proved to be little change in it, so the sheep were still grazing on the rolling hills and on the less precipitous mountain slopes, even though some of those slopes had been burned to a brownish gray by the summer sun.

Retracing the Eastern Shoreline Even the train's schedule was somewhat the same in reverse, including the rest stop at Kaikoura, where I found one wide departure from the previous norm. There I particularly noticed that practically every waitress in the restaurant was surreptitiously studying me as I went about picking out my snack. And it wasn't a case of being so different from the other male passengers, since several of them also sported nondescript beards. Furthermore, those big, fat waitresses appeared to be vying with each other in their efforts to treat me with the greatest rudeness. Such are the traits of homo sapiens, which, despite the dictionary's definition, includes modern woman. It is surprising that those critters haven't jumped all over Noah Webster's grave for his prejudice and for his abrogation of one of their primary civil rights.

From Kaikoura north, the terrain soon became so rough that the views through the windows on the left side of the train were limited to steep mountain slopes, whereas those on the right side occasionally revealed beautiful seascapes. Unfortunately my seat companion had preempted the window seat, so I was forced to peer past her head to view them. The advantage of the window seat had been wasted on her, since she slept through most of the trip. Of course, I had seen almost all of the seascapes before, but I never tire of beautiful scenery.

When the rails wandered farther inland, the scenery deteriorated to wasteland, so I began to read some of the obviously contrived episodes in a recently published New Zealand *Reader's Digest*. Periodically, my eyes alternated between the windows on both sides of the train, and they accidentally discovered still another form of entertainment.

The seat immediately behind the one directly to my left was occupied by a man and a woman, both of whom appeared to be slightly more than thirty-five years old. Since they were a well-matched pair, I immediately assumed that they were man and wife.

But that assumption was quickly set aside when I overheard the woman say, "But my brother told my husband that that wouldn't work, so he finally gave up the idea."

An involuntary turn of my head allowed me to reassess the situation, but my eyes found everything in order. The woman, who sat alongside the aisle, was primly knitting a woolen something or other, whose completed portion was folded on her lap, and the man sat with his right hand resting on the uppermost right knee of his crossed legs. They were relatively handsome people for their age, but most New Zealanders are relatively handsome at any age. My initial inspection was only a glance; then my eyes returned to the printed page while José and Pancho agreed that the duo was a typical example of how two total strangers of different sexes should behave when forced to sit side by side aboard a plodding New Zealand train—or aboard any train, for that matter.

Later, while I was turning to another article, I raised my head and absently looked through the windows on my left. In so doing, my peripheral vision detected that the woman had also crossed her knees and that the toe of her right shoe was pressed against the trouser-clad calf of the man's left leg. Meanwhile, the tempo of her knitting had increased tremendously.

"Humph," Pancho silently remarked. "It looks like there's a couple of lovebirds aboard the train."

"That opinion is based solely on circumstantial evidence," José responded, "so don't be spreading an erroneous scandal."

My attention became absorbed in the printed word, so I may have missed a few chapters of that soap opera, but I overheard no more references to a husband. In fact, the conversation subsided entirely for a while. When I next glanced toward the window on my left, the mountain slopes had pulled away from the railroad, or so it seemed. Simultaneously the knitter withdrew her toe as she uncrossed her legs; then the man swung his crossed legs away from her with an air of rejection. Apparently she sensed the rejection, because she immediately bounced up and down on the thin cushion of the seat and flung her substantial fanny solidly against his right thigh.

It was an old game that I had observed many times and even engaged in during my youth, but those people were old enough to know better. Besides, the game merely kindles fires that such people should not jointly quench.

My eyes returned to the printed page while my mind recalled my first experience with a similar woman. It occurred during the early thirties—the flirty thirties it has been called, but I have detected no appreciable increase in conservatism during the last fifty years. In fact, the actions of those two strangers seemed to indicate that such behavior is international in scope. Nevertheless, this particular incident occurred during the time when I was attending a midcontinent state university. That particular afternoon I had not only squandered a precious quarter for admission to a motion-picture theater, but I was about to squander an even more precious two hours of study time before I was to report to the place of my part-time employment. Since it was the matinee hour, the theater wasn't crowded, so I readily found an aisle seat among several unoccupied seats.

Shortly after I was seated, the dim outline of a feminine figure came to a stop in the aisle beside me, and a low voice murmured, "Pardon me, please."

Obediently, I struggled to my feet, and before I could step into the aisle to allow the newcomer free passage, her soft body squeezed past me and settled into the adjacent seat. Since there were vacant seats beyond the adjacent one, I resented the intrusion. In fact, my seat was surrounded on three sides by vacant seats. The least that she could have done was to take the seat beyond the adjacent one so that both of us would have been more at ease, because those old, wooden seats with cast-iron fittings were set much too close together. That became very apparent when the newcomer's left arm was thrust softly against my right arm; consequently, I was forced to sit stiffly erect, whereas before her arrival I had been spilling comfortably over the armrest into the area of the adjacent seat.

I had scarcely recovered my interest in the developments on the screen when my neighbor revealingly crossed her legs and allowed the toe of her right shoe to subtly nudge my right corduroy trouser leg. After a brief study of the problem, I chose to ignore it, assuming that the toe would be withdrawn when she next shifted position. As I had suspected, she did shift her position but to an even closer proximity, and the toe began to swing rhythmically against the corduroy trouser leg.

Suddenly I began to suspect that the actions were intentional, and the suspicion gave me pause, because no woman had ever deliberately attempted to tease me before, at least not so obviously. Of course, I considered withdrawing my leg, but I was young and very naive, so I adventurously left it in place and waited to see what would happen next. If I had been even half-smart, I would have withdrawn my leg and never allowed another woman to get that close to it again. As it was, the creature soon got around to pressing her knee firmly against mine. Fortunately, my blood vessels were strong and flexible, because my hot blood was bubbling up to a bursting pressure, and the increased pressure of her soft shoulder against my solidly muscled arm did not relieve that stress one bit.

Some self-styled authorities on the subject of romance have claimed that men are the most romantic of the two sexes, and they may be correct in that claim. In any event, at that particular time in my history I proved to be no exception to the claim. Since the area was dimly lighted, I couldn't distinctly see my amorous neighbor, so my mind began to conjure up a veritable vision of a lithe, young beauty, possibly a couple of years younger than I, and one who, for some inexplicable reason, was drawn passionately to me—and only to me. Of course, I should have realized that it had to be only a dream, because never before had such a creature indicated that she was about to swoon from an all-consuming passion for me.

That picture was still on my mental screen when the light on the big screen faded and the house lights flicked on. Of course, I immediately turned to fit that picture to the real article, and it was totally destroyed when the harsh house lights revealed a pudgy creature with slack, putty-colored features and lackluster eyes. To my eager young eyes, she was a dowdy, old woman who must have been pushing thirty. Such are the things from which dreams can grow in the dim light of a motion-picture theater.

The flashback was interrupted by a sudden outburst from the woman on my left, who shouted, "Oh, surely you can see them!"

I involuntarily looked at her just as she thrust the knitting needles toward the window as if she were pointing out something that should have been of great interest to her seat companion. Simultaneously she leaned toward him and gently brushed one point of her upper anatomy against his shoulder while I self-consciously turned away.

"No, not there!" I heard her shout. "Over here!"

And my eyes not only treacherously ignored my will, but they turned toward the couple just in time to see her propel herself toward the man with the knitting needles outstretched as if she were about to stab him, and she did stab him, but not with the needles, because they were pressed against the window in a pointing gesture.

Smiling philosophically, I turned my eyes toward Lake Grassmere on the right just as José suggested, "Since the lake is relatively close to Blenheim and since that progressive town is not far from Picton, the trip should soon be completed."

"Seemingly, that fact is bearing heavily on the mind of the man to our left," Pancho rejoined, "because he's beginning to strongly press a previous suggestion that we failed to overhear. It seems to concern an unscheduled stop in Picton."

Then, almost in synch with Pancho's reasoning, I heard the man say, "Picton would make a particularly noice overnoight stop, since it's not only a pritty town, but it has some good ristaurants."

Looking surreptitiously toward the woman, who was knitting furiously, I concluded that the smug, self-satisfied expression on her flushed features seemed to indicate that she had gained her goal, whatever it was.

Meanwhile, the man veered away from that subject to another seemingly unconnected one. "Since Oy'm a man of action," he muttered somewhat obscurely, "Oy'm not one to fool around with a lot of words. When I want something, I go roight aftah it."

"That's the right tack," José silently applauded him. "Lead her to believe that you are overcome with passion."

"Yeah," Pancho agreed. "That's the approach that Al always employed when he was on the loose."

The voices gradually faded from my consciousness as I recalled a certain blind date, whom I had agreed to escort to a movie in the company of an associate named Arnie, whose date had dug up my date. Actually, *dug up* were not the proper terms, because she was considerably younger than I, and she wasn't blind, but she did wear spectacles, which were much more decorative than mine. She was slender and nicely put together, but her angular features were typical of a blind date.

Despite her lack of sex appeal, my sense of fair play compelled me to be as gallant and entertaining as my limited capabilities permitted. Therefore, when Arnie elected to drive directly from the theater onto some of the unlighted country roads that surrounded that city in central Kansas, I assumed that I was expected to make some amorous advances. And I did, but I didn't press my accelerator to the floorboard until shortly after Arnie parked the new Packard along the shoulder of one of the most remote of those dark country roads.

According to the results from my initial experiments with the opposite sex, a man should always start from engine idle and accelerate to one hundred miles per hour within six seconds, but the rate of acceleration should conform to that designated by a parabolic curve. So my rate wasn't far advanced by the time that Arnie turned off the ignition, but it zoomed practically straight up from that point on. In fact, I was literally showering the poor girl's pouty lips and angular features with pseudo-passionate kisses.

Finally, my lady carefully untangled our spectacles, pulled away, peered at me through the dim light afforded by the August moon, and exclaimed, "Wow! You're really up tight, Al. I feel sorry for you."

Detecting a subtle stir in the front seat, I paused in my lechery long enough to exchange dim smiles with Arnie; then I pulled her toward me and resumed accelerating.

Within a few brief minutes, she pulled away again, gulped a lungful of air, and exclaimed, "Whew! You must be suffering. I really do feel sorry for you, Al." Then, after removing her spectacles and straightening their frames, she stared speculatively at me. Meanwhile, I nervously considered the possibility that she might decide to alleviate my pain on the spot, so I immediately resolved to ease up on the accelerator.

Nevertheless, she was still sorry for me after Arnie dropped us off at her apartment, but I wasn't actually suffering. I have never bought the popular claim that a man needs special attention from a woman from time to time. Of course, I would never denigrate such attention, but I suspect that the claim is an old rake's tale that some men employ to influence particularly gullible women. And some women may employ it to justify voluntary, even eager submission.

For a brief moment the sounds of the two voices returned from across the aisle to my consciousness; then they faded away again as my mind voluntarily retrieved a thirty-five-year-old scene aboard an airliner that was winging its way from Atlanta to Los Angeles. Since my associate and I had booked our flight late, the craft was so crowded that we were forced to accept separate seats. My seat proved to be the forward member of a pair of opposed bench seats, located just aft of the right side of a bulkhead. The seat faced aft, but I didn't mind that because I had the entire seat to myself.

Opposite me were a pudgy, sixteen-year-old girl and a pudgy, middle-aged woman who had reluctantly removed her stocking-clad feet from the edge of my seat-to-be when I arrived. It was an awkward, ill-conceived arrangement in which I felt compelled to avoid the eyes of the woman and the girl by staring through the adjacent window; consequently, I failed to note that, sometime shortly after takeoff, the woman had again placed one of her feet against the edge of my seat.

My first intimation of its presence was induced by a yielding of the seat's coarse fabric when she thrust it against the seat while adjusting her position on the opposite seat. Suspecting that she had deliberately made the adjustment to attract my attention to its presence, I covertly watched for further developments. Soon she readjusted her position, and, in so doing, she moved the closest foot closer to me and dropped the other one onto the thinly carpeted floor.

To relieve my eyes from the constant strain of staring at the brilliant, white clouds below, I turned my head from the nearby window and pointed it toward a more distant, opposite window, where I was rewarded with another view of brilliant, white clouds. That view was momentarily obscured by a passing feminine figure. After my eyes automatically adjusted their range to it, they noted the speculative stare that the slender, young stewardess cast at the gradually intruding foot as she passed. During a subsequent trip she probably noted that the foot had crept a bit closer to the seat of my trousers, which, being a woman of the world and a likely minion of Big Brother, she probably had been expecting.

Meanwhile, I stolidly observed the dual developments with the intense interest of a fully committed amateur psychologist who was anything but an innocent "bysitter," since I obviously could have stopped the charade by moving away from those eager toes. According to my analysis, I was a pawn in a game wherein one of the three players wasn't even aware that a third player was involved, and the third player had been enjoined by Big Brother to maintain a close surveillance over the situation. Consequently, if the game were allowed to progress too far, the second player might become a not-so-innocent victim of Big Brother.

I had forsaken such games many years before, but an evil impulse drove me to make as much of the situation as possible. Obviously it provided an ideal opportunity to strike back at Big Brother through his mindless emissary, so I thrust one of my size-eleven oxfords against the edge of the opposite seat, pushed myself back on my seat, casually withdrew the oxford, and crossed my legs.

As I had expected, the woman apparently interpreted the move as one of collaboration, since her stocking-clad toes were suddenly threatening home base. Instantly I deeply regretted the move, because she was obviously responding to strong, primeval impulses without considering the impact of those responses on her teenaged daughter, who sat stiffly aware of her mother's gross activities.

I was about to move away from those aggressive toes when the other amateur psychologist cruised by and took quick stock of the situation. Seconds later she returned and whispered a message to the woman that left her with an uneasy expression. After the stewardess left, she leaned toward her daughter and whispered a message to her; then both women arose and disappeared in the direction of what could have been the rest room, but I deeply doubted that that was their destination.

Sometime later, when they returned, the daughter appeared to be suffering from traumatic shock and her mother seemed to be extremely distraught. After they had seated themselves, the woman hurriedly fished a handkerchief from her bag and pressed it against her eyes.

"I can't help myself," she blubbered, almost as if she were explaining a heretofore undefined problem to the world at large.

My uneasy eyes quickly turned away from her bleary eyes and drawn features, paused briefly on the daughter's stark eyes, and hurriedly sought refuge in the cloud layer laying far below. Even though I have always despised people who are incapable of controlling their emotions and their actions, I felt a certain empathy for the two unhappy creatures, especially for the daughter, who obviously was another innocent victim of the clumsy machinations of Big Brother. I bitterly castigated myself for involuntarily setting the woman up and allowing her to get out of hand just to satisfy a lifelong grudge. Actually, I was as much to blame for her mental stress as was Big Brother, because I had deliberately abetted her action, albeit surreptitiously and very briefly. If true justice were to have been rendered, I should have been the one who was summoned and admonished.

Very likely that mother-daughter relationship was damaged beyond repair by the woman's thoughtless, self-centered actions. I've never forgotten the stark, pain-filled eyes of that teenaged girl. In fact, I resolved on the spot never to be a party to another such incident, and I never have been. Despite Big Brother's persistent persecution, there are much better ways to combat that profligate beast.

My mind drifted far afield for some time; then it zeroed in on another, more recent scene aboard a jumbo jet. I had been assigned to a seat located on the left side of the craft near its front entrance. A gray-haired woman was seated to my left, and there was a vacant seat on my right. Just before takeoff, a slender, perky, little stewardess paused in the aisle beside the seat on my right and stared silently at the magazine that I had absently tossed onto it.

Finally she leaned forward and said, "I'll be sitting here during takeoff."

"Oh!" I exclaimed and belatedly snatched the magazine from the seat. "I assumed that the seat was to remain vacant."

"It will be throughout most of the flight," she said. Then, dropping onto it, she solidly thrust her soft shoulder against my firmer one and lightly jabbed my right rib cage with her sharp left elbow while she collected the ends of her seat belt. Then she turned toward me and pressed a firm, little, bosom-high projection against my shoulder as she extended her right hand overhead.

"I'm turning on more air," she explained, twisting the air valve and staring intently into my startled eyes. Meanwhile, the projection penetrated deeper and deeper into my shoulder. I numbly nodded acceptance of the subterfuge while Pancho silently decried her obvious lack of a bra.

After the plane was airborne and the stewardess left to help prepare and distribute the evening meals, my other seat companion inquired, "Are you going to Los Angeles?"

"Yes," I replied.

"I'm going on to Ontario," she volunteered.

I decided that she must be the talkative type; therefore, to keep the conversational ball in the air, I inquired, "Do you live there?"

"No," she replied, "I live in Indiana. I'm going to Ontario to visit my daughter and her family."

"Very likely you'll enjoy that," I suggested inanely.

"Yes, I'm really anticipating seeing them," she agreed enthusiastically, "but I hated to leave my husband, because he's an invalid, and he depends so much on me."

"Oh," I murmured. "I'm sorry for both of you."

"It's a cross that both of us must bear," she granted with the air of a born martyr.

Eventually the discussion was interrupted by the arrival of our meals. In the process of consuming them, we accidentally bumped elbows several times because of the constricted space. At least I assumed that it was accidental, because both of us had advanced beyond the flirtatious age. Besides, she had an invalid husband, and I had a steady girlfriend to whom I had been true in every respect for more than twelve years.

"Do you live in Los Angeles?" she asked after the trays were removed.

"Not in the city itself," I replied. "I live in Topanga Canyon, which is located about thirty miles northwest of the L.A. city hall."

"Then you must have been away on a business trip," she surmised.

"Sort of," I admitted. "Actually, I work for a consulting engineering firm, which has assigned me to the McDonnell-Douglas Company in St. Louis."

"Then you've been away for a long time," she ventured. With such questions she managed to keep the conversation going throughout most of the trip.

Finally, the "Fasten Seat Belts" sign flashed on, and the whine of the turbines dropped to a more subdued level. Then the little stewardess returned, dropped into the adjacent seat, solidly thrust her soft shoulder against my firmer one, and lightly jabbed my right rib cage with her sharp left elbow while she collected the ends of her seat belt. Since the plane was about to land, she didn't adjust the air valve, but there was no reason for her to do so excepting the one that had compelled her to do it in the first place.

After the craft landed and finally rolled to a stop beside the terminal, she jumped to her feet, reached overhead, and opened the horizontally hinged door of the stowage compartment. From it she removed the jacket of her uniform and dumped it on the seat beside me. Then she reached for the partially buttoned front of her thin blouse and either accidentally or deliberately pulled the last button free. Needless to say, a pair of her most intimate possessions escaped from concealment, but she quickly corralled them.

"Wow!" I exclaimed. "This airline really provides a very complete service, even a floor show."

Jauntily tucking them behind the edges of the blouse, she nonchalantly buttoned it, picked up the jacket, and slipped into it. Meanwhile, a glance at my other seat companion revealed that her soft, red lips had dropped slackly open, and her pale-blue eyes registered complete disbelief in what they had observed. Very likely that prim, midcontinent lady had a juicy story to report to her daughter when she arrived at her destination, but I'll bet that it wasn't reported in the presence of her grandchildren.

According to amateur psychologist José, "Once more that episode indicates that one of Big Brother's minions has malfunctioned, but in the opposite direction from the minion in the previous episode."

"Without doubt," Pancho entrained, "the last minion fitted into Big Brother's stable very well, because she must have possessed the same profligate philosophies that he possesses."

"Of course, that incident could have happened in any other society," José observed, "including that of New Zealand, but I'm not fully convinced that any of the straight-laced Kiwis would ever behave in that manner."

During the remainder of the train ride, I failed to learn who won the game across the aisle from me, because the slender grandmother awoke, glanced through the adjacent window, removed her spectacles, rubbed the sleep from her eyes, and replaced the spectacles. Meanwhile, I turned to the next page, silently read the teaser beneath the title of the new article, and snickered derisively.

Since she looked at me me with a question in her eyes, I felt compelled to explain: "According to this article, New Zealanders don't like pancakes." Then, with another derisive snicker, I asked, "How could the author arrive at such a conclusion? I haven't seen one pancake during my entire three months' stay in New Zealand. Therefore, if New Zealanders have never eaten pancakes, how can he justify such a claim?"

After an uncertain smile, she murmured, "Oy suspect that many New Zealandahs have nivah eaten pancakes, so they don't really know whethah they loike them oah not."

With that statement to guide me, I began to suspect that she might be one of those very passive women who never disagrees with anybody. In fact, she had the wary expression of one who never fully commits herself on any issue. Then I set out to prove that philosophy by archly inquiring, "Do you like pancakes?"

After thoughtfully clasping both hands together with their forefingers extended to form what could have passed for a church steeple, she thoughtfully shoved the steeple up under her chin and finally murmured, "Moy daughtah loikes them."

Smiling tolerantly, I countered, "But you don't like them?"

Nervously unclasping and clasping her hands, she wrung them tortuously in her lap and finally screwed up enough courage to meekly reply, "Will, not viry much."

I laughed outright, because I had proved my philosophy. Well, I had proved it to my own satisfaction at least.

The laugh must have relaxed her, because she began to slowly emerge from her shell. "But some people have to learn to loike some koinds of food," she protested.

"True," I conceded. "Therefore, if your daughter is the only member of your family who has learned to like pancakes, that author may be correct in his claim."

"But I suspect that my daughter isn't the only New Zealandah who loikes pancakes," she rejoined.

"Then you are saying that this author may not be correct in his claim," I ventured with a teasing smile.

"Will," she began, again unclasping and clasping her hands while frowning deeply like someone who is mentally seeking an avenue of escape, "he may be pahtly corrict in his clime."

I smiled at the thought that her conclusion brought to mind: the ancient cliché that no one can be partly pregnant, least of all, an author. An authoress, maybe, but never an author. But I decided to allow her to escape, because such thoughts couldn't withstand the rigors of exposure to such a naive stranger; besides, I didn't even know her name.

Then I turned and smiled at her, because she had not only found an avenue of escape, but she had made no attempt to force her opinions on me. Suddenly my mind told me that, despite her reluctance to commit herself, she was my kind of person. Besides, I've always catered to the meek, because they are supposed to inherit the earth. Since the pearly gates may be closed to me, I've constantly sought for a reasonably comfortable sanctuary from Hades, so I always try to befriend the meek. Perhaps some of them will have enough guts, collectively, to grant asylum to me on this earth when the boom is finally lowered. As previously mentioned, I particularly dislike hot climates.

At Picton the transfer from the railway station to and through the New Zealand Rail Ferries Terminal should have been accomplished without incident, but Big Brother would not be denied his pound of flesh. However, cruel experience had taught me to be alert at all times, so I didn't flinch when the piercing whistle sounded from my left as I rounded a turn in the long, concrete ramp that led down toward the wide opening in the wall beyond it. My grim eyes swept the scene before me and duly noted, first, the small family that had preceded me by about twenty paces and, next, the tall man in a handsome uniform, who was staring at two men in coveralls as if expecting their approval of his lip service. Since I had surged far ahead of the bulk of the passengers, there could be little doubt as to whom that whistle had been directed.

Meanwhile, the tall man turned away from the two maintenance men with a self-satisfied smile and strode egotistically up the ramp while my eyes measured the height of his rangy, well-balanced frame at about six feet five inches. The self-satisfied smile was still in place when he came into close range, but it quickly faded under the impact of my cold, challenging stare. Incredibly, the man appeared to expect me to respond in a friendly manner to his dastardly stab in the back, but I had never responded in a friendly manner to such an act in my life, especially when the perpetrator was a member of one of Big Brother's ill-advised squadrons.

One hundred years ago, in the American West, the man's act would have generated a shoot-out, and I was in the mood to call him out even though I didn't have a gun and couldn't have seen clearly enough to hit a red barn with one. According to my standards, any real man should be prepared to defend his honor with his life. Unfortunately, it is no longer a factor in the character of the average American male.

As usual, the never dormant Vesuvius within me boiled over as I lumbered along the endless passageways toward the ferry. "It's truly a harsh conclusion to draw about the character of any woman," Pancho mused, "especially about one who must have been tall and beautiful. But that big guy's mother had to be a real dog to produce one of Big Brother's mongrel pups."

"It's amazing how easily some characters blend into Big Brother's foul program," José responded.

Picton to Wellington

From the terminal at the end of Picton's deepwater port, the huge ferry moved slowly into Queen Charlotte Sound and increased its speed to about fifteen knots. Even though the oaken benches in the forward end of the passengers' quarters on the top deck of the vessel afforded the advantage of an overview through the clear plate glass of a wide window, I soon forsook the bench for the rail. During the previous trip I had found it to be much more pleasurable to stand there and visually absorb the unobstructed views of the lushly verdant slopes that progressively dipped deeply into the sound not more than two hundred yards distant. Since the breeze was rather chilly, I wasn't crowded by other passengers, but two Australian men paused on my right and briefly engaged me in a boisterous conversation while a tall, slender young man lounged on the rail to my left and listened to the repartee.

After the Australians left to join their families within the glazed enclosure, the young man moved nearer and asked, "Are you from America?"

Since my source had been discussed during the previous conversation, I was sure that he already knew the answer to the question. Nevertheless, I assumed that he was using the question as an introduction to another conversation, so I replied, "Yes, I am."

"What part?" he rejoined.

"Well, I suppose the answer to that question should be the North American continent," I responded with a chuckle. "For example, I spent my childhood on the plains of Saskatchewan and my boyhood in Vancouver, British Columbia."

"I've been told that British Columbia is very beautiful," he ventured.

"It is," I said, "but New Zealand is every bit as beautiful in its way."

He savored the opinion briefly before stating: "Then you are a Canadian."

"Not entirely," I answered somewhat obscurely. "I've lived in the United States during the last sixty years."

"Aw, Al," Pancho interposed, "you are deliberately trying to leave the impression that you are a Canadian gone wrong."

"And wisely so," José injected. "After all, the term *ugly American* still survives among many of our foreign neighbors."

"But to exhibit shame of his American heritage, . . ." Pancho rejoined incompletely.

In response to the man's questioning gaze, I grunted, "Huh?" Then I guiltily begged his pardon.

"I asked, 'In what part of America do you live, mister . . . ?' " he courteously answered.

"Tyrrell," I interjected. "But call me Al."

"I'm pleased to make your acquaintance, Al," he murmured, entrusting a strong right hand to me. "Most people call me Robby—for Robin."

After completing the introductory amenities, I evasively answered: "I've lived in several different parts of the U.S., Robby."

He may have sensed that he was being too inquisitive, since he paused and thoughtfully studied my features, so I contritely said, "I came most directly to Auckland from Honolulu, Hawaii."

"So you are from Hawaii," he murmured.

"Not really," I confessed. "A Hawaiian airliner picked me up in Los Angeles and deposited me in Honolulu on the first leg of my intended trip around the world."

"Oh, I would like to do that," he murmured wistfully.

"Most recently I've been living in Fullerton," I finally admitted. "It's a small city located about thirty miles southeast of downtown Los Angeles."

"So you have deliberately avoided admitting to this naive, clear-eyed, young New Zealander that you practically live within the city limits of the sin-pocked 'City of the Angels,'" José interjected derisively. But I refused to allow the remark to sidetrack me again.

"Then you must have been to Hollywood," Robby remarked with an air of instant interest.

"Many times," I admitted.

"Is it as beautiful and exciting as its history and name imply?" he asked.

After studying his sparkling eyes for an instant, I regretfully shook my head and answered, "You would be deeply disappointed by Hollywood. It has become a dirty adjunct of an equally dirty Los Angeles with row on row of grimy, old business blocks and turn-of-the-century homes. In my opinion, large parts of both Hollywood and Los Angeles should be interred without a prayer."

"Ohhh," he exhaled with an air of distinct disappointment. "From the movies, I've always believed that Hollywood must be a very glamorous place what with all of those beautiful movie stars . . . and Grauman's Chinese Theater."

"Few of those stars live or work in Hollywood," I said. "Furthermore, to my knowledge, Grauman's Chinese has not functioned as a theater for many years."

"Nevertheless, I would like to see it and Hollywood," he insisted.

Registering a tolerant smile, I pointed out: "That worldwide curiosity directs a lot of tourist dollars into the coffers of both Hollywood and Beverly Hills."

After nodding pensively, he asked, "What parts of New Zealand have you seen?" Apparently he suspected that a similar curiosity had drawn me to the shores of his islands.

"A small part of the North Island," I replied. "And I've traversed most of the principal rails and many of the main thoroughfares of the South Island. However, I've spent the last ten weeks in Dunedin."

"Oh!" he exclaimed. "I've been attending the university in Dunedin."

"Do you mean that university with the Gothic clock tower that overlooks the slate roofs of those big, bluestone buildings?" I inquired.

With a proud nod, he informed me: "That's the University of Otago, which was founded in 1878."

"Obviously it is a fine, well-established school," I remarked. "But what type of studies are you pursuing?"

"I'm studying to become a teacher," he answered.

Upon turning my head to study the man's features, I found that he had unintentionally aided me by removing his straw hat because the force of the westerly wind had increased after the ferry passed from the sound into the strait. The wind toyed energetically with his straight brown hair and forced him to squint slightly when he faced into it, but mostly it chilled both of us.

He had cradled the hat under one arm, but I could still see both of its ornate bands, one of which circumscribed the base of its high crown while the other one decorated the rolled edge of its wide brim. It was a striking hat, and I suspected that the man had selected it to draw attention to himself. Furthermore, it must have been the attention of the opposite sex that he sought, because he had arrived at that vulnerable age. It was something that I fully understood, because I had been there, too, but I had never owned such a striking hat. Maybe my luck with the opposite sex would have been better if I had possessed one.

Satisfied with my study, I said, "You should make a fine teacher, Robby; that is, if you stick to your studies, and you must do that. Unfortunately, we have a terrible educational system in our country, and you may have already detected some of it in my words."

He was obviously pleased by the compliment, so that leverage may have influenced his opinion. "No!" he exclaimed. "You appear to be very well educated."

"I certainly hope that I am," I muttered. "However, I received my elementary education in Canada, so I may have had an advantage over many of my American classmates. Furthermore, I've continued to educate myself throughout my life, so that may also have helped."

"Actually, I don't have much of an education," he confessed shyly. "I was raised on a farm near Gore, so I've never had much opportunity to educate myself."

"But you appear to have learned the right things," I responded. "Too many of our modern teachers have never been taught basic morality, so how can they properly guide the upcoming generations?" Without permitting a response, I charged onward: "Furthermore, too much of the teacher's time is consumed in trying to fit students into modern society, a society whose moral values have deteriorated to the point where none of the upcoming generations should be fitted into it."

"According to the telly, there doesn't appear to be a lot of difference between our societies," he ventured.

"That's because your government selects the material that's displayed on your television screens," I pointed out. "You should see some of the trash that's displayed on our TV screens. On second thought, I withdraw that statement, because you shouldn't see it; in fact, nobody should see it. Some of it is so foul that even I become embarrassed and turn the *bleeped* TV off."

"I suppose that some things do get a bit out of hand in a big, progressive country," he suggested. "But America is the only nation to place men on the moon, so its technology has to be the most advanced in the world. Nevertheless, like Russia, it has made some bad mistakes, such as the fiery death of the three *Apollo* astronauts and the seven others who were killed in the shuttle's disaster."

"I happened to have worked on both of those programs," I volunteered, " and. . . ."

"You did!" he interjected. "What did you do?"

"On the *Apollo* program I was employed by the prime contractor as an engineer, specifically a research specialist on fluid systems," I replied.

"Then you must have known something about what caused that fire," he suggested. "The one in which the three astronauts perished."

"It didn't take a fluid systems specialist to determine how hazardous some of those nonmetallic materials were in the presence of pure oxygen," I muttered. "In fact, many of the people in our facility were painfully aware of the problem. For example, the engineer who shared my office informed me that he had run tests on some of those materials in a pure oxygen atmosphere and found that what eventually happened could happen, so he forwarded the test report to the governmental agency that was monitoring the program."

"And what did the agency do with report?" he asked.

"Probably the same thing that most government agencies do in such situations," I growled. "Apparently it shelved the report."

"So three astronauts were consumed by fire," he murmured with a scandalized expression.

Following an emphatic nod, I phlegmatically stated, "Apparently, there was a lack of competent engineering or the astronauts were expendable as well as combustible."

"What horrible negligence!" he exclaimed. "Why wasn't somebody made to account for it?"

"Bureaucratic politics is an insurmountable barrier to such action," I answered. "In fact, according to some of the media, that government agency even blamed the prime contractor for the accident."

"Why didn't the contractor disprove it by presenting your associate's report to the media?" he asked.

"Probably because the prime contractor wanted an inside track on further contracts from that agency," I retorted succinctly. "And the prime contractor has acquired some very lush space plums since that time."

"So that government agency bought the prime contractor's silence with more contracts," he muttered.

"So it would seem," I granted. "In the U.S. there's a popular cliché, which seems to apply to that case. However, instead of knowing **where** the body was buried, the prime contractor may have gained considerable leverage by knowing **why** those three bodies were buried."

"Then the failure of the shuttle may also have been due to bureaucratic negligence," he postulated.

"Possibly," I murmured. "But I came aboard that program a bit late, so I had to accept an engineering position in one of the sections of ground support equipment systems. During my orientation tour, I discovered several reasons why the shuttle could have encountered problems during its operational phases. One of them was the system of tiles (the bird's feathers) that insulates the craft's structure from the intense heat generated during its reentry into the atmosphere. In addition to the system's great cost, I discovered that its installation is incredibly time consuming. I also discovered that they are very susceptible to damage by rain, hail, and various contaminants, including those common to the hands of the installers. For those reasons alone, I declared on the spot that the shuttle was an impractical system and that it should be canceled before any more funds were wasted on it."

"Why wasn't it canceled?" he countered.

With a derisive chuckle, I answered, "There were several very good reasons, but one of the biggest ones concerned personal economics."

"Personal economics," he murmured.

"Yes," I retorted. "At the time I was speaking to a man named Griffith, who was my supervisor, and he was not going to transmit my opinion any further, since canceling the shuttle would have not only canceled my job but his as well. In fact, I noted at the time how cautiously he looked about to see if anyone of importance were within audiorange of my words. I'm sure that many of the other engineers on that program realized how incredibly impractical the shuttle program was, but it provided very lucrative employment for them and for numerous highly paid wheels."

"Perhaps the problem of cost can be overcome in time," he suggested. "After all, the idea of using a launch vehicle over and over seems sound."

"But not at the cost involved," I insisted. "However, since so much money has been invested in it, the main reason for continuing the shuttle program is to provide certain military forces a space bus with which to service the satellites of various defense systems. It could serve the scientific community in a similar fashion but not for its impractical space station. That should never be built."

"Maybe things would have gone smoother if smarter people had been placed in charge at the beginning of the shuttle program," Robby ventured with a smile.

"Well," I began thoughtfully, "the man who became chief engineer on the shuttle worked with me on the B-70 bomber, so I know something of his capabilities."

"What do you think of them?" he inquired.

"As a man, I liked and respected him," I replied.

"How about his capabilities as an engineer?" he persisted.

"I don't know for sure," I admitted. "But I do know that he had spent considerable time at the plant in Detroit where the B-70 hydraulic pumps were being designed, built, and tested. And I know that he and the two hydraulic engineers, who had preceded me as resident engineers, failed to solve a major problem in the design of the pumps, which I solved within six weeks after my arrival there."

"Perhaps you should have been made the chief engineer on the shuttle program," he ventured.

My abrupt laugh caused him to turn startled eyes on me. "Unfortunately, most of the engineers in high positions have won them through members of the family, through friends, or through the practice of astute politics," I muttered. "Even if I had the qualifications for such a position, and I don't have them, I could not have gained the position, because I have never had any family leverage or any influential friends, and my political potential has been rendered absolutely nil for reasons that are too complex to explain in a few words."

"But how do you account for the shuttle's disaster?" he rejoined.

"With thousands of pounds of highly combustible liquids aboard, the shuttle was designed for such a disaster," I replied. "In fact, I was surprised that it survived as long as it did. And I was surprised that the failure didn't occur on the launch pad, where the entire launch facility would have been destroyed, along with the shuttle, at a tremendous cost."

"But the use of those liquids must have been mandatory to its successful operation," he protested. "Otherwise safer liquids would have been employed."

"Safer fuels, such as the so-called solid fuels, could have been employed," I admitted, "but they would have greatly increased the sizes and costs of both the shuttle and its auxiliary launching modules."

"But they wouldn't have killed those astronauts," he posited.

"Possibly," I conceded. "However, large quantities of relatively less combustible fuels are still hazardous. And the human element is the most unpredictable factor in the use of any fuel, no matter how hazardous it is."

"But surely people can be trained to use even hazardous liquids successfully," he said. "Apparently everything had been in order until the launch of the last shuttle."

"There are many thousands of components in the electrical and mechanical systems of the shuttle and in its launch facilities," I droned, "and all of the flight-critical ones require periodic inspections—by humans. As you well know, there has never been a perfect human being on this earth." Then, after assessing the protest in his eyes, I added, "At least not within the last nineteen hundred and fifty years."

"But I've read that there are backup systems to forestall such failures," he said.

"True," I said, "but they are limited to only some of the most vital systems or their components, and even they are not accident-free."

"So you say that the shuttle should be canceled," he murmured musingly.

"Not now," I rejoined. "It has a potential of several military applications. Besides, I believe that my previous statement was something to the effect that it should have been canceled on the spot, but that was before it was fully designed and built."

Nodding absently, he turned and peered intently into the wisps of mist that partially shrouded the wind-tossed water to our right. "Isn't that the North Island?" he inquired with an air of growing excitement.

I peered in the same direction and detected just a faint outline of a landmass. "Some of it does appear to be hiding beyond the fog," I conceded, "so we should be arriving at the ferry terminal very soon."

"This is sort of exciting, because I've never been to the North Island before!" he burst forth. "In fact, this is the first time that I've ever stood on anything other than the South Island." And he stamped one foot against the deck; then, with an expression of embarrassment, he laughed at the juvenile act.

To relieve his embarrassment, I slapped the nearest of his well-muscled shoulders and said, "But you've been fortunate to have lived in one of the few remaining garden spots of the world, so you've had no reason to venture abroad."

Settling back against the rail, I looked thoughtfully at his well-formed features. "He appears to have a lot going for him," José submitted, "but I wonder in what respects Big Brother might warp and blight his life during the next fifty years."

"Very likely," Pancho began, "a Big Brother reinforced by new toys, such as computers and communication satellites, poses a serious threat to Robin's future, even in remote New Zealand."

"Maybe not," José rejoined. "A smaller population may be able to control the beast; that is, if that population can survive the debilitating effects of socialism."

A blast of cold wind tore at our clothes, and Robby shivered perceptibly as he glanced across one shoulder toward the enclosed area beyond the windows. Suddenly his attention appeared to become fixed on something or someone. Intuitively, I whipped about and detected the faint outline of a figure as it rapidly faded away from just beyond the window into the dim reaches of the passenger quarters. When Robby turned about, I was stolidly studying the turbulent waters far below the rail.

Looking apologetically at me, he said, "I have to go now, but I've thoroughly enjoyed our conversation. I sincerely hope to meet you again, maybe in America, even." And he thrust forth a firm right hand.

"I hope so, too, but time and tide wait for no man," I quoted enigmatically, accepting the hand.

After he had departed, I huddled over the rail and stared blindly at the cold, gray waves far below it. Even the screaming of the gulls and their antic dives into the wake of the vessel didn't distract me.

"Why?" Pancho mused. "Why should anybody, even a moron like Big Brother, consider Al to be a threat to anybody, especially to a grown man?"

"How unfortunate that a naive young man like Robin should be exposed to such seamy philosophies," José chimed in. "There can be no doubt, whatsoever, that Big Brother should be castrated."

"Yeah," Pancho agreed, "and the wounds should be deeply cauterized—with acid."

18

Wellington to Auckland

A shuttle bus conveyed me from the ferry terminal to Wellington's railway station, where I went directly to the ticket counter. There a large, matronly woman fixed her eyes on my bearded features and attempted to make a perfect donkey of herself—well, not quite perfect, but she did make an issue of my request to exchange my coach accommodations for a sleeper. There appeared to be some other things about me that she resented, too, but I had showered that morning, so the lack of a shower could not have been one of them, and I could only speculate on the nature of the others.

When she finally presented the sleeper ticket to me in exchange for the coach ticket and some more of the country's colorful currency, I deliberately thanked her with more than my usual courtesy in an attempt to impress on her that she had behaved like a clod. Since the effort appeared to be wasted on her, she must have been accustomed to behaving like a clod and an imperfect donkey.

After depositing my suitcase on the luggage counter, I carried my briefcase into an adjoining hall and set it against one of the walls. Then, removing the ticket from my shirt pocket, I carefully studied the various inputs that had been scribbled on it.

Under "Travel Code," the numerals *6260* had been inscribed, but I was unable to detect anything unusual about them. However, the numerals *13* had been inscribed under "Remarks," and since they possessed a bad reputation in America, I immediately suspected the woman of dark and nefarious intentions.

Indubitably I had misinterpreted many similar situations in the past, and I realized that this might be another one; nevertheless, like the average human being, I judged her to be guilty until proved innocent. If the latter should prove to be the case, then, like the average human being, I would probably nonchalantly shrug my shoulders and say, "So what?" Besides, my constant efforts to ferret out Big Brother's not-so-subtle maneuvers had always added a certain zest to my otherwise mundane existence, so I have never allowed my failures to dim the pleasures of my successes. Too often my interpretations had proved to be accurate, and those apparent triumphs served to boost my faltering ego, despite the constant denigrations of Big Brother and his minions.

Thrusting aside one of the bevy of large, oaken doors in the wall between the station's waiting area and its boarding area, I found myself on a wide, concrete apron. Since Wellington Station was a railway terminal, the rails for each train terminated at a bumper that abutted the apron. A visual sweep of the area failed to reveal any means of directing passengers to their trains, so I veered toward a trio of men in uniforms, who appeared to be conductors, and came to a skidding stop beside them.

In response to my questioning eyes, the tall man who stood facing me inquired, "Can I help you, sir?"

"Possibly you can," I replied. "Can you direct me to the sleeper train that's scheduled to depart for Auckland within the next half hour?"

Pointing toward the end car of a train standing against a bumper somewhat farther along the apron, he said, "That should be the Northerner, moy man."

"Thank you," I murmured. Then, after setting off toward it, my rapid strides abruptly became a sprint, because the end car of the train began to move slowly away from the bumper.

After I swung onto the long, concrete platform that stood between my objective and another pair of rails, a voice from directly behind me breathlessly called, "Oy'm sorry, moy man, but they've moved yoah trine onto the nixt tracks."

When I applied my brakes, the tall conductor pulled up behind me, placed his big left hand on my right shoulder, thrust his right arm past my left shoulder, and pointed toward a train whose rear car was located all of one hundred feet from its bumper. "That should be it," he rumbled.

"Why didn't they move it all of the way back against its bumper, like the others?" I protested with some rancor.

Glancing down at my flushed features, he shrugged his shoulders like Pierre from Paree and amiably responded, "I really don't know. Mybe they just wanted to be differint."

It was such an illogical response that I broke into an involuntary laugh, whereupon the man grinned widely, raised his ham of a hand from my shoulder, and slapped it down so solidly on the selfsame shoulder that my fillings rattled in their sockets.

After turning in the direction of his confederates, he called back, "Have a noice trip to Auckland."

I would have had to step down from the platform and cross the rails on which the train stood to get onto its concrete boarding platform. Therefore, I wisely returned to the apron, rounded the bumper, and trudged along the boarding platform to the designated sleeper car, where I came to a stop about five feet behind the uniformed man who appeared to be responsible for the car and its passengers. Setting the briefcase on the platform, I stood erect and expelled a sigh of relief. As I had expected, the conductor turned about and glanced toward me; then his eyes returned to my features for a second visit, but I had not expected him to deliberately turn about and walk away from me.

"Perhaps his mind is pondering some big problem," Pancho suggested.

"If he has a mind," José added. Whichever the case, the man soon reappeared with his head inclined toward the platform while his eyes appeared to be searching its surface for the proverbial needle in a haystack.

As he was about to pass in front of me, I thrust forth my ticket and growled, "This **is** my car, is it not?"

After peering down at the ticket, he glanced toward the slender figure of a uniformed Maori woman who was strolling toward us. "Present it to that young lady," he growled in turn and resumed his inspection of the platform.

"Apparently you unintentionally demeaned his status by requesting that he perform a service below his station in the pecking order," José remarked, "or perhaps it's the man's nature to be rude to passengers."

Nevertheless, I waited until the woman arrived and presented the ticket to her. While she stood studying it, I insisted, "I don't really warrant that classification." She turned puzzled, dark eyes to me, so I pointed to the numerals within the "Remarks" box and added, "That's an unjust designation, and I deeply resent it."

Apparently her mind was in low gear, or mine was on the wrong track, because her eyes remained puzzled while she silently turned about and led me up the car's steps and around a corner to my compartment. It proved to be the first one to the right of the narrow hallway that extended the full length of the car. After she left, I stood in the middle of the small cubicle and peered balefully through one of its two windows at the conductor, who had assumed a standing position on the platform opposite the doorway through which we had entered the car.

As I suspected, the woman headed directly toward the conductor, thrust the ticket before his eyes, and asked a question that I failed to read from her lips. Glancing briefly at the ticket, he fixed his eyes on hers and spoke through tight lips for several seconds, so I was unable to determine the nature of his monologue, but the woman's features began to acquire a rather pained expression.

"Apparently Al's interpretation of those numerals was correct," José surmised.

"Past performances of a similar nature seem to bear out that opinion," Pancho conceded.

Responding to the exchange with a nod, I then reinspected the hallway, whose external wall was lined with panel-high windows. The paneling of that wall and of the opposite wall with its several doors were finished in glossy mahogany. Then I reversed my field and took stock of the compartment. A distance of some seven feet separated the open doorway from the opposite windows, and the distance from the forward wall behind the nicely upholstered seat to the aft wall must have been about five feet. True, it was snug, but there was a bit more: A small, curtained closet was partially obscured by the open door, and just beyond the closet was a narrower door.

When I pushed the narrower door open, a small bathroom was revealed. It could not have been more than three feet deep by four feet long, and the small, stainless steel water closet on the right dominated most of the floor space. A tiny, stainless steel lavatory was turned up about a horizontal hinge on the wall, and directly above it was an equally tiny cabinet whose door bore a small mirror. Above the mirror a chrome-plated shower head projected from the wall. Despite the room's minuscule proportions, it contained the essentials, even a chrome-plated towel support and a paper dispenser. I was about to close the door when my eyes detected a small sign that advised bathers to close the door tightly while showering. Then I noticed the door seals and the drain in the middle of the stainless steel floor.

"Hmm," I mumbled, "the Northerner is really loaded for *bare*."

After closing the bathroom door, I casually studied the upper berth, which was latched up in place over the upholstered bench seat, both of which extended the full length of the compartment. Then I stowed the briefcase in one corner of the closet and seated myself beside the window so that I could keep abreast of any new developments.

Several passengers now traipsed about the platform while luggage carts and similar small vehicles were being moved to and fro. Eventually the conductor cruised into view, and our gazes immediately clashed like two sabers. For some reason he then took up a temporary post almost directly beneath my window. There was nothing particularly unusual about that with the exception of his weird whistle, which invariably began just as he cruised into my view and stopped just as he cruised out of it. Aside from its intended purpose, the whistle indicated that the man had no ear for music, but his ear may not have been so much at fault as his pucker. And there may have been a *sound* reason for that: Possibly some disenchanted listener, like myself, had bent it out of shape for him.

Even Pancho got into the act. "Despite the size of this city," he sleepily injected, "it's just a *whistle-stop*."

As the train slowly moved from the station, my mind began to review some of the other incidents that had transpired between Dunedin and Wellington.

"Al is to be congratulated on his ability to analyze Big Brother's psychology and to predict his behavior," José remarked.

"Obviously the monster has made his presence known with a vengeance," Pancho chimed in. "And it may have been a desire for vengeance that's behind his most recent overtures."

"Vengeance for what?" José inquired.

"Perhaps Wilfred conveyed to some of the monster's local associates the fact that, early on, Al not only detected Big Brother's presence, but he openly defied the monster's CIA and FBI in Wilfred's presence," Pancho postulated.

Dreamily, my mind drifted back almost thirty years to a scene in a small, dimly lighted apartment. It was the home of a lady friend whose name might have been Flora, but it wasn't—not quite. We were in the middle of a discussion regarding the San Diego police department, where she had once been employed.

Suddenly she burst forth: "Some of those guys are low-down scum!" Then, squaring her shoulders and thrusting forth her chin as if defying an unseen assailant, she asked, "Would you believe that I had to fight off more than one of those guys to keep from being dragged into what we called the back room?"

Despite my surprise, I tried to play down the drama by saying, "More than one guy does seem to be a bit much."

Thrusting a thumb and forefinger against my cheek, she gently pinched it. "Not at one time, dummy!" she retorted. "Different guys at several different times."

"Aw, they were just teasing you," I said.

"No, they weren't," she insisted. "In fact, there was some talk about one of the girls who **wasn't** a fighter, so I know they weren't teasing. No way! They meant business."

"But that must have been idle gossip," I rejoined. "No civil servant would ever jeopardize his or her position and a lush pension by committing a stupid act like that."

"Two of them did," she insisted, "and I could have been another one if I hadn't fought back and freed myself."

"I don't blame the man," I responded. "In fact, I have an overwhelming compulsion to drag you into your bedroom right now."

She immediately jumped to her feet, all five feet of her, and her eyes dared me. "What's stopping you?" she demanded. "Have I ever fought you off?"

Ignoring the question, I pulled her onto the sofa beside me and said, "I suppose that some scum may have infiltrated the police department. After all, it's common knowledge that police departments tend to attract some very undesirable characters."

"You'd better not let them hear you say that," she warned me. "And you'd better tip your hat to the cops, because they expect people to do that mentally if not physically."

"They'll have to earn my respect first," I rebounded.

"You'd better do it anyway," she advised me, absently studying my features at close range.

"Never!" I retorted sharply.

After registering a startled expression, she murmured, "Well, that makes no-never-mind. What I want to know is: Am I going to have to drag you into my bedroom?"

What should a man do with a woman like that?

He should?

Great! That's what I did.

About nine o'clock the Maori woman appeared in the open doorway of the compartment and inquired, "Kin Oy mike up the buths now? Oah would you rathah wite a whoile?"

"Now is as good a time as any," I answered. Arising from my seat beside the window, I moved toward the hallway.

After stepping aside to allow me to pass, she called after me, "Oy'll be jist a minit."

"Take your time," I responded, assuming a position beside the open doorway with my back against the wall.

While I peered through the opposite window at the passing landscape, sharp sounds, such as those made by the unlocking and locking of latches, erupted from within the compartment. Within "jist a minit" the woman stepped through the doorway into the hall and said, "It's riddy."

I swung myself around the door jamb into the compartment and found that the available space had shrunk to about one-third of its previous size. The seat had been replaced with a three-foot-wide berth with two pillows, a pair of sheets, and a comforter. Furthermore, the upper berth had been lowered into a horizontal position, and it possessed a similar supply of sleeping accoutrements plus a small ladder that extended from the berth's near edge to the floor.

After seating myself at the far end of the lower berth, I was in the process of removing my shoes when the sounds of a tentative tap-tap-tap escaped from the inner panel of the closed door.

"*Entrez-vous*," I called.

The door swung open, and the familiar dark visage was revealed. "Oy foahgot to infoahm you that anothah passingah will be sharin' yoah compahtmint from Palmahton to Auckland," she murmured.

"Man or woman?" I countered with a sly smile.

She shot a scandalized glance toward me; then, realizing that I was teasing her, she smilingly replied, "A gintleman."

"I don't mind sharing it with a man," I said, "but I don't know whether I can stand a gentleman."

After looking uncertainly at me for an instant, she responded to my teasing smile with a smile.

"By the way," I resumed, "I'm writing a book about my travels abroad, so I have to collect a lot of trivia, such as the names of some of the people whom I meet along the way. Would you mind stating your name?"

With a shake of her head, she replied, "My name is Mary."

While leaning forward and extracting a pencil and a pad from my briefcase, I asked, "Mary what?"

"Mary Fletchah," she answered.

"Hmm, Mary Fletcher," I mumbled. Meanwhile, my mind pondered the possibility that she might not be all Maori after all. Then the question behind the farce surfaced: "What's the conductor's name?"

"Oy don't know," she replied with a frown. "This is moy fust trip with him, but Oy kin ask."

"I would like to know his name," I admitted.

"Oy'll git it foah you," she promised, allowing the spring-loaded door to swing closed behind her.

It was a warm night, so I shed my shoes, socks, and shirt, but I refused to part with my jeans, because Mary would be showing that gentleman to his berth at a later hour. In fact, her now-familiar tap-tap-tap resounded from the inner wall of the door about two hours later.

"Come in!" I called.

"Oy'm sorry to awaken you," she apologized, pushing the door open, "but Oy have to install a new passingah."

"That's no problem," I responded, hurriedly pulling a wrinkled shirt over my bare shoulders.

"I also am very sorry to disturb your slumbers," the mellow tones of man's voice called from beyond the woman's right shoulder. Then the tall, slender figure of a young man squeezed past her with a battered briefcase in one hand and a duffel bag in the other one. With fluid grace, he dropped the bag against the open door and set the briefcase opposite mine in the small closet. Then, extending his right hand toward me, he said, "I'm Henry Mercier."

While reaching for the hand, I thrust my feet onto the floor and endeavored to stand, but he insisted, "Don't bother to stand, because these circumstances don't warrant such social amenities."

"That's okay by me," I retorted, collapsing onto the berth with a laugh. "My name is Tyrrell; however, since you are obviously an American, you can call me Al."

"I'm pleased to know you, Al," he said, adding his left hand to the top of the handshake. "Please allow me to brush my teeth and do a few other small chores; then both of us can get some sleep."

"Of course," I said.

Meanwhile, Mary stood silently in the open doorway with a strange and somewhat bemused expression on her dark features. It seemed to indicate that she was harboring secret thoughts about this particular arrangement, an arrangement that she appeared not quite to comprehend.

Finally she looked at me and said, "Oy obtained the conductah's nime."

"Oh, that's great!" I exclaimed. Then, quickly fishing a pencil and a pad from my briefcase, I returned to the edge of the berth and asked, "What's his name?"

"Jim Elvinson," she replied.

"How is his last name spelled?" I inquired.

"*E-l-v-i-n-s-o-n,*" she slowly marched the letters forth.

"Hmm," I mumbled thoughtfully. "That sounds like a Scandinavian name to me, but it could be English, I suppose."

"I don't know anything about him," she said, "but Oy suspict that he's a New Zealandah."

Then, looking at the newcomer with that strange, almost commiserating expression, she said, "Oy hope you enjoy a noice rist, Mistah Mercieah."

"Thank you," he replied, as she reached for the door handle and glanced down at the duffel bag. "But let's leave everything as it is," he added, "because it's a very warm night, and that bag will block the door open so that we can get some cooling air through here."

"Second the motion," I added.

"Good noight to both of you," she called back after disappearing into the hallway.

"Good night," we chorused.

Then Henry turned toward me and requested, "Please excuse me while I wash off some of this grime before I retire."

"Of course," I replied as my mind continued to ponder Mary's strange behavior.

"Where are you from, Al?" Henry called through the partially open doorway of the bathroom.

"Fullerton, California," I replied.

"I've been spending summers—our winters, that is—at Claremont College in Southern California," he continued to call to me. "Currently I'm attempting to get a doctoral degree in geography at the University of Western Australia."

"That sounds great," I rejoined. "I would've liked to have remained in school long enough to be called a doctor of something or other. But what does a doctor of geography do for a living? Teach college students geography?"

"Well, geography isn't the whole picture," he replied. "I'm also an economist. Presently I'm returning from a three-week assignment in New Zealand, during which I've been trying to determine the advisability of converting some of the country's pastures back to forests."

"That sounds extremely interesting to me," I called back to him. "About three months ago I shared a seat on a bus with a young Dutch student who had been working for one of this country's large timber companies. According to him, New Zealand has already taken some steps in that direction."

"That's still another approach," Henry responded between the swipes of his toothbrush. "I've been working with some members of the Tree Crops Association, and they are considering some of the nut trees, such as walnut, hazelnut, and pecan, which are not well known in this country."

"As you probably know, most of those trees do very well in Southern California, where the climate is extremely dry," I said. "But how well will they do in this relatively damp climate?"

"That's the problem," he admitted, pushing the door open. "Considerable research will have to be done to determine how well specific nut trees respond to New Zealand's various climates. Like California, this country has several different types of climates; consequently, it may be necessary to determine which climate is most compatible with a specific nut tree."

Following a short session over the duffel bag, he turned about and silently climbed the ladder to the upper berth. After awkwardly pulling his legs over its edge, he resumed: "Apparently the timber companies have been experimenting with many different types of trees from which lumber can be produced. Presently they seem to have zeroed in on fir and pine trees, such as Monterey and Radiata, which have been acquired from Canada, Chile, and Northern California. But the association is trying to escape from a monoculture by widely diversifying its tree culture. It is even considering the American honey locust as a source of food for animals."

"What part of the tree is to be used for fodder?" I inquired.

"The pods," he replied.

"Hmm," I mumbled. "I've never heard of them being used that way."

"Of course, the economics and culture of such a food source have yet to be determined," he pointed out.

"How does a doctoral degree in geography fit into this type of research?" I asked.

"This is a different aspect of geography," he explained patiently. "It deals with land-use and microclimates, such as those encountered in the Third World nations."

"But New Zealand is certainly no Third World nation," I protested.

"I was assigned to New Zealand because the association has a problem," he explained. "Furthermore, that problem is relatively close to my base of operations in Perth."

"In what other countries have you conducted such research?" I asked.

"Well, not many," he confessed. "However, I've spent some time around Camarillo, California, some more time in Central America, five months in Australia, and three weeks here."

I sensed the birth of a smile. After resolutely aborting it, I said, "True, that's just a start; however, with more training and experience, no doubt you'll be able to advise land-use managers on plant culture in all parts of the world."

"I certainly hope so," he said, "because I do like to travel."

"But plants and their compatible climates surely don't constitute the entire picture," I protested. "What other problems do you have to solve?"

"Of course, soil is a very important factor," he responded promptly.

"Of course," I granted. "And I should have remembered that, because I was raised on a farm."

"According to some authorities," he resumed, "land-uses have been assigned values from one to ten: One through three are good enough for agricultural purposes, such as the growing of food crops; four through six support the grazing of various types of animals, such as sheep; and certain types of trees can be grown on land whose values range from seven through nine."

Possibly I erred by automatically concluding that land-use value ten covered the mining of various ores and construction materials. In fact, I should have verified that conclusion; instead, I said, "But I've seen sheep grazing among trees. How does that land-use fit into the picture?"

"That's unusual," he rejoined, "because sheep damage trees. However, those may have been native trees that were deliberately left in the pasture for animal cover when the land was cleared."

After considering the answer for a moment, I mumbled, "Hmm, that may have been the case." And the discussion paused until I inquired, "What do you know about the plants that produce kiwi fruit?"

"Not very much," he admitted. "However, I happen to know that the fruit was developed from a Chinese gooseberry, which is a small, hard fruit that grows wild in its native country. In fact, that's what it was called here until about nineteen fifty, when some enterprising North Island growers decided to call it 'kiwi' after the flightless native bird. Possibly the bird's brown, hairlike feathers influenced that decision, because the exterior of the fruit resembles it somewhat."

"Do the trees grow on hillsides like avocado trees do?" I asked.

"Not all avocado trees grow on hillsides," he reminded me. "Most of the kiwi fruit is grown near Te Puke on a flat coastal plain."

"Never heard of it," I murmured.

"It's located on the north coast of this island," he stated. "In fact, it's almost straight north of our present geographic location." After a brief pause, he asked,

"Have you been to Rotorua and its various thermal areas?"

"Yeah," I answered.

"Then you were within twenty miles of kiwi fruit country," he said. "But the fruit doesn't grow on trees; it grows on vines that often grow to the size of small trees. Most of the vineyards are surrounded by hedges to protect the vines and the fruit from strong winds."

"Why was Te Puke selected as the site of such a lucrative agricultural development?" I persisted.

"It wasn't selected," he replied. "Like Topsy, 'it jist growed.' That particular coastal plain is covered by a thick layer of volcanic ash, so the soil is extremely rich, and that may have had some bearing on its development as a fruit center."

"Number one on your land-use scale," I ventured.

"Probably," he granted, "but I really don't know that, because I've never seen it."

I cast a questioning glance toward the curved lower surface of the upper berth. Then Pancho answered the question: "He must have read about it in a book or a magazine."

Silence descended on the tiny conclave for some time. Finally he called, "Where are you going when we get to Auckland?"

"I have a six-month Australian visa," I answered. "But if I do go there, I doubt that I'll stay very long."

Typically, I was evading the question, because there was the possibility that the man had been briefed by Big Brother and deliberately planted in my compartment so that he could pump such information from me. Of course, that appeared to be a wild shot in the dark, even to me, but it was not without some merit, because there obviously were many more male Kiwi passengers who could have been assigned to that specific compartment; besides, such incidents had occurred before. Regardless of whether the possibility was logical or not, I certainly did not intend to chance assisting the monster in his illegal activities in any way.

"Why not?" he belatedly inquired.

Momentarily, it seemed that the man had read my mind. Then I remembered my statement to the effect that I doubted that I would spend much time in Australia. "Well, I'm reasonably sure that no part of Australia can begin to match the beauty of New Zealand," I replied. "And since all cities are pretty much alike, it seems unlikely that I'll find one in Australia that will entice me to remain."

Of course, I could have truthfully admitted that, by remaining there for some time, I could expect only to encounter another problem similar to the one that had developed in Musselburgh, but he would never have understood that without a long historical review of Big Brother's activities.

"Did you hear me, Al?" Henry interjected into my thoughts.

"No," I ruefully admitted. "I'm sorry, but I must have been woolgathering."

"Do you plan to cross the continent?" he repeated.

"Possibly," I replied, even though it was my fixed intention to do so.

"If you do, you'll be coming to Perth," he said. "When you arrive, look me up, and we'll go out to dinner together."

"That would be nice," I murmured, realizing that the simple statement had blasted my suspicions into eternity. Suddenly Henry appeared to be one of those human gems that is so rarely encountered in los Estados Unidos, and I had been blessed by the incredible good fortune of encountering him on the opposite side of the world.

Then he proceeded to prove my reassessment by asking, "Do you have a pencil and some paper handy?"

"Yes," I replied. Then, hurriedly tumbling off of the berth, I quickly removed the items from my briefcase, returned to it, and seated myself on the edge of it.

Peering over the edge of his berth, Henry said, "I'll give you my telephone number so you can call me when you arrive. Then, if our plans should happen to require my address, I'll give that to you over the phone."

"Fine!" I exclaimed. Turning back the cover of the pad, I looked expectantly upward.

There was a long pause while he peered intently downward. "Say!" he exclaimed. "That's very good. Are you an artist?"

Glancing down at the pad, I discovered that it had opened to a sketch that I had rendered of Jim for the sole purpose of refreshing my memory of his appearance when the time came for me to enumerate some of his misdeeds. After quickly flipping the sheet over to a fresh one, I looked up at the tousled head and mildly answered, "Not really; however, some so-called authorities on the subject have claimed that I do or that I did have considerable artistic talent."

"I have to agree!" he exclaimed. "Isn't that a likeness of the conductor?"

"After that compliment, I would be a fool to deny it, even if it were not," I retorted with a smile. And he responded with an amiable grin.

After dictating the telephone number, he insisted, "Be sure to call me, because I would like to discuss your trip across Australia with you, especially if you travel by train. Everybody should make that trip at least once in his life."

"Is it all that great?" I asked skeptically.

"Well," he drawled, "let's say that it's very unusual. Actually, you'll find that the train is like an oasis in a vast desert. The Nullarbor Plain is really a desert, you know."

"I suspected as much," I said. "After all, the name corresponds to the Latin words for no trees."

"It is treeless," he granted.

"What about wild animals?" I queried.

"You might see some 'roos," he replied. Then, sensing my confusion, he added, "Kangaroos, that is."

"Do you mean that they can be viewed from the train?" I asked incredulously.

"Yeah," he replied, "but you should look for them behind bushes or scrub. As you implied, they are very timid creatures, so they'll try to hide from the train."

"I may make that trip," I muttered with a strong suspicion that, by saying so, I was self-destructing.

I fully realized that I might be trusting the handsome, young stranger too far with my plans. In fact, I sensed that my actions might be abrogating a long-established policy of never revealing my hand to Big Brother or to anyone who might deliberately or inadvertently reveal it to him. Among other things, that policy advocated that Big Brother's train be derailed, or at least sidetracked, by any legitimate means available to me. But several recent incidents indicated that he was on the same train with me, so that policy could produce some drastic consequences for me.

Meanwhile, my cell mate was crawling down the ladder. "If you do make that trip, be sure to call me when you get to Perth," he insisted. After rummaging through his briefcase for several seconds, he softly exhaled, "Ah! There you are, you elusive little beggar." Then, with a pencil and some sheets of paper clasped in one hand, he cautiously struggled up the ladder to his dovecote and perched on the edge of it momentarily. Looking down from it at me, he said, "I hope you don't mind my keeping the light on for a few more minutes. This meeting proved to be a very productive one, and I'm too excited about it to go right to sleep, so I would like to jot down some of its more salient parameters."

"Jot as long as you like," I mumbled from beneath the arm that I had placed over my eyes to block out the stabbing light rays. "I'm not likely to go back to sleep very soon."

"However, if you have something on your mind that you particularly want to discuss," he resumed, "keep right on talking."

Almost compulsively, my arm jerked away from my eyes and left them staring starkly into the stabbing light rays. After a moment's consideration of the strange suggestion, my arm slowly slid back into position.

"Don't be so *bleeped* suspicious," José exhorted me. "Very likely he was just being courteous by pointing out that he wasn't deliberately turning off the conversational spigot while he immersed himself in that report. Besides, if he actually were trying to pump the details of your plans from you, he certainly would have been more circumspect about it. Obviously, he's no dummy."

Pancho must have been sound asleep, because there was no rejoinder from him. In fact, there was only the occasional rustle of sheets of paper from above for some time, so I almost dropped off to sleep.

Abruptly I was aroused from a state of torpor by a voice softly calling, "Al."

My arm leaped from my eyes and left them staring blearily into the same light rays, that is, the same source of light but different rays. "Huh?" José frantically injected into my growing consciousness. "I wonder what he wants."

"One can't be too careful of the strangers that one meets under these circumstances," Pancho observed sleepily. "One of Wilfred's co-workers had a problem with just such a character aboard one of these very same sleeper trains."

"Yes, Henry," I replied weakly.

"Oh, Al!" moaned José. "That may have been the wrong answer under the circumstances."

"I hope I didn't waken you," Henry apologized, "but I did call softly so I wouldn't waken you if you were asleep. However, since you are awake, I would like to discuss some aspects of this meeting with you; that is, if you don't mind."

I was so relieved that I immediately retorted, "Of course, I don't mind!"

"I've been thinking that the crux of this problem lies in the lap of the association," he resumed. "Obviously, it must be induced to finance the research that's required to determine how well different nut trees will grow and produce in several of this country's applicable microclimates."

After a moment's meditation, I said, "Henry, I'm never one to advocate any form of socialism, because there's too much evidence that it doesn't work, but this is one of the rare instances when I suspect that the government should be the sponsor of this particular research program. After all, practically the entire population would benefit from it, so society should pay for it through the offices of the government. Besides, the association may not possess sufficient funds to pursue such a far-reaching program."

There was a prolonged silence while the man apparently digested the proposal. "Al, I suspect that you are right!" he burst forth. "That's a terrific suggestion, and I'm going to make a note of it." Then, following the sounds of a series of pencil scratchings on rumpled paper, he added, "I'm going to present that idea to the people at the university when I get back to Perth. They should love it."

"That guy would make a great P.R. man," José suggested.

"Yeah," Pancho agreed, "but he would make a better politician. Did you notice how he already has Al eating out of his hand, and that man is no easy beast to corral."

"You guys shut up!" I growled savagely.

"I beg your pardon," Henry called. "I didn't quite hear what you said."

"Huh," I grunted while both sides of my brain scrambled to cover up my faux pas. "You must have heard me clear my throat," I suggested.

"You corrupt prevaricator!" the lads chorused.

"Oh!" Henry exhaled with a yawn. "Well, now that the research problem has been solved, I can go to sleep."

"Me too!" the lads chorused, and silence finally prevailed.

Vaguely, I heard the remote squeal of brakes at the same instant that my supine body rolled against the wall behind the berth. With a final screech, all motion ceased. Then the sounds of distant footfalls, interspersed by friendly greetings, were wafted to my ears by the soft somnolent airwaves. As full consciousness slowly returned to my mind, I detected the sounds of a body stirring in the upper berth. Extending one hand to the nearest window blind, I raised it a few inches to see if my new buddy and I should actually be awake at this hour. The small station's lamps were still lit, but an aureate glow in the sky above distant buildings seemed to indicate that the sun might be lurking just over the horizon, so I assumed that the morning had actually dawned.

"Good morning, Al," Henry called from directly above me.

After painfully twisting the arthritic joints in my neck just far enough to peer up at him, I replied, "Good morning, Henry. Did you sleep well?"

"I must have," he muttered, moving back from the edge of his loft. "I don't remember a thing after I knocked off last night."

Shortly after I had laundered my beard and Henry had washed and shaved, a tentative tap-tap-tap sounded from the door. Henry pivoted from his suddenly arrested stance in the middle of the constricted floor space and opened the door to Mary's dark features.

"Good moahnin'," she greeted us with a scintillating smile. "Kin Oy mike up yoah buths now?"

"Yes," we jointly responded. After squeezing past her into the hallway, we assumed similar positions against the wall and stared through the opposite windows at the telegraph poles, which had resumed their incessant march.

"New Zealand is one of the last frontiers," Henry murmured. "It was first inhabited by seafaring Polynesians about one thousand years before the first white man reached its shores."

"Yeah," I agreed, "and that man must have been Captain Cook."

"No, it wasn't," he responded with a placating glance. "Abel Tasman preceded him by a few years. In fact, his voyage of discovery brought him to the western shores of these islands back in sixteen forty-two."

"One hundred fifty years after Columbus discovered America," I muttered. "So New Zealand really is one of the last frontiers."

Following an absent nod, he resumed: "And the white man encountered about the same type of opposition from the natives that the early settlers encountered from the American Indians. In fact, several of Tasman's men were killed by the natives when they attempted to go ashore. Nevertheless, he claimed the land for Holland and named it Staten Landt, but the name was soon changed to Nieuw Zeeland when the islands were proclaimed to be a Dutch province. At that time the Netherlands was a very acquisitive nation."

"So that's how the name was derived," I remarked. "Where did you learn that? In some geography or history class?"

Glancing at me with a faint smile, he shrugged his shoulders and answered, "I don't remember, but I read a lot, so it could be the fallout from one of my reading sessions."

I nodded understandingly. "According to some of my reading," I said, "Captain Cook was followed by whalers, sealers, traders, and missionaries. Then, in eighteen forty, all-powerful Great Britain declared sovereignty over the islands and promptly conned the Maori chiefs into signing a treaty in which they pledged allegiance to the crown for the rights to certain lands—for the same lands, in fact, that the chiefs' antecedents had possessed for about one thousand years."

"That sounds like what happened to the American Indians," Henry muttered. And I nodded.

After Mary exited, I stepped away from the wall, and he followed me back into the compartment. With it restored to a semblance of order, we set about preparing for the train's arrival in Auckland. In so doing, Henry picked up his boxlike little briefcase, and one side of it broke free, allowing its contents to spill onto the floor.

He stood stock-still and looked at the mess in dismay. "Wye, you miserable beast!" he exclaimed. Then, kneeling beside it, he turned the case's open side up and began to collect and stuff the scattered sheets of paper into it while bitterly protesting, "The least you could've done was to have waited until I got back to Perth."

I was beginning to suspect that Henry had assigned living intelligences to some of his possessions, since he had addressed his evasive pencil in a similar manner when searching for it within the same case during the preceding candlelit hours.

After the contents had been restored, he picked up the errant side, which consisted of a single sheet of plastic-covered cardboard, and ruefully inspected it.

"A few pieces of strong adhesive tape might be the answer," I suggested from the seat beside the window.

"I should buy a new one," he murmured absently, "but this student's finances don't permit such expenditures at this time."

My sympathy was so deeply stirred that I looked purposefully toward my sturdy, twenty-year-old briefcase, which still stood proudly upright, despite the fact that it contained a net weight of slightly less than one metric ton—at least it always seemed to be that heavy whenever I lifted it.

"Now don't propose a trade," Pancho insisted. "What would you do with all of the stuff that you've collected during this trip? Besides, you probably would lose all of your notes through the side of that thing before you could buy a new one in Auckland."

"Don't add to the poor man's embarrassment," José chimed in. "He appears to be made of the right stuff, so he should survive. After all, you survived under similar conditions."

Since such arguments consume time, too much time passed, and the opportunity to become an altruist also passed, so we parted on the station's platform with a firm handshake.

"Don't forget to call me when you get to Perth," he called back to me.

"I won't," I promised, waving him onward. I was not about to try to match those long, lithe steps with a one-ton load in my right hand.

Auckland Airport Again

From Auckland Station I journeyed by shuttle bus via Beach Road and the Southern Motorway to the Auckland International Airport. At the curb in front of it, I picked up my bags, passed through the airport's entrance into the ground level facilities, and came to an abrupt stop in front of the Continental Airlines ticket counter. There I dropped both bags and my lower jaw onto the floor. Not only was the immediate area unlighted, but it was totally devoid of service personnel, and there wasn't another prospective airline passenger within fifty feet of it. Then I saw the "CLOSED" sign.

"Huh," I grunted. "The least that they should have done was to provide directions to the new location."

Glances in all of the other directions convinced me that I was almost surrounded by Air New Zealand ticket counters, so I picked up the bags, trudged to the nearest of the counters, and set the bags on the floor in front of it. Behind it a relatively young man was busily completing the identification and transfer of some luggage to a conveyor belt.

When the task was finally completed, he turned to me and asked, "Can I help you?"

While submitting the Continental Airlines ticket to him, I asked, "Can you point out to me the new location of this airline's ticket counter?"

After accepting the ticket, he studied it briefly, turned toward another agent, who was serving a customer, and interjected, "Do you know where this man can find Continental?"

Across one shoulder the other agent replied, "Their offices are located at the top of the stairs." Then his eyes turned toward me, and they remained fixed on me for several seconds.

Meanwhile, the first agent said, "Those stairs are located beyond the end of that wall." Then, after pointing across my right shoulder to the wall, he added, "The people in that office must approve your ticket before we can help you."

I picked up the luggage and moved toward the end of the wall while my mind puzzled over the last part of his statement. Beyond the end of the wall the stairway came into view, but I wasn't fully satisfied with all that I had learned during that brief exchange. Resorting to a tried and proven artifice, I stopped in the middle of the floor, set the bags on it, placed both palms on the small of my back and slowly swiveled my shoulders while my eyes swept through a 270-degree arc. In the process, I saw that my second informant's customer had departed, so he had drifted to the side of the first one, and both men were staring in my direction. Grimly, I picked up the bags.

"So Big Brother is aboard and regrettably in charge of the situation," José concluded.

In the office at the top of the stairs I received a similar stare from the man to whom I presented the ticket. And the man who affixed his approval to it also prefaced the operation with a stare. Meanwhile, Pancho concluded, "Continental has become a defunct airline."

"Where do I go from here?" I inquired of the signer.

"Air New Zealand should honor it," he replied in clipped words.

Back at the Air New Zealand ticket counter, I elected to approach the second of the two agents, but I learned no more from the closer association, except that I would have to wait until the morrow for the next available flight to Sydney.

As I was about to leave, he added, "Since the caterers are on strike, no food will be served aboard the flight. But you'll be reimbursed for that inconvenience with a twenty-dollar bill when you board the aircraft."

"Twenty dollars for one of those meals," I murmured incredulously. "I'll bet that you receive no complaints about that deal. It's a gem."

I must have struck a sensitive nerve, because his eyes wavered perceptibly before they turned away from my incredulous eyes.

Airways Motor Inn At the Travelers' Information Centre a rather mature woman with a pleasant mien obtained a reservation for me at the Airways Motor Inn. In accordance with her directions, I dragged my luggage through one of the several doors at the airport's entrance to the bus stop, where the inn's shuttle bus picked me up.

After registering for a night's lodging under the cold eyes of the young woman at the inn's desk, I picked up my luggage and began the trek to my room. En route, I noticed that directly opposite the desk was the entrance to an inviting dining room. After recovering from a shower, I made myself reasonably presentable and journeyed to the dining room for a belated breakfast. There I found that, even though my presence had increased the clientele to a total of three males, there was a conspicuous lack of service personnel.

I must have waited five minutes before a young Maori woman appeared and asked, "Do you wish breakfast?"

In addition to being hungry, I had been subjected to a needlessly long wait, so she could not have missed the inherent criticism in my blunt, "Yes!"

"I'm sorry that you had to wait," she murmured, "but I'm the only one on duty. The other girl called in sick, so I have to do her work as well as mine."

"Don't concern yourself about the wait," I responded sympathetically. Then, after reviewing the uncrowded roomscape, I less sympathetically added, "I'm in no great hurry—just starved to death."

"Well, we can certainly take care of that problem," she rejoined. "Where would you like to sit?"

Once more my eyes swept the vacant tables and returned to hers with a whimsical expression.

"True. Excepting two tables, you have an unlimited choice," she responded with a smile.

"How about that corner table?" I inquired. "It's located close to the kitchen, which will make your task a bit easier."

"That's thoughtful of you," she observed, leading me toward it. As I seated myself, she tendered a menu with the words: "I'll return for your order as soon as I see what the desk clerk wants."

As the fates decreed, my location permitted me to look through the open doorway and across the lobby toward the desk, where the clerk indolently lounged with her eyes on me; however, they quickly flitted away when my eyes came to bear on them. Soon after the dark-skinned hostess arrived there, I deliberately glanced up from the menu and encountered not one but a pair of eyes, which quickly turned away from mine.

When the hostess returned to take my order, her demeanor had completely changed from casually pleasant to deliberately cold and aloof. Some minutes after she entered the kitchen with the order, an equally dark-skinned young man swung the kitchen door open, came to a stop, and turned his eyes directly toward me.

Characteristically, I returned his gaze so coldly that he obviously became discomfited and darted back into the kitchen.

Several minutes later the hostess, closely followed by the same man, reentered the room and strode rapidly to the lobby, where a conference with the desk clerk ensued. After it terminated, the hostess returned to her post while the man departed in the direction of the porte cochere. Some time later he passed through the dining room and entered the kitchen. After a mere minute had passed, he pushed the kitchen door open and marched to my table with the handle of a steaming pot of coffee clutched in one brown hand.

When I silently shook my head in response to the question in his dark eyes, he stood for almost a minute as if undecided what his next move should be. Finally he did an about turn and retraced his steps.

How strange, I thought. That hostess-waitress must have remembered that I had previously rejected her offer of coffee, so why did she send him to me with that coffeepot?

Meanwhile, a heavyset, middle-aged man entered the dining room, looked in my direction, strode to one of the booths that lined the opposite wall, and seated himself so that he had an unobstructed view of my table. Then, without asking me whether I wished something more, the hostess returned to my table with the check. In fact, neither the neat uniform nor its white, lace trim appeared to need any starch, because there was so much starch in her legs that her knees refused to bend when she stalked haughtily away.

I spent several of the daylight hours in my room recording some of my most outstanding misadventures during the previous twenty-four hours. The brunch sufficed until almost dusk; however, when the dinner hour arrived, I was in no mood to be exposed to another ordeal like the one I had suffered through during the brunch. Therefore, I struck out from the inn along a wide, sweeping thoroughfare that took me to a fast-food restaurant similar to America's McDonalds, where I enjoyed a sandwich and a glass of milk without any apparent notice or harassment from the personnel.

There were several other early patrons in the dining room when I entered it the following morning. Without a word of greeting, the same hostess escorted me to the same table, laid a menu on it, left to seat another patron, and returned to take my order.

When she arrived with my breakfast, I asked, "What's the function of that man who brought the coffeepot to me last time?"

"He has lots of them," she replied, "but he was hired to drive the bus."

"Oh," I remarked artlessly. "I suspected that he was a bartender, because he wore an apron."

"He helps around here some," she said. "Why are you inquiring about him?"

"I'm writing what may turn out to be a travelogue covering my current trip around the world," I answered. "For example, I've already noted some of my experiences while I was having breakfast yesterday."

"What experiences?" she countered.

"That particular man's strange behavior, for one," I replied. "Furthermore, there was the heavy conference that you two conducted with the desk clerk, plus the unexplained presence of that man." And I gestured toward the same heavyset man who had just entered the room. She silently watched while the man returned to the same booth and seated himself facing us, but she offered no explanations.

"It appears that my presence has stirred up an awful lot of furor around here," I muttered, "and I haven't done a thing to create it."

"That's what you people always claim," she burst forth involuntarily. "You always claim that you didn't do it, but there has to be some evidence that you did, or there wouldn't have been any charges."

Swinging startled eyes toward her taut features, I protested, "But no official charges for any crime worse than unintentionally running a red light have ever been leveled against me, so why all of this fuss in a restaurant that's located practically halfway around the world from that red light?"

She must have found the pattern of the carpet intensely interesting, because she lowered her eyes and closely studied it while slowly turning about and strolling toward the kitchen. Suddenly, as if in response to a second thought, she veered to the booth where the heavyset man sat. After settling onto its nearest seat, she placed her arms on the table and tightly clasped her hands. From that point on, they engaged in a prolonged conversation. Meanwhile, I particularly noted that neither party looked in my direction, but I strongly suspected that the conversation concerned me.

When she returned to my table with the check, she appeared to be much more at ease. She even looked directly into my eyes when she murmured, "I sincerely hope that you have a very nice trip around the world."

"Thank you," I replied. "I've been hoping for that throughout some nine thousand miles of intermittent travel, but my hopes haven't been realized. Furthermore, I suspect that they won't be realized as long as people behave like people instead of like human beings."

Once more her eyes sought the solace of the carpet; therefore, I sensed that I had overstepped her line of propriety, so I hurriedly attempted to correct the situation.

"By the way," I began, "you speak English very well. In fact, you have scarcely any dialect."

Looking up with a pleased smile, she said, "I try very hard. Actually, that may be why I have this job."

"Do you work a split shift?" I inquired, quickly adding, "I happened to notice that you were still here when I left the inn about seven o'clock last evening, so you must work a split shift."

"I don't work a split shift," she responded with a deep frown. "I work twelve hours out of every twenty-four-hour day."

"No!" I exclaimed commiseratingly. "I've been led to believe that there are laws against that sort of slavery. There are in my country."

"There are here, too," she said grimly.

"Would you mind giving me your name?" I inquired rather tentatively. "I use a lot of dialogue in my writing, so I would like to be able to use your name should I decide to include some of our conversations in my travelogue."

Abruptly her dark eyes glowed with excitement. "Do you mean that you might put what I have said in print?"

"Why not?" I countered.

"My name is Rachel," she burst forth. "Rachel Clark."

While I jotted her name on the receipt that the desk clerk had tendered to me the previous morning, a persistent smile played with my lips. Apparently people the world over yearn to see their words in print, and I'm no exception; however, I have a very important mission in life that inexorably drives me toward that end.

After breakfast I still had time to waste before the scheduled departure of the shuttle bus, so I wasted it in one of the lobby's few easy chairs with a pencil poised over a notebook that rested on its upholstered right arm. Typically, the words were indecipherable by anyone else, but that effectively eliminated the need of a code to defeat Big Brother and his kind. Eventually I noticed that several of the inn's patrons and their luggage had collected in the entrance, so I moved my luggage alongside the stack just as the bus stopped beside it. During the trip the dark-skinned bus driver appeared to be particularly anxious to win my approval. Since my heart rebelled at holding a grudge against such an inoffensive individual, I dropped a sizable tip into his palm after accepting my luggage from him at the airport. But I suspect that he appreciated much more the smile that accompanied it. Big Brother has confused so many good-hearted people all over this blighted world.

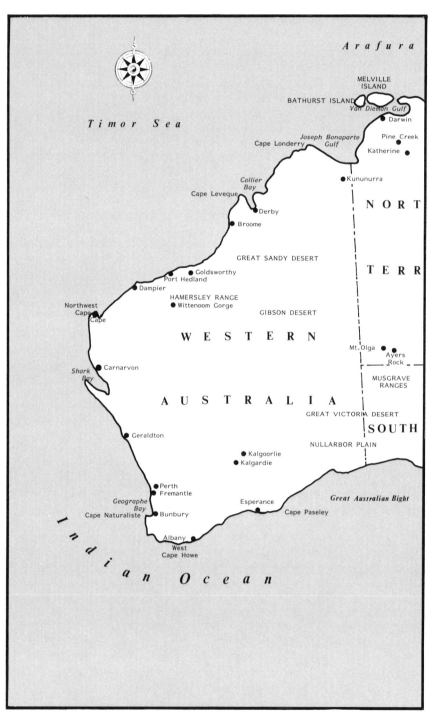

Map of the Western Part of Austrailia

Map of the Eastern Part of Australia

19

Auckland to Sydney

As usual, I was forced to endure a momentary wait just before boarding the airplane, but I had expected it. I had not been assigned to a window seat, but that didn't disturb me at the time, because there was only seawater between Auckland and Sydney, a span of more than one thousand miles of it. Nevertheless, when the craft began to circle above Sydney in preparation for its approach to the airport, I deeply regretted the lack of a window seat. By sharply craning my arthritic neck, I was able to catch a few fleeting glimpses of the fabulous water wonderland below. They were enough for me to realize that the approach to the city and its harbor provided one of the most beautiful views from an aircraft that I had ever experienced. Fortunately, I was surrounded by Australians, and one member of the duo in the seat behind mine unintentionally provided me with a veritable "Cook's Tour" of the city and its intricate waterways.

He introduced it by excitedly exclaiming, "Theah's Elizabeth Bye!"

"Wheah?" inquired his companion.

"Roight theah nixt to the Captain Cook Gravin' Dock," he replied.

"That's roight," agreed the other man, "because Woolloomooloo Bye ixtinds inland jist beyond it."

"And theah is the Botanic Gahdins with Fahm Cove in the cintah," my guide resumed. "Ah-ha!" he exclaimed. "And the Opera House is still on the point. Ah-ha! Nobody has moved a thing since we lift."

"Nobody could move the Opera House," his mate protested. "It's solid concrete."

"And theah is Circulah Key Styshun, wheah all the ferries dock," my informant continued imperturbably.

If I hadn't spent some time in Auckland, I would never have known that the man was discussing Circular Quay Station. Fortunately, a tactful Kiwi had informed me that down under the word *quay* is not pronounced *kay*, like so many Americans pronounce it; it is pronounced *key*, like the dictionary indicates it.

"And theah's the bridge," my man informed me indirectly.

"It's not jist the bridge," objected his companion. "It's the Sydney Hahbah Bridge, one o' the most spectaculah bridges in the world."

"But it's not as spectaculah as the Golden Gite Bridge," observed my tour guide.

"Aw, that's a suspinsion bridge," observed the other man contemptuously. "Oy'm talkin' about a real man's bridge, loike the one dirictly below us."

Apparently my man decided to change the subject, because he next said, "Theah's the Dahlin' Whaves, and we ah about to floy ovah the Cintral Styshun."

So much for a Cook's Tour of Sydney and its environs—in the vernacular yet. But the pilot must have been more intent on landing the aircraft than in providing a tour, since he pointed its nose down and set it on the tarmac of the Sydney International Airport with scarcely a bounce. Meanwhile, I hurriedly collected the forms that were supposed to get me past the Australian Immigration Authority.

Sydney

From the point where the airplane docked, a series of tunnels and corridors fed the foreign passengers into the terminal. Eventually, they fed into a wide, open area across which a line of high, two-by-three-foot desks were located at equal intervals. Each desk was manned by one or more immigration agents, and just beyond them several more agents formed a formidable and conspicuous barrier to potential gate-crashers. I immediately wondered why so small a space should be considered to be a threat to Australia's security when the nation possesses the longest unsecured coastline of any nation. Whatever the logic, if any, the security forces were there, so we aliens formed fifty- to seventy-five-foot-long lines in front of the desks. After the first few passengers were processed from each of the lines, it became very apparent that those at the rear ends of the lines would be standing in line a long time.

As usual, I was carrying my heavily loaded briefcase (nothing could part me from its precious contents), and its weight applied so much strain on my arm that I lowered it to the concrete floor with a grateful sigh. While I casually studied some of the other passengers, my attention was attracted to a somewhat more than middle-aged man and woman standing about three positions behind me. Obviously their loud American voices had attracted the attention of many other passengers. I, for one, suspected that their voices may have been deliberately pitched at such high decibel levels to inform the world at large of their many travels about that large world. Apparently they also wished to impress all and sundry of their wealth and social position by casually dropping many names of the rich and famous as well as the names of some of the world's most prominent watering holes and cultural centers, such as London, Paris, and Rome. Meanwhile, my eyes wandered from the couple and scanned the expressions of some of the silent bystanders while I wondered if the terms *ugly Americans* were also circulating through their minds.

Since the passengers in front of me had advanced a bit closer toward the barrier, I picked up my briefcase and stepped forward. Meanwhile, the couple behind me continued to regale everyone within shouting range about their exciting lives in Philadelphia and Washington, D.C.

In the interim my eyes had been studying the features and expressions of the agents who stood beyond the high desks. If they were trying to be inconspicuous, they had failed, because the chubby American woman suddenly changed the subject and focused the attention of practically everybody on them.

"Would you look at that line of agents!" she exclaimed. "It looks like the lines of Gestapo agents we used to see in newspapers and magazines during the Second World War."

"They are the local Gestapo," said her obese partner, "and they are to see that no undesirable aliens enter the country, so I may have to see Australia by myself."

"Oh, Mort!" she exclaimed with a raucous laugh, poking his big paunch. Then her mascara-laden eyelids widened, exposing much of her prominent orbs, which swept the faces of the standees within the immediate area as if seeking to determine how well the man's torpid humor had been received. Then she added, "But you won't see my picture tacked to any post office wall."

"They're probably looking for some of those characters as well as for international crooks," Mort suggested.

"But our crooks become international crooks as soon as they arrive here," she observed. And again her eyes made the circuit to determine how well her assumed humor had been received.

"They are looking for crooks regardless of their origins," Mort retorted. "No doubt their departures were noted at the sources by government agents, who forwarded their descriptions to these guys."

"And there are the passports and visas," José silently interjected. "They may serve as abbreviated reports on Big Brother's histories of the bearers."

"Yeah," agreed Pancho, "codes could easily be incorporated into those long serial numbers."

Then the woman's loud tones swept away the competition. "Nevertheless, they look like they know what they are doing," she said, "and they are really giving everybody the once-over."

"How much nicer it would be if those agents were stationed behind one-way glass panels," José suggested.

"But that would fool nobody," Pancho objected.

"Of course, it would fool nobody," José conceded, "but innocent travelers would be spared the embarrassment of direct scrutinies, whereas the features of known criminals could be studied in detail and their identities verified from photographs."

Meantime, through the medium of my peripheral vision, I resumed my study of the agents' features and actions. Eventually I detected one of them progressively studying the features of the passengers in my row. His gaze slid smoothly over the passengers in front of me, but when it came to me it steadied to a long, sustained stare until my eyes deliberately met it. Then his eyes quickly darted away, but their reaction had not been that of a casual observer.

"So once more Big Brother has preceded us to another remote city down under the equator," Pancho concluded.

But I wasn't satisfied with just one triumph, so my eyes zeroed in on the only woman in the line. She should have been a more difficult subject, but she didn't prove to be, despite the highly vaunted ability of women to employ their peripheral visions so much more effectively than men do. First off, I fixed my eyes on one of the other agents in a manner that enabled me to watch her from the corner of one eye while I appeared to be studying the other agent. Finally her eyes began a steady survey of the passengers in front of my line, and, to my great chagrin, they passed right over me to the next individual. Suddenly, as if in response to an afterthought, they returned to my features and fixed on them, but my eyes met hers with almost a physical impact. Like the eyes of the previous agent, her eyes quickly darted away, but they were escaping, not just passing.

"So," José began, "our previous convictions have been reinforced."

"Apparently our research in Australia is to be much easier than it was in New Zealand," Pancho opined.

When I advanced to the prescribed position beside the desk and presented my passport to the agent, he opened it to my picture and looked at it; then, turning to me, he asked, "Where do you plan to stay in Australia, Mr. Terril?"

"I have made no specific plans," I replied, "other than to search for a nice, quiet place to continue some writing."

"You are a writer?" he countered with searching eyes.

"Just a would-be writer," I responded with a smile. "But I'm wondering why you don't pronounce the name of your country *Austreyelia* like other Australians do?"

With a slightly derisive smile, he muttered, "Apparently you've been listening to Paul Hogan." Then, returning the passport to me, he added, "Have a nice stay in Australia."

Advancing from there to some low tables, I recovered my luggage from one of several indifferent inspectors, who waved me on, so they must have considered me to be a harmless old American who would never think of smuggling gold, diamonds, or dope into a foreign country. But my innocent mien had fooled them, because I legally passed almost two hundred pounds of dope right past their unsuspecting eyes.

After exchanging some U.S. dollars for Aussie dollars at a conveniently located branch bank, I went in search of the Tourist Information Centre and found it in a far corner of the terminal. While pausing at the edge of the carpeted domain, I allowed my gaze to sweep across the three desks and several easy chairs. Then my eyes were arrested by a beckoning gesture from a rather large woman seated at the desk on my right.

When I approached the desk, she inquired, "May I assist you in some manner?"

"Possibly you can," I replied, "that is, if you assist visitors in locating lodging."

"Yes, we do that," she replied. "What kind of lodging do you have in mind?"

"Something that's clean, relatively modern, and economical," I replied.

"There are several hotels within the immediate area," she said. "However, there are some outlying motels, too. Do you particularly want a hotel?"

"No," I answered. "In fact, I prefer motels. Often they are less costly than hotels."

She nodded understandingly, reached for the telephone, gestured toward the array of easy chairs, and suggested, "Why don't you relax for a few minutes while I call some of the likely candidates."

I responded with a nod while my eyes futilely sought for a vacant easy chair. Turning about, I retreated to one of the evenly spaced oaken benches that stood nearby on the marble floor of the waiting area. After placing my bags beside one end of it, I seated myself and began to study the people within the centre's carpeted area. Two of the three desks were occupied by women, and the paper-cluttered surface of the third one seemed to indicate that it had been occupied, but its occupant didn't appear to be in the scene. A family of four and its luggage were gathered about two of the easy chairs, and two senior gentlemen, one in the uniform of a security guard, were ensconced in adjacent chairs.

From the corner of one eye, I noticed that the eyes of the man in uniform had fixed on me briefly; then he turned them toward the man beside him and said something that induced the other man to turn and look in my direction. Several minutes later the man in uniform arose and strode to the side of the desk, where my lady was still speaking into the telephone. When she returned the instrument to its cradle, he leaned forward and spoke to her; meantime her eyes slowly rotated toward me. Then he turned about and returned to his chair.

"So," Pancho remarked, "the plot continues in its usual pattern, and. . . ." But the woman's beckoning forefinger forestalled any other conclusions.

When I approached the desk, she presented a small card to me and said, "This will introduce you to the people at the Eastside Motel. They will send a shuttle bus to pick you up within about fifteen minutes." Meanwhile, her eyes were carefully studying every detail of my bearded features.

"Thank you very much," I responded rather formally. Then, wheeling about, I returned to the bench.

Thirty minutes later I returned to the desk and asked, "Did that party at the Eastside Motel really mean fifteen minutes?"

Following a quick glance at a small clock, she sharply exclaimed, "Apparently not! I'll call again and find out what the problem is."

"Thank you," I responded formally and returned to my post.

About two minutes later she appeared in front of me, and I automatically got to my feet. "The bus should be here for you very soon," she said. "It was on an errand to the city and got caught in heavy traffic."

"I've been exposed to some of the world's heaviest auto traffic," I said, "so I fully understand the problem."

"I'm sure it won't be long now," she said confidently, withdrawing in the direction of her desk as I slumped back onto the hard, wooden bench.

About five minutes later she reappeared before me and stated, "Still another problem has arisen, so you are to take a cab from here to the motel, and the desk clerk will pay for it when you arrive there."

"And where do I find a cab?" I countered.

"Go out the entrance on your left," she instructed me with a gesture, "and you'll probably find several of them at the curb."

"Thank you again," I muttered, picking up my luggage.

There were three taxicabs standing at the curb, so I didn't lack for transportation. Of course, I selected the first one, since a small riot probably would have followed if I had not.

"Wheah to?" the driver asked as he was about to insert my bags into the boot.

"The Eastside Motel," I answered. "Do you know where it's located?"

A pained expression crossed his angular features. "Yis," he answered, "but Oy don't go theah." Then, immediately and firmly, he deposited my bags at my feet.

"Well, who does?" I countered, as equal parts of consternation and suspicion surged into both sides of my brain, which began to argue about whether or not Sydney taxi drivers had a legal right to be choosy about where they delivered their passengers.

He looked back at a dark-complexioned man with straight, black hair who lounged against one door of the next cab, gestured toward him, and indifferently replied, "That cab droivah will tyke you theah."

The other driver's dark, lackluster eyes suddenly came to life, and his laxly suspended hands convulsively pushed his reedlike body away from the door so precipitously that he advanced on us at a rapid trot.

The first driver pointed imperiously toward my luggage and said, "This man wants to go to Kensington. Do you know wheah that is?"

The other man's dark head nodded vigorously.

"Oy have to pick up a customah on the othah soide of the city," he informed the newcomer, "so it isn't practical foah me to tyke him." Then, turning on his heels, he stalked back to the side of his vehicle and opened its rear door for a couple whom

I had preceded by some twenty paces.

My new driver picked up my briefcase and toted it to the boot of his vehicle while I stared in disbelief at the larger bag. Reluctantly, I picked it up and followed him while one side of my brain claimed to the the other side that the first driver must have lied either to my driver or to me, because his stories to each of us didn't match. During the interim I concluded that my driver's selection of bags had been justified, because my two hundred pounds must have exceeded his weight by almost 100 percent; however, I must have been three times as old as he.

As we were about to get under way, he asked, "Where do you want to go?" in an accent foreign to both my American ear and to my Kiwi-adapted ear.

"The Eastside Motel," I replied. "Do you know where it's located?" From his unsure expression, I assumed that he didn't recognize the name. "According to this card, it is located at 147 Anzac Parade," I added. "Do you know where that is?"

He silently nodded.

"Are you a native of Australia?" I asked.

"No," he replied. "I came here from India sivin months ago."

"Then you are an immigrant," I ventured. And he silently nodded.

By the time that we had been under way for several minutes, I was surprised to discover that we were passing the terminal for the second time but in the opposite direction. Since I had been liberally exposed to the chicanery practiced by many American taxicab drivers, I decided that the man should be warned of the circumstances, so I said, "When we get to the motel, the desk clerk will pay you for this trip. Even though I don't know which is the shortest route, I suspect that the desk clerk will."

The information was greeted with stolid silence, so I concluded that there must have been a reason for the second trip past the terminal. Later, however, I concluded that he had overshot our destination by about a half mile since I recognized some buildings while we were returning to it on a parallel course.

The cab pulled onto a narrow, concrete driveway on the left side of the beige-colored, brick facade of a three-story wood-frame structure and stopped beneath the skimpy superstructure of its porte cochere. This time the little man elected to carry the suitcase, probably to influence the magnitude of the tip, but the task proved to be too much for him. After watching him stagger under its load for several steps, my conscience forced me to move alongside the bag and add my left hand to its handle; consequently, since he was a full ten inches shorter than I, he also got a lift. But it wasn't that big a deal for me, because I had already carried those bags halfway around the world, or so it seemed. In any event, I scarcely noticed the added weight of the Indian, possibly because he was spinning his wheels like a pair of propeller blades.

From the porte cochere several concrete steps led up to a wide, concrete landing, which introduced us into the lobby through a pair of glazed doors. Immediately to our left, a high, L-shaped, wooden counter enclosed an area containing a mechanical calculator, a cash register, and a well-molded woman of some thirty-two summers.

"Good day," she greeted me, as I lowered the bags and the cab driver to the floor in front of the counter. "You must be Mr. Terril."

"Right on both counts," I responded facetiously.

Her features registered a smile, but her eyes remained unexpressive. "While you are registering," she resumed, "let me pay this man." Then she thrust a pen into my right hand, pushed a pad of forms toward me, and turned to the cab driver. I had just lettered my name when I heard her sharp protest, "Eleven dollars!" Then, in lower tones, she added, "I never pay more than eight dollars for that trip." When I looked up, she turned the sparkling anger in her eyes toward mine, so I hurriedly looked down at the form and added my home address to it.

"But this place is a long way from the terminal," the driver protested. "It's worth eleven dollars."

"I never have to pay more than eight dollars," she insisted, "and that's all I'll pay you." Then she moved purposefully toward the cash register.

"No, the charge is eleven dollars," he insisted. "I have to collect that much, or I'll have to pay the difference."

"That's not so!" she almost screamed. "There's no way anybody can determine how much you were paid for this trip."

"Yes, there is," he insisted. "It shows on the meter." Then, sensing some leverage, he added, "That's why you have to pay eleven dollars; the meter shows that much. Come, I'll show you."

"That proves nothing!" she shouted angrily. "I'm not going to pay you eleven dollars for the roundabout route you deliberately took to run up the meter. I'll give you nine dollars and not a tuppence more."

Meanwhile, I added the city, state, and "U.S.A." to my home address while the cash register chirped amiably and extended the cash drawer. Then, chancing an upward glance, I observed the man's rapidly disappearing back just as the woman shouted, "And you won't get more than eight dollars next time!"

I had already concluded that, even though I admired that woman and particularly wanted her to be on my side of any conflict, now was not a good time for some of my excruciatingly funny humor or any other warped pleasantries, so I silently paid the forty-five-dollar charge, accepted the key to my room, and dragged my luggage across the lobby to the lift. Meanwhile, through an open doorway, I noticed the end of a bar, which fronted on the aisle that provided access between the lobby and the front entrance. And I particularly noted the small dining room tucked between the aisle, the lobby, and the partial walls that outlined them.

After a nap and a refreshing shower, I descended to the lobby and ventured into the dining room, where I was greeted by no greeter. I was about to depart when a stocky, young oriental man pushed open what proved to be the kitchen door and inquired, "Can I serve you?"

"Are you open for business at this hour?" I countered with a sweeping gesture toward the untenanted dining area.

"Yes," he replied. "What can I get for you?"

"I missed lunch," I confessed. "Do you happen to have a light something or other that will fill the resultant void?"

"Yes," he answered. Then he reeled off a number of hot meals that would have far exceeded the limits of the void.

"What do you have in the form of a dessert?" I finally inquired. "A pudding, perhaps?"

"I have some rice pudding," he replied.

"That's what I want!" I exclaimed. "How about fixing me up with a big bowl of it?"

"Apparently you like rice pudding," he responded with a broad smile.

"Yeah, that I do!" I retorted enthusiastically. "I've always liked it ever since my boyhood, when my grandmother often served it as a dessert. However, it also may be due to my oriental ancestry."

"Oriental ancestry?" he murmured with a bemused expression. Then, detecting the smile lurking in my eyes, he responded with another broad smile. "I'll get the rice pudding for you right away," he promised, moving toward the kitchen. Coming to an abrupt stop, he turned about, smiled inanely, made a sweeping gesture with one hand, and added, "You may sit wherever you like."

The pudding proved to be creamier than my grandmother's puddings; nevertheless, it was delicious. I was about to finish dispatching it when the chef-waiter appeared beside the table. "That was absolutely delectable!" I exclaimed.

His dark, almond-shaped eyes displayed shattered pieces of futilely suppressed pleasure. "Would you like another bowl of it?" he eagerly inquired. "That one would never take the place of a lunch."

"No," I answered, "some of a good thing can be divine, but too much of it can be . . . just too much."

In response to his puzzled stare, I added: "You may not have heard that ancient oriental proverb before, but it's a direct quote from one of my oriental ancestors."

His moon-shaped face broke into a smile. After it slowly faded away, he said, "You are too much of a humorist to be of oriental ancestry. I suspect that you are an American." Then he broke one of the Orient's most strict rules by patting my shoulder. Suddenly I felt at home—in a normal environment.

A bus conveyed me from the motel to Queens Square, which was bordered by the greenswards of Hyde Park on the south and the Domain on the north. From there a short stroll along Market Street brought me to Castlereagh Street and a view of Sydney Tower, whose slender, circular elegance literally pierced the blue, sun-shot sky. According to the tourist guide that I had obtained at the motel's desk, the cylindrical section near the top of the structure housed restaurants on each of two levels, but I was too cheap to spend the few bucks that would gain access for me to one of those towering viewpoints. However, since I had already viewed the entire city from a much higher elevation, there was no logical reason for me to repeat the experience from a much lower elevation.

From the base of the tower I returned to Queens Square and strolled north along Macquarie past Sydney Hospital and Parliament House to the State Library of New South Wales. The library proved to be a massive structure that must have been designed to impress the viewer, and I was suitably impressed.

When I entered the building through one of a bank of massive oaken doors, I was fully prepared to detect the first unwary move by any of the library's personnel, and I struck pay dirt immediately. Near the entrance a gray-haired woman was seated behind a low counter. Since some hip-high rails seemed to indicate that incoming patrons were required to pass in front of the counter, I paused in front of the woman and asked, "As a tourist, am I entitled to use the library?"

"It's for the use of everyone," she replied with a cool, appraising stare. Simultaneously, my peripheral vision caught a fleeting glimpse of a much younger, blonde woman in the act of excitedly gesturing toward me while her eyes alerted another young woman, who was seated at an opposite desk.

Fixing a piercing stare on her eyes, I said, "That isn't a very neat way to cement congenial international relations." Apparently the attack had been properly directed, because both of them immediately became deeply engrossed in their work. However, since the fingers of the blonde's left hand were nervously tapping the top of her desk and the tapping became progressively more rapid the longer I stared at her, I suspected that she was watching me from the remote reaches of her peripheral vision.

Finally, redirecting my attention to the older woman, I asked, "Can you tell me where I should look for a history of this fair city?"

"There should be some of those books on the far wall," she replied with a gesture toward the rear of the huge room.

"Thank you very much," I murmured.

With a pair of sharp glances at the two young women, I turned away and strolled along a central aisle toward my objective. Meanwhile, my eyes rotated from a study of the high ceiling to the long mezzanine on my left, which supported numerous stacks of books. At the rear of the room I found that a male attendant presided over the immediate area, so I solicited his assistance in finding the bookshelf containing the sources I sought. Shortly after my arrival he responded to the older woman's beckoning forefinger, and the duo conferred for several minutes. When he returned, I particularly sensed a new attitude on his part, so both José and Pancho assumed that Big Brother's message had been transmitted to him.

After leaving the library, I resorted to randomly selected bus rides to acquaint myself with the city. At the end of the second tour I decided to return to the motel's restaurant for dinner. From the bus stop I approached its front entrance and came upon a newly posted sign indicating that the restaurant was under new management.

Even though the meal proved to be very tasty, the place was lightly patronized, so I wasn't distracted from my study of the restaurant's personnel. While I was consuming the rice-pudding dessert, a young oriental man strolled through the entrance and took up a post behind the bar. It may have been the anxieties commonly associated with starting a new business that induced him to scan the room as if counting the customers or it may have been some other reason, but I particularly noticed that when his eyes finally settled on me, they lingered awhile.

"How incredible!" Pancho exclaimed silently.

Uncharacteristically, I didn't stare back, possibly because his partner had treated me like a normal human being; besides, I was not yet fully convinced of the accuracy of my diagnosis. After a brief interval his chef-waiter partner joined him at one end of the bar, and I particularly observed the low-toned exchange that induced the chef-waiter to turn his head and look at me.

"And that convinced Al," José injected.

After paying the barman for the meal, I deliberately strolled past the waiter-chef, who was still posted at the end of the bar. I courteously returned his "Good night," even though it had not been a good night for me. And I successfully ignored his curious stare, because it has always been difficult for me to return rudeness for a kindness, even after that kindness has been followed by an unintentional rudeness.

Meanwhile, Pancho seconded his partner: "How incredible!"

With a Sydney Tour Guide tucked into a jacket pocket, I opened the door of Room 215 early in that fifth morning of February, stepped through the opening into the hall, closed and locked the door; then, after traversing the hallway to the lift, I arbitrarily chose to descend the winding stairway to the lobby. A glance toward the closed doorway of the manager's quarters seemed to indicate that I was, indeed, an early bird.

But I was not the earliest bird in that city of some three million souls, because the bus was almost fully loaded. On approaching the driver, I paused and said, "I'll be seating myself directly behind you, so will you please inform me when the bus reaches Alfred Street?"

"That's the ind of the loine," he replied, "so git off whin ivirybody ilse gits off."

"Thank you," I said, settling onto the seat behind him.

According to a map in the guide, the bus must have traveled along Flinders and Oxford Streets; then it must have turned right onto College Street. Furthermore, it must have passed the Australian Museum, St. Mary's Cathedral, Sydney Hospital, Parliament House, and the State Library of New South Wales, but I was so busy trying to orient myself that I failed to identify them. But I had already seen most of them from ground level, so it was no great loss; besides, I had many more important reasons for being in Sydney, and one of them included a tour of the Sydney Opera House.

As the driver had predicted, the bus did stop at Alfred Street, and all of the passengers did leave the vehicle. After stepping down from it, I looked warily up at the lowering black clouds tinged with streaks of gray and decided that discretion was the better part of valor, so I set out at a trot.

"You'd better step it up a bit," José urged.

"Yeah," Pancho added, "that seventy-foot-long wooden roof was constructed over the sidewalk for a pur. . . ."

"Yeah," José interjected, "as a shelter. And we well know what those gray streaks in the clouds mean in midcontinent America."

"Naw, it wouldn't do that in Australia," I protested aloud.

Then, just before I ducked beneath the wooden roof, an ice-cold raindrop struck my bald pate and splashed across an area the size of a Mexican dollar.

"You almost made it," José commented, but I paid no heed, because I had just escaped a virtual downpour.

While standing beside another escapee, a relatively young man in a working-man's togs, I silently watched the curbs fill with rushing rainwater.

After several minutes the man looked whimsically at me and exclaimed, "Wot a bloody blahst!" Then, almost as if on cue, the huge raindrops turned into large, crystal-white balls, which struck the pavement and bounced jubilantly in all directions.

"Bouncing, white water!" I exclaimed with a teasing glance toward the short, broad-shouldered man.

"That's hile!" he protested. "Ain't ye nivah seen hile befoah?"

"Yes," I replied. "In fact, it has been claimed that hailstones as large as baseballs have fallen on some parts of the central plains of America, but I've never seen any that large."

After his skeptical eyes had carefully studied mine for a moment, he inquired, "American, eh?" And I nodded.

"Possibly he had the misfortune to encounter one or more Texans," Pancho suggested, "hence his doubts about the size of those hailstones."

"But Al was merely reporting what he had gained from media reports of prodigiously large hailstones," José protested.

"But we've never seen hailstones larger than a quarter of a dollar in diameter," Pancho rejoined, "so those reporters may have been Texans."

Suddenly the downpour stopped, almost as if the bearded man upstairs had turned off a valve. Then the sun burst through some of the more wispy clouds with a brilliance that dazzled the eyes. Since there were only the puddles to avoid, I dashed alongside what I suspected to be a projection of Hunter Street toward my towering objective on Bennelong Point about three hundred yards distant. Initially I did encounter a few errant raindrops, but I was more concerned about traversing those three hundred unsheltered yards before that unpredictable weatherman again turned on the valve.

Just as its pictures indicated, the structure and its simulated sails were massive, but I was more impressed by the lavish waste of reinforced concrete than by its magnificence. I was too early for even the first guided tour, so I substituted my own tour. Consequently, I didn't see the Concert Hall, which seats 2,700 people, or the Opera Theatre, which seats 1,500. But I did peek into some of the smaller units, such as the Drama Theatre with 550 seats, the Cinema with 420, and the Recording Hall with 300.

Actually, I was disappointed by the building, if it can really be called one, what with towering, concrete sails surmounting the basic steel-reinforced, concrete structure. I suspected that more reinforcing steel and concrete had been placed in that behemoth than in all of the dams in the Los Angeles flood control basin. Unfortunately, like the Opera House, they have never served a purpose sufficient to justify the costs of their construction. But the Opera House may have been a political pork barrel too.

According to what I overheard from more knowledgeable bystanders, Joern Utzon was the original designer of the Opera House. After several years of research on the many unusual construction problems entailed, construction was finally started in 1959. Since its completion, it has housed orchestral concerts, operas, ballets, dramas, jazz concerts, miscellaneous choral groups, and various types of conventions.

From the Opera House I slowly retraced my steps to Alfred Street. There I redirected them toward the Circular Quay Station, where I paused to ponder the purchase of a ticket for a trip aboard one of the several ferries, the hydrofoil, or a tram. The problem proved to be so monumental that I decided that I would ride the red Sydney Explorer bus. Unfortunately, I never did so, because pangs of hunger sidetracked me.

From the station I turned right on Pitt Street and wandered into the area identified as The Rocks, where I became somewhat disoriented. Therefore, I may not have actually been in The Rocks when I saw the sign "American Pancakes" in the second-story window of a large, red-brick building. My stomach instantly shouted, "That's for me!" Then it practically led me to the entrance of the building and up a flight of rustic, wooden stairs to the second floor, where we came upon an attractive young woman standing behind an *un*rustic counter with an electronic cash register on one end of it. As we approached closer to her, I sensed that she was studying my features much more intently than the situation warranted.

Of course, she broke the silent deadlock with the usual: "Can I help you?"

"Yes," I replied with a thoughtful mien. "I would like to sample some of your pancakes."

Silently selecting a menu from a rack, she led me to a table for four and placed the menu beside the nearest plate. "I'll return for your order in a minute," she promised. Then she veered diagonally toward the swinging door of the kitchen. Several minutes later a relatively young man pushed the kitchen door open and stood staring at me until my artillery drove him to cover.

"So we also have the incredible here," Pancho remarked.

Following the incident the young woman pushed open the door and advanced toward me with an order pad in one hand.

After coming to a stop beside the table, she raised the pad, poised a pencil over it, and, in ice-cold tones, inquired, "Have you decided what you want?"

"Yes," I retorted in equally cold tones. "As I told you, I would still like to sample some of your pancakes." Then I added a supercilious smile, which was intended to infuriate her as much as she had infuriated me.

"Well," she began impatiently, "what do you have in mind, specifically?"

"Make it a stack of cakes and one egg over easy," I murmured with a deep sigh.

As she stalked toward the kitchen, I felt so weary of the constant conflict that I yearned to leave the place and seek out some secluded spot where I could complete my self-appointed tasks. Obviously, such a program was impossible, because that was what I had in mind when I set up shop in Dunedin, and the conflict—the war, that is—had continued.

If Kiwi pancakes are anything like the pancakes that I partially consumed in that Sydney restaurant, I can fully comprehend why the Kiwis don't like them. But I have encountered pancakes of equally low caliber along many of the highways and byways of the U.S. of A. Lots of talent and experience are required to whip up a batch of pancake batter from scratch, gauge the heat properly, and guard the product during its cooking cycle. Very few commercial establishments possess either the talent, the experience, or the time to process the delicacies properly like grandma did. But her pancakes were a product of pride and love—pride in her skill and love for those for whom she prepared them.

Nevertheless, after that nerve-jarring reception my ulcer may have been in no mood to accept even a batch of grandma's light and golden beauties. Certainly that particular reception was only one stress attack, but it probably expanded the ulcer a smidgen beyond the limits created by the thousands of other such stress attacks that eventually had built up the ulcer to its current critical size.

From the restaurant I found my way back to Pitt Street, but several construction projects interfered with my progress through The Rocks, so I missed several points of interest during my trek toward the southern abutment of the Sydney Harbor Bridge. Most of those projects, I was to learn, were sponsored by the government of New South Wales during its restoration of the birthplace of Australia for the 1988 Bicentennial.

For the tourist, The Rocks Visitor's Centre on George Street offered site displays, maps, and guided hiking tours through the area. At one time that centre was a coroner's court. Currently, horse-drawn carriages and hansom cabs allowed the visitor to enjoy leisurely views of the colonial buildings, but I chose to investigate the area's true character by scrambling up its steep hills, cobblestone streets, and stairways, over which the horse-drawn vehicles couldn't travel. Besides, no fare was involved.

On Circular Quay West I found Cadman's Cottage, which had been built in 1816. It is Sydney's oldest existing house; however, it had been converted into a museum that covered the growth of Sydney Cove between 1788 and 1820. Campbell's Storehouse consisted of golden sandstone warehouses that dated back to 1838 and currently housed restaurants, pubs, stores, and the Australian Wine Cellar.

After continuing several hundred feet beyond the junction of George and Pitt Streets, I came upon the abutment of the Sydney Harbor Bridge. Since I had spent some time in the bridge department of one of America's midcontinent states during the early part of my engineering career, I was fascinated by the three-mile-long structure whose arch towered 440 feet above sea level. I could only guess at the dimensions and the number of pilings that had been driven into the earth to support not only the massive abutment but approximately one-half the weight of the huge steel and concrete structure, which extended across the harbor to the opposite abutment. There had to be many of them, because the structure of the bridge must have outweighed the structures of similar suspension bridges by a considerable amount.

From the abutment I slowly continued along the waterfront to Pier One, where I tarried long enough to discover a nice restaurant on the second level, so I filed that bit of information in the most accessible recesses of my mind for future reference. I also discovered that the pier housed a large assortment of small shops, which were arranged in a manner similar to that of an arcade or a small shopping mall. Obviously they were designed to appeal to the tourist, so I followed the bent of the many other tourists by wending my way through several of the aisles. Among them were some very unusual handcrafted items, such as native jewelry, native clothing, and exotic pottery. And there were opals, lots and lots of opals. There also were beautifully finished sheepskins, and several boutiques displayed the latest in ladies' apparel. One shop displayed ancient nautical wares or duplicates thereof. A few of the shops purveyed numerous tourist teasers, such as lavishly attired dolls, seashells, or highly polished brass and copper items, plus some artifacts. One shop even displayed jars of homemade jams, jellies, and preserves.

Everything progressed smoothly until I arrived at a particularly beautiful display window and began feasting my eyes on its array of opal jewelry. Then I got into trouble. Well, not really, just sort of. Actually, I was pondering the possibilities of finding a suitable item for my lady, while both sides of my brain were arguing about whether it was within the scope of my budget, when a middle-aged lady paused beside me and fixed fascinated eyes on the display. My casual glance revealed a handsome creature luxuriously attired in accordance with the latest fashions.

We had been standing there for almost a minute when an evil genie compelled me to say: "I'm shopping for an opal for my lady, but I haven't found one within my price range."

As I had expected, she looked toward me with an expression that seemed to inquire, "What is your price range, stranger?"

So I replied, "A dollar ninety-eight."

Then her eyes turned toward a beautiful opal brooch in the display, and, sheeplike, my eyes followed them to the $600 price tag beside it. After rotating her stylish coiffeur ninety degrees, her eyes slowly traveled from my bald head and untrimmed beard to the torn and travel-stained jacket; then they continued down the faded blue jeans to my scuffed, down-at-heel Hush Puppies. Abruptly, she whirled about and took off at a rapid pace, but there was no apparent reason for the furtive glance that she tossed back across one well-formed shoulder.

"Humph," Pancho mused. "These Aussies have no sense of humor a-tall. She behaved as if she suspected Al's sanity."

"But she didn't see him paying any six hundred dollars for a highly polished piece of soft, varicolored Australian rock," José loyally injected. "A body would have to be very crazy, indeed, to do that."

Eventually the structures of Pier One gave way to concrete wharves surmounted by modern warehouses. Nevertheless, I ventured ever onward and finally came to the end of a pier, where further travel would not only have been very wet but sheer folly. After seating myself so that my legs dangled over the end of the pier, I was in a fine position to peer down into the relatively clear, blue-green water or to watch the activities of a lone fisherman, whose line was suspended from a nearby vantage point.

He was relatively young, about thirty, and both tall and slender. He wore no hat atop his shock of sun-bleached, light-brown hair; consequently, a battalion of reddish-brown freckles marched from one sunburned ear across lightly tanned, angular features to the opposite ear.

"Good dye," he greeted me with an air of easy informality.

"Good day," I agreed. "How is the fishing?"

"Nuthin' so fah," he replied, "but it alwyes has bin a bit iffy off o' this point."

"What do you normally catch?" I asked. "Baramundi or sea bass, perhaps?"

"No," he replied. "Neitha. Baramundi is a whoite fish that's shipped into Sydney from noahtheastern watahs."

"What about the John Dory?" I persisted, reminding myself not to again expose my total ignorance of the subject by suggesting the answer, especially since I had obtained the names of those fish from a tourist guide.

Nodding approvingly, he answered, "John Dory is a delicate whoite fish tat's often obtained from these watahs."

"North American restaurants used to serve a lot of Australian lobster tails," I volunteered. "Where were they found?"

"They must have been owah cryfish, which taste a lot loike shrimp and lobstah," he replied. "Unfoahtunately, theah has been so much demand foah thim that the supply bekime threatened, so the provinces invoked laws to protict thim. In fact, we would consume most of the available supply owahsilves if they had not become so costly. One reason foah their hoy cost is the hoy cost o' fishin' loicinses levied boy provinces such as Victoria and South Austreyelia. Foah ixample, almost half a million dollahs in annual fees ah pide boy the ownahs of the thuty-noine trawlahs that ah loicinsed to fish foah prawns in Spinsah Gulf."

"Where is Spencer Gulf located?" I asked.

"Poaht Augusta is at the noath ind of it," he answered. Then, to allay my obvious confusion, he added, "Wist of Adelaide on the coast of South Austreyelia." A quick glance confirmed that I was finally aboard, so he resumed: "Furthamoah, the law limits the numbah of pots that a lobstahman can sit."

"First you called them crayfish," I protested. "Then you called them prawns, and now you are calling them lobsters. Which are they?"

"We used to call thim cryfish," he replied, "but you Yanks exhibited such an overwhilming appetite foah lobstahs that we took to calling thim rock lobstahs."

"In other words, if we can't tell the difference between them and lobsters, you Aussies are not about to point out the difference to us," I ventured.

The freckles undulated like golden gulls on the crests of indolent tan waves while they rode out the wrinkles created by his infectious grin. "We really don't cayah wot they ah called as long as you Yanks continue to pie such exhorbitant proices foah thim," he rejoined.

"Then the Australian government is indirectly boosting the price by restricting the supply," I suggested.

"No," he answered, "the provincial governmints ah controlling the supply so that greedy fishahmin don't destroy it entoirely. Foah ixample, they issue C-shiped, bronze timplates to the fishahmin foah theah use in diterminin' whethah the smallah lobstahs ah mahkitable."

"But some fishermen must ignore such controls," I said.

"Yis, we have some of thim and some poachahs, too," he granted. "And theah ah some who ignoah the lobstah's breedin' cycle and still othahs who scripe the iggs off of the females and sell thim." After noting my puzzlement, he explained, "The females carry their fertiloized iggs outsoide theah bodies undah theah tiles. The law requyahs that femile lobstahs and theah undisturbed iggs be tossed back into the sea so that anothah crop of lobstahs can divilop."

"Do you find any abalone in these waters?" I inquired.

"Lots of black-lip and green-lip abs ah found in Watahloo Bye," he replied.

"And where is that?" I inquired.

"Neah Elliston off o' the Grite Austreyelian Boight," he replied.

"And that also is off the coast of South Australia," I ventured.

"Yis," he replied.

"It seems to me that most of your good fishing waters are located off of that coast," I observed.

"Not intoirely," he replied. "Those watahs ah cold, so they attract lots o' edible fish and crustacea."

Suddenly the man started and peered intently at the point where his line entered the water; finally, regretfully shaking his head, he turned back to me and said, "It appeahs that all Oy'm goin' to catch todye ah some wives tossed up by the vygrant breezes."

"Maybe your luck will change if I leave," I suggested, raising my legs and swinging them onto the concrete.

As I arose, he protested, "No, yoah prisince has nothing to do with it. In fact, this is a typical dye. Besoides, Oy rayally catch anything but old rubbah boots heah."

"From that remark I suspect that you've been reading too many American comic strips," I suggested, tentatively moving away.

In response to his infectious grin, the freckles chased each other across the tanned undulations of his features like tiny dervishes. "Oy injoyed owah conversation," he called to me, as I moved away.

Stopping abruptly, I slowly turned toward him and muttered, "I did too, much more than you'll ever know." While I was turning away, a parting glance revealed that a gang of puzzled wrinkles had tumbled the freckles on his brow.

"Obviously he'll never understand that statement," Pancho mused, as I finally got under way.

"Nobody will ever fully understand why we obtain so much pleasure from these all-too-rare intervals when we manage to escape from Big Brother's artificial world." José added.

"Yeah," Pancho agreed. "Especially times like this one when we can indulge in normal communications with people whose minds haven't been contaminated and warped by who knows what kinds of inputs."

By various steep byways I tortuously made my way up through an old residential area to a small grocery store. There I purchased a cold soft drink and lounged against a showcase while consuming it. The store wasn't that cool; in fact, its ambient temperature probably exceeded that of the balmy air outside the open doorway. Since the proprietor had subjected my bearded countenance to a sharp scrutiny when I paid for the drink, I deliberately hung around and watched for more evidence that he might have been exposed to Big Brother's handiwork. After draining the last drop of liquid from the bottle, I set it on the wooden counter in front of him and moved slowly toward the open doorway.

"Thank you!" he called after me. "Come again."

With a nod I passed through the doorway, turned to my right along the badly fractured sidewalk, and resumed climbing. Meanwhile, the two sides of my brain were arguing about the results of my research. "It may have been Al's accent that caused the man to stare at him," Pancho finally opined. And I sided with the opinion.

Somehow I ended up high on Lower Fort Street. After a brief rest, I again turned upgrade and climbed past several dilapidated buildings to the street's intersection with Argyle Street. Following another rest stop, I turned and looked downgrade through the aperture afforded by the Bradfield Highway overpass toward the quay, located some three or four blocks beyond it.

From behind me a voice abruptly inquired, "Are you lost?"

Whirling about, I beheld a slender, middle-aged man, who stood rocking on the heels of carefully polished, brown oxfords while his smiling eyes inspected my startled features.

"No, not entirely," I replied after casually noting his neat, lightweight business suit and the matching necktie clipped to the front of his white shirt. "But I have a desperate need for something to protect my bald pate from this subtropical sun, so I could use some help in locating the business district of this burgeoning burg."

He fixed a level gaze on mine—level in that the primary elements of both gazes were about the same distance from the sidewalk. "Well," he began, "I suppose that you might find what you want on George Street."

"And where would that be?" I asked.

"Straight down this street," he answered. "However, since I'm going that way, I'll walk along with you, if you like, and I'll point it out to you when we get within view of it." Then my mind noted the lack of a heavy Aussie accent.

"That's kind of you," I murmured. Meanwhile, my eyes were studying the rough rock wall that towered above the opposite side of the street. Pointing to it, I asked, "Isn't that limestone?"

He turned and looked across one shoulder toward the rugged, roughly cut surface. "Yes, it is," he answered. "In fact, most of this section of the city rests on an upthrust layer of limestone." Then, pointing toward its upper edge, he asked, "Have you been on top yet?"

"No," I replied. "I finished a climb from sea level just this minute."

"It isn't much farther to the top," he said. "A footpath winds from Argyle Place up to the observatory, where one can get a nice view of The Rocks and Sydney Harbor. It might be worth your effort."

After looking thoughtfully up at the gently waving bushes that overhung the wall's topmost edges, I reluctantly shook my head and said, "That climb will have to wait until another day." Following a brief silence, I added, "I'll bet that without modern rock drills and blasting powder that wall wasn't cut in a day."

"It was cut with hand tools by convict laborers during the middle of the eighteenth century," he volunteered. "In fact, most of the early work on The Rocks was done with convict labor."

"I read somewhere that Australia was settled by convicts, who were shipped from England about that time," I said.

"The first fleet of ships arrived here in seventeen eighty-eight," he responded, as we involuntarily joined in a military step that rapidly carried us down Argyle Street. After a short silence, he added: "And tents were pitched along Sydney Cove to house them and their guards."

"Where is Sydney Cove located?" I asked.

"We are headed directly toward it," he replied. "It is now called Circular Quay, but the city's name was derived from it. Some of Sydney's first buildings were constructed just this side of the quay on The Rocks, but the area soon deteriorated into a slum peopled by prostitutes, press gangs, and criminals."

"Yeah, I've been touring some of those buildings and cobblestone streets," I said. "If you were visiting the city for the first time, like I am, where would you go next?"

After pondering the question for a moment, he countered, "Have you been to Taronga Park Zoo?"

I shook my head.

"You might enjoy a visit there," he suggested. "It has a large assortment of Australian animals, such as kangaroos, koalas, emus, and the platypus."

"That sounds like a good suggestion." I granted.

"You can get there from the Circular Quay by bus," he added. Then he slowed to a stop, so I followed suit. "In addition to that, you might consider one of the ferry rides. The trip to Manly and back shouldn't take more than an hour, and it would give you a good view of the city from the harbor."

"That also sounds like a good suggestion," I said.

"I turn off here," he explained. "I'm sorry that I failed to properly introduce myself, but I'm usually called Bill."

"It has been my pleasure to know you for this brief moment, Bill," I said, accepting the extended right hand. "Belated as it is, I'm usually called Al. Thank you so much for your information and advice."

"Oh, Al!" he called after me, as if responding to an afterthought. "You'll find George Street at the next intersection."

"Thanks again, Bill," I called back.

Turning about, he jauntily raised his right hand and called, "I hope you enjoy your stay in Australia."

"Hmm," José mused, as I resumed walking. "We might just do that, Bill, if we're lucky enough to run into many people like you."

"It's unlikely that he descended from a convict," Pancho opined. "From his behavior it's much more logical to suspect that he evolved from a very fine set of genes."

Somewhere among the tall buildings in the business district, I chanced upon a sign that advertised the services of hairstylists. After following a series of arrows up a flight of stairs to the second floor, I strolled into what appeared to be a deserted curl and purl establishment. Besides the several cubicles containing various different types of hairdressing equipment, there were three barber chairs at the rear end of a large cul-de-sac, so my mission seemed not to have been in vain; however, there wasn't a mechanic in the entire scene. In fact, from the various hurriedly cast-off aprons and such, I gathered that they had fled in haste, apparently to indulge their appetites, since the hands of a clock pointed to 12:17.

The sounds of leather softly scuffing against plastic floor covering drew my eyes toward the dimly lighted recess to my left, from which a trim, handsome man of about thirty was emerging. A white smock hung across his broad shoulders and extended almost to the rear pockets of his brown, tweed trousers, and an unobtrusive necktie was neatly pinned to the front of his crisp, white shirt. He was a somewhat more rugged duplicate of men whom I had observed through the windows of women's hairdressing emporiums in America, but he missed being as dapper and debonair as they by a wide margin.

"Good dye," he greeted me. "Can I be of service?" Meanwhile, he subjected my bearded countenance to a preoccupied study.

Typically, I instantly rebelled and even glanced purposefully toward the stairway, but a dire need of a barber's services induced me to ask, "Do you service beards?"

Even to me the words sounded as if I were requesting something akin to an oil change, and the barber must have received the same impression, because he smiled faintly before asking, "Would you loike a trim?"

"Yeah," I replied, "from my Adam's apple all of the way up to the bald spot."

He swung toward the first of the barber chairs, which stood at an obtuse corner formed by the junction of two walls. Then, with a minuscule bow, he gestured toward the chair with the palm of his right hand turned away from his right knee and with the tips of its fingers pointed rigidly toward the floor. I carefully restrained a smile, because the actions reminded me so much of an ancient American cartoon, wherein, with a similarly sweeping gesture, one character turns to another one and says, "After you, my dear Gaston."

After I was seated in the chair and hog-tied in place, he inquired, "How would you like the beard trimmed?"

After deeply pondering the question, I said, "It really should be shaved off." Then, with both pairs of eyes locked, I resumed pondering. Finally I shook my head and muttered, "No, that wouldn't be fair to Big Brother."

The intensity of his stare increased momentarily; then it seemed that a veil was drawn across his eyes as he cautiously inquired, "What do you mean?"

"Well," I began with a grim smile, "a beard can serve two opposite purposes: It can partially hide the identity of a man, or it can serve as a means of readily identifying him. Since this one hasn't served very well as camouflage, it would be unfair to the enemy to complicate the game for him by removing it, so please trim it but not too closely."

Apparently the remarks shook the man, because he volunteered not one word throughout the operation until he endeavored to untangle a particularly curly part of the beard. "Uhm," he grunted. "It's extremely thick."

"Yeah," I responded, "it would be nice if some of it would automatically transfer to the top of my head."

From that point on he uttered only the words, "Thank you," when I presented a dollar tip to him. As I was leaving the area, a sweeping glance verified my suspicion that he would be thoughtfully staring after me.

"Yeah," Pancho conceded, "that guy definitely knew what Al was talking about."

"That's debatable," rejoined José. But they voluntarily dropped the subject. After all, everything that evolved from that pair was debatable.

After purchasing a beanie from Fletcher Jones, Australia's finest clothiers (according to the receipt), I walked all of the way back to Pier One. There I found the restaurant on the second level to be somewhat ritzy. Furthermore, most of its clientele was rather formally attired, at least as viewed by the eyes of a shoddily attired ancient mariner from the suburbs of Los Angeles.

The bearded host seated me at a small table midway of the large dining room, placed a menu in my hands, returned to his post, and signaled to the waiter. From that point in time my attention was confined almost exclusively to his activities and to those of the slender, dark-complexioned waiter. The host appeared to have survived thirty-five austral summers, and the waiter may have survived thirty of them. Of course, either one of them could have descended from a convict or from a camp follower or from both; consequently, that heritage, plus a hard life on The Rocks may have aged them far beyond their years. Both men were attired in suits: That of the waiter had been neatly cut and assembled from a dark, closely woven fabric, whereas the host had chosen his from a loosely woven, brown fabric that may have never been pressed after it was assembled and placed on the hanger by its tailor.

After the waiter responded to the host's beckoning forefinger, the host placed one arm about his shoulders and spoke confidentially to him. Meanwhile, the waiter's dark eyes turned toward me; then they darted furtively away when his gaze met mine.

The waiter took my order and delivered it after a reasonable lapse of time. When he was about to leave the table, I looked up at him and asked, "What was the big deal with the host when I first arrived?"

He started slightly, and the small, black moustache above his upper lip began to dance uneasily like a globule of water on a red-hot stove. "I don't know what you mean," he responded nervously; meanwhile, his eyes turned to and seemed to beseech those of the remote host for rescue from this madman.

In fact, he appeared so eager to escape that I bowed my head in defeat and growled, "Forget it!"

Minutes later I detected an eye signal from the waiter to the host, and the two men soon disappeared behind a shoulder-high flower box. I couldn't determine what transpired there, but shortly after they returned to the scene, the host meandered to my table and unctuously inquired, "Is there anything more that we can serve you?"

My right eye stared thoughtfully into one of his eyes, while the left one studied the activities of the waiter, who was alertly watching from across the room. "No," I finally replied, "but compliment the chef for me, because that was one of the most delicious seafood coquilles that I've ever consumed."

"Thank you," he responded with an ingratiating smile. "I'll inform the chef."

Within minutes he returned to the table with a silver tray bearing the check and set it on the table. Pausing beside my chair and resting one arm lightly on my right shoulder, he leaned forward to my right ear and said, "I hope that you'll return."

Since I had heard rumors about how many of the *boys* find employment in restaurants, I almost cringed. I've never "cottoned" to men, even normal ones, who get too cozy with me. Of course, psychiatrists could make considerable hay from that reaction, but the fad opinions of their profession change from day to day, so what do they know of human behavior?

After leaving the restaurant, I visited the zoo. Unfortunately for the zoo, my several visits to the San Diego Zoo had spoiled me, so I gave short shrift to Bill's zoo. Nevertheless, I strode into the Circular Quay Station and purchased a ferry ticket to Manly. Despite the fact that I was equally unimpressed with Manly, the trip to and from that point proved to be particularly pleasurable. The views of Sydney and its Opera House from the ferry were fully as impressive as Bill had implied they would be.

The dinner hour was at hand when the bus cruised past the entrance of the motel's oriental restaurant and dropped me nearby. Even though it was the only readily accessible dining spot, I couldn't force myself to return to it, so I strode along the street to a tiny Italian grocery store. There I had previously purchased a cold soft drink and engaged in a friendly discussion of world politics with its short, middle-aged Italian proprietor. This time, however, I immediately sensed that the atmosphere was no longer friendly, so I turned about and headed back toward the motel. En route, I happened to notice what would pass for a small town drugstore in America, so I crossed the street and entered it.

Since there was no one to serve me, I was about to leave when a remote voice called, "Can I help you?"

Upon turning about, I saw that a tall, well-built, middle-aged man was strolling toward me from a doorway at the rear of the store. As he moved along the opposite side of the counter, his eyes fixed on my features, and they remained fixed on them, so I stubbornly resolved to go to bed hungry. Nevertheless, I courteously replied, "No, I guess not. I was looking for a place where I might get what we call a malted milk."

"I can fix one for you," he volunteered.

"But I don't want to interrupt what you were doing for such a small sale," I protested.

"I was merely visiting with my wife," he rejoined. "What flavor would you like?"

"Make it easy on yourself," I said.

"You are an American, eh?" he surmised, busying himself with a chrome-plated canister.

"Yeah," I grudgingly granted.

"Staying at the motel, eh?" he persisted while slipping the canister into the mixer.

Shooting a sharp glance at him, I civilly admitted to staying there.

The roar of the mixer precluded any further communications. Upon switching it off, he stated: "My wife came from a neighboring country."

"Oh, Canada no doubt," I responded confidently.

"No," he replied. "Peru."

After shooting another sharp glance at him, I conceded, "Peru could be called a remote neighbor of the U.S., I suppose."

Removing the canister from the mixer, he placed it in my extended hands and said, "While you're working on this I'll go get my wife and introduce her to you."

Scooping a package of wafers from a display rack, I called, "Please add these to the bill." Then he glanced across one shoulder toward the package in my extended hand and nodded.

"It appears that he wants to display his wife to Al," José telegraphed to Pancho.

"Yeah," Pancho responded, "and I'll bet that she's a brand new one."

"Probably," José conceded. "But what Al doesn't know is that he is also to be displayed."

"You guys can it!" I interjected savagely. "This has happened too often for me not to recognize that instantly."

After several minutes had passed, Pancho cautiously suggested, "He's probably briefing her, hence the delay."

"She could be powdering her nose," José observed.

When the man did finally return, he was followed by a tawny-skinned, dark-eyed beauty. Coming to a stop opposite me, he then extended one hand to her, and she responded to it by gliding to a stop beside him. Momentarily, his eyes caressed her finely molded features and nubile body; then they turned toward me, and, almost reverently, he murmured, "This is my wife, Maria."

Both José and Pancho were so busy collecting and assessing behavioral data that there was a brief pause until I finally responded to their urgings by saying, "This is a great pleasure, Maria. My name is Albert—Alberto in your country."

"The pleasure is mutual," she responded with scarcely any accent. Meanwhile, her opaque eyes were intently studying my bearded features.

It was disconcerting, to say the least; therefore, more to break the ensuing silence than anything else, I asked, "*¿Habla usted español, Maria* (Do you speak Spanish, Maria)?"

"*Si, senor,*" she responded delightedly. "*¿Desea usted hablarme en español* (Do you wish to speak to me in Spanish)?"

"Not really," I admitted ruefully, "but I understand some of it." Immediately she began to spout Spanish while I answered or commented in English, and her husband silently listened. Apparently she sensed that he was being excluded unintentionally from the conversation, so she said, "Alberto, you understand Spanish very well."

But I reversed the trend by stating, "*Usted es muy bondadosa* (You are very kind)." Nevertheless, she continued to employ English throughout the remainder of the discussion, which I considered to be very considerate of her under the circumstances.

Typically, I was anxious to escape from the situation as quickly as possible, so I said, "Since I plan to leave for Melbourne in the morning, I should hit the sack early. But I've thoroughly enjoyed meeting you people, and I particularly enjoyed discussing with you, Maria, some of the mutually familiar parts of our Northern Hemisphere."

"But it's early yet," she demurred.

"*El tren sale por la manana* (The train leaves in the morning)," I reminded her, moving slowly toward the doorway.

"*¡Muy bien!*" she called to me; then, waving a slender arm, she added, "*Adios.*"

"Enjoy your stay in Australia," the man called after me.

"Why do these people always say that?" José mused, as I strode toward the motel. "After all, their reactions to Big Brother's misinformation are the primary reasons why we can't enjoy our stay here."

"And that poor woman," Pancho injected. "She's so starved for the familiar sounds of her native language that I have to wonder if she is enjoying her stay here."

"Very likely she sold herself to that fascinated older man to gain a more luxurious life-style," José chimed in. "I doubt that he could have won an equally youthful local beauty. She probably boosts his ego through the stratosphere. Consequently, the famous quotation, 'What fools we mortals be?' seems to apply to him in particular."

When I entered the motel, the manager was standing behind the counter. "Good evening, Mr. Terril," she opened.

After responding in kind, I paused in front of the counter and studied the bold, green lettering on the business cards neatly stacked in the clear, plastic box that stood on it.

"I wonder if she's one of 'Mine Hosts: The Crawfords,'" Pancho wondered.

"Apparently she is," José volunteered, "or she wouldn't have fought so fiercely with the cab driver about the fare."

Meanwhile, I turned to her and said, "You were right about the cab driver running up the meter. I've been meaning to tell you before, but no opportunity presented itself. I suspected right off that he was deliberately running up the meter when we passed the terminal a second time. I even warned him that he would have to deal with the motel when he got here, but he seemed unconcerned about it."

Nodding sagely, she murmured, "We don't usually have that kind of trouble with our own people."

Involuntarily, my bearded lips split into a wide grin. "But I must have had some of that kind of trouble with one of our own people," I said. "The driver of the first cab that I was about to take refused to come here when he learned that the Eastside Motel was to be our destination."

A startled expression flashed across her pretty features as she thoughtfully lowered her head and stared at the countertop. Finally, looking up from it, she suggested, "Maybe they are learning that they can't cheat us. We've accurately determined the distance from here to the terminal, and it doesn't warrant a charge of more than eight dollars."

I was about to humorously suggest that it might be farther traveling from the terminal to the motel, but I wisely refrained, because my far-out humor had not been faring well in Australia.

With a smile on my lips, I said, "That driver not only overran the far end of the trip, but he overran this end of it by about half a mile. I'm sure of that, because I recognized some buildings that we had previously passed." And she nodded knowingly. "In one sense I should have done a better job of warning him about running up the meter," I resumed, withdrawing my wallet. "Therefore, I'll pay the difference between what you paid him and the eight dollars."

"No!" she shouted. "You are a stranger, so how could you know what route the man should take?"

"But I did know what he was doing," I rejoined.

"Well, you must be smarter than most visitors," she murmured. "Nevertheless, the man has been paid, and that's the end of the matter."

From the sparkle in her eyes, I concluded that she meant it. However, while I was replacing the leather, my mind was formulating another proposition. "By the way," I began, "I've noticed that my presence here has attracted a lot of attention, and I would like to learn why."

"Why do you say that?" she countered sharply.

"I have some very good reasons for the statement," I retorted, "and they are based on some rather acute observations."

"I still don't know what you are talking about," she protested.

"That's what a New Zealand motel manager claimed, too," I muttered, "but he involuntarily revealed some interesting information to me, so he did know what I was talking about. I'm hoping that you will do likewise, because Big Brother can't be suppressed by the countermeasures of a lone rebel. The combined efforts of a great many rebels are required. Furthermore, it is to the advantage of everyone to cooperate in this matter, because I've found that Big Brother's tentacles extend into many governments, including yours."

"What did the motel manager reveal?" she countered. "What do you suspect that I can reveal to you?"

"Of course, I can only speculate on what you can reveal," I replied, "but I strongly suspect that you can reveal information such as whether you were called and warned of my arrival. Or, if not that, whether the many public service types of businesses, such as this one, have been alerted to my presence in this country. That's the kind of information that I need to combat Big Brother effectively."

"The only call I received was from the Tourist Information Centre," she replied, "and that was to reserve lodgings for you. I don't know why you are asking all of these questions. Are you an international criminal or something?"

"Not to my knowledge," I replied. "In fact, I've never been indicted for anything, nor have I ever been in court, except to be granted a divorce."

"Then why are you asking all of these questions?" she countered.

"Because I have several reasons to suspect that you have been fed a lot of misinformation about me," I growled. Then my eyes challenged hers, but they refused to meet mine.

"Okay," I resumed, "if you believe in fair play at all, you will tell me what channels were employed when you were contacted regarding me."

Momentarily she stared at me with a guilty half-smile as if mesmerized. "I can't," she murmured. Then, apparently realizing the implications of the involuntary response, she added, "I don't know what you are talking about."

"But you do," I insisted. "In fact, you almost committed yourself just now. If you would only cooperate with me, I could determine the source or sources of my problem, and that would help me to counterattack it or them."

The guilty half-smile returned; then, ruefully shaking her head, she whispered, "You are really something. No wonder you have a problem."

"Then you refuse to help?" I countered.

"I can't," she responded. "I mean, how can I? I don't even know what you are talking about."

With a dejected nod, I muttered, "That's par for the course," and turned wearily toward the lift.

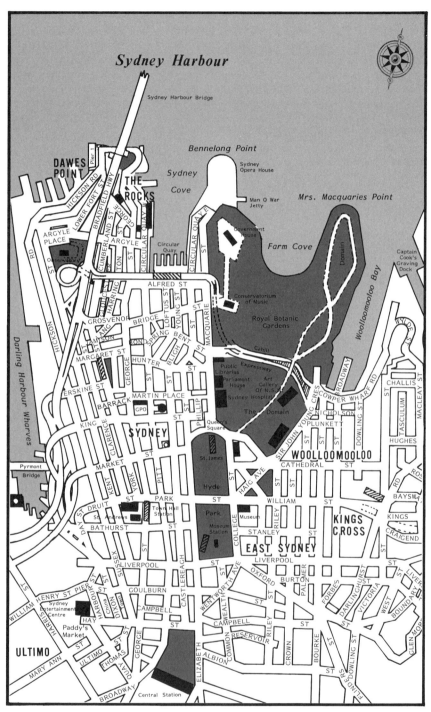

Map of Sydney

20

Sydney to Melbourne

When the Intercapital Express pulled out of Sydney's Central Station, I was the sole occupant of one of the long, cloth-upholstered bench seats that graced the left side of the train. Since all of the seats faced aft, I concluded that Railways of Australia had responded logically to reports that, during accidents, such seating arrangements netted fewer injuries to passengers. Initially my position beside the window provided little more than views of the disheveled industrial districts and dilapidated housing areas that commonly straddle the railroads of large cities. With nothing more exciting to do, I relaxed and watched the slender, red-headed conductor as he slowly advanced along the aisle while collecting the tickets. When he finally arrived in my immediate area, I was fully prepared, so I didn't miss the man's protracted stare in my direction just before he stepped forward to the side of my seat and extended a hand for my ticket.

Even though the train was touted as an express, there was a bit of stop and go before it finally got rolling. During the second of those stops I acquired a seat partner: a somewhat voluptuous young woman who may have been thirty. She was clad in a sheath of beige lace that overlay a lightweight but more obscure member whose color nicely complemented that of the sheath. Nevertheless, the ensemble was so thin that it literally clung to her thighs. The undergarment terminated several inches above her trim kneecaps, so the view may have been mildly titillating to men of her generation. Possibly it was intended to titilate; if so, it was done with reasonable tact.

Since the rails paralleled the Great Dividing Range, the scenery improved after the train escaped from the more dominating scars created by man. Even then the scenery was not particularly spectacular; however, the towering eucalyptus trees and the clusters of bushes superimposed on the tumbled terrain possessed a certain characteristic flair. Meanwhile, my new seat companion propped both knees high against the back of the seat in front of us, leaned back, and closed her eyes, so there was no lack of scenery on either side of the window.

Somewhat later the conductor came along the aisle collecting the tickets of the new arrivals. When he stopped alongside our seat, not only did his eyes appear to be irresistibly drawn to the seductively exposed knees, but his red eyebrows began to jump about his freckled forehead like a pair of sexually excited grasshoppers. Finally he reached forth and tapped . . . no, not a knee but her shoulder.

She started, opened her eyes, hurriedly pulled the sheath down over her knees, and lowered them to a sitting position.

"Ticket, please," he muttered.

After he punched the ticket and continued onward, she turned to me and inquired, "Do you know whether the diner is open?"

"Several minutes before the last stop there was some sort of an announcement," I replied, "but I ignored most of it, so I'm sorry to say that I don't know."

After pondering the statement briefly, she nodded her head and said, "I think that I'll gamble on it." Getting to her feet, she collected her purse and took off toward the front of the car.

I returned to watching the scenery for several minutes until I was distracted, and I do mean distracted: First, the conductor reappeared alongside the seat in front of me for some inexplicable reason; then, clad in a tan uniform, a ravishing blonde, and I do mean ravishing, appeared beside him. Her eyes seemed to be searching for something or someone but without apparent success. Finally she cast an interrogative look toward the conductor, whose expressive red eyebrows immediately responded like a pair of railroad semaphores. They must have conveyed some kind of message to her, because she abruptly turned and looked directly at me. However, when her china-blue eyes impinged on my exasperated gaze, they quickly turned away. Then the duo moved toward the front of the car as if a mission had been accomplished.

While I resumed my study of the landscape, several of the nearby passengers arose sporadically and straggled forth in the same direction. Several of them soon returned with small packages of food. Even though I sensed no hunger pangs, I stood up, stretched cramped muscles, stepped into the aisle, and strolled forward. After passing the rest rooms, the aisle led me to a heavy, spring-loaded door, which finally yielded to my persistent efforts. Then I passed through the opening, crossed over the steel plate that covered the car coupling, and continued on into the next car.

The curved surface of a mahogany-paneled wall immediately forced me into an aisle that skirted the left side of the car to a point where the full wall gave way to a pony wall. From that point about a dozen passengers had formed a horseshoe-shaped line whose other end terminated in front of a commissary, which was housed between the pony wall and the far side of the car.

Since I've always hated to wait in line for any service, I was about to return to my seat when Pancho observed, "You'll be sitting in line along with a whole train full of passengers during most of the trip to Melbourne, so what's the difference?"

"The only difference is sitting instead of standing," José added.

The logic was irrefutable, so I pulled up behind the last man in the line and slowly followed him around the base of the horseshoe to the far wall of the car, where a brief wait induced me to turn and lean back against it. About two minutes later the ravishing blonde appeared in the aisle through which I had passed. She was a tall girl, so her long, swinging stride brought her to the end of the line in short order. After pausing momentarily to assess the space between me and the curved projection of the pony wall, she raised her eyes to mine, and their lines of sight passed right through my eyes like a pair of parallel laser beams. In fact, her eyes reacted to mine as if her mind were on another planet, but I quickly discovered that her body wasn't.

As I pressed my back against the wall to allow her to pass, she moved purposefully forward, slid her left hand under my right arm and pulled herself so tightly against me that I would have had to be dead not to feel the two punctures that

A Native Aussie Loafing on the Job

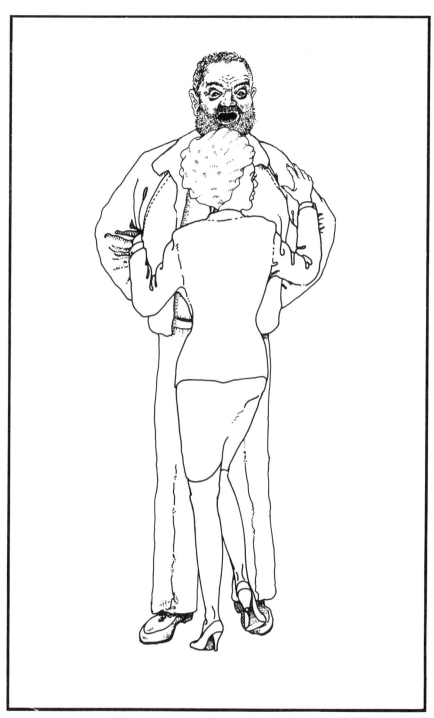

The Brazen Brat In Action

literally seared my chest. Then, for some unfathomable reason, she paused with one slender knee thrust between my not-so-slender knees before slowly pulling away. And I *sware* that, following the sounds of two sharp pops, there was the soft rustle of bed linen. Then, incredible as it seemed, she swept seductively past the other passengers with the greatest of ease and plenty of clearance. I was so dazed by the incident that I just stood there and stared at the space between me and the pony wall—a good twenty inches.

My preoccupation with space was interrupted by the man behind me, who tactfully murmured, "You ah nixt, suh."

"Oh, yeah!" I exclaimed with a guilty glance toward the eight feet of vacated space that separated me from the counter of the commissary. "Pardon me for sleeping."

I must have been suffering from shock for a considerable time, because I've never been able to recall what I purchased and where I consumed it. In fact, my first recollection of returning consciousness was a growing awareness of being seated beside the window just before my seat partner returned.

She seemed to be in a particularly talkative mood, because she cast aimlessly about in several different conversational fields before I observed, "You don't seem to have an Australian accent. Are you a native of this country?"

After a tumbling nod of her brown curls, she said, "My apparent lack of an accent may be due to the fact that my father is a university professor."

"Then you are a college graduate," I unwisely assumed.

With a rueful shake of the brown curls, she answered, "No, but I've been exposed to that kind of environment practically all of my life."

"Then you probably are not an indirect descendant of one of those early convicts," I ventured with a smile.

"No," she responded with a matching smile, "my ancestors were Poles."

"How did they ever manage to break away from the North Pole and migrate down here to the South Pole?" I inquired.

"Probably the same way that most of the other immigrants found their way down here," she suggested.

"I've read that most of the Australian population evolved from British ancestors," I rejoined. "According to one of my sources, one hundred sixty thousand British convicts founded this nation."

"But most of those convicts were men," she protested with a chuckle, "so they must not have been the sole source of our thirteen million people."

"Hmm," I mumbled thoughtfully. "That's right. So how did they overcome that problem?"

"It has never been fully overcome in some of the most remote areas," she replied. "In fact, there is less than one woman to every two men in many of those areas. However, in answer to your question, some of those convicts took aborigine wives, and. . . ."

"But that must have thrust some of the aborigine men out into the cold, dark night without blankets," I protested. "Didn't they take up their boomerangs or whatever and try to reclaim those women?"

"I doubt that they did," she murmured. "They are a pretty peaceful lot."

"But didn't England try to colonize this new land?" I inquired.

"Australia practically colonized itself," she replied. "Of course, colonization did start with the shipment of the convicts, the guards, and their families to Sydney. From there it expanded north to Brisbane and south to Melbourne, Hobart, and

Adelaide. Consequently, about three-fourths of the population is concentrated on the east coast."

"Didn't the British government attempt to colonize the country with free men as well as convicts?" I persisted.

"Not really," she answered. "In fact, the government demanded such high prices for land that colonization was discouraged. Many of the people who did migrate from England were from urban areas, so they were repelled by the arid outback. Many Irish farmers ventured into it, but they had always been blessed with ample rainfall, so most of them ended up on the coast, too."

"Why hasn't the government irrigated some of that desert?" I asked. "After all, California would be nothing but a desert without its massive irrigation systems."

"We don't have that many large rivers," she replied. "We've used some of the water from the Murray River, but much of the irrigated land doesn't lend itself to the growth of grains and forage crops. At best, it's suited to raising sheep and cattle. Without irrigation water, it takes an awful lot of land to support just one animal."

With an understanding nod, I suggested, "Perhaps Australia should concentrate on developing its natural resources. After all, it isn't logical to employ costly irrigation systems in an unfavorable agricultural environment when most of the nation's largest markets are located halfway around the world.

"Recently we've concentrated on mining our large deposits of iron ore," she said. "Unfortunately, the far-flung nature of such resources handicaps us, but our railroad systems have been strategically planned to overcome that problem. In fact, Australia has more rail service per capita than does any other nation in the world. Actually, our isolated ports are closer to more large Third World ports than to a port of any progressive country except Japan. Some of our cities are even closer to such ports than to each other; for example, Perth is closer to Jakarta than to Sydney, and Darwin is closer to Singapore than to Melbourne."

"It was unfortunate that the railroads between some of your principal cities were not properly coordinated," I volunteered. "According to something I read, the rails between some of the more remote cities were often set at different widths, because none of the decision makers ever considered the possibility that the rails might be extended and combined into a national railway system. Therefore, when the last of those systems were finally combined in nineteen sixty, it had been necessary to replace many of the railroads and scrap their associated equipment."

"As you know," she rebounded with a defensive gleam in her eyes, "Australia's first settlers were convicts, mostly hard-core criminals, who were dumped along Sydney Harbor. Later free settlers from the British Isles settled in what are now Melbourne, Hobart, and Adelaide. Obviously, with Perth located clear across a continent whose area is equal to that of the contiguous United States, our cultural and political centers were so few and widely separated that they tended to develop independently. Besides, with the central government located eleven thousand miles away in London and with communications so poor at that time, the settlers became very independent and defiant of authority, so the governing members of each settlement made their own decisions."

"There can be no doubt that those convicts were defiant of authority, all right," I responded with a chuckle. "In fact, that may have been the primary reason why the British government shipped them halfway around the world."

"Australians used to be ashamed of their heritage," she said, "but now they tend to view it with a certain rueful pride."

"Australians are fortunate to have only one hundred eighty thousand aborigines to contend with," I suggested. "That's less than two percent of the population. Twelve percent of the American population is black, and I can only guess at how many yellow, brown, and red-skinned people there are, but they have to constitute a sizable proportion of the population, too."

"So your population has developed into a potpourri," she rejoined. "Australia has acquired considerable numbers of ethnic types, too. In fact, the northern provinces wanted to import Asians for labor at one time, but the southern provinces voted the proposition down."

"They were very wise," I murmured.

She cast an enigmatic glance toward me, so I defensively added, "Despite the claims of impractical liberals, intermixing the races doesn't work; furthermore, the mixing of religious groups doesn't work, and intermixing of the sexes has created tremendous problems all over the world."

She fixed startled eyes on my eyes; then, perceiving the smile in them, she laughed outright. "Nevertheless, other races and nationalities did come here," she resumed. "During the early days Afghans served as camel drivers in the outback, Italian and Portuguese fishermen appeared in some of the ports and stayed, and many of the Chinese coolies, who were employed during several of the gold rushes, never left. More recently there has been a heavy influx of immigrants from India."

"They have been invading Canada, too," I said, "and many of the Canadians are up in arms about it."

After an energetic nod, she added, "Many Australians resent them, too."

"Why do governments continue to create conditions that always result in friction between the races and often create national chaos?" I inquired with a searching stare.

Apparently she didn't know the answer, or she was too tactful to disagree with my politics, because there was no response. After several minutes of thoughtful silence, she asked, "Have you been to Alice Springs yet?"

"No," I replied. "The name of that town has been mentioned to me several times lately. What makes it so special?"

"Well," she drawled, "It's located in the Red Centre along with some of the best scenery in the outback, and it has some nice lodges."

"What's the Red Centre?" I persisted.

"It's called 'Red' because of the bright vermilion color of the soil," she replied, "and it's called 'Centre' because it's located at the geographic centre of the continent."

"Hmm," I mumbled. "That's logical. And I suppose that its main attraction to tourists is its proximity to Ayers Rock."

"Ayers Rock is in Uluru National Park, which also is located in the Red Centre, but the park is two hundred eighty miles southwest of Alice Springs."

"It is!" I exclaimed. "I've been laboring under the impression that it was practically next door to Alice Springs. By the way, I've been informed that Ayers Rock is the largest monolith in the world. Can you verify that?"

"Well, I can't personally verify that it's the largest rock of its type in the world," she replied, "but its periphery measures about five and one-half miles, and its highest point stands more than eleven hundred feet above the surrounding terrain."

"Hmm," I mumbled. "I'm sure that it's bigger in all of its dimensions than Stone Mountain, Georgia, but Stone Mountain may be the largest granite monolith in the world if Ayers Rock is composed of another material."

"Ayers Rock is composed of heavily eroded, red sandstone," she said.

"Okay," I muttered. "Then the Georgians won't have to change their literature, even if their rock is limestone."

"The Olgas are located seventeen miles from Ayers Rock," she resumed, "but they are close to the mountain range from which they were carved, so they are composed of a highly compressed mixture of river-washed sand and rocks called conglomerate."

"You seem to know an awful lot about rocks," I muttered.

"I have a friend who is a geologist," she said, "and he has taken me on some of his field trips, so I've learned a bit about rocks."

"Ohhh," I murmured with a sly smile. "Has he shown you any *diamonds* yet?"

She either missed my implication or ignored it. "In either case," she answered, "Australia has just gotten into diamonds. The annual production of the Argyle mines is about thirty million carats from a main body of ore that is predicted to last for about twenty years. But this country is the source of some ninety percent of the world's finest opals."

"How enlightening!" I exclaimed. "Until this minute I had the impression that Brazil was the principal source of opals."

"Some opals are mined there," she conceded, "but Mexico produces more of them."

"Since the Europeans didn't discover the Americas until fourteen ninety-two, and they didn't sight the northern tip of Australia until sixteen six, opals must be strictly a product of the new worlds, yours and mine," I suggested.

"Well," she began, as if weighing the most tactful way to correct an associate's error, "opals actually are one of the world's oldest gemstones."

"Please pardon my ignorance," I pleaded glumly.

Courteously bowing her curls, she resumed, "According to some historians, opals date back to four hundred B.C., and their principal sources were some Hungarian mines, which were finally closed down about nineteen thirty."

"You are an amazing source of information," I murmured.

"Of opals, perhaps," she responded with a smile, "but most Australians know the opal story. To many of them, it is part of their daily lives."

"But do they know what makes them so precious?" I countered.

"People make them precious, of course," she retorted with a smile. "Many of them spend long hours in hot, dingy mines prying the ore loose from a very reluctant mother lode; then other people spend more hours determining how best to separate the gems from the host rocks and. . . ."

"Which are of volcanic origin, no doubt," I interjected, "so they have to be as hard as basalt."

She shook her head. "Australian deposits are different from the sources in the Americas because they are of sedimentary origins," she resumed. "Consequently, most of them are found in veins, crevices, and other cavities within one hundred twenty feet of the earth's surface. In fact, Australian opals are composed of hydrated silica."

"Then they can't be very hard," I assumed.

"They can't be as hard as diamonds for several reasons," she granted, "and one of them is water, which constitutes some ten percent of their composition."

"Then they have to be amorphous," I insisted, "not crystalline; consequently, their colors must be variable."

She nodded. "Their colors are dependent on the diffraction of white light from the inner walls of the voids within wee silica spheres," she said, "and those colors vary with the distribution and sizes of the spheres."

"Are opals widely distributed?" I asked.

"Somewhat," she replied. "The first Australian opals were discovered about eighteen ninety in an area now called White Cliffs. That area is located just over the Great Dividing Range from where we are now." And she gestured toward the high, irregular horizon visible through the somewhat remote windows on our left. "But the biggest fields where opals are currently mined include Lightning Ridge, which is located near White Cliffs in New South Wales; Coober Peddy and Mintabie in the southeastern part of South Australia; and Guilpie in South West Queensland."

After a brief pause she resumed, "The Halley's Comet Stone, a two-thousand-carat black opal, was found at Lightning Ridge in nineteen eighty-five. Since its value has been estimated at three million dollars, the mining of opals is still big business in Australia."

"What are the most dominating colors?" I inquired.

"All of the colors in the rainbow," she replied. "In one area of South Australia they range from clear white to opaque white. In an area of Queensland opals are found in ironstone boulders, which consist of an iron-stained sandstone, and they often display a dark array of all colors. Some of the most popular opals are found in the vicinity of Lightning Ridge. Like the Halley's Comet Stone, they are black opals, but they are capable of displaying many different colors against a background of seemingly black or gray potch."

We became absorbed in our individual thoughts for several minutes until I broke the silence. "Some time back you mentioned the Great Dividing Range," I said, "but I haven't seen any really high mountains yet."

"Well," she began, "the Eastern Highlands, along which the train is now traveling, were of mainly marine origin, but some of them were terrestrial."

"I assume you're telling me that much of this continent was raised from the bottom of the sea," I said, "but some of the upper levels projected above the sea before that slow event began."

With a crisp nod she resumed, "The upper Proterozoic rocks, where the earliest down warps occurred, permitted the accumulation and concentration of considerable mineralization: not only in the highlands but in several other parts of the continent."

"I detect the influence of that geologist again," I interposed.

After a smug smile, she resumed, "Consequently, that's how most of the gold, lead, zinc, and uranium deposits evolved. Some lacustrine and volcanic deposits were laid down over the eastern part of the continent; in fact, mountains were upthrust during each period of the Paleozoic era. The highest of the upthrust rock strata created the Snowy Mountains and the Victorian Alps as well as the precipitous scarp edge that lies above the hills of the coastal plain. In some areas massive, horizontal sandstone strata were disrupted." After pausing and gesturing behind us, she added, "Including some of the Blue Mountains."

"Where did the mineralization occur?" I inquired.

"In parts of New England, Manaro, and West Victoria, the older rocks, such as Cambrian, Ordovician, and Silurian, contain metalliferous deposits," she replied. "Some Jurassic coal and considerable quantities of brown coal are found in Victoria."

"But the latter are hydrocarbons," I pointed out.

"Oh, yes, that's correct," she agreed with a vigorous nod. "Back to minerals, seventy percent of the iron ore is taken from the Middleback Ranges, and a wee bit is obtained from the Yampi Islands. It has been estimated that there's a reserve of two billion tons of high-grade hematite in the Hamersley Range of Western Australia alone. Much of the ore is shipped from the port of Dampier and from Port Hedland."

"To what points is it shipped?" I asked.

"To Japanese ports mostly," she answered.

"But doesn't Australia manufacture any steel at all?" I protested.

"Some," she replied. "Most of it at Port Kembla in New South Wales."

"Somewhere I read that considerable gold is still mined here," I said. "Where?"

"Ninety percent of it is mined in Western Australia," she answered. "Most of it is taken from the many mines in the Kalgoorlie-Boulder region. Since eighteen twenty-three there have been several gold rushes in widely separated areas, one in eighteen thirty-four and another in eighteen forty-one, but they proved to be small finds. There was one at Summerhill Creek in eighteen fifty-one; furthermore, there were finds at such places as Wyalong, Ophir, and Sofala, which is in Victoria."

"You've done a fine job of giving me a thumbnail sketch of Australia's geology," I said. "I only hope that my notes will cover half of it."

"Why would you want to keep notes of such information?" she inquired with questioning eyes.

"No, I'm not crazy," I responded with a smile. "I hope to employ those notes in writing a book of my adventures abroad."

Following a thoughtful pause, she suggested, "Then perhaps you should note that Australia's geography was greatly affected by the Quaternary glaciation period, which ended about fifteen thousand years ago."

"If erosion is ignored, how could that have affected the geography of this continent?" I asked.

"Aside from erosion caused by runoffs from melting snow and ice, it did substantially change the geography of the continent," she replied. "For example, as the glacial shield and the polar ice caps melted, the level of the sea rose and inundated thousands of valleys, including what is now Sydney Harbor. Furthermore, the great glacier must have influenced the limestone structure of the Nullarbor Plain, because the artesian basin beneath it is interwoven with thousands of complex channels and caves, some of which are connected to the surface by blowholes."

"How were they discovered?" I inquired. "When pits were dug for railroad ballast?"

"No," she responded with a level gaze. "They were discovered by one of Western Australia's government agents, who went there to investigate reports of an invasion by an army of rabbits from the south."

"An invasion of what?" I exploded incredulously. "Do Australian rabbits also wield boomerangs?"

After a convulsive giggle, she retorted, "No!" Then, with visions of boomerang-wielding rabbits in her eyes, she giggled again and finally resumed: "After almost falling into some of those blowholes, the agent reported that they appeared to be cavities in the earth and the underlying limestone, that they varied in size from about one foot in diameter to huge pits large enough for trees to take root and grow, and that they occasionally spewed forth cold air."

"Why didn't the residents connect conduits to them and air-condition their homes?" I inquired with a wry grin.

"At that time about the only residents were kangaroos and emus," she replied. "Besides, some of those holes inhaled air instead of expelling it."

"So that agent could have been sucked right down into hell's kitchen," I ventured.

"Apparently that didn't happen, because he did write the report," she observed. "But while the members of his party were stumbling around in the dark, some of them did almost fall into blowholes hidden by ground cover."

My eyes studied hers thoughtfully for a moment; then I asked, "By some mischance, did that agent happen to be from Texas?"

"No, he was an Australian," she responded with a puzzled expression. "Why?"

"Because that story sounds just like some of the stuff that comes out of Texas." Then, after thoughtful study, I asked, "You wouldn't try to kid a naive old man, would you?"

My smile must have been infectious, because she cheerfully returned it with an energetic shake of her curls and insisted, "I've told you only what was reported. Furthermore, the agent claimed that those blowholes must be connected to the ocean, which is over sixty miles away."

"Aw!" I exclaimed incredulously. "How did he arrive at that ridiculous conclusion?"

"He claimed that the sounds of running water issued from some of the blowholes, that sounds like those of a speeding train issued from others, and that sounds like those of an approaching hurricane came from still others."

With an amiable shake of my head, I insisted, "I'll bet that guy migrated here from Texas, because that's the same sort of tall tale that a Texan would tell."

After a thought-filled silence, she murmured, "Yes, some Australians can tell pretty tall tales, too. For example, one man reported seeing a flying saucer last week."

"Oh-ho!" I exclaimed. "That's one of my favorite tall tales. But it's surprising how many people believe that flying saucers actually exist; some fifty-one percent of them, according to one poll." Then, turning my eyes to hers, I added: "That's spelled *p-o-l-l* not *p-o-l-e*."

"Some *polls* do indicate a strong belief in UFOs," she responded with a rather serious mien.

As she had intended, no doubt, I fumbled the interpretation of the pun, so I contritely protested, "I didn't intend to crush any toes."

"If you'll go back and take a look at the spelling of the word *polls*, you'll find that my toes are still intact," she rejoined with a condescending smile.

"Huh?" I grunted. Then the light dawned, so I extended my forefinger and marked a mythical *l* on the rear surface of the seat ahead of us.

After accepting the implied accolade with a smile, she resumed: "However, I strongly suspect that the toes of the man who claimed to have seen the flying saucer were badly bent, because the trooper who accepted his report exhibited considerable skepticism about it on the telly."

"Some so-called psychiatrists claim that the people who are most inclined to sight those wayward wheelbarrows are often very religious," I ventured with a probing gaze.

"Very likely those psychiatrists are atheists," she countered with a probing stare.

To deliberately misquote an old cliché, to be forewarned is to be forewarned, so I decided to avoid such controversial references in the future. Nevertheless, I didn't entirely forsake the subject. "Possibly they are atheists," I conceded, "but some of those psychiatrists generate and promote philosophies of human behavior that are as far-out as the beliefs of people who claim to have seen flying saucers or of people who have committed themselves to Buddhism or Mohammedanism."

"I suspect that atheism may be a religion to some people," she suggested with another probing stare.

"Just as the philosophies of the origin and future of the earth and all other celestial bodies have become the religion of many of our physicists?" I suggested.

"Theirs can't be a very sound religion," she demurred, "since so many of their beliefs change radically from time to time."

With an approving nod, I added, "Which tends to indicate that people are inclined to believe almost any claim as long as it is sufficiently strange and illogical. That's why gossips can inflict so much havoc."

"Well," she began with a chuckle, "there's a wide difference between theories regarding the birth and death of the universe and the lowest form of human communication, but I agree with your conclusion."

The speed of the train had slowed for one of the several sizable urban areas that immediately preceded its destination, so I particularly noted some of its relatively large buildings. Meanwhile, I sensed an apparent interest on the part of my seat companion; therefore, being the inherently courteous child that I am, I pushed my shoulders stiffly against the back of the seat so that she also could view them.

"Oh, what a shame!" she exclaimed.

After visually rechecking the largely industrial scene, I shot a questioning glance toward her.

"That beautiful, old building," she informed me mournfully.

"Which one?" I asked, turning my head and probing the scene.

"The building that's being demolished," she replied.

In response to another questioning glance, she leaned toward me, thrust her left hand past my left shoulder, and, sans knitting needles, pointed toward the building. Then, totally without warning, she pressed closer and stabbed my shoulder, not just once but several times, as she continued to point, stab, and state, "They didn't have to demolish that beautiful building. They could've renovated it and saved so much cost." Then, with an inscrutable expression, she pulled away and settled back against the seat.

"Hmm," I mumbled distractedly. "Modern societies have become so wasteful—and so unpredictable."

"It's not only the waste but the destruction of beautiful landmarks into which some fine architects have invested their very souls," she responded in the same mournful tones.

I was not particularly impressed with the so-called beauty of the old warehouse; in fact, I strongly suspected that it had served solely as a ploy for that flanking attack. Suspecting that she might have a thing for architects as well as for geologists, I eagerly sought to align myself with the architects by stating, "I spent part of my life designing and building homes."

"You have delved into a bit of almost everything, haven't you?" she asked.

After carefully pondering her use of the word *delved*, I decided that it was an innocent one, so I answered, "Yes, in addition to various kinds of engineering, including civil, structural, mechanical, and aerospace, I've been a general contractor and a technical writer."

"You must have lived a very interesting life," she suggested.

"Well," I drawled, "I suppose that everybody's life is interesting to the one who is living it, and mine has not been boring, but it could have been much happier."

Unaccountably, her expression displayed considerable concern and sympathy as she softly inquired, "But you are enjoying your trip abroad, aren't you?"

"I have especially enjoyed this particular trip," I responded gallantly.

Pleasure lighted her features as she extended her right hand and gently patted my left paw. Then she lapsed into deep meditation for several minutes while I watched her from the corner of my left eye. Finally she reached for her bag and dug a postcard and a felt-tipped pen from it.

"What's your given name?" she inquired while removing the pen's cap.

"Albert," I responded with searching eyes.

"Thank you," she murmured, absently turning the card over.

Meanwhile, directing my attention to what was transpiring beyond the window, I watched the landscape become increasingly urban. Several minutes later she nudged my left arm, so I turned from the window to her.

"I have something for you, Albert," she murmured, shyly presenting the card to me.

"A card for me!" I exclaimed and incredulously accepted it as my mind gyrated in confusion.

It bore an artist's impressionistic rendering of Circular Quay. A pair of parallel, brown piers outlined a patch of green water in which a white ship lounged, and the blue structural members of the Sydney Harbor bridge's arch curved gracefully above the ship's white superstructure.

"How uniquely beautiful!" I exclaimed.

"It's a print of a pastel done by Grace Cossington Smith in 1933," she informed me with raised eyebrows. "It's called the 'Great White Ship at Circular Quay,' and it hangs in the Australian National Gallery."

Upon turning the card over, I found the following message inscribed in bold script: *To Albert, Bon voyage and bonne chance. Plaxy*

Suddenly my eyes misted. It had been many years since anyone had extended even the smallest token of kindness to me, and the woman's simple gesture moved me more than I was willing to admit or express.

"Oh," I began with a gulp, desperately searching my mind for appropriate words. "How utterly nice!" Then, impulsively extending my left hand, I clasped her right hand in it and said, "You'll never know how much I appreciate this. I'm going to place this card among my most treasured souvenirs."

Meanwhile, her uncertain smile seemed to indicate that she couldn't quite comprehend why such a small token should excite such a large response, so I picked a reason right off of the top of my bald head and explained: "As they say, the value of the gift doesn't count as much as the thought behind it."

"I'm pleased that you are pleased," she murmured.

Once more my eyes returned to the signature. "Is your name pronounced the way that it's written?" I asked.

In support of a nod, she added: "It's a Polish name."

"It's a beautiful name," I murmured, "and I'll never forget it."

"Some people have found it easy to forget," she responded wistfully.

I hurriedly tried to divert her mind from possibly painful memories with light nonsense. "Usually I employ association to assist me in remembering names," I said. "For example, since I've used lots of Plexiglas in aerospace designs, I'll probably always rememeber Plexiglas, so Plexi equals Plaxy."

She responded with a somewhat glassy stare followed by a doubtful one, while my mind was arriving at the firm conclusion that, even though Plaxy might not be receptive of my particular brand of humor, she certainly had a lot of class.

To divert her mind from the stupid remark as well as to gain information, I said, "By the way, do you happen to know of any good places to stay in Melbourne?"

She glanced sharply at me; then, seeming to conclude that the question was an innocent one, she answered, "The Victoria Hotel is a nice place to stay, and it's not too expensive. In fact, I usually stay there whenever I'm in Melbourne."

Following a brief consideration of the information, I muttered, "That sounds like a good bet." Seconds later I added, "In fact, I'll call there this evening." And she turned such a strange expression to me that I was startled by it.

Some minutes later, after the lads finished sorting the various possible reasons for it, Pancho suggested, "Very likely she has been briefed by Big Brother, so she must have misinterpreted your slightly ambiguous statement to mean that you intended to call her at the hotel."

"When, in fact, you intended to call the desk clerk to reserve a room," José added. "It would be a logical conclusion after Big Brother planted so many seeds of doubt in her mind."

That explanation completely submerged my previous pleasure, so I sat in sullen silence during the remainder of the trip through Melbourne's suburbs.

When the train finally came to a stop at the station, I turned to her and said, "Victorian protocol would dictate that I assist you from the train, but I suspect that the circumstances dictate otherwise." From her point of view it may have seemed to be a strange statement, but I was viewing the situation from a background in which the somber figure of Big Brother had lurked for half a century, so the statement fitted my mental picture.

Possibly her point of view was distorted by the same hulking shadow, because she coolly replied, "No, I can manage very nicely." And there seemed to be an air of urgency in her actions as she collected her few belongings and joined the first passengers in their exodus.

As was my wont, I waited until the stragglers passed; then, picking up the briefcase, I followed them from the train onto the platform.

Melbourne

Upon arriving in the station, I warily approached one of the public telephones with the intention of calling the desk clerk at the Victoria Hotel, but I was so daunted by the unfamiliar directory and the instrument that I decided to gamble on a room being available when I arrived there.

Several taxicabs were available in front of the station, so I nodded to the middle-aged driver of the first one and helped him load the luggage. Then he asked, "Wheah to, mite?"

"Well," I began, "I don't have a reservation at the Victoria Hotel, but let's try it anyway."

With a thoughtful nod, he muttered, "That's up on Little Collins Strait."

After assuming our respective places, I leaned back against the seat and subjected the man to a quick study. Aside from being somewhat shorter than I, he possessed a heavier bone structure, which may have created an illusion that he was bigger than he actually was. Like many of the Australian males that I had observed, his features were underlaid by heavy bones and a square jaw, so the words *angular features* were in order.

During my travels I had found that local cab drivers were often fine sources of information regarding the principal points of interest and their histories; therefore, to generate some of that information, I began with a compound question: "Melbourne doesn't have the wealth of waterways that Sydney has, does it?"

"Huh," he grunted. "The only watahwye Milbourne has is the Yarra Rivah, and it's so bloody muddy it has to flow upsoide down."

After an overdone laugh, I felt justified in adding: "I've been told that Melbourne was settled by free men. Is that so?"

"Yis, and a few free women, too," he responded with a sly glance. Then, with an uproarious laugh, he added, "And some women who weren't free."

And I joined in it—but more for political reasons than because the remark was so amusing. When I could make myself heard, I said, "I've read that Melbourne has a rather large Chinatown. Is that true?"

"Aye," he granted. "That would be down on Little Burke Strait. It has been theah since the middle o' the last cintury. Would ye be wantin' to see it?"

"No, not now," I replied. "But that isn't the only ethnic group in the city, is it?"

"No, theah ah siviral moah," he answered. "The Greek siction is located in the cintah o' the city on Lonsdale Strait, the Eyetalians congregated along Lyon Strait, and the Turks chose Sydney Road."

After absently watching the interplay of lights and shadows on the buildings and vehicles for a few minutes, I gestured toward one of the big green and yellow trams and asked, "Do those things give you much competition?"

"They go all ovah the city," he retorted with a long stare, which seemed to imply that the statement should sufficiently answer the question.

Following a nod, I veered to the subject: "Some of these buildings appear to be very old."

"Some o' thim ah," he affirmed, "but not loik London. Milbourne was a quiet, provincial town with just a few clapboard buildin's until the gold rush in eighteen fifty-one, whin the population doubled, and it has doubled siviral toimes since but not in such rapid succission."

"I didn't know that gold was found here," I said.

"The gold was found about one hundrid moiles inland," he informed me. "Howivah, much o' it found its wye into the city in the foahm of fancy homes and buildin's. We'll see some o' thim on the wye. In fact, theah is one roight theah." And he dramatically pointed toward the front of a relatively small building with ornate, iron railings about a partially circumscribing balcony.

"That reminds me of some of the older buildings in Mobile, Alabama," I murmured.

"Wheah's that?" he asked.

"It's located near the Gulf of Mexico in the United States," I replied.

"Oy picked you foah a Yank!" he exclaimed with a self-satisfied smirk.

I nodded absently, and we traveled in silence until he volunteered, "The Flindahs Strait Styshun, Queen Victoria Mahkit, and siviral o' the fiahhouses lind an old-fashioned flavoah to Milbourne." Then, as an afterthought, he added, "And some o' the depahtmint stoahs also contribute to it."

"I've seen a lot of 'BYO' signs," I murmured absently.

"Bring yoah own liquah," he informed me succinctly with an alert glance.

"I suspected as much," I said. "Some of the restaurants of New Zealand employ the same practice."

Suddenly the cab turned left from a narrow street onto another narrow street for a moment; then it turned left onto an even narrower street. Possibly it only seemed narrower, since the one-way traffic was further impeded by a line of parked cars that stood almost bumper-to-bumper alongside a neatly maintained old building. The driver quickly applied the brakes to slow the rate of the cab's descent on the sharp downgrade.

"As usual, theah's no plice to put the cab!" he exclaimed with an exasperated air.

"Is that the hotel?" I inquired with a gesture toward the old building on our left.

"Yis," he replied, "and they haven't provided any plice foah us cabbies to stop."

"How about that narrow alley on our right?" I suggested with another gesture.

"No, Oy can't," he began. Then he abruptly swung the vehicle into the alley and brought it to a quick stop. "Oy'm sorry," he muttered, "but Oy'll have to go roight out." Then he quickly swung open the door and stepped onto the pavement.

Since there was an air of extreme emergency in his actions, I hurriedly opened the door, stepped onto the pavement, and went to the rear of the cab, where he was already pulling my bags from the boot. Meantime I quickly extracted a sufficient number of one-dollar bills from my wallet to cover the fare and the tip. And I thrust them toward him just as the reason for the emergency appeared in the uniform-clad figure of a heavyset young woman, who fixed a pair of cold eyes on the driver's wary eyes.

"Oy'm leavin' roight awye!" he shouted to her. And he did.

Meanwhile, I peered thoughtfully through the dusk at the bulky apparition and tried to justify the unseemly fuss. Finally I picked up my luggage and started across the street just as she turned her baleful attention on me. Suddenly the situation struck me as so ridiculously unreasonable that a charge of fury surged through me, so I stopped dead in my tracks and pointed a pair of eyes at her that dared her to give me a ticket for jaywalking. Then I turned away and strode defiantly across the narrow thoroughfare.

"Apparently stupidity is found in bureaucracies all over the world," José fumed.

"Yeah," Pancho joined in. "Why is it that societies always select their dumbest members to enforce dumb laws?"

"Because the lawmakers are dumb, you dummy," José retorted.

The lobby of the Victoria reflected the structure's age, but it was neat and clean. I strode to the desk on my left and paid forty-three Australian dollars to one of two middle-aged, cold-eyed female desk clerks for the use of Room 145 during the rapidly encroaching night of 7 February 1986.

In the small bathroom that adjoined the room, I washed the roughest soil from my hands and beard. Then I returned to the lobby, cornered the ancient bellman, and asked, "Is there a good restaurant in this area?"

From his post beside the base of the beautiful central stairway, he stepped to the adjacent oaken newel post, pointed toward a glazed door in the far wall, and said, "That doah lits into a small areawye that leads to a foine ristaurant."

While peering at it, I reached into a pocket for a coin; however, upon turning to give it to him, I found that he had returned to his post. I shook my head in disbelief, because an American bellman would have been standing there with both hands outstretched.

After passing through the doorway into the areaway, I found that an opposite door opened into the restaurant, where a brief pause permitted me to study the layout. Then I advanced to the cashier's counter on my left, stopped in front of the relatively young, blond hostess-cashier, and asked, "Am I too late for dinner?"

"No," she answered rather formally. Then, with a preoccupied air, she selected a menu from a nearby rack and led me toward the far side of the room. Meanwhile, from the corner of my left eye, I particularly noticed that the man behind the bar must not have been very busy, because he fixed his eyes on me and continued to stare at me until my peripheral vision lost him as we followed the aisle around a right-hand turn. At the table the blonde placed the menu beside a dinner plate and formally stated, "Your waitress will be with you in a minute."

"Thank you," I responded in the same formal manner.

While she was returning to her post, I seated myself and carefully studied the reflections from the large, plate glass window directly ahead of me and found that it effectively reproduced a dim, mirrorlike view of the room behind me. When the blonde turned the corner, I saw that the barman was still staring at the back of my head. Then he was abruptly blotted out of the picture by the trim figure of an oncoming waitress, who cruised to a stop beside my table.

As I looked up at her, she said, "Good evening," in a very familiar dialect. "How can I serve you?"

I leaned back against the chair and shot a second, more appraising glance at her pretty features and the soft, light-brown hair that framed them. "Good evening," I responded. "From what part of midcontinent U.S.A. did you derive?"

"Oh, you are an American?" she countered.

"Yes," I confessed, "but what are you doing in Australia?"

"I'm a schoolteacher," she answered. "I work here during the summer season."

"But this is February," I observed with a smile. "That is a winter month."

Responding with a tolerant smile, she inquired, "What are you doing in Melbourne, may I ask?"

"I'm on my way around the world, and Mel . . . ," I started to explain.

"Please excuse me," she interjected. "If you've been traveling all day, you must be famished, so allow me to place your order; then we can talk."

"Fine," I murmured with my eyes on the menu. "What do you recommend?"

"Everything," she replied. Then, in response to my questioning eyes, she added, "The food here is very good, even according to American standards. In fact, Melbourne has some of the best restaurants in Australia."

"Great!" I exclaimed. "Then I'll have the roast lamb." Looking up at her, I explained, "Habitually, I select the local specialties; otherwise I would miss sensing an important part of each environment through which I pass."

"Lamb is certainly a popular dish in Australia," she assured me. "I'll place your order right away so that I can bring it to you before you starve."

When she served the meal, I exclaimed, "Humm yumm! This does look good!"

"I surely hope you like it," she murmured.

Since she appeared to be lingering, I inquired, "How long have you been in Australia?"

"Eleven years," she replied.

I carefully studied her features and decided that, despite her statement, she didn't appear to be over thirty. Meanwhile, I cleared the first bite from my mouth, swallowed it, and asked, "Have you never wanted to return?"

"I've thought of it," she admitted, "but I've invested too much time in this school system to sacrifice it on an impulse."

"Besides, you probably have a lot of Australian friends by this time," I suggested.

"I have some," she granted. "But where do you plan to go from here?"

"According to my visa, I'm permitted to spend six months in this country," I replied, "and I've been considering spending most of it in Tasmania. What can you tell me about Hobart and its environs?"

"It's a nice little city," she answered. "A lot of English people settled there years ago. Of course, it is rather remote and isolated, so it's a very quiet place. Even the tourists seem to behave themselves better there than they do in Melbourne."

"It sounds like the kind of place where I would like to spend the next six months," I muttered.

"It's just a short hop from Melbourne," she said. "The least you should do is fly over and see if you like it. You really shouldn't leave this area without seeing Tasmania and some of its outback."

"That's a fine sales pitch," I said.

Meanwhile, her eyes had been wandering about the room. "Please excuse me for a moment," she requested. "I suspect that I should make a tour of my station."

"Of course," I murmured.

By the time she returned, I had finished the repast, so she asked, "Can I get something more? A dessert or a drink, perhaps?"

I was enjoying the association tremendously, and, even though my physical needs were satisfied, I didn't want to break it off and return to the lonely, unfriendly walls of the hotel room, so I said, "I could do with a cold drink."

After she departed, my eyes peered absently through the large window toward the dim activities on Little Collins Street; then they automatically adjusted to the window's mirror effect as she approached the bar and left the order. As she was about to turn away, the barman called her back to the bar, where they conversed briefly. Finally turning away from the bar, she looked toward the rear of my head and then wandered thoughtfully toward the table of another customer.

Meanwhile, the barman moved around one corner of the bar and finally came to a stop beside my table. "You ordered a drink, sir?" he inquired with a probing stare.

It may have been his rude stare, his cold calculating attitude, or both that incensed me so much; in any event, while repeating the order, I returned the rude stare to him in an even more frigid condition.

After a ten-minute wait, I signaled to the waitress. When she arrived at the table, I said, "If that drink hasn't been made yet, please cancel the order."

"I'm sorry," she murmured with averted eyes, "but the barman must have forgotten to deliver it. I'll see what happened to it."

Once more I employed the window to watch the scene at the bar, where the waitress spent several minutes in a deep conversation with the barman. Finally she returned with the drink and coldly set it before me.

"Thank you," I growled. Then, looking up into her antagonistic eyes, I added, "The barman must have had a very interesting story to tell during that session."

"What do you mean?" she countered with a shocked expression. "I just placed the order and came right back."

"Not according to what I saw," I retorted, pointing to the mirrorlike reflection from the window.

Her quick glance elicited a startled expression that instantly turned to one of anger. "Well, what else could you expect when a man like you. . . ." Then she stopped, whirled about, strode rapidly along the aisle to the turn, and disappeared into a limbo beyond the scope of my makeshift mirror.

A few minutes later a well-built, middle-aged man emerged from the limbo and strode toward the bar, where he conversed for several minutes with the man behind it. Somewhat later the same man appeared beside my table with the dinner check, a very concerned mien, and the question, "Was the food satisfactory?"

"It was excellent," I replied. "In fact, I enjoyed the dinner hour very much— most of it, that is."

His eyes dropped momentarily, so I suspected that I had scored, but he was such a pleasant chap that I was unable to unload onto him any of the vitriol that still boiled within me. Instead, I picked up the check and headed toward the cashier's counter. As I passed the bar, my hard stare netted me nothing, because the barman was very deliberately avoiding my eyes.

In that state of mind, I must have left the table without leaving a tip. While tossing and turning between the bed's sheets, I was unable to remember leaving one.

"If so, it was unintentional," Pancho reminded me.

"After all," José joined in, "the initially nice young lady wasn't responsible for subsequent developments."

"And neither was the barman, for that matter," Pancho injected at that point. "In fact, he also was a mere pawn of an incredibly unscrupulous and vicious international combine."

"But the woman's words, 'a man like you,' continue to bug Al," José rejoined. "They seem to imply the same meaning as Wilfred's words, 'You are a terrible man.' "

"Apparently Big Brother is deliberately trying to destroy us in every nook and cranny of this massive globe," Pancho suggested.

"And he appears to be employing every available evil and corrupt device to accomplish his unscrupulous goal," José added.

"But those two people didn't exhibit very much intelligence by baldly accepting his vicious claims, whatever they are," Pancho mused. "Especially when they could see for themselves that Al exhibited no unusual characteristics, whatever they are supposed to be."

Several other decisions were made during that storm-tossed conference: First off, there would be no trip to Tasmania; furthermore, I didn't intend to spend any more time in Australia than was required to transport myself across the continent. And I concurred fully with José's conclusion: "Obviously the people of Australia are different from those of New Zealand, so there may be something in the claims of some scientists that the genes are compelling factors in the behavior of people."

And I wholeheartedly accepted Pancho's opinion: "The genes of the current stock of Australians, particularly the bureaucrats, must contain a heavy charge of the same sadistic characteristics that prevailed among those early convicts."

Early in the following morning I deposited my heavy bags alongside the curb and stood back against the wall of the hotel to wait for the next available cab. Meanwhile, the slender little bellman, who may have been as old as I, eyed them possessively while he stood at the curb and watched for cruising cabs. My second inspection verified my suspicion that he was the same bellman who had directed me to the restaurant, so he may have been the Victoria's only bellman and doorman.

In response to his whistle, a cab swung against the curb, and he energetically loaded the luggage of two men who appeared to be salesmen. Then he looked toward me and called, "The nixt one will be yoahs."

Responding with a nod, I moved forward beside my luggage. Following a brief wait a cab swung around the adjacent corner and continued more slowly along the downgrade. Meanwhile, the doorman stepped out into the street, placed a nickel-plated whistle to his lips, and loudly exercised it. Then, in response to the doorman's beckoning, the cabdriver swung the vehicle against the curb directly in front of me.

Almost before I could move from my tracks, the doorman darted to my luggage and grasped both of them. His frail figure bent under the load, but he did get them off of the sidewalk during one faltering step.

"Here, let me help you with those," I muttered, as I literally had to tear the largest one from his grasp.

"No, Oy kin handle both of thim!" he protested, and he actually tried to recover it.

"Let me have it," I insisted, gently pulling it away from him. Then I led the way to the rear of the cab.

After they were loaded in the boot, he turned to me and insisted, "Oy could have handled both of thim. Oy handle thim all o' the toime. Besoides, you must be as old as Oy am."

I smiled tolerantly and silently placed a bill in his hand, because I didn't have the heart to point out to him that I was twice as big as he.

21

Melbourne to Port Pirie

Melbourne to Adelaide

I was still in a dark mood when I boarded the train early the following morning. I made no notes throughout the twelve-hour trip; nevertheless, much later I was able to clearly recall that the railroad passed through some grazing country beyond Ballarat. Then it traveled through the highly productive wheat belt of West Victoria before crossing the Murray River and passing through the Mount Lofty ranges, which are located in the general vicinity of Adelaide.

About midway of the trip, a twelve-inch-diameter aqueduct began to parallel one side of the railroad right of way and continued along one side or the other until the railroad crossed the Murray River, the source of the aqueduct's irrigation water. By that time the steel pipe's diameter had increased twofold.

Most of those twelve hours were expended in an ongoing mental struggle, wherein I attempted to employ logic in the solution of my problem. As usual, the time was wasted, because no one has ever successfully employed logic in the solution of an illogical problem. Nevertheless, every time that I had encountered a new set of circumstances, such as the one in the restaurant, I had tried to attack the problem from the overview afforded by the new experience. Unfortunately, there had never been sufficient bits and pieces to provide more than a partial solution. But those partial solutions had provided me with a sort of mosaic, call it a jigsaw puzzle, which had assumed the shape of a dark and sinister figure sans many of the puzzle's most vital components. However, enough of the figure had been revealed by the many different experiences to substantiate my suspicions that it was George Orwell's Big Brother who crouched so threateningly in the dim shadows surrounding me.

Adelaide Several taxicabs were parked in front of Keswick, Adelaide's Rail Passenger Terminal, so I selected the lead cab and helped the driver stow my luggage in its boot.

"Wheah ah we bound, mite?" he inquired after we were seated.

"Well," I began thoughtfully, "that's a good question, but I'm going to rely on you to supply the answer."

"Yis?" he hissed with a startled expression.

"Yes," I retorted. "What I want is a good, clean, motel for about thirty dollars. Can you take me to one without driving to Timbuktu?"

"Will," he drawled, "Oy suppose so. In what paht of the city would you loik it to be lokited?"

"Any part," I replied, "as long as it's not in the limehouse district."

"Hmm," he mumbled. "Oy don't believe we have one o' thim."

"Since the reference was to the one in London, I believe you," I said.

"Thin Oy couldn't git you theah boy bidtoime," he burst forth with a laugh.

He was so delighted with his humor that I also chuckled, but, as usual, my amusement was derived more from the man than from the remark.

"But don't let any of my stupid statements induce you to go beyond the city limits," I warned him.

"It won't be fah," he promised.

Apparently the man's definition of the word *far* must have been tempered by his impression of distance gained from a lifetime on the Nullarbor Plain, because it seemed that we traveled clear across the relatively small city of Adelaide before he finally said, "That'll be it on yoah lift. If you don't loik that one, we kin go a bit fathah to anothah one."

Without even a glance toward the motel, I hurriedly said, "This will be fine."

After paying the fare and adding a tip for the man's sense of humor, I picked up my bags and carried them into the small lobby of the motel. There I found a relatively mature couple, whose male member was lounging impatiently against a small, panel-high counter, which projected a few inches beyond the base of a small opening in the wall that separated the lobby from the office. Practically everything was correspondingly smal excepting the heavyset woman who stood beside the man.

Shifting her weight from one big foot to the other one, she impatiently grumbled, "What evah happened to him?"

Before the man could reply, a matronly woman appeared on the opposite side of the opening and explained, "Oy'm sorry, but Mr. Thrussell was unexpectedly called away, so Oy'll hilp you."

Meanwhile, I selected a glaringly red business card from a small metal container on the opposite end of the counter and studied it. In its upper left-hand corner were the words *Under New Management*, and the name, Clarice Motel, dominated the center of it. The next line bore the words *Accommodation Reasonable Rates*, followed by *Singles from $20.00—Doubles from $26.00*. And directly beneath that line was the word *Managers*, followed by the names Bert and Sheila Throussell. In the lower left-hand corner was the address, 220 Hutt Street, Adelaide; and the opposite corner bore the words *Fully Licensed Restaurant, Continental Breakfast Included in Price*.

After the couple left, I moved forward to the counter, and Sheila inquired, "Can Oy hilp you?"

"I would like a single room for one night, please," was my response.

While she was laboriously inscribing my name on a registration form, a relatively handsome man of middle age appeared behind her and peered across her left shoulder at the product of her efforts with a sort of bemused expression on his cleanly shaven features. After she completed the last letter of my name, his gaze switched sharply toward my bearded features, and his expression quickly changed to one of deep thought.

"That will be thirty-two dollahs," Sheila murmured. And I submitted two twenty-dollar bills to her. After dropping a handful of bills and some small coins into my extended palm, she pointed toward a door in the far wall of the lobby and said, "That doah leads to a court, and room thirty-foah is located on the fah soide of it."

"Thank you," I responded pensively. Then, pocketing the change, I picked up the luggage and surged toward the door.

Suddenly Bert burst through the doorway beside the opening and suggested, "Lit me hilp you with those bags."

"No, thank you," I answered. "But I could use a little help with the door." After passing through the opening, I called back, "Thank you."

Meanwhile, both sides of my brain had begun to argue about whether Bert had recognized me, and, if so, from what source? From a picture like those of wanted criminals commonly posted in American post offices?

In the small, neatly appointed room, I placed the luggage against one wall. Then, digging the receipt out of my jacket pocket, I carefully studied it.

"Apparently this is not one of the twenty-dollar singles," Pancho suggested. "Either that or we were charged thirty-two dollars for one of them."

After glancing about the snug quarters, I pondered the possibility of squeezing two average-sized people into it, and José quickly concluded, "It might prove to be a fit that would appeal to only a young and very amorous couple."

Then my eyes returned to the receipt, and Pancho exclaimed, "Hey! Let's demand a rebate, because that *bleeped* woman left an *r* out of our name. No wonder Bert was looking across her shoulder with such a bemused expression. At least one member of the new management has to be a novice."

Since I wasn't hungry, dinner was skipped; therefore, early the next morning I was ready for the continental breakfast, but it wasn't ready for me. I was the first to enter the small, hexagonal breakfast room. In fact, I arrived so early that the dawn's early light had not yet managed to penetrate the film of dew on the glass panes that graced the pair of French doors letting onto the adjacent courtyard. A half-dozen sets of small dining tables and chairs were scattered about the room, and a somewhat larger table stood against one wall. At the rear of the larger table an electric hot plate supported a pair of clear-glass urns, from which twin tendrils of steam indicated the approximate temperature of the water they contained. Stacked in front of the hot plate was an assortment of dry cereals, small packages of coffee, dehydrated cream and milk, and some sugar and sugar substitutes. A small pitcher contained a thin, milklike liquid that could have passed for white water.

Despite my months down under, I had never been exposed to such an array of dry cereals or synthetic foodstuffs before, so I fumbled the ball badly. First off, I assumed that the flaky stuff in an open container was cornflakes, so I spilled some of it into one of the bowls stacked on the table. Then I added a coarse, sugarlike substance to the top of it and confidently poured over it what appeared to be milk. In spite of the fact that it began to snap, crackle, and pop in a familiar fashion, I must have been 100 percent wrong in every selection, because the stuff in that bowl turned into the most unappetizing mess that I had ever beheld. Nevertheless, I gave it the benefit of the doubt and cautiously tasted it. Then, picking up the bowl, I firmly placed it on a remote corner of the large table.

After I had assembled what appeared to be a typical down under continental breakfast, consisting of wheat flakes sprinkled with sugar and inundated by some of the so-called milk, another tenant entered the room and expertly prepared his continental breakfast in jig time.

"Apparently some experience helps," José observed.

"Plus some intelligence," Pancho added.

While I was wrapping myself around the last crumbled flake of my repast, Sheila entered the room, stepped to the larger table, and inspected its stock. Right off she detected that isolated bowl, picked it up, peered incredulously at its contents, and looked accusingly around the room. I felt reasonably secure in the knowledge that there were two potential culprits; however, for some unfathomable reason, her eyes passed right over the other guy and zeroed in on me. Maybe that *bleeped* woman was smarter than I had given her credit for being.

I really should have inspected the stuff in that bowl before I left, because I had a hunch that it may have set up like a batch of the finest construction-grade concrete. The world could certainly use a fine, low-cost construction-grade concrete.

I decided to return to Keswick by taxicab. This time, however, I was content to go by way of Robin's barn, so to speak, because I wanted to see some of Plaxy's home town.

The business district was relatively small, but it contained a number of mercantile establishments and modern office buildings, none of which exceeded thirty floors in height. Like America's New England, the residences were not large, but every one of them was attractive and neatly maintained. Without doubt Americans could learn a lot about community planning and its maintenance from the inhabitants of the lands down under.

At first the cab driver seemed to be in a somewhat somnolent state; however, with some prodding, he finally got around to covering some of the features of the city along with a bit of its history.

"Adelaide, sometimes called the Garden City, is the capital of South Austreyelia," he began flamboyantly.

"What is its population?" I asked.

"About one million people," he replied. "In fact, three-fourths of this province's population is concintrited in Adelaide."

"But none of its early colonists were convicts, were they?" I countered.

"Roight," he replied with a proud lift of his chin. "According to a decree in eighteen thirty-two, South Austreyelia was to become a model stite composed intoirely of free men. In eighteen thirty-six eight shiploads of colonists arroived heah, followed by John Hindsmarsh, owah first governor. At that time land could be purchased foah twilve shillings per acre."

"But what could be grown on it, and where could it be sold even if it did grow?" I inquired skeptically.

"Most o' what the colonists grew, they consumed," he answered, "but there were many exportable products, such as timbahs, wood bahk, sealskins, droyed fish, whale oil, and salt."

"So Adelaide is a seaport?" I suggested in questioning tones.

"The city is located between the Gulf Saint Vincent to the west and the Mount Lofty Ringes to the east," he replied, "and it is divided into north and south sictions boy the Torrens Rivah." But he failed to answer my question and state that the river was or was not navigable.

At the Keswick Rail Passenger Terminal I found that there was no way that I could book direct passage from Adelaide to Perth for that day, so I purchased a ticket that reserved Seat 21 in Car 1 on an Australian National train, which was scheduled to depart for Port Pirie at 12:40 P.M.

Since a three-hour wait was involved, I seated myself on one of the oaken benches in the waiting area of the terminal, dug from my briefcase a pad and a pencil, and began to record several of the episodes of the past several days. Unfortunately, the shouts, shrieks, and screams of two quarreling brats constantly interrupted my train of thought, so the product of my efforts really served no good purpose.

Adelaide to Port Pirie

The train? Actually, it could scarcely be called a train, since, in addition to the engine, there were only two coaches. There must not have been more than ten passengers in Car 1, so the trip could not have been financially rewarding. Since the Australian railway systems are operated by each province through which they pass, there was no one agency to worry about the economics of the trip. Like American bureaucrats, Australian bureaucrats never worry about such things, because the taxpayers pay for all cost overruns, and the taxpayers don't worry about such things, because they pay the bureaucrats to worry about them.

The conductor reminded me of the conductor of the Wellington-to-Auckland train in that he also was middle-aged, ruggedly constructed, and equipped with angular features. Furthermore, he went about his duties in the same bored, preoccupied manner. Therefore, since I had suffered so much at the hands of that New Zealander, I watched the man like a hawk, and my efforts were rewarded; that is, if a stab in the back can be called a reward.

I had been assigned to one of the cloth-upholstered bench seats on the left side of the car. Unlike the Intercapital Daylight Express, all of the train's seats faced forward. Since I was the seat's only occupant, I preempted the end by the window. From it I could have tossed a pebble either fore or aft without striking another human being excepting the somewhat more than middle-aged couple in the seat directly ahead of me.

Shortly after the train left Keswick Station, the conductor entered the car through the doorway in its forward end and advanced along the aisle with that peculiar side-to-side sway which seems to characterize the in-transit strides of train conductors all over the landmasses of this topsy-turvy world. After collecting the tickets, he returned to the big, gray-haired man in the aisle seat ahead of my seat and conferred briefly with him. Then he resumed the side-to-side sway toward the doorway in the forward end of the car. Meanwhile, the other man arose and followed him through the doorway and the interconnecting walkway into the next car.

About five minutes later the head and shoulders of the big man reappeared beyond the high, glass panel in the door, and he set one shoulder against the door. Then, pausing, he turned as if to communicate with someone in the background of the interconnecting walkway. Several seconds later he turned his head and looked through the glass panel at me; then, after he turned his head toward the background, his lips appeared to direct a statement to it.

Finally the conductor emerged from the background, looked through the window at me, and said something to the big man that caused him to laugh uproariously. Unfortunately, they stood in a dimly lighted area, so I was unable to read their lips, but there could be no doubt about who was the subject of their discussion. At that point it broke off, and the conductor disappeared into the background. Meanwhile, the big man pushed the door open and moved through the opening toward his seat.

Stopping beside the seat, he looked drolly down at the woman, whose frizzled gray hair was just perceptible to me above the back of the seat.

"Yuh know," he murmured, "we had to come all o' the wye to South

Austreyelia to have to give wye to an American. . . ." Then, bowing his head, he lowered his voice, so I failed to overhear the remainder of the remark.

Incredibly, the woman immediately squirmed about and thrust her head higher so that she could peer at my bearded beauty across the back of the seat. Meanwhile, I alternately graced both pairs of eyes with my coldest go-to-*bleep* stares. Of course, the woman returned to the position from which she should never have departed.

Meanwhile, the man turned malicious eyes toward her and callously inquired, "Did you get a big thrill out o' that?" Then he slumped down beside her.

Typically, I sat and stewed up a fury that threatened to blow a hole through my balding pate. Meanwhile, the lads tried to transfer some sense to that hot head.

Right off Pancho warned, "Watch your step, Al. It would be both illogical and unwise for you to lose your cool in Australia."

"Yeah," José concurred. "Big Brother would love that, because he could then legitimately toss you into a padded cell."

"Or into an unpadded one," Pancho observed. "That's what Big Brother Ivanovich always does to dissidents. And who is to say that the system doesn't work?"

"And who is to say that Big Brother Sam would do anything different?" José added.

"Console yourself with the thought that we've always hated idiots," Pancho advised, "never poor, benighted imbeciles, who are not responsible for their acts, but the bona fide idiot, who fondly nurtures the opinion that his intellect is superior to others when his actions indicate that he doesn't even possess such a commodity."

"All of us hate those two guys with a burning passion," José promised loyally.

"What else can we do?" Pancho entrained. "Apparently they haven't broken any laws excepting the laws of logic."

"All that we could employ in our defense would be a series of our logical observations," José insisted. "And no court in any country would ever accept them as grounds for legal action in defense of physical reprisals."

"Yep," Pancho agreed. "As usual, Big Brother has enlisted the eager collaboration of a couple of bystanders to continue his illegal attacks on us."

My fury finally subsided to the boiling point, so I slowly became aware of the small, railside lake beyond my window and the black swans that cruised so majestically on it. Then I heard the woman ahead of me exclaim, "Look at the swans! Wye, they ah so close to the trine that the loight tips on theah rid bills ah visible. It's a wondah that the noise of the trine didn't froighten them into floight."

"A whoile back Oy saw a floight o' Cape Barren geese," the man responded more loudly. "Viry loikely they wuh headin' foah one o' the coastal inlits. And theah's supposed to be pilicans along this coast, too."

"Oh, look at the flock of galahs!" she exclaimed.

"We have thim, too," he responded indifferently. "In fact, they ah to be found all ovah the continint."

Meanwhile, I opened my briefcase and removed a copy of *Australian Flora and Fauna* from it. On page 12 I found a picture of such a bird, but it was identified only as one of Australia's cockatoos. Later I found some words in another source that described the bird as a crested pink-and-gray parrot, so let's say that it belongs to either the *parrotoo* or the *cockarot* family.

Somewhat later I overheard the man say, "We should be gittin' into Crystal Brook pritty soon."

"Is that a big town?" the woman inquired.

"No," he rumbled, "it's just a small country town, a junction of railroad loines, in fact. That's wheah this railroad joins the Sydney-to-Perth railroad."

"Thin Poaht Pirie must not be much fahthah," she suggested.

"Not much fahthah," he granted. "Not moah than anothah twinty-foive kilomitahs anywye."

"Thin we should be intering the Flindahs Ringe pretty soon," she speculated.

"Not until we cross the Rocky Rivah," he rejoined.

Meanwhile, I remembered that according to the ticket agent at Adelaide, Port Pirie was the jumping off place, so I anxiously waited to see how far I had to jump.

Port Pirie As soon as the train pulled to a stop alongside the long, wide concrete platform that constituted the most outstanding feature of the town's railroad station, I descended onto it. After traveling almost a hundred yards toward the small, wood-frame station at the far end of the platform, I decided that my suitcase must have been unloaded at about the same point where I unloaded myself. Returning to the spot, I found the suitcase aboard a low, wood-frame, four-wheel, flatbed wagon that was being connected to a small tractor, so I presented my stub to one of the two operatives and retrieved it. Several steps later I regretted that impulsive act, because the wood-frame building at the near end of the concrete platform proved to be a warehouse, not the luggage storage area that I had suspected it to be, so the tractor-drawn luggage wagon eventually ended up at the passenger station, where I was bound. Consequently, I needlessly lugged that *bleeped* suitcase some four hundred feet. What was that deal about hating idiots? Yeah, I really hated myself by the time that I finally arrived at the station.

However, before getting well under way, I happened to come upon the conductor. Stopping nearby, I lowered my bags to the pavement and said, "Since I'm planning to write a travelogue on my trip through Australia, I would like to obtain your name so that I can plug it into the travelogue when I get around to describing the trip from Adelaide to Port Pirie."

"Moy name is Black," he replied.

Actually, he included his given name; however, under the circumstances, I suspect that *black* is all that is necessary to describe fully a man who voluntarily stabbed a total stranger in the back with one of Big Brother's filthy, blood-caked stilettos.

Nevertheless, after courteously thanking him, I asked, "Can you tell me where the business district of this burg is located?"

"Shuah," he replied. "It's just beyond that yillow sign." And he pointed along the platform to an object that loomed about one thousand feet beyond the station.

"Is that where the hotels are located?" I persisted.

"What hotils?" he countered with a puzzled expression.

"Do you mean to imply that there are no hotels in this crazy town?" I asked incredulously. "Where do travelers find lodging?"

"What travelahs and what lodging?" he countered with an evil grin. Apparently relenting, he added, "People mostly sty at the pub."

"And where's the pub?" I inquired with a sudden sense of the infinitude of utter futility.

"It's just beyond that yillow sign, loike I showed you," he answered.

"The business district is the pub!" I practically screamed.

"Oah vicy versy," he responded with another evil grin.

I actually lugged those heavy bags all of the way past the side of the station to the far end of that concrete platform, and I would have stepped down from it onto the battle-scarred roadway, but Pancho suddenly shouted, "Stop!"

Of course, I stopped, because a truck could have been thundering along that rough pavement. But a quick glance indicated that there wasn't a vehicle of any kind in sight, so I was about to step down from it again when José shouted, "Stop!"

"Okay, guys," I muttered, setting the bags on the end of the platform. "What gives?"

"You don't want to commit yourself to a night in a sleazy room over a pub in a backwater town like this," insisted Pancho.

"Yeah," agreed José. "Besides, where would you find properly prepared food?"

"Probably in the pub," I retorted. "After all, it is the business center."

"And with what kind of characters would you be associating in the meantime?" inquired Pancho.

"Very likely I would be associating with some nice human beings like myself," I replied impatiently.

"You have to be kidding!" exclaimed José. "Have you forgotten how sadistic the people in a small town can be?"

"Or how raffish a bar full of clannish drunks can be?" added Pancho.

"No," I responded, "but practically all people possess some sadistic tendencies; besides, I don't have to associate with either the people of this small town or a bar full of clannish drunks."

"But you just said that you would probably dine in the pub," protested José.

"And what do you think would happen after the barman's eyes *glommed* onto you while one of the waitresses was seating you at a table in the dining area of that pub?" interposed Pancho.

"Probably about the same thing that happened in that Melbourne restaurant," suggested José.

"Moreover, this time the barman would probably regale the drunks at one end of the bar with one of Big Brother's dirty stories," observed Pancho, "and before he could get to the other end of the bar with a variation of the same story, the first set of drunks would be after you."

"And you are too old to take on ten drunks at one time, anymore," observed José.

"Whadya mean ten drunks at one time . . . anymore?" countered Pancho.

"Well," José began uneasily, "Al has always claimed that he could whip any ten drunks at a given time."

"Yeah, that's what he has claimed," Pancho caustically conceded, "but most drunks rarely ever get **that** drunk."

"Nevertheless, it could turn out to be a life-or-death issue," José insisted. "After all, our man becomes pretty rabid when he finally gets mad."

"Yeah," granted Pancho, "and we shouldn't forget that time when it took the entire football team to pull him off of the big high school bully, who foolishly accused him of being yellow for discontinuing football because of a pair of football knees that slipped out of joint every time he turned sharply on them."

"Yeah," agreed José. "He was battering that poor, misguided guy's head against the sun-baked earth so hard that it was almost split and spilled his. . . ."

"Naw!" interjected Pancho. "He didn't have any."

This time, however, it could be **his** head that's being battered against a **pub** floor, and it could be us that are bein' spilled, so it could be a matter of life and death—ours."

"That's what I already said!" protested José. "Why do you always try to steal my thunder?"

"Consequently, we don't want the next 'face on the bar room floor' to be Al's," resumed Pancho imperturbably. "We are much too closely related to him to relish that."

"Cool it!" I interjected sharply. "After thinking it over, I've decided to try to get a ticket on the next train out of here, so there may not be any reason to discuss this matter further."

After that argument there may have been a bit of blood in my eye when I entered the waiting room of the railroad station. So I purposefully approached the panel-high opening beyond which a lone ticket agent presided from within the depths of an upholstered swivel chair. Since only one very young couple had preceded me, I had not long to wait.

When I stepped before the window, the agent muttered, "Wot kin Oy do foah yuh, suh?" Meanwhile, his eyes studied me from within deep recesses formed by a set of fleshy cheekbones and a pair of overhanging, straw-colored brows.

A quick counterstudy revealed a physique that could have been mistaken for that of a slob; however, not one pound of the three hundred pounds of approximately thirty-year-old human flesh sagged one iota, but the baling wire–reinforced swivel chair did.

"I would like to purchase passage to Perth," I replied as my eyes took stock of the man's closely cropped, straw-colored hair.

"Whin do yuh want to leave?" he inquired.

"As soon as possible," I replied.

"Loike t'dye?" he asked.

"Sooner if possible," I retorted whimsically.

The man's thick lips spread into a pleased smile. Meanwhile, the freckles on both sides of them vied for survival space with freshly sprouted, golden whiskers.

"Oy'm sorry," he responded with a friendly smile, "but Oy don't have any dirict connictions with the powahs above, so the bist Oy kin do is t' sill yuh a tickit for t'dye."

"That's good enough!" I retorted.

The man's smile turned into a chuckle as he slowly reached for a pad of forms and began to complete the topmost form with a stubby lead pencil that periodically became lost among his thick fingers. Apparently he considered me to be some sort of a comedian, therefore a friend, so I was not about to tell him that those words just happened to come out that way. Furthermore, I was not about to admit that I was in desperate need of a friend like him, one who could get me out of town before nightfall.

After some highly technical manipulations of the stubby lead pencil, he looked up at me and said, "That will be three hundred fifty-one dollahs and fifty cints."

The impact of the statement lifted my elbows off of the narrow counter and set me back a couple of paces. Then I reached for my wallet and doubtfully muttered, "Suppose I don't have that much Australian money."

"It's a moighty long walk to Puth," he responded implacably.

"How much would coach fare cost?" I asked.

"Only fust class fayahs on this trine," he retorted.

"Can you change some American traveler's checks to Australian currency?" I inquired.

"Oy don't know what the ixchinge rite is," he replied.

"Aren't there some business people in town who could tell you what it is?" I asked.

"Hmm," he mumbled thoughtfully, "mybe. Oy'll see what Oy kin foind out." And one huge, freckled hand slowly reached for the adjacent telephone.

Several calls later he muttered, "Oy'm gittin' a woide divergence of opinions."

"This is beginning to sound like America," I said impulsively. "And those divergences of opinion usually net somebody other than me a fat financial gain."

Following a perceptible wince the big man frowned pensively. After several more calls he placed the instrument on its cradle, looked up at me, and said, "Will, Oy have two differint rites."

"How much different?" I asked.

After another session with the stubby lead pencil, he looked up at me and answered, "About ilivin dollahs wuth."

"Hmm," I mumbled thoughtfully. "I'll save much more than that in board and lodging by spending the night on the train, so figure the highest rate."

After fixing thoughtful eyes on me for a moment, he then inquired, "Ah yuh shoah that it's all roight?"

Eagerly nodding, I presented several bills and some traveler's checks to him and answered, "I'm sure that it's all right, because this may be a matter of life and death."

He turned startled eyes toward me, but he was much too poised to inquire regarding the reasons for that involuntary statement. If he had asked, I would have told him the truth: that two very close friends had advised me to take the next train to Perth for the good of my health. But no one warned me that the train trip might be detrimental to my health or that I might be caught between Big Brother and the deep, blue sea.

I had carried my luggage about one hundred feet along the platform toward the boarding area when the nearest intercom requested, "Will Mistah Terril please retuhn to the ticket office!"

"Now what?" I muttered. After reversing the field, I beheld the huge agent thundering along the platform toward me as fast as his clumsy, wide-track wheels would permit.

When he came within audio range, he called out, "Oy called anothah pahty and was told that the lowah rite may be the roight one." Then he came to a screeching stop in front of me, exhaled a boiler full of highly compressed steam, and added, "If yuh'll give me yoah home addriss, Oy'll forward the diffirince to yuh."

I was literally struck dumb with wonder and admiration. The last time that I had been directly exposed to an obviously honest man, I had been fifty years younger, and the man had been a midcontinent farmer who didn't even know what the words *financial deviousness* and *chicanery* meant.

Even I could sense the admiration in my eyes as I retorted, "No! If there is any difference, you keep it. I owe you that much for all the time you've spent in research on this problem."

"But that's moy job," he protested. "Oy'll be glad to forwahd it to yuh, if yuh'll only give me. . . ."

"No, put it in your pocket," I insisted.

"Ah yuh shoah that it's okye?" he persisted.

"Yes, yes, it is okay," I responded impatiently. "And thank you for your very fine cooperation in this matter."

"Thank yuh, suh," he muttered. "And Oy hope yuh have a noice trip to Puth."

As we turned our backs on each other, Pancho began, "Hmm." Then he musingly resumed, "There's not one chance in a thousand that we would have encountered that kind of a man in the States—even in the Bible Belt."

"Yeah," José agreed. "That guy may be a rough, country lad, but he possesses the heart and soul of a gentleman; he's a real gem of a man, in fact. And Al involuntarily questioned his integrity." Meanwhile, I mentally cringed.

"He owes the man an apology," Pancho insisted. "After all, who knows more than he about how it feels to have one's integrity unjustly impugned?"

"I hope that there's an eleven-dollar difference," José rejoined. "But nothing can fully compensate the man for that unjust attack on his integrity."

During the hour-long wait I studied the immediate environs and quickly arrived at the conclusion that the ticket agent in Melbourne was right: Port Pirie was the jumping off place. In addition to the port and its bevy of grain elevators, there were some small businesses, some homes, and the pub. To the east, inland scrub covered rolling hills that eventually melded with the Flinders Range, and the cold waters of Spencer Gulf effectively precluded any jumping off on the west side. With the barren coastal plain and the Great Australian Bight to the south, only Port Augusta and the Nullarbor Plain remained, so the agent must have been referring to the plain.

Tiring of the environs, I began to study the railroad personnel in the area, most of whom appeared to be local yokels. Since the frequency of their evasive glances far exceeded the interest normally warranted by the presence of a gray-bearded stranger, I concluded that my decision to avoid a layover at the pub was well founded.

22

———————————◀●▶———————————

Port Pirie to Kalgoorlie

Just before five o'clock I strode alongside the train to the conductor and presented my ticket to him. "Can you direct me to this compartment?" I asked.

"I can do better than that," he cheerfully replied. "I'll escort you to it." After leading me to the first compartment in Car 1, he opened the door for me and said, "The man with whom you'll be sharing this compartment slept in the upper berth last night, so you'll have the lower one."

"Great!" I exclaimed. "But I wonder why he selected the upper berth when he had a choice of either of them."

The man merely shook his grizzled head with a bemused smile, so I began to suspect that my new cell mate might be something of a character.

"The first sitting for dinner will be called in about one hour," he informed me. "And a ticket for either the first or second sitting will be issued to you shortly before that time. Choice of the sitting is yours."

"Thank you," I responded to his departing back.

It was almost six o'clock when the figure of a tall, ruggedly built man blocked out most of the light that flowed from the adjoining hallway through the open doorway. The dimmed light and the sounds of a body in motion caused me to turn away from the window for a quick study of the source, but the source forestalled it by advancing toward me with a large, outstretched right hand.

"I assume that you are sharing this compartment with me," he said. "My name is Jerry." And he added a surname, but that has been omitted to protect a nice guy from any scurrilous attacks by vicious gossips, such as Big Brother.

Arising, I met him halfway, including my full name. "But you can call me Al," I suggested.

"Okay, Al," he said. "Where do you hail from?"

After telling him, I inquired, "And where are you from, Jerry?"

"Dallas," he replied.

"But not directly, I'll bet," I said. "There isn't even a token of a Texas accent."

"I wasn't born in Texas," he admitted, settling onto the other end of the seat. "I spent twenty years in the service, so I probably have a sort of universal accent."

"Me, too," I rejoined. "I was raised on the plains of Canada; however, since that time I've lived in many of the states but mostly in California."

A man clad in the uniform of a railway employee paused in the open doorway.

"Please pardon me, gentlemen," he interposed. "Which sittings would you prefer?"

"I prefer the first one," Jerry replied.

"I also prefer the first one," I added.

"Fine," the man murmured, presenting a small card to each of us. "Please respond promptly to the dinner call, because we don't want to delay the diners of the second sitting." With that, he exited.

I studied the card, which was about the size of the average business card, and found that its light-blue color was overlaid by dark-blue printing. Below the words *Dining Car Service* were the words *First Sitting*, and opposite them were the redundant characters *1st.*

Meanwhile, Jerry was busily changing from a pair of tennis shorts into a pair of slacks, so I assumed that shorts as dinner attire must be frowned upon by the dining car society of Australia.

Following a critical glance at my worn blue jeans and the soiled cuffs of my faded, blue windbreaker, I looked at Jerry and said, "I don't have anything with me but these, a sport jacket, and some slacks; furthermore, I don't even own a tuxedo. If I must change into my slacks and jacket just to join those people in the dining car, then I'll have to go hungry, because I refuse to do it."

He glanced amiably at me, grinned widely, and said, "Don't worry about it. Some of those people will be wearing about the same type of garb you are, so don't worry about it."

"I won't worry about it," I promised. "If somebody wants to worry about it, let it be the Australian fuddy duddy in white tie and tails."

Since Jerry didn't offer to accompany me to the dining car, I assumed that he was otherwise occupied. Upon arriving there, I found that he was already seated with two other men and an attractive woman with straw-colored hair, all of whom appeared to be about forty years old.

The three minutes leeway that I had allowed him proved to be almost too much, because I was one of the last diners to be seated. The dining car's host did the deed, and he did it so smoothly that I immediately suspected him of dealing from a stacked deck. But I even admitted to myself that that was carrying suspicions too far; nevertheless, the man did channel the other three diners into their respective chairs with a flourish that required instantaneous decisions if not a stacked deck.

I was assigned to a window seat that faced aft, and a relatively young man was seated opposite me. An attractive young woman was seated beside him, and an elderly woman, who must have been about my age, was seated to my right. As I pondered the seating arrangement, I admitted to myself that the middle-aged host must be a very talented man, indeed. Meanwhile, my gaze touched the linen-clad tabletop with its sparkling array of cutlery and dinnerware; then it came to rest on the eyes of the other man.

"I suppose we should introduce ourselves," he suggested in a familiar accent. "My name is Allan." And he included a surname, but it has been omitted to protect the guilty. Then, glancing toward the young woman, he added, "This is my wife, Jane."

"I'm glad to know you, Allan and Jane," I murmured. "You may call me Al," and my sweeping gaze included the lady beside me.

"I'm Joan," she responded in tones so low that I failed to hear the name. Nevertheless, from careful attention to the ensuing conversation, I managed to gain it.

A conversation continued for some time. When it finally stalled, I inquired,

"From what part of the United States did you people come, Allan?"

"I'm from Tucson, Arizona," he replied, "but Jane is from Australia."

"Then you live here now," I persisted.

"Yes," he replied.

To include the quiet-mannered lady beside me in the conversation, I inquired, "And where do you live, may I ask?"

"Sydney," she answered in the same low tones.

"How nice that must be," I murmured. "I spent two days there, and I was very impressed by the city."

Then Jane interjected a question regarding the part of the city in which Joan lived, so I applied myself to what proved to be a much better meal than any of those that I have encountered aboard many different American airliners. I deliberately retired into the conversational background throughout most of the meal for the same reason that I usually withdraw from such gymnastics, but justification for it was not to materialize until the next meal.

With a gentle shove from the tactful host, we first-sitting diners made way for the second sitting. En route through the club lounge to the compartment, I was startled to see the couple that had occupied the seat ahead of me in the coach of the previous train.

"Hmm," mumbled José. "I wonder how long it'll take that loud-mouthed character to circulate the words that conductor Black transmitted from Big Brother to him, whatever they were." But a careful surveillance of the duo indicated that neither of them had observed me, so Big Brother must have employed another form of Mr. Black to do the dirty work that brought about some subsequent developments.

My roommate's large frame was distributed over much of the central part of the seat when I returned, so I suggested, "Since I've occupied the window seat throughout most of the evening, why don't you take a turn on it, Jerry."

"No, you sit there," he retorted. "I'll be leaving pretty soon anyway." Then he moved aside, so I squeezed past him and collapsed onto the seat.

"How high are you stacked, Jerry?" I asked.

"I'm six-two," he replied.

"And a bit over two hundred," I guessed.

"Two fifteen," he admitted and ruefully patted a budding paunch.

"You are approaching the age when that will continue to grow, despite every conceivable effort to counteract it," I predicted. And since he didn't volunteer the information, I mentally pegged him at about forty-two. "What did you do in the service, Jerry?" I asked.

"Aircraft maintenance," he answered. "I was in the U.S. Air Force."

"We have associated backgrounds," I observed. "Some thirty-five of my most productive years in aerospace engineering were spent in the design of aircraft, including fighter craft, bombers, and airliners. Consequently, if you have encountered any access problems, I may have been responsible for some of them."

He smiled faintly. Apparently he was too tactful to venture into those uncharted waters.

"What do you do for a living?" I asked. Then, without allowing him to answer, I added, "Assuming that you are on a vacation from some sort of employment."

"I'm a truck driver," he answered.

"A truck driver!" I exclaimed. "You don't look like any truck driver I've ever seen."

A pleased smile hovered around his lips as he muttered, "Let's say that I'm a man who happens to drive a truck for a living."

"Let's do," I responded. "After all, too many of us acquire preconceived opinions about how people in different trades and professions should look and act, and I've tactlessly followed that bent. If you had been wearing a white smock when we met, very likely I would have suspected you of being a doctor."

"I suppose that clothes do make the man," he suggested.

"Not necessarily," I rejoined. "Mechanics who work in clean rooms wear white smocks similar to those worn by doctors, so a smock could make either a mechanic or a doctor, depending on the reactions of the beholder."

"Then clothes do make the man," he insisted, "at least in the eyes of the beholder."

"A very astute observation," I responded with a chuckle. "I can see that I'll have to adhere closely to the rules of logic in my dealings with you."

"Where do you plan to go when you get to Perth?" he asked.

Since the question was a wide departure from the subject at hand, I reacted cautiously to it. "I have no definite plans," I answered evasively. "I may stay in or near Perth for a while; that is, if I find that I like the area and it likes me."

He nodded absently, ruffled the light-brown hair on his right forearm with his left palm, and arose. "I think I'll go to the lounge and have a beer," he muttered. Then, looking down at me, he asked, "Would you like to join me?"

"No, thank you, Jerry," I replied. "I'll sit here at this window until nightfall and keep a wary eye on the landscape for unwary kangaroos."

Turning toward the doorway with a preoccupied air, he ducked his head, probably from habit, and strode through the opening into the dimly lighted hallway.

My vigil paid off almost immediately, but it wasn't an unwary kangaroo that I sighted through the rapidly gathering dusk; it was a very wary emu. And it was making rapid tracks alongside a distant fence that enclosed one of the last wheat farms of the area. In fact, its rapid passage was what attracted my attention to it. At first, I suspected it of being an ostrich until I remembered that those largest of flightless birds are natives of only Africa and Arabia. Nevertheless, the combination of dusk and distance limited my view of the bird to merely its outline, so it could have been a vagrant ostrich or even an illegal alien. Eventually the dimness blended into darkness, so I removed a pad and a mechanical lead pencil from my briefcase and became immersed in recording the various incidents of the day.

Soon those efforts were interrupted by a uniformed trainman, who stopped in the open doorway and inquired, "May oy mike up the berths, suh?"

"Yes, of course," I replied, "but allow me one minute to put things in order." After doing so, I stepped into the hallway and waited while he performed the task.

Jerry returned about eleven o'clock. "I'm sorry to awaken you, Al," he apologized, bustling around the cramped quarters, washing his teeth, and preparing himself for the remainder of the night.

"Consider it no problem, Jerry," I insisted. "I'm a light sleeper, so no one could possibly enter this cubicle without awakening me."

But his apology may have been justified, because two hours after he had climbed into his lofty sack and immediately slipped into slumber land, I was still counting sheep, and they weren't the ghostly creatures that a more imaginative mind might have incongruously viewed upon the Nullarbor Plain through the shade-covered window. Advanced age may have had something to do with it, but an overactive mind may have been more at fault. In any case, after viewing the emu and awakening to Jerry's entrance, I was left with only ennui and lassitude.

After the usual morning ablutions, Jerry and I surged toward the dining car at the first summoning ding of the breakfast ding-dong. The hurry and scurry of the passengers reminded me of hogs frantically responding to their feeding call. Consequently, on very short notice, the dining car personnel had trained us hogs well.

At first blush that metaphor may have applied more to me than to the other members of our table, because I was the first to arrive, but I may have been saved that embarrassment by still another embarrassment. Joan was only a few steps behind me, but Allan and Jane could be classified only as late arrivals, and they were closely followed by a grim-faced host who appeared to be literally pushing them toward our table. In fact, the duo looked like they had just lost an argument to the man and were being pushed into a situation that they were extremely reluctant to accept.

Of course, there were the usual good mornings, but there was a distinct difference in the manner in which they were rendered. In fact, there was a perceptible chilliness in the atmosphere, and I don't mean the ambient atmosphere. Consequently, I wearily concluded that Big Brother must have communicated one of his weird messages to my youthful associates, albeit indirectly.

During the previous meal Joan had been been rather reserved and quiet, but now she had become almost the life of a very dull party. At the time I suspected that she also may have noticed the apparent reluctance of the couple to join us and that she may have been trying to compensate for their obvious shortcomings. In any event, she endeared herself to me by supporting a very limited conversation, one that might have died without her sturdy support, since I rarely force my words onto anybody who doesn't wish to associate with me. But this case proved to be an exception, since I chose to tease those two simple-minded young adults.

"Allan," I began, "I'm not sure that I approve of your marriage to Jane."

Allan's lower jaw suddenly stopped chewing, and his eyes seemed to be magnetically attracted to my malicious ones. Meanwhile, a dark storm began to collect in Jane's clear eyes. Even Joan paused with a piece of toast midway to her mouth and tossed a startled glance at me.

"Well," I slowly resumed in a deliberate attempt to build up the negative effect, which was rapidly reaching explosive proportions. "It just doesn't seem right to mix good, old, American blood with the blood of another race like that of an Australian. You should have considered the many problems that will confront your offspring."

Joan chuckled outright, and Allan's eyes lost some of their hard sheen. But Jane knew how to meet such an attack: She abruptly exclaimed, "Oh, look! There goes a wallaby." And she pointed toward a patch of scrambled scenery that had just been repeated some one hundred feet beyond the windowpane.

Since that time I have decided that it was impossible for any creature to have dwelt in that particular patch of scenery. In fact, I seriously doubt that there was a wallaby within a hundred miles of the patch; therefore, that gal must have descended from one of those early convicts who may have been charged by some English lord with ruining one of his lordship's favorite punch lines, so the culprit ended up on The Rocks along Sydney Cove.

Upon returning to the compartment, I found Jerry sprawled on the near end of the seat, so I gratefully squeezed past him to the one beside the window.

In the process I inquired, "Did you happen to see a wallaby from your dining car window?"

He shook his head. Then I contritely interposed, "No, of course, you wouldn't have seen it, because you were seated on the opposite side of the car."

"We should be seeing some 'roos, though," he suggested. "There are supposed to be a lot of them along this stretch of track." Then, to allay any doubts regarding the subject matter, he added, "Kangaroos, that is."

"We probably passed Tarcoola during the night," I remarked, "so we must've passed beyond the sheep country by now."

Following an absent nod, he said, "Tarcoola is the junction of the Chan with the Trans Australian. Chan is the other name of the Central Australian Railway, which goes north to Alice Springs. It was placed in service in nineteen eighty, so it's practically new. I was thinking of bidding on that side trip, but I suspected that it would be a very boring ride through nothing but wastelands; besides, I wasn't too sure that Alice Springs would have much to offer, so I finally passed."

"What more does this line have to offer?" I countered with a chuckle.

"According to the brochure, it has had much more to offer," he said. "So far we've passed wheat fields, sheep lands, a couple of large lakes, some mulga, plus some salt and blue bush. The scenery has been consistently different."

"True," I conceded, "but we passed most of that last night. This morning we are confronted by nothing more than a vast, open limestone plateau, and that scenery is not supposed to vary throughout the next several hundreds of miles."

"It's hard to believe," he murmured, "but people actually live out there on that barren plateau; however, they keep pretty close to the railroad."

"I've noticed that the railroad agency is replacing the jarrah wood ties with steel-reinforced, concrete ties," I said, "so the construction crews have to be located on site, even if those locations are no more than work camps. When I worked in the civil engineering department of a railway company almost fifty years ago, both the railroad's construction crews and its maintenance crews were usually located near their work."

"The same policy is followed here," Jerry said. "In fact, small houses with galvanized sheet metal roofs are provided to workers with families. If you watch closely, you'll see some of them from time to time."

"That fits the pattern that I remember," I submitted. "But most of our maintenance men lived in the small towns through which the railroad passed."

"So do these," he responded with a laugh. "Those four or five shacks that house the families of the workers constitute an entire town."

"I assume that a supply train makes periodic trips to provide them with the usual necessities, such as food and beverages," I ventured.

"Yeah," he responded with a chuckle, "they call it the 'Tea and Sugar Train.' It even carries a minister to guide them and to tie an occasional marital knot."

"How about divorces?" I countered with a smile.

"I suspect that they have to go to a city for the untying ceremonies," he surmised. "Possibly they agree to disagree without the benefits of legal badinage."

"I wonder what type of person would accept employment in such isolated locations," I muttered with a shake of my head.

"According to what I've heard in the lounge car," he began, "like the French Foreign Legion, those crews are made up of men from all over the world. Some of them are ex-convicts, and a lot of them are social misfits, but many of them have been born into that life, so they know of nothing better."

"A typical example of psychological conditioning," I suggested. "With a little mental conditioning, human beings can withstand all sorts of rigors, for example, the living conditions of the Eskimos, the Siberians, and the Tibetans."

After absently nodding, he appeared to become lost in thought for some time, so I turned my attention to the rapidly deteriorating landscape.

Finally he arose, glanced toward me, and muttered, "Well, it's beer time. Would you like to join me?"

"No, thank you, Jerry," I replied. "I'm not much of a beer drinker."

Was it relief that I detected on his well-molded features as he passed through the open doorway? I wasn't sure, but it made sense that even a nice guy might feel burdened by the company of a much older man, especially one overhung by Big Brother's dark shadow.

It may have been speculations regarding the lives of those hardy people of the outback that caused my mind to flash back through sixty-five years to the scene of some of my earliest schooling. The focal point was a small, one-room schoolhouse that stood on one corner of a rural road intersection near the middle of the forty-eight contiguous United States. I remembered it well, particularly the country roads, which always became so muddy after a heavy rain that a neighbor's three sons, my two younger sisters, and I chose to walk along the weed-grown shoulders to avoid being bogged down in the mud during our treks to and from the schoolhouse.

One day in early spring, immediately after the students had been dismissed, the six of us struck out in a group from the school yard for our respective homes. Typically, we four boys forged ahead while my sisters straggled behind us. From time to time I would look back to ensure that they were not falling too far behind. In such cases I was prone to drag my feet a bit, which usually slowed the entire forward echelon. Two of the brothers were somewhat older than my buddy and I, and they were given to lording their seniority over us. It may have been that tendency which induced the oldest boy to try to impart some supposed sexual lore to us younger lads after we had traveled about halfway from the white schoolhouse toward my grandparent's farmhouse.

I don't remember what brought the subject up, but I vividly remember the older boy's lascivious expression when he confidentially inquired, "Do you know what makes babies?" Then he looked back over his shoulder to verify that my sisters were outside of the audio range.

Of course, I didn't know the answer, so I answered, "No."

"Well," he began, "you've seen a bull climb onto a cow, haven't you?"

"No," I admitted reluctantly, "but I've seen a dog climb onto another dog." However, I failed to inform him that I had never been allowed to follow one of those trysts to completion, because grandpa invariably picked up a clod and effectively discouraged the affair.

"Well," he resumed with an expression which seemed to imply that he was about to reveal one of the world's most closely guarded secrets, "babies are made the same way." Then he proceeded to describe the union in glowing four-letter words; however, of the male's two potential targets, the boy selected the wrong one. Apparently he had observed the copulation of a pair of farm animals from a distance, hence the error.

Of course, none of us boys had any illusions about babies being brought by the stork, but none of the details of procreation had been explained to any of us. However, I have never forgotten the embarrassed expression on my buddy's fair features as his brother crudely and erroneously described his concept of how babies are made.

It was to be many a moon before that concept would be set straight in my young mind. In fact, my grandfather was confronted by an opportunity that could have corrected it, but he wisely chose to avoid it.

It came about this way: One evening my grandfather and I strolled from the farmhouse through the gate of the large farmyard to greet a neighbor who had just arrived aboard a grain wagon, from which the upper sideboards had been removed. The elderly neighbor lounged on a worn, wooden seat whose leaf springs were mounted on the forward end of the lower sideboards of the wagon. As he brought the team to an easy stop about midway of the yard by a gentle pull on the two leather reins in his work-hardened hands, grandfather genially shouted, "Hullo, John!"

"Hullo, Will," John responded. "How be ye?"

"Tol'able, tol'able," Will replied. "How's everybuddy at yore house?"

"Tol'able," John replied, " 'ceptin' 'Tilda. Her awthritis is botherin' her agin."

"Too bad, too bad," Will muttered. "Farm work may be a bit too hard for her now. Maybe yuh should sell out and move into town, John."

"I've considered it," John admitted, "but what would I do with all o' that time on my hands?"

"You could just take it easy for a change," Will suggested. Then, with a glance toward the big bay stallion, whose halter rope was tied to one of the wagon's rear corner fittings, he added, "So this is yore pride and joy, hey?"

"Yep," John replied with a proud glance at the rugged animal. "He's goin' on six, now. Jist gittin' into his prime."

"You claimed over the phone that he's a big one, and he shore is," Will muttered.

"Shall we git to it?" John suggested. "I haven't slopped the hogs yet, and I don't want to have to stumble 'round in the dark while I do it."

"Why don't ye tie yore team to that gatepost near the corner of the barn?" Will suggested. "The mare is in the barn."

John nodded; then, lightly flipping the reins, he added, "Giddup."

While the wagon was rolling slowly toward the gatepost, I cast a mystified glance at the stallion. Then, turning toward Will, I asked, "Why is that big horse tied to the back of John's wagon, grandpa?"

The slender old man turned his deep-blue eyes thoughtfully on me and slowly replied, "Well, I asked John to bring him here to breed one of my mares, so he brought him the easiest way he could."

He must have rightly suspected that I didn't know the definition of the word *breed*, because he employed it in a self-assured manner. Of course, his attitude was justified, because they didn't teach sex education in schools during those times. In fact, the prevailing philosophy seemed to be directed more toward protecting the innocence of children than toward destroying it.

After a long, pensive pause, he looked down at me and asked, "Isn't it gittin' a bit cold out here for ye?"

"No," I replied, desperately trying to control an inadvertent shiver. "Aren't we going to watch John breed that mare?"

His eyes did a double take, and a wry smile tortured his gray moustache into a crude semblance of a twisted Fuller Brush. "No, that ain't possible," he murmured. "Why don't you pick up an armful of wood at the woodpile and put it in the wood bin for grandma. Besides, it's too cold out here for you."

His tone was gentle, but I had learned that whenever grandpa's eyes acquired that firm expression, he was not to be opposed, so I reluctantly headed for the woodpile.

Actually, I've never observed the process of breeding a mare, but it should not be long before it will be displayed on television screens. After all, many TV programmers seem to be obsessed with displaying the copulation of animals, especially wild animals. When it is finally displayed, I'll turn to another station like I always do when subjects that demonstrate the inherent bad judgment of my countrymen are televised. But I deeply regret that so many innocent children will be exposed to such crude and unnecessary subjects.

Within four months the scene had shifted to a granary at the west end of a red barn that stood in a Canadian farmyard some seven miles from the center of Regina, Saskatchewan. To gain access to the freshly threshed wheat, my two sisters and I had been forced to crawl over several 1- x 12-inch boards, which had been nailed across the lower part of the granary's only doorway to keep the highly piled grain from flowing through the opening onto the barn's earthen floor. It was a warm day in the latter part of August, and we found the grain to be cool and pleasant to loll in. However, since the grain seemed to slump down two steps for every step upward, I soon tired of trying to climb to the peak of the pile, so I turned purposefully toward the opening.

"Where are you going?" Alice, my younger sister, called.

"Down by the creek," I replied.

"Wait for us!" she shouted, struggling toward me on slender little legs that threatened to disappear into the loose grain with each faltering step. Suddenly she stopped and stared critically at her older sister, who was sprawled on the tumbled slope with her legs spread wide and with the fingers of one hand probing experimentally beneath the innermost edge of one leg of her homemade bloomers. "Hazel, what on earth are you doing?" she protested with an embarrassed glance at me. The other girl ignored us while she grimaced and continued to dig.

After watching what must have been an endless chore for several seconds, I finally said, "What you need is a cork."

Alice, who usually treated her only brother with a certain amount of respect and, at times, even with admiration, fixed disapproving eyes on me.

That only incited me to an even more daring remark. "And I know how it can be corked," I muttered as I faked a move toward the older child but stopped just short of her.

She stopped probing, looked up at me, then daringly pulled her dress higher and laid back on the grain while Alice's features registered an eight on the Richter scale. Not to be outdone, I sprawled crosswise on her for an instant; then, struggling upright, I plowed through the grain toward the opening.

"Wait for me!" Alice called.

After crawling through the opening and dropping onto the earthen floor, I tolerantly turned about, reached up, slid her forty pounds across the barrier, and set her feet onto terra firma.

"Wait for me!" the other girl called, but she was big enough to manage on her own, so I clutched the child's small hand, and we struck out for the creek, where there were more interesting things to do, such as prodding an occasional frog into the water or watching the sandpipers skittering through the shallows.

Since that time I've often wondered whether my mother had mentioned the birds and the bees to that girl at such an early age or whether the girl had reacted out of sheer lassitude. Furthermore, I've wondered whether a misinformed boy, such as that one, could reach the procreative age and err so radically during his first tryst with an equally uninformed partner. Of course, such a combination of possibilities must have been unlikely, even during those times, but I merely wondered. Maybe a serpent would have interceded and set them straight, but suppose that the tryst occurred in New Zealand, where there are no serpents. Then it could have ended up in disaster; that is, if those are the proper words to describe such a situation.

Almost three years later the scene had shifted to the third floor of a house located at 167 East 132nd Street in Vancouver, British Columbia. Actually, the third floor was a loft, which I, as the twelve-year-old man of the house, had finished and painted. The work had netted two large bedrooms, and the existing stairway ended in my bedroom. Adjacent to the stairway's upper landing, a doorway provided access to the second bedroom.

As the scene was set for that particular moment, I was about to return from my bedroom to the basement and stoke the furnace with some slabs of bark-encrusted Douglas fir; however, when I was about to pass the open doorway of the other bedroom, my older sister called, "Albert!"

I glanced through the opening and saw that her nightgown scarcely covered the still childlike body, which was sprawled carelessly across the bed.

I paused, placed one hand high against the doorjamb, and impatiently answered, "Yes."

"Do you remember what we did in that old granary?" she inquired with a simper.

After casting a puzzled glance at her, I muttered, "I don't remember doing anything."

"We didn't," she admitted, "but we could have."

Then, sensing the invitation in her smiling eyes, I frowned deeply, because incest was not permitted by my code of ethics. Meanwhile, from my mother's room on the second floor I heard the sounds of urgent whispering, which were followed by the sounds of Alice's light footfalls on the carpeted floor of the interconnecting hallway. In turn, their impacts on the uncarpeted, wooden steps of the stairway resounded through the stairwell. They paused as she reached the intermediate landing; then she hurriedly rounded the corner with her wide, blue eyes directed apprehensively upward. When they met my stolid stare, they relaxed into a relieved smile, and the tension appeared to flow from her slight frame. Since I blocked the doorway to the bedroom, she came to a stop before me and continued to look smilingly into my eyes.

"You know me better that that, even if mom doesn't," I growled.

Then I stepped away from the doorway; however, before passing me, she paused, ducked her head as if in thought, looked up at me, nodded emphatically, and continued toward her obviously discomfited roommate.

We understood each other, that little sister and I, but I never came to understand the older one. Apparently we were not only formed in vastly different molds but fired in very different furnaces. For instance, I later gathered from innuendos cast by schoolmates that she must have implied that we had completed a union in that granary, an act that not even the most sexually precocious children could accomplish at such an early age. Besides, at that time I was still laboring under a misconception regarding the proper target, so I would have corked the wrong one. Consequently, there never was any incest in my immediate family.

In fact, a member of an organization sponsored by our church proved to be the first adult to officially correct my concept of the birds and the bees. He was the counselor of the Wolf Pack, and I distinctly remember the expressions of embarrassment that flooded the features of the other Wolf Cubs when those revelations were being made, so I have always viewed the incident as a definite invasion of our individual privacies. But it may have saved me from the greater embarrassment of unintentionally committing sodomy during my first sexual venture.

There were to be more instances when I would be unjustly accused of behavior unbecoming to a gentleman and a scholar. However, after so many accusations of equal caliber and inaccuracy, I have come to the conclusion that if there were only more scholars and gentlemen in the world, such accusations would be more readily recognized in their true light.

With such reminiscences the morning passed quickly. When I arrived in the dining car for the midday meal, I immediately hooked a forefinger in the top buttonhole of the host's jacket and said, "Please place me at another table, because I strongly suspect that two of the people at that table are very unhappy with the present arrangement. Make it a table by myself if you can."

Apparently I caught the man "in his *unaware*," because, after hemming and hawing momentarily, he hurriedly thrust me onto a nearby aisle chair at a table where three relatively young men were seated. Meanwhile, a quick glance had confirmed my suspicions that there was, in fact, a small table at which I could have been seated by myself, but I didn't protest. Nevertheless, I fully intended to do so as soon as someone else became a reluctant associate. If it was necessary to maintain social equilibrium, I was prepared go hungry throughout the remainder of the trip.

The trio must have been a sophisticated lot, because they took my presence pretty much in stride, but there were no introductions. Furthermore, I was never included in their conversations, but it wasn't a very talkative group. Nevertheless, I did learn a bit about Australia by carefully listening to a few of their exchanges.

The first of those exchanges erupted from the man directly opposite me, who mourned, "Not one tray on the whole *bleeped* pline throughout the intoyah moahnin'."

"And we won't see any until tomorrow moahnin'," stated the man beside me.

"Theah wuh some beautiful mountain ash trays in Victoria," remarked the third man wistfully.

"They ah the tallest hahdwood trays in the world," remarked the man to my right, "and theah numbahs ixtind cleah down into Tasmania."

"The Sydney blue gums and alpine ash git fairly tall, too," remarked the man opposite me.

"Eucalyptus trays throive will in tropical areahs, wheah the mine rinefall comes in the summah," said the fourth man, "and they also do will in coolah cloimates with wintah rines."

"Yis," agreed the man in front of me, "the eucalyptus trays dominate most of Austreyelia's forists."

"Theah ah sivinty genera and neahly three thousand species o' thim," volunteered the man beside me. Hmm, I thought, these fellows appear to be very well versed in the flora of their country.

But the man at the far corner of the table laughed derisively. "You blokes ahen't foolin' me one bit," he said. "You got all of that troipe from the pamphlet called *Rile Across Austreyelia*."

"Oy did not," retorted the man beside me. Then, with a chuckle, he confessed, "Oy got most of it from a pamphlet that Oy filched from the Sydney Loibrary."

As usual, Jerry was sprawled in the middle of the seat when I arrived in the compartment.

"Slide over against the window, Jerry, and keep your eyes peeled for kangaroos," I commanded.

"Apparently this isn't very good kangaroo country," he muttered, moving toward the window.

I settled onto the near end of the seat and suggested, "Since you must have boarded the train at Sydney, you probably came directly to this country from the States, hey?"

"No, I didn't," he answered. After squaring his big frame on the seat, he spread his legs, leaned forward, rested an elbow on each knee, clasped his big hands, and resumed, "I met an attractive young woman en route, so I detoured with her to her parents' home near Gore, which is located on the southeastern part of New Zealand's South Island."

"Oh, yeah," I interjected. "It happened to be on my route to Dunedin."

"I spent a month there," he muttered. Then, following a short pause, he added, "I might have stayed even longer, but New Zealand is pretty strict about enforcing its visiting privileges. Nevertheless, I suspect that I could have married the gal and stayed there for the rest of my life."

"You might have done a lot worse," I observed. "New Zealanders are just about the nicest people that I've ever encountered." Then, after pausing and reconsidering the statement in the light of some of my recent experiences there, I modified it: "Of course, there are some real stinkers among them, but I suspect that there are fewer stinkers per hundred Kiwis than there are among most of the other societies aboard this globe."

"Yeah, I found them to be very nice, too," he said. "In fact, the woman's parents suggested that I get a visa and return for a longer stay."

"Maybe they had visions of a new son-in-law," I suggested.

"Maybe," he conceded, "but I had one marriage turn bad on me, so I don't intend to plunge into another one right away."

"How long have you been divorced?" I inquired.

"Two years," he answered. Then, after pausing and absently studying the knuckles of his clasped hands, he continued, "I'll never understand my ex-wife. All she wanted was to be free to shack up with another guy, and that's all she's been doing for the last two years."

"At least she waited until she was free to do so," I observed. But he didn't respond to the statement, so I don't know that she waited. Of course, as Pancho observed at the time, that wasn't any of my *bleeped* business. After a short silence I said, "It seems that practically the entire female race tends to be attracted to particularly promiscuous men or to men who are reputed to be promiscuous."

"Women do seem to be pretty tolerant," he admitted.

"They have to be," I retorted. "Otherwise they would never put up with any of us guys."

Since he glanced toward me with a smile, I assumed that I had succeeded in prying him loose from a period of deep-blue despondency.

Then, turning my eyes toward the scene beyond the window, I involuntarily exclaimed, "Say! There appears to be a lot more growth out there."

"There are supposed to be belts of myall, mulga, and mallee in this area," he remarked.

Most of the words were unknown to me, but I was in no mood to reveal my ignorance, so I suggested, "Some of it looks like it might be kangaroo grass."

"Perhaps it is," he conceded, "but this area is still underlaid by a massive layer of limestone, which is so near the surface that there isn't sufficient topsoil to support the growth of much vegetation, even when there is enough rain to start it."

"I understand that the edge of that limestone plate has been so ravaged by the breakers along the Great Australian Bight that the shoreline has been eroded into vertical cliffs, often towering three hundred feet above them," I ventured.

"True," he granted. "According to one of the fellows in the lounge, some of the harder limestone off Port Campbell has successfully withstood the onslaught of those waves, so huge limestone pinnacles, called the 'Twelve Apostles,' stand hundreds of feet off the shore along with rubble from the associated limestone strata."

"That seems to attest to the power of wind and water over matter," I suggested.

"And to the resistance of some of that matter to them," he countered.

After my pensive nod we lapsed into a long silence. Finally he resumed: "The great white shark also ranges through those waters. It's the largest flesh-eating fish in the seas and one of the world's greatest predators."

"But it is found in other waters, too," I observed.

After a nod he added, "But not as commonly as along this coast."

"What do you suppose attracts such sharks to this coast?" I inquired.

"I've been told that the sea lions particularly attract them to the shorelines of small islands and partially submerged rocks off this coast," he replied.

"Then there has to be something to attract the sea lions to this coast, or they wouldn't be here," I muttered.

"There are lots of different fish and crustacea in those waters, plus some dolphins," he said.

"Since the the Australians fish the gulfs and bays of this coast for western king prawns, the water must not be very deep," I observed.

"According to what I've heard," he began, "they fish for abalone in depths of about ninety feet, but the delicacy is usually found in only the more sheltered areas, such as the bays and on the lee sides of small islands. Several miles from the shore the continental shelf breaks off to about six hundred feet, from where it ultimately plunges more than a mile to the bottom of the ocean."

"I wonder if there are any fish in those depths," I muttered.

"They wouldn't be edible if there were," he rejoined. "Along the continental shelf there are several types of fish, including everything from starfish and leafy sea dragons to huge cuttlefish, squids, and octopuses. Some of them are deadly; for example, even though the blue-ringed octopus is small, its bite can kill a man."

"What about this leafy sea dragon?" I began.

"Oh, that's nothing more than a small relative of the sea horse," he interjected. "It's usually found on weedy bottoms or within heavy growths of kelp."

Seemingly we had exhausted the subject, because we subsided into silence for several minutes. Eventually Jerry stirred, arose, turned, and looked down at me.

"So you hear the call of a wild beer," I ventured.

"Yeah, I can use one," he muttered.

In response to the question in his eyes, I answered, "No. As usual, I'll forego the pleasure."

"You are welcome to join us," he insisted with a smile.

"Naw, I would only beat your time with that luscious blonde," I retorted.

Turning away with a smile, he moved to the open doorway, automatically lowered his head, and stepped through it into the hallway.

Shortly before the dinner announcement was sounded, Jerry returned, rather deliberately closed the door after him, and immediately made the usual changes in his attire. Just minutes before the signal for the first sitting was sounded, there were the sounds of many people bustling along the aisle past the closed door. Among the several voices, some were raised in boisterous but unintelligible objections.

Suddenly a woman's shrill, clarion tones inquired, "But why did we have to leave the lounge?"

Jerry's eyes darted quickly toward mine and just as quickly veered away from them. Then the dinner gong sounded, and we burst through the doorway into the aisle with Jerry running interference for me, but we encountered no tacklers or blockers.

As we thundered through the club lounge, I called to him: "I wonder why nobody is waiting in here for the second sitting. Usually it's full." He glanced sharply back at me but continued onward without replying.

José pondered the problem all of the way into the diner, where he finally suggested, "That change of policy in the lounge, along with the woman's shrill question, may indicate that our austral Big Brother may have reluctantly made that change of policy in the interests of justice and fair play."

"Ha!" Pancho responded. "That's totally out of character for Big Brother, so forget it."

As usual, the dinner table was relatively quiet, but the man diagonally across the table from me uncharacteristically started the conversation: "Aftah foah hundrid and sivinty kilometahs o' strite rileroad, it's koinda noice to sinse even a small bind from toime to toime."

"That's the longist stritch o' strite rileroad in the world," responded the man beside me.

"Theah's a moite moah grass now," volunteered the other man, "and theah's a bit o' salt and blue bush too."

"To the south theah's nothin' but open, bluestone plateau," interjected the man opposite me, "but we should be runnin' into some myall and bulloak pritty soon."

"Pritty soon we'll be crossin' the hoyist point in the loin at foah hundrid foah metahs above sea livil," announced the man beside me.

"That's about thirteen hundrid sivinty feet above sea livil, mite," the man at the far corner directed to me.

"Thanks, mate," I responded with a grin. And I seemed to sense more cordiality among them after the sally.

"We should be in Kalgoorlie by this evenin'," he suggested to the man beside me.

Meanwhile, the dining car host paused beside the table, and my quick glance confirmed my suspicion that his intent eyes were carefully inspecting the service at each table.

To attract his attention, I said, "Sir." And when he looked down at me, I added, "In my opinion you deserve a compliment for the dispatch and efficiency with which you perform your many tasks. Furthermore, your establishment serves the most palatable meals that I've consumed aboard any public transportation system."

For an instant the man's visage seemed to glow with pleasure. Then his inherent sense of propriety appeared to assert itself, because he executed an almost imperceptible bow and said, "Thank you, sir. It's noice whin people recognize the fact that we ah troyin' to do owah bist."

Shortly thereafter the members of the first sitting arose almost en masse and began to pick their individual ways through the car toward their respective compartments or to seats in the practically deserted lounge. Meanwhile, a rather mature couple had just become ensconced on the upholstered bench that extended along one wall of the lounge, and my alert eyes immediately detected the male member's tug on his lady's sleeve after his eyes settled on my bearded features.

After I entered the compartment and assumed my post beside the window, Jerry returned, but he didn't waste any time in small talk. In fact, he entered the tiny bathroom and pulled the door closed. In rapid sequence there were the scrubbing sounds of a toothbrush, the buzz of an electric razor, and the characteristic sounds of a shower. Then there was a brief silence, during which the man apparently toweled himself, combed his dark-brown hair, and pulled on a pair of shorts. Finally he pushed the small door open with a swish that wafted the aroma of a fine cologne to my nostrils. Pausing momentarily for a last inspection of the handsome reflection from the small mirror, he then sidled through the narrow doorway into the compartment. After donning a fresh sport shirt and a pair of gray slacks, he pulled a pair of socks over his big feet and tucked the two assemblies into a pair of sizable brown oxfords.

Then he arose, glanced absently at me, muttered, "Well, I'll be seein' yuh," and moved purposefully toward the open doorway. Seemingly his mind was so preoccupied with his mission that he forgot to duck his head as he strode through the opening, but his carefully waved locks cleared the header by a safe margin.

Then I arose, swung the door closed, and returned to my post beside the window, where the scenery had changed only slightly throughout most of the trip across the Nullarbor Plain. However, according to the strip map, there should have been some salmon gums and some salt and blue bush in the area, but I would not have recognized them, because they are only native to Australia.

Kalgoorlie Also according to the strip map, Kalgoorlie has a population of 21,010, which started 15 June 1893 with the discovery of gold in the general area. On 19 January 1903 a pipeline reached the settlement from Mundaring, about 340 miles distant, but the standard-gage railroad lines were not linked until 3 August 1968, so its growth was slow.

After the train came to a stop beside the station, a view of the surroundings convinced me that its growth would continue to be slow. However, even though those surroundings were shrouded in semidarkness, the street lights revealed patches of sand-colored soil whose surfaces were as dry and barren as the surface of the Nullarbor Plain. From that brief inspection I concluded that most of Australia's outback must be a never-never land comparable to some of Southern California's most remote wastelands.

A more detailed inspection revealed a typical small city that appeared to be supported solely by local mining activities. But one neatly devised main street did accommodate several reasonably large, red-brick buildings, one of which sported a tower with the faces of small-caliber Big Ben clocks mounted on two of its four sides, so there must have been some associated business activities. From those limited views I decided that the city had a certain appeal. In fact, I might have enjoyed a week-long visit there under normal circumstances. Some day I may even return there for that visit provided that the inhabitants are not offended by these disparaging words.

23

◄(❋)►

Kalgoorlie to Perth

After the new train crew set the electro-mechanical system on its way, I stared at the repetitious landscape until my mind finally rebelled and involuntarily returned to another of my older sister's machinations.

The family had returned from Vancouver to my grandparents' farm. From there it had been transplanted onto an old homestead near one corner of an uncle's farm located in the northern part of the state. It was a practical move in that my uncle had no son, and I had grown to a size that made me an asset in helping him plow corn, milk cows, put up hay, and perform many of the other routine tasks that had become so burdensome for him.

The grist for my sister's mill may have started to form about one hour before dusk one evening in late August. Another stripling and I had returned from a neighbor's farm to my uncle's farm after a hot, tiring day of putting up alfalfa hay. Actually, there was no logical reason why both of us should have gone all of the way to the far end of the pasture to herd the cattle back to the corral when one of us could have accomplished the task with ease. In fact, the cattle usually returned to the corral on their own at dusk, but we had finished haying a bit early, so we decided to do the chores a bit early.

Nevertheless, there we were at the far end of the pasture, prodding the placid animals into their homeward journey, when I called to my colleague, "Hey, Art! Since I'm almost home, why don't you drive them to the corral so that I won't have to walk all of the way back here?"

"Nuthin' doin'!" he retorted. "With yore uncle in town for the evenin', I refuse to be stuck with milking all of these cows."

Meanwhile, I had noticed that my older sister was standing on the rear porch of the nearby wood-frame farmhouse in which we lived. I wasn't surprised to see her there, because she usually appeared in the scene whenever one of the local youths showed up. What's more, I suspected that she would continue to watch us until we disappeared around the upcoming bluff.

Accepting the other lad's refusal with an air of amiable resignation, I reached down, picked up a flat stone, and whipped it expertly along the surface of the shallow creek that meandered through the pasture. As expected, it hopped a half-dozen times and sank through the clear water to the bottom.

Then I called, "Hey, Art! Are you going to the rodeo?"

"My dad wouldn't miss it for the world," he replied as his prodding activities moved him somewhat closer to me.

"My uncle has mentioned going to it, too," I said.

At that particular instant one of the cows suddenly crowded close behind the one ahead of her and tried to mount her.

"Hey, stop that!" I shouted.

"She's in heat," Art informed me.

"I know that," I retorted contemptuously. "I'm merely trying to keep her from exciting the whole herd."

"Well, I didn't know whether you knew it or not," Art responded with an injured air, "what with you being from the city and all."

"But why won't the other one allow her to climb on?" I asked.

"Because she's not in heat," he replied contemptuously. "Actually, the one that's in heat won't respond to anything but a bull," he added with a knowledgeable air, "but she don't mind letting any bull in the vicinity know what she has on her mind."

"Aw, I'll bet that I can get aboard one of them," I boasted. "Watch me ride that big, red heifer."

Then, accelerating from a walking start to full speed in five long steps, I slapped both hands on either side of her tailbone and landed astride the middle of her back. The startled animal immediately leaped sideways and deposited me solidly on my hip pockets in the soft, green grass.

"Ho-ho-ho!" Art shouted delightedly. "You'll never make it on the rodeo circuit. Wye, even a heifer kin throw you."

I got gingerly to my feet, cautiously tested the rear end of my fuselage, and limped slowly toward him. Then, with challenging eyes, I muttered, "I don't see you doing any better."

"Wye, anybody kin do better than that," he retorted.

Suddenly the animal in heat tried to mount still another member of the herd. "Hmm," Art mumbled. "Yore uncle ought to take that cow over to Bill's place. He's got a real good bull."

Then, for some inexplicable animal reason, the heifer tried to mount one of the other cows.

"Why did she decide to get into the act?" I asked irritably. "Surely she's not in heat, too."

"Naw," he responded, "she don't even know what she's doing. All she knows is that all the other cows are doin' it, so she wants to be in style. But watch me show you how to ride her rodeo style."

Then he hurtled forward, made a belated leap at the rear of the animal, failed to gain sufficient altitude, and collapsed against the heifer's rump with both arms desperately grasping at its sleek hips. Meanwhile, the startled animal tensed and then leaped forward. Simultaneously, there was a deep, explosive sound from its tail end as its rear legs kicked backward, leaving Art sprawled on the grass.

I hurried toward him to determine if he had been seriously hurt by the stupid, boyish prank. However, upon viewing his condition, I quickly applied my brakes. He got slowly to his feet with an incredulous expression and began to wipe with both hands at the greenish-brown mess that covered the front of his faded, blue overalls all of the way up to the bib.

His befuddled eyes appeared to be so numb with shock and so full of embarrassment that I became convulsed with laughter. Collapsing onto the grass,

I rolled from side to side in the ecstasy of my merriment. In fact, I almost "came a cropper," too. Fortunately, Art's suddenly hopeful expression reminded me that much of the pasture was contaminated in a like manner. Under the circumstances that begrimed character would never have warned me of the hazard, so I hurriedly scrambled to my feet. Meanwhile, he turned like a zombie with his dripping hands outstretched and stalked to the edge of the stream, which had spread out over the particularly flat area to a depth of about six inches.

After several minutes he had restored a modicum of cleanliness to the overalls by splashing handfuls of water against the front of them. Therefore, I really shouldn't have done what I did, but a little green demon screamed for me to do it, so I slipped up behind him and sent him sprawling face down into the water.

Fortunately for me, Art was a rather passive individual, or I might have ended up with a bloody nose. But the act was more of a success than a debacle, because the atmosphere was so hot and dry that the overalls were both relatively clean and dry by the time that we arrived at the corral. In fact, the climate in that midcontinent area is something that every living human being should avoid.

After opening the corral gate and allowing the cows to find their stalls in the barn, we fed them their rations of corn, milked them, and ran the milk through the cream separator. From the creamery we went to the feed lot, threw some alfalfa hay into the bunkers, and spread some corn in the feeders for the fattening steers. Since the horses had already been fed and turned loose into the pasture, we were then free to return to our respective homes.

Meanwhile, back at the ranch, my older sister must have been bending our mother's ear with her interpretation of what had transpired in the pasture, because there was a distinct air of disapproval in the air when I returned. As usual, Alice had been burying her snub nose in a book, so she could not have been less concerned about what was happening out on the range. But I wouldn't have asked her what had transpired during my absence even if she had known, because I had merely participated in an escapade that was typical of most normal, agile, red-blooded farm boys of thirteen.

As the scene faded from my mind, my eyes turned toward the car window and detected a few glimmers of light from several small buildings; then there was nothing but the black night. Meanwhile, the engineer sounded a long, mournful greeting to the members of that lonely outpost.

Once more my mind retrieved a subsequent scene from the same era of the past. Just before school resumed in the autumn, my uncle and I cut several milk cows from his herd and drove them to the small corral at the old homestead, where he informed me that the twenty-year-old saddle pony, which I had been riding, was to be included in the transfer. We also unloaded some corn into the weathered, old barn's small granary and piled some alfalfa hay alongside the wooden rails of the corral fence. Then the addition of a few hogs and some chickens completed the ranch scene.

From that time on I fed the livestock, maintained their various living quarters, walked 1 1/2 miles to school five days of each week, and worked at my uncle's ranch every Saturday. For a boy who had just turned fourteen, I was busier than the average bear.

My uncle's feedlot was in constant need of repairs because of the lunging and rooting activities of the livestock. Not only were the fat steers constantly breaking down bunkers, feeders, and rail fences, but the more agile hogs were forever rooting out holes under the hog-wire fences and escaping through them.

While we were filling in one of those holes, my uncle, who was the strong, silent type, erupted in a fit of frustration and suddenly shouted, "I don't see why these *bleepty-bleep* dumb hawgs have to keep diggin' their way out! Shorely they kin see there's more to eat in the lot than there is outside it during this time of the year."

"Maybe they are just typical Americans who love their freedom," I suggested.

My uncle didn't have much of a sense of humor, so I should have stopped there. Despite the skeptical glance that he tossed at me, I foolishly continued: "Besides, if they are so dumb, how come we can't keep them contained?"

It took almost a minute for the import of the question to penetrate both of our thick skulls, and it must have dawned on us simultaneously, because my eyes glanced up from my shovel toward the man's blue eyes just as they caught fire. Since I fully expected him to swing his shovel at me, I tensed for instant flight. Fortunately, he must have realized that the remark was not directed exclusively to him, so he cooled off quickly. But he never mentioned "*bleepty-bleep* dumb hawgs" again, not in my presence anyway.

One evening about dusk I opened the corral gate at the old homestead and allowed the milk cows to find their respective stalls in the barn, where their rations of corn were already in the feed boxes. Since the open barn door didn't dispel much of the darkness in the structure, I lighted a kerosene lantern and placed it on the straw-covered, earthen floor so I could see to locate the milk faucets.

The milking progressed in routine fashion until I got to the last animal, a large holstein, which was a particularly nervous and irritable critter. Furthermore, she had acquired a cut on one teat, probably from a stray strand of barbed wire. After carefully cleaning the appendages, I really should have applied some ointment to the damaged one; however, realizing that a call to the evening meal was imminent, I attempted to hurry the operation. That was my second mistake, since as soon as I squeezed the injured appendage, the creature switched her tail and savagely brought her right rear foot forward, propelling the pail against me and the stool. Not only did the kick upset me and the stool, but it spilled a large quantity of milk onto the earthen floor. Meanwhile, the empty milk pail rebounded from my left shin and caromed into the lantern. That was my first mistake, because a similar accident around the turn of the century is reputed to have started the great Chicago fire, so I should never have placed it there.

After hurriedly righting the lantern, I lifted it and placed its bail over a harness hook, where it should have been placed in the first place. Then I furiously and loudly described the critter's unlikely canine ancestors in lurid details clear back to the first generation. After carefully working some ointment into the wound, I substituted a clean milk pail and stubbornly returned to the task. She must have sensed that she had sinned, because she didn't kick again, but she did raise the same foot and switch her tail as a warning several times. I reacted appropriately by cautiously extracting just enough milk from that particular quadrant of the udder to preclude its becoming painfully gorged before the morning session. Then I applied some more ointment to the wound.

Next I looped the bails of the milk pails over other harness hooks and placed the wooden box against the opposite side of the five-foot-high wooden wall that separated the holstein's stall from the vacant one adjoining the far side of it. Just as I was about to release the animals from their stanchions and herd them into the corral, I decided to perform a rather urgent task, so I stepped into the vacant stall and prepared to relieve myself. Pausing in the act, I looked malevolently across the shoulder-high wall between the two stalls toward the holstein, impulsively stepped up onto the wooden box, and shot a spiteful stream across the wall onto the back of the animal, which moved about uneasily under the crude, unseemly barrage.

By chance, I glanced across the stall's wall toward the barn door just as my older sister ducked out of sight. No doubt she had come to inform me that the evening meal was awaiting my presence, since that was her part of the evening routine. From early childhood I had been taught to be modest, so I was appropriately embarrassed by the misadventure, but it never occurred to me that it could be misinterpreted for anything but what it was, even in the dim light afforded by the remote lantern.

By the time that I had washed up, the incident had faded from my mind, so I appeared at the dining table in relatively high spirits, since I had only to separate the cream from the milk after the meal. But I was greeted by a strange silence. Characteristically, my younger sister never spoke unless somebody spoke to her, so her silence was understandable, but my older sister and our mother were constantly exchanging the latest gossip; therefore, their silence was not so readily understandable. Of course, I quickly decided that it must be due to my inadvertent exposure; however, since it had been inadvertent, I chose to ignore their silence. Besides, the shadows in the barn had been so deep that my privacy had been almost assured.

About fifty years later I was employed in the Ground Support Equipment Group of one of the largest aerospace companies in the Los Angeles area. I had accepted the engineering position at a large downgrade in rating since only three more years of service with that particular company would qualify me for a company pension before being forced to retire at the age of sixty-five.

The group was located on the ground floor of an old aircraft hangar that had been converted into engineering offices. An adjacent group consisted of manufacturing support personnel, and many of them were anything but assets to our society. One of them, a big, buxom blonde was . . . well, leave it at gross and uncouth, for want of sufficient four-letter words to describe her adequately.

There were several sallies besides hers from that area during the time that I was forced to remain there to gain my goal, and one of them came in the form of an extended moo, to which there were several titters from the immediate vicinity surrounding me.

Some of my colleagues may have collaborated in the titters, because several of them were of a like caliber, but I was particularly shocked to overhear one of the less likely ones callously observe, "Yeah, they dig up practically everything when they investigate somebody for a security clearance."

My justifiable rage caused me literally to grind my teeth in frustration, because the government agency that investigated my background not only must have accepted unsubstantiated rumors, but it must have been instrumental in transmitting those rumors to the people in that manufacturing group, which, of course, constituted slander.

Slowly my thoughts returned to the there and then, as my eyes absently peered through the window at the shadowy landscape.

"That could be it," Pancho suggested.

"That could have been what Wilfred was referring to when he said, 'Albert, you are a terrible man,' " José volunteered. And I nodded.

Later I was to discover an even more obscene and equally fallacious claim against me, which may have been what he was referring to. Unfortunately, we little people have no weapons other than the pen with which to fight the claims of Big Brother.

Since the scenery was blanketed by darkness and there was only the remote hum of the train to entertain me, my thoughts momentarily returned to the scene in the club lounge wherein the man had tugged at his mate's sleeve as I passed. There had been so many similar incidents throughout my life, all of them totally unjustified. Then my memory automatically shifted to one that had occurred almost fifty years earlier.

The scene was set in the comfortable, nicely appointed living room of a home located in a small suburb of a midcontinent city. I was seated with three other people about a card table under the subdued light shed by a pair of floor lamps. Just after the mythical curtain was raised, a tall, handsome young woman opened a door in the far wall of the room and moved quietly across the deeply carpeted floor toward an open doorway that revealed the dim outlines of kitchen components.

"Hi, Ruth!" I called to her. "Who is the lucky fellow this evening?"

She paused momentarily and smiled superficially. "This time I happen to be going to a sort of sorority meeting," she replied. "Actually, it's a young business-women's meeting."

"Drive carefully, dear," interjected the mature, heavyset woman seated opposite me.

Meanwhile, the spare, elongated frame of the middle-aged man to my left was perched awkwardly on a straight-back chair. The man's lean legs were crossed, and his left arm was cocked akimbo while he studied the cards fanned out in his right hand. He glanced at Ruth and smiled fondly at her; then his eyes returned to the cards.

"Well," Ruth began undecidedly, "enjoy your pinochle game." Then she continued toward the kitchen door.

"Good night, Ruth," called the dark-haired young woman to my right. "I hope you enjoy the meeting."

Ruth's long strides had already carried her through the open doorway, but a remote "good night, all" drifted back into the room.

The big woman absently tucked a tendril of fading blonde hair into place, looked sharply toward the younger woman, and said, "You haven't lost any time from work during the last six months, have you?"

The younger woman's dark eyes turned toward the other woman's probing, light-blue eyes with a puzzled expression. "No," she finally replied, "not more than a day or two for an occasional migraine headache. Why?"

"Why don't we get on with the game!" the other man's deep tones interjected sharply, and his thin, dark moustache literally bristled at his mate.

She looked defiantly at him and set her fleshy jaws. Then, turning toward the other woman, she answered, "Well, just after your secret marriage to Al, the lady next door . . . ," and she paused to gesture toward one wall of the room before adding, "claimed that you were pregnant. But that can't be, because you don't look like you're pregnant."

The other woman was silent for several seconds; finally she murmured, "No, I wasn't pregnant then, and I'm not pregnant now." Then, glancing mischievously at me, she added, "At least I hope not, because we can't afford for me to become pregnant yet."

The older woman's eyes turned toward mine and widened perceptibly. Apparently the fury that had exploded within me must have boiled up into my eyes, so there was ample reason for her reaction, because the "lady next door" was my mother.

"That's why we were secretly married," I growled. "We couldn't afford all of the stupid rituals that go with getting married."

The other man turned scalding eyes on his mate and shouted, "Let's get on with the game!" Then he cast a sympathetic glance in my direction.

A knock at the compartment's door dissolved the scene, so I shook my head to clear it from my mind and called, "Enter!"

A trainman pushed the door open and asked, "Would yuh moind if Oy mide up the berths now?"

"No, of course not," I answered, rising and moving toward the doorway.

After he had completed the task, I had no alternative but to retire for the night. But my mind not only refused to retire; it refused to condemn me for never forgiving my mother for expressing her unfounded suspicions. In fact, I never looked upon her as my mother from that time on. Of course, I continued to serve her as a dutiful son, because my code demanded it of me, but the mother-son relationship was destroyed, and I suspect that she sensed it. Years later, when she passed away from the ravages of cancer, that numbness still prevailed within me, so I felt no compulsion to attend her funeral, which would have entailed only an eighteen-hundred-mile journey.

Some years later, when my older sister suffered the same fate, I felt the same numbness, because she, like my mother, had made similar mistakes. But when my younger sister was taken, I was literally devastated, so I had to be capable of "normal" human emotions.

If, during an investigation of my qualifications for a security clearance, Big Brother happened to pick up my mother's claim along with several other equally erroneous bits of gossip, then he should be greatly embarrassed by these revelations; that is, if he is capable of "normal" human emotions. A full five years passed before my daughter was born, so that would have been a record gestation period, indeed. Actually, my daughter was one of the few chosen firstborns in this iniquitous land of too many freedoms.

It was about two o'clock when Jerry entered the compartment and futilely attempted to visit the bathroom and crawl up to his pad without awakening me. As is so typical of such cases, I tossed and turned for some time while Jerry immediately began to saw logs. Shortly after finally dropping off, I was practically stood on my head by the most horrendous sounds that ever disturbed any man's slumbers. I instantly concluded that it couldn't have been the emergency brakes, because the train was rolling smoothly along at its usual rate. A quick peek around one edge of the blind revealed a sky full of stars, so it couldn't have been thunder. Then it began again: First came sounds like a plumber's helper in use, followed by gurgling and sucking sounds, like those of a swirling pool of water after the plumber's helper has done its bit. But a quick glance toward the bathroom verified that its door was closed. Furthermore, the sounds weren't coming from that direction; they were coming from directly overhead.

"Hmm," José sleepily mumbled. "Jerry must be very tired, indeed, because we've never heard any man snore like that before."

From above there were the sounds of tossing and turning; then one of the man's limbs tumbled over the edge of the berth and hung like some inanimate thing.

"Man, oh man!" José exclaimed. "Is that guy ever exhausted!"

Apparently the movement relieved the problem, because he breathed normally for a while. Then he dragged the inert limb over the edge of the berth and slumped into another supine position. He must have turned onto his back, because the snoring resumed in a big way. In fact, it grew so loud and strepitous that the entire compartment seemed to vibrate.

"Hey, guys!" ejaculated Pancho. "We better do something before the sonic frequencies of those snores reach the harmonic frequency of this car and derail the entire train."

Suddenly a strangling sound brought me into a sitting position. Simultaneously there must have been a similar reaction from above, because there was the sound of something solidly striking the ceiling, followed by an explosion, some gasps, and a very positive "*bleep!*" Then there were the sounds of a body turning and slumping onto the upper berth.

"He couldn't breathe, because he had swallowed his tongue," explained José, "so he jerked upright, bumped his head, explosively expelled his tongue, and gasped for air."

"If you're so *bleeped* smart, how do you explain the *bleep?*" countered Pancho.

"Aw, that's merely code for a four-letter word," replied José.

"The poor guy must have drunk too much beer," suggested Pancho.

"Naw!" retorted José. "How could he become so exhausted just sitting in the lounge drinking beer with two guys and a doll?"

"Maybe the guys decided to retire early," retorted Pancho, "so he and the. . . ."

"That's far enough!" I interjected.

"Well," Pancho persisted, "*irregardless* of what the problem was, be it too much beer or whatever, obviously the poor guy is critically out of condition."

I wasn't the only one in that compartment who could have done with a lot more sleep when the dawn's early light arrived, but I was the only one in that compartment who was up and ready to observe the train's entrance into the city of Perth. It was Kevin, the conductor, who finally got Jerry onto his feet, but it took three stops at the compartment to do it.

After I responded to his first knock, he looked speculatively at me and asked, "How is yoah mite doing this moahnin'?"

"I don't know," I replied. "But he hasn't shown any evidence of life yet." And I particularly noted the preoccupied if not amused expression that crept across the man's well-molded features.

"Will, we gotta git him up," he insisted. "The trine will be pullin' into the styshun in a whoile, and Oy have to cleah out all of the passingahs so that it kin be pulled on into the maintenance yahd."

"Okay," I muttered, despite the thought that suddenly I was jointly responsible for the big brute just because I happened to be his roommate. Nevertheless, I loudly called, "Hey, Jerry!" Then we waited, but the even breathing continued.

"Jerry!" Kevin called, but there was no response. The conductor stepped past me, reached up, and poked the big man's thigh. "Come on, moy man!" he shouted. "Roise and shoine."

"Huh?" Jerry grunted.

"Come on now," Kevin insisted. "Lit's git on with it."

"Ohhh!" Jerry moaned. "It can't be that time yet."

"Yis, it is," Kevin retorted. "Come on and git youahsilf outa theah."

"Okay, okay," Jerry agreed, "but can't you give me just five more minutes?"

Apparently Kevin considered that he had done his duty, since he stepped past me into the hallway. Then, turning about, he commanded, "Keep him movin'. Oy'll be back in a whoile to chick on him."

It's amazing how commanding even the descendants of British convicts can be, almost as commanding as if they were born to be field generals. But I've never been much of a follower. Furthermore, I've never relished being a leader either; therefore,

I suspect that I'm strictly a free spirit. Consequently, Jerry had progressed only as far as the ladder when Kevin returned.

"Come, come, moy man!" Kevin shouted. "The trine will be pulling into Perth viry soon now, and these berths ah not yit mide up."

"All right," Jerry responded, moving slowly down the ladder. "I'll be out of the way pretty soon."

But Kevin wasn't leaving anything to chance: He stood domineeringly at the open doorway while the man went about organizing himself. Meanwhile, I suggested, "There has been quite a change in the landscape since last evening."

"Yis, theah has been a big chinge," Kevin agreed. "Wistirn Austreyelia has a lot goin' foah it. Theah's some sheep just this soide of the boahdah, thin some grine; thin the land improves to the point wheah all koinds of fruits and veggies can be raised." He paused, peered at me, and added, "Keep yoah oys peeled, and you'll see numerous vineyards and wineries jist befoah the trine intahs the city. This cornah o' Wistirn Austreyelia is the gahdin spot o' the intoire country. In the spring theah ah woild flowahs all ovah the plice."

With that and with a tolerant, somewhat amused glance at Jerry, he dashed off—but not for long. He returned with another trainman, who set about restoring order to the compartment irrespective of the cost to Jerry.

"Whoy don't yuh do yoah bit in the lavat'ry, Jerry?" Kevin suggested. To me he added, "Meanwhoile, yuh kin tike a walk through the trine." From his attitude I saw that it wasn't really a suggestion; it was a command. So I followed him as far as the hallway. As previously stated, I'm not much of a follower.

After the maintenance man left, I strolled back into the compartment and assumed my usual position on the seat beside the window. Finally a somewhat refreshed Jerry pushed the lavatory door open and collapsed wearily on the other end of the seat.

"I'm sorry that I snored so loudly last night, Al," he apologized. "I hope that it didn't keep you awake."

"Don't worry about it," I said. Then, in an effort to change the subject and make conversation, I inquired, "What are your plans after we get into Perth?"

"I've been doing some thinking about that trip to Alice Springs," he replied, "but I don't like the thought of another two boring days on the train to Tarcoola; furthermore, there would be two more days to and from the springs."

"When do you have to return to Dallas?" I asked.

"I don't have to return," he replied. "However, if I don't return on schedule, I'll have to send a wire to the boss informing him that I won't be back for a while."

"Well, there's Darwin on the north coast," I suggested, "but you would have to travel by air, since there are no trains into that area. But if you went to Alice Springs, you might be able to travel overland from there to Darwin."

"Probably by camel caravan," he responded dryly. "I've pretty much decided to skip Alice Springs; besides, I suspect that Darwin would be too hot now. But the trip to Alice Springs wouldn't cost much, because I have a long-term rail pass."

"Then there's no good reason why you shouldn't see all of Australia," I ventured.

"I've seen about all of Australia I care to see," he admitted ruefully.

"How about Africa?" I asked.

"Naw," he drawled, "Africa is still too primitive to suit my tastes. If I were to go to any of the Third World nations, it would be one of the local ones, such as Malaysia or Taiwan."

"Taiwan might be nice," I suggested.

"It has become difficult for me to make a choice," he said. "I've been in forty-nine different countries, and I'm not ready to start repeating any of them yet."

"Wow!" I exclaimed. "Forty-nine different countries. Let's see, I've been in only six up to now."

"Well, I spent a lot of time in the air force," he reminded me, "and air force personnel usually travel quite a bit."

"So you did all of that traveling at my expense," I grumbled.

Following a smile he became lost in a preoccupied inspection of his hairy legs. After casually joining in the inspection, I mentally admitted that his shorts presented a relatively attractive physique, but such displays of human hair have never appealed to me. Of course, I've always viewed the matter differently when the hair was firmly lodged on one's head. Then I ruefully stroked the top of my head.

Old social practices are hard to shake regardless of how archaic they have become, so we shook hands in parting. To my mind, the meeting and parting closely compared to two ships that pass at sea: a brief recognition of another person's presence; then never do the twain meet. But I was unaware of how small the city of Perth would prove to be.

Later Kevin also stopped by to shake hands and wish me fair skies. Suddenly he seemed much less a field general and much more a very efficient and likable train master.

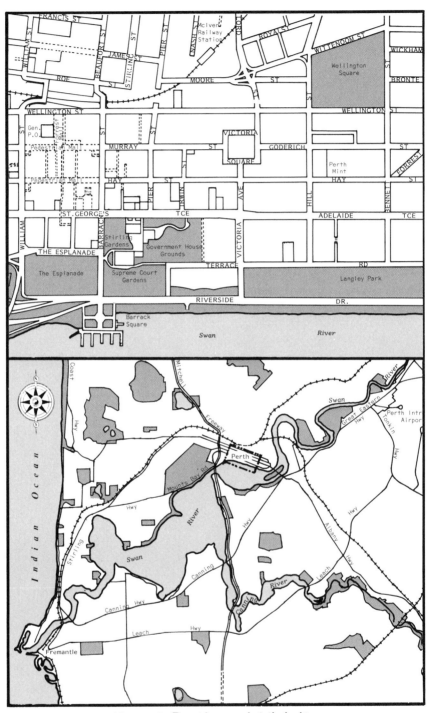

Map of Perth and Vicinity

24

Perth

The taxicab driver contended that the Paradise Hill Hotel, to which he proposed to convey me, was not far from the railroad station. Later I discovered that it was located on Constitution Street in the outermost limits of East Perth and about half a mile from the Swan River. Furthermore, it overlooked two local parks, a race track, and an ancient cemetery that must have received very little maintenance. Nevertheless, as he predicted, it proved to be a comfortable lodging place.

Actually, it wasn't far from the center of the city. In fact, early the following morning, shortly after breakfast in the third-floor dining room, I struck out for the city. From Constitution Street I turned left onto Trafalgar, continued for about one block to its intersection with Wittenoom Street, and crossed it to the corner of a somewhat cluttered but apparently vacant area covered by very dry grass and some rubble. There I came upon another early riser, a slender young man clad in a worn but sharply pressed, gray business suit.

As we were about to pass, I said, "Pardon me, sir, but can you direct me to a street that will take me into the heart of the city?" Then I stopped and looked expectantly at him as he came to a stop in front of me.

A vertical frown wrinkle formed in the middle of his forehead as he pondered the question and absently brushed a strand of straight, light-brown hair from his freckled brow. The frown faded away as he turned blue-gray eyes toward me and, in relatively dialect-free words, suggested, "If you'll accompany me for about two hundrid meters, I'll point out a spot where you can board a bus that'll take you dirictly to the city cintre."

"That'll be great," I said, "provided that it doesn't take you out of your way."

"It won't take me one stip out of my way," he insisted, "but lit's take this shortcut." Then he turned from the sidewalk onto a footpath that appeared to have been beaten hard by countless footfalls. "It cuts diagonally across the East Perth Old Cemetery," he added with a sweeping gesture toward the surrounding area as I followed him onto the path.

On closer inspection I saw that what had appeared to be a large expanse of neglected vacant property was, in fact, an ancient cemetery with dozens of headstones scattered about it. Some of the larger ones were still standing, but none exceeded a height of four feet, and few of them stood upright. Most of the graves had been marked by small, horizontally placed stones, any one of which could have been displaced or pilfered by capricious children, so the path may have crossed the remains of some of Perth's earliest settlers. As we followed the path's meandering course between the larger headstones, that possibility was supported by several inscriptions dating far back into the nineteenth century.

My observations were interrupted by my guide, who called back to me, "You are an American visiting Perth?"

"Yes," I answered.

Then he stopped, turned about, thrust a freckled right hand toward me, and said, "My name is Edward English."

"I'm fortunate to have encountered you, Ed," I said, responding to the firm handclasp and adding my name. "No doubt you are a resident of this fair city, so you must know something of its history and culture."

With a nod he murmured, "Perth was founded on the bank of the Swan River in eighteen twenty-nine, and it bears the name of a much older city in Scotland. It's one of Australia's loveliest cities. Even though Fremantle is bist located for a seaport, Perth is the hub through which most of the agricultural, construction, and mining businiss of this area flows. However, Fremantle is where the America's Cup sits." Then he cast a shy glance toward me as if attempting to determine whether his proud declaration had inadvertently damaged my American pride.

"Many of us Americans are glad that you Australians won that cup," I responded with a smile. "It was won fair and square despite the unethical practices employed by some of the Americans who competed for it. But how far is Fremantle from here?"

"About nineteen kilometers from the city cintre," he replied.

"Hmm," I mumbled whimsically. "That's a little over eleven miles, a bit far for an old man to walk."

"But there are all kinds of transportation to and from Fremantle," he protested.

"By that statement," I began with a smile, "you may have unintentionally exposed yourself to charges of being an accessory to a crime."

"Why so?" he countered with a puzzled expression.

After looking speculatively at him, I drolly answered, "It just occurred to me that since I'm so close to the America's Cup and since we Americans have been unable to retain it by any means, be they fair or foul, it would be a cinch for me to take a cab from here to Fremantle and steal it."

"You touch that beautiful cup, and you'll have iviry Aussie in the country on you," he warned me with a chuckle. Meanwhile, we veered left onto the sidewalk that paralleled Plain Street. "Are you in Perth on business?" he asked.

"No," I replied, "Perth happens to be my last chance to find a compatible place to spend the time remaining on my six-month visa."

"Perth is where you should spind it," he loyally insisted.

"It may be," I agreed.

"From here you can tour much of Wistirn Australia," he pointed out.

"I might tour some of it," I said. "More specifically, however, I'm looking for just a nice, quiet place where I can sit and do some writing."

"Oh, you're a writer!" he exclaimed. And from his expression I gathered that, in his opinion, my position on the totem pole had risen tremendously.

"I'm afraid that I don't really qualify as one yet," I regretfully admitted, "but I've done a lot of technical writing. Currently I'm considering writing a travelogue covering my trip around the world."

"Oh, that should be intiristin'!" he exclaimed with a rapt expression.

Meanwhile, both sides of my brain castigated me for overplaying the role in which fate had cast me. Nevertheless, I unintentionally continued to do so by adding, "Ed, if you have the time, please hold up a minute while I jot down your name, because I may want to inject some of our dialogue into the travelogue."

"I have plenty of time," he responded as we came to a stop.

After locating a folded sheet of typing paper and my mechanical pencil, I scribbled his name along the top of it. Then I inquired, "What do you do for a living, Ed?"

"I'm imployed by the Highway Departmint as a computer programmer in that building" he responded with a gesture toward the large, concrete structure on our left.

"How nice," I remarked, adding the information to his name. "It happens that we have similar backgrounds, because I spent some of the early part of my career as an engineer in the highway departments of three different American states. At that time, however, we were forced to use mechanical calculators in our work."

"Of course, electronic computers work many times faster than they did," he rejoined with a tolerant smile.

"No doubt," I granted, replacing the pencil and stowing the folded slip of paper. (Unfortunately, that paper must have slipped away into the Australian outback; consequently, I've been forced to substitute a name for the man, who behaved like a fine Australian gentleman.)

We resumed walking until Ed came to a stop at the point where the sidewalk intersected with one that paralleled Wellington Street.

"If you'll cross Willington to that far corner," he said, pointing to the objective, "almost any of the buses that stop there will take you to the city cintre, but the Rid Clipper will come along pritty soon, and it's free."

"Thank you for your courtesy, Ed," I muttered, holding forth my right hand.

"It was nothing," he protested, grasping the hand. "As you can see, I didn't have to go a stip out of my way." Turning a thumb toward the huge behemoth that towered over us, he added, "In fact, I'll be at my disk before you can board a bus."

After boarding it, I inadvertently allowed it to overshoot the bus stop at Victoria Square, but the next stop proved to be an even better point from which to begin the two-hour city walk displayed in the pamphlet *Your Guide to Perth & Its Attractions*. From the bus stop I strolled to Murray Street, turned left, and came upon the Post & Telecom Museum. Obviously it was too early in the day to gain admission to the museum, so I continued along Murray past the Old Fire Station and Morton Bay Fig and on to Victoria Square and St. Mary's Cathedral.

From the square I strolled along Victoria Avenue to Hay Street, turned right, and continued on past the Perth Central Fire Station and the Central Law Courts at the Irwin Street intersection to St. George's Hall. At Pier Street a left turn and another short walk netted me the Old Deanery and the Government House, which were located on opposite sides of St. George's Terrace. From there I backtracked alongside Stirling Gardens past Pier and Irwin Streets to the Perth Concert Hall. From the Concert Hall I followed a course across the gardens to Terrace Road, turned right along the road, and trudged all of the way to the Supreme Court and its gardens.

From the Supreme Court, a few more steps carried me across Barrack Street to the Weld Club in the city centre. After a look-see there, I continued along the Esplanade to the Allen Green Conservatory; then, for some unknown reason, except that it was on the guide's map, I returned to St. George's Terrace by way of Howard and turned toward the William Street intersection and the AMP Building. Somewhat farther along St. George's Terrace was The Cloisters, but I chose to omit The Barracks Arch, the Parliament House, and the Old Melbourne Hotel, which were located some distance beyond the limits of the city centre.

In the processes of my mental negotiations, I became disoriented, so I begged the pardon of a passing pedestrian and inquired, "Can you direct me to His Majesty's Theatre?"

"Yis," he replied. "Yuh'll foind it at the cornah of King and Hoy Straits."

After thanking the man, I found King Street and vainly searched its three-block length for an intersection with High Street. Finally I begged another pedestrian's pardon and confronted him with the same question.

"Yis," he replied, "It's the nixt one ovah." And he gestured in the direction from which I had just come.

Frowning deeply, I thanked him. Then, with a mind filled with question marks, I turned about and strolled toward the "nixt one ovah." As I had suspected, a street sign identified it as Hay Street. However, on the opposite corner of the intersection stood His Majesty's Theatre.

"Oh-ho!" Pancho silently screamed. "Now we know how to pronounce the word *hay* Aussie style."

"Humph," José silently grunted. "I knew that all the time."

I never did find London Court, but it may have been swallowed up by the London Court Mall, which was located between St. George's Terrace and Hay Street with Sherwood Court on one end and the Plaza Arcade on the other. From the London Court Mall I found my way to the Hay Street Mall and turned right into the Piccadilly Arcade, which terminated at Murray Street opposite the General Post Office (GPO). Since the GPO fronted on Forrest Place, I crossed Murray Street, entered the huge edifice, and mailed a small package to Fullerton, California.

After accomplishing that small task, I returned to the malls and arcades via the Carillon Centre and began a dispassionate tour of them. Actually, I had no intention of buying anything, but the displays of Australian, European, Asian, and Indonesian merchandise fascinated me. With the passage of time I acquired a pressing yen for a particular type of shop, but I was unable to locate one anywhere. Finally, out of sheer desperation, I decided to appeal to a young woman who was seated in an information booth at one end of the mall.

As I approached the booth, the young woman happened to glance across one shoulder of a matronly woman, who appeared to be requesting information from her, and the young woman's eyes literally clamped onto my bearded features. In fact, she must have been struck dumb by my sex appeal . . . or by something, because the older woman had to repeat her request before the young woman recovered her aplomb and smilingly apologized to her.

After the older woman moved on, I stepped in front of the young woman and immediately concluded that it could not have been my sex appeal that had attracted her attention, because her smile immediately froze as she coldly inquired, "What do you wish to know?"

"Where can I find a rest room?" I retorted. As usual, the request embarrassed me somewhat. In fact, it has always been my opinion that a few young men should be scattered among such booths to answer that type of question for us graduates of the old school.

Apparently she was familiar with such requests, because she leaned forward over the tiny counter and said, "There's one up those stairs." Meanwhile, she was pointing across the mall toward an opening in a wall that was shielded from the sun and the rain by a long, colorful canopy. (But that *canopy* wasn't related to my problem in any way.) "When you get to the top of the stairs," she added, "turn left and continue to the end of the hallway."

So far my mission had been successful, but there was one more card to be played. Upon arriving at the stairway, I quickly turned my head and glanced across one shoulder toward her. As I had suspected, she was staring intently at me, even though a shopper was standing in front of her requesting information.

"I can't determine the source of Al's power over these Australian women," Pancho interjected into my brain waves, "but he surely knocks them dead."

"Yeah," José responded, "like Jack the Ripper."

By the time that I had thoroughly toured the city centre, cashed some traveler's checks, and indulged in a Big Mac, much of the day had passed; nevertheless, I decided to venture farther afield. In the vicinity of William Street I found a bus station that stood alongside Wellington Street. According to a sign posted on one of its walls, there were four clipper buses, each identified by a different color, and each color served a different area of the city; therefore, since I had already patronized the free Red Clipper, I chose to board the equally free Green Clipper. By the time that the round trip was completed, the sun was sitting on the western horizon, so I boarded the first bus to Paradise Hill. Later I was to discover what a Paradise Hell that place could be.

Upon arriving at the inn, I decided to pay in advance for the next night's lodging, so I stepped into the lobby. Unfortunately, I had been preceded by a tall, slender man who appeared to be intent on consuming the entire staff's time, regardless of how many other guests were delayed. The conversation concerned some sort of a play that was to be presented at one of the theaters, possibly His Majesty's Theatre even.

At the instant of my entry, one of the two women behind the desk was inquiring, "Are you a member of the cast?"

"No," he replied, "I assist Laurie with directing the play, and I help coordinate and promote the entire production for her. Laurie is the director of the play, you know," he added with an unction that immediately set my porcelain caps on edge.

In fact, he spoke with such a theatrical flair that I found myself instantly hating him for no other reason. But it may have been my early association with some of the toughest little Canucks west of Hell's Kitchen that caused that reaction. Nevertheless, the man's highly effeminate gestures and his very affected pronunciations of some of the commonest words definitely qualified him as a full-fledged sissy in my book. He appeared to be clad for a dip in the pool, but the way he dramatically swept his terry-cloth robe about his thin, bony shoulders reminded me of some of Shakespeare's most wimpy characters. Possibly he was trying to emulate the appearance of Ben Hur, because the robe didn't extend to his knobby knees. In addition to the knobby knees and big, sandal-encased flat feet, there was another thing about the man that particularly irritated me: There wasn't one hair on his bony chest or his skinny, milk-white, softly muscled legs. As already reported, I despise displays of excessive hair with a passion; nevertheless, that man's carcass would have looked much better to me if it had been covered with a full coat of Neanderthal hair.

Apparently it was his policy to retire to the wings when he could no longer command center stage; consequently, when one of the women looked tentatively at me and inquired, "Can I help you?" he faded away like an old *trooper*—trouper, that is.

After paying for the coming night's lodging, I repaired to the tiny coffee shop that had come to my attention during trips to and from my room. Before entering it, I decided to case the joint through one of its large, plate-glass windows, but my view was obstructed by that tall, ungainly apparition in the swimming trunks and the terry-cloth robe. More and more that robe was beginning to remind me of the villain's cape in one of the silent movies that I had viewed with such fascination as a child. And there was a good reason for the impression, because that forty-five-year-old character was standing in front of the cashier's counter bending the tawny, shell-like ear of a little brunette beauty who probably had not yet seen twenty austral summers.

As I opened the glazed door, he was saying, "Yes, deah, it will be a lovely presentation. If you would like to see it, I'll get a complimentary ticket for you... just name the night. After the performance we might have a midnight snack in some very secluded and romantic spot."

The girl appeared to be fascinated by the character, the actor, and the promoter. From my point of view the man not only possessed a questionable character, but he was a bad actor and a very persistent promoter. In fact, that judgment momentarily induced me to consider entering the scene in the role of a white knight.

With dark eyes glued to the man's sharply chiseled, fair features, which were picturesquely outlined by long, carefully curled blond locks, the girl inquired, "How long will the play run?"

"It's scheduled for only a month, dahling," he replied, "but it has been so well received elsewheah that I'm shuah that our stay will be extended foah anothah month oah even moah."

The saccharin-sweet pseudo-Oxford accent so irritated my mental sensibilities that I involuntarily gritted my teeth and chipped a piece off of one of my porcelain caps, which, even though I'm quite familiar with the word *expectorate*, I promptly spit in the general direction of the Lothario's pedicured toenails.

Finally the mesmerized young woman noticed me; then, coyly looking up at the blond villain, she inquired, "Was there something in particular that you wanted?"

"What a stupid question!" Pancho growled so loudly that I suddenly found both pairs of eyes directed toward me. But those stares had to be happenstance, because I'm the only one who knows what erupts from the two sides of my brain—I hope.

"No, dahling," he responded to her question. "I'm merely touching all of the bases, so I'll be toddling along. Howevah, I'll be seeing you again very soon. That I promise."

Then, with a flourishing sweep of his robe, he exited through the left wing; well, call it the doorway, but I was of a mind to view his departure in the light of flitting away like Liberace if it were not for his obvious and obsessive interest in the entire female race.

Despite Lothario's exhilarating impact, the girl returned to earth promptly. "Now what can I do for you?" she inquired with a saucy glance from beneath dark eyelashes.

"Well, I'm not hungry enough to ride the elevator up to the dining room," I answered, "so what do you have that might whet a lagging appetite?"

"I have some very nice roast beef," she replied. "I could make a tasty sandwich for you from some of it."

After briefly pondering the suggestion, I admitted, "I'm not quite that hungry. What else do you have?"

"Actually, the roast beef is all that I have," she confessed, "but it's very good.

I'm sure I can make a nice sandwich from it that will tease your appetite."

She seemed to be so naive and so eager to please that I agreed, "Okay, make a small roast beef sandwich for me." Then, staring thoughtfully at the remnants within a clear, plastic pastry container that stood on the counter, I added, "And please include a piece of this chocolate cake in the order."

"See, your appetite has been teased, already," she suggested with a smile that literally exuded personality. "How about a cup of hot, freshly brewed coffee?"

"No," I replied with a smile. "Growing boys like me shouldn't drink coffee. But I would like a glass of cold milk."

While I selected the small table at the far end of the small dining area, the sandwich was assembled, placed on a plate, and delivered to me on a tray along with a glass of milk, some cutlery, and a plate bearing a slab of the cake. Obviously, the lass was proud of her expertise, and her dark eyes literally begged for my recognition of it.

"What a lovely sandwich!" I exclaimed. "And what a beautiful piece of cake!" I added belatedly. "Wye, I wouldn't have done as well if I had gone up to that fancy dining room."

Her delighted eyes glowed with pleasure. In fact, it appeared that I had made far more points with the lass in seconds than the much younger promoter had made in minutes. Momentarily I yearned to be even thirty years younger so that I could compete with that phony on even terms, not to win the girl, but to steal her away and protect her from that unscrupulous poacher.

Several minutes later I arose and strode to the counter with the empty glass in one hand and requested, "Will you please refill this glass? I used all of the milk to wash down that luscious sandwich."

"Of course, I'll get more milk for you," she replied, hurrying toward me with an outstretched hand. "But let me put it into a fresh glass." Setting the glass aside, she selected a fresh one from the back bar, swung the refrigerator door open, removed a container, and poured a stream of milk into the glass.

"The restaurants in my country have milk dispensers," I tactlessly observed. "All that one has to do is press the side of the glass against a chrome-plated lever, which actuates a valve that releases the milk through a spout into the glass."

"I suspect that most of our larger restaurants have similar devices," she murmured, "but since we have few requests for milk, we really don't need one."

"Your ancestors must have migrated from the Balkans to this country," I suggested, as she placed the newly filled glass in my extended hand.

"My family came from Greece," she said.

With a dip of my bald head, I said, "How fortunate for Australia." And, just before turning away, I was rewarded with another glowing smile.

I had almost finished the repast when a dark-haired young man pushed open the glazed door and entered the room. I assumed that he was the girl's boyfriend or at least a steady customer, because he immediately disappeared into the farthest reaches of the small kitchen with her. Furthermore, I overheard what I assumed to be the subdued tones of a private conversation. However, after I arose from the table and carried the tray of dishes to the counter, he hurriedly left but not before casting a searching glance in my direction.

"Thank you for bringing the dishes," the girl murmured from the opposite side of the counter, "but I could have picked them up."

"I had to come this way anyway," I muttered, as my eyes searched her features for familiar, telltale tokens of one of Big Brother's scores. Obviously, the sparkling personality had been subdued by the man's visit. Furthermore, her eyes no longer glowed, and when they met mine they veered uneasily away.

"Thank you for a brief respite from evil," I murmured obscurely. Then, turning about, I made my exit from the center of the stage.

"So Big Brother had to get into the act," Pancho suggested as I passed through the doorway.

"What stupid timing!" José exploded. "He should have come while that Lothario was dominating the scene. After all, he is the greatest threat that has entered that coffee shop this evening, unless Big Brother can be considered to be a more qualified candidate, and that's a very likely possibility."

After entering my room, I pulled the door closed and firmly informed them, "You guys be quiet for the next eight hours, because I don't want your stupid yammering to keep me awake all night."

Early the following morning I appeared in the third-floor dining room for breakfast. Since no hostess greeted me and since the entire area was obviously available to me, I selected a table alongside one of the windows in the long line of mullions overlooking the racetrack. But I wasn't the only early riser. Through the window I saw a lone horseman sitting astraddle of a sulky and the long, black tail of a dark-bay gelding. While the man was gently urging the horse along the oval track with occasional slaps of the reins against its back, another horseman, astraddle a similar assemblage, pulled onto the track through an opening in the white rail fence at the far end of the compound and gently urged his gray mare in the direction from which the bay gelding was trotting. Just before the two sulkies were about to meet, the horsemen pulled their steeds to a stop and engaged in a brief conversation.

Simultaneously, the kitchen door swung open, and the same heavyset, matronly woman who had served the previous breakfast to me slowly strolled through the opening. On seeing me, she swung in my direction and said, "Oy'm sorry, but the cook is lite this morning, so we'll have to wite until she arroives."

"I don't mind waiting," I murmured. "It's so quiet and peaceful up here that it's a pleasure to wait." With a gesture toward the two horsemen and their charges, I added, "Besides, I have some entertainment."

She moved closer to the window and looked down at the animated scene while one of the horsemen turned his steed around so that the two sulkies could travel side by side. "Yis," she murmured. "They ah out most iviry moahnin' about this toime exersoizin' theah hosses. Sometoimes theah ah a half-dozen of thim travelin' 'round that track."

We continued to pass the time with similar small talk until the sounds of hard, leather heels against one of the uncarpeted areas of the hardwood floor indicated that the cook might be arriving. Finally the rotund figure of another matronly woman swung around a far corner and headed toward the kitchen door.

Meanwhile, the waitress slowly strolled toward the same door and pushed it open for the oncoming woman, who paused in the opening, glanced at me, and directed some words to the waitress that I failed to hear.

But I did hear the waitress clearly say, "But he seems loike sich a noice man." Apparently the cook was opposed to that opinion because her eyes were flashing, and she was protesting to the waitress in loud whispers as the door swung closed on them.

"So we do run into a smart one once in a while," José ruminated.

"Of course, you are referring to the waitress," Pancho injected. "Unfortunately, there are so few of them."

"Yeah," José agreed. "Life would be so much more pleasant for us if people would only respond to that type of logic instead of responding to the unsubstantiated words of people who cannot possibly know what they are talking about."

When the kitchen finally began to function, the waitress returned to my table and inquired, "What stroikes yoah fancy this moahnin'?"

"Do you have some lean ham?" I asked.

"Will, Oy doubt that any of owah hams kin really be called lean," she responded with a chuckle.

Apparently the cook's words had not influenced the woman's opinion of me one iota, so I relaxed enough to join in the chuckle. "How about some sausages, a brace of fried eggs, and a few pieces of toast?" I asked.

"How would you loike the iggs?" she countered. And I told her.

After serving the meal, the waitress paused beside the table and asked, "Ah you plannin' to spind some toime in Perth?"

Typically, I cautiously stalled: "Well, I've given the matter considerable thought, because I really would like to stay awhile, but I suspect that I'll be moving on pretty soon."

"Ah you on a holidye?" she persisted.

I paused briefly and mentally reviewed the usage of the word *holiday* in both New Zealand and Australia as opposed to its use in America, where time off from employment is called a vacation. "No," I finally replied, "I'm on a trip around the world."

"Oh, how wonderful!" she exclaimed. "Oy wish Oy could do that."

"Some of it hasn't been that wonderful," I muttered darkly. "Some people can be so wrong, and some of those people deliberately go out of their way to create undeserved pain for others."

She fixed sympathetic eyes on mine. Then, moving a step closer, she lightly touched my left shoulder. "Oy suspect Oy know what you mean," she murmured, "but all of us encountah people loike that from toime to toime. Apparently they ah a breed apaht from noahmal people." Then she hurriedly stepped away as if she sensed that she had been guilty of an unintentional impropriety.

"What an astute observation!" I exclaimed. "Unfortunately, too many of those people find their way into professional careers and high political positions. Some of them have acquired overwhelming powers of which the average person has no knowledge whatsoever. For example, I have reason to know that in some respects the Big Brother described in George Orwell's book, *1984*, actually has existed for some time. With the advent of the electronic age he has become tremendously powerful and overbearing. So powerful, in fact, that more rational people may never be able to subdue him."

"I know," she murmured. Then, after a moment of silence, she added, "Even the thought of it mikes my blood run cold. In fact, it terrifoys me!" Then, with her head bowed in thought, she slowly moved toward the kitchen.

When I left the hotel, the morning was still young, so I followed the route through the Old Cemetery and along Plain Street to the bus stop on Wellington Street. After waiting a few minutes, I arbitrarily decided to walk to the city centre. At the far end of Wellington Square I turned left onto Hill Street and strolled along it as far as Hay Street; then, after crossing it, I turned right. On the near side of the Irwin Street intersection, I came upon the Pinnacle Travel Centre, which was located at street level in the corner of an imposing office building. After casing the joint, as Edward G. Robinson was prone to say, I entered it through the Irwin Street doorway, which proved to be the rear entrance of a rather nice office.

From behind a high counter an attractive, dark-haired young woman inquired, "Can I be of service to you, sir?"

"Possibly you can," I replied. "That is, if you are qualified to discuss a proposed travel itinerary through several countries where visas may or may not be required."

"What countries do you wish to visit?" she countered.

"I'm not sure," I confessed, "but the cities that I would like to visit are Jakarta, Singapore, Bangkok, and Colombo."

"Hmm," she mumbled, "I suspect you should be talking to Pat." After stepping from behind the counter, she paused as if in thought; then, turning toward me, she asked, "What is your name, please?" And I told her.

She led me to a flat-top desk that stood in the far corner of the room beside one of the large windows facing the Hay Street scene. A rather chubby, gray-haired woman of some sixty summers was busily presiding over it from a swivel chair.

When she looked up at us with alert, inquiring eyes, the brunette said, "Mister Terril, this is Pat Higgins." Then she turned her gaze on the gray-haired woman and added, "Pat, Mister Terril would like to discuss the visitor's requirements when traveling to several island and Asian cities."

"Please be seated, Mister Terril," Pat requested with a gesture toward the nearest of two upholstered armchairs standing in front of the desk. "What cities do you have in mind?"

After seating myself and repeating the names of the cities to her, I sat back in the chair and studied the nicely attired woman; meanwhile, she stared thoughtfully toward the busy street through the sparkling lenses of a pair of attractively decorated, metal-framed spectacles.

"Well, I don't perceive any problems in traveling to any of those cities," she finally concluded. "However, transportation to one or two of them may prove to be rather costly."

"Of course, cost is an important item," I admitted, "but I don't intend to let it interfere unless it gets completely out of reason."

"How soon would you like to leave?" she asked.

"As soon as feasible," I replied.

"Well, it'll take some time to put such a travel itinerary together," she murmured. "Would you like to make a tour of the city centre or do some window shopping for a while?"

"I'll do both," I replied, rising from the chair.

"Thank you for stopping in, Mister Terril," she called to me as I turned away. "Return in about one hour, and I should have everything organized for you."

After emerging from the travel agency onto the sidewalk along Hay Street, I turned left, paused at the Irwin Street curb, and cautiously assessed the traffic situation.

"Al!" shouted someone from within the oncoming crowd of pedestrians, and Jerry surged forth from the melee with his big right hand thrust toward me. "So you are still in town," he added, energetically shaking my right hand and pummeling my left shoulder. "I suspected that you would be long gone from Perth by now."

"Hi, Jerry," I responded to the friendly manhandler. "Actually, I'm in the process of arranging for my departure."

"With whom?" he countered. "I would like to find my way out of town, too."

"I just left the agency," I answered with a gesture across one shoulder toward the sign on Pinnacle's window.

He glanced at the sign and asked, "Where are you going?"

"At the moment my destinations are in limbo," I answered, "but I should know within the hour."

"Where are you staying?" he persisted.

"At the Paradise Hill Hotel," I answered. "It's sort of a motel located on the east side of town near the Swan River."

"We spent last night in a room at the Crown Hotel," he rejoined. "It was only twenty-six dollars, but it was miserable—cramped, hot, and no air-conditioning whatsoever."

"Oh, yeah, that's the one in the central part of the city that's in the process of being renovated," I responded with a glance across his shoulder toward the dark-haired man who hulked just beyond it. "Mine cost me thirty dollars, but it's equipped with an air conditioner; however, I didn't use it, because there was a cool breeze from the Swan River."

"We had breakfast at the hotel . . . ," he began.

"Undt a big, black cockroach come by our table," interjected the other man.

"Ugh!" I grunted. Then I drolly suggested, "Maybe it was just a very small aboriginal waitress."

"Huh?" he grunted. Then his eyes lighted up. "Oh, yah!" he shouted. "A vaitress vid skinny, black legs." And he laughed uproariously. The picture in my mind was not that amusing, but I was amused by the amusement that the other man had gained from his mental picture, whatever it was.

"By the way," I said, "some of this dialogue is beginning to sound like it should be included in my travelogue. Would you object to giving me your name after we get out of the way of all of these pedestrians?" And I reached into my pockets for the wherewithal to record it as we jointly moved to the corner of the building.

"I'm sorry, Al," Jerry interjected. "I should have introduced you two. Al, this is Al. He was on the train with us."

"Al what?" I countered. "Alastor, Allan, Alden . . . , or Algernon perhaps?"

Al leaned toward me and shouted "Albrecht!" into my right ear.

Fortunately that was the ear whose diaphragm had already been punctured, so it suffered no new damage, but my inner ear vibrated for several seconds after the onslaught.

Meanwhile, I was unable to spell the name, so I jotted the name "Albert" onto one of the margins of the pamphlet *Your Guide to Perth*.

"That isn't quite the way to spell it," Jerry objected in tactful tones.

"No!" Al resumed into the same ear. "Idt iss speldt *a-l-b-r-e-c-h-t!*"

"And your surname," I persisted. "We might as well get it all spelled correctly."

"*K-u-e-m-m-e-r-l-e*," he slowly and loudly spelled out for me.

"Wow!" I exclaimed. "That's quite a name. How do you pronounce it?"

"Kummerly," he and Jerry chorused.

"Hmm," I mumbled. "Just like it's spelled. Al Kummerly. The names are rather euphonious."

"Huh?" Al grunted.

"Where are you from, Al?" I countered.

"From by . . . ," he began and looked appealingly at Jerry.

"He's from a small place near Stuttgart," Jerry interceded. "By the way, Al, when will this book be published?"

"I plan to add my adventures in Australia to the two hundred twenty-three rough draft pages that I've written on New Zealand," I replied, "so it may take a year or more, including rewrites, depending on whether I add some details that I've deliberately omitted up to this point."

"That sounds logical," Jerry muttered.

"Vodt do you wride aboudt?" Al inquired.

"So far I've been describing scenery, cities, people, climates, and a few of my adventures," I answered. "Lately, however, I've been pondering the desirability of including some of my misadventures." Then, with a probing glance at Jerry, I added, "I strongly suspect that Jerry knows what I'm talking about, especially after what transpired during that two-day debacle on the train. Huh, Jerry?"

Jerry stared thoughtfully toward a distant point in the sunlit sky, nodded, and finally admitted, "I suspect that I know what you are talking about."

"In fact, the intrigues that I've encountered in Australia have been the worst ever," I resumed. "Never has Big Brother's presence been so evident, not even in the U.S."

"Is that so?" Jerry murmured thoughtfully.

"Maybe Australian bureaucrats are more domineering than those in other so-called democracies," I suggested.

Again Jerry nodded. "Somebody is probably out to make a name for himself," he suggested, "regardless of whom he hurts in the process." And I nodded.

"What's the title of this book?" he inquired. "I would like to read it when it comes out."

"That does it, Jerry!" I blurted. "That statement has finally convinced me that I should include the misadventures I've been omitting, so the book's title has suddenly changed from *Adventures of an American Abroad* to *Misadventures of an American Abroad.*

"Let me jot that down," Jerry suggested as he futilely searched through his pockets for writing materials.

"I'll make a note of it for you, Jerry," I volunteered, retrieving the required materials from a shirt pocket.

"Include your home address," he requested.

After complying, I said, "I certainly hope that you do read the book, Jerry, even though some of the misadventures may not particularly startle you after what happened on the train. They'll merely complement what you observed there." Meanwhile, the man maintained a tactful silence.

"With so much insight into the true state of affairs in so-called democracies," I resumed sarcastically, "you'll be better prepared to properly evaluate the glowing speeches of political candidates when they boast of the individual's freedom and civil rights under their democratic administrations."

"There's an awful lot of bombast and bull in every politician," Jerry muttered. "Most of that freedom bit is a lot of political hype, but it buys votes." After a pause, he stated, "On the train you mentioned an autobiography. What's the title of that?"

"So far I've been calling it *Saga of Defiance*," I answered, "but a friend has suggested that I call it *The Victim.*" The man's eyes contained a particularly understanding gleam as he silently nodded.

"By the way, where are those destinations in limbo located?" he asked.

After a glance toward Al's confused but alert eyes, I turned to Jerry and answered, "Right now, I'm considering flights to Jakarta, Singapore, Bangkok, and Colombo, which, respectively, are located in Indonesia, the Republic of Singapore, Thailand, and Sri Lanka. To my knowledge, none of those countries requires a visa, so I can enter any of them on my passport. Of course, I'll be spending some of the time en route determining whether what happened here continues to happen in those countries. Furthermore, time consumed by visits to such countries will allow the climate in Europe to warm up a bit before I arrive there."

"I've been considering a flight to Singapore, too," Jerry said. "However, as you know, I've also been thinking of stopping off in Brisbane, but the airline wants an arm and a leg for airfare. One thing for sure: I'm not going back to Sydney on that train. For another, I would have to put a hundred and forty-six dollars alongside my travelpass to do so; consequently, I'll pay the price to fly first, because I couldn't stand another boring trip across that arid plain."

"I can fly for nodding," Al interjected. "I got a ticket in Los Angeles vodt allows me to fly anyver as long as idt iss east or vest."

"And never the twain shall meet," I added with a fleeting glance at Jerry.

"No, nodt by twain," Al insisted earnestly. "By plane."

"That's amazing!" I exclaimed. "How much does such a ticket cost?"

"Yust elewen hundred and nineteen dollars," he replied.

"Wye, that's even less than bus fare for a trip around the equator," I marveled.

"It's fine as long as you can find enough airports in a direct east or west line," Jerry rejoined, "but when you have to fly north or south to get to a particular east or west destination, it probably costs a lot more." Meanwhile, Al cast confused eyes at each of us.

"I'm thinking of hooking up with one of the local tours to see this town," Jerry resumed on a new tack.

"Why don't you do it the economical way?" I countered.

"How iss dodt?" Al interjected.

"All you have to do is make a round trip on each of the colored clippers," I explained, "and you'll have seen much of the city for free."

"How iss dodt?" Al repeated.

"There are four bus routes, whose buses are identified by colors," I began, "and. . . ."

"And there's no charge to ride any of them," Jerry interposed.

"That's right," I said.

"I t'ink I ride dose buses," Al muttered.

"I suspect that I should make a quick trip to the GPO so that I can get back here in time to get the dope on my proposed travel itinerary," I observed pointedly.

"A qvik trip to vodt so that he kin git vodt on vodt?" Al inquired of Jerry with a confused expression.

"He wants to make a quick trip to the Government Post Office, after which he'll return here to receive certain information regarding air travel," Jerry interpreted with a gesture toward the agency.

"Ohhh!" Al exhaled slowly.

Then Jerry extended his hand and said, "Well, it has been nice talking to you again, Al. I think that we should keep in touch."

Al extended a hand and said, "Pleased to meet you, Al."

"Ditto, Al," I responded in kind. "However, during your flights east and west, be sure to keep them separated, because Rudyard Kipling claimed that they should never meet."

With a rare chuckle, Jerry turned away, and Al joined him.

Upon returning from the GPO to the travel agency, I found that Pat had left the office; however, one of the other agents led me to a comfortable armchair, where I waited almost one hour before she finally appeared. Meanwhile, I used the time to observe the other agents' reactions to my presence. Several times I surreptitiously detected the eyes of the dark-haired young woman studying me. Likewise, I noted several instances when the eyes of the only other male were fixed speculatively on me. In each case I chose to test them, and in each case the eyes quickly veered away from my gaze too quickly to conform to normal, disinterested reactions.

When Pat returned, I moved across the room to one of the armchairs in front of her desk.

"I'm sorry that I had to delay you, Mister Terril," she apologized.

"Don't be concerned about it," I murmured. "I used my time to a good advantage."

"Reading?" she speculated.

"No, just sitting here waiting and watching the animals," I replied. "This is quite an animal farm."

She did a quick double take and lowered her eyes from my steady scrutiny. "Well," she opened, "I've been able to get most of the information together on your proposed itinerary, but the flight to Jakarta will cost well over a thousand dollars."

"But Jakarta is located almost directly in line with the flight to Singapore," I protested.

"I know that," she rejoined, "but very few flights are scheduled from here to Jakarta, and none of them are by standard carriers; furthermore, you might have to wait weeks to get on a chartered flight."

"Okay," I began in decisive tones, "let's forget Jakarta."

"That will make it easier," she granted with a sigh of relief. "But Bangkok is a similar fly in the ointment."

"Okay," I said, "so we forget that one, too."

"Then you'll have only a flight directly from Perth to Singapore," she murmured.

"Plus a flight from Singapore to Colombo," I said. "Very likely the authorities in Singapore will require a ticket to my next destination as assurance that I won't be stranded in the Pearl of the Orient."

Since she neither affirmed nor denied the existence of such a requirement, I assumed that there was none. Nevertheless, I decided to allow the order to stand, because I would have to purchase a ticket in Singapore if I didn't purchase one in Perth. Subsequent developments would prove that to be a fortunate decision, indeed.

I was so absorbed in the problem that I failed to sense the hand on my shoulder until its fingers squeezed my sagging shoulder muscles.

"Oh-oh!" exclaimed José. "Finally Big Brother is taking Al into custody."

"On what grounds?" Pancho countered.

"Skip the stupid questions," insisted José. "Just call a lawyer."

But the argument between the incubi was stalled when familiar tones inquired, "How are you doing, Al?"

I glanced from the hand to Jerry's features and answered, "I suspect that we've just put a plan together. How are you doing?"

"I don't know yet," he answered. "We just arrived here to check on some flights." And he gestured toward the nearest high counter, where Al was engaged in a conversation with one of the other agents. "Well, good luck, Al," he added, moving toward the other Al.

"Good luck, Jerry," I muttered and redirected my attention to Pat.

After submitting payment for the tickets, I fixed a steady gaze on the woman's eyes and said, "While I was waiting, there were plenty of opportunities for me to observe the animals in this animal farm, and I've come to the conclusion that some sort of information concerning me must have been conveyed to them and, no doubt, to you as well."

Her uneasy eyes escaped from my gaze and took refuge in the forms, which her suddenly nervous fingers were attempting to separate. "No," she protested. "No one contacted anyone in this office."

"You can be of tremendous help to me if you'll cooperate with me just this once," I persisted. "You can't possibly comprehend how utterly futile it is to try to do battle with an unseen enemy when no one will help reveal him or his nefarious activities."

As if responding to an involuntary impulse, she paused in her scrambled efforts to separate the forms; then, almost reluctantly, she shook her head and repeated, "No one contacted anyone in this office." And she indicated no intention of checking with her staff to verify the claim, so I collected my quota of the tickets, wearily shook my head, and arose.

From the travel agency I thoughtfully strolled through several of the malls and found myself in the vicinity of the bus station, so I crossed Wellington Street to it just as a Red Clipper bus pulled alongside the concrete platform. After boarding it, I seated myself in a vacant seat located near the middle of the vehicle.

At the next stop my eyes detected Jerry's head among the throng of oncoming passengers. In fact, our eyes met simultaneously. Since he moved purposefully toward me, I arose and pointed toward the window seat.

"Apparently you've decided to see the city from the clippers," I said, "so I'll give you the advantage of the window."

"Yeah, after you mentioned them, it did seem like a good idea," Jerry admitted. After settling onto the seat, he asked, "Did you finally get your destinations out of limbo?"

"Yeah," I replied. "Late tomorrow afternoon I'm scheduled to leave for the Pearl of the Orient on Singapore Airlines."

"I haven't made up my mind where to go next or whether to go," he muttered. "But I have a strong inclination to continue traveling."

"Then you'll probably call Dallas and obtain an extension," I ventured.

"Probably," he said. "I love to travel. I suppose that I became hooked on it while in the air force."

"Up to three months ago I had been in just Canada, Cuba, and Mexico in addition to the U.S.," I said, "so this is my first long trip abroad."

After sitting in silence for a few minutes, Jerry said, "I surely hate the thought of having to spend another night in that hot hotel."

"Why don't you get off of the bus with me and take a look at my hotel?" I asked.

"Well," he began thoughtfully, "I'm already committed for tonight; besides, I'll probably be moving out of here right away, too."

Meanwhile, the man pulled at the lower seams of his shorts and spread his hairy legs over a bit more than his fair share of the seat, and I immediately resented the encroachment. Some psychologists will observe that I have a very taut tolerance range, but I could not care less. Nevertheless, in defense of the reaction, I believe that everyone should be entitled to a personal privacy range in any so-called free country, including Australia.

Suddenly I realized that the bus had stopped at Plain Street, so I hurriedly took leave of Jerry and surged toward the front door just as the bus lurched forward.

"Did yuh want Pline Strait?" inquired the middle-aged driver.

"Yes," I replied, "but the next stop will do just as well."

"Yuh should have stahted a bit earliah," he responded in mildly critical tones.

"I was talking to a friend, and I failed to note the stop in time," I murmured contritely.

"Aye, that's easy to do," he granted. "Howivah, Oy'll lit yuh off roight heah to sive yuh half a block."

"Thank you very much," I responded, lunging toward the slowly opening accordion doors on my left.

"Stop!" he screamed. And I came to a stop on the bottom step just as a car flashed past the opening. "Don't step out theah roight now," he commanded as I guiltily looked across one shoulder at him. "Don't ivah froightin me loike that agin, mite," he insisted. "Oy'm gittin' too old foah it. Besoides, Oy'm not supposed to stop heah. In fact, Oy could lose moy job ovah it."

"I'm sorry, mate!" I called to him as I stepped safely onto the pavement. "Thank you for saving my life!"

At the hotel I stepped into the lobby, and an unfamiliar set of nicely molded features met my eyes.

"Good evening," the relatively young woman greeted me in a familiar dialect. "How can I help you this evening?"

"Good evening," I responded with curious eyes. "I was hoping to purchase a map of the city in this office."

"I'm sorry, but we don't have any maps of the city," she replied.

"What part of the U.S. do you hail from?" I inquired.

"Oh, so you noticed," she responded with a wide smile.

"Yep, it's pretty obvious," I rejoined with a matching smile.

"I'm from San Diego," she answered.

"What is a pretty young thing from San Diego doing in Perth, Australia?" I asked.

"I really don't know," she murmured. "Apparently I'm just a crazy, mixed-up kid, because I not only came to Australia, but I married a Chinaman."

"Young lady, you really are a crazy, mixed-up kid!" I retorted before I realized how crass it sounded. But the smile in her eyes didn't fade, so I decided to drop the matter for the nonce and compensate for the unintentional rudeness later.

Since I had broken my fast at a rather early hour and had only a snack at midday, I decided to shower, don my sports attire, and splurge on a square meal. In this case it happened to possess four rough corners, or the equivalent thereof, so it proved to be a painful experience.

When I presented myself to the host in the hotel's third-floor dining room, the scene had not changed appreciably since breakfast. But there were some differences, such as the host, of course, and a lone waiter. Table linens had replaced the paper napkins, and there were a few more pieces of shining cutlery, some sparkling glasses, and a lighted candle on each of the several tables. Even though the only other guests consisted of a young couple, which had been seated alongside one of the windows overlooking the unlighted racetrack, I was seated at a table that was located in a dimly lighted area near the unmanned bar. With certain mental reservations, I arbitrarily concluded that my sports wear was the reason. Actually, I didn't give a *bleep*, because the view from one of those windows would have been obscured by darkness at best, but I was in a mood to be picky.

Since I was in a picky mood, as soon as the host left me alone with my thoughts, I began to regret wasting so much time *dressing* for dinner. In particular, I regretted the shower. Of course, I couldn't undo the shower, but I was seriously considering returning to my room and replacing the sports attire with my more comfortable jeans and windbreaker when, from out of nowhere, the waiter suddenly appeared at my left elbow. Of course, it was pretty dark in my area, so almost anything could have crept out of that murky background, including Big Brother, but I hadn't detected the presence of that critter—not yet anyway.

The relatively young waiter was slender to the point of emaciation, and he was clad in a dark suit that appeared to be black in the dim light. But the dim light didn't conceal his almost tangible obsequiousness, so I immediately typed him as a very nervous person who constantly lived in a state of constant fear verging on sheer panic.

In fact, one side of his mouth twitched nervously as he servilely inquired, "What can I serve you, sir?"

I glanced guiltily toward the still folded menu that lay before me on the table. Extending one hand to it, I asked, "What appears to be particularly appetizing this evening?"

"Will," the man stalled, "that dipinds lahgely on what one loikes, sir."

Obviously, the answer hit the center of the bull's eye. However, since I was in a picky mood, I responded, "True, but surely some of the dishes appear to be more appetizing than others." Then, fixing challenging eyes on his dark eyes, I added, "Don't they?"

Suddenly I was sorry that I had challenged him, because the whites of his eyes rolled up like those of a frightened horse, and he glanced speculatively toward the line of windows and mullions as if about to race toward one of the windows and plunge through it.

"Oy wouldn't know, sir," he responded with a gasp as he nervously wrung his hands. "Oy haven't served any of thim yit."

"Ohhh," I exhaled. Then, after a sympathetic glance at my victim, I said, "Well, I suppose that I'll have to gamble then."

As the waiter left with my order, a man and two women entered the room and approached the host, who greeted them with a familiarity that seemed to indicate a long-standing association. Even though the man's business suit was not formal, its dark-colored cloth seemed to fit the surroundings much better than the gray tweed of my sport jacket. Nevertheless, the host led the man and the stylishly attired women to a table located behind me and somewhat closer to the bar. Of course, that irritated me still more, because I had come to look upon that dimly lighted area as my private domain, a domain that was limited to social outcasts like me who possessed no formal dinner attire. But I was in a particularly picky mood.

Obviously, I could not determine decorously what was transpiring behind me, but it seemed that someone accepted an order for some drinks from the trio. In any case, drinks were eventually delivered. I didn't see who prepared and delivered them, but the service may have incorporated the joint efforts of the host and the waiter. I did observe the arrival of a second man, who was clad in a business suit that compared favorably with my gray-tweed sport jacket, but it wasn't tweed. Nevertheless, the host cordially greeted him and led him to the group behind me, which completed the foursome or, as previously stated, the four rough corners.

Frankly, I can't accurately describe what transpired during the next few minutes, but it seemed that either the host remained in the scene or the waiter reappeared in it, because a third man began to speak in low tones to the foursome. Apparently his subject matter must have been either very confidential or X-rated, because it was couched in extremely low tones. Whatever the theme, when his tones finally subsided, the group burst into ribald laughter; then the sound of his voice faded as if he were departing.

In slightly subdued tones, one of the two men then suggested, "That **would** be a very tender morsel, wouldn't it, Bernie?"

"Don't ask me," the other man retorted. "I don't know."

"You don't?" countered the other man in doubtful tones. "Come on, now, Bernie, fess up." After a brief pause he added, "What do you say, Clarice? Does he know?"

"I wouldn't tell if he did," a feminine voice retorted. And the retort was followed by a gale of laughter.

About that time the host reappeared and moved the group to the table that stood in the corner formed by the kitchen wall and the window wall. Of course, I was immediately irritated by the move, because the man in the informal, gray business suit was being granted a privilege that had been withheld from me and my gray sport coat. But I was in a particularly picky mood, of course.

Fortunately, the table was located in my line of sight; therefore, all that I had to do was to look up from my plate, and I could see what was transpiring between those ghouls, but I couldn't overhear any of the subsequent conversation, if that's what it should be called. Nevertheless, I maintained a strict vigil over them to determine whether their ongoing behavior would conform to the behavior patterns of some of the passengers whom I had encountered on a certain train during its journey through the southern part of Australia.

Only a few minutes had elapsed when the woman on the far side of the table turned her head and looked at me, but she quickly averted her eyes when they met my steady gaze. Several minutes later the woman on the near side of the table actually turned in her chair so that she could look back at me. But she also averted her eyes and returned to the attitude from which she should never have departed. But not once did either of the men look toward me. In fact, they seemed to be deliberately avoiding such attention.

"Has Big Brother committed another of his foul crimes?" inquired José.

"The evidence both before and after the fact appears to support such a conclusion," responded Pancho. With that opinion in my mind, I placed some bills on the check, arose, and moved thoughtfully toward the lift.

During the next morning I attempted to contact Henry Mercier by telephone several times and failed every time. Before leaving for the airport, I tried once more and failed, but I had kept my promise. Apparently the man was away on another field trip.

At the airport I found that, like New Zealand, Australia exacted a final rip-off of twenty dollars from each visitor prior to his departure, and it was euphemistically called a "departure tax."

"It was smart of the government to levy that tax before our departure," Pancho observed.

"Yeah," José agreed. "Some rebellious characters, like Al, might turn around and go home if the tax were levied upon arrival."

"I wonder what would have happened to us if he had refused to pay the tax,"

Pancho posed. "Do you suppose that the Aussie bureaucrats would store us in a cell at even greater cost to Australia?"

"Fortunately for us, he has already paid the tax," José remarked. "Otherwise he might try to determine the answer to that question."

After submitting my receipt for the tax, along with my ticket, and one piece of luggage to a ticket agent, I received the usual stubs and stowed them in my shirt pocket.

Since a large group of passengers choked the departure gate, I impatiently waited while several groups of passengers boarded the craft in accordance to specified blocks of seat numbers. Meanwhile, I noted the usual surreptitious glances from certain airport personnel. When the block bearing my seat number was called, I deliberately waited until most of the line had formed so that I would be located near but not at either end of it.

The line moved continuously until I arrived at the gate. After submitting my ticket to the man at the gate, I deliberately surged forward, but he placed a restraining hand on my right arm and motioned for me to wait. Meanwhile, I sensed the grim smile that touched one corner of my taut lips, but it wasn't a smile of amusement because the sequence had been repeated much too often during my flights across the scarred surface of this old globe to be amusing.

"Now you may go," the gatekeeper finally said, and, with my briefcase in hand, I again surged forward. "No, not you," he curtly advised the party behind me.

"It seems that they are deliberately trying to be as obvious as possible about the routine this time," suggested José.

"So it seems," concurred Pancho. "After all that we've had to endure during this tour, it'll be a great pleasure to shake the red dust of this continent from my feet."

"What on earth are you talking about?" José countered. "You don't have any feet."

"Make it our feet then," retorted his mate laconically.

Meanwhile, I strode across the endless tarmac toward the distant mobile stairway, where preceding passengers were slowly climbing toward the open doorway of the aircraft.

"Hey!" exclaimed Pancho. "Look at that fire engine on our right."

"And look at the bunch of firemen crowded around it," added José. "But why are they looking this way when they should be watching the mechanics fuel the aircraft?"

"How should I know?" countered Pancho. "But they do seem to be deliberately looking in our direction."

"There can be no doubt about it," insisted José. "In fact, the entire crew is looking this way."

Meanwhile, I glanced across one shoulder, and Pancho immediately observed, "Wye, there isn't another passenger within a hundred feet of us."

"Do you suppose that Big Brother has instructed those guys to give Al a special farewell party?" inquired José.

"It surely looks that way," replied Pancho. "If so, I surely hope that they don't say anything to Al when we pass them, because he has been very picky lately, and I, for one, don't want us to spend the rest of our lives on a chain gang in the outback."

"Me either," added José. "But the Australian branch of Big Brother's organization must have built up a tremendous hate during our brief stay. Apparently American mavericks aren't welcome down under."

"I don't see why," protested Pancho. "The Aussies are mavericks too."

"True," agreed José, "but no maverick likes to be defied by another maverick, especially when he senses that he may be in the wrong."

"If any one of those staring, leering characters makes a sound when we pass, we'll end up on that aforesaid chain gang," predicted Pancho with a whimper. "I sense that Al's in a mood to take on the entire rat pack."

After several seconds José exhaled a protracted, "Thank Allah! Nobody got out of line, so we made it."

BOOK 2

LANDS ABOVE THE EQUATOR

25

Perth to Singapore

As requested, I had been assigned to a window seat, but it proved to be located over the wing, so the only view would be wispy, white clouds until the craft reached its cruising altitude; then there would be only the wild blue yonder. After the strange send-off I was in a mood to attribute even the seat assignment to Big Brother and one of his Aussie minions. However, even though the act did seem to fit the pattern of what had been happening to me, I doubted that such was the case.

During most previous flights the seat adjacent to mine had been left vacant, so I wasn't surprised to note that the two seats on my left were still vacant when the maintenance crews began to pull away from the craft. I had just begun to anticipate a flight during which there would be plenty of space for me to sprawl in comfort when my eyes spotted a beautiful, young blonde strolling along the aisle in my direction. One can imagine my consternation and dismay when she paused at the first of **my** three seats and checked the seat numbers. Apparently two of them corresponded to the numbers on the seating passes in her hands, because she nodded absently and turned questioning eyes toward the matronly woman who had come to a stop behind her. In response to the woman's nod, the blonde slipped past the first seat and deposited her sylphlike form on the seat beside me. In the process she gently bumped against me, and I promptly pulled away to allow more space than her ticket really warranted. Meanwhile, she turned apologetic light-blue eyes toward me and smiled with full lips whose natural color had been enhanced only slightly by a matching lipstick. No cosmetics embellished her peaches-and-cream complexion. With a sad shake of my head, I asked myself, why couldn't this have happened to me when I was twenty-five? Suddenly I'm in *luv* at seventy-five.

After liftoff I studied the wispy clouds until they were no more. Then the wild blue yonder quickly bored me, so I resorted to a magazine for entertainment. Occasionally I overheard a subdued exchange of unfamiliar words from the direction of the two women; otherwise all was quiet on the eastern front. After reading everything of interest in the magazine, I closed and rested it on one thigh and again stared pensively through the window at the wild blue yonder. But that bored me even more quickly than it had the first time; therefore, out of sheer desperation, mind you, I decided that for just an instant I would feast my eyes on the ravishing beauty beside me, and I found the blue eyes fixed on the cover of my magazine.

"Would you like to read my magazine?" I volunteered involuntarily.

"No, dank you," she replied in a heavy accent, "I don't read English wery vell."

"What is your homeland?" I asked.

"*De* Netherlands," she replied.

"Oh, Holland," I murmured.

During the ensuing silence I absently tuned in while the two sides of my brain attempted to determine how the name Netherlands had been derived.

"Usually the word *nether* is used to indicate something that's lower, as in *netherworld*," observed José.

"But *netherworld* is just another word for *hell*," protested Pancho, "and that little lady is no devil. In fact, she's a veritable angel."

"In this case the word *nether* translates as *lower*," José patiently explained. "Consequently, the word *Netherlands* translates into *lowerlands*."

"That's the same as claiming that the Netherlands is hell," insisted Pancho, "and I won't have you implying that that beautiful little doll is from hell."

"I didn't imply anything of the kind," retorted José. "In fact, if you had half a brain, you would realize that in this case the word *lowerlands* relates to sea level, so the word *Netherlands* translates into lands lower than sea level. After all, no country has a lower average elevation than Holland."

"Okay, okay!" conceded Pancho. "But I **am** half a brain, you half-wit. Furthermore, hell has a lower average elevation than Holland."

"Cool it, guys!" I exclaimed inadvertently.

"*Wat?*" exhaled the beauty sharply with blue question marks in her eyes.

"Sorry, but I was thinking out loud," I explained inanely.

"*Ztinkin' uit luid?*" she countered with a shocked expression and another pair of blue question marks in her eyes.

"Well, that's not quite what I meant," I responded with an expression that must have been pained since it was painful.

After carefully studying my eyes as if trying to read the thoughts behind them, she said, "*Denken.*" Then, pointing a nicely tapered forefinger toward her smooth forehead as if questioning my sanity, she added, "*Luid.* You mean *denken uit luid. Ja?*" And I stared blankly at her. Actually I really should be forgiven for finally nodding, because the words did sound like thinking aloud, yah.

"At least she has learned how to say *ja*, and that's a step in the right direction," José observed while I silently redigested her words.

Meanwhile, the two women put their heads together, and more of the unfamiliar words were exchanged.

After the conversation terminated, the younger woman turned to me and inquired, "Are you English?"

"No, I'm an American," I replied.

"*Wat* city you *leven?*" she asked.

"I live near Los Angeles," I answered.

"Near Hollywood, too?" she persisted.

"Not far from Hollywood," I granted, mainly because I suspected that saying so might enhance my image in her eyes.

"*Wij* vould like to see Hollyvood," she announced, glancing at the other woman as if for affirmation. The older woman responded by leaning toward her and speaking rapidly in their native tongue. Then the proud beauty turned to me and, as if so instructed, formally stated, "My name iss Anja Coby, *en* dis iss my *moeder.*" Then, after offering a supple hand to me, she added, "*Wij leven* in Apeldoorn, Holland."

"I'm very pleased to know you, Anja," I responded with my heart in my eyes. After adding my name and place of residence, I belatedly bowed my head to her mother.

"Den you haff traveled far, too," Anja surmised.

"I've traveled halfway around the world," I admitted, "but I spent almost three months in New Zealand, so I've been en route for some time. While in New Zealand, I traveled with one of your countrymen throughout most of one day."

"*Wat* city vass he from?" she inquired.

"I'm sorry," I confessed. "I can't recall the name at this time, but it was a big city."

"Amsterdam?" she countered with questioning eyes.

"That's the one!" I exclaimed.

"*Het* iss our biggest city," she murmured.

"He described many of the engineering problems associated with the Ooster-schelde Barrier," I resumed. "Very likely when it's completed, it will be recognized as the greatest engineering feat of all time."

"*Het willen* be vun of *de* mos costly vuns also," she observed with a critical air.

"So you are on your way back to the Netherlands," I suggested.

Nodding absently, she asked, "*Whaahreen* you boundt?"

"Singapore," I answered.

"Oh!" she burst forth with a delighted smile. "*Wij* wisited Singapore before wij come to Australia. *Het* wass a *waar* int'restin' wisit."

"Perhaps you can recommend a hotel in Singapore then," I speculated.

After pondering for a while, she turned to the other woman and conversed briefly with her. Then the other woman leaned toward me and said, "*Wij* stayed at *de* Step-in Hotel, *welk* iss on Bencoolen Street."

"Are its rates reasonable?" I inquired.

She turned questioning blue eyes toward Anja, who joined her in another conference. Finally Anja turned to me and announced, "My *moeder* say *dat de* rates are reasonable, but dondt use *de* dining room, because *de* food iss *niet goed en de* cost iss—should I say, high?"

"Thank you for the information," I said. "For want of any other possibilities, I'll stop there this evening, but I'll dine elsewhere."

The older woman leaned forward again and said, "*Wij* vent to a. . . ." Then she looked appealingly at her daughter.

"Grocery store," Anja substituted.

Energetically nodding her graying reddish-blonde curls, the woman resumed: "*Wij* purchase *brood en kaas, en wij maken* sandwiches."

Anja appeared to be somewhat embarrassed by the revelation of their frugality, so I hurriedly stated, "One has to resort to such devices, because all of the hotels and restaurants are geared to rip off us unwary travelers."

The two women fixed confused stares on each other. Then they launched another conference in their language. Finally Anja turned toward me and inquired, "*Wat* do *de woord* rip off mean?" Following a thoughtful study of the words, I involuntarily started.

"Did you actually employ those crude words while conversing with these highly cultured and refined ladies, Al?" José inquired incredulously.

"Yes, he did," Pancho answered for me. "Now it's up to us to clean up his act."

Finally, with their help, I replied, "The word is a colloquial expression that means to take unfair advantage of someone."

Once more, the women huddled and conferred. Upon emerging from the conference, the older woman directed her attention to me and said, "*Dan* you intended to say dat *een* has to resort to such dewices because *de* hotels *en* restaurants are vaiting to seduce us, *ja*?"

"Well, it sums up to something like that," I reluctantly admitted. And the two women sagely nodded their heads in unison.

After that exchange I was grateful for the ensuing silence, which endured until the "Fasten Seat Belts" sign flicked on. Then the two women exchanged a few words in their language and set their seats for the impact of the upcoming landing.

Meanwhile, Pancho whimsically stated, "*Een hebben* to agree dat *de* reports aboudt *de* parsimony of *de* Dutch people hass *niet* been owerstated."

After the aircraft had rolled to a stop and most of the passengers had deplaned, I arose and followed the two women into the aisle. There, switching the briefcase to my left hand, I accepted the outstretched hand of the older woman.

"You *willen* enchoy Singapore," she insisted.

"I hope so," I responded doubtfully. "May the remainder of your flight home be a smooth one."

"Dondt forget *de* name of *de* hotel," Anja warned me as she extended her hand.

"I won't," I promised. "That is, I won't if I can remember where I placed the paper on which its name is noted."

She chuckled unsurely, so I assumed that, like so many other people, she was not fully convinced that my words were intended to be humorous.

Meanwhile, Pancho observed, "Handshakes are for men, Al. You should have offered to trade it for a kiss."

"Fortunately, he didn't do it!" interjected José. "It might have been too much for him. At his age he should resign himself to just looking at two lips. In this case, Dutch *tulips*."

"Did he squeeze her soft hand a second time as a token of his admiration?" Pancho inquired.

"No, he didn't," José replied, "because I warned him that it might bring on a heart attack or a stroke."

"What the hey!" Pancho protested. "He doesn't want to live forever, and. . . ."

"Maybe not, but I do," injected José succinctly.

Singapore

A Hindu cab driver helped me load my luggage into the trunk of his vehicle; then he asked, "Where do you wish to go, sir?"

"Let's stop at the Step-in Hotel on Bencoolen Street," I replied.

"Have you been to Singapore before, sir?" he inquired, as we crawled into the vehicle.

After staring thoughtfully at the greasy band of his cap for a moment, I cautiously replied, "I haven't been here recently." That was only part of the truth, of course, but I wasn't about to provide an open opportunity for him to crisscross the city to a hotel that might be around the corner, so my implied knowledge of the city was intended as a deterrent.

"A new hotel, called the Strand, is located beside the Step-in," he informed me. "Perhaps you would prefer the newer one."

"Perhaps so," I conceded, "but let's stop at the Step-in first."

Silence prevailed until the brightly lighted marquee of the Strand Hotel loomed ahead. "The Strand is new," he reminded me, "and its rates are low."

"Let's turn into that upcoming driveway and see what the Step-in has to offer," I suggested.

True, it was an old hotel, and its facade was singularly unimpressive when compared to the new but garish front of the Strand. Nevertheless, I ignored the driver's last sales pitch for the Strand, so we unloaded the luggage. Then I paid the fare and tipped him.

"I'll wait awhile in case you decide to go to the Strand," he called to me, as I headed toward the entrance of the hotel.

"This one looks okay to me," I called back to him.

After entering the dimly lighted lobby, I found that a relatively small desk had been set into an *L* on my left. A middle-aged Caucasian couple stood at attention behind it, so I stopped in front of it, lowered the luggage onto the thinly carpeted floor, and asked, "What will a single cost me?"

Both pairs of eyes stared coldly at me, but it was the woman who frigidly replied, "Fifty-two dollars." And it was her attitude more than the rate that turned me off.

"Thank you," I murmured; then, picking up the luggage, I retraced my steps.

"That's much more than the Cobys were charged," Pancho ruminated.

"And that woman certainly acted as if she recognized Al," José chimed in. "Consequently, Big Brother must have preceded us."

"If so," Pancho resumed, "that's only one of many such instances when we may have been charged more than the going rate because of Big Brother's detrimental influence."

"Are they full up?" a voice called from the dimly lighted driveway.

Turning toward its source, I beheld the driver standing patiently beside his vehicle. "No," I replied, "they wanted too much money, so I've decided to go to the Strand."

"I'll take you," he insisted, hurrying toward me.

"No!" I objected, as he tugged at the heavy suitcase. "It's just a few steps, so I'll walk."

"It's such a short distance that I'll take you at no charge," he responded.

That really excited my suspicions: a cab driver who would voluntarily provide any service whatsoever for no charge? That would have created doubts in the most indifferent of minds. But he had already loaded the luggage, so I resigned myself to my fate and climbed into the vehicle.

After adeptly swinging the cab from the driveway onto the adjacent one, he brought it to a stop beneath the ornate porte cochere of the Strand Hotel. Quickly scrambling out of the vehicle, he retrieved the bags from the trunk before I could intervene. Then he made a rather obvious display of carrying both of them into the brightly lighted lobby. But he paid dearly for it, because his back remained bent in the shape of an S-curve long after he lowered them to the floor and accepted the dollar bill that I ruefully tendered to him.

"The greedy lout," José muttered, as I moved toward the long, ornate desk. "Not only did he accept a tip for a trip of one hundred feet that he promised for free, but, by delivering us to these vultures, he's probably clipping us for another ten percent of the upcoming hotel bill."

One of two young and very pretty oriental women greeted me from behind the desk with a good evening.

"Good evening," I repeated. "What's your rate for a single?"

"Fifty-two dollars," she replied in very neat English.

I winced, but I was in no mood to submit to another carnivorous cab driver, so I withdrew my wallet and counted out fifty-two dollars from the Singapore currency that I had acquired at the airport bank.

After the young woman picked up the bills, she looked directly into my eyes and said, "A one-hundred-dollar security deposit is also required." Even I sensed the intensity of my amazed stare, but she held steady under it.

"No, there isn't," I growled, reaching for the bills.

"Doreen," a voice called from beyond the long desk. And, as our eyes gyrated toward its source, I was amazed by the tableau.

An elderly, cross-eyed Chinaman lounged in shirtsleeves on a rickety, straight-back chair, which was precariously tilted back against the wall, and the front of his soiled, white shirt protruded like the pot belly of an overweight Buddha. His wrinkled, threadbare trousers must have been selected to fit his spindly legs, because, even though both the top button and the belt buckle had been freed, they could extend up only as far as the bulbous paunch. Obvious wrinkles in the gray fabric were stretched tautly over his thin thighs. From his knees, however, they flowed freely to the point where they terminated midway of skinny, hairless calves, which were only partially shielded by the crumpled tops of once-white cotton socks. The socks had been stuffed into scuffed, black shoes that appeared to have never been touched by either brush or polish. When our eyes focused on him, he shook his head imperatively at Doreen.

When my gaze returned to her, I swear that I heard a frustrated meow like that of a Siamese cat that I once had the misfortune to know. Furthermore, her eyes reminded me of those of the Siamese cat when, turning them spitefully on me, she literally spit, "Well, okay."

After a few deft scratches of a ballpoint pen, she presented to me a card that had been folded in the middle to reveal the name of the hotel, the city, and the words *Identification Card*, below which my name was inscribed. Then she handed a room key to a young Hindu man whose casual attire didn't even begin to identify him as a bellboy. Before we moved toward the elevator, I looked sharply at the cross-eyed Chinaman and found that he had lapsed into deep meditation or into a deep whatever it is that those stoic Orientals indulge in while their almond-shaped eyes are peering blindly into nothingness.

As I followed the so-called bellboy toward the elevator, a silent voice from left field suggested, "I wonder if that cross-eyed Buddha gets his wires crossed when he meditates."

"Possibly," granted a silent voice from right field. "But I'm more interested in what was behind that China doll's security pitch."

"Yeah," the other field agreed. "What about that? What could that little minx and the cross-eyed Chinaman hope to gain from an uncalled-for security deposit?"

"I don't know," irritably retorted the one from right field. "After all, it was my question. But Al didn't buy it for one second."

From a quick study of the lobby, I concluded that not only was the design lacking in artistry, but short shrift should be granted to both the materials and the workmanship employed in its construction.

I tipped the Hindu for taking charge of my luggage and for opening the door of the room, both of which I was fully capable of doing with relative ease. After his departure, I cased my hard-won domain.

It was typically if not fairly well planned, but the workmanship was atrocious:

The tiles in the bathroom didn't fit properly, the plumbing constantly dripped water, the doors had not been properly fitted to their openings, and the door casings had not been precisely mitered and fitted. For a new structure, its current condition scarcely equaled that of various thirty-year-old hotels in which I had dwelt momentarily. Nevertheless, I didn't intend to allow that to disturb my sleep. And it didn't.

Even though the next morning arrived on Sunday, I arose early, performed a salaam before the shower, emerged from my room, and found my way to the porte cochere, where I roused a sleeping cab driver and instructed him to take me on a short tour of the city.

In general, it looked a lot like many of the Western cities that I had seen, but that was before the populace had begun to infiltrate the streets. In fact, I may have missed much of the flavor of Chinatown by touring it so early in the day. However, the flavor of Saint Andrew's Cathedral, as well as the Supreme Court and Parliament House, could scarcely have been improved by the presence of the largely Chinese populace and a few confused tourists. But the presence of an oriental populace probably would have added some zest to the scenes of two contrasting temples: the Chinese Thian Hock Keng Temple and the Sri Mariamman Hindu place of worship, both of which are located in Chinatown (even though the latter could easily have been set in Little India). And that time of day definitely was not the time to visit The Raffles Hotel, the city's most renowned hotel. There, it is reported that late at night the ghosts of Somerset Maugham and Noel Coward still return by sky sleds or magic carpets to romp through its ancient halls from time to time.

The cab eventually entered one of the main thoroughfares and paused long enough at a traffic light for me to study the surrounding structures. A substantial pedestrians' overpass provided access from the sidewalks to a large Holiday Inn on one side of the thoroughfare and to a large shopping center on the opposite side.

"Let's go back to the Strand Hotel," I suggested to the driver. "I've suddenly decided to remove my luggage from that mail drop and check it into the Holiday Inn. That way, if I have to stay overnight, I'll be set; if I get a flight out, I can pick up my luggage and go directly to the airport."

"As you wish, sir," murmured the middle-aged Caucasian.

After I set my luggage on the carpet in front of the long desk in the lobby of the Strand, a Siamese cat, similar to Doreen, checked me out. In the process, she subjected me to several studious stares, so I assumed that Big Brother must have communicated with her if not with Doreen. Nevertheless, she treated me with the greatest courtesy, which may have been due to the influence of her consistently courteous heritage. In particular, she carefully pointed out to me that, since there had been no outgoing telephone calls, my bill had been paid in full as of the previous evening, and she even pointed out to me where it was indicated on the receipt. At the time I wondered if the cross-eyed Chinaman may have inadvertently, if not deliberately, crossed previous guests, who had, in turn, complained to the authorities. And I wondered whether the efforts of the checkout cat were intended to avoid repeating what may have been an economically painful incident, painful to the Chinaman, that is.

After checking my luggage and acquiring a light breakfast at the Holiday Inn, I left the inn and climbed the wide stairs to the overpass, whose far end deposited me on the second level of the huge shopping mall. Architecturally, I found that it had been treated somewhat like several of the American shopping malls that I had seen. It differed in that, besides typical shops, it housed several businesses, such as insurance companies, branch banks, airlines, and travel agencies. Escalators were the principal medium of communication between the different levels.

While I was studying a directory posted on a huge column near the foot of an escalator, a young Hindu man approached me and said, "Pardon me, sir, but I can be of great service in guiding you through the intricacies of this complex. Where do you wish to go, specifically? Just tell me, and I'll take you there."

I turned away from the directory and looked incredulously at a man who was about my height but much, much thinner. "Why should I require a guide when this directory instructs me where to find what I'm searching for?" I inquired.

Apparently he had encountered that type of response before, because his lips smiled benignly while his dark eyes coolly studied me. "Obviously you are unfamiliar with this complex," he replied, "or you would not be referring to its directory. Not only can I interpret the directory for you, but I will lead you directly to the company that you wish to contact."

The man's command of English both amazed and antagonized me, so much so, in fact, that I suddenly sensed a compulsion to set him back on his heels. So I retorted, "Why should I engage you for a task that I'm fully capable of accomplishing by myself? Besides, I understand English very well."

"True, you may successfully interpret the directions," he granted, "but searching out the business of your choice may prove to be more difficult than you anticipate. I can assist you immeasurably in locating that business. In fact, I can save enough of your valuable time to compensate many times over for my small stipend."

"Thank you for your offer," I responded aloofly, turning toward the escalator, "but I'll try to make do on my own."

"If you change your mind, you'll likely find me here," he called after me. "If not, I will return shortly."

As the escalator carried me upward, Pancho callously observed, "That Hindu's command of the English language surely made Al sound like a man with two left tongues."

"That expression is supposed to be 'like a man with two left feet,' you idiot," José injected acidly.

"How can a man with two left feet even speak?" Pancho countered even more acidly.

"With his tongue and lips, of course, you idiot," was the instant response.

Eventually I reluctantly admitted to myself that the Hindu had been correct in his assessment of the intricacies of the complex. Some of the travel agencies that I sought must have been deliberately hidden, and the skill with which they had been hidden must have taxed even the most devious of the most oriental of oriental minds. Unfortunately, after locating the offices, I found that only one of them, American Express, was open for business. Apparently the Sabbath was being observed by many of Singapore's wide variety of religious groups.

The travel agency proved to be manned almost exclusively by young Chinese women; that is, if *manned* can be successfully applied in such a case. Choosing the path of least resistance, I approached the nearest agent, who was seated behind a small desk.

"May I assist you?" she inquired in impeccable English.

"Can you fix me up with a ticket from Colombo, Sri Lanka, to Athens, Greece?" I asked.

"Please be seated, and I will see what I can do for you," she responded with a gesture toward a nearby armchair.

After we settled several details, such as the travel class and the time of departure, I fully expected to see her pull an abacus from a desk drawer to calculate the cost, but she resorted to the small electronic computer that stood atop one end of her desk.

Finally she looked up at me from the computer's display screen and said, "That amounts to eleven hundred dollars."

"It does!" I exclaimed with an incredulous occidental stare to which she responded with a stoic oriental stare. Finally I added, "It seems that I should see if that price can be improved on."

"As you wish," she murmured.

Unfortunately, while arising to depart, I ignored her smug expression, but I vividly recalled it after futilely attempting to find any other travel agencies open for business. When I returned to purchase the ticket, her expression was still smug, and that also should have given me pause, but I blundered on.

"Surely a company as big as American Express would never deal unethically," suggested José as I strolled across the overpass with the ticket tucked in my shirt pocket.

"It strikes me as odd that the price turned out to be an even eleven hundred bucks," observed Pancho.

The exchanges stopped until I paused beside a newsstand and read the headlines on one of Singapore's newspapers.

"Overcharging by travel agencies to be investigated!" José screamed. "Do you suppose that we've been had?"

"According to that headline, we should be doing some investigating, too," insisted Pancho.

Obstreperously, José insisted, "Naw, we can file a complaint in any American Express office, and all excessive charges will be refunded."

With that thought in mind, I paused in the lobby of the Holiday Inn and picked up a pamphlet that touted a number of sightseeing tours. Since high noon was approaching, I repaired to the Terrace to study it while ingesting some of the tropical goodies that the restaurant featured. But it was not by chance that, shortly after I had been seated at a table, I observed the Chinese table captain in the process of discussing someone in my immediate vicinity with my Chinese waitress, and the only other diners in my immediate vicinity consisted of a woman and two small children.

The pamphlet contained several tantalizing suggestions, including a tour of the scenic east coast. Not only did it describe the delights of a visit to the Buddhist Temple of a Thousand Lights, but it provided a colorful picture of it. In turn, it suggested that the victim compare that temple with the neighboring Dragon Mountain Temple adorned with a rich variety of Chinese deities. It also mentioned a tour of the Changi Prison of World War II fame. But I had never heard of the prison, so I chose to pass up the tour.

Since the tour of the Jurong Bird Park included a visit to the Chinese Gardens, it briefly attracted my attention. According to the pamphlet, the gardens, which emulate the Summer Palace in Beijing, consist of graceful courtyards, pavilions, and pagodas amidst weeping willows and lotus ponds. It rated the Jurong Bird Park as one of the world's best and claimed that its inhabitants include such exotic species as Antarctic penguins, birds of paradise, Australian emus, and Spanish flamingos. It also claimed that the entire bird population amounts to some seven thousand. Even so, my attention continued on to the next suggestion.

Trips to Malacca covered from one to four days at costs ranging from $65 to $220, but I was not in the mood to tarry that long. Then, on an impulse, I paid seventeen Singapore dollars to an attractive young Chinese woman for a round trip to Johore (Johore Bahru), the southernmost town in Malaysia. Since I failed to record her name, I will identify her as Mei-ling, because she is a prominent figure in my next misadventure.

Shortly before departure time Mei-ling circulated among the tourists, most of whom were scattered about the large lobby of the inn, and distributed small cards to them along with instructions for their completion. Minutes before the bus was scheduled to arrive, she collected the tourists into a group and led it to the concrete steps at the entrance of the inn, where she carefully inspected each of the cards. The members of the group, mostly Caucasians, ranged from a youthful couple to several old-timers in my age bracket, and they appeared to be from the four corners of this apparently flat earth.

After everybody was aboard the vehicle, Mei-ling stationed herself at the front of it and stated, "Make very sure that your card is readily available, because you won't be allowed to pass into Malaysia without it. Furthermore, don't misplace or lose it after we cross the border, because the authorities are very strict. In fact, without it, they won't allow you to return. Believe me, you have never really lived until you have spent a night in one of those border jails, so protect your entry card as if your life depends on it."

After the bus finally lurched ahead, it pursued a circuitous route through what must have been one of the seamier parts of the city. It paused briefly at the approach to a causeway while Mei-ling cleared up some emigration matters with a country-man clad in a neat, beige-colored uniform. Then it rolled down the ramp onto a straight causeway that conveyed it about one mile in a northerly direction with the Strait of Malacca on the right and the South China Sea on the left.

Johore

Several hundred feet beyond the end of the causeway the bus came to a stop. In accordance with Mei-ling's instructions, we tourists filed out of the vehicle and formed a line extending from the bus to the first of several windows in the wall of a small, wood-frame structure. After Mei-ling cleared up some matters with one of the brown-skinned immigration officials, who was clad in a wrinkled, poorly fitted, brown uniform, the line slowly advanced.

Upon arriving at one of the windows, I found that the small cubicle beyond it contained a small, brown-skinned man. After appraising my entry card with a bored air, he glanced at my open passport long enough to find the next available space, stamped it, and waved me on. Apparently such is the security practiced by border patrols over most of the world, except that of Australia.

After the passengers reboarded the bus, Mei-ling counted them. "Okay!" she then shouted to the driver. Releasing the brakes, he guided the cumbersome vehicle along several hundred yards of a roughly paved, two-lane thoroughfare that meandered between an assortment of scattered shacks and small, wood-frame buildings.

Meanwhile, Mei-ling announced, "Johore Bahru is the southernmost town in Malaysia, so it is the gateway to this country for people who are traveling from Singapore to the Malay Peninsula. We will first stop at the Sultan's Palace Grounds, which overlook the Straits of Johore."

The stop consumed about twenty minutes, during which we tourists traipsed across the meagerly maintained greensward with Mei-ling, who pointed out and identified several of the tropical plants and shrubberies. Even though she claimed that the sultan was a man of enormous wealth, in my not-too-humble opinion he could have used that wealth to a much better advantage in the design and construction of his Moorish-style, stucco palace with its huge, red-tile roof.

While trudging back across the lawn toward the bus, we came upon a trio of Malaysian youths who were hawking photographs of the palace and its grounds. Coming to a stop at the shoulder of one buyer, I caught a glimpse of one of the obscure and poorly printed photographs, so I declined a request to purchase some similar items.

We next stopped at the Sultan Abu Bakar Mosque, which also was a Moorish-style structure, but it had been constructed entirely of wooden timbers and wide boards. Since none of them had ever been protected from the elements, the wood had weathered to a dark-gray color. Nevertheless, it was a rather artistic effect that added to instead of detracting from the appearance of the octagonal structure. In fact, the walls blended well with the weathered shingles on the triangular segments of the octagonal roof. Very likely the tropical climate was responsible for the large doorways centered on several of the walls, since they must have provided excellent cross-ventilation. The wood-plank floors of both the main structure and the wide platform that surrounded it were raised about four feet above the terrain. Centered on each of the large doorways was a wide, wood-plank stairway that extended from the hard-packed earth to the top of the surrounding platform. To one side of the structure was a relatively small parking lot, where a faded, gray Volvo sedan stood alongside a shiny Rolls-Royce limousine.

I was surprised to see two women strolling toward the mosque, and I was even more surprised to see the sandals that lined one set of its wooden plank steps. Even though it was Sunday, it had never occurred to me that either the Mohammedans or the Buddhists might conduct their religious ceremonies on the Christians' day of worship. However, I was aware that certain religious sects, such as devout Muslims, conduct religious services much more frequently than do even the most devout Christians. As a consequence of that knowledge, I watched with interest as the two oncoming worshipers stopped at the first step, removed their sandals, and placed them neatly at the end of a line of similar footwear. After carefully adjusting their dark clothing, they silently stole on bare feet across the platform into the dim, somber enclosure and seated themselves among others of their kind on the worn, wooden floor.

Mei-ling assembled her charges at the first of the same set of steps employed by the latecomers. Then in low tones she pointed out several of the visually apparent details of the structure and its surroundings. Meanwhile, the resonant tones of a woman's voice droned flatly from a remote point within the dim interior, while I, for one, suspected that its owner was not only the owner of the shiny Rolls-Royce but a member of the sultan's family. I would have liked to have learned more about that speaker and her audience, but Mei-ling was already leading us back to the bus.

The bus next traveled over several poorly surfaced roads and came to a stop alongside a relatively small, wood-frame structure with a low gable roof, which seemed to fit into the pamphlet's description of the Kain Singket Cottage Industry. I joined the other tourists in a trek through its open doorway into a large room that had been created by partially removing the walls of three much smaller rooms. In each of the three cul-de-sacs formed by the partial walls, a brown-skinned woman labored over a loom, each of a slightly different design from the others. High on the walls hung several different products exemplifying both design and workmanship. Apparently visitors were expected to evince interest in the items and to purchase those that appealed to them, but none of the Malaysian women made any sales pitches. In fact, the ever-alert Mei-ling did more to generate interest in the products among her charges than did the entire resident personnel, but the residents may have been confronted by a language barrier.

While several of us were grouped about the largest of the looms, Mei-ling stated, "This equipment is used to weave fine tapestries. Often the designs are so intricate and the threads so compactly drawn that it takes several months to manufacture one complete tapestry."

Then she turned to the operator, who was seated on a wooden bench in front of the equipment, and made a query in words whose phonetics were unfamiliar to me, and the operator responded with similar phonetics.

Redirecting her attention to the group, Mei-ling said, "I am in error about the time. It often takes up to a year to weave one of those fine tapestries."

"How much do they cost?" inquired a member of the group.

"Up to two thousand dollars," she replied promptly.

Immediately, José silently observed, "In U.S. dollars that would be a mere pittance for an annual income."

"But those are Singapore dollars," rejoined Pancho, "so knock off about a third of that pittance."

At even those bargain basement rates there appeared to be no takers for the products, so we moved along to the next, somewhat smaller frame. After pointing out one of the colorful sarongs that were displayed on a nearby wall, Mei-ling discussed its price with a member of the group and drew a blank. Then she became involved in a discussion with the operator, who appeared to be the manager of the industry. Like Mei-ling, she was of small stature but about five years older, and her skin was a light-tan color. Momentarily their conversation appeared to drift into small talk; that is, if small talk is incorporated in that particular Indonesian language. Nevertheless, during the ensuing conversation, Mei-ling's dark eyes met mine briefly while they were absently sweeping the group. Then she leaned a bit closer to the other woman and spoke rapidly for several seconds. Meanwhile, the listener's dark eyes raised from an absent inspection of the fabric in the loom and met mine at the same instant that Mei-ling's eyes focused on them. Instantly both pairs of eyes were averted.

"Oh-ho!" José silently shouted. "Now we are being exposed to ridicule as far from home base as Johore, Malaysia."

"But that exchange can't be used as evidence," Pancho protested. "It's based on just an opinion gained from previous experience, and that would never stand up in a court of law."

"True," José granted, "but how else would you interpret those reactions to Al's counterstare?"

After a brief pause Pancho admitted, "Without doubt it was common gossip that must have derived from Big Brother's cohorts."

"Uh-huh," José silently grunted. "But how does an American go about suing a citizen of Singapore for slandering him to a Malaysian citizen in Johore?"

"Forget it!" retorted Pancho.

After we returned to the bus, it conveyed us past several typical Malay kampongs, which Mei-ling claimed depicted the rural life-style of some of the people. It also stopped at a Muslim cemetery so that we could view it and a royal mausoleum, but the memory of that Chinese woman in the act of passing misinformation to that Malaysian woman had been burned into my mind; consequently, I had lost interest in the tour, so I remained on the bus and pondered.

My mental preoccupation with the scene at the cottage may have been the reason that I could find neither my passport nor the entry card when we arrived at the border. Unfortunately, I had not thought to search for them before I came under the stern scrutiny of one of the inspectors, so I fumbled futilely through the pockets of my jacket and trousers for them. But the ever alert Mei-ling may have saved me from a night in the border jail, because it was she who detected them in my shirt pocket and pointed them out to me. I really don't know which I resented most: her pointing up my absent-mindedness and stupidity or her act at the cottage.

During the return trip the bus stopped at the Kranji War Memorial, which commemorates the twenty-four thousand Singapore people who died in World War II, but I remained in the vehicle and brooded over a current war. Obviously, there are worse fates than death in this vale of tears.

En route from that point to the inn, the bus swung from the highway into a small demonstration plot, where a mere stripling demonstrated how a rubber tree is tapped to yield its latex. Shortly after the youth cut the diagonal groove in the rubber tree's bark, a few drops of the grayish-white liquid emerged from the fresh wound and slowly flowed down into a small aluminum cup that had been suspended beneath its lower end.

From the plot the bus traveled several blocks through the city and finally deposited us at the curb in front of the Holiday Inn. After collecting my luggage, I placed it aboard a cab and instructed the driver to deliver me to the international airport.

At the airport I found the area around the Airlanka ticket counter to be swarming with small, dark-eyed, brown-skinned men. They had been organized into lines, but even the shortest line was almost fifty feet long, so I ruefully carried my luggage to the end of it. In passing alongside it, I absently noticed the interest of a tan-skinned couple whose members appeared to be qualified senior citizens. Seconds after I set the two bags down, the duo moved from several positions ahead of me to a position directly behind me.

While I was puzzling over the deliberate sacrifice, the male member of the combination muttered, "Quite a crowd, eh?"

I turned about to determine whether the words actually had been addressed to me and found a pair of dark eyes peering intently up at my eyes from beneath jet-black eyebrows that contrasted sharply with the man's gray hair. "Yes, it is," I agreed. "However, you must not be a resident of Sri Lanka, because you speak English like an Englishman."

A pleased smile spread across his relatively smooth, light-brown features. "We used to live in Sri Lanka," he said, "but we've been living in London for the last fifteen years. However, you don't speak like an Englishman."

"I'm not English," I admitted. "My home is located near Los Angeles, California."

"How nice," interjected the small, dark-eyed woman at his side.

"Our name is Brown," the man interposed with an outstretched hand. "Mine is Thomas Brown, and this is my wife."

"I'm glad to know you, Mister Brown," I responded, extending my hand. "And I'm pleased to make your acquaintance, madam," I added with just a token of a bow to the lady.

An awkward silence followed; therefore, to keep the conversation going, I asked, "How do you like London as a place to live?"

Suddenly Brown's eyes seemed to be trying to penetrate the mind behind my eyes and determine what ulterior meaning might lie behind that perfectly innocent question.

"We like the people," he finally murmured.

"We love London," chimed the square little woman.

Both of my brain's protégés leaped onto the almost defensive responses and silently protested that my question related only to the climate and the locale, not to racial discrimination.

"Where are you bound?" he asked.

"To Colombo," I replied.

Once more the man fixed his eyes penetratingly on mine. "There may be some things about Sri Lanka that you may not like," he said. "However, I'm not saying that they can't change back."

"Are you implying that its economy has backslid since it obtained its freedom from the British?" I inquired.

With a nod he added, "I fear that the people of Sri Lanka are not yet ready to govern themselves. There is so much internal strife, especially from the Tamils. In fact, the political infighting and constant skirmishes could result in the country being taken over by India, and that would be much worse than when it was under the British thumb."

"Why would India want Sri Lanka?" I asked. "Doesn't it have enough economic problems without acquiring even more?"

"The Tamils originated in India," he replied, "so India's prime minister may use that as an excuse to take over the entire island."

The line of ticket seekers had been maneuvered into the shape of a *U* with one end at the last ticket counter and the other one swung around past it, so my new-found friends and I could look directly along the line of ticket agents. Since my much taller figure stood out in that line of little people, the nearest agent noticed it and fixed thoughtful eyes on me. I immediately mistook his reaction to be typical of one of Big Brother's minions, which it could have been, of course. Nevertheless, in response to my next exploratory glance, he beckoned to me, but the act so confused me that I turned away and pondered various likely reasons for it.

Meanwhile, a similar exploratory glance toward my friends revealed a pair of rather curious expressions, which appeared to indicate that they also had observed the man's gesture. Suddenly I suspected that the agent was inviting me to bypass all of those little people. Furthermore, I suspected that my so-called friends were aware of the practice of favoring passengers with lighter skins, so they had clustered close to me, hoping to ride along on my coattails, so to speak—write, that is.

A second exploratory glance toward the agent netted another beckoning gesture, but something within me abruptly rebelled at such a practice, so I turned away and stared stolidly at the far wall. Minutes later I felt a gentle tap on one shoulder. Turning about, I beheld the relatively tall, tan-skinned agent who had beckoned to me.

"Please come with me," he requested.

I reached down for the handle of the suitcase, but the agent had already picked it up, so I picked up the briefcase and followed him to a point within about six feet of the ticket counter. There he tapped the shoulder of a small, brown-skinned man, who passively stepped backward as if habitually responding to many years of such unspoken demands.

"You shouldn't have to wait in line so long," the agent explained to me with a smile. Then, lowering the suitcase beside me, he returned to his post.

"Thank you," I called to him, but my heart wasn't in the words.

Looking back into the dark eyes of the little man, I sensed a strong impulse to apologize to him for being an unwilling part of the unfair maneuver, but I couldn't find the words; besides, he probably wouldn't have understood them. Then he smiled shyly at me, and my heart broke into little pieces.

After verifying the flight and checking my luggage, I went in search of the appropriate boarding gate. Fanned out in it I found several hardwood benches, so I seated myself at the end of one of them and studied the other passengers as they straggled past the check-in gate. Most of them were small, brown-skinned men who arbitrarily seated themselves on remotely located benches. Meanwhile, I was literally confronted by a young Caucasian couple who took up a position opposite mine. Shortly a middle-aged Caucasian woman deliberately seated herself beside the young Caucasian woman. Minutes later a middle-aged Caucasian couple seated themselves within a few feet of me. Then a tall, elderly Caucasian man seated himself just beyond them. That group was to comprise the white passengers who would board the wide-bodied jet. And all of them had arbitrarily collected about me, apparently because I was white.

Finally my slightly less than brown-skinned friends strolled past the check-in gate and paused to survey the available seating space. As soon as their eyes detected my bearded features, they ignored the ample seating space available among the other brown-skinned people and headed toward the so-called elite.

As soon as the little woman plumped herself down beside me, she said, "Well, you certainly made good time."

"Yes," I muttered, "but there are some things about the Orient that I don't fully understand."

"Things in this part of the world are vastly different from our part of the world," Brown leaned forward and interjected from just beyond her.

"Yes," I repeated, "but there also are some things in our part of the world that I don't fully understand."

"It takes time to change some things," he volunteered philosophically.

"Yes," I repeated, "but I wonder if those changes will be for the better."

Apparently my obscure philosophy confused my listeners, because they lapsed into a silence that endured until, via the PA system, the smooth tones of a man's voice invited us to board the aircraft.

"Well, I hope that you enjoy your visit in Sri Lanka," Brown said, arising and offering his hand. As I arose and accepted it, he repeated, "There may be some things that you won't like about the country." Then he added, "But there are good things about it, too, so be a little tolerant of the bad things and enjoy all of the good things."

"That's a pretty good philosophy," I said. Then with a stiff little bow, I bestowed a parting smile on his mate and added, "I hope that you both enjoy the flight home."

View of Singapore from Johore

26

◀◉▶

Singapore to Colombo

This time out I was not stopped at the gate, and no special committee saw me off. Once aboard the wide-bodied jet, however, my movements were severely hampered by a veritable tangle of small, brown-skinned men. Close contact with some of them generated a strong hope that, as usual, the seat adjacent to mine would prove to be vacant. Fortunately the adjacent seat was still vacant at the time of departure. But the additional space didn't fully overcome the problem, since the ambient atmosphere palpably indicated that many of those little, brown-skinned bodies must not have had ready access to showers.

The craft continued to stand at the gate for some time after its scheduled departure; meanwhile, many of the little devils were constantly popping up from their seats like engine poppets. After each individual popped up, he invariably turned about and stared back at the sea of brown faces. Perhaps they were searching for friends and associates, but I suspected that they popped up to be seen by friends and associates. From the general appearance of the poppets I surmised that many of them were financially incapable of making many such trips; therefore, it may have been something of a status symbol for them to be seen aboard the craft. Whatever the reason, after popping up and successfully locating his objectives, the poppet invariably waved delightedly and unsophisticatedly to them. Actually, they behaved more like a crowd of happy, well-mannered children than like adults.

Following the departure there were none of the usual frills, such as soft or hard drinks and snacks or meals, so Airlanka apparently provided only transportation between Singapore and Colombo. No brilliant sea of city lights greeted the craft when it finally circled over Colombo before slowly settling onto the runway at Katunayaka International Airport. Of course, that was no fault of the airline. The fault may have been due to the time, which was long past the witching hour. Furthermore, assuming that Buddhists and Muslims possess souls, the city is home to only 500,000 souls; consequently, the limited panorama of dim lights may have impressed only the homecoming residents.

Colombo

After the craft landed and taxied onto a site near the terminal, I waited until only a few other stragglers remained, picked up my briefcase, and moved toward the exit.

While cautiously descending the unsteady mobile stairs that had been moved alongside the craft, I looked about, and my introduction to Colombo proved to be anything but impressive. Not only did the structure of the terminal need considerable repair and renewal, but the ground service equipment was in total disarray. After checking the conditions and vintages of the few small aircraft standing about the more remote areas of the field, I resolved to do no island hopping during my stay.

From the silently resting bird, I followed the brown-skinned horde into the terminal through a portal identified by the word *Immigration*. It led into a relatively large room, where the softly chattering passengers had formed long lines before high, pedestal-like desks. At each of the desks the passenger at the front of the line was being interviewed by a relatively tall civilian with a light-brown complexion, and a shorter, brown-skinned man in a poorly fitted, khaki uniform stood at his elbow. Since Sri Lanka was at war with itself, the four or five soldiers could scarcely be considered to be a security force when compared to the security force at Sydney's immigration facility with Australia at war with nobody.

The line moved so slowly that I wearily set my briefcase on the concrete floor beside my right Hush Puppy and began to study the people in the line on my left. Meanwhile, those in the line ahead of me moved forward about two steps, and, before I could reach down and pick up the briefcase, two little, brown-skinned women darted out from directly behind me and ducked into the open space. Having learned my lesson, I placed the briefcase as close as possible to the bare heels of the sari-clad woman ahead of me and carefully monitored the space to ensure that it did not expand to a size that would tantalize any more would-be invaders.

Every interview seemed to be interminable, possibly because some of the individuals appeared to be inadequately documented. Furthermore, the officials approached their tasks with a bored and indifferent attitude, even to the extent of staring absently into space at times. During one such interval I chanced to notice from the corner of one eye that the official at the head of my line was staring speculatively at me; consequently, I immediately jumped to a rash conclusion and turned both baleful eyes on him. He may, however, have been waiting for an opportunity to attract my attention since he immediately beckoned to me. I responded by deliberately looking back at the line behind me. Apparently he decided that I must be a particularly dumb bunny, since he returned indifferently to his task.

Several minutes later I happened to observe a similar gesture by the official at the head of the adjacent line, so my eyes searched the line for its most likely recipient and found a well-dressed and rather pretty young woman with light-brown features. As if expecting the gesture, she immediately stepped out of the line and advanced to the counter, where her passport was stamped with dispatch.

Within a few minutes my eyes again happened to meet the eyes of the official at the head of my line, and again he beckoned to me, and again I resorted to the previous subterfuge. This time, however, he pointed imperatively toward me, so I could no longer ignore the summons. Nevertheless, I felt like a traitor as I strode past those patient little people.

When I stopped beside the high desk and presented my passport to the man, he glanced absently at it. Then, turning to me, he asked, "What took you so long, Mister Terril?"

Momentarily my mind rebelled against a social system which demanded that I bypass all of those little, brown-skinned people just because I possessed a lighter skin than they. Nevertheless, since his eyes remained focused on me as if awaiting

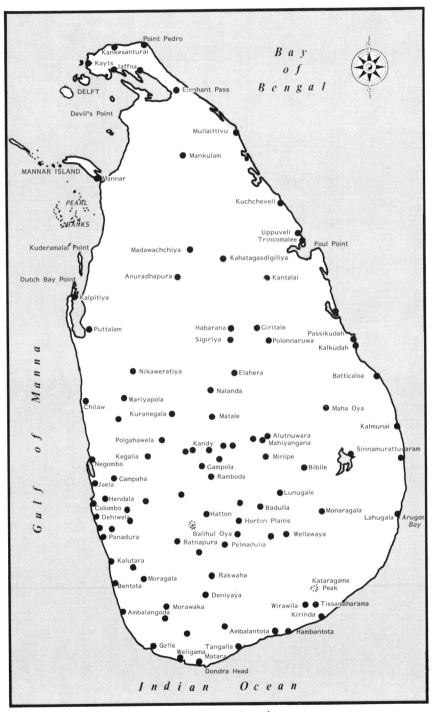

Map of Sri Lanka

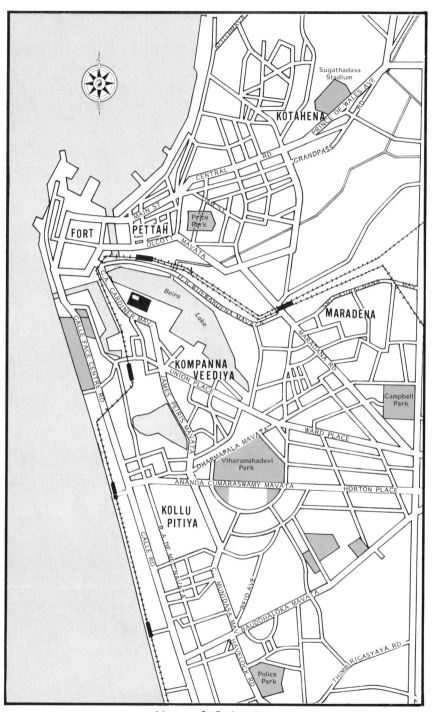

Map of Colombo

an answer and since I wished to enter the country, I mildly answered, "I was a bit late in arriving, so the lines had grown very long."

He stared thoughtfully at me while his mind deciphered my deliberately obscure response. Finally he nodded as if he understood. "Are you here on business or for a visit, sir?" he asked.

"I'm a visitor," I answered.

"How long do you plan to stay?" he inquired.

"Three or four days," I replied.

"How much money do you wish to declare, Mister Terril?" he asked.

After quickly estimating the value of my remaining treasure trove, I answered, "About fifteen hundred American dollars."

Automatically stamping the passport, he returned it to me and said, "I hope you enjoy your stay in Sri Lanka, sir."

Absently accepting it, I looked thoughtfully back at the line of mostly unshod and poorly clothed, brown-skinned people whom I had unwillingly bypassed. Suddenly I couldn't condemn the two little women for surreptitiously inserting their sari-clad bodies into a more advanced vacant space in a line that moved forward so slowly and moved only when and in the order dictated by a higher caste countryman.

"Thank you," I belatedly responded to the man's statement, tucked the booklet into a jacket pocket, and moved pensively onward.

After recovering my luggage, I strode through a short hallway to the top of a stairway, where I stopped and looked down upon a large, elongated waiting area that served many different functions besides the ticketing of passengers and the exchanging of currencies. The sheet metal ceiling was arched and ribbed somewhat like a Quonset hut. Pony walls enclosed several small areas along the far wall. A relatively large mass of humanity was still milling about the central part of the floor, despite the fact that the clock's hands were approaching 2:00 A.M. Most of the men were clad in sarongs; however, some of them wore shirts with sarongs, and others wore shirts with skirts, but all of the clothing was wrinkled if not both wrinkled and dirty. Most of the women wore saris. One Hindu woman was clad in a flowing, silk sari, but my eyes were particularly attracted to the gem that clung to a sidewall of her aquiline nose. Two tall, black-bearded, brown-skinned men wore turbans on their heads, and each was clad in an ensemble that looked very much like a pair of pajamas with an unusually long jacket. Several shorter, tan-skinned men wore tan mufti that could have passed for military uniforms.

In that motley crowd I detected only three other Caucasians and discovered the sensation of being a member of a very small minority. The humid atmosphere bore an almost tangible odor; however, after several hours of incarceration with those little, brown-skinned creatures aboard the aircraft, I wasn't too sure that the other members of the motley crowd were the only contributing factors.

After descending several steps to the main floor, I strode toward a sign at the far end of the building, which bore the words *Travel Service Centre*. There I found a tall, dark-eyed man with a small, black moustache, whose slender stature and near-white skin seemed to imply that he was of Indo-Aryan origin.

"Can I be of service to you?" he inquired in nearly perfect English.

"I would like to obtain the name of a good hotel that's not overly costly," I answered.

"There are several very nice hotels in Colombo," he said. "There are the Hotel Ceylon International, the Hotel Lanka Oberoi, the Hotel Taprobane, and the Hotel Ranmuthu."

Turning a pair of defeated eyes on him, I inquired, "Which of them is most likely to provide the best deal?"

"The best deal definitely is the Ramada Renaissance Hotel Colombo," he replied.

"But you didn't even mention that one," I protested. "I would have immediately recognized the name of an American hotel, so why wasn't it included with the others?"

"I saved the best for the last," he responded with a palpable unction.

I instantly distrusted him but decided to hear him out.

"The Renaissance is a new hotel and the very best that Colombo has to offer," he resumed. "Furthermore, it will cost you only thirty-five American dollars per day, and that is for a room which normally rents for seventy dollars."

I cautiously studied his intent eyes while the left hemisphere of my brain stridently warned, "Watch out, fellah! Don't forget what that Singapore cab driver did to you."

But the man presented himself in such an honest and pleasant manner that I foolishly ignored the warning. "Sounds okay to me," I said. "But how do I get to it? Shuttle bus or taxi?"

"Taxi," he replied. Then he dropped the other shoe: "But the hotel will include a ten percent service charge, which will be added to each day's statement."

"And that's for you," I guessed.

"Yes," he replied.

"Isn't it amazing how accurate one's guesses become after a few experiences like the one I warned you about?" José sounded off tauntingly.

Belatedly, the percentage man asked, "How many days do you plan to stay?"

"Two," I growled.

"But you told the immigration official three or four," protested Pancho.

"Cool it!" injected José. "Can't you see that he would be ripped off for another seven bucks if he stays four days. By now you should know how tight Al is with his money, especially when he's being ripped off."

"Only two," murmured the man with a disappointed expression.

After an absent nod, I muttered, "It appears that I should exchange some American dollars for Sri Lankan currency, but surely no bank is open at this hour."

"Yes, there is one," he insisted. "Just go to the open window in that line of windows." And he pointed a bony, brown forefinger toward the wall along which I had just passed. "Your currency will be exchanged at the rate of twenty-six rupees for each American dollar. But return here, and I will assist you in obtaining a cab!" he called after me.

"Don't bank on it!" José retorted silently.

At the window I came upon another Caucasian who was engaged in a conversation with a short, chubby clerk, whose broad features bore just a hint of brown-skinned heritage. As soon as the Caucasian noticed me, he stepped back from the window and courteously motioned for me to take his place.

"No," I responded, "continue with your transaction. I'm in no great hurry."

"We were merely discussing the advisability of my dealing directly with the Ramada Hotel so that I can save the ten percent service charge," he informed me in an American accent. "After all, I plan to stay six days, so ten percent would amount to a sizable amount."

"There's no reason why you can't call the hotel's desk clerk and request a quotation," I suggested. "If he doesn't raise the ante, you'll have won; if he does, you can still deal with the travel service man, of course."

"Yeah, I guess I could do that," he muttered thoughtfully. "Thanks for the suggestion."

"Do you wish to exchange some American money?" the clerk interjected.

"Yeah, but I would like to exchange these Singapore dollars first," I answered, thrusting several bills toward him.

He silently counted them, tapped a computer several times, and looked at its product; then, reaching into the wooden drawer before him, he withdrew several varicolored— and I do mean *very* colored—bills. After carefully counting them, he placed them before me as I tendered to him a pair of American traveler's checks. While the clerk was repeating the routine, I curiously inspected the brilliantly colored currency and its unfamiliar inscriptions. All told, I received almost 6,000 rupees for the equivalent of some 230 American dollars.

After cramming the bills into my wallet, I turned about and studied the various exits. Since the nearest one was directly across the room from me, I picked up the luggage and trudged toward it.

"I told that ten percenter not to bank on his return," José silently shouted with a gloating chortle.

"Al isn't about to pay ten percent to that guy for just requesting the services of a taxicab driver," remarked Pancho.

Upon arriving at the exit, I thrust the briefcase against one of the two doors, but it refused to open. Then I tried the other one, and it refused to open. Backing off, I set the luggage on the floor, tugged on the first of the two doors, and it refused to open. I was about to tug on the other one when "Mr. Ten Percent" descended upon me like a vulture.

"Those doors are locked," he informed me.

"I've just discovered that," I growled. "But what will the fire marshall say when he discovers it? Hundreds of people could be injured in this firetrap if some absent-minded idiot should inadvertently drop a cigarette into one of the trash bins. In fact, how **does** one get out of this madhouse?"

"I'm sorry for the inconvenience," he responded like someone who had been personally affronted, "but we must keep those doors locked in the interest of national security. Come with me, and I will lead you to a taxicab."

"I'll bet you will," chorused both hemispheres, "just like a lamb to slaughter." Meanwhile, I picked up the luggage.

"The taxi will cost two hundred and fifty rupees, which is about ten American dollars," he resumed. Then, placing a bony hand on the nearest of my straining shoulders, he gently urged me toward another pair of doors located in one corner of the terminal.

In what would normally correspond to a stage whisper, José exclaimed, "Man! Does that guy ever know his currency!"

"Not only his currency but ours, too," observed Pancho. "And it's our currency that he has in mind, you dolt."

"Not all of it," José countered. "But I'll bet eight to five that he ends up with ten percent of it."

When we arrived at the doors, my guide serviced my next few steps by opening and holding one of the doors for me. But that was as far as I got, since several little, brown-skinned men in wrinkled World War I–vintage, khaki uniforms blocked further passage.

"Hey!" exclaimed Pancho. "Those guys are carrying real guns."

"But they may not be loaded," retorted José.

"Maybe so," conceded Pancho, "but those long, cylindrical things in their bandoliers don't look like cheesecake to me."

"They ain't cheesecake," responded José nervously, "so let's pay the ten percent and git the *bleep* outa here."

Mr. Ten Percent did earn his fee, but he did it with relative ease. After stepping around me, he fixed his dark eyes on a particular militiaman, signaled to him with the long, bony forefinger, and waggled it at me. Of course, I eagerly followed the intrepid negotiator through the human barrier to the curb along Airport Way, which paralleled Abdul Cader Road. There I beheld what had to be the strangest assortment of taxicabs ever to be assembled in one spot on the surface of this wobbling world. Some of the finest of the lot appeared to have started out as Volkswagens, from which many of the hoods and doors had been removed. Of course, there were several similar brands, but the vehicle that most struck my fancy was the motorized *trisha*.

From the pavement up it basically consisted of three practically bald, rubber tires mounted on relatively small wheels whose rear axle and front spindle were attached to a horizontal steel frame. Later I was to discover different designs, but this one was powered through a small transmission by the equivalent of a Maytag washing machine motor mounted over the rear axle. A bench seat was located midway of and atop the steel frame, and a sheet metal front panel, surmounted by a small windshield, supported the front of the smaller, horizontal, steel framework to which the tattered fabric top was attached. Vertical members projecting up from the rear corners of the bench seat supported the rear end of the top's framework. A small steering wheel was located on the right side of the vehicle, and since the driver occupied that end of the bench seat, there was space for only one passenger.

Meanwhile, Mr. Ten Percent approached the driver of an ancient Toyota and spoke to him for several seconds in what must have been the local vernacular. Finally the smaller man nodded as if accepting the taller man's terms.

"So the rate has been raised to two hundred fifty rupees," mourned Pancho, "and we're out twenty-five rupees, if not more."

Then Ten Percent returned to me and said, "This driver will take you to the hotel for two hundred fifty rupees. Tipping is optional, but most visitors do it."

"Ho-ho!" chortled Leftie. "I predicted that the man would get his ten percent, and he has obviously manipulated the deal so he will."

"Not only did he get his ten percent," rejoined Rightie, "but he set Al up to tip the driver another ten percent, so the entire rip-off amounts to twenty percent of the basic cost of the trip to that hotel: not bad capitalism for a socialistic society."

Meanwhile, the driver and I had squeezed my luggage into the trunk of the Toyota, so I settled onto the worn seat beside him and unwisely suggested, "Okay, let's take off."

Of course, I was implying that he should launch the vehicle into the wild blue yonder, but I felt reasonably secure in the knowledge that he had not understood the words. Nevertheless, as soon as the reluctant motor exploded into clamorous life, he pressed the accelerator to the floorboard, and the rickety contraption was traveling at top speed by the time that it caromed from a curb on Abdul Cader Road through its unlighted intersection with Jayatilaka Mawatha. It may have been just after it turned south onto the equally unlighted Lotus Road that its dim headlights picked up a figure with an upraised arm standing along the left shoulder of the narrow thoroughfare. It was the type of figure that loomed hugely against the flickering lights of the distant city.

As the vehicle catapulted past the figure, a loud "Hey!" erupted from it, and the driver hurriedly applied the brakes.

"I'll bet that the expression *hey* has the same meaning all over the world," suggested José.

"Maybe so, but did you see the gun in that guy's hands?" countered Pancho in nervous overtones.

"Yeah," José practically whispered. "Do you suppose that he intends to shoot all four of us just because the driver failed to stop in time?"

"Whadya mean by all four of us?" Pancho protested.

"Well, besides the cab driver and Al, there's you and me," José replied. "Doesn't that add up to four?"

Meanwhile, the driver had backed the cab to the side of the militiaman; then the two men exchanged several words that were foreign to three of us. In the dim background beyond the militiaman I detected what appeared to be the outlines of a panel truck and four other militiamen. Finally the militiaman leaned forward and peered closely at my features; then the shadowy line beneath his big, black moustache split into a wide grin, and he cheerfully waved us on. Apparently the color of the features around my full beard didn't qualify me as a brown-skinned threat to him and his government.

Even though wild American Indians are now found principally in the illustrations of history books, I soon discovered that wild Indians still abound in Sri Lanka, at least among its Tamil taxicab drivers. From a standing start that old cab leaped forward to top speed in six seconds, and when it reached more heavily trafficked areas, I began to fear for my life, because it took to erratically weaving in and out between similar vehicles traveling with similar abandon on the narrow, two-lane road. Between weaves it suicidally straddled what would have been a center line if there had been one.

One rule of the road appeared to be that, just before a vehicle passed another vehicle traveling in the same direction, a warning was sounded on the passing vehicle's horn. After such a warning by my cab driver, the alerted driver usually swung his vehicle toward the side of the road—sometimes as much as six inches. Then, ignoring the vehicles hurtling toward us, my driver took us to the center of the road and tore past the other vehicle. Sometimes it seemed impossible for three vehicles to pass simultaneously on that narrow road, but by the grace of Mohammed, Buddha, Allah, or whomever, they succeeded.

Even at that early hour numerous pedestrians were wandering about the road in some of the more populated areas. Another rule of the road appeared to be that, after a driver sounded a warning, the pedestrian was considered to be fair game. In any case the driver invariably chased the pedestrian from the road.

Occasionally we came upon a big, off-white, Brahma bull or an ox wandering indifferently about the road. In several instances they were sacked out along the edge of it, but the drivers always gave them wide berths. It seemed to me that they were treated with much more respect than were the human beings. If it were not because of religious principles, then it must have been because some of those huge critters outweighed the tiny vehicles by a ratio of three to one.

At one point an oncoming wood-frame cart, loaded with what looked like hay, came into view. A pair of huge, wooden wheels, replete with hubs, spokes, and iron rims, supported the cart and provided its mobility. It was drawn by a team of oxen whose yoke supported the otherwise free end of a small timber, which extended from the center of the wooden axle and the cart's substructure.

"What's that thing doing in the middle of the road at this ungodly hour?" José shouted silently.

"It's there because the driver is huddled in the hay sound asleep," retorted Pancho. "In fact, it'll be a miracle if the cab driver doesn't run into that team of oxen."

"He won't dare," José observed. "Cattle are considered to be sacred in this part of the world—at least they are in India; and many of these people are essentially Indians."

At that instant the cab veered from the center of the road to avoid the cart just as the dim lights of another vehicle appeared from behind it. The tires of both vehicles spurted smoke as their drivers desperately attempted to avoid a head-on collision. Since it was obvious that the other driver couldn't change course without piling into the oxen, my driver nonchalantly swung onto the unsurfaced shoulder of the road, and there was just a whisper of a contact as the two vehicles catapulted past each other.

"Whew!" exclaimed Pancho. "That was close."

"You can say that again," responded José.

"Whew!" began Pancho.

"Don't bother," interjected José. "I remember the last part."

"I wonder how Al fared," mused Pancho.

"Oh, he'll be okay as soon as he manages to pry his fingernails from between the bones of his hands," replied José.

Meanwhile, the driver continued to press the accelerator against the floorboard. Since he understood no English, there was no way that I could reason with him, so I crossed my fingers and silently stared at the surrounding evidence of poverty. Even the darkness couldn't conceal the squalor.

Suddenly, still at full speed, the cab veered from the road onto a wide, paved driveway that curved gently toward a large porte cochere, under which it came to an abrupt stop. Just a glimpse of the massive concrete structure beyond it convinced me that Mr. Ten Percent had set me up in a veritable palace consisting of about eight modern floors, which extended several hundred feet along Sir Chittampalam A. Gardiner Mawatha.

As I stepped out of the cab, several small, brown-skinned youths eagerly offered to assist me with my luggage, but the somewhat older doorman shooed them away. Perhaps his small, black moustache justified such actions; if not, then his uniform must have, because its elegant splendor must have surpassed even that of the country's highest military official.

"Greetings," he began. "I trust that you enjoyed your trip to the Renaissance."

"The first flight could have been much better," I conceded; then, somewhat obscurely, I added, "but the second one almost ended up in a hay wagon."

Fixing a wooden-Indian smile and a pair of puzzled, dark eyes on me, he said, "Nevertheless, greetings from the Renaissance."

"Good evening," I muttered, absently digging out my wallet.

"It is now morning, sir," he rejoined.

"Yes, I should have said good morning," I admitted. "After all, it's long past midnight, but before we settle any more trivial details, let me get things straight with this driver."

Withdrawing two colorful bills from my wallet, I thrust them into the cupped hands of the driver. I was about to add two more of a lower denomination to them as a tip when I saw the doorman's watchful eyes widen.

"That's too much," he protested. "The fare is only two hundred fifty rupees, and you already have given him a thousand rupees."

I looked into the driver's mesmerized eyes and watched the regret creep into them as he reluctantly returned the bills to me. After carefully studying both the Sri Lankan and the Arabic numerals displayed on the bills, I looked toward the doorman and ruefully admitted, "You are right. However, I've just acquired this stuff, so I haven't had time to become acquainted with it yet." Selecting two hundred-rupee bills, I placed them in the driver's hands.

"Now give him a fifty-rupee bill, and he'll be paid in full," the doorman suggested. But I added two fifty-rupee bills to the other bills.

"No, that's still too much," the doorman protested, as the driver thrust one of them toward me.

With a vertical palm extended to it, I shook my head and muttered, "That's for being an honest man."

He continued to stare at me with a confused expression until the doorman explained my words to him in the native tongue; then he bestowed a brilliant smile on me.

"But you really should drive much more carefully," I added, and the smile expanded. Meanwhile, the doorman looked on with a stolid expression and tolerantly withheld his counsel.

Since nobody had touched my luggage, I approached it with the intention of moving it out of the doorway, but the doorman placed a restraining hand on my shoulder and said, "I'll take care of it, sir."

For that service I presented a fifty-rupee bill to him while Pancho injected, "We hope that it's a larger tip than the going rate, because he appears to be an honest man."

"We've always endeavored to encourage the growth of that rare characteristic," José chimed. "Besides, he acted in Al's best interests by pointing out his error, so Al should have sweetened the tip to compensate for that."

"Obviously a thousand rupees split down the middle between a dishonest cab driver and an equally dishonest doorman would have been a sizable windfall in Colombo," Pancho resumed. "However, even though all of Al's monetary obligations have been accommodated, he is still in debt: He owes Mr. Ten Percent an apology for suspecting him of unethical business practices."

The long walk from the entrance to the fifty-foot-long hardwood beauty that served as the hotel's reception and service desk was a high-level experience. Not only did I pass the open doorways of such luxurious accommodations as the club lounge and an opulent dining room, plus the plate glass windows of a large coffee shop, but I was dazzled by crystal-bearing chandeliers, floor-to-ceiling front windows, and interior walls sheathed by mirrors and decorative glass. Very likely The Ramada Renaissance Hotel Colombo was intended to be the most luxurious hotel in that tropical paradise. Unfortunately for all concerned, some of the youthful members of one of the most poverty-stricken societies in the world clustered at its entrance hoping to cadge an occasional rupee for a simple service.

Long before arriving at the gleaming front desk, I sensed the impact of three pairs of dark eyes from just beyond it, and their vigil didn't cease until I stopped in front of the first of the slender, immaculately attired figures and met the man's opaque stare.

"Can I be of help?" he inquired in precise English.

"Yes," I responded, unloading several small pieces of paper from my shirt pocket onto the counter. After a brief search I uncovered the introductory slip from Mr. Ten Percent, placed it on the counter in front of him, and added, "I received this from a man who instructed me to submit it to the desk clerk of this hotel."

Meanwhile, one of the other two relatively tall, black-haired men sauntered to his side and peered across the man's left shoulder at the slip. Then, while I narrowly watched, two of them engaged in a long discussion. Meantime, I resolved that, if Big Brother happened to be hiding within one of those identical, well-tailored dark suits, I was determined to detect him. But it proved to be a difficult task because they were as alike as peas in a pod. Since they conferred in a different language, I was forced to depend on interpretations of nuances and innuendos. During the discussion the third man drifted closer to them and listened with apparent interest to what was being said, and that may have been a token, but I was unable to verify it at the moment. Abruptly the second man appeared to make a positive statement to which the first man nodded; then he approached the counter and placed a registration form before me.

On the form were spaces for my surname, both given names, my birth date, where I was born, the country of my choice (nationality), my passport number, its date of issue, and where it was issued. Without doubt that was the most complete registration form that I had ever seen, but Cuba was the only other country in which I had registered for lodging while the country was involved in a civil war.

While supposedly studying the form from the periphery of one eye, I was actually studying the third man, who was lounging against the counter studying me.

"There's no apparent reason for three desk clerks to be on duty at this time in the morning," José observed.

"But we shouldn't ignore the possibility that one or more of them may be a government intelligence agent inserted into the staff to cover the comings and goings of hotel guests who might be connected with the rebels," Pancho countered.

"We also should consider the likelihood that each man may serve in a different capacity," José rejoined.

"I don't buy that," Pancho responded, "because only one of them appears to be actively involved in the functions of the desk. The other two appear to be just standing around and watching."

"True," José agreed. "Then there was that big deal conference; we've never encountered a situation like that before."

"Since there are so many confusing possibilities, we can't draw a logical conclusion regarding Big Brother's guilt, so let's place the decision regarding his potential presence on hold," Pancho suggested.

"Let's do," José suggested. "The number of his weaknesses are legendary, so there'll be other opportunities to determine whether he has preceded us to this island."

"Right!" Pancho silently exclaimed. "Consequently he will involuntarily reveal himself."

After I completed the entries, the clerk inspected the form, marked 653 after "Room No.," and pushed a key across the counter to me. Meanwhile, I looked thoughtfully toward my luggage, which still stood about one hundred feet away in the entrance.

"Your luggage will be delivered to your room by a bellman," the clerk murmured. And I nodded.

"So that's why the doorman wouldn't touch it," remarked José.

"Of course, that's the reason," responded Pancho. "A general never does any menial work; furthermore, that's why Mr. Ten Percent didn't offer to help with the luggage: He considers himself to be of the elite. Only *sojurs* and peons stoop to such tasks in Sri Lanka."

Apparently the clerk had previously spoken to me because he called more loudly, "Sir!" And after I turned and looked at him, he pointed toward the open doors of an elevator and added, "That elevator will take you to the sixth floor."

Hurriedly forsaking the clamor in my head, I strode into the lift and managed to press the correct button without first getting my finger caught between them. At the sixth floor I stepped from the elevator onto a thick carpet that stretched throughout the wide and seemingly endless hallway. From there just a few steps carried me to Room 653.

Even after exposure to all of that opulence, I was still surprised to discover that the room was so spacious. It contained two queen-size beds, a writing table and matching chair, plus all of the items that add so much to the comfort of a bone-tired guest. But rest proved not to be on the immediate agenda, because there were the soft sounds of slowly turning roller bearings along with the whisper of pneumatic tires against the thick pile of the hallway's carpeting, and a four-wheel dolly bearing two pieces of luggage rolled to a stop before the open doorway.

Then a slender, uniformed bellman with a *chocolat au lait* complexion stepped through the opening and said, "Pardon me, sir, but I believe that these are your bags."

"Right," I answered pensively. "Let's see now; maybe we can put them. . . ."

"Allow me," he interjected, taking complete command. After removing a collapsible luggage stand from the large closet, he unfolded and placed it in the most logical location in the room. Then he placed the suitcase on it and set the briefcase on the floor beside it.

Meanwhile, I reached for my wallet, but he raised an admonishing hand and sailed past me to the large windows and carefully adjusted the shades. After deftly wiping a tiny wrinkle from the satiny surface of one of the bed covers, he veered from that point to the large television set, where he unloaded into my ears so many complicated instructions concerning its use that I never did turn the *bleeped* thing on. And I really should have turned it on to familiarize myself with the types of programs that were available to those people. Perhaps it was fortunate that I didn't turn it on, because the programs may have been American soap operas. But he didn't stop at the TV. Oh, no. He had yet to instruct me in the use of the telephone (I should have run into someone like him in New Zealand). But he didn't stop there either. He went on to explain the functions of the relatively uncomplicated lighting system and the shower valves. But he stopped short of explaining the functions of the water closet.

As we were about to leave the beautifully appointed bathroom, he picked up one of the two water bottles from the marble-topped pullman and said, "Drink only the distilled water in these bottles. The water in the tap is not safe to drink." Then he waggled a tan forefinger at me and rephrased the words: "Don't ever drink water from the tap. If you should need more drinking water, just go to the telephone and call room service. Potable water is as close as the telephone."

With that he snapped to attention, and even though his palm was not extended horizontally, I sensed that now was the time, so I greased it. Possibly I overdid it, but I never did become familiar with that fancy currency. During the process I said, "You are a very efficient bellman. Perhaps you should give me your name so that I can call you if I should need something."

"Eardly, sir," he replied, but his voice cracked as he uttered it. Apparently I had shattered his cool, almost supercilious air of efficiency. But I had an unfair advantage, because I had spent some time in Canada, so I was familiar with the British flair for militarylike perfection.

"Eardly is an English name, is it not?" I asked.

"Yes, sir," he replied.

"Thank you, Eardly," I said in tones of dismissal. And he could not have relaxed more quickly or more completely if I had commanded, "Detail dismissed."

At the doorway he paused, looked back at me, and said, "Call me any time. I promise to give you the best of service, sir." And I'm convinced that he would have, too, but I found no need to call him.

Four hours of sleep were scarcely enough; nevertheless, by eight o'clock I was up and showered. On emerging from an elevator into the lobby with the intention of buying another day's sojourn, I found that a heavyset, fiftyish Caucasian man was conferring with one of the two clerks while the other one operated a computer. I came to a stop behind the man just as the clerk excused himself and stepped to the side of the clerk at the computer.

Meanwhile, the guest turned about, focused his eyes on me, and muttered, "I don't see how they do it."

"Do what?" I countered, only because I was sure that the words were exactly what he expected from me.

"Provide such luxurious accommodations at such low rates," he replied. "Why, I can stay here for much less than what it costs me to put up at a mediocre hotel in any of the Common Market nations. Not only do those hotels charge more, but they have none of the amenities, such as a huge pool, an in-house pub, beautiful dining rooms, and a club room, all finished in the most modern decor. Actually there is no reason for me to leave the hotel except to conduct my business, because everything is included on the premises."

"From your enthusiastic words I have to assume that you like it," I responded with a chuckle.

"I love it," he said. "In fact, it has become almost a second home for me. All told, I have spent several months here. Usually I come for two or three weeks at a time, and when I leave, it's like now." He paused, gestured toward the two men at the computer, and added, "It takes a whole roll of computer tape to total my costs. Even so, I get all of this and all of the time that I can spare in that beautiful pool for much less than what the best European accommodations cost."

"I gather that you are a businessman," I ventured.

"No," he replied, "but I'm indirectly involved in business. I'm a consultant for a company in London."

"Would you object to my describing the type of local business for which you are a consultant?" I inquired.

"No, not at all," he responded with a curious glance. "Can you actually do that?"

"First off, you are from the British Isles," I began. "But I obtained that much information from the foregoing discourse." He nodded, so I resumed: "But you didn't tell me that you are a consultant for one or more members of this country's apparel industry."

"How did you do that?" he countered with an air of sudden respect.

"I'm psychic," I replied. Then, in response to his doubt-filled expression, I added, "Of course, that's not so, but I have a friend in the States who was in the apparel industry until countries such as Taiwan, South Korea, and this one began bidding on the labor to manufacture everything from pantyhose to jeans and jackets."

"By the way," he murmured with an outstretched hand, "I'm Adrian Maulsby." And I complemented the introduction.

"Singapore and Hong Kong are pretty active centers, too," he resumed, "but they haven't been able to provide lower costs than this country—at least not lately."

"With enormous improvements in worldwide communication and transportation, no country is isolated anymore," I observed. "Consequently sheer economic survival is dictating that some types of manufacturing be delegated to the hungriest labor pools, and most of them are found in the overpopulated Third World nations."

"Right," he remarked. "Therefore, the rates of pay for pure manual labor in the United Kingdom are being forced lower and lower."

"Likewise in the other highly developed nations," I said. "Like water on uneven terrain, the costs of labor in all nations will eventually seek a common level."

"Plus the costs of transportation and coordination for overseas ventures," the man observed. "It's a bit costly for people like me to coordinate and manage operations like the ones in this country."

"Meanwhile, people in the highly developed nations must become better educated and trained so that they can assume responsible positions in the economic and technical fields," I insisted. "Otherwise they'll be competing with the masses of the Orient and eventually Africa for minimum wages."

"Either that or they'll be demanding that the more efficient and productive members of their societies support them," he responded with a wry expression.

"The rapid growth of Third World populations must be stopped and even reduced," I insisted. "Otherwise many of their people will starve, or they'll invade adjoining nations that have stocks of food and take what they need."

"True," he granted, flexing his thick, softly muscled arms. "The history books are full of attacks on the have nations by the have-not nations."

"Pardon me, sir," the clerk interjected. "We now have a total for you." Adrian cast an apologetic glance toward me, and I nodded amiably, so he turned away, and that was the last time I saw the man.

After completing my mission at the desk, I strolled about twenty paces through the lushly appointed lobby to the heavily glazed entrance of Summerfield's Coffee Shop. After stepping through the wide entryway, I came upon a somewhat voluptuous young hostess, who was clad in an attractive, gray sari. Actually, it is best described as a sarilike garment, since it didn't incorporate the conventional headpiece.

First her exotic, dark eyes greeted me with a prolonged stare; then she murmured, "Good morning."

"Good morning," I responded, despite a sudden conviction that it had just been ruined by the stare.

Selecting a menu from the stack atop a small, mahogany table and gripping the bottom of it with the fingers of both hands, she held it upright against her bosom. Meanwhile, she was looking pensively toward the tall, well-built figure of the young man who was striding purposefully from the dining area toward us. After he pulled up in front of us, his right hand automatically accepted the menu while the other one adjusted the left lapel of his well-fitted, gray jacket. All the while his eyes were studying my features.

"Please follow me," he muttered. Turning about, he led me to a table within a sea of tables and chairs, mostly unoccupied.

After placing the menu on the table, he murmured, "Your waitress will be here shortly."

"Thank you," I said and absently seated myself.

Like the hostess, the waitress possessed a tan-colored complexion, but she was clad in a neat, gray uniform. "Are you ready to order, sir?" she inquired in excellent English.

"Yes, I am," I replied. "However, since I'm writing a travelogue, I like to record the names of the people whom I encounter, so do you object to telling me your given name?"

"It's right here," she responded with a gesture toward the small nameplate on the upper left side of a full but otherwise plain bodice.

"I'm sorry, Sandra," I muttered. "I should have noticed it, since waitresses' names are commonly displayed in that manner."

"There is no reason to be sorry," she demurred. "Are you an author? What do you write about?"

For a sound reason I chose to answer only the last question. "About people, their customs, and some of the dialogues that I share with them," I replied. "For instance, I may decide to describe you and what we are now discussing."

"And will you use my name?" she inquired wistfully.

"Of course I will," I replied. "I would have to use it to describe our dialogue accurately. Consequently I'll jot your name in this little notebook so that I can find it when I need it."

Removing the booklet from my shirt pocket, I opened it and prepared to inscribe her name while she stared at the page across my left shoulder and slowly spelled *s-a-n-d-r-a* for me. Obviously she was taking no chances that her name would be misspelled or omitted for any reason whatsoever.

"Thank you, Sandra," I murmured. "Now, how about that breakfast?"

"Oh, yes!" she exclaimed as if suddenly descending from a much higher plane. "What would you like?"

"Ham and one egg, with the egg over easy," I replied. "Do you know what I mean by over easy?"

"Oh, yes," she replied. "We serve guests from all over the world, so we have become quite familiar with such requests. You want the egg over lightly." And I nodded while looking doubtfully up at her.

But both the ham and the egg were cooked to the point of perfection; however, the slices of three fresh, ripe, tropical fruits that cohabited with them placed that breakfast on an interstellar plane. In spite of my inability to identify all of them, I later learned that they could have been any combination of papaya, pineapple, passion fruit, banana, mango, rambutan, guava, soursap, or any one of several sweet melons, all of which are grown on that particular tropical island. During another breakfast I did identify a slice of banana, but it had ripened on the tree, so its flavor was far superior to that of any of the Central American bananas that I had consumed in America.

Observing Sandra in conference with two other waitresses, I began to suspect that my tropical paradise was about to be overcast by the dark shadow of Big Brother. But the suspicion was denied for the moment when one of the two other girls brought a cup of coffee to the table. Her physical structure was so similar to that of Sandra that I would have failed to notice the difference if she had not conspicuously displayed her nameplate as she set the cup and saucer before me.

After a quick glance at the coffee, I looked up at her and muttered, "Oh, thank you, Margaret," even though I had not ordered coffee.

"You are welcome," she responded with a bit of that oriental charm that so endears those little people to most Westerners. "Can I get something else for you?" Her intense solicitude struck me as incongruous until I recalled that she had been a member of the conference. Then, with a rare display of ingenuity, I retrieved the notebook and ostentatiously looked at her nameplate. While I was jotting the name in it, she stood beside my chair and silently beamed at me.

It could not have been more than three minutes before the third waitress appeared at my shoulder with a pot of steaming hot coffee and demurely inquired, "Would you like your coffee warmed, sir?"

I glanced toward the untouched cup and then at her just as she looked at it.

"But would you like for me to refill it with hot coffee?" she inquired in pleading tones.

To avoid a scalding contact, I had intentionally allowed the dark-brown liquid to cool, but I couldn't refuse those soft, pleading eyes, so I murmured, "That's very thoughtful of you, Betty."

Then, very deliberately, I reached for the notebook. Meanwhile, the poor girl almost splashed some of the hot coffee on my hand while watching me inscribe her name in it. Since Betty could have passed for a slender, small-boned English girl, her Caucasian heritage must have dominated.

While Betty was away replacing the cup and its saucerful of spilled coffee with fresh chinaware, Sandra returned and asked, "Is there anything more that I can get for you?"

"No, thank you, Sandra," I replied, "but thank you for the fine service. In fact, I don't recall ever having such attentive service."

Her glowing dark eyes matched her smile as, with a slight bow, she moved slowly backward. In doing so she almost backed into the tall, young host who was bearing down on her like a boiling storm cloud. I suspected that he had been watching developments from afar and had decided to put a stop to all of the special service. In any case he immediately sequestered Sandra and, with a furtive glance at me, sharply importuned her in their native tongue. But she didn't take kindly to the treatment. In fact, from one of my most surreptitious glances I gathered that his storm had begotten one.

Seconds later I heard her defiantly call, "Tsk! tsk! tsk! Lincoln," as he stomped away.

Nevertheless, when she returned with the check there was a much more formal air in her bearing. After she left, Pancho injected, "So Big Brother's tentacles extend all of the way into Colombo."

"That last scene wasn't the only evidence of his presence," observed his mate. "How about the desk clerk's long stare across the computer while Al was talking to that business consultant?"

With that I deposited a large tip, arose, and trudged slowly toward the cashier's counter, but I didn't fail to notice that all three of those naive girls now avoided my searching gaze.

From the entrance of the hotel a stroll in an easterly direction along Sir Chittampalam A. Gardiner Mawatha netted no intersecting streets, so I turned about and retraced my steps to the hotel and extended them as far as the point where D.R. Wijewardhana Mawatha intersected with it. There I turned about and again retraced my steps to the hotel. After looking in on most of the first floor's public accommodations, I rode the elevator up to the sixth floor and entered my room. Seating myself at the writing desk, I began to expand my notes up to and including the most current of my misadventures.

About three o'clock I backed away from the desk, stiffly arose, and wandered to the exterior wall of the room. There I discovered that the two large windows overlooked the translucent water of a large swimming pool and the turbid waters of Lake Beira, whose shoreline abutted one wall of the pool. While the broad, beige figure of a lone bather, clad in a beige swim ensemble, splashed listlessly in the pool, the waves created by her efforts sharply reflected the rays of the tropical sun. Fortunately the sun's rays had been filtered by humid haze; otherwise the ambient temperature would have zoomed to 130 degrees Fahrenheit instead of the current 90 degrees. Meanwhile, the room's thermostat stood at a comfortable 70 degrees.

Then my gaze rested on the figures of two small men, who were in the act of pushing off an ancient, unpainted, flat-bottom boat from the far shore of the lake. After it was launched, one of the men seated himself on a horizontal plank located about midway of the boat and manned the oars, while the second man seated himself on a similar plank that spanned the craft's boxlike aft end. Since it seemed likely that they would break out some fishing gear shortly after launching the boat, I continued to watch them. When the craft had almost reached the middle of the lake, the man at its aft end apparently called to the rower, because the rower stopped, turned, and looked back at the other man just as he excitedly pointed to the bottom of the boat. After a brief conference the men exchanged positions. Then, while the new rower stepped up the rowing rate, the other man extracted what appeared to be a rusty, one-gallon container from beneath the aft plank and began to scoop water from the bottom of the boat and cast it overboard. When the craft had traversed about three-quarters of the distance to the opposite shore, there was another hurried conference, after which the men again exchanged tasks. Then they resumed rowing and bailing at an even more accelerated rate. When the prow of the craft finally was driven onto the near shore, the rower slumped forward on the oars while the other man dropped the container and collapsed onto the aft plank.

While I stood smiling at that bit of life's drama, José suddenly observed, "I would like the answers to three questions about that voyage: First off, did those guys plan to fish from that so-called boat? Next, did they venture forth on a pleasure cruise? Or did they cross the lake in that boat just to save the few extra steps involved in walking along its shore?"

"Apparently it was the latter," his mate replied. "If so, they succeeded in saving some steps all right, but at a tremendous expenditure of physical energy. At the rate that the water was leaking into that boat, they had a good thing going for them though, because they should have been able to fish directly through the bottom of it."

"One thing for sure," José resumed, "they'll learn to swim before they make another voyage across the lake in that tub."

"Let that be the last opinion on the subject," I interjected, "because I intend to sack out for a while."

With that picture still in mind, I did sack out and became locked into a dream during which I was bouncing along over the surface of that lake in a hydroplane at 250 miles per hour. Meanwhile, the nose of the craft was constantly dipping into the water and splashing gobs of the stuff into the cockpit with each bounce. Unfortunately I was unable to find a rusty, one-gallon bailing bucket; consequently my head popped through the disturbed surface of the lake two times, but I couldn't recall the third one. After returning to consciousness, I was unable to determine how I managed to sleep through the evening and the entire night without even getting my feet wet. I must have been immersed in a very deep sleep, indeed, but, fortunately for me, I had not been asleep in the deep.

Even though the morning was relatively new when I stepped through the open doorway of the coffee shop, the same hostess was standing at her post. And she repeated the same routine, including the selection of a menu, which she again held upright against her bosom, until Lincoln appeared and assumed possession of it—the menu, that is.

"Ayubowan," he murmured, turning to one of the two tables within the decorative alcove that faced the entrance.

"That must translate into an English good morning," I speculated from behind him.

A smile lightly touched his fleshy, off-white features as he turned to me and gestured with one long arm toward the table on our right. "It is a greeting," he conceded, handing the menu to me as I settled onto the richly upholstered bench seat that faced the entrance.

"What is your given name?" I inquired.

"My Sinhalese surname is Mahan," he replied.

"But Sandra, Margaret, and Betty are not Sinhalese names," I guessed.

"That's correct," he said. "Those are English names. At one time this country was governed by the British, and during that time some of the people of Ceylon gave their children English names, but the Sinhalese continued to give their children Sinhalese names."

Momentarily, my mind toyed with the name *Lincoln*, which had sprung so spitefully from Sandra's lips during the previous morning; however, since he seemed to be so proud of his Sinhalese heritage, I restrained an impulse to mention the name to him.

Like someone who was reciting from a book, he resumed: "The people of Sri Lanka consist of several ethnic groups, such as the Sinhalese, who are of Indo-Aryan origin; the Tamils, who are of Dravidian origin; and the Burghers. The Burghers are descendants of Portuguese and Dutch settlers, who arrived here during the forepart of the seventeenth century. There also are some Moors, who are of Arabic origin, and a few Eurasians and Malays. Actually the population of Sri Lanka is a potpourri somewhat like that of America."

"That's regrettable," I blurted. Then, in response to his questioning gaze, I explained, "It guarantees constant conflict between the ethnic groups."

After thoughtfully fixing his eyes on mine for an instant, he said, "True, it has proved to be a source of trouble in this country. That's why soldiers have been assigned to guard the airport, the banks, and other points sensitive to the economic welfare of the country and to the safety of its people. It can no longer be denied that the Tamils have become a serious threat to the future of this independent socialist republic."

"Did the problem evolve from religious differences?" I inquired.

His eyes wavered unsurely for a moment. "Well," he began, "not entirely, but it may be a small factor. Early on, the Tamils migrated to the northern end of Ceylon from the Tamil Nadu area of India, which lies along the nearby coast of the continent. Now, after all of those years, they want to establish a Tamil state with its own laws and economy. As far as religion is concerned, most of this island's fifteen million people are Buddhists, so religions don't begin to cause the problems they do in countries such as Ireland."

There may have been a ray of respect in my eyes as they studied the man's intent eyes, because he certainly seemed to be very knowledgeable. Then my attention turned to the rather rectangular little hostess. With a nod in her direction, I asked, "What is our lady's name?"

"Ashanti," he replied. Then, anticipating my next question, he added, "She is Sinhalese, of course."

I nodded as my mind toyed with the likelihood that the Sinhalese controlled most of the higher posts in this land of unequal opportunities.

"If you like, I'll take your order and have one of the waitresses serve it," he suggested. I repeated the previous order, and he departed.

Since the waitress who served it so impersonally was new to me, I assumed that Mahan, alias Lincoln, had found one whom he could influence just as Big Brother must have influenced him. Briefly I was plunged into a deep dudgeon, but Sandra saved my day by belatedly appearing with a steaming coffeepot.

"Ayubowan," I greeted her.

"Good morning," she responded with a scintillating smile. "Would you like a cup of coffee?"

I had deliberately omitted coffee from my initial order, but I refused to deny the little renegade an opportunity to make more points with me.

"Yes, I would love to have a cup of coffee," I replied. "You've been so kind to this old man that I'm going to give you top billing in one of my chapters."

Her tawny features literally beamed delight as she turned up the cup and poured the steaming brown stuff into it. "I'll return and warm it up for you a bit later," she promised. Then, with a defiant glance at the distant Mahan, she returned to her post.

"Of course, Al and Sandra are expressing their defiance in different ways for different reasons," Pancho injected. "If hers doesn't express a difference in opinion with Mahan regarding Al, then it's intended solely to see her name in print. But Al's defiance has been directed toward Big Brother through his pawns for half a century."

"And that's just," José insisted. "According to an ancient cliché, a man is known by the company he keeps. Therefore, those stupid pawns have been just as qualified to receive Al's counterattacks as has their mentor, but it would be much more satisfactory to me if he directed his attacks at the source of the problem."

From the coffee shop I strolled to the hotel's entrance and passively permitted the doorman to summon a cab for me. Momentarily, I had come to the conclusion that fighting the ten percenters required too much effort, so I had decided to tolerate the system, and I was amazed by my reward.

"A Mercedes," I muttered incredulously, as the cab rolled smoothly to a stop beneath the porte cochere.

"Yes, sir!" retorted the doorman as he proudly opened the cab's rear door for me. I was so stunned that I almost forgot to tip him.

"Ver vould you like to go?" inquired a gruff voice from the direction of the driver's seat.

"Do you know where the American Express office is located?" I countered.

"Dere iss vun down near *der* vater front," he muttered.

"That must be it," I assumed. "Surely there can't be more than one of them in this isolated city. But I suggest that you take a route that will permit me to see some of the city."

"Vell, vee could go by way of Janidhipathi Mawatha," he suggested.

"You know the city, so you make that decision," I said.

A Sketch of One of Sigiriya's Famous Frescoes

Clock Tower of the Fort

We wandered along several streets, but the man wasn't much of a tour guide, so most of what I saw was unidentified. However, my previous impression of the city's outskirts was not greatly improved by my impression of its business district. En route, we passed the President's House and several other prominent buildings, and we paused so that I could view the Clock Tower, which stood in the Fort among several masonry buildings. Since the Clock Tower reflected the British love of such towers, I assumed that they must have constructed it and most of the buildings within the Fort.

Finally the cab stopped at an intersection where the streets diverged at awkward angles. Pointing toward a building on the opposite corner of the street, the driver said, "Dot iss ver you vill find *der* American Express office."

"How much do I owe you?" I inquired, leaning forward to get at my wallet.

"Vell, I haff driven aboudt three miles," he answered thoughtfully. "*Der* law allows only *der* usual rate, but I leave it to you; pay me vot you like."

I gathered that he was pleading for a large tip, which is strictly against my religion, but my eyes appreciatively scanned the handsome interior of the luxurious vehicle and then zeroed in on his eyes. "Are you implying that you have to compete on even terms with all of those decrepit little cabs and *trishas*?" I asked. He nodded so ruefully that I probably exceeded common sense by a large margin when I selected the bills for payment of the fare.

Upon arriving in front of my objective, I found a pair of glazed doors. Pulling one of them open, I strode into a somewhat dusty foyer and came to an abrupt stop in front of a small, flat-top desk. Seated behind it in a swivel chair was a small man with a small, black moustache superimposed upon light-brown features.

Looking up from some paperwork, he arose and rather hostilely inquired, "Whom do you wish to see?"

"I would like to discuss an overcharge for an airline ticket with an appropriate party," I replied.

"Please state the nature of your business," he requested.

"Wye, I just did that," I muttered somewhat truculently.

After a wince the little fellow bowed his head as if defeated by the demands of his position. Meanwhile, I subdued the remorse that welled up in my chest and more kindly suggested, "Perhaps we can find someone in your office who can handle my problem."

Reluctantly he turned toward the half-dozen, dust-laden steps that led up to a large office on our left, and I silently followed him. Eventually a middle-aged Caucasian woman responded to his tentative call, and she quickly decided that I was in the wrong American Express office.

Back at street level the little man's attitude returned to that of a big-time executive, but I carefully avoided destroying his confidence for a second time while he gave me detailed instructions about which buses would take me to the appropriate American Express office. As soon as he mentioned the word *bus*, my mind blanked out on the instructions and flipped to a scene in my memory bank, wherein the bus was crammed with unclean, little, brown-skinned bodies. Consequently I was forced to inquire, "What's the name of the street on which I'll find that office?"

"I told you to get off the bus at the Eurasian Bank," he responded impatiently, "and you'll find the office nearby in the Mackinnons Building."

Since the man appeared to be acquainted with only local landmarks, I murmured, "Thanks for your help," and departed before, in sheer exasperation, that budding entrepreneur tossed me out onto the street.

Initially I had planned to flag another taxicab, but that proved to be more difficult than anticipated, so I finally decided to see the city from its sidewalks while searching for the office on my own. On my own soon appeared to be the only way that I would find it, because the first two brown-skinned men that I accosted didn't understand English.

While I was striding along a sidewalk, a young woman suddenly appeared alongside and thrust before me what had to be the world's smallest baby. Involuntarily I came to a stop and stared at them. The childlike woman was neatly clad in a sari, and the baby was clothed in a jerkin, about which a thin blanket had been literally bound and tied as far up its body as its armpits permitted. With dark eyes carefully averted, the woman murmured a few unintelligible words; then, with several stabbing motions of a small forefinger, she pointed insistently toward the baby's midsection. I was so confused that I just stared at the child until its mother flipped it against her bosom and padded away on bare feet to make a similar plea to another pedestrian. Apparently the child's head was so small and light in weight that it required little support since the mother's small hands provided none whatsoever. In fact, she handled the tiny child like a rag doll.

After that incident I swung into a back street that appeared to be more of an alley than a street. Pedestrians dominated its traffic, and the term *street people* immediately sprung to my mind, because they appeared to be such a poverty-stricken lot. At the street's intersection with another narrow street I came upon a crowd of the street people. Most of them were standing, but some of them had assumed comfortable sitting or lounging postures about the periphery of a high pile of coconuts that had been deposited against the curb near the corner of a decrepit, old building. Since the nuts were still enclosed within their green husks, I assumed that they had been freshly picked. After being picked, they may have been loaded into a vehicle, possibly an ox cart, and delivered during the cool, wee hours of the morning to that street corner.

Suddenly I sensed that not only had my coming been noted, but it had been anticipated, since several pairs of dark eyes were leveled in my direction. Meanwhile, other eyes were directed toward a slender man who may not have been more than six feet tall, but he towered over the adjacent bystanders. When I was about ten feet from the gathering, as if on schedule, a bystander selected one of the green, husk-encased nuts from the pile and tossed it to the tall man, who fielded it nicely with his left hand. Then, with his left forearm held upright and with a calculating glance at me from the corner of one dark eye, he raised the bush knife in his right hand from alongside his thigh and cleanly cleaved the green husk, nut and all, shearing away the upper part of it.

The cool, clean precision of the act caused me to stop and stare apprehensively toward the parts of the husk and nut that remained in his left hand. As far as I could determine, the tips of his fingers remained unscathed, even though the blade must have passed within a small fraction of an inch of them. Then that character placed the cleaved edge of the nut against his lips and tilted its bottom up; then his big Adam's apple bobbed rhythmically up and down between the sinews of his throat as he gulped down the thambili (liquid from the king coconut). Meanwhile, some of the bystanders watched in open admiration, while others looked expectantly toward me.

Of course, I realized that the operation was a come-on for the grizzled, old tourist who had strolled along that alley behind my beard. And I was sorely tempted to sample the liquid, but the sanitary conditions failed to meet my standards, so I absently picked my way through the fringes of the group and almost fell over the tiny woman with the doll-like baby. Even though I had escaped her previous plea, this time she seemed determined to win. Again she presented that human doll and frantically gestured toward it while sputtering unintelligibly in her native tongue. Meanwhile, she refused to look directly at me, but the baby's beady little eyes stared intently at me, so it couldn't have been a rag doll. Truly, the woman's actions were strange, but she must have been reasonably smart, since both she and the child appeared to be cleanly and carefully maintained. Once more I was tempted, but giving alms is against my religion, so that woman-child failed because of an old man's fanatical religious principles. Besides, I was surrounded by a horde of equally qualified recipients.

From that narrow back street I returned to the main thoroughfare, but few of its intersecting streets were identified, so I finally attempted to describe my problem to a man with light-brown features who wore a light-brown business suit, and he managed to redirect me toward the Eurasian Bank. While I was endeavoring to follow his directions without the aid of street signs, a tall, middle-aged man with pale features emerged from the throng of little, brown-skinned pedestrians, and our eyes locked momentarily as we passed. I was so surprised to see a member of my race that I stopped and looked back to verify the fact and found that the other man had done likewise. Simultaneously we smiled, exchanged friendly waves, and continued on our separate ways. After that exchange I better understood the attitudes of members of ethnic groups in my country. Why shouldn't they prefer to associate with their own kind? After all, most normal people do.

More by chance than by direction, I stumbled onto a main thoroughfare alongside which several banks and office buildings stood. When I stopped one of the passers-by and requested to be directed to the Eurasian bank, he stared blankly at me until something clicked behind his brown-skinned forehead. Then he delightedly exhaled, "Eurasian," and excitedly gestured toward an indefinite point farther along the street.

Several minutes later I did come upon an unidentified bank, whose entry, like the other banks, was guarded by members of the militia. However, unlike the other banks, this one was guarded by a cordon of them, so it must have been an important financial institution, if not the one I sought.

Even though I hadn't held up a bank for years, I was determined to get into that one by some hook or crook, because its tellers would probably understand my version of the English language. Besides, I wished to exchange some U.S. dollars for some more of that Technicolor currency. Therefore, pausing on the sidewalk before the bank, I carefully cased the joint.

The facade of the ancient building consisted of large, elongated blocks of machine-cut stone, which time had turned to a dark-gray color. The ground-level windows bore iron bars, and the large, recessed entrance had been enclosed by a rough, unpainted wooden structure, consisting of heavy timbers faced with 2- x 12-inch planks. After a careful interrogation by the guards, each of the bank's potential customers was being admitted or denied admittance through a narrow opening at one end of the wooden structure. Getting past those armed guards appeared to be my biggest problem, since they probably wouldn't understand my brand of English or any other kind of English.

While thoroughly psychoanalyzing the stern, brown-skinned visages, I detected the weakest link of the cordon. One of the guards broke under my piercing gaze and squeezed out an *unguarded* smile. Despite the fact that, like FDR, I hate *wah,* I was about embrace war by taking unfair advantage of that guard's friendly nature. But war is war, so I felt no remorse for what I was about to do to that naive lad. Besides, a friendly fellow like that would be the first to fall during an enemy attack, since he probably would drop his gun and extend his right hand to the first of the attackers, so there was no reason for me to feel remorse. In fact, equipped as they were with what I suspected to be World War I–vintage uniforms and weapons, most of those little characters looked more like potential victims than like soldiers.

Nevertheless, after slowly and cautiously mounting the four concrete steps to the narrow, concrete slab on which the guards stood, I approached my victim and inquired, "How can I get into this bank?"

Of course, if I had any conscience whatsoever, I would have explained my true intentions, but it really didn't matter, because he just stood there and stared at me, so my efforts were wasted. Then my eyes were attracted to his weapon, which was held rather indifferently at parade rest.

"Oh, what a beautiful rifle!" I exclaimed admiringly, impulsively running a forefinger along its gleaming barrel.

In spite of the fact that he had not understood the words, he accurately read my actions and responded with a proud smile. Finally it soaked through my thick skull that I wasn't looking down into the bore of a vintage rifle; I was looking down into the bore of a new shotgun. Abruptly I began to view our lack of communication as a great boon, indeed.

During the process of currying the favor of the friendly *GI,* I had acquired the undivided attention of a very concerned noncommissioned officer. Of course, I had been aware of his concern from the first, since he had been under the surveillance of my left eye on the off-chance that he might be the best one to contact. But I didn't have to contact him, because he contacted me. Actually he first contacted my buddy, who amiably responded to his superior's question with a manual gesture toward his lips. Since my buddy added some unfamiliar words, I assumed that he had informed the man that I had spoken English, so he didn't know the first *bleeped* thing about what the *bleep* I was talking about. The officer turned and fixed questioning eyes on me, so I repeated my previous question to him, but it didn't ring any bells with him either.

Momentarily, we seemed to have reached a impasse. Then, recalling my buddy's gesture to his lips, I thrust my right forefinger toward the officer to attract his attention. But I was careful not to touch him, because I certainly didn't want to be thrown into the brig for assaulting an officer. After gaining his attention, I pointed my forefinger to my chest. Then I pointed to a part of the inner bank, which was perceptible to us through a pair of glazed entry doors beyond the opening in the wooden wall. A dim light appeared in his dark eyes, but I also detected some elements of indecision in them, so I reached for my wallet. Belatedly, I realized that I should never have done that, because he might have suspected that I was reaching for a weapon and shot me on the spot—in several spots *even.* After pointing to the depleted condition of my wallet and again pointing to the scene within the bank, I pantomimed stuffing my wallet with imaginary currency, and he finally understood my problem. Apparently at some point in his career he had been in similar straits, because he smiled understandingly, pushed the door open, and escorted me past another member of his platoon, who was guarding a second pair of glazed doors.

As I breezed past that last barrier toward those vaults full of colorful lucre, I gloated over how easily I had penetrated that closely guarded bank without having to take the shotgun away from that friendly guard. I might have regretted that act for the rest of my life; that is, if there was anything but *rest* left. As I had expected, one of the tellers understood English, so he not only cashed some traveler's checks for me, but he directed me to the Mackinnons Building.

Of course, it's a cinch to locate something when it has been pointed out by someone literally placing his forefinger on it, so I strode across the street to the Mackinnons Building and on into Mackinnons Travel Service, Ltd. There an attractive young woman arose from behind a flat-top desk and tentatively approached me with questioning eyes.

"Good morning," I murmured, as both of us came to a stop and warily eyed each other. "I would like to discuss an overcharge for an airline ticket by your Singapore office."

"What was the nature of the overcharge?" she inquired uneasily.

"I've scribbled a rough analysis of the problem on this sheet of paper," I replied, submitting it to her.

After accepting it, she thoughtfully moved away, placed it atop an adjacent counter, and stared uncomprehendingly at the calculations inscribed on it.

Finally she said, "Please excuse me." In response to the bob of my bald head, she turned away and called to a slender, dark-complexioned man who was seated behind another flat-top desk in a nearby office.

When he arrived, we went through the formalities of an introduction. Then I restated my problem to him, and the woman transferred the sheet of calculations to him.

After looking absently at it, he asked, "Between what points were you to travel?"

"Between Colombo and Athens," I replied.

"And how much were you charged?" he inquired.

"This amount," I replied, pointing to the sum indicated on the sheet.

"Hmm," he mumbled thoughtfully. "That does seem to be excessive, but let me check one of our reference books." After strolling to a bookcase and returning from it with a thick document, he extracted a value from it and mumbled, "Hmm. It is too much."

"How much too much?" I asked.

"Hmm," he mumbled again. "Definitely too much."

"Well," I began, "I wish to clear up the matter before I get too far from this part of the world. Can you do that for me?"

Smiling faintly, he looked off into space. "I suspect that you should wait and take up the matter with your local office," he finally replied. "They are the ones who should investigate it, because it may take a long time."

"Well," I growled, "it surely didn't take that Singapore office long to clip me for about two hundred dollars."

With a sympathetic smile he repeated, "It may be a long time before you get your money—if you get it."

After briefly pondering the statement, I muttered, "That sounds like you suspect that I've been rooked and that American Express is not likely to do anything about it."

"I didn't say that," he protested. But I noticed that he didn't deny the possibility.

"Well," I began indecisively. Then I hurriedly added, "Thanks for your help. I'm sorry to have burdened you with a problem that's out of your jurisdiction."

"I'm glad to have been of some service," he murmured. "I hope that you recover the difference."

"I would feel better about it if the matter were in your hands," I muttered. Then, with a parting salute, I turned thoughtfully away and strode from the office.

"Huh, so Al got took," observed José, as I barged blindly into the crowded street.

"Aw, you shouldn't badger him that way," protested Pancho. "He has been worrying about that two hundred bucks for days."

"Well, at least he learned one thing from the experience," suggested José philosophically.

"What's that?" countered his mate.

"That Karl Malden has been making the wrong sales pitch for years," Pancho replied.

"True," José conceded. "One really should never leave home with it."

"Shut up, you idiots!" I burst forth. "How can I think with all of this yammering going on?"

"Hmm. Sounds like we better cool it," observed José.

"Yeah," agreed Pancho. "But if we are idiots, what does that make him?"

I managed to engage a motorized *trisha* for the trip back to the hotel, where I approached the isolated flat-top desk that stood at the near end of the long reception desk. Fortunately, the attractive little service clerk was still at her post, so I presented my airline ticket to her and requested that she change the destination from Athens to Zurich. Then I repaired to the coffee shop.

Once more Mahan seated me at the table in the alcove facing the entrance, and Pancho instantly volunteered, "He's doing that to keep Al from making time with those little waitresses."

"Naw, Stupid," retorted José. "That Sinhalese guy is smarter than that. He's trying to keep them away from Al."

"All right, Idiot," countered Stupid. "From what so-called premises did you derive that idiotic conclusion?"

"From some very logical ones," retorted Idiot smugly. "Essentially Mahan is trying to prevent those naive, little peasant girls from inadvertently tipping Big Brother's hand to Al."

"How could . . . ," Stupid began, but Mahan strolled back into the area.

After thoughtfully circling it, he stopped beside my table and inquired, "Have you been to the museum at Sir Marcus Fernando Mawatha yet?"

"No," I replied, "but I've been planning to go there and to the Art Gallery at Ananda Cooraraswamy Mawatha."

With an approving nod he said, "That's the conservative one. The Lionel Wendt Gallery exhibits the more contemporary paintings, and the Kalagaraya serves as the permanent Art Gallery of the Alliance de Colombo."

"Hmm," I mumbled. "According to those statements, I have more to see than the remaining time will accommodate."

"If you don't plan to visit Sri Lanka's ancient cities, then you should visit the museum to obtain some idea of the island's culture," he suggested. "After all, that culture began five hundred years before the birth of your Christ."

"I'll go directly to the museum from here," I promised.

After dickering endlessly with a motorized *trisha*'s driver over his demand of thirty rupees for the privilege of transporting me a distance of slightly less than one mile, I finally did make the trip to the museum. After he stopped the contraption at the curb beside the museum, I slipped a fifty-rupee bill into his grubby, brown hands. But I derived no pleasure from the giving; it was what I observed during a glance across one shoulder while striding away that did it. It was the way he shook his confused head and muttered something in his native tongue that did it—something that probably would have translated into *"loco Americano"* in the language of still another brown-skinned people.

No fee was required to enter the large, masonry structure, whose weather-stained exterior indicated a rather advanced age. Nevertheless, several small, brown-skinned men, clad in makeshift uniforms, guarded it and its ancient artifacts from theft or damage. Its bare floors resounded to the footfalls of the few visitors, especially the plank floors of the upper level, which also yielded under them, I found.

Some of the artifacts were thousands of years old. Very likely they were the remnants of ancient cultures that had been unearthed from various sites on the island and carefully closeted for centuries. The old museum was merely the most recent of those closets. Unfortunately there were few indications of the identities, sources, and ages of the items on display. Fortunately most of the few indicators displayed were printed in English.

Among the most ancient of the remnants were pottery, cooking wares, stone mortars, pestles, and stone tools. Some of the exotically colored fabrics must have been woven from strands of jute or hemp to have survived so long. There was a preponderance of weapons, some of them dating back as far as the tenth century. Among the more primitive weapons were spears, swords, battle-axes, and shields. Many of the spears were constructed of a hardwood on which metal heads were mounted. The blades of some of the swords were curved like scimitars; others were straight with two sharp edges. That is, their edges must have been sharp at some time; however, regardless of their sizes, shapes, or materials, all of them had become incredibly corroded.

There were various types of body armor plate whose pallettes, breastplates, tasses, and cuissues were of metal, but some of the more ancient body armor had been fabricated from heavy reeds or small-diameter pieces of bamboo held in place by interwoven lines of jute or hemp.

Apparently the art of weaving had prevailed throughout several centuries, since there were many displays of intricately woven tapestries, saris, and various other types of oriental clothing. Among the displays were some exotically embroidered, moccasinlike slippers with the toes curved up to points, but they must have been the footwear of the gentry, since most of the island's current population still travels on the callous soles of its bare feet.

During my hours-long trek through the various rooms and cul-de-sacs I encountered only two other Caucasians: a young couple who exchanged curious glances with me. Otherwise, the scene was dominated by barefoot mothers with their broods of scantily clad, barefoot children. However, unlike their American counterparts, those children behaved admirably.

Upon returning to the hotel, I decided to indulge in a snack. As usual, Mahan seated me at a table in the alcove opposite the entrance. While I was waiting for my order to be served, he drifted from across the room to the side of my table and inquired, "Did you find the museum interesting?"

"I certainly did," I answered. "Thank you for the suggestion. Some of those exhibits are very old, indeed, but I don't recall seeing any exhibits that demonstrate this society's ability to sculpture marble and stone."

"Nevertheless, some Sri Lankans do have that ability," he responded defensively, "but they specialize in cutting gemstones. In fact, our gem cutters can cut our precious stones to any design that the customer desires, so they do have that ability."

"I didn't intend to imply otherwise," I apologized. "My observation merely concerned the lack of sculptured statues in that museum. But I'm surprised to learn that gemstones are mined here. Very likely they are opals, since they seem to prevail in this part of the world."

"No opals are found here," he said. "But seventeen different varieties of precious and semiprecious stones are mined on the island."

"Amazing!" I exclaimed. "But I had the impression that most precious stones are found in mountainous regions or in regions where volcanoes abounded at one time."

"Sri Lanka is mountainous," he retorted. "Some of its mountains extend up to eight thousand feet above sea level. In fact, most of the tea bushes are grown between the elevations of three and seven thousand feet."

"Of course, tea is the island's principal export," I ventured.

"True," he granted. "But it also exports rubber, coconuts, and spices. In fact, it was the spice industry that first induced European nations to take over this island when it was still Ceylon—that and its gem mines."

"Yeah, they intrigue me, too," I said. "What kinds of gems do they yield?"

"The finest blue sapphires in the world are found in this island's mines," he answered proudly. "In fact, they are second only to the diamond in hardness."

"Blue is one of my favorite colors," I observed absently.

"But the best quality stones are not strictly blue," he interposed. "They are a cornflower blue."

"No doubt they are relatively small," I speculated.

"Some of them are," he granted, "but the largest sapphire stone ever discovered was found on this island, and it weighed a paltry forty-two pounds."

"Paltry!" I exclaimed. "You have to be kidding. Wye, I'll bet that that's the largest gemstone of any type found anywhere."

With a gratified smile he resumed: "Cat's eyes are also found here." Then, in response to my puzzled expression, he added, "The cat's eye is particularly remarkable in that a silvery streak of light appears to travel across the surface of the stone as it is rotated or moved."

"And that forms the pupil of the cat's eye," I suggested.

With a tolerant smile he continued, "The phenomenon is often described by the word *chatoyancy*, which is derived from the French word *chat*, and. . . ."

"And it translates into the English word *cat*," I interjected.

With a nod he added, "The honey-yellow and apple-green cat's eyes are considered to be particularly lucky by some people." After a pause to shift some mental gears, he resumed: "Alexandrite, first discovered about eighteen thirty in the Ural Mountains of Russia, was named for Czar Alexander the Second, but Sri Lanka is the principal source of it now. In natural light it appears to be an olive green, but in artificial light it turns to raspberry red. So far, it is considered to be the third hardest stone."

Meanwhile, two customers had strolled through the entrance, so he excused himself. Upon returning, he resumed: "There are other precious stones common to Sri Lanka, and two of them are the star ruby and the star sapphire, both of which obtain their starlike quality from internal channels and intrusions of submicroscopic size that attract rays of light."

"Possibly they function like small lasers," I speculated.

But he tactfully refrained from commenting on the possibility. Instead, he said,

"Then there also is the yellow sapphire, whose lyrical name in Sinhala means pollen of flowers. Last of the island's most precious gems is the amethyst, which possesses a purple color."

"I'm amazed that this small island produces so many different kinds of gemstones," I muttered.

"But Sri Lanka has a land area of some twenty-five thousand square miles," he protested.

From his thought-filled expression I gathered that he was reconsidering the protest and finding it wanting, since he added: "Nevertheless, it is rated fifth among the best gem-producing areas of the world. South Africa is rated first, of course; then come South America, Burma, and Thailand in that order."

"Thank you for a very informative lecture, Mahan," I said. "Unfortunately, I must move along, or I'll miss my plane."

As I struggled out from behind the table, he extended his right hand and said, "It's a bit early, but I'll wish you a *suba raathriyak wewa* anyway."

"That sounds pretty exotic," I remarked, as I accepted the hand. "What does it mean in English?"

"Good night," he responded with a self-conscious chuckle.

"All of that for just a good night?" I countered drolly. "It may be more lyrical than good night in English, but it uses up a lot more time."

"People in the tropics rarely move as rapidly as those of the Northern and Southern Hemispheres," he responded with another chuckle. "I hope that you have a nice flight." And we parted with a couple of casual salutes.

From the coffee shop I strolled directly to the travel service desk, where I looked down into the pretty brown eyes of the little brunette and inquired, "Did you manage to change the destination of my flight from Athens to Zurich?"

"Yes," she replied, withdrawing the ticket envelope from a desk drawer, "but there's an additional charge."

"Since Zurich is farther north than Athens, that's to be expected," I said, accepting the envelope, to which a neatly inscribed rider had been attached. With a glance at the amount on the rider, I dug out my wallet and matched it with paper of the regime.

"Thank you," she murmured after carefully counting it.

"Thank you for the promptness and efficiency with which you made that change on short notice," I responded. Then, with my eyes glued to the flight schedules printed on the ticket, I absently added, "I suppose that I should line up a cab for the trip to the airport."

"I'll do that for you," she said matter-of-factly.

"No, I'll do it," I insisted. "You've already completed your responsibility. Calling the cab is my responsibility."

"But calling the cab is **my** responsibility," she protested. "I have the cabs. No cab is supposed to go out of here unless I call it."

I stared intensely at her prettily fuming features while a pattern slowly formed in my mind. "But mine will go out of here without your blessing," I retorted rebelliously.

Her eyes stared at the flames in my eyes until they could no longer stand the heat; then they sought refuge in the top of the desk. With that I turned angrily away.

"Man!" exclaimed Pancho. "Did that gal ever tee off Al!"

"Huh!" grunted his mate. "You would have been teed off, too, if somebody tried to tap you for another ten percent after you had been tapped by an agent for ten percent of the hotel bill here, clipped for big bucks by a crooked travel agency in Singapore, and tapped again for ten percent of still another hotel bill by a cab driver. Not only would you yearn to get out of this socialist republic, where every socialist is on the take for a capitalistic ten percent, but you would yearn to get clear out of the Orient."

"Well," Pancho began, "where does that airline ticket take us?"

Too fired up to pay any attention to them, I then bore down on the two clerks at the desk and pulled up against the front of it within a carefully calculated, equal distance between them. "I would like to check out," I muttered, pushing the key across about a foot of the counter.

Two pairs of dark eyes turned apprehensively toward each other. Then one of the men cautiously moved toward the key, picked it up, turned away toward a file, returned with a long computer printout, and placed it on the counter before me. I picked it up and pored over the notations while the man hovered uneasily in the background.

"What is this ten percent for?" I squeaked. Actually it was an involuntary scream, but my voice cracked.

The man warily tilted his head forward into the battle zone until he could see the item to which my forefinger was pointing. "Oh," he murmured, "that's the mandatory ten percent for tips."

"Oh-oh, clear the decks for action, gang!" exclaimed José. "Here we go again!"

"Head for the hills!" shouted Pancho.

But I didn't even wince. By that time I had become too numb to react. I just paid the bill and headed toward the luggage room and my temporarily stored bags. Of course, I had to tip the attendant to retrieve them, but I held it down to an even ten percent.

"Well, everything seems to be under control," José suggested optimistically.

"Better keep under cover a bit longer," warned Pancho. "The fuse may be a bit longer than usual."

Despite the insistent protestations of an otherwise idle bellman, I carried my bags through that plush lobby and on through the entrance, where the doorman inquired, "Has a cab been called for you, sir?"

"No, I'll flag one at the curb," I retorted grimly. And, without pausing, I cruised beyond the porte cochere, across the return driveway and the cracked sidewalk to the curb at the side of Sir Chittampalam A. Gardiner Mawatha.

It wasn't as easy as flagging a cab in New York, even during the rush hour, because the drivers merely cast puzzled glances toward me and continued to push their little jalopies to the limit. Finally one of them did heed my beckoning gesture and swung his palpitating tin steed onto the driveway. Too far onto the driveway, it proved to be, because the doorman got to him first. And he proceeded to lay some instructions on the driver in Sinhalese or some other language equally unintelligible to me.

Normally it would have been unintelligible to me, but I was laboring under extreme stress. Since my psyche was working overtime, my mind clearly interpreted the words: "Look, fellah," the doorman said, "we have a good thing goin' here. Every driver who leaves this driveway with a passenger drops ten percent of the fare on my palm when he returns, so don't forget to stop on your return trip, or I'll blackball yuh."

That may have been the gist of the instructions, but it isn't intended to be construed as a factual interpretation. From the resigned expression on the driver's swarthy features and his silent acceptance of the instructions, I gathered that one of us was stuck for 10 percent. Of course, I was the most likely candidate, since I had not yet received a quotation from the driver. The doorman had aptly forestalled that.

After silently helping me load the luggage, the driver shot a questioning glance at me.

"I want to go to the airport," I responded with an appropriate gesture. Since he nodded, I assumed that he would move out in the right direction. And he did.

The man's tail must have been parked too close to the Toyota's afterburner, because he took off like his sarong was afire. I won't even try to describe that horrible trip because mere words can't do it. The only other experience in my life that can be even remotely compared to it was the trip from the airport, and the trip to it easily doubled the near disasters of that one. However, there were no cattle or ox carts on the road, thank Allah, or there would have been some beef burgers strung along it. Of that I'm sure. Apparently the driver was trying to make up sufficient time to compensate for the 10 percent that the doorman was laying on him. There had to be a logical reason for his insane driving. On the other hand, maybe there was no reason, because Sri Lanka does lie within the inscrutable Orient.

When the cab arrived at the airport, we found that between us we were unable to raise sufficient change to either pay the 250-rupee fare or to change one of my 1,000-rupee bills. Finally, with many gestures, I managed to explain to the man that I would go to the terminal and obtain change for a bill from the bank. But he may not have fully understood my intentions; consequently, he cautiously accompanied me to the terminal's central entrance, whose doors were not only unlocked but wide open at that hour. Of course, a pair of guards confronted us, but one of them spotted the airline ticket in my shirt pocket and motioned me on, and the other one refused admittance to the driver. While impatiently waiting for the chubby little bank clerk to make change, I glanced across one shoulder toward the open doorway, where the little driver anxiously waited. Apparently he didn't fully trust me, and I grimly wondered if some profligate Caucasian might have employed a similar tactic to beat him out of a fare.

But this time fortune had smiled on him, because I not only returned with the fare, but I sweetened the pot with a fifty-rupee note. Because of the circumstances he was forced to accept it silently, but his delighted smile was enough reward. His happiness must have been contagious, because both guards favored me with approving smiles. Of course, it's against my religion to buy either favor or approval, but I was merely spreading a little goodwill to compensate for some unprincipled member of my race who may have taken advantage of that passive little fellow.

At the ticket counter I was forced to pay a departure tax. After disposing of that and checking my luggage, I still had time to waste, so I took up a position at a relatively inconspicuous point and began to study the milling throng. As before, I found that it was mostly composed of small, poorly dressed, brown-skinned people. But I did spot several men who wore well-cut, tan suits that appeared to be identical in design, so they could have been uniforms, but they bore no military insignia. In practically every case the color of the man's skin was no darker than that of his suit, so I assumed that the men in those suits must be of a higher caste than were their darker, barefoot countrymen.

Among the various barriers to the boarding gate was a line of immigration officials; however, since I was leaving the country, my passport was cheerfully stamped. Then I remembered my Sri Lankan currency, so I turned back to the official and said, "I forgot to exchange some of your currency. May I still do that?"

Tolerantly pointing back to a man behind the grille of a nearby window, he replied, "That man will exchange it for you, but you must go no farther than that window."

"Thank you," I murmured, turning away and mentally applauding the courteous cooperation of the Sri Lankan officials.

At the grilled window I stopped, dug out my stock of Technicolor currency, and presented it to the clerk. After a brief wait I fixed a questioning gaze on the man's expectant eyes.

"The receipt, sir," he responded. "I must have the receipt."

Then my mind retrieved the scene in the bank, when I had interrupted the clerk while he was completing that receipt to inquire regarding the location of the Mackinnons Building. Even if he did finally complete it, I never saw it again. "But I never received a receipt for that particular exchange," I protested. "The bank clerk forgot to give it to me."

He stared suspiciously at me for an instant, shook his head, and firmly stated, "I must have the receipt before I can exchange the money." Then he pushed the notes toward me.

"What is this?" I asked angrily. "Another government rip-off?"

His dark eyes glistened as he passively replied, "I'm sorry, sir, but that's the rule."

"Then this money has no real value without a receipt," I growled savagely. "So why doesn't the government just issue receipts and skip the currency?" I inquired illogically.

"I don't know," he responded uneasily, "but that's the rule."

"I have a rule, too," I retorted. "I'm writing a book about my experiences abroad, and I promise you that I'll include this incident in it. No one, not even a foreign government, takes advantage of me and escapes unscathed. In fact, potential tourists should be warned against this type of trickery."

His eyes wavered under my angry glare. "What kind of a book are you writing?" he inquired uneasily.

"A travelogue," I replied. "Usually the writer suggests to the reader where to go for the best deals. In this case I am going to recommend that travelers skip Sri Lanka, because the currency is suspect."

Meanwhile, my mind was churning with thoughts of how discourteous and uncooperative the Sri Lankan officials were. Then I whipped around and charged past the startled immigration officer so rapidly that his mouth dropped open in amazement.

"Wow!" exclaimed José. "Al surely blew his top that time."

"Not so loud," cautioned Pancho. "He's still steaming."

"He shouldn't have beat on that poor guy so hard," suggested José. "He was only abiding by the rules; besides, it was Al's fault that he didn't receive the receipt. That bank clerk would have given it to him if Al hadn't taken off so quickly after he learned where the Mackinnons Building was located."

"Well, you know how Al is . . . ," Pancho began on a philosophical note. "He's a pretty stable guy until somebody treats him unfairly. No doubt he'll cool off and write that money off for what it is worth, which is nothing."

"But he'll put the incident in the book, won't he?" José asked.

"Yep," was the prompt response. "He always keeps his promises."

"If it's physically possible," added José.

27

Colombo to Zurich

Colombo to Geneva

Once more there was no committee to see me off, but Big Brother's Sri Lanka branch may have possessed a more normal psyche than his other branches. At least it may have been less sadistic than the branch that saw me off at the Perth International Airport. Even though only some 60 percent of the seating capacity of the craft was occupied, I had been assigned to a seat in the central part of it with a vacant seat on either side of me. After it settled onto the landing strip at Calcutta's airport, I unlocked my seat belt and moved to a vacant seat beside a window so that I could view the general area and watch the maintenance activities in the immediate vicinity. Like Colombo, it was an unimpressive sight. Not only was most of the maintenance equipment very old and in need of repair, but the terminal and its outlying facilities were in need of maintenance attention, and the entire area was poorly lighted.

When I returned to my seat, I found that a small, dark-eyed man with a light-brown complexion and graying hair had occupied the seat on my left, so I assumed that he was a native of India. Just minutes after takeoff the craft's internal lighting systems were either doused or dimmed, so most of the passengers who had not already done so pushed back their seats and tucked in their heavy blankets for the remainder of the night. As usual, my mind remained alert in the unfamiliar environment, but it finally responded to the drone of the engines and an increasingly insistent weariness.

Even so, the indirect glow of the sun was just breaking across the eastern horizon when I awoke. Simultaneously, I sensed that the adjacent passenger was also awake. As soon as he sensed that I was awake, he sat upright, raised his seat, neatly folded his blanket, and looked about for a place to stow it.

"Let's place it on this unoccupied seat," I suggested with an outstretched hand.

"Thank you," he responded and surrendered it.

After attempting to erase some of the wrinkles from his conservatively cut business suit, he pulled a briefcase from beneath the seat in front of him and removed a packet containing several sheets of bond typing paper stapled in its upper left-hand corner. When my eyes involuntarily wandered to the English words typed on the top sheet, I deliberately turned them away. After the man flipped over the top sheet and began studying the material on the next one, my eyes stubbornly turned to it and zeroed in on one particular paragraph, through which several engineering equations were scattered, and I was hooked. Finally I forced my eyes away from the equations, which dealt intriguingly with the manipulation of hot gases. Since they were familiar equations, I was able to follow them to their inevitable conclusions, so they became even more intriguing, but I firmly resisted any further temptations to peek. After completing a review of the material, the man leaned forward, returned the packet to the briefcase; then he sat back against the seat, raised one forearm, and peered pensively at his wristwatch.

Simultaneously the public address system burped; then the captain announced, "I'm sorry to report that the airport at Zurich is snowbound; however, the airport at Geneva is open, so we'll change our course and land there. For those passengers who must go to Zurich, rail passes will be issued at the Geneva terminal. Again I'm sorry for this inconvenience, but the situation is in the hands of a much higher authority than ours."

Automatically my eyes sought those of my dismayed fellow passenger. "And you have to be in Zurich at a specified time for a meeting," I volunteered.

"Yes," he replied. "This is a terrible inconvenience for me. Of course, I'll have to get to a telephone as soon as possible and notify some people of the delay."

"They'll understand," I insisted. "After all, they live in that environment."

After looking at me and at my casual attire, he asked, "But it won't inconvenience you, will it?"

"No," I responded with a chuckle. "I'm on a world tour, so it will merely add a few more miles to the tour. In fact, I'll gain a free train trip from Geneva to Zurich, so the weatherman has been on my side this time." With a droll smile, I added, "But I didn't bribe him."

The expression on the man's dark features remained unchanged, but I consoled myself with the knowledge that the people of India are not renowned for their sense of humor.

"Hmm," Pancho silently mumbled. "I didn't know that Al had any Indian ancestors."

"Watch it!" José warned. "He's apt to give you a fat lip."

"Who has lips?" Pancho responded nonchalantly.

"Are you retired?" the man beside me solemnly inquired.

"Yes," I answered. "I retired from an engineering position in the American aerospace industry. But I couldn't avoid noticing that you must be an engineer, too."

"Yes, I am," he responded with an outstretched right hand. "My name is Hasu Sheth. I'm with Airoil-Flaregas of India."

After I completed my part of the formality, he slipped one hand beneath a lapel of his jacket, retrieved a small card from a card case, presented it to me, and said, "This is my card."

"Thank you," I said. "Of course, I no longer have any need of a business card, so I can't reciprocate in kind. Nevertheless, since I'm writing a travelogue about this trip, your card may prove to be very convenient."

"Oh, you are also a writer?" he inquired.

"I've done a lot of technical writing," I answered, "but this is my first foray into the journalistic field."

"I sincerely hope that you meet with great success," he murmured, as the craft's huge tires mildly protested to a couple of contacts with the runway and settled onto it with a solid thump.

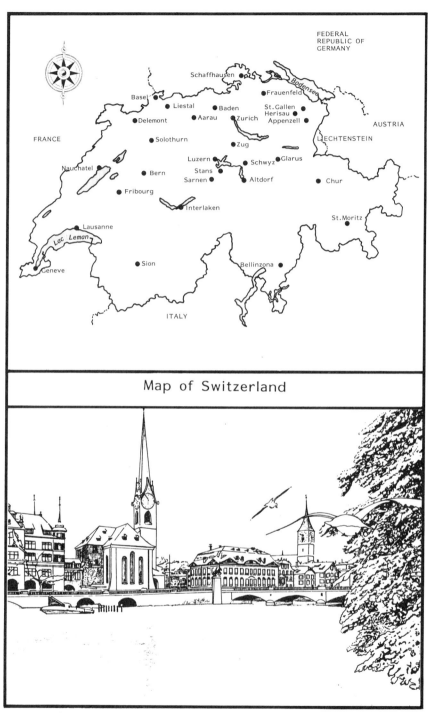

Map of Switzerland

A Wintery View of Zurich and the Limmat

"And I hope that this misfortune doesn't create a major problem for you," I responded.

"I'm sorry to leave so abruptly," he muttered while hurriedly unlocking his seat belt, "but I must hurry."

"I understand," I rejoined, as he injected himself into the aisle. "Since snow occasionally falls on most of the Northern and Southern Hemispheres, I've been confronted with many similar problems."

Geneva   After merging with the throng in Geneva's air terminal, I found that some of the passengers were behaving rather rudely and abrasively. I particularly noticed it in the area of the terminal where the train tickets were being issued. More specifically, I noticed it in the behavior of two stocky, dark-complexioned men who looked to be thirty or more, so they were old enough to know better. Even though they consulted each other in fluent French, they may have been Italians since, to no one in particular, they kept chanting, "This change in destination caused us to miss our flight from Zurich to Milan, so we don't want train tickets to Zurich; we want plane tickets for the next flight from here to Milan."

Meanwhile, they pushed and shouldered their way past me and several of the passengers ahead of me to the relatively young blonde who was issuing the tickets. There, in French, they loudly made the same demands.

If they were Italians, then they must have spoken Italian in addition to French and English. Therefore, since I am hard pressed to communicate intelligently in one language, it may have been jealousy that compelled me to view them in such a critical light. But the ability to communicate in several languages doesn't necessarily indicate that an individual is cultured. Courtesy and kindness to others are fairly reliable gauges of that. Consequently, upon my arrival before the distraught blonde, I dribbled courtesy and kindness all over her to compensate her for having to fend off the demands of the two self-centered men while she served other customers with prior rights.

Geneva to Zurich

Despite my inability to speak French, I remembered enough of the language from my tortuous high school days to encounter no problems whatsoever in following the French directions on the station's walls to the Zurich train. But the English equivalents beneath them were helpful, too.

Since considerable drama has been constructed about some exotic trains in literature, such as the Orient Express, which starred in *Murder on the Orient Express*, I chose to dub that Zurich train "The Swiss Cheese Express."

For some reason that wasn't apparent to me, José quickly came to my defense with the words: "Despite the name's failure to imply something exotic and exciting, it probably suits Al's sense of drama."

"Okay, so he has a warped sense of drama," Pancho chimed in. "But we know how stubborn he can be, too, so the name of the train is still The Swiss Cheese Express."

"To our knowledge no one was murdered on it during that particular trip," José rejoined, "and. . . ."

"And no one was mugged on it," Pancho interjected. "But two stupid human beings became involved in some juvenile shoves and pushes."

"We're getting ahead of the story," José silently protested. "That is, if it can be called a story."

Apparently no seats were assigned, because my ticket indicated neither a seat number nor a car number, so I boarded the nearest car and selected a seat that could accommodate only one passenger. Opposite it was a similar seat, and across the aisle were two opposite bench seats capable of accommodating four passengers. Since there appeared to be no storage accommodations for my luggage, I stacked it about me so that another passenger could use the opposite seat.

Shortly after I was in place, a slender, nattily attired, middle-aged man stopped in the intervening aisle and lowered two large suitcases onto the coarsely carpeted floor. After casting a supercilious glance toward me and my worn attire, he picked up one of the suitcases, rotated it to a horizontal attitude, and carefully placed it on one of the unoccupied seats. Then, placing the second one in a like manner at the end of the first one, he seated himself in the middle of the seat opposite them. Right off I decided that fate had dealt a bad hand to me by placing that particular passenger in that particular pair of seats. Within just seconds I had acquired a strong dislike for the man, for his fine, tailor-made suit, and for his gray, felt hat with the feather in its black band. In particular, I disliked the way he looked down his nose at me, so I resentfully turned my head and peered through the window at the activities of the workmen alongside the train. Even though the sun shone hazily, their expelled breaths formed wisps of steam as they hustled about the cold, concrete platform and loaded cold parcels aboard what must have been a cold express-mail car.

Finally my gaze turned involuntarily from the window to those beautiful suitcases. Not only were they perfectly matched in size and shape, but their rich leather literally shouted great cost. Unfortunately the dark eyes of the man caught me in the act. Once detected, I could no more avoid those supercilious eyes than the victim of a cobra can avoid the snake's hypnotic eyes. Uncrossing his legs, he carefully pulled the seams of his trousers straight, leaned toward the nearest of the beauties, and flicked an imaginary speck of dust from its softly glowing surface. Then he turned toward me with a contemptuous sneer, and the spell was abruptly broken, because I found that I no longer disliked the man; I passionately hated him.

As soon as the train cleared the city limits, the man in the cab of the diesel electric engine must have advanced the throttle to full speed, because its line of eight cars practically flew through the snow-dusted countryside. The rails must have been welded and ground to produce such a smooth ride, and every member of the railroad maintenance crew must have served his apprenticeship in the Swiss Watchmaker's Guild to be able to maintain such uniform track levels and super elevations.

At the first stop one of the oncoming passengers paused in the aisle beside me and stared speculatively at the two bags. Then he looked toward their proud owner and gruffly muttered some German words. The other man mutely shrugged his shoulders and gestured toward the bags and the space beside him as if implying that nothing could be done about the situation.

The man in the aisle was not only bigger, but he was much more ruggedly constructed than the would-be dog in the manger, so I wasn't surprised to hear him rumble some more German words that sounded like a command. Apparently the dog in the manger decided that the big mastiff might bite, because he abruptly arose and moved one of the suitcases to the seat beside him.

But the big mastiff was not satisfied with just half a loaf, and he must have said as much in German, since the dog in the manger immediately arose and stacked the second suitcase on the first one. Then the big mastiff seated himself in the middle of the vacated seat and stared balefully at his victim, who sat huddled like a whipped dog beside the two suitcases.

Of course, I could have added a supercilious sneer to the big man's stare, but that would have been something like a small dog barking at the dog in the manger after the big mastiff had whupped him, so I just sat there and admired the big brute. For some reason I had acquired a deep and abiding love for him; meanwhile, my hate for the man opposite him had subsided to contempt.

Geneva is located at the western end of Lake Geneva, which projects into the southwestern corner of Switzerland. About two hundred miles of well-engineered rails find their way from Geneva past Bern, the capital, through some of the world's finest pastoral scenery to Zurich, which lies near the border between the tiny nation and Germany.

Beyond Geneva the sky became increasingly overcast, and the landscape was partially obscured by snow flurries, so much of the trip's scenic potential was lost to me. Without doubt a sunny summer day would have been preferable, but some winter scenes can be just as spectacular as summer scenes, especially in Switzerland. Despite the overcast skies, there were uniquely Swiss farm dwellings, barns, occasional chalets, and a few small villages to attract my attention. As the train advanced in a northeasterly direction, the depth of the snow increased, and the heavy deposits of snow on the roofs, the rolling countryside, and the groves of pine trees added considerably to what would have been a veritable winter wonderland in bright sunlight.

At the outskirts of Zurich the train slowed its rate of travel, so I was forced to view the shoddy underclothing of a large European city in the depths of a winter storm. Despite the fact that the snow probably covered many of the city's scenic sins, those railside views reminded me somewhat of the views commonly found alongside the rails in American smokestack cities, such as Cleveland and Pittsburgh.

I had become so absorbed in viewing the rapidly changing scene that I was the last passenger to open the spring-loaded door at the forward end of the car. It was just as well, because an altercation was under way on the platform at the top of the steps leading down to the station's concrete platform. Since the passageway was obstructed by the two passengers involved in the altercation, no one was leaving the train, so I set my suitcase against the door to hold it open. Then, swinging the briefcase in front of me, I grasped its handle with both hands and waited for the problem to be resolved.

Right off I saw that the dapper passenger from across the aisle appeared to be one of the principals, and the other one was a tall, callow youth with a shock of curly, blond hair who may have been seventeen years old. At that particular instant the youth was thrusting the end of his right forefinger against the tip of his nose with such force that several of its blond hairs were exposed. In the process he said, "You think that because you are wealthy, you can turn up your nose at everybody else."

Consequently, I concluded that once more my private hate had been influencing people and making friends. Since the man responded in German, the nature of his words was lost to me, but many of the impatiently waiting passengers fixed critical eyes on him, so I assumed that they understood the words and considered them to be lacking in culture.

But there was one amusing aspect of the situation: The argument was being conducted in two different languages, and neither of the wranglers appeared to understand the other one's words. Nevertheless, each of them seemed to accurately sense the other one's desire to denigrate him. But the youth possessed one advantage in that he bore no luggage, so his arms were free to gesture tellingly. Meanwhile, the other man stood with one of those beautiful suitcases in each hand and responded with a flow of German words that, according to the expressions of some of the bystanders, must have been rapidly progressing from uncultured to uncouth.

After the youth's grotesque display, he moved toward the steps, but the man lowered one suitcase and employed the freed hand to pull him back. In response to the youth's shocked expression, the man gestured magnanimously toward a young woman and nodded his head for her to precede them. Apparently the woman was only too glad to escape from the charade, because she literally bolted down the steps. And the youth attempted to follow her, but the man roughly grasped his arm and pulled him back. Then, picking up the suitcase, he roughly thrust himself ahead of the big lad. In the process he almost tumbled down the steps; however, much to my chagrin, he managed to right himself at the last instant. Since the blockade had been broken, the other passengers surged onto the station's platform, and I followed suit. Meanwhile, the youth had wandered somewhat far afield in his effort to relocate the other aggressor, and it was from directly behind me that he finally sighted him.

"Hey!" he shouted to the man. "Who is calling your mother now?"

The words didn't fit any indirect insult with which I was familiar, but I suspected that the boy was implying that the man's mother had been a call girl or the equivalent thereof. Perhaps the words possessed certain European connotations with which I was unfamiliar—and with which I preferred to remain unfamiliar.

The oaf was so intent on keeping his eyes on his adversary that, like a big, awkward St. Bernard puppy, he staggered about in a long, unbuttoned topcoat and accidentally bumped into me.

"Uh!" he grunted. Then, with but a glance at me from light-blue eyes, he staggered onward, still intent on harassing his adversary.

"That certainly was a display of very cloddish behavior," José interjected heatedly.

"Think nothing of it," Pancho responded. "Very likely he's just an awkward English schoolboy whose parents have sent on a tour of the continent between school sessions to keep him out of their hair."

"I meant the way they mishandled the treatment of that young lady," José rejoined.

"Yeah," agreed Pancho. "Apparently neither of those idiots know anything about etiquette, because one of them should have preceded her down those steps and. . . ."

"And assisted her to ensure . . . ," interjected José.

"And assisted her to ensure that she didn't fall," added his buddy.

"Yeah," agreed José. "Furthermore, if that lady had been about to climb those steps, those idiots should have allowed her to precede them; then one of them should have followed her up the steps to ensure. . . ."

"To ensure that she didn't fall," interjected his buddy.

"Apparently neither one of you idiots know that the best books on etiquette frown darkly on one party interrupting another one during a discussion," I interrupted them.

Zurich From the station platform, I moved into what appeared to be the railroad station, but it was unlike any such station that I had ever seen. Looking up, I saw that, inset between the cold, gray, steel rafters of the towering gable roof were hundreds of small, glass panels. Within the station's cold, gray walls were only cold, gray, steel columns, beams, and girders. Apparently the waiting room and the ticket counters were enclosed beyond the cold, gray internal wall along which I strode. Meanwhile, several small vehicles—luggage trucks and tractors—maneuvered about the open area and over the rails imbedded in the concrete floor.

It seemed that I had walked a country mile by the time that the rails and I arrived at the towering opening in the far end of the structure. Moving close to one of the internal walls, I set the luggage against it and paused to rest my arms and assess the situation. But the gusts of air that swept through that great opening must have come directly from the snow-encrusted peaks of the Alps, because they pierced my light topcoat like the business ends of icicles, so I hurriedly picked up the luggage and set to it once more. On rounding one side of the opening, I spied several taxicabs standing at a nearby curb, but my tear-filled eyes fixed on the sign of a hotel that stood on a nearby street corner. Bowing my bald head to the piercingly cold blast, I forged onward over the longest two blocks of snow-encrusted sidewalk that I had ever traversed.

Shouldering my way through the hotel's entrance into its small foyer, I paused at the open doorway of the lobby and allowed my bleary eyes to find the middle-aged man and woman, who were posted behind the small reception desk located in a cul-de-sac on my left. Even though my weary arm muscles practically screamed for a break in the action, I managed to extract enough BTUs from them to carry the luggage across the intervening space.

Dropping the luggage on the floor at the base of the desk, I looked from one hostile visage to the other one and inquired, "What's your rate for a single?"

"We have no vacancies," the woman retorted aloofly.

"Thank you," I murmured. Then, picking up the luggage, I began to retrace my steps.

"Brr!" rumbled José. "I don't know which is colder: the wind or that woman's attitude."

"Her attitude was no colder than the stare that she fixed on Al as we moved across that lobby," observed Pancho. "Furthermore, if there are no vacancies, then why are two people required at the desk just to inform potential guests of the situation?"

"I suspect that Big Brother not only has preceded us into this alcove of the Arctic," José replied, "but he must have left a pair of brass knuckles with each of those whom he contacted."

After setting the luggage on the sidewalk, I fished Hasu's business card from my wallet and began to study the names and addresses of the four hotels that he had so obligingly listed on the back of it for me.

"No rooms awailable in *der* hotel?" inquired a voice in guttural tones.

I shot an appraising glance toward the inquisitor and responded with a nod. Then my eyes steadied and narrowed under the burly man's penetrating stare.

After advancing a step closer, he muttered, "My cab and I are at your disposal, sir."

My eyes pensively engaged his gray ones again until they uneasily fled. Incredible as it seemed, the man appeared to have recognized me.

Characteristically, I decided to investigate the matter further, so I asked, "Is the Hotel Stoller far from here?"

With a shrug of his broad shoulders, he muttered, "No, iss not far. Iss joost off of Hardstrasse on Badenerstrasse."

That meant nothing to me, but I had already decided to gamble, so I said, "Yes, I would like to engage you and your cab to take me to that hotel."

He quickly picked up the bags and carried them to the rear of a black vehicle parked beside a nearby curb. Raising the trunk's cover, he lifted the bags and stowed them in it as easily as if they had been loaded with feathers. Meanwhile, I stood by and wistfully yearned to be about thirty-five, too.

After a run of several blocks along the snow-covered surfaces of various streets, the driver swung the vehicle from Badenerstrasse onto a snow-covered parking area beside a small portico, which extended out from the front of a towering, well-preserved old building to the ice-covered sidewalk that paralleled Badenerstrasse. After he brought the cab to a stop, I opened the door beside me and said, "Please wait here while I check at the desk." Then, slamming the door closed, I skated precariously across the ice-covered sidewalk to the connecting sidewalk beneath the portico, which had been cleared of snow and ice as far as the pair of glazed doors at the hotel's entrance. About six feet beyond the entrance I was confronted by a low, twelve-foot-long counter that enclosed a cul-de-sac in one corner of the small lobby. A man who appeared to have survived some forty-five Zurich winters arose from a desk in the far corner of the cul-de-sac and approached the counter with a strange expression on his even features, so I braced myself for another rejection.

Nevertheless, with a pseudo-air of confidence, I inquired, "What's your rate for a single?"

"Ninety-five francs," he responded with a slight German accent.

"Okay, it's a deal," I said. "But a cab is waiting for me, so I'll return shortly." After turning about and thrusting open one of the double doors, I hurried down a couple of steps and along the sidewalk to the ice-covered sidewalk. There I came to a stop and cautiously studied its surface.

"Iss one awailable?" called the driver.

I nodded and slowly moved onto the treacherous ice.

"No, don't come onto *der* ice!" he shouted. "I vill bring your bags."

For a big man, despite the handicap imposed by the bags, he traversed the tricky surface with relative ease. While I held one of the glazed doors open, he marched into the lobby with them, set them beside the counter, turned, and looked expectantly at me.

"Huh!" I grunted. "Since I haven't exchanged any of my money for francs yet, it looks like you are out of luck," I added with a teasing smile.

His eyes wavered for just an instant; then they steadied into a faint smile as he muttered, "Then I vill take vun of your bags."

"Don't do that," I protested. "In that suitcase there's a heavy sweater that I must have to keep me from freezing to death in this frigid climate. Maybe this man can change some American money for me."

In response to my questioning eyes, the desk clerk nodded, so I withdrew my wallet. In return for a hundred-dollar traveler's check, my palm was crossed by several bills bearing unfamiliar monetary designations.

After I paid the fare and tipped the driver, he looked at me with a pleased expression and said, "*Dank* you. You haff been wery generous."

"That's not my nature," I retorted, "so your good fortune may be due to my unfamiliarity with your currency."

"*Dank* you again," he muttered, turning about and opening one of the glazed doors. There he paused momentarily, turned his head, and exchanged expressive stares with the desk clerk before continuing onward.

After I registered, an ancient bellman emerged from the dimly lighted background and carried my bags to the lift. Actually he appeared to be more of a handyman than a bellman; nevertheless, he held the lift's door open for me like any good bellman should. While squeezing into the tiny enclosure, I discovered several probable reasons why the Europeans call them lifts instead of elevators: First off, it was no larger than an old-fashioned American telephone booth; furthermore, it traveled upward very slowly and jerkily, so I soon became convinced that, from the wheelhouse on the roof, another handyman must be lifting the lift by means of a block and tackle. Besides, it was much too cozy for two fat, old men. In fact, it may have posed a problem for the management, because almost any smart, young man could figure out how to make the contraption trap him and an attractive young blonde between floors.

The room proved to be large enough to accommodate two standard double beds, but those beds were equipped with the most complicated combination of linens and blankets that I have ever seen. I never did figure out how to employ those complex components properly, but I finally managed to get by with them. Even though the Swiss people are exalted for their precise workmanship, don't believe it, because nothing in the bathroom functioned properly except the water closet, and it trickled water continuously, so it didn't function properly either. Of course, those malfunctions were all that I uncovered during a brief residence. There may have been others.

Despite the snowbanks, I resolved to see the city, and that was how I happened to be aboard a *Strassenbahnwagen* (tram), which I fervently hoped would take me uptown. If not, then I was willing to settle for downtown. Of course, the tram's destination was displayed on its exterior, but it was in German; furthermore, none of the waiting passengers understood my requests for information. So those were the reasons that I didn't know whether the tram was traveling into town or out of town. But I wasn't deeply concerned about which direction it was traveling, since I was relatively sure to see some of the city in either case.

Immediately after boarding the tram, I looked for the conductor, but the motorman appeared to be the only railroad man aboard the crowded vehicle. Since he was isolated within a cubicle at its forward end, it was obvious that he couldn't collect any fares. Meanwhile, that carload of plump, middle-aged, female shoppers either sat or stood and stared silently into space while I thought how quiet and serene this world would be if all women behaved that way. Every one of the creatures appeared to be deeply involved in her own thoughts, so I was unable to catch the eye of any of them and inquire regarding payment of the fare. Furthermore, their mothers may have warned them to beware of strangers, particularly of men with gray beards, because one of the beards might prove to be a blue beard that had been dyed gray.

Finally I worked up enough courage to step toward a heavyset woman and inquire, "Is the transportation on this bus free?"

She started slightly and stepped back a bit, almost as if she had just settled back onto earth from a trip to one of those ultramodern space stations. Then the blank expression in her blue eyes was replaced by a cold, calculating one as she peered intently at my beard, which, to her space-adapted eyes, may have taken on a bluish hue.

I waited expectantly for her answer, but she just stood there on her conservative heels and stared at me, so I asked, "Do you understand English?"

Obviously she didn't, because she didn't answer, so I fished out my wallet and extracted a Swiss note from it. With the note and wallet clutched in my left hand, and smiling inanely, I pointed my right forefinger to the note. Then, after pointing to my brisket, I pointed to the top of the nearest seat and inanely inquired, "Free?"

Suddenly the blue eyes lighted up. "Ja!" she shouted. "Free!"

I courteously bowed my head and, from force of habit, murmured, "Thank you," even though I was already aware that she didn't understand English.

The exchange must have attracted the attention of the lads, because Pancho inquired, "I wonder if she actually understood the nature of that question. Or did she misinterpret it and shout, '*Ja*! Free!' out of exuberant anticipation."

"Hmm," José mumbled. "Perhaps Al did miss a bet by failing to follow up on that response."

Meanwhile, with time to pass, I removed a small, blue booklet from a pocket of my topcoat and attempted to interpret the words at the top of its cover. The title, *Zurich News*, didn't prove to be very difficult, and beneath it, the words *Wochen-Bulletin, 15.-21. Februar, Mit Stadtplan* proved to be fairly easy because of their similarity to the adjacent English words: "Weekly Bulletin, February 1986, With City Guide."

"If only they had included a similar English translation for this tram's destination, we would know which way it's traveling," José observed wistfully.

When I attempted to open the booklet, the complexity of its construction really impressed me. Not only did it automatically open to the centerfold, but the centerfold voluntarily unfolded to reveal a map that covered several areas of the city, including *Industriequartier, Aussersihl, Hottingen, Fluntern, Oberstrass, Unterstrass*, and *Wipkingen*. But I never was able to get it to do that again; therefore, even though a Swiss watchmaker must have designed it, I concluded that it didn't function properly, so the Swiss may have to appeal to the Japanese for similar maps that do perform reliably.

According to the map, I must have boarded the *Strassenbahnwagen* at *Albisrie-derplatz*, from where it continued along *Badenerstrasse* to its intersection with *Birmonsdorferstrasse*. There I followed several of the shoppers down the steps and became lost for several hours among throngs of people, each of whom mutely shook his head when I requested assistance. Eventually, happening upon a particularly enticing display in the window of a bake shop, I entered it—more to escape from the cold wind than to make any purchases—but the delectable Swiss goodies proved to be irresistible, so I purchased a half-dozen sweet rolls. Shortly after leaving the shop, my stomach protested so vehemently about having been ignored during the morning that I took refuge in the secluded entryway of a vacated shop and broke one of the cardinal rules of good etiquette by champing on the rolls in public. Not only that, but I consumed all six of them.

By that time I had become so chilled that I decided to forego viewing the city's points of interest until the snow flurries ceased to obscure them, so I returned to *Albisriederplatz* on the *Strassenbahnwagen*. From there I hurried to the hotel and submitted myself to another claustrophobic ascent in the tiny lift from the lobby to the third floor. Of course, the sweet rolls had destroyed all hunger pangs; therefore, even though nightfall was still a couple of hours distant, I sacked out for the night and immediately surrendered to Morpheus.

About five minutes later I suddenly jerked upright on the bed, stared blindly into the surrounding darkness, and listened intently. And my alertness was rewarded.

"But that can't be," José protested.

"But it has to be," Pancho insisted. "That map indicated that the central part of the city is located southeast of the hotel, so Al really went downtown instead of uptown."

"But he was also going east . . . ," José began.

"You guys stop your *bleeped* yammering so I can get some sleep," I interjected. Then I dropped back onto the bed and pulled the covers over my head, but that didn't do any good, of course.

About ten o'clock in the following morning, I boarded the *Strassenbahnwagen* at *Albisriederplatz* with full expectations of being transported to the central part of the city. Once more the car was full of plump, well-dressed women; however, standing some six feet from me was one rather raw-boned number who appeared to be about sixty years old. For support, her bony right hand clutched the chrome-plated, steel pole that guarded the inboard corner of the side exit's shallow stairwell. It was her distraught stare that first attracted my attention to her, but I soon redirected my eyes to the same map that I had studied during the previous trip.

From it I discovered that the huge railroad station, through which I had traipsed during the early part of the previous day, must have been the *Hauptbahnhof*, the main or central station, which straddled the *Sihi* and abutted the *Limmat*, a river that flows into the *Zürichsee*. North of the *Hauptbahnhof* stood the *Schweizerisches Landesmuseum* and the *Platzpromenade*.

Suddenly, still clutching the pole, the woman lunged forward one step and shouted several German words, as if in response to an unseen interrogator. Apparently the words startled her as much as they did the people about her, because her dull eyes abruptly glinted with awareness. Then, bowing her head in an abashed manner, she attempted to hide behind that slender pole. But she need not have been so concerned, because there were only carefully hidden expressions of sympathy in the eyes of those outwardly cold and indifferent people.

Meanwhile, I deliberately searched for points of interest on the opposite side of the map. Among them I selected the *Opernhaus*, the *Kunsthaus (Heimplatz)* or the Museum of Fine Arts, and the churches: *Grossmünster*, *Fraumünster*, and St. Peter. Unfortunately the fates decreed that I would see none of them.

When I left the warmth of the tram, the lowering sky threatened dire consequences if I didn't return to the tram, but I stubbornly struck out in search of a bank in that banking capital of the world. According to the pamphlet a few banks were to be found along Badenerstrasse, and that was where I found two banks, in which I was informed that it would take from a week to ten days for funds to be transferred from my bank in Fullerton to a local bank. After trying several other banks, including the Union Bank of Switzerland, I received the same response. By chance I happened onto an American Express office, and, despite my unhappy experience with the one in Singapore, I ventured into it and netted a similar answer.

From there, without success, I endeavored to relocate the bakery that I had previously patronized. Spying a group of heavily clothed people that had gathered alongside a building to await the coming of a tram, I swung toward it, stopped in front of a burly man of somewhat mature years, and inquired, "Do you happen to know of a bakery in this general area?"

He stared at me so blankly that I felt compelled to ask, "Do you understand English?"

The word *English* must have turned the tide, because he squeezed forth the first smile that I had seen in two days, and it was an embarrassed smile at that. Then he vigorously shook his head.

Eventually I came to the conclusion that, if some of my funds could not be immediately transferred from America to support further adventures on the Continent, I would shake the snow off my Hush Puppies and board an airplane back to home base, where such funds were readily available. Even though I was so cold that my teeth chattered like jackhammers, I went in search of the American Express office, but they must have moved the *bleeped* thing, because I failed to find it in what I believed to be the area in which it had previously been located. Furthermore, the *bleeped* map confused me, because I was unable to keep it properly oriented with the various street corners on which I stood while studying it and shivering uncontrollably. Of course, the snow on the streets may have contributed somewhat to that confusion, because there was no snow on the map excepting an occasional snowflake. Actually my confusion may have been due entirely to the cold, which had converted the two Jellolike masses in my head into solids.

In a mood verging on desperation, I entered one of the towering edifices of high finance and approached a meticulously attired banker, who must have been enjoying his middle years in relative luxury.

"Where have they hidden the American Express office?" I inquired of him. "I found it earlier in the day, but I've been unable to locate it again, so they must have moved it."

After a brief study he almost smiled as he arose from behind his fine mahogany desk and grasped my elbow in his left hand. "Come with me," he said, "and I'll point it out to you."

I realized that he was trying to get me out of his hair, but he was genteel about it. Even so, that was the first time that I had ever been thrown out of a banker's office. Beyond the entrance he gently pulled me to a stop on the nicely finished cut-stone slab, pointed toward a nearby street corner, and said, "Cross this street to that corner, turn right, and go past two intersections. Then turn left on the far side of the next intersection, and you'll find the office within about two hundred meters."

"Thank you very much," I murmured. "You have generously contributed several minutes of your valuable time to assist a stranded wayfarer, and it is appreciated much more than you may suspect. Unfortunately, in this largely German-speaking city, English-speaking business people, like you, are about the only sources of information to which a tourist who speaks only English can appeal."

"I am glad to have been of assistance," he murmured with almost a smile.

At the American Express office I quickly sensed recognition, but José reluctantly conceded, "The tokens of recognition may have evolved from our previous visit. After all, there were only three young women in the office, so there couldn't have been many customers since we left."

For the first time in several years, I opted to utilize my credit card for a purchase. But I didn't submit it until I had obtained and compared the costs of three different routes from Zurich to Los Angeles. Ultimately I settled on a flight from Zurich to London. From there a second flight would complete my trip around the world to the City of the Angels.

As I opened the glazed door of the warm office and headed into the bitterly cold wind, José observed, "That young woman seemed to be even colder and less friendly than what appears to be normal for these cold, unfriendly people."

"Yeah, I noticed that, too," responded Pancho, "but it may be just the critter's nature."

"I doubt it," rejoined José. "I'm convinced that she has been briefed by Big Brother."

"Perhaps so," granted Pancho, "but let's terminate this discussion, because that frigid blast on Al's bald head makes my blood run cold."

"Yeah, mine, too," conceded José. "Why don't we con him into buying one of those big fur caps?" Since there was no response from the other side, it must have congealed into a solid.

By the time that I had located a point from which to board the *Strassenbahnwagen*, I was practically frozen. Furthermore, I was beginning to exhibit all the symptoms of impending pneumonia, so I scrambled aboard the first tram that stopped there. Fortunately, it also stopped at the *Albisriederplatz*. From there I sprinted to the hotel, only to be confronted by another erratic trip to the third floor in the mailing tube.

Even though I had skipped both breakfast and lunch, I decided against a trip in a cab to one of Zurich's reputedly fine Swiss restaurants. Nevertheless, after showering, I donned my slacks, jacket, and the usual accessories; then I chanced another trip down to the lobby in that incredible mailing tube. While striding past the desk, I detected the clerk's steady stare and monitored it from the corner of one eye all of the way to the doorway of the dining room.

A short, swart waiter seated me at a table for two, which was located against the wall immediately to the right of the doorway. It was one of about six such tables that stood on the same level as the doorway. Across a three-foot wall, it overlooked the main dining room, whose floor was about four feet lower than that of the upper level, so it provided a fine vantage point for the diner who faced in that direction. And I chose to face the dining room, but not because I'm a nosy fellow. Normally I could not care less about the activities of the people about me, but I had learned from bitter experience that those activities are rarely normal. Consequently, I was fully prepared for anything that might develop, or so I mistakenly believed.

After the waiter left to place my order, I began to study the general layout of the lower area. Below and slightly to the right of me, a relatively young couple occupied a booth that consisted of a plain, wooden table plus a pair of wooden seats and backs austerely upholstered in a bilious, gold, plastic material. Apparently it was the last of several similar booths that lined the small cul-de-sac partially obscured by the wall on my right. The man and woman also must have ordered, because their eyes were casually assessing the other diners, too. I even sensed the momentary touch of their gazes, and a sweeping scan of the room permitted my peripheral vision to verify that their gazes were, in fact, casual. With my elbows propped improperly on the table, I relaxed under the influence of the unusual normalcy of the situation while the fingers of my right hand toyed with my ragged beard.

A narrow aisle passed between the young couple's booth and the partial wall before me. Then it intersected with a longer aisle that extended directly ahead of me and along another wall aligned with the wall on my right. About midway of the lower dining area, another aisle projected from the long aisle to a partially enclosed stairwell that led down into what must have been the kitchen. Several dining tables, attended by from four to six chairs, were scattered about the large room and the stairwell. A balding man of about fifty appeared to be the *Krippe* or manager of the dining room. A somewhat more than mature woman with faded, blonde hair and a very blond young man were serving the diners on the lower level. They may have been his *Frau* and their *Sohn*, since the trio functioned like a family.

Actually I wasn't surprised when the desk clerk appeared from the obscured part of the cul-de-sac. But my eyes never left his stocky figure as he turned the corner, strolled along the longer aisle, turned from it toward the stairwell, and collected the trio about him.

"Of the hundreds of Big Brother's contemptible minions that we've observed in action," José injected into my thoughts, "that black-browed vulture exhibits more of the cult's evil characteristics than any ten of the others."

"Amen!" Pancho chimed.

It was a brief meeting, but I didn't fail to observe the long stare that the blond pretty-boy directed up toward my table. After the meeting disbanded, he accompanied the clerk during his return trip. As they approached the point where the aisles intersected in front of me, his light-blue eyes boldly challenged my stormy, dark-blue ones until they could no longer withstand the flashes of lightning that flickered from mine to his, so they flitted away like frightened doves.

Apparently the two young people in the booth below me were known to the blond blade, because he had lingered over taking their order. After returning from the deeper recesses of the cul-de-sac, he stopped and chatted with them in German for several minutes. Meanwhile, I observed several surreptitious glances from them, so I had to conclude that he was spreading the word, or an expansion of the word, that had been conveyed to him by the desk clerk. After he left, my careful surveillance verified that the surreptitious gazes were repeated, but they lacked the casual characteristics of the previous gazes.

Sometime after my meal was served, I paused during its consumption to watch Big Brother's blond tyro. At the time he stood with a tray balanced on one hand and conversed with a ruggedly constructed, middle-aged man who was seated at the near end of a large table. Apparently its five other diners also were known to the youth, since he often directed his remarks to them. Suddenly I was startled to see the middle-aged man turn about and stare back across the room toward me while the eyes of the other diners, mostly women, became riveted on me. As usual, I met the onslaught head on, and they quickly lowered their eyes or turned them away. Meanwhile, the blond town crier glanced in my direction and abruptly departed in the direction of the stairwell.

Several minutes later the *Frau* emerged from the stairwell with a heavily laden tray held firmly before her by both hands, and the *Sohn* followed her with a similar tray. While approaching the turn in front of me, the *Sohn's* eyes chanced to meet my intent orbs, and he immediately lowered his eyes. No doubt the youth had come to realize that I was aware of his scandalous behavior, and he was unsure of how best to respond to the problem. Nevertheless, he came up with a most unusual solution to it, but I suspect that it was more of an involuntary response than a planned one.

During the duo's next trip, the young man carefully avoided my eyes. After coming within my audio range, he looked at the woman and said, "This one prefers boys."

The woman's gaze immediately veered upward to mine; then they turned guiltily away, so there could be little doubt of who was intended to be the victim of the attack. Furthermore, since he had used English in lieu of German, which had been employed exclusively before, there could be no doubt about who was intended to be the victim.

But those crude words didn't even pause at my audio receptors; they continued on into my skull and ricocheted from its inner walls like small cannonballs. And the sounds of their impacts continued to reverberate through it like the lingering tones of bells in a cathedral tower. But they created no physical pain, because I was too numb from shock to feel pain. In fact, several minutes passed before I could collect my mental faculties; meanwhile, a murderous rage had built up in me.

Nevertheless, I placed the correct number of francs on the check and remembered to add a tip for the waiter. Then, raising my eyes from the currency, I looked directly into the blue eyes of a ravishing young blonde, who was seated at the adjacent table. She must have arrived during my moment of stress, since under normal circumstances no man of any age would ever fail to observe the arrival of so beautiful a female of the same species. Our gazes locked and continued to cling; meanwhile, the lashes around her blue eyes gradually widened as if she were becoming wary of the raging fires that burned within my eyes. If those had been physical fires, I'm sure they would have seared that lovely head and its luxurious, blonde curls, its lightly penciled eyebrows, and its inconspicuously marked red lips. My body must have been numb, indeed, since it scarcely sensed the instant that our gazes were wrenched apart when I suddenly moved my chair back from the table, arose, and turned toward the doorway. As the door responded to my tug, I glanced over one shoulder and found that her eyes were still staring after me with an expression of intense wonder.

Obviously I was in no mood to stop at the desk, but I did, so the clerk arose from the flat-top desk and aproached me. In response to his silent presence, I muttered, "Since I'll be leaving very early in the morning, I wish to pay up to date."

He nodded, moved to a file, thumbed through its contents, withdrew a statement, and presented it to me, but his murky eyes never met my level gaze.

After I submitted the payment, he returned some change to me and said automatically, "I hope that you have enjoyed your stay at the Hotel Stoller."

"I don't understand how anyone could have the guts to make such a statement so soon after creating an evil mess, such as the one that you deliberately created for me in that dining room not more than ten minutes ago," I growled in deep, bass tones while my left forefinger stabbed viciously in the direction of the dining room.

From the sound of those tones, I sensed that I was close to the breaking point; therefore, to avoid losing control of myself, I turned bitterly away. Once more my years of self-discipline had paid off, because, angry as I was, I still realized that, despite the obvious justification of a physical attack, it would be used against me when I finally got around to confronting Big Brother. But those years might have been wasted if, while at the desk, my eyes had detected the supercilious smile that they observed from in front of the slowly opening doorway of the lift when I stepped aside to allow it to disgorge two passengers. Fortunately for me, the same pair of passengers blocked direct access to the desk during the moment when I was infused with an overwhelming impulse to charge back and beat the clerk's insolent features to a pulp. Very likely I would have played right into the eager hands of the source of the problem if I had yielded to the impulse.

As soon as my head struck the pillow, my mind involuntarily began at the beginning of its index and carefully searched through it for some incident or set of circumstances that might have led Big Brother to make one of the greatest errors in his error-prone existence. It meticulously studied every male associate from puberty on—boyhood chum, high school buddy, and university friend, but it found nothing. Loren Isley was my only close associate at the university level, and he eventually became the president of a great university, so that relationship could not be suspect. During my civil engineering career there were no close associates; likewise during my aerospace career. I was much too busy during my years as a builder to have close associates, and after I retired there was only Charlie, but not even an idiot would ever connect him to such a decadent practice. Therefore, there was no apparent reason for the remark: "He prefers boys." In fact, it was such a vicious and shocking attack that I will never forget it.

My mind stubbornly retraced its steps, and it almost passed over the only possibility, but it was so absurd that it scarcely warranted consideration. Nevertheless, a finger of my flickering memory pressed a computer key that displayed a dimly lighted scene in a popular night spot located in one of a large city's major hotels. I was seated on a nicely upholstered bench that curved continuously along one side of a large, lushly carpeted floor, on the far side of which was a matching bench. In front of me an untouched cocktail glass stood on a cocktail table. Several other cocktail tables, accompanied by pairs of chairs, were scattered about the carpeted floor. Most of the benches and chairs were occupied by couples, but I was alone. Beyond the carpeted floor was a small dance floor, at one end of which was a four-foot-high platform, where a six-piece orchestra held forth; meanwhile, its leader rendered a popular song.

Suddenly the name *Al* was introduced into the song by the somewhat short and rather swarthy singer, but I ignored it because several other Als also frequented the night spot. But the singer's dark-haired sister happened to be seated at a nearby table, and, slowly turning her head, she fixed curious dark eyes on my features for several seconds.

Surely that man can't be serenading me, I thought, but the name was repeated by the blandly smiling singer. Still other heads covertly turned in my direction, so I was forced to suspect that not only was he serenading me, but some of the surrounding listeners were capable of suspecting that I might have something going with him. Just the suspicions made me furious. Each time that the name was repeated, I progressively became more angry, but my anger was not directed so much toward the pixilated singer as toward the idiots who were so ready to connect me to him.

After the music stopped, the leader began a routine that had become familiar to me during many previous visits. At first I had assumed that during the intermissions the man actually was straightening the orchestra's equipment when he moved about the edge of the platform with his back to the patrons. Unfortunately for the man, like so many other rank amateurs, I rather fancied myself to be something of a psychologist, so I had reluctantly arrived at the conclusion that those oft-repeated actions must be the product of an overwhelming compulsion to parade his rather sizable derriere before that motley crowd. But I had more than just those observations on which to base my suspicions: I also had observed the reactions of a tall, slender member of the orchestra to that *tour de farce*, and he always exhibited the same embarrassment for the man that I sensed in myself.

After completing his round, the leader stepped down from the platform and made several genial comments to various patrons as he moved between the tables. Finally he stopped beside my table.

"Hello, Al," he murmured with a wide smile. "How are you doing this evening?"

Gaylord wasn't the man's name, nor was his name like it in any way; however, I choose to use it because it suits the plot.

"Fine, thank you, Gay," I replied, "but I could do with a lot less notoriety."

"But I was just singing 'hello' to a friend," he protested.

Since we hadn't exchanged even one word until a short time before that meeting, we could not have been considered to be friends in any sense of the word, but my mind rebelled at making an issue of the statement.

"I've decided to drop your house plans, Gay," I said rather abruptly.

"Oh," he responded with a concerned expression. "Why? Surely not because I used your name in a song?"

He had struck my cherry-red iron with an unerring hammer, but my anger was no longer hot enough for me to deliberately burn him. "No, Gay," I lied. "I just can't find enough free time to do the job right, and I refuse to do it unless I can do it right. Nevertheless, I'm making a gift of these preliminary plans to you, so my decision won't cost you anything." Then I plucked a roll of vellums from the seat beside me and placed them on the table.

"Oh, no, Al," he protested. "I want you to finish the plans." Then he studied my eyes for a moment and added, "Won't you reconsider your decision?"

But even I could see that he already knew the answer, so I merely shook my head. Then he absently picked up the roll and murmured, "I'm very sorry, Al, but thank you for the plans." And he strolled away with his head bowed in thought.

Actually I had brought the plans with me for the specific purpose of discussing some changes with him, but that stupid song had forced me to change my mind. Nevertheless, my sense of fair play would never permit me to cost the man either time or money, irrespective of his morals, so I had sacrificed many hours of my spare time to get off the hook. Moreover, I was determined to avoid placing myself in a compromising position—a position in which Big Brother could make another of his stupid mistakes. Obviously, he had made it anyway, and it appeared to be a deliberate act.

"Apparently he had been lurking in the background, hoping against hope for an opportunity to totally destroy us," José injected into my bedtime reverie, "and we didn't know that he had succeeded until that dim-witted youth compulsively revealed it to us."

"No wonder Wilfred claimed that Al is terrible man," Pancho observed.

"I would view a man with a similar reputation in the same light," José mused, "but I would never confront him with it, because I happen to know how much in error such reputations can be."

"For many years we've known that Big Brother was a purveyor of common gossip," Pancho rejoined, "but it never occurred to me that he would stoop to deliberate lies and deceit to gain his nefarious goals, whatever they are."

"But the evidence that he did is apparent," José observed, "because that youth isn't smart enough to volunteer such slander."

"There can be no doubt regarding the source of the lad's cruel remark," Pancho insisted. "Of course, he is chargeable for his crime, but the lowest criminal has to be the one who generated that false claim, and no punishment can be too great for such a criminal."

"But who punishes Big Brother?" José countered.

I had been tossing and turning with every turn of the problem for hours; finally I sat up and stared blindly into the darkness.

"One thing for sure," Pancho began, "our reputation has been irrevocably destroyed. But I propose that we never surrender to that evil monster, because somebody has to stand up to him, and I'm less likely to yield under the stress of combat than is almost anybody else in this world."

"Change the I to we," José interjected, "and you've got something."

"During the ongoing battle I'll shed even more of Al's red blood," Pancho resumed indomitably, "but I may be able to strike some telling blows, too, and let flow some of Big Brother's black blood."

"There's little doubt that we're too old to win the war," José presumed, "but in response to adequate publicity younger and more virile men may take up the torch of true freedom and really burn his tail with it."

"I certainly hope so," Pancho responded. "Left unchecked, Big Brother will eventually dominate the entire world much like George Orwell predicted in his book *1984*." Then I slumped back onto the bed, but I didn't sleep—not one second throughout the entire night.

28

Zurich to Los Angeles

Zurich to London

At the curb in front of the airport, the atmosphere was cold, cold, cold, and the overcast sky was gray, gray, gray, so I paid the taxicab driver and quickly moved into the warm terminal. Then I checked my luggage, exchanged some currencies, boarded the aircraft, and took possession of my window seat without observing any of the usual side effects of my presence.

When Swissair's sturdy craft burst through the sulking clouds, the rays of the easterly sun momentarily blinded my eyes, so I directed them downward at the tops of the heretofore gray clouds. And they were dazzled by the softly diffused light reflected upward by a billowing bed of what appeared to be the finest of white gossamer.

"Oh, look at the Alps!" exclaimed a woman in delighted tones.

Immediately my eyes eagerly scanned the farthest reaches of the soft, white bed within the limits of the window frame, but they detected no Alps. Then, turning my head toward the opposite window, I saw the scintillating white peaks projecting majestically above the same layer of wispy, white gossamer.

"That's typical of Al," José observed caustically.

"What's typical of him this time?" countered his mate.

"He requested a window seat so that he could see the Alps," was the response, "and he didn't even consider which was the best side of the craft from which to view them."

The autopilot must have been set on a direct course to London, since the towering peaks remained in view for a long time before they finally merged with the horizon. Meanwhile, the magic carpet glided smoothly over the southern edge of West Germany and skirted the border between France and Belgium. Since both countries were covered with snow, I doubt that the border would have been visible even if there had been no cloud cover. Of course, some know-it-all readers will contend that phantom lines can't be seen under any conditions, but they are not as fortunate as some of us who have been specially endowed. A similar cloud cover obscured the English Channel, so I wasn't able to confirm its existence either. And I wouldn't have known that London was also covered by snow if I had not seen some of the surrounding landscape after the plane penetrated the cloud cover and began to circle Heathrow Airport.

London   Despite the snow, I would have preferred to have delayed my departure for a few days to visit some of the city's historical sites, but my funds were at ebb tide; furthermore, the severe cold acquired in Zurich threatened to become an even greater problem, so I decided against it.

To board the airplane that was to transport me from London to Los Angeles, I was forced to pass through British immigration and board a shuttle bus to a second terminal. Based on previous experiences, I expected to detect several tokens of Big Brother's precedence while passing through the terminal, but I failed to detect even one. In particular, I expected to score with the official who was to inspect my passport, but the friendly, fiftyish man just glanced at it and stamped it; then, without even looking at me, he cheerfully wished me "happy landings." After so many unhappy landings, I found such a reaction to be encouraging, even exhilarating, since it appeared that I had finally come upon a country where Big Brother didn't dominate the bureaucracy.

But I've always been thorough in my research, whether it be technical or otherwise. Therefore, after the trip to the second terminal, I attempted to attract the usual recognition there, but I continued to draw a blank in every familiar subterfuge, even when I submitted my ticket for verification. José and Pancho were ecstatically delighted with the initial results of the research, but I still was unconvinced. After carefully studying the agents at the British Airways ticket counter, I discovered that one woman wasn't serving any customers, so I submitted my ticket to her again, and she verified that it was in order, of course. In the process, however, I observed a familiar reserve, an observation that had served me well in the past, especially when women had been exposed to Big Brother's decadent influence. Of course, it was a quick check, and I could have misinterpreted her behavior, but I strongly suspected that I had scored.

Sometime I would like to return to London to verify that quick check; that is, if it can be verified. Who knows but what Prime Minister Thatcher has driven Big Brother out of the British Isles. After all, she has exhibited considerably more intelligence than have American politicians and bureaucrats. Furthermore, George Orwell was much closer to her, to the Parliament, and to the British bureaucrats than he was to their peers in any other country, so his book *1984* may have left a greater impression on the British bureaucrats.

London to Los Angeles

I was assigned to a window seat on the left side of the big, wide-bodied jet, but it was located over the aft part of the wing, so I couldn't have seen anything of consequence even if there had been anything of consequence to see. The big bird habitually flew the Great Circle Route, which traverses the lengths of England, Scotland, and some of the North Sea. Then it swings in a westerly direction over the North Atlantic Ocean, passing below Iceland and Greenland before veering toward Canada. Both England and Scotland were covered by a blanket of snow, and much of the North Atlantic also bore a heavy burden of ice and snow, so the location of my seat really didn't matter, or so it seemed at the time.

The seat to my right was unoccupied, but a short, dark-eyed, matronly woman with a light-brown complexion slouched in the aisle seat beyond it. She wasn't the type of woman who normally attracts a man's attention, especially the attention of a seventy-five-year-old man, so I didn't really notice her until she slipped a small, light-brown hand into a voluminous cloth handbag and extracted a thin, hardback book. It wasn't the type of book that normally attracts my attention either, but when she opened it to a page marker, I was startled by line after line of what appeared to be chicken scratches instead of the usual printed characters. Of course, those are archaic terms, at best, but they happen to be particularly applicable in this case.

Apparently the symbols meant something to her, because she settled back against the seat and began to decipher those chicken scratches as rapidly as I read printed English. I quickly ruled out both ancient and modern Greek, and the symbols appeared too plain to be Hebrew. They seemed to be similar to some Sanskrit symbols that I had once seen on an ancient Indic document displayed in a large museum. Of course, I was aware that Sanskrit had not been in use for hundreds of years, so I continued to ponder the likely source of those strange symbols.

Meanwhile, from my occasional glimpses of the North Atlantic I gathered that ice covered most of it, because there were just a few dark streaks of open water in its far-reaching, snow-clad surface. After the craft passed over the northern part of Labrador, the surface of Hudson Bay came into view. Since it proved to be devoid of streaks of open water, I assumed that the seawater in that partially landlocked basin had frozen to a great depth.

At about that point on the map I decided to take a walk, as my grandpappy was prone to say. After unlocking my seat belt, I arose, stepped into the space in front of the unoccupied seat, and stared thoughtfully down at the preoccupied reader.

"I'm sorry to inconvenience you, madam," I murmured, "but will you please excuse me?"

With a slight start she glanced up at me, unlocked her seat belt, arose, and silently stepped into the aisle.

"Thank you," I muttered, stepping into the aisle.

On arriving before my objective, I found that a relatively young, black-haired woman was apparently waiting for the small sign on the nearby door to change from "Occupied" to "Vacant." Meanhile, her small, dark-haired son was poking an exploratory forefinger along the door's hinge line. Momentarily I considered returning to my seat, but thoughts of the unnecessary inconvenience to my neighbor scratched the consideration, so I lounged against the side of an unoccupied seat in the immediate vicinity.

The sign changed to Vacant when the occupant unlocked the door and exited, but the woman ignored it. After some time had expired, I gestured toward the sign and said, "That one is available."

Turning her dark eyes toward me, she first frowned and then shook her jet-black curls. I tried to determine the reason for her reaction, but none of my determinations seemed to fit the situation.

Meanwhile, the child approached her and murmured something. Then she looked irritably at me as if I were the source of the problem, whatever it was, and growled, "I wish whoever is in the bathroom would clear out of it."

"But that one is available," I protested with another gesture toward the Vacant sign.

Staring balefully up into my eyes, she retorted, "I know, but I want the bathroom."

Gradually our gazes unlocked; then, with a shrug, I muttered, "Okay, since this one's available, I'll take it."

Meantime Pancho mused, "I wonder if this particular aircraft is equipped with a special bathroom, one that incorporates a sunken tub even."

While I doubtfully shook my head, José concluded, "That I'll have to see to believe."

When I returned to the side of the older woman, I said, "Please excuse me again." She arose and silently stepped into the aisle.

"Thank you again," I added. And she flashed a quick smile at me.

After we were seated, she leaned across the vacant seat and, in heavily accented tones, inquired, "Do you live in Los Angeles?"

"No," I replied. "I live in Fullerton, which is a satellite of Los Angeles."

With a nod she said, "Some members of my family live in Pasadena, and I am going to visit them for a while." After a brief silence, she archly inquired, "Is Fullerton far from Pasadena?"

"No," I answered. "It can't be more than twenty miles from Pasadena."

After nodding her graying black curls energetically, she picked up the book and opened it to the page marker, which dropped onto her lap.

"Pardon my unseemly curiosity," I requested, "but do you mind telling me what language is represented by the symbols in that book?"

"Of course not," she responded with a smile. "They are Arabic." However, those were not her exact words, but I have chosen to avoid the exact words because of certain extenuating circumstances that are about to be revealed.

Failing to restrain an impulse to exercise some of my slapstick humor, I suggested, "Then the title of the book could be *The Arabian Nights Entertainments or Stories from the Thousand and One Nights*."

"No," she responded with a tolerant smile. "It was written by one of my country's leaders." And she named the country. "My husband is assistant to one of the ministers," she added. And she named the ministry. Then she coyly inquired, "Do you have some paper?"

I plucked the British Airways boarding pass from my shirt pocket and presented it to her with its blank side uppermost.

"Thank you," she murmured. After separating a ballpoint pen from the clutter within the cavernous cloth bag, she made some inscriptions on the pass and returned it to me. A name was inscribed on it in letters that appeared to be a combination of lower-case Gothic and English script.

"That's your family name?" I inquired.

"No," she replied with another coy smile, extending a small hand to recover it. "That is my given name."

After relinquishing it to her, I leaned across the intervening space and watched while she inscribed alongside the so-called given name the word *name* and enclosed it within parentheses. Directly below it she inscribed another name, and alongside it she inscribed the word *family* and enclosed it within parenthesis.

"Thank you," I murmured after she returned the pass to me.

Silently repeating the coy smile, she reopened the book while I tucked the pass into my briefcase with a sense of mild satisfaction. Sitting back against the seat, I resumed studying the few views of the snow-clad terrain that the clouds accorded me. Meanwhile, the thought never occurred to me that certain circumstances might dictate that I should never use those names and titles in my travelogue.

Some time later two familiar voices roused me from a deep reverie. Absently turning my eyes toward their sources, I saw that the dark-haired young woman and the small boy had paused beside the woman, and it was the two women who were conversing. Still later the voices roused me again, and I found that the duo had returned to the side of the woman. Even though the two women were conversing in a foreign tongue, it seemed to me that the older woman was protesting that she really didn't have to go, while the younger woman, who greatly resembled the older one, seemed to be insisting that she accompany her. Meanwhile, the younger woman cast a couple of wary glances toward me, and they immediately impinged on my ever-alert mental faculties like tocsins; consequently, I prepared myself to be particularly observant when the trio returned.

Whatever the problem, it consumed considerable time; however, contrary to my expectations, the older woman returned alone. Unfortunately that provided fewer clues for me to pursue, but I did detect a notable difference in her attitude, and it matched the differences observed in other people under similar circumstances during past battles with Big Brother. In particular, I noticed that she made no more attempts to engage me in a conversation, but her dark eyes often turned toward me. Furthermore, she seemed to be unduly restless, often twisting first one way, then another, in her seat and suddenly bouncing up and down on it for no apparent reason except to attract my attention. Over the years I had encountered many similar situations, so I possessed sufficient experience in the subject's behavior to readily detect and identify it. Since I had carefully schooled myself in feminine psychology, I was confident of my ability to control the particular subject's tendencies. Consequently, I carefully refrained from any direct glances in her direction, but I kept abreast of her ever-changing activities via my peripheral vision. According to my amateur psychology, those activities might provide clues regarding what had transpired during the session with her daughter—and with whomever else might have been involved.

Meanwhile, José observed, "I suspect that someone observed both the transfer of those names to Al and the visit of the younger woman. Very likely that observer mistook the use to which he might put the names and. . . ."

"In fact," Pancho interjected, "the observer may have jumped to the conclusion that Al and the woman were planning a rendezvous; therefore. . . ."

"Therefore," José interrupted, "a clumsy move was made through the medium of the younger woman to foreclose on those mistaken plans."

"But the countermeasures appear to be backfiring," Pancho resumed delightedly. "If a victim has ever been ripe for the plucking, that dark-eyed woman certainly is."

"But Al isn't interested—now, later, or ever," insisted José.

Inadvertently the woman eventually succeeded in attracting my attention, but it was due entirely to her persistence and gross conduct. The incident occurred during one of those intervals when I turned my head away from the tiring scene beyond the window and looked forward. Apparently the star of that seductive production was set to act immediately, because she suddenly bounced up on the seat and swept her ugly, plaid skirt high on her thick thighs. I turned my head away very quickly, but the damage appeared to be irreparable, since, like a bird of prey, she remained poised for a repeat performance. Meanwhile, I stubbornly pointed my eyes toward the window and the boring snowscapes of Manitoba. After she settled back against the seat and reopened the book, I eventually detected the change of attitude and cautiously turned my head partially forward to relax the strained muscles in the back of my neck. To relax the cramped muscles in my thighs, I crossed my legs in such a way that the toe of my left Hush Puppy dangled about six inches into the space in front of the vacant seat.

Within seconds she shed her slippers, revealingly flipped her right leg over its partner, and swung her toe to within a tantalizing two inches of my poor, innocent

Hush Puppy. Obviously she was inviting a surreptitious contact, but I was determined not to be trapped into her silly game, even by chance, much less cooperate in it. Perhaps I would have yielded at twenty-five, or even at thirty-five, but at seventy-five such behavior would have indicated a total lack of character. And that woman, likely the grandmother of a small, dark-haired boy, had to be depraved to offer the opportunity.

Meanwhile, I was confronted with the problem of removing the toe of my Hush Puppy from its precarious position without accidentally striking her toe and without causing her to lose face. She should not be left with a sense of rejection, because I had painful memories of how spiteful a rejected woman can become, almost as hateful, in fact, as the proverbial woman scorned. There was no way for me to predict what that strange woman from east of Suez might do if she even suspected that she had been rejected. To her it could be the equivalent of a woman scorned.

Such were the thoughts of that Don Juan of seventy-five just before he very cautiously withdrew the Hush Puppy and recrossed his legs with both toes stowed safely within his seat's domain. In the process he barked a shin on a projection of the seat ahead of him, and he ruefully wondered why it could not have been the Hush Puppy. After all, it would have been in character for it to *bark*.

Almost instantly the woman recrossed her legs with the stocking-clad toe of her left foot dangling about six inches into the aisle, where a passing passenger soon bumped into it. But she refused to withdraw it, so I concluded that she felt rejected—therefore, a woman scorned. And I began to fear for my life, because those Arabian women are noted for their capacity to hate. But I survived as far as Edmonton, Alberta, where the pilot apparently decided against any further flights of fancy (almost to the Arctic Circle), since he turned the craft's nose toward Los Angeles and tossed another shovelful of coal onto the fire under the boiler.

When the craft passed over Bakersfield, it looked like I was going to make it unscathed all of the way into the City of the Angels, so I relaxed a bit. But it proved to be too much and too soon. While I was readying my briefcase for the coming exodus at the Los Angeles airport, the tires of the main landing gear's wheels screeched briefly during an initial contact with the runway, and I mentally complimented the pilot on the skill with which he had started them rolling. In perfect conjunction with their final impact, that crude creature on my right raised her plaid skirt all of the way up to her waist and calmly adjusted her panty hose. Then she cast a sultry glance toward my incredulous eyes and slowly lowered the skirt with a final pat as if she were complimenting it for a job well done.

So intense is the hate of a woman rejected that I'm sure she intended to knock me dead with that last-minute maneuver, and she almost succeeded, because I remember fearfully counting every one of the seven beats that my heart skipped. By the count of five I was fully convinced that I had come to the end of the line, despite the fact that my heart consistently skips two or three beats from time to time. However, it wasn't excitement that stopped my heart; it was the gross bad taste of that vulgar exhibitionist.

"As for the reason behind the extreme change in the woman's behavior after she returned from being dragged away by her insistent daughter, your guess may be as good as mine," Pancho opined.

"Irrespective of what the reason was, the woman's reactions substantially indicated that it had to be totally out of perspective," José rejoined. "In fact, such errors in other people's judgment have been cluttering Al's life for the last fifty years."

"I grant that Big Brother may be too dumb to recognize his errors," Pancho resumed, "but I am even more inclined to suspect that he is deliberately ignoring them."

But that wench had not yet completed her attacks on me. While I stood in front of my seat and impatiently waited for her to arise from her seat and move into the aisle, she cast frequent glances toward the rear of the craft. Finally the younger woman and her child appeared in the line of departing passengers. After they paused beside her, she looked up soulfully into the other woman's dark eyes and began to chatter in a foreign tongue. Meantime, the other woman leaned forward, placed an arm across the back of her seat, and gazed balefully across the woman's head at me as she apparently questioned her in the same tongue. Then the seated woman stared pitifully up into her inquisitor's eyes and replied at length. Meanwhile, the younger woman turned challenging eyes on me, but my eyes met them defiantly. She must not have expected to encounter someone who was prepared for a confrontation, because she quickly averted her eyes, grasped the seated woman's right arm, and hurriedly assisted her into the aisle. While pushing the older woman precipitously ahead of her with one arm, she pulled the child after her with the other one. Abruptly turning her head, she fired a parting glare at me from glittering, black orbs.

"Maybe Al should have surrendered to that old witch and her stupid game," José suggested.

"Very likely he would have fared much better in the eyes of her daughter, and who knows what other eyes," Pancho rejoined, "because the words that she spouted so spitefully to her daughter had to carry an ocean of vengeance."

"Nevertheless, Al retains his dignity, or what remains of it," José observed. "Certainly he would never sanction its being sullied by contact with such a creature, regardless of the vengeful aftermath."

"Later Big Brother will probably listen to reports of her morbid fabrications with delight while gleefully rubbing the scaly backs of his clawlike hands in eager anticipation of the next opportunity to spread a new, malicious rumor," Pancho remarked.

Anaheim-Fullerton Area   In front of the British Airways segment of the L.A. terminal, I boarded one of the shuttle buses that have been traveling between LAX and the Disneyland Hotel for years. About forty-five minutes later the hands of the clock on the vehicle's instrument panel were approaching three o'clock when I passed it on my way down the steps onto the bus terminal's platform, which adjoins the hotel's property.

Having partaken of no nourishment for several hours, I strode toward the nearest restaurant. At its glazed entrance, I lowered the suitcase onto the concrete sidewalk, swung the heavy, spring-loaded, glazed door open, hurriedly jerked the suitcase from the sidewalk, thrust it through the opening, shouldered aside the persistent door, and squeezed myself and the briefcase through the narrow opening. Then I paused, briefly studied the layout, strode to the cashier's counter, dropped the luggage beside it, and exhaled a long sigh of relief.

"Heavy, huh?" cheerfully suggested the pretty, young woman beyond it. I laughed outright, and she responded with a stare from a pair of puzzled, brown eyes.

"Of course, you didn't intend for that remark to be funny, and by itself it wasn't funny," I explained. "But it reminded me of an identical remark, which, in the proper context, was funny. At least it was funny to me, even though I was the victim."

"Well," she began with a speculative expression, "since things have been rather dull around here this afternoon, I could use a good laugh, so why don't you tell me about it?"

A sweeping glance verified the lack of patronage, so I fixed my eyes on hers and said, "Okay, you've brung it on yourself, so here goes: Once upon a time. . . ." Then I stopped and interjected, "All stories are supposed to start with once upon a time, you know."

"Not the stories that are told around here," she retorted with a rueful laugh.

After submitting a sympathetic smile, I resumed, "It happened while I was having a piece of steel construction equipment built in a small, two-man machine shop. During one phase of the work the mechanic placed a long, steel pipe on a workbench and welded several shorter pieces of steel to it. Then for some reason— probably to go to lunch—he left the shop through the rear door. Meanwhile, I entered through the front door. Recognizing the component, I immediately picked it up and just as immediately dropped it onto the concrete floor, where it resonated like the bells of St. Mary's Cathedral. The unusual clatter awakened the irascible old owner of the shop from his noon nap, so he came to the doorway of his small office, peered sleepily over the edges of his rimless spectacles at the freshly welded assembly, and casually inquired, "Heavy, huh?"

"Was it heavy?" she inquired with a puzzled expression.

"Not very," I responded with a sense of defeat. "But it was hotter than *bleep!*"

"Oh!" she exclaimed, clapping a palm over her mouth. "Now I understand what you meant." And she giggled delightedly. In fact, she became so delighted with her mental picture of the episode that she continued to giggle behind the palm while her other hand clutched the sleeve of my jacket and twisted its nylon cloth convulsively. After partially recovering her aplomb, she wiped the tears from her eyes and exclaimed, "You have a marvelous sense of humor!"

"Don't credit me with a sense of humor," I responded lugubriously. "I just fumbled a very simple, true story. You are the one with the sense of humor, because you could still see the humor in my botched up story after I explained it to you."

"No," she insisted, as she continued to clutch my sleeve. "What was so funny was the way that you answered my question with 'Not very, but it was hotter than *bleep!*'" And she became convulsed by laughter again.

It's amazing how much a young woman with a soft touch can boost the ego of an old man. But that didn't happen to be one of the reasons for my presence, so I asked, "Is there a telephone on the premises?"

"I'm sorry that we don't have one," she replied, "but there's one in the entryway of the building midway of the curve. Come, and I'll show you where it's located." Then she led me to the glazed doorway and pointed it out to me.

After completing the telephone call, I returned to the restaurant and seated myself at the counter, where, at my request, a heavyset, fortyish waitress served to me a piece of pie and a glass of milk, along with a prolonged stare, but the stare was her idea. Since there was a dearth of customers at that time of day, she then chose to while away some time at the cashier's counter by engaging the congenial young woman in a conversation. Suddenly suspicions regarding the subject matter of that conversation erupted in my mind after I covertly detected some familiar tokens. Typically, I had deliberately presented the appearance of staring in a preoccupied manner through the glazed entry while watching them from the corner of one eye. Meanwhile, my mind pondered the recurring problem. Suddenly I yearned to be free of the constant slander that flowed so freely from the foul mouths of Big Brother's millions of minions.

"Of course, the trip abroad was intended to provide Al with an opportunity to find a country . . . ," Pancho began.

"Where a worthy pioneer could spend his declining years free from the evil monster's corrupt influences," José interjected.

"However, the trip's failure was not unexpected," Pancho added.

"But I sense that the waitress's stab in Al's back has proved to be the proverbial straw," José observed.

Savagely pushing the half-consumed pie away, I swung my Hush Puppies around, stepped down from the stool, and set them in motion. After jerking my bags from their slumbers beside a nearby booth, I strode to the cashier's counter, dropped them beside it, slammed the check on it, and extracted my wallet. My erstwhile friend shot an evasive glance toward me as I tendered a five-dollar bill; then she silently performed the usual functions on the electronic cash register while the waitress lounged indolently against the counter and stared at me. I responded briefly with a defiant glare, but I was in no mood for a war of nerves, so I accepted my change, picked up the luggage, and angrily made my exit.

As the glazed door swung closed behind me, Pancho observed, "I don't blame him for getting mad. Like all of the others, that big gal didn't know what the *bleep* she was talking about."

"Yeah," José agreed. "Welcome home, Al. Welcome back to the land of freedom."

LC responded quickly to my request for a lift from the Disneyland Hotel to our home. Since neither of us is very demonstrative, the meeting was not an emotional one; however, I suspected that we were equally pleased to be together again.

After several months, during which I expanded my writing activities, LC decided that she would like to invest some of her vacation time in a trip to Vancouver, British Columbia, where Expo 86 was in session. Consequently, I was elected to purchase the airline tickets.

After I entered the well-appointed offices housed within the small glass palace of the travel agency, my eyes were greeted by the smiling, brown eyes of a plump, young woman. At the moment she presided over the twenty-foot-long counter that extended from a receptionist's unoccupied desk to an ornate cashier's counter.

"Good morning, sir," she greeted me. "How can I help you?"

"I would like to do business with you," I claimed with a teasing smile, "but I previously submitted my problem to another young lady, who is processing it, so I suspect that I should continue with her."

"What is her name?" she asked.

"I don't remember," I ruefully confessed, "but a flower bears the same name." Then, after a thought-filled pause, I slyly inquired, "Could it be Sunflower maybe?"

She stared suspiciously at me for an instant. Then, with a delighted giggle, she countered, "Could it be Violet maybe?"

"Right on!" I exclaimed with a pseudo-innocent smile.

"Sunflower!" she called across one rounded shoulder toward the dimly lighted area at the rear of the establishment. Then, after a brief wait and a giggle, she repeated, "Sunflower!"

A rustling sound emanated from the dimness, followed by the outline of a figure which, as it advanced toward us, evolved into a tall, dark-eyed young woman whose pretty features bore a puzzled expression.

"This gentleman would like to confer with you," explained the buxom lass with another giggle.

"Good morning, Violet," I greeted her. "I'm sorry that I was unable to remember your name. You may remember that several months ago I filed a request for a refund on an overcharge for an airline ticket issued by your Singapore office. But before we discuss that matter, I would like to obtain two airline tickets for passage to and from Salt Lake City."

"Oh, yes," she responded with a thoughtful inspection of the carpeted floor. "I remember that request. You must be Mr. Terril."

"You remember names very well," I observed.

"When do you wish to depart for Salt Lake City?" she asked.

"The time is negotiable," I replied, "but the days are not."

The session with Violet and the computer, which stood nearby on the counter, consumed considerable time, but she finally extracted an acceptable flight schedule and a somewhat less acceptable bottom line from it, so I presented a check to her in exchange for the tickets.

Then, with probing eyes, I inquired, "Now how about that refund?"

After a pause during which mental gears seemed to mesh, she answered, "Don't forget that Singapore countered your request with a request for the original receipt. Then you submitted the receipt to us, and we sent it to Singapore. Now we are waiting for Singapore's response."

"But it has been over three months since I made that request," I protested. "I'm beginning to suspect that Singapore doesn't intend to respond to it."

"Of course, I can't predict when Singapore will respond or what the response will be," she murmured with evasively shuttling eyes. "But they will respond; that I promise."

"I'm convinced that Singapore will claim that there has been no overcharge," I said. "Consequently, I've already prepared an attack on the corporation, which will be included in the travelogue that I previously mentioned to you."

"Why should you attack the corporation?" she countered. "The Singapore office is responsible for the overcharge; that is, if there was one."

"Because the corporation is morally responsible for the business ethics of all of its branch offices," I retorted. "Consequently, it should have ruled on the validity of my claim, not Singapore. If Singapore does respond negatively to my request, which my logic predicts will be the case, then I have to assume that the corporation is indifferent to its moral responsibilities."

"What's the nature of this so-called attack?" she inquired with skeptical eyes.

I smiled pensively while my mind slowly assembled the words. "For years Karl Malden has been making the wrong pitch," I chanted, "because you really should leave home without it."

She bowed her head and subjected the computer's keyboard to a deep study while I slowly retreated toward the door. As it responded to my push, I glanced across one shoulder toward her just as she looked up from the keyboard at her buxom associate and exclaimed, "Oh, gawd!"

BOOK 3

EXPO 86

29

Ontario to Coeur d'Alene

Ontario to Salt Lake City

Our residence in Fullerton was located a bit farther from the Ontario airport than from the Los Angeles airport, but LC and I chose to depart from Ontario since it was more accessible than heavily congested LAX. Besides, we viewed Ontario's long-term auto parking rates much more favorably. After checking our luggage at the America West counter, we repaired to the gate designated on our boarding passes. There we were withheld from boarding the aircraft until the last boarding call, because we had been assigned to seats 1B and 1C, which were supposed to be the first two seats beyond the entrance of the Boeing 737 aircraft.

LC preceded me into the craft, and, after checking the numbers above the first two seats, she turned to me and protested, "But there is no seat 1C."

"Then you may have to walk to Salt Lake City," I responded nonchalantly.

"What seems to be the problem?" a voice harshly interjected from directly behind us.

I turned about and found that the tall, black steward, who had been checking the passengers' boarding passes at the entrance, had left his post and was frowning down on us. "Somebody must have made a mistake," I retorted in equally harsh tones. "The seat number on this lady's pass doesn't correspond to any of those on the aircraft."

He rudely snatched the pass from her hand. Then, after briefly comparing the seat designations, he thrust it toward her and commanded, "Take that seat." And with a long forefinger, he dramatically pointed toward seat 1A.

When she moved toward it, I said, "No, I'll take that one. You take seat 1B."

"But it won't provide enough leg space for you," she again protested. Nevertheless, I silently guided her to 1B, which afforded the greatest comfort.

After we were seated, I thoughtfully studied the rangy, athletically built, young, black man, who stood just inboard of the entrance and checked the boarding passes of the latecomers. Finally he stepped to the door, closed and latched it, turned about, lowered a jump seat from its position on the forward bulkhead directly opposite my seat, and slumped onto it. Meanwhile, from behind us a somewhat voluptuous, young, black stewardess swung along the aisle toward the bulkhead and smiled coyly at the steward as she approached him.

"Hi," he greeted her.

"Hi," she responded with a coquettish giggle. Then, performing essentially the same operations on the adjacent jump seat, she seated herself beside him and added, "I'm Gloria."

"I'm Tony," he responded as they engaged their respective seat belts.

"Oh, I'm really bushed!" she exclaimed after the fittings of her seat belt snapped home.

"That's an odd statement," Pancho interjected into my mind. "I distinctly heard her tell him that she is Gloria."

"She could be Gloria Bushed," suggested his mate.

"Apparently she's a bushed Gloria," Pancho responded in silent tones that brooked no counter. Of course, I was the only victim of the exchanges.

"Out late with your husband?" inquired the steward in leading tones.

"No, just out late," she responded with another giggle. "I'm divorced."

"I'm tired, too," he muttered. "In fact, when I get home, I am going right to bed and sleep the clock around; that is, if I can keep my daughter out of my room."

"Oh, what a beautiful ring!" she exclaimed, caressingly running the fingers of her right hand along the side of his left hand to the finger on which an ornate ring sparkled. "Did you get it for football?"

"No, for track," he replied. "My coach gave it to me."

"Probably a sprinter," José suggested as my eyes studied the long, muscular limbs vaguely outlined beneath the dark fabric of the man's trim trousers.

"Al was a sprinter, too," Pancho remarked, "but his coach never gave him a costly ring."

"Furthermore, Al and his teammates had to buy their own socks and track shoes," José rejoined.

"And their grades always had to be up to snuff," Pancho added.

"Yeah," José responded. "I wonder if his grades had to be up to snuff, too."

While I surreptitiously watched the duo, the man placed his left hand on the woman's right thigh, and she responded with an eager smile. But the contact appeared to be intended not only to excite her but to gain her attention, because he gestured toward me with his head, and she responded to the gesture with a knowing leer.

"I got hooked up with one of them once," he muttered. "In fact, I went back to that *bleep* three times before I had enough."

Suddenly the man's evil implications filled me with a deep disgust for him, which was closely followed by an intense revulsion when the woman proceeded to create even more horror in my mind with a revelation of her moral depravity.

"I had a similar experience one time when I was in Washington, D.C.," she rejoined. "It was at a party." Then she paused and studied his expression as if trying to determine whether he fully comprehended the nature of that party. "Man, what a party that turned out to be!" she caroled. "I've never had so much fun in my whole life." Then, in an apparent attempt to add emphasis, starting on a high note, she exclaimed, "It was so much fun!" Then she stared into his eyes as if inviting still more revelations of voluntary degeneracy.

"Obviously Big Brother hasn't missed any tricks," José observed. "In Switzerland it was sodomy; here it's another form of perversion. Has he no character at all?"

"The answer to that is too obvious to warrant an answer," Pancho retorted. "I would like to point out that anybody who voluntarily submits to such an act is just as queer as his partner. After all, there are no one-way streets in *queerdom*."

"But those two idiots don't consider themselves to be queers," José observed.

"Of course, they don't," retorted his partner, "but they are just as much in error about that as the black man was in accepting Big Brother's claims, whatever they were."

"Obviously, the reason for his ready acceptance of those claims, whatever they were, involves his inherent capability of engaging in such acts himself," José retorted.

"But surely every moral American should be deeply disturbed by Big Brother's part in the development of this soul-searing scene," Pancho rejoined.

"Amen!" exclaimed José.

From thirty-eight thousand feet above sea level, the russet waters of the tumbling Colorado River were scarcely visible without the aid of binoculars, but the walls of its narrow, mile-deep gorges, their irregular floors, and the soaring walls of its barren canyon still loomed impressively below the aircraft. Within a few more minutes the Zion National Monument and the nearby Bryce Canyon proved to be of insufficient size to readily attract my attention. In fact, I would have missed them if the pilot had not described their general locations over the public address system as the aircraft passed between them. But I didn't miss the huge, open-pit copper mine where man had cut a huge gash through a mountain that overlooks the southern end of the Great Salt Lake.

Minutes later the big bird landed on the tarmac at the Salt Lake City airport where, for just a signature, National Car Rental provided us with a Eurosport car with scarcely three thousand miles on its speedometer.

Salt Lake City to Montpelier

From the airport we drove north on a U.S. highway; however, shortly before leaving the environs of Salt Lake City, we swung from the highway onto a street that provided access to the parking lot of a relatively large restaurant. At ten o'clock during that particular Saturday morning it was patronized by only two middle-aged couples. A plump, middle-aged waitress selected two middle-aged menus from a rack at the end of the cashier's counter and led us to a middle-aged booth that stood against the far wall, where she indifferently dropped the menus onto the table. Apparently the wall separated the dining room from the kitchen, since the sounds of colliding pots and pans were quite audible to us.

We had almost completed our repast when my peripheral vision detected the preoccupied stare of a tall man of forty-something, who stood at the cash register. As he stepped aside, another man was revealed, and both of them appeared to be listening closely to what the cashier was saying. From the cashier's counter the men moved somewhat surreptitiously to the opposite corner of the room, where they assumed loitering attitudes and engaged in a desultory discussion. Meanwhile, an unguarded guarded glance from the shortest of them warned me that they may have been assailing my civil rights, so my surveillance increased tenfold.

They may have been partners in the business, and they may have been brothers, but their matching black moustaches may have created a false impression of a family resemblance. They may have selected that particular vantage point because they habitually employed it, but I suspected that they selected it because of its unob-structed view of our booth. And that suspicion seemed to be supported by the fact that the shortest of the two men turned his gaze away from my alert gaze and murmured some words to his companion, which induced him to stare toward me as if he were viewing the eighth wonder of the world. Then the other man added his stare to it, so I discarded any semblance of subtlety and boldly met their stares with a particularly icy one. The shortest man immediately averted his eyes, turned, and moved away toward the cash register, but the other man held fast momentarily. Then, with an expression of resentment, he also yielded, but he deliberately strode across the room in the direction of our booth while my eyes openly challenged him. But he lacked the manhood for a direct confrontation. His forte was the low, cowardly, off-key whistle, the typical response of a so-called man—especially a man of Big Brother's caliber.

Apparently LC failed to observe the incident. Even if she had, it is unlikely that she would have interpreted it in its intended light. That relieved my mind considerably, because I certainly didn't want any of my personal problems to spill over onto her. But I wasn't through with that tall bird with the warped beak.

After picking up the check and rising, I looked down at LC and suggested, "While I'm paying the check, why don't you go to the little girls' room, because such opportunities will be spaced far apart in the wilds of Utah."

She silently nodded, arose, followed me to the cashier's counter, and continued onward when I stopped in front of it. Meanwhile, a teenage busboy lounged over a publication of some sort at the far end of it. The slender cashier must have been watching us from the doorway of the kitchen, into which the two men had disappeared, because she was already on the way to her post. After coldly accepting the check and a twenty-dollar bill from me, she laid the change on the counter without meeting my probing gaze. The behavior was too familiar to me, but I was so emotionally charged up that there wasn't sufficient space within me for resentment to expand further.

"Do you know the tall man with the moustache who just left the far corner of the room?" I inquired with deceptive mildness.

"What about him?" she countered glacially.

"I just wondered if he is one of your local queers," I muttered.

"I didn't see him," she retorted, even though she had just left the doorway through which he had passed. "I don't have the slightest idea what you are talking about."

"Well, I certainly do," I retorted. "In my opinion any man who whistles at another man, like he just did, has to be as queer as a three-dollar bill."

"I don't know what you are talking about," she repeated angrily with a covert glance at the busboy.

After a cynical glance at her, I regretfully checked the tense figure of the boy from the corner of one eye, turned away, and strode into the foyer just as LC emerged from a doorway in its far wall.

While we strolled from the entrance toward the car, Pancho suggested, "I'll bet that the whistler was the cashier's husband, and the busboy was a product of the union."

"There's an uncharacteristic element of reason in that suggestion," his partner agreed reluctantly. "Many of the businesses in the American outback are operated by families."

"But Al didn't intend for that lad to be caught in his counterattack," Pancho insisted loyally. "Unfortunately many innocent bystanders have been injured because of Big Brother's attacks on him."

"Yeah," his mate granted, "but this counterattack was justified, because that big guy really is queer."

"Of course, he is," Pancho retorted. "After all, he committed a sadistic act, and practically everybody knows that sadism is one of the primary facets of *queerdom*."

From the parking lot we returned to the U.S. highway and resumed our trek north through Ogden to Brigham City. There Uncle Sam's highway took off in two different directions, but we didn't hesitate. We veered onto the northeasterly leg, which, according to the road map, would take us to Logan, Utah. Meanwhile, the scrub-covered, rolling terrain had acquired a few clusters of small pine trees, and the picturesque, snow-capped mountains appeared to have moved much closer to us, but we had moved closer to them, of course.

At Ladybird Park, which is located just north of Logan, we paused briefly to savor the lush beauty of the rolling terrain that nestled so peacefully at the base of one of the towering, snow-covered peaks. LC triggered a couple of snapshots of the terrain, but mankind has yet to develop photographic equipment capable of producing nature's beauty in the same colors, perspectives, and magnitudes as those perceived by the human eye. Later we discovered that the hazy atmosphere and the cloud-laden sky had detrimentally affected the product.

From the small city park the highway resumed climbing to a 7,805-foot pass; then it rapidly descended to tiny Garden City on the west bank of Bear Lake, which straddles the Utah-Idaho border. From there it continued across the border and touched Paris, Idaho. Just beyond that point we stopped briefly alongside the Bear River and endeavored to capture on film some of the grandeur of the tumbled, snow-clad horizon with the river in the foreground.

In Montpelier we checked into the Best Western Crest Motel and immediately left it to dine at the Matador Restaurante, where we received attentive and courteous service from a tall, brunette waitress. Despite that and the fact that there was no musical interlude, I detected several of the typical tokens indicating that Big Brother had preceded us to that isolated small town.

Montpelier to South Yellowstone

After a quiet night and a light breakfast, we resumed our journey in a northeasterly direction to Geneva, located just west of the Utah-Wyoming border. Midway between Geneva, Idaho, and Smoot, Wyoming, we stopped alongside the highway to admire the distant, snow-clad peaks of the Salt River Range. According to the highway map, 11,418-foot Wyoming Peak stood just east of the southern end of that range, so those shimmering peaks had to be pretty tall in the saddle to obscure so prominent a landmark.

After we resumed the journey, the highway gradually swung north until it paralleled the range. Meanwhile, it lightly touched Smoot, Afton, and Thayne before crossing the Snake River at its confluence with the Palisades Reservoir. There it turned east and followed the meandering river in a northeasterly direction until it crossed the river at Hobart Junction, where we forsook it in favor of another highway that followed the sinuous course of the Snake River north through Jackson and into the Grand Teton National Park.

Unfortunately I had listened too attentively to the words of a TV commentator, who had raved through most of a "60 Minutes" program about the scenic wonders of the Grand Tetons and the Jackson Hole area; consequently, my expectations were so high that some of the area proved to be a great disappointment to me. In fact, we passed through Jackson into the park before we realized that we had traversed a main thoroughfare of one of the most highly touted tourist meccas in the nation.

But the Grand Tetons didn't disappoint me in the least. And I quickly arrived at the conclusion that they should disappoint no one because some of those lofty peaks appeared to pierce the floor of heaven itself. And I said as much to LC at the time. Since that time, however, I have done some research on the heights of mountains and found that I also may have been guilty of raving.

I discovered that Grand Teton's peak is only 13,770 feet above sea level, and it is the highest of the Tetons. The heights of several mountains within the continental United States surpass that height. Among them are Colorado's Pike's Peak, Northern California's Mount Shasta, Washington's Mount Rainier, and Southern California's Mount Whitney, whose 14,995-foot peak is the highest of the lot. Hawaii's Mauna Kea and its Mauna Loa are just a few feet higher than the Grand Teton, but Alaska's Mount McKinley surpasses its height by more than one mile, and Nepal's Mount Everest towers over it by more than three miles. Consequently, I have concluded that the name *Grand Tetons* should be changed to *Petit Boutons*, which are French words that translate into "Little Pimples," whereas the French words *Grand Tetons* translate into "Great Teats." Obviously, the latter is a misnomer, but it seems to be more euphonic than *Petit Boutons*.

Yellowstone National Park At Moran we turned the little car onto still another U.S. highway, which swung past the east side of Jackson Lake, and continued onward to the south entrance of Yellowstone National Park. By flashing my Golden Age Passport before the eyes of the attendant, we managed to avoid the two-dollar fee. But before advancing farther into the park, I parked the car in front of a nearby information board, on which a map displayed the park's roads and their current conditions.

After studying it for several minutes, I looked at my companion and inquired, "Well, Dolly, where to now?"

"Most of the roads into the northern part of the park are still closed," she responded unhappily, "and I particularly wanted to see the bears during this trip."

"It seems to me that the bears should still be hibernating," I re-marked.

"But it's spring," she protested. "Surely they've left their dens by now."

"It's spring at this elevation," I granted, "but the higher slopes, where the bears are holed up, must be covered by snow, so they have to be sawing logs. After all, there's no good reason for them to come out of their dens, because there's no food value in snow, and that's all they would find to eat."

"Well, let's go as far as we can," she suggested. "Maybe some of the bears with insomnia will have migrated to lower levels by this time."

"Humph!" I grunted. "Now we have bears with insomnia. Next we'll have somnambulistic bears."

Her dark eyes expressed so much disappointment that I reluctantly released the brakes, and the car moved forward and upward toward that winterland. As indicated by the information board, the road climbed rapidly; meanwhile, the patches of snow beneath the pine trees quickly combined into a uniform snowpack that grew higher and higher about their trunks. Eventually we came to a small turnout, whose surface had been cleared of snow, so we ducked into it long enough for LC to expose one frame of film with the car standing against the backdrop of a ten-foot wall of snow. However, about ten feet beyond that wall of snow there was a steep back slope; furthermore, a snowplow may have discharged much of the snow from the roadway onto the back slope, so the picture probably conveyed a false impression. But there must have been about four feet of snow on the level, and that's on the level, *honest Injun.*

At West Thumb, which is located on the west bank of Yellowstone Lake, I parked the car in front of a small general store with a fast-food counter. After purchasing two hot dogs, we consumed the food in the car. Then I maneuvered the vehicle into an adjacent parking area overlooking the lake, where LC braved the cold mountain air long enough to focus the camera on one of the columns of steam that were spewing forth from several vents along the bank of the snow-covered, ice-locked lake.

Meanwhile, José suggested, "Incredible as it seems, Big Brother must have paid a visit to the two middle-aged gents in that remote store on this so-called roof of the continent."

"If you're referring to their none-too-subtle exchanges of glances while the boss was waiting for the hot dogs, I have to agree," conceded his mate. "But I wonder which of his vicious stories was laid on them."

"It doesn't really matter," retorted José, "because the net result is always slander, whichever it was."

From the parking lot at West Thumb we followed another two-lane road along the shore of the lake to its north end and turned onto an intersecting, two-lane road that followed the Yellowstone River in a northerly direction to the Upper and Lower Falls. Despite the lack of suitable sunlight, LC photographed the less spectacular of the two falls, which dropped the river's burden of spring rains and melted snow into a 109-foot, spray-shrouded chasm. Meanwhile, with a thunderous roar, the other one plunged over a 300-foot drop into a similar chasm.

From the falls the road continued to climb, and the surrounding snow became progressively deeper. Finally the dark-gray, asphalt pavement disappeared beneath a huge pile of the white stuff, but a sign bearing the redundant words *Road Closed* had been neatly planted in the middle of it.

After the vehicle rolled to a stop against the spongy barrier, I looked obliquely at my lady and observed, "Apparently the road maintenance crew could no longer *bear* the burden of its battle with the Storm King, so there's no more *bare* roadway."

"But the big board at the gate indicated that this road is closed to through traffic," she countered in accusing tones.

"Yeah, it's closed, all right," I agreed, shifting the control lever into reverse, "but the reason for coming this far was to see if we could find some bears with insomnia, and I haven't seen even a bear track, much less a wakeful bear or even a sleep-walking bear."

"Of course, you haven't seen any bear tracks, because the bears are still hibernating," she responded with a superior air. "After all, they are smart enough to know that snow isn't fattening, so they won't leave their cozy dens until the snow has melted. Then they'll come out and search for food."

I turned an incredulous pair of eyes on her and immediately redirected them to the rearview mirror, which was desperately warning me that the car was about to back into a six-foot snowbank while I was jockeying it about for the return trip. Despite their obvious assets, women can be extremely irritating at times.

Meanwhile, she absently murmured, "There appears to be a lot more snow now than there was during our last Memorial Day visit."

"Memorial Day is a bit too early for your fuzzy friends," I said. "Next time we'll give them another month in which to crawl out of their dens and rub the sleep from their eyes."

We backtracked several miles to an intersecting road, where I brought the car to a stop so that we could read a sign, which promised that the intersecting road would deliver us to Old Faithful among various other unusual sites.

"Let's do go to Old Faithful," LC urged. "Maybe we'll arrive in time to get some pictures during its next regurgitation. Unfortunately during our last visit the camera jammed just as it regurgitated. Remember?"

"Uh-huh," I grunted. "But did you intend to use the word *regurgitation?*" I inquired with a wry smile.

"Well, that's what it does," she insisted with a defensive air. "The surface water from the rains and melting snow seeps down through the siliceous gravel and through the fissures in the rhyolite bedrock to a level where a heat source from deep within the earth raises its temperature to the boiling point. Since the hot water and the steam are restricted from descending any lower, they expand upward through similar strata of siliceous gravel and fissures of rhyolite. But their only avenue of escape is a vent through the concretelike surface of the top layer of siliceous gravel, which has been sealed by countless deposits of silica from the reactions of the geyser." She paused, tilted her head back so that she could look down her nose at me, and added, "In other words, it acts like a pressure cooker. If that isn't the same as regurgitation, then I don't know what the word means."

"It sounds like regurgitation to me," I responded with a chuckle. "But you'd better not go public with the term, because the park's public relations department will be jumping all over you." After staring thoughtfully at her for several seconds, I asked, "By the way, how do you happen to know about the geology of *geezers?*"

"I read about it in one of the park's pamphlets," she replied. "But the word is pronounced *guyzers*, not *geezers.*"

After tendering a tolerant smile, I directed my attention to the winding thoroughfare as the little car eagerly responded to the downgrade.

After a few miles of tortuous travel, the snow and pine trees gave way to an occasional meadow or a flat area, where streamers of steam curled lazily upward from several points. Eventually we came upon a small, hydrothermally active basin, to which a boardwalk led from a small parking area that adjoined the road. Handrails had been added to the sides of the walk to prevent visitors, such as children and adults with the minds of children, from walking into or even falling into the pools of boiling water.

Since I had seen the exhibit during our previous visit, I elected to remain in the car, which was parked near the end of the walk. A small herd of buffalos (American bison) grazed placidly on the fresh, green grass that had sprung up on the bottom of the adjacent ditch and its gently slanted back slope. For several minutes LC sat with her right arm on the open window's ledge and uneasily eyed the animals. Meanwhile, she appeared to be pondering the advisability of risking a buffalo stampede just to photograph a pool of boiling water. From where I sat, the mission wasn't even worthy of consideration. Finally she collected enough courage to open the door; then, with a furtive glance toward the nearest beast, she leaped out of the car and scampered to the end of the walk. From that point she nonchalantly proceeded along its semicircular configuration, as I pondered the amazing confidence instilled in her by a flimsy handrail that could not have stalled a charging buffalo for one microsecond. Nevertheless, she followed it to the far side of the caldron, where it terminated in a rail-enclosed viewpoint.

Meanwhile, I sat and watched a burly bull buffalo move steadily toward the near end of the walk as he harvested the lush grass at the bottom of the adjacent ditch.

A Terrorist in Action

Consequently, when LC returned to the end of the walk, he had consumed the current crop and was standing there belligerently swinging his massive head from side to side while searching for greener pastures. She stared apprehensively at him, but he ignored her. Then she looked appealingly at me, and I also should have ignored her.

Instead, I called: "Place the camera on the rail and take a picture of the brute."

After skeptically studying his curved horns and massive shoulders for a moment, she did as I had suggested. Then her eyes appealed to me again.

"Aw, he won't bother you," I responded, "but give him plenty of leeway when you go around him."

She nervously inched forward toward the end of the structure; then, after a brief interval of indecision, she dashed madly around the beast just as he snorted and tossed his head about threateningly. My heroine instantly screeched and bolted toward the car, whose nearest door I had obligingly pushed open.

"There's no reason for all of that hurry-scurry," I protested mildly upon her arrival.

"Yes, there was," she retorted breathlessly, slumping onto the seat. "And that's the last time I'll ever take your advice when I am confronted by danger, because that beast was about to take after me."

"Naw, he wasn't mad at you," I responded derisively. "He was mad at that guy. See?" And I pointed toward a smaller bull that the big bull was eyeing malevolently while continuing to shake his big head. The big bull seemed to resent the other bull's poaching activities on his grassy back slope. Abruptly lowering his head, with a grunt he launched his heavy body headfirst at the side of the offender. There was the sound of a solid thump, but the poacher was already leaving town, so no major damage was incurred. Obviously the poacher was an independent character, because he yielded just a few feet of space; then, placidly lowering his head, he resumed grazing. Nevertheless, he kept one respectful eye on the big bull while that possessive character began to harvest the greener grass on **his** back slope.

During the hurried trip through the most active hydrothermal areas, we passed several striking features, such as silex springs, fumaroles, paint pots, and small geysers, but we suffered no great loss, because we had previously visited the sites. However, we did pause briefly beside the road to study an adjoining, meadowlike setting where streamers of steam spiraled slowly upward from widely separated sources while some thirty American elks grazed between them. By that time the sun had long since passed its zenith, so we sped past the Firehole River Area. Despite our haste we failed to escape the characteristic odor of hydrogen sulfide gas at many of the exhibits, and it sharply impressed on us the close proximity of the so-called nether regions to the surfaces over which we traveled.

In response to my pained expression as we passed one of them, LC callously observed, "You might as well get used to that odor, because you'll be exposed to an awful lot of it during the hereafter."

How can a man cope with a such a woman?

Finally, in response to a road sign bearing the words *Old Faithful*, I turned the car from the main thoroughfare onto a road that soon terminated in a parking lot at the rear of a towering lodge.

After I brought it to a stop, LC grasped the camera and suggested, "Let's use the last frame on this roll for a shot of the lodge, because I don't want to be caught short when Old Faithful blows his stack this time."

"Okay," I agreed. And she thrust the camera toward me.

In response to my questioning stare, she murmured, "You are the architect and the builder, so you should know which will be the best view of the structure."

Reluctantly accepting the gadget, I crawled out of the car and moved toward a potentially advantageous position on the sidewalk in front of the car. Raising the camera, I peered through the viewfinder at the massive, wooden structure. Even from a distance of approximately three hundred feet, I was forced to adjust the zoom lens to include the wing that I was attempting to photograph, but the view of its steeply pitched, gable roof failed to satisfy my so-called artistic sense, so I moved laterally until it was satisfied. Finally I pressed the shutter button, but there was no responding click. Then I tried to advance the film, but the lever refused to yield.

With that I turned toward LC and called: "Hey! This pile of junk has locked up again. Do you suppose that it's about to frustrate us a second time?"

"Here, let me try it," she commanded, pulling up beside me. And I surrendered it to her.

After inspecting the positions of the visible controls, she pressed the shutter button, but there was no response. Then she attempted to advance the film, but it refused to advance.

"Hmm," I mumbled. "It appears that we have spent a bundle on a Japanese camera that's no better than the usual American product."

"It'll work," she insisted. "It worked fine until you tried to operate it. In fact, it hasn't locked up like this for a long time."

"That's because we haven't used it for a long time," I retorted.

"I'll figure out how to make it work," she predicted confidently.

"That I'll have to see to believe," I retorted. And that was when I made my big mistake.

She silently studied the assembly for a moment; then, after abruptly nodding her head, she began to unscrew the fastener that retained the camera in its leather carrying case. When the case fell free from the camera, a small button in the rear surface of the camera was revealed.

A sense of defeat settled over me like a shroud, because I had forgotten that obscured button, so I had to stand there and ruefully anticipate what was about to happen. Of course, she pressed the button, extracted the rewind handle, rolled the film onto its spool, and removed it from the camera with a triumphant flourish. "See!" she crowed. "It does work when you know how."

In my opinion it is completely out of character for any chick to crow, because only roosters and crows crow. However, I don't know how the pecking order goes among those noisy black fowls, but I suspect that both sexes crow; in fact, both of them would have to crow to make so much noise, so a chick crow could crow, but LC is neither a rooster nor a crow, so she should never crow.

Obviously I had to act quickly or lose what little control over her that I still possessed, so I snatched the roll of film from her hand and eagerly inspected its free end for evidence of damage. Unfortunately the end was intact, and, in spite of the force that I had so impatiently applied to the advance lever, none of the perforations had been deformed; consequently, I couldn't even claim unfairly that she had forcibly removed the film from the camera. Silently I returned the roll to her— silently because no man should ever attach any importance to a woman's triumph, especially when she possesses superior mechanical ability.

We entered the lodge through one of its rear doors and strolled slowly along a wide corridor to the central part of the building, which, despite its rustic decor, immediately reminded me of the rotunda of a state capitol building where I once worked as a highway engineer. We infiltrated a group of other visitors and joined in their vertebrae-cracking visual inspection of the exposed wooden trusses that supported the so-called rotunda's wooden roof, which must have towered almost fifty feet above the floor.

"I had forgotten how very old it appears to be," LC murmured. "How old do you suppose it is?"

"That's difficult to determine because of its rustic characteristics," I replied, "but I doubt that it's older than Old Faithful."

"Aw, that's no comparison," she retorted derisively. "Why, Old Faithful must be hundreds of years old."

"Of course, no one knows how long Old Faithful has been faithful," I said. "But some self-appointed authorities on the subject claim that it may have been here during the Ice Age."

"No kidding," she responded skeptically.

"No kidding," I seconded.

"Do you suppose that this building could be one hundred years old?" she inquired.

"It may not be as old as it appears to be," I replied, "but it could be as old as I am."

A predatory gleam leaped into her brown eyes. "Aw, it can't be that old," she insisted.

Then she stepped to the side of a bark-stripped tree trunk, which served as one of the columns that supported the mezzanine, and stroked an imaginary numeral *1* on its rough surface. As an afterthought she added an imaginary serif to each of its imaginary ends. Then she had the unmitigated gall to smile demurely into my wrathful eyes.

"So you weren't content with just insulting me," I growled. "You had to rub salt in the wound."

After a particularly pleased smile, she suggested, "Actually it may not be as old as it appears, because the *au natural* poles and the saw-sized timbers and planks may have been deliberately employed to give the building an antique appearance."

"A rustic appearance," I suggested absently.

Deliberately ignoring the suggestion, she pointed upward and said, "The use of those tree trunks with their branches still intact is clever." Then, glancing toward me, she added, "I mean those trunks with the two opposed branches that serve as braces between the tree trunk and the beam."

"The use is not clever," I retorted. "Unique, perhaps, but not clever, because there are spaces at the points where the so-called braces connect to the beam, so the braces can't transmit any load from the beam to the tree trunk even if those small limbs were capable of carrying a load of any magnitude. The beams and the columns had to be designed to support the entire load of the mezzanine, so those stupid branches were incorporated only for effect—and they affect me very negatively. The least that the builders could have done was to properly miter and block those limbs at the beam."

"I think they are clever," she retorted. And after studying her stubborn expression, I wisely dropped the subject.

In part, her observation was correct in that practically all of the building's internal structure and trim consisted of unfinished products of the forest, excepting the hardwood flooring, whose wide tongue-in-groove boards had been recently sanded, varnished, and waxed. But some of the concessions, which fronted onto the so-called rotunda, had been fabricated from plate glass and chrome-plated metal trim, so they were out of synch with the dominant decor.

Following the purchase of a roll of film at one of the concessions, we strolled to the entrance, whose heavy, oaken doors bore beveled, plate glass that brilliantly reflected the light rays from the ornately rustic chandeliers. I tugged mightily on one of the massive doors, and the ease with which it swung open startled me. Then I followed LC through the opening onto a wide concrete slab and down some concrete steps into another parking area.

LC immediately cast an accusing glance across one shoulder toward me and said, "It would have saved a lot of unnecessary steps if you had parked the car here."

"True," I admitted. "But that crazy car was tired, so it deliberately selected another route that allowed it to park in the nearest parking space."

She cast another glance toward me and shook her head with the air of a martyr, because my penchant for blaming my shortcomings on the behavior of inanimate things was not unknown to her. Unfortunately I presumed to lead the way to our objective, which I assumed to be the somewhat distant, low, flat-topped knoll whose gently rounded shoulders had been colorfully decorated by algae. Typically the algae fed on chemicals deposited by the many streamlets that trickled down its shoulders into a moatlike depression. We eventually arrived at a woven-wire fence that guarded the depression, which proved to be the course of a small stream, and we immediately exchanged puzzled stares.

"I don't recognize this area a-tall," I muttered, "but this mound has to be the one from which Old Faithful erupts."

"I don't recognize it either," LC murmured, "but I'm sure that some bleachers were located between the lodge and the geyser." Looking back at the lodge, she added, "But the bleachers were much closer to the lodge than this is."

"But this has to be the site," I insisted. "Look at the the big column of steam that's rising from the center of the mound."

She looked in the direction to which I was pointing; then she looked back at the lodge and shook her head with a baffled air. For a moment she studied the boardwalk paralleling the fence; then she turned and walked thoughtfully along it. Meanwhile, I tagged along with an occasional glance through the fence at the unfamiliar stream. We had almost arrived at the point where the boardwalk intersected with another one when a tall, young woman turned from the intersecting walk onto it.

When her long strides were about to carry her past us, I said, "Please pardon me, miss, but can you point out to us the location of the Old Faithful geyser?"

"Yes, I can," she responded with a pleasant smile. "It's located right over there."

As my eyes turned in the direction that she pointed, I immediately recognized the site: another low knoll spouting a streamer of steam from a port located about midway between us and one wing of the lodge.

"Thank you," I murmured, casting a guilty glance toward my companion. "But why is so much steam rising from this area?" And I pointed to the adjacent knoll.

"That steam is being produced by a number of geysers," the young woman replied. "In fact, there are dozens of them over there. If you'd like to learn more about them, pick up one of the pamphlets that the park's services group has placed in the box located just this side of the point where the walks intersect. It costs only a quarter, and it helps tremendously during the tour of that particular area."

"Thank you again," I murmured. "Actually this is not the first time that we've visited the park, but things look so different." And I cast another guilty-laden glance toward my partner and smiled inanely at her.

"No doubt many changes have been made since your last visit," suggested the other woman. "In fact, materials for still another walk have been dumped just beyond that intersection, so still more changes are projected."

While anxiously pushing LC toward the intersection, I said, "Thank you still again, but we should not miss Old Faithful's upcoming eruption, because the rapidly declining sun may be too low on the horizon for us to photograh it."

"There's no need for you to hurry," she called to us. "It erupted less than thirty minutes ago, so you have plenty of time to get set for the next one."

I expressed my appreciation for the additional information with a smile that literally strained my facial muscles and then urged LC onward with a gentle nudge. After we were safely out of the audio range of our informant, I said, "It's amazing how friendly and helpful some strangers can be. Suddenly I'm considering spending the remainder of my life associating only with strangers."

Following a thought-filled pause, LC murmured, "That gal is both too tall and too young for you." Then, after several steps, she added, "So you intend to give up all of your friends, including me."

"Not you, Dolly," I muttered, as I locked her right arm about my left arm and gently squeezed it. "Since you are my only friend, I won't have to give up any friends when I begin associating only with strangers."

She studied my eyes with an inscrutable expression for a moment. Then, thoughtfully looking down at the passing panorama of wooden boards, she asked, "What changed the length of the interval between Old Faithful's eruptions?"

"Well," I began slowly, "despite the claims of some rather opinionated geologists, I strongly suspect that nobody really knows. But Old Faithful may have decided to join the United Brotherhood of American Geysers."

She stopped abruptly, which forced me to do likewise, of course. Then she turned and stared at me as if I had just crawled forth from one of those hot, odoriferous caverns beneath the soles of our shoes. Finally she shook her head sadly, gently disengaged our arms, and silently resumed walking, but her actions spoke louder than words.

I cautiously hurried to her side and defensively protested, "But that's usually what happens when one joins a union. The union always demands lower production rates from its members so that more dues-paying members can be employed; consequently, Old Faithful has been forced to produce fewer eruptions during the last twenty-five years."

"But what do the geologists claim is the reason for the extended interval?" she countered.

"Some of them claim that the physical characteristics of the reservoirs and channels, which supply the hot water to the geyser, were altered by the earthquake," I replied. "But, of course, they don't really know."

"That makes sense," she murmured.

"What makes sense?" I asked. "The fact that they really don't know?" She must have been preoccupied or something, because she didn't even answer.

I made the mistake of arriving at the little wooden box first; however, that did permit me to discover for myself that it was mounted at a convenient height atop a wooden post and that its plywood top was sloped down from its horizontal hinge to ensure that the drainage from rain and melting snow would flow away from it. I immediately raised the top and looked expectantly into the box.

"Huh!" I grunted when LC pulled up beside me. "No pamphlets. In fact, this must not be the right box, because there's no coin slot."

"Yes, there is," she insisted. "It's right there. See?" And she pointed to the end of a piece of one-inch-diameter pipe, across which a small piece of sheet metal had been welded.

"Hmm," I mumbled. "So the coin is supposed to slip through the slot in that piece of sheet metal, then. . . ."

"Then it drops down through the pipe into this sheet metal coin box," she interjected, thrusting her right hand beneath the wooden box and patting one side of the coin box. "They have assumed that everybody is honest as far as the pamphlets are concerned, so they have placed them in the wooden box with the expectation that everyone will slip a quarter into the slot before taking one of them."

"The fools!" I exploded. "I'll bet my kingdom in Hades that there aren't two quarters in that coin box; meanwhile, all of the pamphlets have been removed from the wooden box."

Then I proceeded to make a production of a simulated study of the obviously impregnable coin box. Finally, with exaggerated reluctance, I shook my head and said, "Oh, well, there's probably no more than a couple of quarters in the *bleeped* thing anyway."

"Whom do you think you are kidding?" she challenged me with smiling eyes. "More than once I've stood by while you pointed out an error in change to a clerk. In fact, I recall that one of those errors involved a ten-dollar bill."

"But I couldn't let the guy clip me for a whole ten bucks," I protested.

She exhaled a short, exasperated laugh, shook her head, and turned away toward the intersecting boardwalk.

"Huh!" I grunted. "Some Canadians have no sense of humor whatsoever."

She quickly turned and retorted, "Obviously some Americans don't have a sense of humor at all."

By the time that I had drawn abreast of her, we could see the source of Old Faithful's steam on our right. But about 150 feet of mostly wet and disheveled terrain separated it from us, so we were relatively safe from an unscheduled exposure to a scalding shower. It was a desolate scene, which strongly reminded me of moonscapes that I had observed on a television screen many years before. The principal differences were the steam, of course, and the facade of the lodge in the background.

"I don't see how we missed it," LC murmured. "It was so close to the lodge, yet we walked so far." Then, turning from the scene toward me, she asked, "Why did you lead me so far afield when you knew very well that the geyser is located very near the lodge?"

"From the entrance of the lodge the other site looked a lot like this one," I responded defensively.

"But it obviously was too far from the lodge," she persisted. "Surely you must have realized that it was too far away to be the site of Old Faithful."

"Since that site looked like the one we were seeking, I just kept on going," I replied peevishly.

"Even when it obviously was too far away to be the right one?" she countered.

"Well, they could have moved the *bleeped* thing," I muttered.

"They what!" she exclaimed with an incredulous expression.

"Well, there must be plumbers around here to service the plumbing in the lodge, so they could have moved it," I insisted with a teasing grin.

After staring briefly at me, she murmured, "You are absolutely impossible."

With that, she linked her left arm with my right arm, and we sauntered onward as nonchalantly as if a potential confrontation had not been circumvented by an impossible human being.

En route to the bleachers we encountered a beggar. He was a perky, little fellow clad in a light-brown fur coat, along the back of which a darker brown stripe stretched from his shoulders to his tailbone. As soon as he noticed us, it became evident that he was a beggar, because he immediately bounded across the grass to the side of the boardwalk, where he stopped, stood upright, and extended his forepaws toward us in a supplicating attitude.

"Oh, how cute!" LC exclaimed. "Let's take a picture of him standing upright like that."

Then he dropped down onto all four feet, pointed his nose toward us, and appeared to be sampling the air currents to determine if we actually had some peanuts. Possibly he had been conned by other heartless camera buffs.

"All right," I reluctantly agreed, "but be ready to snap the shot when I entice him to stand upright."

Then I kneeled alongside the boardwalk and extended the thumb and forefinger of my right hand as if they contained a goodie, and he immediately stood upright with his forepaws cupped to receive it. Unfortunately, LC had forgotten to advance the film, so she missed a perfect pose, since the little fellow held it just long enough for him to discover that I was attempting to defraud him. Then he settled onto all four feet. Apparently he could be conned only once by the same con man, because he refused to return for another disappointment, so LC had to be content with a view of his left side as he sat on his haunches with his fuzzy, dark-brown tail curled behind his arched back like a question mark.

Meanwhile, a four-year-old boy invaded the scene and eagerly sought to establish a lifelong friendship with the tiny creature. From some distance behind us, his father called: "Billy! Billy! Don't bother the little ground squirrel, because those people are trying to take a picture of it."

Actually the child's fascination with the animal would have provided an endearing picture in itself, but such pictures are best preserved in the minds of the beholders, since none of man's ingenious gimmicks is capable of reproducing the aura of happiness and joy that such a child exhibits when he first discovers another of Mother Nature's gems.

I looked at the frustrated father and thrust the palms of both hands toward him in a stalling gesture. The man must have properly interpreted the gesture, since he nodded and smiled the smile of a man who has discovered that he is unable to fully cope with the demands of parenthood.

As he strolled past us, he called, "Billy!" But the lad ignored him. "Billy!" he repeated, and he received the same response. Then, in obviously bribing tones, he called, "Come, Billy! Let's go farther up the walk. There are even bigger animals up there."

The boy looked up from his crouched position near the squirrel, and my eyes followed his startled gaze to a large, dark-brown rodent, which, at a distance of not more than a hundred feet, was scuttling across the boardwalk. The boy leaped up so suddenly that he frightened the tiny ground squirrel; consequently, he hurriedly darted away and dived into his burrow. Meanwhile, the lad dashed past his father toward the more intriguing animal while the man anxiously called, "Billy! Billy! Be careful, because it might bite you."

I immediately recognized the species from a previous visit. At that time a couple of the creatures had ventured forth from beneath the wooden platform, which supported the wooden benches that served the dozens of spectators who periodically collected there to view the next eruption of the geyser.

As we followed the venturesome child along the boardwalk, LC exclaimed, "Look! The platform has been extended to twice its previous length." After obeying the command, I nodded.

"And look at all of the marmots!" she exclaimed. "There must be dozens of them." Then she fixed her eyes thoughtfully on mine and murmured, "There were only two of them when we were here before. Where did they all come from?" Then, detecting the cannibalistic gleam in my eyes, she hurriedly insisted, "Don't answer that question."

"I was about to say that they must have migrated from other areas," I responded with an offended air.

"Pardon my bluntness," she retorted, "but I deeply doubt that statement. I suspect that you were about to say that the stork brought them or something to that effect."

"If that's the case, then the people who manage the park should require that the concessionaires add a pill to each package of peanuts that they sell to the visitors," I muttered. "These varmints have been multiplying like—like people."

"Aw, the nut vendors should never do that," she retorted.

"Why not?" I asked.

"Because some of the visitors might happen to consume the pills instead of feeding them to the animals," she answered.

"And what's so bad about that?" I countered.

After pondering the question briefly, she replied, "In view of the human population explosion, there appears to be nothing bad about it."

We actually caught a woman in the act of bribing a marmot to stand up on its rear feet by offering it nuts from a small container, and the little glutton was eagerly collaborating with her while a man was attempting to record the crime on photosensitive film. And, without any conscience whatsoever, LC stole a shot of the animal.

Even though the sun was approaching the horizon, a relatively large number of people had collected on the platform or seated themselves on its benches to witness the geyser's performance. Meanwhile, LC and I found that one end of a nearby bench was unoccupied, so we zipped up our jackets against the sharp mountain breezes and occupied it. Even though few of the visitors were acquainted, there was an air of comradery among them, which led them to beg and grant information about the geyser at will.

During the exchanges a voice from our right inquired, "When is Old Faithful supposed to spout?"

And a voice from the background volunteered, "Five-fourteen."

"Plus or minus ten minutes," suggested the first voice.

"Plus or minus ten minutes," agreed the second voice.

"With a twenty-minute margin of error Old Faithful seems to be a misnomer," I remarked to my companion.

"The fact that it always performs relatively close to a schedule should warrant the name," LC observed.

I nodded because the observation was logical, more logical than usual, in fact.

As the minute hand of LC's wristwatch approached five o'clock, she huddled beside me on that hard, wooden bench and scanned the scattered clouds fearfully lest one of them should zoom across the face of the declining sun before Old Faithful's moment of triumph. In fact, one cloud did blot out the sunlight just as the geyser hiccuped, but that amounted to only a few spurts of hot water and a belch of steam.

Simultaneously an excitable male viewer shouted, "There it goes!"

"No," interposed a veteran male viewer, "that's just the first of a few preliminary rumbles. It'll endure several of those labor pains before the geyser is born."

But the sun shown brightly on the column of boiling water and steam as it spurted high into the atmosphere and expanded into just a cloud of steam that billowed higher and higher.

"How high does it go?" inquired the voice of a male viewer from the background.

"I don't know for sure," another such voice responded, "but it looks like it must be up there between one hundred and one hundred fifty feet."

"How long does it last?" inquired another bystander.

"They say about two and one-half minutes," answered the voice of a female viewer.

"Did you get it?" I inquired of LC after the surging water and steam had subsided.

"Did I get it!" she gloated. Then, with a glance at the frame indicator, she added, "I got six shots of it in different stages."

"Then you should be happy," I muttered, as I arose to join the milling people.

"I would be if a bear and two little cubs had been standing in front of the geyser," she murmured.

I whipped a sharp glance toward her, and she immediately raised a restraining palm. "Please don't strike me." she pleaded. "I'll go peacefully." Then, in domineering tones, she added, "Surely you are aware that it's against the law for you to strike me."

"True," I conceded. Then, after looking speculatively at her for a moment, I added, "According to one of my uncles, it's against the law to strike an idiot."

Actually I may have been saved from a fate worse than death by the intervention of a complete stranger. After stepping down from the edge of the platform, I turned about to assist LC; then the heavy tones of a man's voice inquired, " 'ow long did you 'ave to wite?"

Despite my assumption that the question must have been directed to someone else, I glanced toward its source and found that the speaker was a man accompanied by a woman within the same midforties age bracket. Furthermore, he obviously had directed the question to me.

"We had to wait about thirty minutes," I replied.

"We got heah just as she blew," he volunteered with a delighted laugh. "It was almost as if she shiduled the event foah owah binifit."

"You were very fortunate," I murmured. "By the way, from what part of Australia did you come?"

"We ah from London, England," he responded with a chuckle.

With a rueful glance toward my companion, I muttered, "That was a miss of some ten thousand miles, but the dialects are very similar."

"Yis, they ah," agreed the man. Then, with a pair of friendly smiles and waves, he and his companion hurried onward.

"Every time that I hear a British accent my mind has become conditioned to suspect the presence of an Aussie or a Kiwi," I murmured.

"That could become a minor problem," LC suggested. "After all, British people have been scattered all over the world. But few Canadians have British accents."

"True," I agreed. "Unfortunately, their speech has been strongly influenced by ours."

Shortly after we began the return trip, LC exclaimed, "Oh, look! There's the Paint Pot. I would like to see it again."

"Okay, then you shall see it," I muttered, swinging the car into a space in a parking area that paralleled the roadway.

"Let's pick up a pamphlet on it," she suggested, as we strolled from the car toward the end of the boardwalk that led to our objective. "There's a box at this end of the walk."

"Yeah," I agreed. "And I'll pick up a bit of change at the same time."

"On second thought, I'll pick up the pamphlet," she said. Pausing, she began one of her interminable searches through her bag for a coin.

"No, I'll pick it up," I insisted. Coming to a stop beside the box, I hurriedly raised the lid to forestall any further discussion of the matter.

"Here's a quarter," she called, hurrying toward me with it in one outstretched hand.

"We don't need no quarter," I retorted while surreptitiously inserting a quarter into the slot. Then, quickly withdrawing a pamphlet, I allowed the top to drop back into place with a loud bang. Unfortunately, the loud bang failed to coincide perfectly with the *boeing* of the coin when it struck the bottom of the coin box.

"Ah-hah!" she exclaimed triumphantly. "That proves what I have known all along."

"What proves what?" I countered.

"The sound of that coin dropping into the coin box proves that you are one of the phoniest crooks in the world," she retorted.

"You don't have to insult me just because I'm inept," I protested. "You could give me some credit for trying."

After an approving smile, she then spoiled the whole thing by a frown followed by a negative shake of her head.

"I don't know why I continue to put up with such a negative woman," I murmured, "but I suppose it's because she's the only woman who'll put up with me." However, the remark was wasted.

Upon opening the pamphlet to its first page, I immediately exploded, "What a roarin' rip-off! From the first I suspected that I should just pick this thing up and walk away."

"Why?" she inquired, as she crowded close to me in an effort to determine the reason for the explosion.

"We intended to pick up a pamphlet. Right?" I asked.

"Right," she granted. "And that's what we got, isn't it?"

"No!" I retorted. "It's a leaflet. It practically says so right here," I insisted, stabbing viciously at it with a forefinger. Then I added, "See there? This thing identifies that thing back there as a leaflet box, so this has to be a lousy leaflet. I'm going back there and get my money back."

"No, you are not going back there," she insisted while her right hand firmly clutched at the front of my shirt.

"No?" I inquired mildly.

"No!" she responded firmly. Then, like a tolerant mother cajoling a petulant child, she added, "Actually you are far ahead in the deal, because a leaflet is much better than a pamphlet."

"Is that so?" I countered with a bemused smile. "Then I actually outsmarted the establishment, didn't I?"

After pensively studying my eyes for a moment, she murmured, "I suspect that outsmarting the establishment is important to you. I certainly hope that you don't try to con anybody else the way you do me, because some people are dumb enough to take such nonsense seriously."

"I never permit the stupidity of other human beings to interfere with my entertainment at their expense," I responded nonchalantly.

Her expression appeared to indicate a deep desire to advise me further on that subject, but she released the front of my shirt and lightly brushed away the wrinkles; then, reaching for the leaflet, she requested, "Let me take a peek at that thing."

"If I do, I'll never see it again," I predicted, withholding it from her. "If you want one, I'll get one for you, but you can't have mine."

"Since you paid for that one with kitty money, I have a half interest in it," she retorted impatiently, "so let me see it."

"Okay, since you are insisting on even-steven, I'll give you half of it," I said, turning to the leaflet's centerfold and grasping both sides of it in a tearing attitude.

"Don't tear it in two!" she commanded. "There's no reason why both of us can't use it."

"But another one doesn't have to cost anything," I protested. "All that I have to do is to walk back to that box, lift the lid, and take a leaflet. It's as simple as that."

"But that would be stealing," she insisted.

"No, it wouldn't," I retorted. "When we return from the tour of these exhibits, I'll replace the leaflet, and everything will be perfectly kosher."

"But that doesn't seem quite right," she persisted.

"But it is quite right," I insisted. "In the back of this leaflet I happened to notice this statement." Then I turned to the statement and added, "Here. Read this."

Aloud, she read, "Please return this leaflet to the box, or you may purchase it by leaving twenty-five cents in the coin receptacle."

I realized that I had overplayed my hand as soon as I detected the fiery glow in her brown eyes; consequently, when she imperatively held forth one hand, I surrendered the leaflet as gracefully as I could under the circumstances.

"Thank you," she said much too politely.

"I'll lay you eight to five that I'll never see that thing again," I muttered. "If that proves to be the case, I'll have been bilked out of my share of that quarter." I had to say something, because I couldn't allow her to get away with that imperious attitude scot-free.

"I'll see that you get your fair share," she promised. Then, with sparkling eyes, she added, "Besides, these leaflets are intended for use by people who can read."

Wisely ignoring the pitch, I had surged about three paces ahead of her when she shouted, "Stop!"

"Stop what?" I inquired after stopping and turning about.

"Just stop, because we have to go back," she replied, turning about with her eyes fixed intently on the leaflet.

"For another leaflet?" I asked.

"No, we have to go back to see an exhibit that we missed." Then she beckoned to me with a forefinger, and I responded with an overt air of eagerness.

Pulling up beside her, I hopefully inquired, "What do you have in mind?"

But the innuendo was lost to her, or she deliberately ignored it. "Look at all of that algae," she said, gesturing to an area beyond the adjacent guardrail.

"So I see a few trickles of hot water that eventually flow below this boardwalk," I observed caustically. "What's so startling about that?"

"But aren't those ribbons of colors startling?" she countered, pointing a forefinger toward the tiny rivulets. "Those particular colors are produced by tiny plants called algae, which are commonly found in ponds, streams, and wetlands throughout the world."

"If so, then why are we wasting valuable vacation time and money on a trip to Yellowstone when we could see the same thing in California?" I asked.

"Because Yellowstone's hydrothermal activity makes it different from most of the other areas of the world," she replied. "As for California, most of it is a desert."

"But there's a big, fat ocean along one side of it," I observed.

"True," she conceded, "but California's wetlands don't display the variety of colors that appear in these streamlets."

"The colors range from green to orange," I observed. "So what?"

"If you'll reach down and touch some of that green algae with your forefinger, you'll learn what," she predicted. I stared doubtfully at the steaming water that gently washed the green-colored soil and exchanged glances with her. "Well, what are you waiting for?" she asked belligerently. "Touch the algae and learn something about nature."

Glancing toward the wisps of steam, I murmured, "Regardless of what I'm supposed to learn, I'll take your word for it."

"It's perfectly safe for you to touch this algae," she said, "but you should never touch it in some of the other hot springs, because some types of algae can survive in temperatures up to one hundred sixty-seven degrees Fahrenheit. Actually, the colors of the algae indicate the temperature of the water. For example, orange indicates an environment with a higher temperature than green does. Some of the colors in and around hot springs are produced by strands of yellow or pink bacteria in water at temperatures up to one hundred ninety-five degrees Fahrenheit, which is just below its boiling point."

"But the boiling point of water is two hundred twelve degrees Fahrenheit at sea level," I pointed out.

"Yes, this leaflet covers that," she admitted, "but at this elevation, it's one hundred ninety-eight degrees Fahrenheit. It indicates that chemical deposits of sulfur, iron oxides, arsenic sulfides, and several other substances add vivid colors to some of the areas around hot springs, such as those of the Norris Geyser Basin."

"It's so nice to be able to read," I observed pointedly, but she ignored the observation.

We strolled about forty paces along the boardwalk and came to a pool of steaming water, which was the principal source of the hot water that flowed beneath the boardwalk at the point where we had last stopped.

"This is the Silex Spring," my tour guide informed me. "Deep within the earth beneath us molten rock constantly transmits heat upward through solid rock to ground water that has penetrated to such depths. Consequently, the water becomes very hot and expands upward through fractures in the rock and through channels in glacial gravel. Then it bubbles up through an opening in the surface of the earth as a hot spring."

"But what prevents the hot water from seeping away through the glacial gravel?" I asked.

She turned back to the previous page, carefully studied it, and answered, "Apparently sinter confines the water within the vent."

"And what is the definition of the word *sinter*?" I persisted.

"Hmm," she murmured after another search. "It isn't defined here."

"It's the siliceous or calcareous material that's commonly deposited by hot water within and about the vents of springs and geysers," I loftily informed her. "It forms a compact layer that is more impervious to water than are the surrounding materials."

"Not bad," she murmured.

"Sometimes it pays to be illiterate," I responded somewhat obscurely.

She flashed a brilliant smile at me; however, as usual, she was merely toying with me, because she countered: "In that definition you employed two other words that are equally foreign to me. Where only one word confused me before, now there are two. You are better at creating problems than at solving them. Maybe you should become a politician."

"Stop this stupid nonsense and get on with the show," I muttered darkly.

After lingering through a self-satisfied smile, she resumed: "Very hot water has the property of lower viscosity than water has at much lower temperatures; therefore, it flows more rapidly through restrictive fissures and channels. Furthermore, it more readily dissolves tremendous amounts of silica, a common component of volcanic rocks, so fissures and channels are constantly being enlarged, thereby providing even greater freedom of flow."

She looked at me as if expecting a comment, but I was playing the part of a bored scientist, so she continued: "Elements such as lithium, fluorine, arsenic, and boron are often dissolved from the earth's substances by hot water, which carries them upward to the surface. There they are deposited on the walls of the spring or in associated runoff channels. Silica, or silex, as it is often called, is a gray-to-white substance that also permeates the walls of springs and their runoff channels."

Momentarily our gazes met, so I interjected, "We really should go on to the next exhibit, because the sun is sitting on an adjacent mountaintop. Soon, it'll drop down behind it, and you'll be unable to read that stuff."

"But I'm not reading it," she protested. "I'm paraphrasing it."

Typically I didn't try to debate the fact that she couldn't read it and paraphrase it after the sun had set, because she would have presented one of the world's most illogical reasons why she could do just that.

"This is the exhibit that I particularly wanted to see," LC said, as we began to climb the sloping boardwalk toward a sign that bore the words *Fountain Paint Pot*.

"What's the pitch on it?" I asked.

"There's no pitch on it," she replied. "It is just mud."

"You'll be buried in mud if you don't answer that question properly," I growled, purposefully grasping her left arm.

"Eek!" she screeched. "Unhand me, you villain. I'll submit to your will."

"Very well, fair maiden," I said. "Then give me the pitch on it, or I'll take that thing away from you."

Peering briefly at the leaflet, she then murmured, "Apparently we'll find the muds to be thin and watery because of the current abundance of surface water. Later in the summer, when there's less surface water, the muds become very thick; consequently, the bubbling action, caused by steam from an underlying source, changes with the increased viscosity of the mud. For that reason visitors are forewarned to be wary of bursting bubbles, which can lob big gobs of mud over the guardrail."

When we finally came to a stop beside the guardrail that encircled the puddles of bubbling mud, I grunted, "Yep, the muds are thin and watery."

"I wonder what elements compose the different colored muds," she murmured.

"If that leaflet is worth its purchase price, it'll tell you," I said.

After a superficial glance at it, she mumbled, "Hmm. It doesn't **tell** me a thing!" I glared at her while she smiled benignly up at me.

"However, according to the printed matter," she smugly resumed, "the muds are composed of fine clay and particles of silica, created by the chemical composition of the minerals within the rocks and by pulverization that's due to the abrasion of hard particles." Then, casting a sly glance at me, she added, "So it appears that we got our money's worth, after all."

"But what's the composition of the clay?" I asked. "Clays differ throughout the world."

"So you suspect that you've cornered me," she retorted. With gloating eyes, she triumphantly announced, "But I have the answer."

I responded with a weak smile.

"The local rhyolite is of volcanic origin and resembles granite," she began, "but its crystals are so small that they cannot be visually detected without optical aids. Primarily it consists of silicon and feldspar. In time, environmental acids break down the feldspar into hydrous aluminum silicate, which is a clay called kaolinite. In its pure form the clay is white; however, when contaminated by iron oxides, its color changes into various shades of orange, pink, and red."

"That's a pretty big quarter's worth," I granted reluctantly, "but let's move on to the next one."

"That would be the Leather Pool," LC said. "Let's do stop there, because that name intrigues me."

"Okay," I agreed, "but your real reason for stopping there is to demonstrate your reading ability."

"How did you discover that?" she countered with unconvincing candor.

"Oh-ho!" I exclaimed. "I know every one of your artifices. They are as transparent as. . . ."

"As that mud back there," she interjected.

And I smiled the smile of a man who is accustomed to smiling in the face of inevitable defeat.

"Hot springs are in a constant state of flux," she read.

"That's a new state to me," I interposed. "Is it a fifty-third state, or is it located in another country?"

"It'll be your state if you don't stop interrupting me!" she retorted sharply.

I submitted an approving smile while she matched it with a pleased one.

"Such changes occur gradually," she resumed, "but abrupt changes are introduced by earthquakes. In nineteen fifty-nine the Hebgen Lake earthquake changed the Leather Pool to its current condition. Before the quake the pool's water temperature of one hundred forty-three degrees Fahrenheit permitted a brown, leatherlike algae to grow around its periphery. After the quake the water temperature rose to the boiling point, which killed the brown algae, and the current water temperature is still too high to support algal life."

"Possibly the earthquake shifted some glacial gravel deposits, thereby exposing the ground water to much hotter rock formations," I suggested.

"Essentially that's what these words imply," she granted with an approving glance.

"In other words, that leaflet contains information that you could obtain directly from me," I suggested with a deliberate air of egotism.

She refused to be baited; however, after displaying an inscrutable smile, she silently resumed reading while we followed the boardwalk around the first half of a semicircle toward a fumarole on the far side of the exhibit.

Finally we stopped beside the fumarole, and she began: "According to the leaflet, when surface water from rain or melted snow penetrates the earth to depths where it comes in contact with very hot rock formations, it flashes into steam. Consequently, a two-thousand-fold increase in volume creates sufficient fluid pressure to drive some of the combined gases from vents in the earth's surface, such as this one."

"Huh!" I grunted. "That thing is about as productive as some of our congressmen."

"Perhaps they would accomplish more by resorting to steam instead of hot air," she suggested.

"Why?" I countered.

"With steam they could lay down the equivalent of a smoke screen and really confuse their constituents," she answered.

"That's not necessary," I rejoined, "because a simple non sequitur serves them just as well."

"Now you have confused me," she murmured.

"Originally those were Latin words for a conclusion that doesn't follow from its premises," I explained. "For example, an incumbent insists that his constituents should vote for him because his political opponent is much more qualified to serve them than he is."

"But that doesn't make sense," she protested.

"Neither do some candidates for political offices," I retorted, "but there are enough illogical voters to elect them and even reelect them."

"This is no place to be discussing politics," she said. "Come on," she commanded, grasping my right arm and pulling me along the boardwalk. "I want to see the Red Spouter."

"Maybe I should pass up this one, because I can't stand the sight of blood," I observed. But, like any other sane person, she ignored the remark.

"According to report, this spring came into being during the nineteen fifty-nine earthquake," she stated. "It changes radically throughout the seasons. During. . . ."

"Just like somebody I know," I interjected. "A Dr. Jekyl one minute, and a Mistress Hyde the next minute."

"Before I was so rudely interrupted," she retorted, "I was about to say that during the summer it functions as a fumarole, but from late fall to the following summer it spouts brilliant, red water."

"Why?" I asked.

After responding, "It doesn't say," she hurriedly added, "There are no words of explanation in this leaflet."

"Hmm," I mumbled thoughtfully. "I suspect that during the winter there's sufficient surface water to make it perform normally, whereas during the summer there is insufficient water to dilute the color, so it spouts red."

"But why would there be so much red at any time?" she asked.

"There may be a large deposit of iron oxide through which one or more of its channels pass," I suggested.

"But you have no proof of that, do you?" she countered, stabbing a forefinger into the right side of my brisket.

"Don't do that!" I objected. "It hurts."

"No, it doesn't," she insisted. "More than likely that's a ticklish spot."

Of course, I could never admit it, because I would be persecuted forevermore. Nevertheless, she gently rubbed the offended area, which netted about the same response from my brisket as the stab, but I didn't dare admit it.

"The Volcanic Tableland is a pretty tall name for such a flat surface," I muttered, as we paused to study the terrain in the foreground. "What's so unique about it?"

"Well, listen carefully, and I'll explain it to you in words that even you can understand," she replied. "But pay attention to what I say, because I don't intend to repeat any of it."

"You don't have to make such a big production of it," I protested. "Get on with it, and don't give me any more guff."

"The present landscape began some seventy million years ago," she began. "At that time the earth's local crust was bent, fractured, and heaved upward into high mountain ranges, such as the Gallatin Mountains." And she pointed toward the not-so-distant skyline.

"Who says?" says I.

"Says I," she said. "Besides, those claims are printed on this white page in black ink." Then she fixed a challenging gaze on my skeptical features, but I refused to accept it. "Volcanic ash and fragments of rock were showered over the entire region," she resumed, "and lava flowed across the terrain to form the bulk of the Yellowstone plateau." Then, pointing to the immediate horizon, she melodramatically added, "In fact, you can see the tops of the cooled lava flows along the skyline of the Purple Mountains and the Central Plateau."

"What cornball would believe that tripe," I erupted, but she ignored the outburst.

"Eventually, ice buried the ruptured land," she stated. "In fact, a massive ice cap covered the center of the park, and glaciers spread out from it across the plateau and into the valleys of the Firehole, Gibbon, and Madison Rivers."

"Prove it," I commanded, but she ignored me.

"Hot springs at the edges of the lava flow were overrun by the encroaching ice, which melted so rapidly that great heaps of gravel were formed."

"How?" I asked.

"It doesn't explain how it took place," she admitted, "but I assume that some of the hot rocks shattered because of the extreme temperature differentials."

"Not bad for a woman," I granted reluctantly, "but no male geologist would buy it—especially from a woman. Very likely geologists would favor the grinding of hard rock fragments against softer rocks under the tremendous forces created by movements of the massive glaciers."

"Well, whatever," she responded with a shrug. "According to this leaflet the Porcupine Hills are merely heaps of such gravel deposits. In fact, during cold days steam can still be detected rising from the hot springs beneath that gravel."

"I presume that the Porcupine Hills are the tree-clad hills in the foreground," I ventured.

"The same," she answered. "Now from here we go on to bigger and better things."

"No doubt they'll be *geezers*," I said.

"*Guyzers*," she responded with a frown. "In fact, there are some on the right side of the boardwalk. Since there's a boardwalk out to them, let's go see them."

"Huh-uh," I grunted. "But you go, if you wish, while I wait here. As far as I'm concerned, a *geezer* is a *geezer*, and I've seen the biggest of them already."

"No," she said, "let's skip them and continue around the curve." After traveling about ninety feet, she added, "The first one on our right is called the Fountain. Just beyond it is Morning and nearby is Spasm Geyser, so I suppose that their names were selected in accordance with their behavioral characteristics."

"Do you understand the hydraulics of a *geezer*?" I inquired.

"It's in here," she insisted. "According to this theory violently boiling water within a geyser's plumbing system is believed to provide the motive force for its eruptions. However, the exact conditions that initiate the eruptions are not known, but it has been suggested that steam bubbles may form as the water rises; consequently, the pressure on the water is decreased."

"That's not clear," I protested. "One of the more likely ways for the pressure on the water to decrease would be for the bubbles of steam to migrate to the surface of the water and burst."

"But why would they migrate to the surface?" she asked.

"They would be driven upward by the greater pressure at the bottom of the water," I replied. "Water pressure increases in direct proportion to the weight of its overlying volume."

"I still don't see why the bubbles would be driven to the surface," she protested. "After all, they are surrounded by water pressure."

"But the water pressure at the top surface of the bubble is less than that at its lower surface," I explained. "Visualize a hollow sphere in a liquid; then visualize a horizontal plane through the center of that sphere. Next, visualize the sphere's two horizontal tangents. Obviously the liquid pressure below the horizontal plane between the tangents is greater than the liquid pressure above it because the liquid pressure on the lower surface of the bubble is equal to the weight of its volume of water plus the weight of the volume of water that bears against the bubble's upper surface. Consequently, the pressure on the upper surface of the bubble is half as great as that of the lower surface."

"If you are trying to con me," she responded with a confused expression, "don't."

"Grant that the pressure on the lower surface of the bubble is greater than that on the upper surface," I requested. "Then the bubble is pushed upward by the difference in the forces. As the bubble rises, the surrounding liquid pressure lessens, so the bubble increases in size to balance its internal steam pressure with the external liquid pressure. And its expansion continues all of the way to the surface, where it bursts and releases a minuscule amount of fluid pressure (energy) to the atmosphere. When that amount of fluid pressure is multiplied by millions of bubbles, a lot of water pressure is reduced."

"Then you agree with this theory," she suggested.

"Not necessarily," I replied cautiously. "I merely attempted to clarify that statement."

"Don't blame me for it," she retorted. "I just relayed it from this leaflet to you."

"I haven't blamed anybody—yet," I muttered.

Favoring me with a tolerant smile, she resumed: "When the bubbles become large enough and collect in sufficient quantities, they block the water from flowing around them; consequently, the water at the top of column is thrust up and through the geyser's vent into the atmosphere."

"That isn't very clear, either," I objected, "but I suspect that I know what they are trying to explain."

"But there's more," she said. "The vented water reduces the internal pressure on the remaining water."

"True," I agreed. "Less volume, less pressure, so the water begins to boil again."

"And the steam from it expands rapidly, thereby thrusting more water through the vent," she added. "The intervals of violently boiling water, expanding steam, and eruptions of steam and water are repeated until all of the water has been depleted."

"It's beginning to shape up," I conceded reluctantly, "but there's a much simpler explanation to the phenomenon."

"I'm not through yet," she protested.

"You just think you're not through yet," I muttered, slowly moving onward.

But she refused to be circumvented. "Variations in the behavior of geysers are influenced by differences in the available water," she called after me, "not only by the temperatures of the underlying rocks but by the nature of each subterranean plumbing system."

"The temperature and proximity of the hot rocks probably influence their behaviors most of all," I rejoined, coming to a stop.

She glanced up from the leaflet and said, "That theory may be supported by the following statement: The difference between a hot spring and a geyser lies in the ability of a hot spring to allow large bubbles of steam to flow through the water to its surface."

"In other words, the orifice may be the deciding factor as to whether the water flows like a hot spring or erupts like a geyser," I suggested.

"In still other words," she resumed, "the water in a hot spring bubbles up and flows freely, whereas that of a geyser erupts and spurts somewhat like a percolator, but with uncharacteristic clouds of steam."

"Not bad," I granted, waiting for her to join me.

Pointing toward a column of water and steam located some distance from the boardwalk, she melodramatically exclaimed, "That's Clepsydra!"

Following a momentary pause to study the geyser, I muttered, "But it's playing constantly, so why is it called Clepsydra?"

"Blame it on the earthquake," she murmured, peering intently at the leaflet. "Before the quake it spurted frequently from its central vent; immediately after the quake it erupted steadily; since that time the geyser's behavior has been modified to the extent that it ceases to play during the eruption of nearby Fountain Geyser."

She looked up from the leaflet and asked, "What does its constant playing have to do with its name?"

"None," I retorted. "The word *clepsydra* is defined as a means of measuring time by the regulated flow of water through an orifice, so the name doesn't apply."

"How did you happen to know that?" she inquired.

"Oh, it's just one of those things," I responded airily. "Some of us are blessed with knowledge, and others have to read it. I may have inherited it from one of my Latin or Greek ancestors."

"You have no such ancestors," she retorted. "In fact, the only foreigner in your family tree had to be the devil."

I assumed the role of the injured innocent and played it to the hilt, but she ignored the effort.

"Furthermore," she added, "you probably obtained that definition from a dictionary, but you're going to be hard-pressed to come by a dictionary in the hereafter, because paper burns."

As we were about to stroll past Jelly Geyser, LC suddenly shouted, "Stop!"

I applied my brakes so quickly that her bowed, preoccupied head crashed into my right shoulder. "What gives?" I asked. "I didn't see a stop sign."

She ruefully rubbed her forehead and adjusted her spectacles; then, pointing to the gray-white surface of the upcoming gentle slope, she dramatically announced, "That's sinter. It has been deposited by runoff water from the hot springs and geysers that we've been passing during this trek."

"I'm not particularly impressed," I said. "In fact, it's very similar to the wetted surface of one of California's dry lake beds."

"You should be impressed," she retorted, "because it may have taken a thousand years for the water to build up that much sinter."

Following another pensive inspection of the scene, I concluded, "It wasn't worth the effort."

"There are several hot spring basins between here and Old Faithful," she read, "and sinter is slowly building up on the shoulders of them. Nine miles of the Firehole Valley are plated with sinter, the first of which probably was deposited while the ice of the glacial period was retreating."

"Hmm," I mumbled. "By this time it should be pretty thick."

"But it's not thick," she said. "In fact, it's so thin and fragile that it often cracks when people step on it."

"Hmm," I repeated. "So that's the reason for this elaborate system of board-walks."

"That's one of them," she granted. "Another is to keep people from crashing through a fragile surface into a pool of boiling water."

We moved onward some one hundred feet to a point where LC insisted on stopping to study the barren scene. Meanwhile, I stared speculatively at some of the denuded trunks and stumps of several lodge-pole pine trees and finally volunteered, "The trees must have been killed by the action of the chemicals and minerals."

"According to the leaflet," she said, "they were drowned by runoff water from the hot springs. Furthermore, fresh sinter was deposited about the bases of the trees' trunks and their roots, so some of the wood has been petrified."

"I stand by my statement," I insisted, "and that leaflet indirectly supports it, because the minerals must have sealed the pores of the wood, thereby first killing the tree; then they preserved it long enough for the tree to become fully permeated and petrified."

"This document states that parts of the trees have been petrified," she observed. "In my opinion, there's no reason why they couldn't have been petrified after they were drowned, so I support its statements."

"That so-called document was published by one of the government's bureau-cracies," I growled, "so it must have been written by a bureaucrat. Since bureaucrats notoriously err, I suspect that those trees died of old age."

"Such a negative attitude," she murmured aloofly. "I don't know why I put up with such a negative man."

"The answer to that is easy," I responded. "No other man will put up with you."

From the Paint Pot we pointed the nose of the car in a northwesterly direction along the same road to its junction with another road at the small settlement of Madison, where we turned in a westerly direction. After about fourteen miles of travel through a forest of lodge-pole pine trees, we caught just a glimpse of the Madison River on our right just before passing through the west gate of the park.

West Yellowstone Several blocks beyond the gate the road intersected with a federal highway at the point where it made a right-angle bend. We could have continued west through the south side of tiny West Yellowstone, but we chose to turn north on the same highway, since it served as the other main thoroughfare of the town. After rolling about one hundred yards and making a sharp right turn, we found ourselves on the driveway of the Desert Inn, a so-so Best Western Motel. Previously, however, we had discovered that most of the lodges in that remote community were so-so.

Later we dined at the Big Western Pine, formerly the Rustler's Roost, located on the second floor of another motel some two blocks west of the Desert Inn. Early the following morning we broke our fast at the Coachman's Inn, which served a creditable meal of ham, eggs, and buttermilk pancakes. Those associations were accomplished without incident, but I sensed a familiar, forbidding, dark cloud in each of the establishments, so Big Brother must have preceded us.

West Yellowstone to Coeur d'Alene

From West Yellowstone we traveled due north to an intersection with another federal highway, which veered in a northeasterly direction around Hebgen Lake. There several people had lost their lives when a large part of a mountain slumped across the Madison River during the 1959 earthquake. After more than a quarter-century, the scars on the tumbled landscape appeared to be as fresh as those of yesteryear. Since the highway had been neatly routed over the huge, naturally formed earthen dam, most of the changes appeared to have been made by man.

Some distance beyond the lake we stopped beside the highway to photograph a herd of domesticated deer that grazed peacefully in the pastoral foreground of some beautiful, snow-capped mountains, which must have been components of the Madison Range. From that point we continued onward past the small towns of Ennis and Harrison to a Y in the highway, whose northeasterly leg conveyed us to still another federal highway, which led us in a northwesterly direction past the town of Whitehall and into the city of Butte, Montana.

Butte In Butte we enjoyed a fine lunch at Terri's restaurant, where, despite the fact that the manager was very attentive and pleasant, I particularly sensed the presence of the familiar, dark cloud. There appeared to be no logical reason for the man's attitude unless he was attempting to compensate for the extremely cold and unfriendly attitude of the buxom waitress, who, after a life that must have spanned about fifty-five years, should have been smarter. From Terri's we set out in search of the World Museum of Mining, but that proved to be a major undertaking, because no one seemed to know where it was located. Finally, after my mental state had reached a high level of frustration verging on desperation, I parked the car just west of Harrison Avenue on the north side of Cobban Street.

Then, turning to LC, I grimly said, "Very likely I'll be right back." From the car, I strolled east along Cobban Street to Harrison Avenue and the entrance of Fran Johnson's Sport Shop.

"Good afternoon," a tall, personable young man greeted me as I entered the establishment. "Can I assist you in some way?"

"Possibly," I allowed with a wry smile. "But there's likely to be no profit in the deal."

He fixed calculating eyes on me and guessed, "You are a stranger, and you're lost in Butte."

"That's pretty close," I admitted. "However, I'm trying to locate the World Museum of Mining, but nobody seems to know where it is located. Can you direct me to it?"

After pondering the question briefly, he said, "I know where it's located. That is, I could take you right to it, but I don't know how to direct you to it, except to tell you that it's located on top of the hill."

"Yeah, that's what other people have been telling me," I responded, "but Butte stands on a very big hill."

Nodding understandingly, he turned to another young clerk and inquired, "Do you know where the mining museum is located?"

"Well," he began pensively, "it's located on top of the hill behind Montana Tech."

"But where is Montana Tech located?" I asked.

The two men exchanged glances. Then my first informant turned back to me and said, "Either one of us could drive right to it, but. . . ."

"But you would use landmarks," I interjected with a chuckle. "That's the way I usually find my way around the city in which I live, but I'm not familiar with Butte's landmarks. However, I've already used too much of your time, so I'll struggle along as well as I can by myself. Thank you for trying to help."

While I was turning away, my first informant clutched my left arm and said, "Wait a minute. We may have something back here. Let's go and see."

With an imperative gesture, he turned about and strode toward the far corner of the store, while I hopefully tagged along. He stopped beside a remote display rack and, after a quick inspection of the items on it, scooped up a gold-colored folder.

"Yes, we do have something here," he murmured, alertly peering at it. "But let's go where both of us can see this thing." Then he led me to the side of a glazed display counter and spread the folder on top of it. "We are here," he said, circling the intersection of Cobban and Harrison with a ballpoint pen. Then, in response to his questioning glance, I nodded, so he added, "And Montana Tech is here." And he placed another circle around a point in the upper left-hand corner of the small map of the city. "From here go north on Harrison to Granite, then turn left on it past the university, and you can't possibly miss the museum. However, the road that curves from here down to it is unsurfaced," and he indicated it with a scrawled pen line, "so don't stop until you come to the end of it, because that's where the museum is located. Okay?" And I nodded, so he folded the pamphlet and slid it across the smooth surface to me.

"How much do I owe you for that map?" I asked, reaching for my wallet.

"Nothing," he replied. "They are free. I'm glad I finally remembered that we have them."

"But you have used a lot of your valuable time, and I insist on reimbursing you for part of it," I insisted, offering a one-dollar bill to him.

"Naw, I can't take that," he protested, shoving my hand away. "It's our policy to serve our customers."

"But I'm not a customer," I pointed out, "and I'm not likely to ever be one, since I'm just passing through the city. Here, if you won't take it for the store, put it in your pocket."

"Thank you, but I can't do that either," he responded with a chuckle. From his expression I suddenly realized that he meant it.

"By now you must realize how much I appreciate your help," I called to him, as he turned away and began to stroll back to his post.

"I'm glad that I was able to help," he responded with a pleased smile. "Have a nice day."

While I was pushing open the big door, Pancho suggested, "If this had been L.A., that clerk would have feigned reluctance to accept the gratuity, but both of his hands would have been extended with their palms cupped."

"If it had been New York," José added, "he would have greedily snatched the bill from Al's hand."

"Yeah, it certainly is nice to be among real people again," observed his mate.

"True," granted José. "But I wonder how that young fellow would have reacted if Big Brother had preceded us into that store."

"Why wonder?" countered his partner. "There are thousands of precedents from which an accurate conclusion can be drawn; consequently, the obvious answer is very negatively."

Just beyond the university the car settled into a pair of dusty ruts that guided it around a sweeping curve and down a slope to a weather-beaten, wooden gate, where I brought it to a reluctant stop. Across the top of the gate we could see a massive headframe that towered over what I assumed to be the vertical shaft of an old mine. Nearby a gabled roof overhung the board-and-batt siding of a large, wood-frame building, on which the words *World Museum of Mining* stood out in stark, white letters. Finally my eyes detected the padlock on the chain that secured the unpainted end frame of a gate to an unpainted 6- x 6-inch wooden gatepost. From there my gaze wandered upward to the placard on the wall above it. Then I looked uneasily at LC.

"What day of the week is today?" she posed.

"I'm not sure," I answered evasively, "but yesterday was Sunday. Of that I'm sure."

"Well, that doesn't make today Tuesday," she retorted bitterly.

"I know, I know," I responded in mollifying tones. "And it's very unfortunate, since that sign still indicates that the museum is closed every Monday during this season."

"They could have placed that information on the sign that's posted alongside the highway," she observed with considerable rancor. "As it is, we've wasted a lot of time searching for this place."

"Never mind," I murmured. "We won't leave this city until we have uncovered some of its brawling history."

"But I particularly wanted to see that mine and the museum," she protested like a pouting child.

"Well, tomorrow is Tuesday," I observed pointedly.

"No, it isn't that important," she insisted. "It doesn't make sense to stay overnight just to see an old, abandoned copper mine."

"According to this folder," I murmured, "the museum features unusual exhibits of mining equipment and some of the paraphernalia employed by the early settlers in this area. It's located on a thirty-acre mine site with over thirty exhibit buildings, and it is open from nine to nine daily, June to Labor Day, and, excepting Mondays, ten to five during the rest of the year. However, it's closed December through February. Free admission."

"You aren't making the situation any easier," she observed. "I would love to see it."

"There's the Copper King Mansion," I suggested. "But it seems that they should have spelled Copper with a capital *K* in this case." Then I resumed reading: "It is a thirty-two-room, red-brick structure designed to connote Victorian elegance from its intimate billiard room to its sixty-foot-long ballroom." Pausing briefly, I wistfully added, "I've never been intimate in a billiard room."

"And you never will be," she responded. "Not with me at least."

"Well, that covers the Copper King Mansion," I muttered. "Too bad, too, because the walls and ceilings of many of its rooms are frescoed or paneled and trimmed with many fine woods." After another brief pause I added, "I wonder if that intimate billiard room was equipped with. . . ."

"Very likely it was," LC interjected. "After all, Butte has been a mining town for more than one hundred years."

"And it presents that kind of an image," I responded with a sweeping gesture toward the dozens of old headers that stood over abandoned mines interspersed by many weathered dwellings, all of which crowded the sharply sloping terrain. "Furthermore, this folder states that Butte is perched on the richest hill on earth." Then, after a pause to ponder, I added, "Apparently all of these mine shafts have been replaced by open pit mines. According to this thing, at one time the Berkeley Pit was the largest of its type in the world, but mining operations were discontinued there in nineteen eighty-two, when they were moved to the Southeast Berkeley."

"That must be the huge, new cut that we observed when we entered the city," she suggested. And I nodded.

After a brief silence she suggested, "Perhaps we can find that ore shop whose sign we noticed on the way into town."

"We can try," I agreed.

Unfortunately, we did find it, and it cost me a pile of greenbacks, since LC found a number of copper mementos that struck her fancy, and, as usual, she just happened to have left her money in her other purse. That excuse has cost me a fortune over the years. But the store proved to be a copper mine in itself, because it contained bins filled with various types of copper ore. Furthermore, one of the two little old ladies who operated it knew not only all of the ores' geological names, but how and from what sources they were obtained. And the walls of one of the display rooms were literally papered with ancient, black-and-white photographs of both the people and the equipment employed during some of the mine's earliest operations.

Butte to Coeur d'Alene

Upon leaving the ore shop, we found that we should shake the red dust of Butte from the tires in a quick exodus, so I pressed firmly on the car's accelerator. After rapidly passing Anaconda and continuing on through Deer Lodge, Garrison, and Drummand, the car paused in the city of Missoula—but not long. After passing Huson, Superior, St. Regis, and De Borgia, it climbed to the 4,738-foot level of Lookout Pass at the Montana-Idaho border. From there it rolled downgrade through Mullan, Wallace, Kellogg, and Cataldo to the small city of Coeur d'Alene.

Coeur d'Alene As the car rolled into it, we briefly considered spending the night in the new, 340-room, eighteen-story resort complex called the Coeur d'Alene, of all things. It was reputed to be the most lavishly appointed hotel in the Pacific Northwest, but seventy-five dollars seemed a bit wasteful for just a place to sleep. Consequently, we decided to spend half that sum for a room at the mediocre Pines Motel and then spend our savings on a fine dinner at the Coeur d'Alene's Dockside Restaurant.

The substitutions worked out rather well, because we greatly enjoyed the repast. It was fortunate, however, that LC didn't detect the dark cloud that shrouded the fine linens, the sparkling glassware, and the glistening cutlery. Apparently Big Brother has a strong taste for such luxuries, too. At least I easily detected his unclean presence, and it spoiled my appetite. After the dinner only darkness shrouded us throughout the night in the small motel room, but we were just as unconscious there as we would have been in one of the big hotel's beds at twice the price.

For some strange reason, when we returned to the Dockside for breakfast, I failed to detect the dark cloud, despite the fact that a bank of nature's clouds hung threateningly over the hotel and the lake. They even dropped a few sprinkles of rain on us while we were touring the fine marina that surrounded two sides of the hotel.

In the adjacent parking lot we found that disaster had rained on the car. And it had rained on us, too, because a folded sheet of paper had been lodged between the windshield and one of its wiper blades. After removing it and crawling into the car, I studied it briefly and then exchanged some somber glances with my partner in crime.

"What is it?" she asked, even though she obviously suspected the answer.

"It's a notice of a parking violation," I answered glumly.

"Why here, of all places?" she asked.

"Because we're not permitted to park here," I retorted impatiently.

"I still don't see why," she protested. "There's no sign to that effect."

"Yes, there is," I retorted.

"Where?" she countered with an incredulous expression. "I can't see it."

"It's bolted to the top of that steel pole," I answered, gesturing toward the pole that stood beside the car's left, front fender.

She leaned forward, looked up through the top of the windshield, and exhaled, "Ohhh! But that isn't readily visible to motorists."

"I know, I know," I responded irritably. "It's not the five dollars that I resent so much; it's the principle involved—or the lack of principle, I should have said."

"Obviously, it's a tourist trap!" she exclaimed. And her tones dripped vitriol.

"Right!" I agreed. "And this is one tourist who'll never spend another penny in Coeur d'Alene. Granted, the lake and its surroundings constitute one of the most beautiful settings in this country, and I don't intend to deprive myself of the pleasure of viewing it again, but I'll never spend another sou within these city limits."

"Hmm," she mumbled. "If I remember correctly, a sou is a French coin that's valued at much less than our penny." She paused, smiled at me, and added, "That's cutting it pretty fine, isn't it?"

"If the city fathers don't like it, let them *sou* me," I growled dispassionately.

30

Coeur d'Alene to Vancouver

Coeur d'Alene to Wenatchee

From the motel's parking lot we moved almost directly onto a federal highway that led us in a westerly direction across the Idaho-Washington border through Opportunity (someday I'm going back to sample some of that) to the city of Spokane. There we chose another federal highway that continued almost due west, through the rangelands and the fields of grain that dominate the areas about Reardan and Davenport, to Wilbur, where we parked the car in front of a western-style restaurant.

While we were waiting for our sandwiches, I casually watched for a token of the usual dark cloud, and I quickly found it in the attitudes of the middle-aged fry cook and the plump waitress, who may have been man and mate. It wasn't readily apparent, but a half-smart character with fifty years of experience in such nonmeteorological observations could readily detect it, and I did.

Meanwhile a heavyset man who must have been as old as I seated himself in a straight-back chair at the table to my left. His location permitted his pale-blue eyes to peer diagonally across his table at me, and he allowed them to do so from time to time. He was clad in worn but neat western-style attire, and a western-style straw hat was tilted comfortably away from his furrowed brow in a manner which seemed to imply that it had never been removed for any reason, least of all in a public place. In fact, he may have worn it into the sack, because its bent and battered brim appeared to have suffered through all of the vicissitudes of a western man's lifetime.

When the waitress casually approached him, he inquired, "Has Joe been in yet?"

"No," she replied. After a pause, during which her eyes studied his eyes expectantly, she asked, "Do you want something?"

After pondering the question, he muttered, "No, not now. Joe's supposed to show up, so I'll wait until he gits here."

With an absent nod she left to serve two roughly clad men who were seated at a table in the far corner of the plainly decorated and dimly lighted dining room. By the time that I had consumed about half of my huge, roast beef sandwich, the old man signaled to the waitress, and she approached him with apparent reluctance.

"I guess I'll go on without Joe," he informed her.

"All right," she murmured. "What would you like?"

After pondering the question, he looked up at her and countered, "What do you have?"

"Wait just a minute," she responded, "and I'll get a menu for you." Several seconds later she returned and thrust an open menu before him.

After studing it intently for a moment, he looked up at her and asked, "Will you read it to me? I came off without my glasses."

"All of it?" she countered with a stricken expression.

"Well, no," he replied uneasily. "What's the special?"

"Breaded veal cutlets," she answered.

A pained expression flitted across his weather-beaten features. "No, it can't be that," he objected. "I forgot my teeth, so it has to be something that I can eat with my. . . ." Apparently he was unwilling to use the word *gums*, so he finally added, "Without them."

"How about a bowl of soup?" she inquired.

Another pained expression passed across his rugged features. "Naw," he grunted. "Why don't you just fix something for me that I can eat?"

Momentarily, exasperation threatened to destroy her passive features, so she quickly averted her face to hide them from him. In so doing, her eyes chanced to meet mine just as an involuntary smile tugged at my lips.

Fortunately, her moving body briefly blocked the man's view of me, but his alert eyes must have detected part of the smile. As soon as she left, he fixed his eyes on mine and, with a sheepish grin, needlessly explained, "I forgot my teeth."

I nodded, but a compulsion to compensate for the fatuous smile forced me to say, "My grandpappy used to do that. He claimed that for years he constantly carried them with him in the left-hand, rear pocket of his blue denim overalls until one time when he sat down on them, and they bit him. After that he rarely carried them with him, so he was always forgetting them."

The old man stared at me so long and so thoughtfully that I resolved never again to exercise my so-called sense of humor, especially on a strange stranger. I can lay the blame for that story on my grandpappy, but it was only my boyish laughter that rang out across the dinner table when he told it, so my warped sense of humor may have been at fault. However, the other members of the family may have heard it before, of course.

The old man's eyes continued to peer unblinkingly at me. Finally he said, "I was to meet somebody here for lunch, but he hasn't showed up yit." I responded with a restrained nod.

Then, as if talking to himself, he added, "Joe knows that I would never stick him with the check, even though I threatened to last time. I always pay my way, but some people seem to think it's smart to take advantage of their friends." I continued to maintain a tactful silence.

"I'm worth a lot more than he is," he continued to ruminate. "For some reason, some people like to hang out with people who have money, but I've never been that way. I always pay my way."

I began to suspect that Joe was a sponger and that the old man had become aware of it and called him on it.

"And I always expect everybody else to pay his way too," he added.

So Joe had been faced with the prospect of paying for his own lunch, I surmised, and that's why he didn't show up today. So his erstwhile buddy was presiding over a lonely meal because he was too proud to buy Joe's companionship.

"But the governmint don't look at things that way," the man's deep tones interjected into my thoughts. Then, after a long stare, he asked, "Ain't that so?"

I glanced toward LC for support, and she granted to me the smallest of sympathetic smiles, so I looked the old man in the eye and firmly stated, "That's so. In fact, the government—namely, the Congress—demands that the productive taxpayers of this so-called land of freedom shall pay the ways of all of the sleazy, indigent voters so that they'll reciprocate by voting the congressmen back into office, where they can repeat and increase those unfair demands on us productive citizens."

An expression of pleased wonder crept into the man's watery, old eyes. "I've never heerd it put in just those words," he muttered, "but they are right on, as the people on TV say. Too many lazy people are living off the governmint, and there are too few of us productive taxpayers to support the governmint's endless demands. Pretty soon our towering national debt is going to come tumbling down onto our heads, and all of us are going to suffer, including those of us who have worked all of our lives and saved enough money to ensure a secure retirement under normal conditions. By that time our money won't be worth a *bleep*." Then he cast an apologetic glance at LC.

Abruptly I viewed the man with more respect. Obviously he was old and garrulous as well as partially blind and toothless, but he wasn't dumb in any sense of the word. No doubt he was lonely and craved companionship. That was something I could fully comprehend, since I had spent the last fifty years of my life under Big Brother's unfriendly mantle, so I considered myself to be an authority on loneliness. Suddenly a burning sympathy for him welled up from deep within my chest.

"Have you finished your lunch?" LC interjected tactfully.

"Huh?" I grunted. Then I glanced toward her and saw that she was tentatively holding the check in one hand, so I automatically deduced the nature of her inquiry. "Yes," I replied, "but I doubt that you really intend to pay for our lunch." Then I smiled to let her know that she didn't fit into Joe's category.

As I arose, my neighbor interjected, "It was nice talking to you." Then he wistfully added, "Maybe we can git together sometime." And he must have forgotten his condition, because he dealt me a big, toothless smile.

"Possibly we can," I said. "After all, who knows what the fates have in store for us. Meantime have a nice day."

As we strolled toward the cash register, gruff tones belatedly called, "And you have a nice day too."

When I opened the door, a quick glance across one shoulder confirmed my suspicion that the man had deliberately delayed gumming his food until we left, but the bent brim of his hat hid my tolerant smile from his faded vision. We had a lot in common, that old man and I, and we could have been friends, but Big Brother would never have permitted that.

It was a relatively short run from Wilbur to Grand Coulee, where we spent about an hour inspecting and photographing the massive, steel-reinforced, concrete dam from various vantage points. The dam was no mystery to me, since I had served some time with the U.S. Army Corps of Engineers during its design and during construction of the flood control system in the Los Angeles River basin. But the designs of dams such as the Sepulveda, the Tujunga, and the Santa Fe are not to be compared to the monumental Grand Coulee Dam or to the Chief Joseph Dam, which is located in the Bridgeport area.

In Bridgeport we turned onto a road that pursued a southwesterly direction through apple orchards alongside the Columbia River. After inspecting LC's property in Chelan, we continued along the west side of the Columbia River to Wenatchee.

Wenatchee Midway of the small city, we checked into the Chieftan Motel, where LC immediately availed herself of the telephone to communicate with her sister, Louise, whose home was located north of the city's outskirts.

During the hour-long conversation I lay on one of the two double beds and mentally marveled at the range of subject matter that two close sisters could cover in that time. Eventually they agreed to terminate the conversation for the nonce and resume it over coffee at one of the Chieftan's dining tables during the following morning. Just before LC returned the instrument to its cradle, she suggested that Louise bring any members of her immediate family who would like to join us at the breakfast table. Then I began to mentally berate myself for having allowed my personal cloud to overshadow her life. But the damage had been done, so recriminations served no logical purpose; besides, it was Big Brother's fault.

Actually, it was the behavior of Louise's husband, Frank, that particularly irritated me, because he had broken LC's tender heart every time that he had declined one of her invitations to join one of our dinner parties during our infrequent visits in the area. To my knowledge, he had declined every invitation since we had joined forces. In fact, the first and only time that had I met the tall, arrogant man was during a quick visit to the Norton home in 1984, while we were remodeling the house on LC's property in Chelan.

Apparently it was his day to behave like a normal human being, since I detected no reason for the negative reputation that the man had acquired among the Canadian males of LC's immediate family. I respected the opinions of those men, because men are usually good judges of the characters of men whereas women are notorious failures in that respect. At the time I had mentally noted that Frank was a man whose behavior with women other than his wife would bear watching. Some time later my suspicions were justified.

But there was another reason for my suspicions of the man's character, and it derived from a TV report on some wife-beating cases in the L.A. area. At the time LC had grimly remarked that she had seen a man strike his wife more than once, and each time the act had filled her with fury and revulsion toward him. Of course, those statements didn't pin the onus on Frank, but many of his reported behavioral characteristics seemed to fit the picture. Besides, I gathered that Louise invariably had to obtain his permission before every rendezvous with us, so I concluded that he was captain of the Norton ship. But one Captain Bligh throughout history is enough, be it literary or otherwise.

Furthermore, Frank is the type of man who attempts to prove his manhood once every fall by venturing forth into the wilds with a high-powered rifle to slaughter defenseless wild animals, such as deer. In my opinion, any man who is that sadistic has to be capable of beating his wife. However, that opinion covers only those so-called men who slaughter wild animals for sport, not those men whose economic status dictates that they must perform such acts to refurbish the family's larder or protect their livestock.

We dined on prime rib in the Chieftan's popular dining room, and, as usual, a dark cloud hung over our table, but LC didn't appear to notice it. Nevertheless, several of the restaurant's personnel seemed to be intent on pleasing us, and their efforts could not have been attributed to lagging patronage, because people were waiting in the foyer for dining tables to be vacated.

Early on, from a remote corner of the cleverly divided dining room, a sharp, birdlike whistle sounded. Of course, the health department would never have sanctioned the housing of a bird in such an environment, so I assumed that the sound must have evolved from the lips of a bored busboy who imagined himself to be a bird imitator or something. But the poor misguided youth may have been endowed with a bird brain, because the whistle was not repeated, so the management must have frowned on exhibitions of such birdbrained behavior.

Promptly at seven o'clock of the following morning, LC and I strolled through the entrance of the Chieftan's dining room into the foyer, and, while selecting a pair of menus from a nearby rack, the same slender, middle-aged host of the previous evening greeted us with a pleasant, "Good morning. Breakfast for two?"

"Eventually there'll be three," LC replied. "However, the third party may have already arrived. If so, she probably has requested that you inform us of her arrival."

The lenses of the man's metal-framed spectacles reflected sharp flashes of light from a nearby lamp as he shook his head. "Apparently she hasn't arrived yet," he said. "Meanwhile, would you like to be seated and have some coffee while you wait?"

She turned questioning eyes toward me, and I nodded, even though I rarely drink the stuff. With that he led us down a couple of carpeted steps to a trio of tables that were tucked into a space partly defined by a slightly curved pony wall. Attached to the wall was one lushly upholstered bench, which served the far sides of the dining tables, and a pair of captain's chairs stood along the near sides of each of them. LC squeezed between the ends of the first two tables, settled onto the bench, and relaxed against its resilient back while I selected the nearest of the two chairs.

"Your waitress will be with you shortly," the man promised, placing three menus on the table. Then he returned to his post.

Some time after the coffee had been served, the waitress returned with a pot of hot coffee. LC accepted a refill; meanwhile I stared at the cold, opaque surface of the liquid near the rim of my cup and wondered how any sane person could become addicted to such a poisonous brew.

After the waitress departed, the host appeared behind the adjacent chair, fixed his eyes on my companion, and inquired, "Are you LC?"

"Yes," she answered.

"Your sister just called and said that she has been unavoidably detained," he informed her, "so she'll be about thirty minutes late."

"Thank you for the message," she responded. "I'm sorry that this arrangement has created such a nuisance for you."

"No problem," he claimed, "but would you like another cup of coffee?"

"No, thank you," she replied. "I just received one."

Meanwhile his alert eyes detected my obviously cold, untouched beverage, and they fixed accusingly on mine as he turned away.

"Don't let the man's attitude disturb you," Pancho instructed me. "Since you've indulged in few of the popular human vices and in none of the unpopular ones, you'll never be accepted by any part of society, so learn to live with it."

During the ensuing twenty minutes we participated in the usual desultory chitchat that close associates commonly employ while marking time. After one brief interval of silence, LC murmured, "Please excuse me for a few minutes." Then she arose and departed.

Minutes later a soft hand clutched the top of my right shoulder, and a feminine voice shouted into my right ear, "Hi, Al!" Then the fleshy features of a middle-aged woman were thrust before my eyes, and a pair of dark eyes peered closely at my features as, with a hearty laugh, she inquired, "You are Al, aren't you?"

"Hello, Louise," I responded, but my efforts to rise were thwarted by the heavy weight on my right shoulder until the woman removed it and squeezed part of it into the adjacent chair.

"Yes, I'm Al," I admitted. "However, if this thin moustache is confusing, you would never have recognized me from behind the full beard that I was sporting when I returned from abroad."

After expressing a mechanical smile, she inquired, "Where's Sister?"

"Apparently she tired of my company," I replied. "Therefore, just before you arrived, she excused herself and took off in that direction." Then I gestured toward a hallway.

"Oh!" she remarked with an enlightened expression. "Coffee usually affects me that way too. But she shouldn't be away long." Then her eyes lighted up. "In fact, there she is now."

Suddenly LC's left arm brushed past my right ear as it collaborated with her right arm in a hurried attempt to encircle the big woman's shoulders. While her lips were pressed against the woman's dark hair, they softly murmured, "Dear Louise. How are you?"

By the time that LC had pulled away, squeezed between the tables, and seated herself, her eyes were spilling tears. While my eyes carefully sought horizons far beyond the restaurant's opaque walls, the bulky woman leaned forward and buried her chubby arms under her ample bosom as she peered at her sister with an expression of tolerant curiosity.

"Be it funerals, new arrivals, departures, or weddings," she murmured fondly, "they always draw tears."

With bowed head, LC gulped, wiped her eyes with a crumpled, white hanky, placed it to her nose, and sniffled. Then she looked up at her sister, smiled beautifully, and protested, "But it's so nice to see you, Louise."

"It's so nice to see you, too, Sis," Louise responded, as her soft hands involuntarily darted from their cover and clasped the firmer ones.

Abruptly releasing them, she withdrew a voluminous bag of coarse, woven fabric from her capacious lap and extracted a small, knitted sweater from it. Then, placing it on the table, she lovingly spread it and flattened it with the palms of her hands so that three little, brown bears were sharply perceptible to us as they marched along the front of the wide, white stripe that circumscribed the midsection of the garment.

"I splurged a bit," she confessed. "I went out and bought a two-thousand-dollar knitting machine." Pausing briefly, she fondled the fabric in the vicinity of the elfin figures. "But I still have to learn how to use the machine more efficiently," she added. "Nevertheless, I've knitted five of these things and averaged about one hour per unit, but I should be able to do better. I have to do better, because they won't sell to the stores for more than five dollars."

"The materials shouldn't be costly," LC suggested.

"No," she said, "but they would cost much less if I could buy them in bulk lots."

LC raised the garment so that she could view it more closely. "It's cute," she murmured. "It should sell very well."

"It will, it will," Louise insisted. "In fact, it has to, because I don't know how much longer Frank's ulcer will permit him to work."

"Pardon me," the tall, dark-haired waitress interjected from behind my chair. "Are you people ready to order?"

After glancing at each of the unopened menus, I looked across a shoulder toward her and requested, "Please give us two more minutes." After the two women hurriedly opened their menus, I added, "Make that five minutes."

"That won't be necessary," Louise insisted loudly. "All I want is a Danish."

"How about you, LC?" I inquired.

Following a moment's study she murmured, "I'm not quite ready, so give me a minute."

"Make it five minutes," I instructed the waitress. She smiled sympathetically at me and went to serve the customers at the adjacent table.

"I have a number of other patterns that I intend to try," resumed Louise. "And any one of them could go like wildfire."

LC looked up from the menu and suggested, "Perhaps you should try all of them on a small scale and push the ones that prove to be the most promising."

"That's a good idea," the other woman responded. "In fact, I can hardly wait to get started."

They were still enthusiastically exchanging ideas when the waitress returned and tentatively inquired, "Are you ready to order now?"

"My order is still the same," Louise interposed. "A Danish and a cup of coffee, and I already have the coffee, of course."

"How about you, LC?" I asked.

"Uhm," she responded, self-consciously redirecting her eyes to the menu. Then she looked apologetically across my shoulder at the waitress and requested, "Please give me one more minute."

I squirmed about so that I could see the waitress, who looked down into my eyes and suggested, "Maybe I should return a bit later."

"Why don't you take the other orders while she is making up her mind," I suggested.

"Okay," she agreed, retrieving an order pad from an apron pocket and supporting it on the palm of one hand. After poising a pencil in the fingers of the other hand, she looked expectantly at me.

"As previously stated," I began, "this lady would like a Danish in addition to the coffee that she is consuming. I would like one egg, a piece of ham, some hash-browned potatoes, and a couple of pieces of toast—over easy on the egg."

"That's the same as the special," she murmured.

"Okay, call it a special then," I retorted.

"That's what I was considering," LC interjected.

"Okay, then make that two orders plus the coffees," I muttered while the waitress peered quizzically into my eyes. Then I added, "Obviously we could have ordered some time ago if I had only remembered the right combination."

After flashing an understanding smile, she left to place the orders. Meanwhile, the host was seating a relatively elderly couple at the third table just as Louise turned to me and loudly remarked, "I see where that queer, Freud, has come under fire again."

I sensed a puzzled frown above my eyes as they studied her heavy features. Then I asked, "Who says that Freud was queer?"

"Well, perhaps he wasn't queer in the usual sense," she granted, "but he certainly had some very strange psychological philosophies."

"True," I agreed, as my peripheral vision carefully absorbed the newcomers' intent stares. "Apparently Freud was obsessed with some personal psychological experiences, which may have led him to assume that the behavior of all men is influenced by his (Freud's) pet Oedipus complex."

"But most of the middle-class European children were not raised by their mothers during those times," she protested. "They were raised by servants, governesses, or tutors, so how could the males of that era acquire the so-called Oedipus complex? Many of them never saw their mothers."

"Very likely you read the same article that I did," I said. "However, Freud may have been an exception in that he may have been reared by a particularly doting mother; consequently, he may have acquired such a complex."

"If that was the reason for Freud's obsession, then it may be the reason why so many men of this era have emotional problems," she suggested. "They may have been too close to their doting mothers."

"I doubt that," I rejoined. "Most of the current stock of males have been reared by baby-sitters, part-time servants, or by child care centers and orphanages, so their environment has differed very little from that of Freud's time. However, the high divorce rate has created a vast number of matriarchies, especially in the ghettos."

"But there has to be some reason for the vast number of weirdos out there," she insisted.

"No doubt there's a multitude of reasons," I said, "but I doubt that Freud had a handle on any of them. In my opinion most of those queers got that way at an early age by associating with hard-core members of that strange society. The best way to reduce that influence is to isolate such people from normal society."

"Apparently you suspect that Freud's psychological philosophies are clear off base," she suggested.

"At least as far off base as the philosophies of most of our current stock of psychologists and psychiatrists are," I responded with an enigmatic smile.

According to her expression the statement received her full attention for a moment. Then she concluded, "That's pretty far off base, because many of those people still adhere to Freud's philosophies, and they really should be much smarter than that."

"Despite what the politicians tell them, most people are not very smart," I said. "That's made very apparent by the politicians that they elect to office. Add to that the hundreds of different religious doctrines to which they subscribe, and it becomes quite obvious that most people are not very smart, especially when some of those religious doctrines involve voodooism and devil worship. Then we have those stupid characters who are convinced that their particular physiological makeups are adaptable to only unusual sexual practices."

"They are queer," she declared loudly and positively. "But people aren't the only ones," she insisted. "I had a queer kitten once."

Both sides of my brain hurriedly searched for some device by which to derail her train of thought, because I had heard the story before, and I detested it, but they reacted too slowly.

"In a way, I suppose that I served as a sort of surrogate mother to it," she began, "psychologically, that is. Maybe it never matured psychologically." She paused, apparently to organize her thoughts. "When I held it close," she resumed, cupping and positioning her hands as if they held an imaginary kitten high on her bosom, "it would crawl up and place its tiny forepaws on my face. Then it would lie there and watch me very closely as long as I watched it; however, as soon as I looked away, it would thrust its little mouth between its forepaws and go suck, suck, suck while pumping its forepaws like it was nursing." She paused again and looked toward LC; then she looked at me and stridently exclaimed, "It was so cute!"

"And it was so sick," I muttered with undisguised disgust. "But it had to be conditioned to such behavior, because no normal kitten voluntarily behaves like that."

"But it wasn't a normal kitten," she insisted. "In fact, it continued to behave that way long after its normal nursing phase. It was just a weird kitten, and there was nothing that I could do about it."

My mind instantly suggested that she could have stopped collaborating with it, but I substituted, "You could have placed it in a gunnysack and dropped it into the river."

Almost deliberately, she turned toward LC and reintroduced the subject of knitting. Meanwhile my mind backtracked through almost seventy years to a wintry scene, a scene in which three small children were trudging down the steep slope of a farmyard access road that led from a stately, wood-frame farmhouse to an adjacent, unsurfaced country road.

Characteristically, the boy bore the bulk of the burden, while his younger sisters clung to the sack more for support than to assist him as they negotiated the icy slope. At the point where the roads intersected, they stopped and lowered the sack onto the frozen roadway so that the boy could adjust his grip on it. Simultaneously, a few faint mews sounded from within it, and the smaller of the two girls extended one mittened hand and gently patted the tiny bodies outlined by the coarse, jute surface.

"Don't cry, little babies," she murmured. Then her big, misty eyes turned to her brother. "Do we really have to drown them?" she asked in pleading tones.

"That's what grandma told us to do," her sister interjected.

Meanwhile the boy's blue eyes stared stonily through the lacy network of nude ash and cottonwood limbs at the steel superstructure of the bridge, which, in his mind's eye, loomed like a gross, malformed gallows against the gray, overcast sky. Finally he raised the sack and resumed his awkward gait, while the girls formed an abbreviated line behind him. Shortly the sounds of their footfalls on the heavy timbers of the bridge rebounded faintly, despite the fact that the sounds of horses hoofs and the jouncing passage of buggy wheels over their uneven surfaces could be heard in the farmhouse. In fact, that was how grandma kept abreast of the neighbors' activities: that and the handsome, oaken telephone that hung on the kitchen wall near the window, through which she discreetly peeked at passers-by while silently listening to the latest gossip on the party line.

About midway of the bridge, the boy turned toward the railing on its downstream side. As he pulled up beside it, the older girl immediately thrust her head between the steel rails and peered curiously at the muddy water of the Blue River as it slowly flowed from beneath the structure.

"Don't lean so far out!" the boy warned her. "You might fall into the river."

Characteristically, she fixed resentful eyes on him and leaned still farther over the gently churning water.

"It looks so cold," her sister interjected.

"It is cold," she retorted. "Can't you see the ice along the bank?"

Once more, the smaller child looked up at her brother and asked, "Do we have to drown them?"

"Of course, we do," the other girl interjected.

The smaller child's eyes misted, but she held firmly to her self-imposed course by proposing, "We could untie the knot and leave the sack in the bushes."

Meanwhile the boy toyed pensively with the knotted twine. "No, we can't do that," he finally concluded. "They would starve to death if they didn't freeze to death first." Then he looked down at the turbid water and muttered, "But that water looks so cold."

Sensing an uncommitted ally, the younger child pleaded, "Let's not drown them."

"We have to drown them," the older girl interjected. "Grandma told us to drown them. Here, let me do it," she entreated, tugging eagerly at the sack.

For an instant the boy appeared about to yield, but he suddenly shouted, "No! Grandma told me to do it, and I'll do it." Then he clumsily hurled the sack over the railing and morosely watched as its living cargo struck the water and careened along on the crest of the current.

"But it didn't sink!" the older girl protested.

"Maybe the twine will loosen, and they'll escape after all," the other girl hopefully suggested as the sack veered toward the far bank at the river's bend.

Meanwhile, her brother continued to stare at the sack until it disappeared around the bend.

After that harrowing experience, the boy firmly resolved never to allow himself to be drafted into drowning another kitten. And he never did, despite several occasions when he was sorely tempted to stuff a female feline of the genus *Homo sapiens* into a gunnysack, along with a few rocks, and drop it into a river, preferably one with cold, muddy water in it.

My reverie was shattered by the waitress, who inquired, "Would any of you people like more coffee?"

Ignoring the duet of "No, thank yous," I absently considered the possibility that we were being gently nudged toward the exit. It appeared to be a distinct possibility, because we had long since consumed our respective meals. Nevertheless, Louise resumed her account of how she was stripping the Internal Revenue Service of some of its ill-gotten gains.

"I read a lot," she said. "In fact, I read up to one hundred books every year. But it doesn't cost me all that much, since, after reading them, I take them to the city library and receive a fifty percent credit for each donation. Then I subtract the credit from my income taxes."

"Are those books hardcovers?" I interjected.

"No, of course not," she responded with an expression that clearly questioned my intelligence. "Hardcovers are much too expensive; besides, paperbacks contain the same words, so why pay four prices for hardcovers?"

The lurid images that I had recently observed on the covers of paperback books displayed in a local market leaped onto my mental videoscreen, so I inquired, "What kind of books do you read? Who are your favorite authors?"

"I don't have any favorites," she replied. "I read everything in print. In fact," she resumed with a lewd chuckle, "I've found some of it to be pretty wild."

"Don't you find some of that stuff pretty repulsive?" I countered.

"No," she replied. "True, some of the authors go pretty far, but they are only telling it the way it is."

"But many of those authors deliberately cater to the baser instincts of their readers," I protested. "In fact, some of them must generate their so-called literature in old-fashioned privies. Since this is supposed to be a modern and somewhat cultured society, such privies should be completely out of vogue."

"I've always learned something from everything I've read," she responded coldly.

"I don't see how anybody can learn anything of a constructive nature from authors who punctuate their sentences with blasphemous or obscene words and who employ vicious, immoral plots," I said. "Practically everybody is capable of evil thoughts, but I, for one, refuse to involve myself in them or to permit some weird author to generate them in my mind."

The big woman deliberately turned toward her sister and began one of her interminable stories, but years of such rejections had inured me to them. In this case I had fully expected the reaction, because it is a well-known psychological axiom that, if one wishes to be accepted into a society, one must tolerate the weaknesses and idiosyncrasies of one's associates.

Once more, the waitress appeared and anxiously inquired, "Does anyone want more coffee?"

"No," I volunteered for everybody. "But do we have the check yet?"

"Yes," she replied. "I left it some time ago."

Since the reply had pointed overtones, I glanced at LC and suggested, "Perhaps we should be moving along." And she nodded agreement.

"But Mitch had become tired of having those people overflow onto his property," Louise resumed, "so he went down there and really told them off. Of course, he had been around Frank long enough to be able to do that in style, so he got pretty loud."

"Who were the people?" I interposed. "Itinerants?"

"No," she replied. "They were his Mormon neighbors."

"That's odd," I muttered. "I've always found the Mormons to be very considerate people."

"Well, these weren't," she retorted. "For example, they told Mitch that God intended the land for the use of all of the people, and they were talking about Mitch's land when they said it. When Mitch came home and told Frank about it, Frank said, 'Tell those *bleep-bleeped* hippies to get their *bleepin'* stuff off your property, or I'll go down there and make them move it off under the business end of a shotgun.'"

Almost immediately the host appeared and asked, "Would anybody like more coffee?"

"No, thank you," I replied, arising. "We are about to leave."

After pausing at the cashier's counter, I herded my tiny flock through the doorway. Then LC suggested, "Let's go to the motel room and visit for a while."

"That sounds like a good idea," Louise responded, so I silently accepted the inevitable.

While I strolled alongside the chattering women, José erupted: "I suspect that that host was about to evict us."

"Naw," his mate retorted. "What ever gave you that wild idea?"

"Well, Louise is not one to operate at low key," he replied, "and she certainly didn't delete any of Frank's punctuation from her description of Mitch's problem, so the host had a good reason to act."

"Come to think of it," his mate retorted, "I suspect that the host was about to evict us."

"That's what I said!" José retorted caustically.

At the motel room the two women immediately preempted the only chairs, so

I moved to the most remote of the double beds and stretched out on it.

During the ensuing conversation the droning sounds of the voices lulled me into a stupor, from which I finally emerged to hear LC ask, "But has she been able to control her diabetes?"

"Yes," Louise replied. "Ever since I first developed the technique for controlling it, she has adhered very closely to it." Stopping momentarily, she glanced in my direction and asked, "By the way, what does Al do to control his diabetes?"

"Nothing," I interjected abruptly.

"Oh, but you shouldn't allow it to ruin your health," she protested, turning her attention fully on me, "especially when it's so easy to control if you know how. What you should do is get one of the kits that consist of. . . ."

"You and LC are two of a kind," I rudely interrupted her. "Both of you are hooked on gimmicks and gadgets."

"But you have to have your head stuck in the sand to ignore such a simple solution to your problem," she retorted angrily. "All that's involved is a small pinprick at the end of a finger, and the kit does the rest. Any normal diabetic would do that much to protect his health."

"But Al doesn't have a critical case of diabetes," LC interjected defensively. "The doctor merely advised him to watch his diet."

"Uh, uhm, oh, I see," grunted the big woman.

"I wouldn't even be aware of it if a token of it had not appeared during a routine physical examination about two years ago," I interposed. "In fact, I've deliberately scheduled such checkups for years, because my father was afflicted by the disease during his declining years."

"Well, I have to anticipate it, too," Louise growled. "After all, I have a diabetic daughter."

"Yes, I know that," I said. "LC has been describing your battles with it, and I congratulate you on your apparent success with it."

Obviously the accord had been destroyed by the woman's outburst, but it was she who suggested, "Well, you guys probably want to get started on your way to Vancouver, so I better get out of here."

Since neither LC nor I denied the accuracy of the suggestion, she slowly arose, and LC followed suit while I rolled to the side of the bed and stood up. At the open doorway one of her pudgy hands involuntarily reached forth and convulsively squeezed one of LC's loosely folded arms.

"Well, Sis," she murmured, "it has been great seeing you again, even for just this short time. I hope that you have fun at Expo Eighty-six."

"It should be very interesting," LC responded with dewy eyes. "Be sure to take care of yourself, Louise."

Meantime one of two women who may have been members of the motel's maintenance staff called from a nearby doorway to Louise with an air of familiarity, but I failed to catch the words.

Nevertheless, Louise responded with a blunt, "No!"

Then, with nary a glance in my direction, she moved ponderously toward her vehicle.

Wenatchee to Hope

The system of international highways over which we planned to travel to Expo 86 required that we return to Chelan. From there we continued northeast along the

Columbia River's numerous man-made lakes, through Pateros, to the point where the Okanogan River flows into the Columbia. After crossing to the east side of the Okanogan, the highway turned north alongside the river and clung to it through the town of Okanogan and as far as Omak, where we stopped for a light lunch.

From Omak we resumed traveling in a northerly direction through Tonasket and Oroville to Osoyoos, British Columbia, which is located just beyond the international boundary. There we turned west onto a relatively good Canadian highway that eventually veered northwest along the east side of the Similkameen River, which the highway followed through Keremeos and Hedley to Princeton before crossing to the other side. Just west of Princeton, the river turned sharply south, and the highway followed suit. More or less it paralleled the river's course almost to its source in the Manning Provincial Park. Then both the highway and the river gradually swung into a northwesterly direction, but only the highway continued through somewhat rugged terrain toward Hope, British Columbia.

Hope Obviously it was a small town; nevertheless, we committed ourselves to a night in one of the new Royal Lodge's neat motel rooms for about twenty-eight Canadian dollars (less than sixteen U.S. dollars). Considering that the equivalent lodging below the border would have cost almost three times as much, it was an incredible bargain.

In response to LC's inquiry, the friendly woman who managed the lodge suggested that we dine at one of the two restaurants in the immediate vicinity. So we crossed the highway, as directed, and strolled east past a service station toward the entrance of a nondescript dining establishment. It may have been identified, but I failed to note its identity. Nevertheless, we came to a stop at the entrance and exchanged skeptical glances.

"The manager admitted that it isn't a very prepossessing place," LC murmured, "but she claimed that the food is good."

"Usually it's wise to obtain more than one opinion," I muttered, "but a consensus is difficult to come by when the only other sources are people who are associated with either another restaurant or a service station, so let's gamble on it."

After passing through the unembellished entrance, we came to a stop beside the cash register, which stood on the near end of an L-shaped counter that formed a cul-de-sac with the wall. From that point I began to study the layout. Austere wooden booths obscured most of the two far walls of the small dining room, and several dining tables attended by straight-back chairs dominated the foreground. Midway of the wall on our left was a transfer counter, above which a rectangular opening revealed much of the kitchen. A narrow walkway separated the transfer counter from the adjacent dining counter, in front of which several evenly spaced stools stood in a line. Most of the stools were occupied by men of various vintages, all of whom wore western-style attire.

I turned about and glanced toward the cul-de-sac to determine whether the cashier-hostess had returned to her post, but it remained vacant. Another inspection of the dining room revealed that its entire staff consisted of three very young women. One was serving a foursome ensconced in a booth; another was busily clearing used dinnerware from one of the vacated dining tables; and the third, a slender, dark-haired young woman, stood in the walkway opposite a young man who was seated near the far end of the counter.

We waited patiently for one of the girls to break free and seat us, but they ignored us. Finally I moved to a more conspicuous spot at the near end of the counter and leaned back against an unoccupied stool while my companion moved alongside me.

After a long wait LC sighed wearily, shifted her weight from one foot to the other, and murmured, "They certainly are poorly organized."

"What else can you expect?" I countered. "Practically all of them are teenagers."

Simultaneously the dark-haired young woman emerged from the near end of the counter, paused, and glanced toward us with an air of irritation and indecision. Finally she approached us with an unfriendly gleam in her dark eyes and said, "A table will be ready in just a minute."

Of course, there could have been several reasons for her attitude. For the moment I chose to assume that there was only one: that she had overheard our disparaging remarks. Therefore, I turned on my most disarming smile and murmured, "Thank you."

Since she turned about and retreated into the cul-de-sac, I assumed that she was the cashier. Later it became very apparent that she wasn't the hostess, because she didn't volunteer to seat us even after two tables had been reset.

At that point I looked dourly at LC and growled, "It must be every man for himself." Then I stalked toward the nearest of the two tables. Sensing that she wasn't following me, I stopped, turned about, and asked, "Aren't you coming?"

She responded by advancing slowly to me while my eyes sharply probed hers. "Well," she began in defensive tones, "you said, 'it must be every man for himself,' and I'm no man."

"At the moment I'm sorry that you aren't," I retorted. "I have yet to strike a woman," I added darkly, "but you stress my tolerance beyond all reasonable limits." And she responded with a delighted chuckle.

Meanwhile I chanced to glance across the top of her carefully curled, dark-brown hair and encountered an intent, dark-eyed stare from within the cul-de-sac. It was a very familiar one, in fact, and the quickness with which it was averted suddenly supported some previous suspicions.

"Let's take the table at the far side of the dining area," I suggested, deliberately passing by my initial objective.

After leading her to a chair at the end of the more remote table, I withdrew the chair and steadied it for her as she settled onto it. From the vantage point that I selected on the far side of the table, not only was it possible for me to observe the activities of the cashier but those of practically everybody in the room excepting the diners in the booth behind me.

But I didn't take immediate advantage of it, because Pancho observed, "So Big Brother's slimy tentacles have extended all of the way from his befouled lair to this remote, little frontier town in Canada."

"This is not the time," I mumbled, "so be quiet."

"I beg your pardon," LC interjected.

Smiling apologetically, I said, "Don't pay any attention to my absent-minded maundering. Apparently I've taken to talking to myself in my old age."

She responded with a skeptical expression, so I changed the subject: "By the way, I don't recall hearing those words since I left Canada over sixty years ago."

"What words?" she countered.

"The words *I beg your pardon*," I replied.

"Well," she began pensively, "I suppose that when we ex-Canadians return to Canada we automatically return to Canadian courtesies."

"It sounded rather nice," I murmured. "Much nicer than the typical American's 'Huh?' " And she chuckled softly.

Then she also changed the subject: "I do believe that finally we are about to receive some attention from a waitress."

The plump, blonde girl could not have been more than eighteen years old; however, she wore not only a small diamond ring but a plain wedding band.

"May I take your order?" she inquired.

"May we have a menu?" I countered.

"We don't have menus," she replied, "but I can tell you what we are serving this evening."

I cast a startled glance toward LC, who was so shaken by the revelation that she failed to remember the trio of options that the girl reeled off to us.

"Please repeat what you just said," she requested. And the girl cheerfully did so.

I don't remember either what we ordered or whether it was palatable, because I was intently watching for some expected developments. But the food must have been reasonably satisfactory, or I surely would have remembered it.

Shortly after ordering, I noticed that the initial amiability of our buxom waitress had deteriorated into an air of preoccupied aloofness, so I assumed that Big Brother's message had been conveyed to her during one of her trips to the cashier's counter. At the suspected instance, my eyes had missed neither the cashier's imperative beckon to her nor the girl's involuntary glance across one round shoulder toward me as she listened to the cashier's message.

About the time that our dinners were delivered, a ruggedly built, clean-shaven man of about fifty-five entered the room. After pausing at the end of the counter and tipping up the wide brim of his weathered, light-brown Stetson hat from his deeply furrowed brow, he studied the seating situation at the counter. Then he stalked along behind the line of seated patrons and mounted the last stool.

Immediately my intuition nudged me, so I carefully studied the broad, leather-jacketed back on which the brim of the Stetson rested while the man sat hunched over the counter with his elbows thrust outward. Apparently local etiquette permitted headgear in public places, because the Stetson was not the only hat still in place. I had failed to note the man's features when he entered, and they were no longer visible, of course, but the bulging blue jeans were prominently visible as well as the faded, light-brown, western-style boots, whose eroded heels and warped soles bore ample evidence of recent contact with a clay-colored mud. A number of keys were tightly clustered on a large, metal ring that was attached to the man's wide leather belt directly above the right hip pocket of his jeans.

"Probably keys to handcuffs and to the local lockup," I mumbled absently.

"I beg your pardon," LC repeated.

"I advised you to ignore such remarks," I responded with a false air of cheerful well-being.

"But it isn't characteristic of you to talk to yourself," she protested.

"Age changes everybody," I muttered philosophically. But she must not have bought the statement, because her eyes contained a suspicious expression as she returned to her meal.

The man was scarcely seated before the cashier scurried along the walkway and stopped in front of him. He must have been expecting her, because he didn't look up when she arrived. Nevertheless, they immediately became engaged in a long conversation, during which she removed a bowl of soup from the transfer counter and placed it before him without interrupting the flow of words.

Shortly after the cashier returned to her post, the man turned his head and stared across his right shoulder at me. Typically, I stared back at the heavily lined features and the red-rimmed eyes until he finally turned away.

"That man is no frequenter of friendly pubs where only beer and ale are dispensed," flashed Pancho.

"A solitary drinker of strong whiskey is he," José chimed, "and those ruddy, deeply eroded features blatantly declare it."

"So much for one man's brain and its opinions," I mumbled. LC looked up from her plate for an instant; she then thoughtfully resumed her meal.

The man must have resented my challenging eyes, since scarcely a minute passed before he glanced malevolently back at me, picked up the bowl of soup, and scuttled crablike from the stool to the vacant booth on my right. There appeared to be an ulterior motive behind the move, because he had gained the advantage of being able to study me inconspicuously, whereas I was unable to reciprocate without deliberately turning my head to do so. Obviously he had reversed the strategic advantage. Nevertheless, I had missed his primary objective entirely because a low, off-key whistle suddenly erupted from the booth. To say that I was startled would be the understatement of the century. Of course, I couldn't turn my head to verify that he, in fact, was the source, because that would indicate that the vicious ploy had scored. However, from the farthest reaches of my peripheral vision, I readily detected the intense eagerness in his baleful eyes.

"Incredible!" exclaimed José. "It's absolutely incredible that an officer of the law should so blatantly break it."

"Aw, come off it!" retorted his partner. "He's one of Big Brother's black dragons, so what else can you expect?"

Meanwhile LC pushed back her plate and said, "I'm stuffed like an owl. I can't eat one more bite." Then she glanced at my plate and added, "It must have been pretty good, because you ate all of it."

"Merely from force of habit," I responded. "As a boy, I was trained to clean up my plate. Besides, I've been thinking."

"I suspected as much," she said. "You've been unusually quiet during the meal."

I sensed a twinge of conscience, so my mind cast about for a logical rejoinder, but it failed in its quest, so I inanely repeated, "I've been thinking."

"You're always thinking," she murmured tolerantly. "Knock off for the evening. Let's turn in right away so that we can get an early start in the morning."

After a nod, I thoughtfully arose and, from force of habit, went to assist her, but my thoughts had been constructive, so I was prepared to look across her curls toward the aggressor at the same time. But he must have anticipated the move, since he was staring off into space.

The cashier aloofly accepted the bill that I tendered to her in payment and coldly returned a bill and some change to me. As I moved toward the open doorway, the bill fluttered from my hand to the floor, and LC immediately stepped forward to retrieve it for me.

"I'll get it!" I sharply insisted and quickly kneeled to do so. In the process I deliberately looked directly across the room into the malicious eyes of the transgressor. Suddenly I literally froze in that position, because a dark hulk appeared to be crouching behind him with one huge paw resting on the man's left shoulder.

"Can that be Big Brother?" Pancho flashed incredulously.

Breaking free from the paralytic effect of the scene, I stood upright with the bill dangling laxly in my right hand; then everything fell into its proper perspective.

"That hulk was merely a shadow cast by the opposite side of the booth," José informed me. "The huge paw was produced by a similar shadow, but I would've sworn that it gave that guy's shoulder two congratulatory pats before it disappeared."

Then my eyes sought for LC and found her stalking haughtily through the doorway, so I hurried to assist her from the top of the high, concrete slab down to the surface of the asphalt pavement. In the process I discovered that her body was as rigid as that of a cigar store Indian.

"I'm sorry that I spoke so sharply," I apologized. "But I can't have you serving as my personal handmaiden. It would make me appear to be old and infirm."

Manifestly, the words were well chosen. "But you don't look your age," she protested, "and you certainly are not infirm."

Meanwhile Pancho insisted, "Actually, he should have been the one to pick up that bill, because he deliberately dropped it."

"Yeah, that was a devious ploy," José conceded, "and it was my idea."

"Why did you come up with a stupid recommendation like that?" countered his partner.

"It was a calculated maneuver to permit Al to observe the transgressor's behavior at that particular instant," José explained. "Man! Did it ever pay off!"

Since it had been a long, tiring day, we returned to the motel room, donned our pajamas, and crawled into the double bed. And LC immediately slipped into slumber land, but I tossed and turned for several hours. Meanwhile, the two sides of my brain ineffectively reviewed Big Brother's last attack through the usual medium of one of his black dragons. But they refused to stop with just reviews; they planned a counterattack.

At one point Pancho observed, "Obviously a counterattack is justified because Big Brother's black dragons are as great a threat to every American's freedom and civil rights as the red dragons of the Big Red Bear have proved to be for the average Russian."

"Seemingly, George Orwell possessed a prescience of what was to come," José rejoined, "because he brilliantly described the threat of the coming electronic age to the freedom of the masses."

Eventually, without either one defining the nature of the suggested counterattack, silence prevailed within the ivory tower.

Hope to Chilliwack

From knowledge gained during a previous journey into the heartland of British Columbia, we recalled that the Trans-Canada Highway and the glacially chilled waters of the Thompson River converge on Lytton from the east just before entering the Fraser River canyon. Our tattered, old road map not only verified those facts, but it triggered memories of the highway's route south along the eastern wall of the Fraser River gorge, which is almost as deep as the Grand Canyon. Eventually the highway passes alongside a 140-foot-deep concrete flume at Hell's Gate, through which over 50 million gallons of clear mountain water thunder during each minute of every midsummer day. Fortunately the boulder-strewn channel of the lower rapids subdues much of that tremendous burst of kinetic energy as the river boisterously continues south.

Meanwhile the highway crosses to the west wall of the canyon and passes through a small town where, about the middle of the last century, a Hudson Bay trading post flourished during the gold rush. At Hope the highway crosses the river again as it bends toward the southwest, and it keeps abreast of the river's sinuous course for several miles.

As a consequence of that knowledge, we weren't surprised when, shortly after our early morning departure from the Royal Lodge, the car rolled onto the Trans-Canada highway. But we were surprised by the many enchanting vistas of the river as it meandered along the relatively flat canyon floor between the sheer rock walls and steep, tree-covered slopes of the towering Cascade Mountains.

After a long silence I said, "I wonder why I wasn't more impressed by the beauty of this scenery when we passed through this canyon before."

"Because it was raining at the time," LC promptly replied. "Remember?"

But I wasn't permitted to reply, because the car suddenly rounded a wall of sheared rock, and a scene of ethereal beauty was revealed to us.

"Just look at those fleecy, sun-pierced clouds!" LC burst forth. "See how some of them appear to drift heedlessly down against the mottled, green mountainside and languorously disappear between the treetops. Meanwhile, other clouds seem to deliberately dip down and caress the sparkling surface of the river. Isn't it fantastically beautiful?"

"Even more beautiful than the finest oriental tapestry," I granted. "But those clouds are likely the remnants of a fog bank that moved up the river from the delta during the night."

"Aw, fog would never reach this far inland, would it?" she protested.

"This area is not that far from the Strait of Georgia," I replied. "In fact, it may be no more than sixty miles from the delta, which is often fogbound after nightfall at this time of year. At least that used to be the case some sixty-five years ago, when I lived in Vancouver."

A skeptical expression still lingered at the edges of her even features, but she habitually employed tact, so the subject was adroitly changed. "Aren't those clusters of pristine tree leaves absolutely divine!" she exclaimed ecstatically, pointing toward the high limbs of a tree.

An appreciative smile sprung to my lips as I replied, "Since that question is more of a statement than a question, it really doesn't warrant an answer. However, I wonder why, after the pines and Douglas firs were removed, the Canadian logging companies were permitted to allow deciduous trees to take over these choice timberlands. Such trees possess little or no commercial value."

"That may be so," she conceded, "but they do add a lot of variety and beauty to the landscape. See how nicely the colors of their leaves blend with the darker greens of the pines and firs."

"Mother Nature has a fine eye for color combinations," I admitted. "In fact, this particular area possesses many more such combinations and more intrinsic beauty than any of the comparable areas through which I passed during my New Zealand safari."

"Most countries have a few beauty spots," she murmured. "Wye, even some parts of Southern California are beautiful during the rainy season."

"True," I agreed, "but too often no rain falls on its continuous inland desert. And so little rain falls along the coast that the people in Los Angeles would be in dire straits without the water imported from the Owens Valley and the Colorado River.

Then, after receiving a nod of acknowledgment, I added, "No doubt beauty exists all over this blue, green, and sand-colored sphere, but I suspect that more of it is concentrated on the southern part of British Columbia than on any other part of it."

In the meantime she had been intently studying an element of the landscape that dominated the floor of the canyon between the highway and the river, so I turned my head to determine its nature. Simultaneously she said, "Look at that long, high pile of gravel."

"I've already seen it," I retorted. "What about it?"

"Did you notice how level and smooth the top of it is?" Then, with an uncharacteristic air of assurance, she added, "The river must have deposited it there during the Ice Age, which ended about ten thousand years ago, so it has been there for a long time."

"I strongly suspect that, when time is measured in the terms of geological ages, it was deposited there only yesterday," I suggested. "Actually, men on carryalls and bulldozers deposited it there when they built that dike several years ago."

"Dike!" she exclaimed incredulously. "Why would a dike be built in this wilderness?"

Fortunately, José knew the answer, so I replied, "The lower canyon of the Fraser River is so low and so flat, relative to the river's channel, that dikes have been constructed alongside the channel to protect adjacent properties."

"What properties?" she protested. "Wye, we haven't seen one house, or even a barn, since we left Hope."

"But the dikes were constructed to protect other types of property," I replied. "In nineteen forty-eight, particularly heavy runoffs from the ice fields and the watersheds in the upper reaches of the Fraser River drainage system caused this part of the river to overflow many of the dikes that had been constructed alongside it. Parts of both railroads and this highway were inundated. Consequently, not only were the dikes repaired, but more materials were added to the tops of them."

"Well, I would certainly think so," she remarked with a respectful glance toward the levee, which abruptly ended against the slope of an encroaching bluff. "The river does appear to be very wide and deep—when we can see it."

"That eight-hundred-fifty-mile-long channel drains an area almost as large as the state of Oregon," I informed her. "And it carries fifty times as much annual water as the Rio Grande does."

"How do you happen to know so much about this particular river?" she inquired with searching eyes.

"You must be aware of how much time I spend reading during the evenings, while the TV set is grinding out its usual quota of inane soaps and endless commercials," I responded.

After pondering awhile, she said, "Then maybe you can tell me why these mountain slopes appear to spring right out of the canyon's floor."

Several seconds elapsed before I answered, "Maybe I can. First off, we already know that, relative to the river, the canyon's floor is rather low and flat. Of course, there has to be a logical reason for that, and I suspect that it derives from the Ice Age, when the oceans had to be much lower than they are now. At that time much of their water was trapped in the massive ice shields that extended from the poles across most of every continent excepting Australia."

"But how could that affect this canyon's floor?" she asked.

"Be patient, my child," I responded condescendingly, gently patting her left knee. "During the Ice Age the mouth of the river had to drop with the sea level;

therefore, much of the canyon's rock floor eroded away and was swept into the Strait of Georgia."

"The river's channel would have become deeper," she granted, "but the canyon's floor would not have been affected."

"Oh, but it would have been affected," I insisted. "Not only would the water from the melting ice have eroded the riverbanks, but every river tends to meander throughout its lifetime; consequently, the floor of the entire canyon would have eroded away to about the same level."

"Okay," she conceded. "So the entire floor eroded away. What I want to know is why these steep mountain slopes appear to leap right out of the canyon floor, and you haven't explained that to me."

"But I've explained only half of the cycle," I objected. "Eventually the environment became warmer; therefore, during each summer more ice melted than was created during the previous winter."

"Okay," she agreed. "So the ice gradually melted away. Eventually . . . end of Ice Age. Then what?"

"During the time that it was melting," I resumed, "the levels of the oceans gradually increased, so the higher waves in the Strait of Georgia began to push the sand and gravel back into the mouth of the river. And the river responded by backfilling its constantly migrating upstream channel with freshly eroded materials. Since it often overflowed its channel and deposited more and more sand against the slopes of the surrounding mountains. . . ."

"And that's why the mountain slopes appear to spring right out of the canyon's floor," she interjected. "The river deposited sand and silt higher and higher on the canyon's floor."

"Yeah," I responded with expectant eyes.

"Well," she exhaled slowly, "it **is** a logical explanation."

"Thank you," I murmured, very deliberately patting a nonexisting curl into place against my topknot and adjusting the nonexisting knot of a nonexisting necktie.

She watched my actions with an air of increasing suspicion. "By the way," she began, "from what source did you draw that little gem?"

"Actually, I didn't read it," I replied. "It's my own analysis of the problem drawn from many different sources of information." Then I blew on the fingernails of my right hand and lightly buffed them on my denim-clad right knee.

After nodding thoughtfully, she murmured, "I suspected as much." Meanwhile I stared warily at her until she again broke the silence. "But wasn't this canyon covered by a two- to five-thousand-foot mantle of solid ice during that epoch?"

"That's what some scientists claim," I admitted.

"Then how could the river have accomplished so much under the terrific pressure of all of that ice?" she countered.

"Hmm," I mumbled, while both sides of my brain frantically searched for a logical answer. Finally I lamely answered, "But there wasn't that much ice at the beginning and the end of the Ice Age, so it could have taken place during those times."

"But the sea level was lowest during the peak of the Ice Age," she rejoined.

"Hmm, that's right," I mumbled.

"Wouldn't it have been more logical to consider the erosive actions of the glaciers on the canyon's walls," she asked. "No doubt they were constantly shifting along the rocky faces of the mountains. In the process they loosened rocks and ground them against more solid rocks under tremendous pressure." She paused, stared speculatively at me, and archly asked, "Couldn't that material on the canyon's floor have been crushed and deposited by those huge glaciers?"

Shooting a startled glance toward her, I reluctantly replied, "Yes, I suppose so." But I refused to add that the possibility had never occurred to me.

Of course, I should never have volunteered my solution to her problem because I was very familiar with her inclination to question every one of my words. Conversely, she invariably accepted every printed word as if it were cut into polished granite. Apparently she has never realized that printed words are the products of fallible human beings like me.

In the interim she had been absently studying the scintillating surface of the river as it swung majestically around a bend. Finally she said, "The rate that the salmon population is being decimated frightens me. Sometimes I hate the human race and its destructive nature."

"Apparently some of Canada's efforts to rescue them are paying off," I ventured. "According to one report, last year's runs of humpback and sockeye salmon exceeded all previous runs for several decades."

"How did the king salmon fare?" she asked.

"I don't know," I admitted. "In fact, I know very little about that variety, but I happen to know that it's the favorite of commercial fishermen."

"It is also called chinook salmon," she informed me.

"Chinook is the name of a warm, moist breeze that occasionally passes through the Seattle area," I muttered.

"And it is also the name of an Indian tribe," she said. "At weights of up to one hundred twenty-five pounds, the chinook salmon is the largest member of the salmon family, but they usually weigh less than forty pounds."

"That's still a lot of fish," I remarked. "How do they get that *weigh*?"

"Well," she began pensively, "I suppose that a relatively long life span is one reason, and most of that, about two to eight years, is spent in the Pacific Ocean ranging from California to Alaska."

"When do they spawn?" I asked.

"Two different times," she answered. "Some of them move into the rivers to spawn as early as March; others wait until early August."

"If I am reincarnated as a male fish, I surely hope that it's as a king salmon so that I can make two spawning runs," I responded with an oblique glance.

"You would, too," she retorted caustically. "That is, if you could. But you couldn't, because after the first run you would be dead, dead, dead."

"Hmm," I mumbled. "That's what I learned from an article on salmon. According to it a salmon surely leads a hard life. As a minnow. . . ."

"Fingerling is a better word," she interjected.

"Okay, as a fingerling," I resumed, "a salmon has to hide from his cannibalistic big brothers; then, after a precarious existence in the ocean, he has to struggle upstream against all kinds of odds, including rapids and sharp rocks, to the scene of his birth. There, after one glorious fling with a female of the species, he turns belly up. What a miserable life!"

"Actually, they never really mate," she murmured, peering up at me through dark lashes, "at least not in the usual sense."

"That's adding insult to injury," I somberly remarked.

"After the female arrives at the headwaters of the tributary or lake in which she hatched," LC resumed, "she scoops out a nest, a so-called redd, in the gravel of its bed. There she lays a quantity of eggs, which a passing male fertilizes. Subsequently, she may lay several other clutches of eggs in the nest, and each of them may be fertilized by a different male."

"The profligate Virgo," I muttered. "Unfortunately, female salmon appear to have copied the behavior of female *Homo sapiens* with one vital exception." And she fixed suspicious eyes on me.

"In fact," she began again, "a female salmon may lay as many as five thousand eggs before she calls it a day—a lifetime, that is."

After a brief silence she asked, "Do you happen to know why the sockeye salmon were so named? Was it because of the way their eyes are set?"

"Even though the eyes of some salmon become deeply recessed during the run, that's not the reason for the name," I replied. "The term *sockeye* is the white man's misinterpretation of the Salishan word *sukkeh*, which is the Indian name of the Fraser River's blueback or red salmon. It is a commercial fish, usually weighing between four and six pounds. And it is found in coastal waters from Oregon to Alaska."

"The humpback salmon," she began. "What kind of a salmon is it?"

"It is the pink variety," I replied. "At its two-year maturity it weighs from three to ten pounds. Most commonly it is found along the California coast, where, unlike other salmon, it spawns in the sand just above high tide."

"There are more types of salmon than I suspected," she murmured.

"There are others," I said. "For example, there's the chum or dog salmon, which, after attaining maturity at four years, weighs from five to ten pounds. And there are the coho, or silver salmon, which are found in the ocean and in streams from California to Alaska. At maturity they weigh from five to ten pounds, and they spawn from November to February. However, after the lampreys were evicted from the Great Lakes, some coho salmon were transplanted in them."

"What are lampreys?" she asked.

"A lamprey is an eel-like fish, some species of which attach themselves to other fish and suck their body fluids from them," I replied.

"Ugh!" she grunted.

Smiling sympathetically, I resumed: "There's also the kokanee, which is a sort of landlocked salmon in that it inhabits lakes."

After one of her prolonged studies she inquired, "By some chance, did all of that data evolve from one of your so-called analyses?"

"Nope," I answered. But her teasing smile softened the effect of the uncharacteristic attack.

"That report about the increased population of sockeye and humpbacks may have applied to the Fraser River," she conceded, "but it couldn't have applied to any other major river, because all of them have been dammed."

"The Grand Coulee is equipped with fish ladders," I reminded her.

"True," she agreed, "but they have never functioned very well. In fact, most of the Columbia River's salmon population has been destroyed by its dams. Therefore, the Canadian government should never dam the Fraser River. In fact, it would be a criminal act to dam that beautiful river."

"I doubt that hydraulic engineers are smart enough to design dams that can effectively accommodate the three and one-half million fish that annually return from the ocean to their spawning sands in the Fraser's tributaries and lakes," I said. "Therefore, this continent's last potential source of great hydroelectric power may never be harnessed."

"I certainly hope so," she murmured. "The last of the wild and free rivers should remain that way."

Chilliwack Without breaking any speed laws or any of Canada's aviation laws, we flew past Cheam View and touched down in the parking lot of a luxurious, new complex that adjoined the highway in the outskirts of Chilliwack. There we broke our fast at a table located beside one of the large, sunlit windows in the "abc family Restaurant." Even though I encountered no incident like the one at Hope, I quickly discovered that Big Brother had already planted his evil seeds there.

As usual, actions of the staff members tipped me off: for example, the surreptitious glances of our tall, mature waitress; the protractive stare of the younger, overfed waitress, who made a special trip into our area and hurriedly ducked out of it when she detected my cool, analytical stare; likewise, the aloof attitude of the preoccupied hostess-cashier who accepted payment for the meal. However, there were other unrelated and interesting byplays during the meal.

"Look at that big Salvation Army car!" exclaimed LC. "And it's relatively new, too."

Obediently, I looked through the adjacent window in the direction of the nearby parking lot. True, it was a big car: a luxurious station wagon on which the words *Salvation Army* were inscribed in sweeping script. Of the two tall men who stood at an open front door conversing animatedly, the tallest not only was big and rangy, but he was decked out in a carefully pressed uniform that would have turned former Filipino President Ferdinand Marcos green with envy.

"That big brute must be a wheel," I insisted.

"Even so, that's a lot of splash for a Salvation Army officer," she rejoined. "Especially in Canada."

"It certainly is a far cry from the threadbare hand-me-downs that the members of the Salvation Army wore during my boyhood," I muttered. "But the leaders of many religious groups appear to be living it up these days. Practically all of the evangelists on TV behave like multimillionaires."

"I would love to know what rank he holds," she murmured wistfully.

"Do you want me to ask him?" I inquired teasingly.

"No, of course not, you clown," she responded with a playful slap on the fingers of my clasped hands, which were parked illegally on the table.

"It's just as well," I said. "Very likely he's married." And I received another splat.

Chilliwack to Vancouver

But that wasn't the only physical abuse that I was to suffer at her hands during the morning. It was while we were approaching the bridge which conveys Highway 1 across the Fraser River at Coquitlam that I made the second mistake. "Apparently Simon Fraser was terribly upset when he arrived at the site of the upcoming bridge," I volunteered after a long silence.

"Why?" she asked.

"He spent several months exploring this river for the British government under the illusion that it was the Columbia," I replied, "so you can imagine his chagrin when he arrived at this bridge and found the words Fraser River posted on it."

"But how did he ... ?" she began. Then her left palm suddenly whacked my right knee. "Wye, that bridge wasn't even there then!" she exclaimed. "You deliberately set me up for that, you monster. Why do you do such things to me?" And she raised a fist threateningly.

"It was an honest mistake," I claimed, experimentally flexing my knee. "But you should be more careful where you hit me, because this is my braking leg. If this fractured knee should fail in an emergency, you'll have only yourself to blame if we end up in the river."

Ignoring the statement, she inquired, "By the way, why did Simon Fraser make such a stupid mistake?"

"He probably forgot to include a good topographical map among his supplies," I suggested with an air of sincerity.

Turning incredulous eyes on me, she raised her fist again and said, "If you don't stop that nonsense, I'll. . . ." Then, lowering the fist, she passively inquired, "If Fraser didn't explore the Columbia, who did?"

"Another Northwest Company trapper named David Thompson," I replied.

"Then he probably discovered the Thompson River, too," she surmised.

"He never even saw the Thompson River," I responded with a chuckle. "His buddy Simon Fraser discovered it and named it for him."

She fixed brown eyes on my eyes and exclaimed, "You're kidding me again!" In response to the solemn shake of my head, she settled back and remained quiet for some time.

When we were about midway of the Port Mann Bridge, I reopened the subject of bridges: "Obviously, this is a relatively new bridge, so it couldn't have been here when I lived in Vancouver."

"Then how did people cross the river?" she inquired. "On ferries?"

"Not to my knowledge," I replied. "If I remember correctly, the Pottutto Bridge was the only gateway to the Vancouver area from the southeast. During the early twenties Grandpa and Grandma Severns must have driven their old Dodge touring car across it when they came to visit us at one sixty-seven East Thirty-third Street. I particularly remember grandpa's words after my mother dried her happy tears and asked, 'Did you have any trouble finding us?'

"His deep blue eyes literally sparkled with pride as he hitched up his trousers with his wrists to relieve the strain on his suspenders and absently ran one callous palm across his bristling gray moustache. 'No,' he replied. 'We jest barged right through New Westminister to the King's Highway and follered it to yore street. We didn't have no trouble a-tall.' "

"The King's Highway?" LC countered.

"Yeah," I responded with a fond smile. "He never did get the name *Kingsway* straight. Furthermore, I never attempted to correct him."

She turned questioning eyes on me, so I defensively responded, "Well, during his boyhood he and his family lived in a small settlement on the Ohio frontier, so he never received more than a fourth-grade education. Naturally, he was a bit sensitive about it; besides, I knew what he was talking about, so why should I make a big issue about something of little importance?" She nodded absently and peered pensively into space.

After a momentary silence, I added, "Even though he never weighed more than one hundred thirty-five pounds and stood an erect five feet six inches high, inside that frail frame dwelled the heart of one *bleep* of a big man."

After turning sharply toward me and peering intently up into my eyes, she impulsively patted the knee that she had so recently ravaged. Then she turned away and stared thoughtfully at the scenery.

Vancouver From Coquitlam the highway continued west past Burnaby Lake to the Burnaby-Vancouver city limits, where it turned north. As we approached the Second Narrows Bridge, my companion suddenly broke a long silence with the words, "We don't want to cross into North Vancouver, do we?"

"We may be able to find less costly lodging there," I suggested.

"True," she agreed.

After trying several motels and one hotel, I glowered darkly at the last one and said, "Let's go directly to Expo Eighty-six and see as much of it as we can by nightfall. Then let's take off across the border. Finding a motel there may not be such a problem."

"Let's do," she urged.

For several reasons our route proved to be anything but a direct one. Since our location provided an overview of Burrard Inlet, LC had reason to exclaim, "Oh, look at that rusty old cargo vessel." Pointing to it, she added, "I would love to have a picture of it."

That was how we happened to be down at the waterfront, where I discovered the enormous grain elevator that first refused to fit within the viewfinder. It wasn't picturesque, just huge and unusual. A string of orange-colored grain cars stood along its near side, and a large cargo vessel lounged along the opposite side. A few hundred feet west of it we came upon two small container vessels, one of which was the *Klondike*, from which heavy hawsers extended to the adjacent wharf. And the camera's shutter clicked once more.

We returned to the car and drove it across the Lion's Gate Bridge and on into Stanley Park, where my preoccupied study of the scenery was interrupted by LC's question: "Does it look familiar to you?"

"Not very familiar," I answered. "As a twelve-year-old boy, I came here often during sunny Sunday afternoons to join hundreds of other Vancouverites in the seven-mile hike around the park. At that time there was no suspension bridge across the First Narrows, and there was no highway through the park, just narrow footpaths. It was beautiful then."

"A seven-mile hike!" she burst forth.

"Yes, a seven-mile hike," I repeated. "Many of the people didn't own automobiles then, so most of the more remote residents traveled to the park by streetcar or proudly walked to it and then walked around it. They were great walkers, those early Vancouverites. If they weren't walking around Stanley Park on a nice Sunday afternoon, it was because they had already walked across town to church, and some of them boasted of doing both. Many of the real old-timers, those with the gray-thatched roofs, not only walked two miles to church, but they returned on 'shank's ponies,' as grandpa was prone to say."

"They must have taken a lot of showers," LC suggested.

"Showers!" I retorted with a derisive chuckle. "I doubt that they took as many as they should have, because showers weren't as readily available then as they are now. In fact, I suspect that a Saturday night bath served most of them for the week whether they needed it or not."

"Whether they needed it or not!" she exclaimed. "You have to be kidding."

Ignoring the charge, I pointed to a body of water on our right and said, "I'll always remember one particularly pleasant first of July evening, when I sprawled on the grass alongside the Lost Lagoon and watched the sun set. The atmosphere was so still that the water in the lagoon was as smooth as glass. In fact, I was so enthralled by the beauty of the setting—the surrounding Douglas fir trees, the bushes and flower beds, and the reflection of the setting sun on the mirrorlike surface of the water—that I remained there until the fireworks were set off. And I have never been one to wait very long for anything."

"I know," she murmured with an oblique glance, but I ignored it. "No doubt," she resumed, "the fireworks display was viewed by about equal numbers of Canadians and Americans, because Dominion Day and Independence Day are only three days apart."

"Even then, our countrymen surged across the border into this small corner of paradise," I agreed. "Consequently, many of them may have unintentionally collaborated with me in watching the sharp reflections of rockets, aerial bombs, and flares from the lagoon as they exploded brilliantly against the background of a velvety, dark-purple sky while a faint afterglow lingered along the western horizon."

"We are on Georgia Street now," she informed me. "According to this map, Expo Eighty-six is straight ahead of us."

"Perhaps we should leave the car in one of these parking lots and take a cab to Expo Eighty-six," I suggested. "In what part of the downtown area are we?"

"I don't know," she replied, "but Thurow should be the next cross street."

"Isn't that a parking lot up there?" I inquired with a gesture to our right.

"It looks like one," she replied.

"Then let's see if we can get into it," I muttered, swinging the car onto Thurow Street and almost instantly onto Alberni Street.

For six Canadian dollars we received a parking ticket on which were printed the words *Place Face Up On Dash; otherwise, car may be towed away at your expense.*

From the parking lot we strolled back to Georgia Street and turned right. At the Burrard Street intersection I stopped, looked back, and exclaimed, "Man! That's one long block. I forgot that Vancouver has some very long blocks, but I remember the name of this street."

"Where do you suppose we should go to find a cab?" LC asked.

"Probably to the front of a big hotel," I surmised, "but I don't remember where any of them are located."

After passing Hornby Street, we turned right on Howe Street and just happened onto two cabs. Fortunately only the first one had been claimed, so we boarded the second one.

"Where do you nice people want to go?" inquired the plump, fiftyish oriental woman.

"Directly to Expo Eighty-six," I replied.

"I can't go very directly, because this is a one-way street," she said, "but I'll go as directly as I can."

"We shouldn't expect any more than that," I murmured.

"Where are you from?" she inquired.

With a quick glance at me, LC replied, "From the Los Angeles area."

"Oh, that must be a beautiful place," responded the driver.

"I'm very sure that Vancouver has a big edge on it," I interjected.

"I love Vancouver," she murmured. "That is, until it rains for weeks at a time, but most of the rain falls during the winter. Our summers are beautiful: Some rain falls, and there are some clouds, but even they are beautiful."

"I know," I said. "I lived here as a boy."

"I've been here twenty years," she resumed, "and I've loved every minute of it."

"How long have you driven a cab?" LC asked.

"Most of that time, it seems," she answered with a chuckle. "But I can't complain, because I have my own company now."

While LC and I were exchanging approving glances, she interposed, "If you like, I'll drop you off at the Stadium Gate, since it's centrally located relative to the principal exhibits.

"We accept your suggestion," I said, "and we thank you for being so considerate."

Several minutes later the vehicle slowed smoothly to a stop. Then I extended the payment plus a liberal tip to her. As she turned to accept them, she murmured, "Thank you. I hope that you enjoy your visit to Expo Eighty-six."

"You started us off very well," I murmured. "I hope that you have an extremely lucrative day."

"Eh?" she responded.

"Have a busy day," I substituted, squeezing through the doorway.

"Oh, thank you," she responded with a smile and a wave. "I just hope that I can keep up with it." Then the cab spurted away.

"What an interesting Chinese woman!" LC exclaimed.

"And apparently a very competent one," I remarked. "If she is an example of Canada's average minority citizen, then some of our minority citizens should hang their heads in shame for making so many demands on our government—on you and me."

31

—◖◉◗—

Expo 86

My bemused eyes slowly turned away from the rapidly accelerating taxicab and focused on the entrance of our objective. Obviously, our captivating little driver had delivered us to the correct address, since several sets of large, artistically tumbled, azure-blue symbols over the entrance attested to the fact that it was, indeed, EXPO 86. To aid the viewer further, they were conspicuously located above the long, arched roofs that spanned the spaces between the several small, azure-blue cubicles that served as box offices. Enclosed within neat, white borders on the front of each cubicle was a tabulation in white characters that displayed the admission rates for adults and children in both English and French.

Even though the overall design impressed me, I was disenchanted by a combination of mismanagement and confused staff members, which held up long lines of impatient visitors until past mid-morning. Finally the gears began to turn, and the visitors moved slowly forward to the tune of clicking turnstiles. In due time we arrived at an opening in one wall of a cubicle, where a businesslike gentleman promptly surrendered two tickets to me in exchange for forty Canadian dollars. As we continued slowly onward, I pondered the reason for a particular set of words that adorned the faces of the tickets. Suddenly a man's hand reached forth from beside a turnstile, plucked the tickets from my hand, deftly tore off both of the stubs, and thrust the remnants back into my hand.

As we continued past the ticket taker, I turned to LC and asked, "Do you suppose that those words mean what I think they do?"

"What words mean what?" she countered, plucking the remnants from my hand; then, after briefly studying them, she thrust them back into my hand.

"Crownlife insuring your Expo Eighty-six visit," I answered.

"Obviously, Crownlife has insured Expo Eighty-six for the duration of its advertised run," she said. "And the French words *Billet d'une Journée* correspond to the English words *One-day Ticket*."

"You are a veritable fountain of information," I said teasingly. "Without your help I would never have known that my interpretation of those words was correct."

After looking thoughtfully at me for a moment, she said, "Apparently Canada is confronted by much the same problem that the U.S. has encountered, and that is. . . ."

"And that is a minority group that stubbornly refuses to learn to read, write, and speak the national language," I inserted. "Both governments should ensure that every one of their citizens is literate in the national language. They also should require that all immigrants be fully conversant with the national language before they are allowed to enter the country."

"But the province of Quebec was a French colony long before the British took possession of it in seventeen fifty-nine," she protested. "Nevertheless, I agree that all French-Canadians should be conversant with the English language. After all, many Europeans can communicate in several different languages, primarily because they've found that it's to their economic and social advantage."

"Unfortunately many of the members of some of our minority groups are incredibly lazy," I muttered. "Furthermore. . . ."

"Oh, look!" she exclaimed. "A monorail train is about to pass over us on that elevated track. I must get a picture of it." But the sleek, aluminum cars glided past before she could properly focus the camera. "Oh, darn!" she ranted. "That would have made such a good picture, but I missed it."

"Wait a few minutes," I advised her. "Another one will come by pretty soon. There has to be more than one train. One train would never be capable of accommodating so many people."

"True," she agreed. "Meanwhile, I'll adjust the camera for a shot from this specific spot." I nodded with a thoughtful mien and resumed studying the festive decorations in the background.

"They certainly haven't stinted on banners and pennants," I mumbled.

"I beg your pardon," LC murmured, peering intently through the viewfinder at the monorail.

"It wasn't of sufficient importance to repeat," I said. "But you'd better get set, because I hear the sounds of another train."

Carefully steadying the camera on the target area, she murmured, "I hear it, too." Fortunately the train slowed when it became the target. "Oh, you living doll!" she exclaimed, actuating the camera shutter. Then, looking triumphantly at me, she exulted, "I think I got a good one that time."

"Great," I grunted. "But let's move along, because we may be able to find a place where we can book a ride on one of those things before the crowd becomes too big."

"I would like that," she murmured, allowing the camera to dangle on its strap. Then, practically in my left ear, she shouted, "That train's stopping at a station over there near the Thailand building! Wasn't it smart of the designers to locate it so close to the gate?"

After cringing from the impact of the booming tones, I restrained an impulse to point out that it was an obvious location for the station. Then, after silently veering toward it, I stopped short of the lead-on ramp, which was jammed with waiting passengers. "A thirty-minute wait!" I burst forth with a gesture toward a sign that had been suspended from the end of the railing. "Come, let's go see some of the exhibits. We'll ride the monorail train when we don't have to wait so long to board it."

En route to the major exhibits, we passed several lines of waiting visitors, including one in front of the Expo Theatre, to which I pointed and said, "We can go to a theater in Los Angeles almost any time."

"When did we last go to a theater?" LC called from about two steps behind me.

Abruptly I stopped and flashed a startled smile toward her. "The last one that I remember was when, in the company of the Stones, we listened to the dulcet tones of Beverly Sills at the Dorothy Chandler Pavilion. Many years before that we went to one drive-in movie, and those two times represent the sum of our theater-going experiences during the last eighteen years."

Laughing lightly, she concurred, "Yes, let's not waste any time in a theater today. There are too many more interesting things to see."

Australia II

"And that's one of them!" I blurted. "I must see that."

"What must you see?" she inquired, peering along my line of sight.

"That sailing sloop over there by the Australian building," I replied.

She looked past one corner of the building toward the lightly ruffled surface of False Creek and protested, "I can't see any sloop."

"It isn't a seagoing sloop," I growled. "It's standing at this end of the building. Look for a sleek, white hull with gold trim along its deck line."

"Do you mean that thing standing on a pedestal?" she asked.

"That's it," I answered. "Isn't it a beauty?"

"Well, uh, uhm," she replied. Then she apparently decided against expressing any further opinions on the subject.

"I suspect that it's merely a scaled-down model of the Australia II," I said. "Remember? The one that won the America's Cup last year?"

"Uh-huh," she responded disinterestedly.

"Charlie and I had a long discussion regarding its winged keel," I resumed, "and that one looks exactly like the one I described to him, so I have to get a picture of it."

"You mean that you and Charlie had an argument about the design of that keel," she rejoined, "so you intend to get a snapshot of it to prove your point."

I deliberately ignored her claim. After all, she had struck the target dead center, so what could I say? But I didn't intend to allow that to deter me from obtaining my evidence, so I hurried toward the exhibit.

"Hey!" she called after me. "Wait up a minute. That sloop can't go anywhere while it's mounted on the pedestal; besides, it isn't even equipped with sails."

"I want to get a shot of it before some stupid cloud wanders across the face of the sun," I muttered.

"You might as well wait for me," she responded indomitably, "because I have the camera."

"Oh, yeah," I mumbled. So I impatiently waited for her with an air of defeat.

Despite physical and feminine hindrances, I obtained my evidence. Then we wandered into the adjacent building and viewed some of the other exhibits—exhibits that had been transported so far from that land down under the equator to that land so high above the equator.

Transportation

Shortly after leaving the building, we came upon a large plaza, about which were displayed many different types of transportation, both new and old.

"Just look at that exotic pachyderm!" I exclaimed.

"Look at what?" inquired my companion.

"That member of the genus *Elephas maximas*," I replied.

"And you had the temerity to deride immigrants who are not conversant in the national language," she responded derisively. "To me, that's merely a life-size, wooden model of an elephant. But isn't the natural wood finish beautiful?"

"It's well done," I conceded, "but that's a model of a particular type of pachyderm, an Indian elephant. To my knowledge, no African elephant has ever been domesticated."

"Are all such elephants equipped with two pairs of big, wooden disk wheels?" she inquired with a teasing smile.

"Those wheels and the wooden pins that retain them on their big wooden axles remind me of similar devices that I saw on ox carts in Sri Lanka," I replied. "Very likely those wheels were included in this design more to facilitate its movement than to provide decoration. If the exhibit were not so big, it would look very much like a child's toy."

"An awful lot of time must have been consumed in weaving the elaborate tapestries that are draped so nicely across its broad back and wide forehead," she remarked.

"Especially where so many different colors have been intermingled," I suggested. "There also is a multitude of colorful tassels and other ornaments."

"And the canopy over that artistically decorated burden on its back is very colorful, too," she added.

"Possibly that so-called burden was intended to represent a means of conveying one or more passengers," I said. "In this case they may have been royal passengers. Large wicker baskets were employed as mounts for wealthy sportsmen when they still hunted tigers in India from the backs of elephants at the turn of the century."

Beyond the elephant we found a lavishly decorated, brown Gypsy caravan equipped with four yellow wagon wheels, whose wooden spokes had been neatly detailed with red lines. Attached to the front axle was a pair of equally yellow shafts, between which a lifelike model of a white horse stood resplendent in a set of shiny, black harness.

In the background stood numerous other relics of the era when horsepower was truly horsepower. Among them was an assortment of ancient velocipedes, motorcycles, and motor cars, but they had been propelled by mechanical horsepower.

UFO-H_2O

While I was studying one of the aged autos, LC suddenly shouted, "Look at the flying saucer!"

Since the subject of flying saucers was an archaic joke between us, I immediately shouted, "Where? Where?" and turned around and around within a tight circle. Meanwhile my eyes frantically scanned the cloud-strewn sky.

"Not up there," she retorted with a suspicious expression. "Over there about ten feet above the center of the plaza." Then she pointed dramatically toward an object that could have passed for two massive aluminum saucers fitted rim to rim.

"Hmm," I mumbled, "I wonder how they manage to stow all four of those long landing gears in the craft."

"Those aren't landing gears," she informed me in patronizing tones. "They are slightly tilted posts that have been planted in the concrete to support the flying saucer."

"Hmm," I repeated. "If so, then that pilot made a beautiful, pinpoint landing."

She stared stonily at me for an instant, but enthusiasm compelled her to ask, "Did you happen to notice the pilot?"

"Do you mean that sphere projecting from the upper hatch at the center of the vehicle?" I countered.

"That's his head," she informed me. "Isn't it cute?"

After studying the monstrosity for several seconds, I replied, "It is if one can call a head cute when it has a flanged hole for a mouth, two trumpetlike ears, and no eyes at all."

"But it has eyes," she insisted. "Its eyeballs are located on the ends of the two long, slender antennas that project from the top of its head."

"Ah, so!" I exclaimed. "What a terrific advantage!"

"Why so?" she countered.

"I've missed seeing so many beautiful *femmes* just because I can't see through the back of my head," I answered.

"If I ever catch you looking at another woman, I'll fix you so that you can't see through the front of your head," she declared while threatening my eyes with the forefinger and little finger that projected from her right fist.

"As you well know, Al," Pancho droned, "you can ignore such threats."

With that misinformation in mind, I casually watched a passing cutie from the extremities of my peripheral vision until the same two threatening fingers appeared before my eyes.

"Of course, LC doesn't really mind that typical male response to feminine beauty," José observed. "After all, she realizes that Al selected her from the pack."

"Yeah," Pancho chimed. "She's just making sure that he don't trade her in for three twenty-year-olds."

Meanwhile LC returned to a thought-filled study of the pilot. "I wonder why it just sits there," she said. "I would like to see some action."

"Me, too," I agreed. "Any second I've been expecting the *bleeped* UFO to take off, and I wouldn't miss that for anything in the world."

At first she appeared about to ignore my sally; then she confidently assured me, "It won't take off, not while it is still connected to the city's water supply anyway."

"Why did you make that ridiculous statement?" I asked, as we moved closer to the craft.

"Apparently, you haven't seen its name," she replied.

"No, I haven't seen it," I admitted. "Where's it located?"

"On that metal plaque along the front edge of the saucer," she answered. "See it?"

"UFO H two O," I read aloud. "But that doesn't prove that the flying saucer is connected to the city's water supply," I objected. "In fact, those symbols probably represent something other than water to space creatures."

"Haven't you seen those sporadic spurts of liquid from some of the portholes?" she countered. "Furthermore, why are all of those little kids dashing back and forth beneath it and screaming like a bunch of banshees?"

"They could be trying to avoid being kidnapped by the space creatures," I volunteered.

After a brief pause for thought, she caustically countered, "What does any normal child do when it is struck by a stream of water, especially in the spirit of play?"

"We have no proof that those spurts of liquid are streams of water," I insisted. "They may be streams of a strong space nectar, and that may be the reason for the wild screams. Those kids could be intoxicated."

"Oh!" she exclaimed sharply. "You are impossible."

"That's not so," I retorted; then I slyly suggested, "If you doubt me, try me."

After ignoring the retort, she deliberately directed her entire attention to the craft.

"Hmm," I mumbled. "UFO H two O is a very unusual name for a flying saucer. Do you suppose that it's a seagoing tub?"

"It could be," she conceded. "That makes about as much sense as some of your other suppositions."

"Be tolerant of genius, Dolly," I demurred. "After all, many other great minds have generated some equally strange philosophies, such as the all-too-common beliefs that the moon travels around the earth, that long ago the continents broke away from a contiguous landmass and migrated across an internal sea of molten magma to their present locations, and that the earth is actually round or oblate, not flat, as it appears to be."

But she had become weary of the charade, so she changed the subject. "Look at that little two-year-old in the blue, denim overalls," she commanded. "Isn't he darling?"

Since I always avoid recognitions of the more attractive attributes of other men, I ignored the question, but the brat's antics attracted my gaze like a strong magnet. At the time he was stretching his sturdy little frame to the ultimate limits of its flexibility in an effort to position his lips over the outlet of a water fountain that stood alongside the UFO. Even though he had fully actuated the handle, the water refused to flow. Nevertheless, he patiently waited, and some water finally did trickle from it. He immediately thrust his closed lips closer to the outlet.

"Obviously he's thirsty," I observed.

"Watch closely," she insisted. Then, after an expectant pause, she added, "That must be a trick water fountain." Simultaneously, a large gout of the stuff splashed against the child's face.

He jerked sharply away from it, calmly blinked, and thrust his lips against the remaining trickle. He seemed to be laboring under the illusion that his lips had to be in position before the fountain would function. At the very instant that the fountain's flow appeared to have returned to normalcy, another great gout of water spurted forth, and the lad involuntarily recoiled, tentatively ran his tongue over his dripping lips, and calmly returned them to a state of readiness.

"I have to doubt that he is thirsty," she burst forth with a chuckle. "In fact, he's probably waterlogged."

"Likely so," I agreed with a matching chuckle. "Actually he's playing Russian roulette with a wayward water fountain."

"And he's delighted every time he loses," she murmured. Then, after blotting mascara-stained tears of amusement from her eyes, she added, "But what a wonderful way to entertain children."

Highway 86

After leaving the UFO to the other children, we moved toward the Japan building. As soon as we saw the crowd of Caucasians that had collected at its entrance, we continued on to the next exhibit, which proved to be as unusual as UFO-H_2O.

From a height of about twenty feet, the six-inch-thick, thirty-foot-wide concrete slab of so-called Highway 86 dropped down in two smoothly contoured ramps to the level of the surrounding pavement. Then it rose in a similar manner. Not only did it incorporate four lanes, but a four-foot-high steel railing guarded each side against inadvertent accidents—visitor accidents, not vehicular accidents, because each vehicle was fixed firmly in place along one of the four lanes with adequate fore and aft spaces between it and adjacent vehicles (even though their respective velocities were zero). The simulated traffic consisted of an amazing assortment of automobiles, recreational vehicles, trucks, motorcycles, and almost every other mobile toy employed on highways by mankind. Every external surface of each vehicle had received a coat of dove-gray paint, including the glazed and chrome-plated parts. Closer inspection revealed that most of the vehicles must have been expropriated from the local junkyards, so the paint may have been applied to cover a multitude of imperfections.

After thoroughly surveying the lifelike scene, we stood idly by and watched the activities of other visitors. Eventually our attention was drawn to a couple accompanied by a boy and a slender girl, who may have been eight and six years old, respectively. The apparent father of the children was standing beside a dove-gray convertible, staring speculatively at it while his left hand toyed with the flap of the camera case, which was supported against his left hip point by the loop of a strap that hung diagonally across his body from his right shoulder.

"Percy!" he called. "Come and get behind the steering wheel of this MG, and I'll take a picture of you driving it."

Meanwhile the lad was toying with the handlebars of a dove-gray motorcycle. Next he and his attention wandered to the prow of an adjacent, dove-gray sailing sloop, which was mounted on a dove-gray trailer with no apparent means of locomotion, dove-gray or otherwise.

"Come on, Percy!" the man called in pleading tones. "Get into this car so that I can take a picture of you."

"Let him make his own selection," the woman demurred.

Casting a frustrated glance toward us, the man moved to the side of the motorcycle. "Okay, Percy!" he called. "If you prefer this motorcycle, come here, and I'll take a picture of you on it."

But Percy had descended to the side of an even smaller dove-gray vehicle, which he was inspecting with avid interest. The man expended one incredulous stare on the boy and the vehicle; then he climbed up the ramp to the prow of the dove-gray sloop and looked down on the lad. In tones verging on anguish, he called, "Come up here, Percy, and I'll take a picture of you on the prow of this boat. It'll make a nice memento of Expo Eighty-six."

"I suspect that he has made his selection," the woman called to the man.

Reluctantly, the frustrated photographer clumped down the ramp and joined the woman and the girl, who had gathered about the lad and the vehicle.

"Surely you don't want a picture of you in that thing?" he inquired.

The boy bowed his head, smiled weakly; then, resolutely raising his head, he nodded vigorously.

"Take the picture," commanded the woman. "I, for one, want a picture of him in that contraption, because it's the last thing in this world that anybody would ever expect to see on a highway."

"Take a picture of me in it, too!" screeched the girl in shrill soprano tones.

"Okay, Percy," muttered the photographer with a very defeated air. "Get into it!"

A delighted smile lit up the lad's dark-blue eyes as he scrambled into the so-called contraption.

"Stretch out your legs," the man instructed him, "and place your arms on the armrests."

Obediently, the boy extended the toes of his heavy, leather shoes toward the toe bar, which he failed to reach by no less than six inches. Then he placed both arms as instructed, which made him look like a huddled little bird with its wings extended. The woman approached him, adjusted the collar of his multicolored sweater, fussed over the rolled tops of his heavy, woolen, three-quarter-length socks, pulled one leg of his tan-colored pants down to a point above his bony knee so that it matched the other one, and bestowed a glowing smile on him.

For some reason Percy's eyes flicked toward mine, and the flesh around them crinkled into a self-conscious smile. Of course, I was morally bound to reinforce his self-esteem, so I smiled back at him. Any real man would have done as much for a nice boy with reddish-tan hair, a face full of freckles, and knobby, red knees.

Satisfied with the setting, the photographer snapped the shutter. Then, turning ruefully toward us, he shrugged his shoulders and said, "I can only imagine what our dinner guests will say when Percy shows this picture to them and proudly says, 'This is a picture of me in a wheelchair on Highway Eighty-six.' "

We laughed in unison, but LC placed it in its true perspective by inquiring, "Where else would one ever see a boy in a dove-gray wheelchair cruising along a highway but in Expo Eighty-six?"

Unfortunately photographic film often tends to amplify a subject's least favorable physical features while it subdues and even hides some of the favorable ones, especially the inner ones. Consequently, the forthcoming print of Percy's snapshot may have received some unfavorable mental reviews by the family's dinner guests. Fortunately close family members often possess notable blind spots concerning the physical faults of their loved ones; therefore, that print may have been suitably enlarged, framed, and hung above the mantle of the fireplace.

Skyride

After studying the exhibits in the Yugoslavia-Romania building, we deliberately set our course toward the Pavilion of Promise. However, an adjacent Skyride station attracted our attention, so we unintentionally passed by the pavilion. Unlike the monorail stations, passengers were moving quite rapidly through the Skyride station. Just seconds after arriving, we were introduced into a skycar by an attendant, and the car was whisked some forty feet aloft at the lower end of a six-foot steel rod, which was suspended from an offsetting steel fitting on a multistrand steel cable.

The endless steel cable was supported at infrequent intervals by large, steel pulleys attached to the ends of twelve-foot-long horizontal crossbars, which were symmetrically mounted to the tops of several large-diameter steel towers. While our skycar moved slowly south, several other skycars moved slowly past it in the opposite direction on the parallel leg of the endless cable system. During the half-mile trip, the skycars passed above several concessions and exhibits scattered along the eastern shoreline of False Creek. En route, the system frequently stopped to allow other passengers to board or alight from it; consequently, our eyes were treated to several stationary, unobstructed views of False Creek and its environs.

During one such stop I turned to LC and said, "This basin, including its waterways and the emplacements along it, has been vastly improved from the way it was when I lived here. Many a time I walked along the Granville Street Bridge and peered down from one of its rails at the drab lumber mills, the rusty railroad tracks, the discarded equipment, and the dilapidated industrial shops and warehouses that littered the shoreline of False Creek as it was then."

"Why was it called False Creek?" she asked. "It looks more like a river than a creek."

"It is neither," I replied. "Actually it's an arm of English Bay. It may have been dredged out, because the water appears to be deeper than I remember it to be. In fact, the present scene disproves the old adage that one can't make a silk purse from a sow's ear, because, from a sow's ear, False Creek has become a silk purse."

"Aw, it couldn't have been that bad," she opined.

"It was worse," I insisted. "Not only were there large expanses of shallow, brackish water to contend with, but there were hundreds of rotting logs plus the pollutants from several factories and mills. At times the various odors added up to one horrendous stench, especially when the fog drifted slowly inland from English Bay. Now the scene is clean and serene."

While LC's eyes feasted on the sparkling, blue waterway, she appeared to become lost in reverie, but the resumption of motion jolted her back to reality and moved her to say, "It's so beautiful, but we've been very fortunate in that the weather has been unusually sunny for this area."

"True," I agreed. "And I have some early memories of the typical winter weather of this area—all of them wet."

Following a short silence she said, "I've looked all over this site, and I've found no sails, or the so-called angel's wings, of the highly publicized Canada Pavilion. Have you seen them?"

"No," I answered. "And we aren't likely to see them unless we can hook a ride on one of the monorail trains, because that pavilion is located about one mile north of here on Burrard Inlet. From pictures of it I assume that its designers attempted to simulate the sail-like roof structure of Sydney's world-famous Opera House, but they wisely used Teflon-coated fabric instead of the prodigiously costly concrete that the Australians employed."

"But the fabric will never last," she protested.

"True," I agreed. "But how long will Expo Eighty-six last?"

"I don't know," she admitted, "but it can't last beyond nineteen eighty-six and still be an ongoing Expo Eighty-six."

With a pensive nod, I said, "According to something that I read, the people behind this extravaganza hope to employ it to reduce British Columbia's current unemployment rate of twelve percent by attracting to the area numerous commercial enterprises from abroad."

"Mostly from south of the border, no doubt," she surmised.

With another nod I added, "According to that same article, Vancouver is called the Peace Capital of Canada. In fact, the city fathers even went so far as to invite the world's peace leaders here in April to attend their Centennial Peace and Disarmament Symposium."

"Knowing people, I doubt that they'll accomplish very much," she responded scoffingly.

"Probably so," I agreed, "but I wonder what will happen if the energy of the peacemakers ever equals the energy of the warmakers."

"A stalemate, I hope," she suggested.

"If so, then I would join the warmakers," I murmured teasingly.

"Why?" she asked.

"They would have guns with which to defend me from some of those vicious peacemakers," I answered. "Some of those guys are dangerous."

"Hmm," she mumbled. "It certainly looks like peace is an unattainable dream."

"It is as long as there are people on this tortured planet," I averred.

"There's supposed to be a four-million-dollar People-to-People Peace Pavilion here," she murmured. "I don't recall seeing it. Do you?"

"Not for sure," I replied, "but it could be the Pavilion of Promise, which we passed up to board this thing."

"Promises, promises," she wailed. "That's all we ever get, never anything concrete."

Smiling faintly, I returned to a previous subject: "According to my source, Vancouver's mayor claims that this city has no slums or indigents. He also claims that its inhabitants are safe on the city's streets every hour of the day or night. But he does admit to the presence of some crimes, such as petty theft and drug addictions."

"It's surprising that there aren't more major crimes in a port city like this one," she remarked.

"Especially in a city that's located so near the U.S. border," I added grimly.

A thump sounded from directly above the skycar; then it began to descend. "That must have been the sound of the landing gear dropping into place," LC suggested.

"That sound came from above this craft," I retorted. "Who ever heard of a landing gear being located on top of an aircraft?"

Squirming uneasily, she murmured, "I was only teasing."

"I know," I said. "So was I. Seriously, though, that sound must have been produced by the hanger's attachment as it rode past the last set of pulleys."

Since the craft's motion was gradually slowing, she ignored the explanation and prepared to disembark.

Oriental Exhibits Plus

From the station we emerged into an entirely different world, an oriental world, beautifully decked out in brown, gold, white, and fire-engine red. Colorful banners, gently curved, red-tile gable roofs, and one large, geodesic sphere blotted out most of the view of the not-so-distant mountains. Directly to our right was a building that housed items exhibited by the People's Republic of China. At least a sign in neat English and perky Chinese characters claimed that to be the case, so we followed several other visitors into it to verify the claim.

A Stroll

Following a jaunt across the narrow mall to the Folklife Festival, we moved along to the Northwest Territories exhibits. From there we decided to walk back beneath the Skyride's dangling cars. In the process we discovered that the geodesic sphere housed the Expo Centre. We also discovered that its structure consisted of interconnected aluminum tubing, or so it appeared. Each hexagon was reinforced by a network of similar but smaller tubing. Over the upper hemisphere the frugal Canadians had placed sheets of a polyethylenelike material to shed the frequent rains; otherwise the sphere was open to the elements.

Just beyond the sphere a monorail train station seemed to beckon to us, and, like those ancient mariners who responded to the gestures and calls of the seductive sirens on the rocks, we responded, and our ship was sunk by the sign at the end of the ramp: "1-hour and 30-minute wait for next available train."

"At this rate we'll never get to the Canada Pavilion," LC remarked peevishly.

"True," I agreed. "At this rate we would have to wait an hour and thirty minutes for a ten-minute ride, after which we would stroll through the pavilion for about an hour; then we would have to wait another hour and thirty minutes or more for another ten-minute ride. All told, that amounts to about four hours and twenty minutes."

"And we would have seen only the Canada Pavilion," she added. "If we continue to limit our stay to one day, then we should remain here and see whatever there is to see."

"We can walk to and from that pavilion in forty minutes," I pointed out.

"Oh, no, we can't!" she exclaimed. "Already I'm too fatty-gewed for that."

"Out of simple-minded curiosity, let's see how long we will have to wait for a monorail train when we get to the station at the Stadium Gate," I proposed.

"It'll be two hours," she predicted. "Would you like to bet that it'll be less?"

I ignored the challenge and wisely so, because an attendant was in the process of changing the sign on the ramp to two hours when we arrived there.

The Sri Lanka Building

As we swung southwest of the gate around the so-called washrooms, I motioned toward a sign and said, "Let's see what Sri Lanka is exhibiting."

"Let's do," she agreed. "In fact, I insist that we do."

As we entered the open doorway, soft, contralto tones called, "Can I be of assistance to you people?"

We stopped as one and turned as one toward the attractive, dark-eyed young woman who stood just beyond the heavily glazed showcase on our right.

"I doubt it," I answered. "We are interested in what Sri Lanka is exhibiting, only because I was in Colombo not more than three months ago."

"Oh, how wonderful!" she exclaimed. "I'm from Colombo."

I studied the woman's slender, relatively tall figure and well-shaped head, topped by luxurious, dark-brown hair, and suggested, "You also are from Sinhalese parents, I'll bet."

"Yes," she admitted proudly. "How did you guess?"

"I didn't guess," I answered with a smile. "While I was in Colombo, I found that the Sinhalese people are usually taller than Sri Lankans who derive from other ancestors, and you fit that category."

Looking at the glittering display within the showcase, I inquired, "What kind of gems are those? Sapphires?"

"Some of them are sapphires," she responded with a sweeping gesture toward a particular display that literally invited us to see for ourselves.

LC immediately evinced so much interest in the gems that I leaned across the top of the showcase and confidentially murmured, "If you have something for about a dollar ninety-five, you may be able to do some business with us."

"Stop trying to impress her," LC commanded from beside my shoulder. "You know very well that you never carry that much money with you."

"Then there's no reason why we should waste any more of the lady's valuable time," I retorted, "so let's move on."

"Wait up one minute, mister," she called, grasping my departing right arm. "I would like to know what these things cost." Then she pointed her right forefinger unerringly toward what had to be the most costly pair of earrings of the lot.

"Oh-oh!" I exclaimed apprehensively. Peeking from beneath my brows at the saleswoman, I pleaded, "Please don't tell her."

She looked searchingly into my capricious eyes. Then, with a confident smile and the air of a conspirator, she leaned across the counter toward her and whispered the price.

LC stiffened slightly, shuddered perceptibly, and murmured, "This man is right. We really should be moving on." Gripping my arm more tightly, she pushed me into the stream of passers-by.

"It has been nice talking to you," the woman called after us. "Have a nice day at Expo Eighty-six."

In response LC turned and replied, "Thank you for your tolerance."

"You didn't have to say that," I protested. "She's paid to tolerate people like us." And I received an inscrutable smile in exchange.

With some ingenious maneuvering born of experience, I managed to steer her past several other showcases, loaded with similar baubles, which had obviously been designed to weaken the wills of women like her.

Tiptoeing through the Tulips

On the way to more exhibits we happened upon one of several circular planters that decorated the area.

"Aren't those dark-red tulips fabulous!" LC exclaimed.

Ignoring the question, I indulgently followed her to the bench-high, circular, concrete curb that contained them. Characteristically fondling them, she ran one hand up a thick stem and cupped the lush blossom in her palm while sampling its fragrance. "They are so lovely," she murmured.

"Seat yourself on that curb, and I'll snap a shot of you beautiful posies," I suggested.

"No, let me take a picture of you with them," she countered.

"You know how much I dislike being photographed," I retorted.

"I don't see why," she said. "You are very photogenic."

"I have some very good reasons," I responded evasively. "For example, after the film is developed, you and everybody else will be terribly shocked to find a total blank in that part of the scene that was occupied by yours truly."

"I can readily understand why that would apply to the space above your shoulders," she retorted, "but there's no apparent reason why the rest of you shouldn't photograph."

After submitting to the ordeal, I silently turned away and aimlessly strolled in the same direction that we had been pursuing.

Typically, she mistakenly assumed that I was parading a pique, so she hurried to my side and coyly inquired, "Where are we going now?"

"Well," I began meditatively, "since we've been in direct contact with several Canadian provinces during our early years, we would gain very little by viewing their exhibits."

"True," she agreed. Then, after transferring the site map to me, she pointed to a specific area and said, "Meanwhile we can spot check the following buildings: Spain, Belgium, Italy, France, and the Federal Republic of Germany.

"We can do that," I conceded, "but we can continue to pass up those buildings whose entrances are blocked by masses of perspiring human flesh."

Responding to the words with an ingratiating smile, she added, "On the same basis, we can see the exhibits of Barbados, Costa Rica, Norway, Hong Kong, and Hungary. They also are close by."

A Pirate Ship, Yet!

While looking toward the adjacent waterfront, I nodded absent agreement.

Upon turning her eyes in the same direction, she impulsively suggested, "And we can take a closer look at that sailing sloop, if you like."

"It isn't a sailing sloop," I muttered. "It's a beautiful replica of a bona fide sailing vessel, circa sixteen hundred. And it looks very much like the ships manned by pirates depicted in some of the books that I read during my boyhood in this selfsame city."

"It could be a copy of a pirate ship," she suggested tentatively.

"No, that can't be," I insisted. "Excepting naval vessels, sailing vessels were designed and built for the exclusive purpose of transporting people and cargo. Unfortunately many of them were commandeered by mutineers, renegades, and cutthroats, who then employed them to attack and plunder merchant ships at sea. Consequently, there never were any so-called pirate ships, only pirates on stolen ships."

"But almost any sailing ship could have been adapted for piracy by the addition of cannons and grappling hooks to its deck," she protested stridently. "Wouldn't those changes have made it a pirate ship?"

Surprised by her outburst, I gently patted one defiant shoulder and with a particularly benign attitude admitted, "That's very logical. I never suspected you of being an authority on sailing vessels."

"Humph," she grunted. "I'm an authority on lots of things that you don't know about."

"Such as knitting and tatting," I suggested teasingly.

"More than those things," she flared. "For example, I happen to know that this ship is equipped with three masts, and the mast on its front end. . . ."

"On its forward end," I interposed.

After frowning malevolently at me, she repeated, "And the one on its front end is called the foremast. Furthermore, those groups of parallel ropes stretched from the sides of the ship to the middle of each mast are called rigging. And those small, horizontal pieces of wood attached at equal intervals to the rigging are used by the sailors to climb from the deck up to the booms when they are furling the sails."

"Those so-called ropes, or rigging, also serve to support the masts when the ship is under full sail," I added cautiously.

"So they have a secondary purpose," she retorted jauntily. "Actually you are no more of an authority on sailing ships than I am. In fact, I'll bet that you don't even know which side of that ship is its lee side."

After pensively studying her for a moment, I raised my right hand, thrust its forefinger into my mouth without actually wetting it, removed it, and held it aloft. Then I pointed to the far side of the ship and said, "It's that side."

"Correct. It's the left side of the ship," she murmured with an air of increased respect. "But what did wetting your forefinger have to do with determining that?"

"It didn't determine that," I answered. "From it I was able to determine the source of the wind. In this case it is coming from English Bay. Since the leeward side of a ship is always the side that's opposite the direction from which the wind is coming, the lee side of any ship can be either its left- or right-hand side."

"Oh-ho!" she exclaimed. "For years I've labored under the misconception that the lee side of a ship is always its left side."

"The left side of a ship is called the larboard or port side," I informed her, "and that applies only when the ship is viewed as we are viewing this one, from its stern toward its bow. The opposite or right side of a ship is called the starboard side."

"Apparently, with some exceptions, you would have fitted into the era of windjammers very well," she responded with uncharacteristic graciousness.

Having learned from experience that such moods were of short duration, I watched her warily but finally conceded, "Yeah, I probably would've fitted in quite well with One-eyed Jack, Harry the Hook, and Peg-leg Pete. Maybe I should take to the sea and become a modern-day pirate."

"No, you really shouldn't," she stated flatly. "Aside from the fact that you don't have an ounce of pirate blood in you, you are terribly susceptible to seasickness. Remember?"

I turned sharply on her and growled, "The least that you can do is to stay out of my dreams."

"I don't want to stay out of your dreams," she responded with an elaborate flutter of her dark eyelashes. "What I'm trying to do is to keep you from launching yourself into a sea of nightmares."

Munich Festhaus

What with traveling from building to building and traipsing along the aisles within them, we must have covered more than eight miles by the time that we arrived at the Festhaus Garten.

From LC's weary expression, I concluded that she yearned for a place to sit, so I suggested, "Why don't we go sit on one of those benches, place our elbows on the interconnected tabletop, and order a pair of beers?"

"Let's do!" she exclaimed. "I'm **so** tired of walking."

"Okay," I exhaled with a sigh. "Where shall it be?"

After a brief survey of the crowded benches, she said, "There doesn't appear to be any space available to us."

"There may be just enough space at the end of that bench near the center of the garden," I said, maneuvering her to it.

"Oh!" she exclaimed after slumping onto it. "Never has a hard, wooden plank felt so soft and comfortable."

"Obviously you have allowed yourself to become pretty soft in certain areas," I remarked with a teasing study of the most prominent area.

"Why should I worry?" she countered. "You just admitted that it's pretty." I could have observed that the use of the word *pretty* wasn't intended to be interpreted in that sense, but I wisely refrained.

For human beings, Canadians are relatively smart, so the beer was cold. That was fortunate, because I doubt that I could have downed a stein of warm beer even as an excuse to sit on the bench.

"Hmm," LC mumbled. "It tastes so good. I must have been very thirsty, because I don't particularly like beer."

"I know," I responded with an oblique glance, "and that's one of your few virtues."

Her left elbow struck my right elbow sharply, and a sizable slurp of the libation splashed over the rim of the stein onto my right hand. As I quickly turned accusing eyes on her, her eyes defied me. "You had that coming," she growled. I had no other recourse but to mop it up myself, since she didn't volunteer to help, but she did reluctantly toss a spare paper napkin my way.

Meanwhile her eyes avidly scanned the wooden tables, the wooden trellises, the colorful umbrellas, and their associated supporting structures. "It's so quaint!" she exclaimed.

"But it isn't Bavarian quaint," I rejoined, stuffing the wet napkin into my empty stein. "It might be considered to be North American quaint, but it should never be compared with Bavarian-beer-garden quaint."

"I wasn't comparing it with anything," she retorted. "Besides, when did you see a Bavarian beer garden?"

"You know very well that I've never been in Bavaria," I replied.

"Then how can you establish yourself as an authority on Bavarian beer gardens?" she countered.

Since past experiences indicated that supercilious arrogance particularly irritated her, I applied a heavy load of supercilious arrogance and responded, "It's easy for those of us with talent. Besides, I've seen pictures of such gardens, and they were quite different from this one. For example, the gable roofs were much steeper than the roof on that big, stucco and wood-frame structure. Wye, its pitch can't be more than four to twelve, whereas the pitches of many Bavarian roofs must be closer to twelve to eight."

"But lots of snow falls on the Bavarian roofs," she objected. "Vancouver rarely gets more than a few inches of snow, so there's no logical reason for a greater pitch for the roof of that building."

"But it's the extreme pitch that makes Bavarian buildings so quaint," I stated.

"To me this building is quaint," she insisted.

I studied the stubborn set of her jaw and wisely conceded, "Okay, so it is quaint. But does just one German parent qualify you to tell me whether those words constitute a man's name?" Then I pointed to an area high on the building's wall where two words were centered beneath two light-brown banners that bore the words *Munich Festhaus*.

"Hmm," she mumbled. "Georg Reiss. Yes, they probably represent a man's name, possibly the concessionaire's name."

For some time we lolled in the sun and indulged in the human distraction of people watching. Finally, with a speculative glance at LC, I inquired, "Have you finished your beer?"

"Yes," she replied. "But do we have to leave so soon?"

After registering a sympathetic smile, I replied, "We do if we expect to see much more of this extravaganza today."

"Why don't you take a picture of this?" she suggested with a sweeping gesture.

Fixing suspicious eyes on her, I charged, "You are stalling for more bench time; otherwise **you** would have volunteered to take the picture. I can always tell when you are trying to con me."

"I'm still tired," she confessed.

Involuntarily my right hand reached forward and patted her shoulder; then I scooped up the camera from the top of the table. After snapping a couple of shots, I returned to the table and sternly commanded, "Come on, Dolly. Let's get with it."

"Ohhh!" she groaned during an attempt to rise. "Every one of my joints has set up like concrete. I can't move an inch." Then she raised one hand and a pair of eyes that pleaded for assistance.

Tolerantly, I grasped the hand and pulled her to an upright attitude. "Come on," I urged. "It can't be all that bad."

A Cloud in the Sky

Locking my left arm about her right arm, I swung her smoothly over the bench and toward the rear of the area. Then my eyes detected the steady gaze of a tall, relatively young man who was standing just beyond the rear limits of the beer garden. Of course, his gaze could have been attracted by my companion, whose actions might have been mistaken as evidence of intoxication. But his gaze wasn't directed toward her; it was directed toward me. Furthermore, there were familiar tokens of recognition in the man's eyes, but I had never seen him before.

It could have been a series of coincidences, of course, but a dark cloud began to cross the face of the sun at the same instant that a similar one began to creep across my heretofore happy state of mind. Meanwhile LC had been discussing a subject that I had missed completely, because both sides of my brain were spinning in their shell. While LC continued her monologue, we turned almost in front of the man and strolled onward. After traveling about fifteen paces, I abruptly stopped and looked back across my left shoulder. As expected, I encountered the same steady gaze; however, the man immediately turned away, but the promptness of his action merely confirmed my previous suspicions.

"That cloud mass bodes ill for Expo Eighty-six," I muttered, swinging LC around to view it.

"Oh, so that's what you stopped for," she murmured, leaning wearily against our locked arms.

"Yeah," I rumbled. "We probably should keep an eye on those clouds and be ready to leave in a hurry. If they should drop some rain on us, we'll be forever getting a taxi out of here."

So we stood there and watched the rapidly gathering clouds. Suddenly the sunlight faded to a dim, gray sheen, and my eyes involuntarily fixed on a point high above the man's head where a particularly dark blob had collected.

Meanwhile Pancho burst forth: "Look at the clouds on either side of that dark blob. They look like two huge wings about hulking shoulders on either side of an evil and particularly ugly head."

"Yeah," José agreed. "And from each of them a thick streamer extends forward with what seems to be a clawlike hand on the near end of it."

"And those clawlike hands are stretched out toward the Festhaus Garten," Pancho rejoined.

"Those clawlike hands are stretched out toward us," insisted his mate nervously.

"And note how the huge chest and the long, gaunt lower body seem to project from the blob and the shoulders clear across the mountains," Pancho observed.

"Yeah," José repeated. "And a pair of goatlike legs appears to trail from that body far beyond the mountains, possibly beyond the border."

"But they can't be goatlike legs," Pancho objected. "Goats don't have long, forked tails."

"Do you know what that gross figure reminds me of?" José asked.

"Yeah," Pancho answered. "But demons don't dwell in the heavens."

A Demon In the Sky

An Earthly Demon

"People will be greatly surprised to discover where that particular demon dwells," José observed succinctly.

"Oh!" exclaimed his partner. "Are you implying that that mean, vicious looking creature is . . . ?"

"Yeah," interjected José. "That mean, vicious looking creature must be Big Brother." Then both of them lapsed into shocked silence.

"Oh, that dark cloud mass looks cold!" LC exclaimed with an involuntary shiver.

"It is," I muttered, "and it's completely insensitive."

Her expression exhibited a total lack of comprehension; however, her vanity apparently refused to allow her to request clarification. After several minutes we involuntarily swung around and resumed our journey.

After taking a few steps, she looked back across her right shoulder and exclaimed, "Look! The sun is shining again."

I looked back across my left shoulder and remarked, "That's because the strange looking cloud has withdrawn behind the mountains." But my eyes didn't miss the baleful glare from the blob on the hulk that crouched just beyond the mountain ridge overlooking North Vancouver.

"It may have been driven to this area by a strong offshore wind," she surmised. "But it must have been driven back inland by a much stronger onshore wind."

While I strolled pensively onward, José silently insisted, "But nothing is stronger than the evil that that particular cloud embodies.

An Earthly Demon?

Meanwhile my mind toyed with likely reasons for the presence of the man at the Munich Festhaus. Finally I absently murmured, "He appeared to be too nice a guy to be a member of that gang."

"I beg your pardon," LC countered.

My mind emerged from its preoccupied state with a start, and I hurriedly said, "It was nothing of importance, Dolly. I was just doing some woolgathering again."

"You were talking to yourself again," she insisted. "I wish that. . . ." Leaving the sentence unfinished, she pulled me to a stop and shouted, "Look! There's a demon waiting for you."

Immediately looking up toward the mountain ridge, I encountered a dark, malevolent glare from what appeared to be a waiting demon.

"Not up there," she commanded. "Over here on earth where no reputable demon should be." And she pointed to one corner of a heavily glazed building.

While I stared incredulously at the exotic figure, José claimed, "That ain't no demon. That's a pussycat compared to the demon beyond the ridge."

In turn, I claimed, "That ain't no demon." Fortunately I stopped just in time because LC would never have understood the remainder of José's statement.

"It surely looks like a demon," she said.

"It appears to be a larger-than-life model of an ancient Korean warrior," I suggested.

After referring to the site map, she exclaimed, "How unusual!" Then, casting a very deliberate glance toward me, she added, "You appear to be right this time, because it is standing at one corner of the Korean building. In fact, there are two demons. See?" And she pointed beyond the corner toward another so-called demon.

"I've heard of Siamese twins," I muttered, "but I've never heard of Korean twins."

"These twins are different in several respects," she remarked. "For example, the Siamese twins were physically attached from birth. These twins are normal in that respect. But what's that long, round thing in front of this one, the thing that he is holding with both hands?"

After a particularly enigmatic stare, I replied, "No doubt you mean the thing that's planted on the pedestal in front of him at parade rest. That's his automatic rifle."

"Don't be ridiculous!" she commanded. "According to the elaborate decorative details, he has to represent a sixth- or seventh-century something or other."

"Then will you concede that it's a heavy weapon?" I countered. "A weapon intended for use as a club?"

"That sounds reasonable," she conceded, "but he has to be a pretty perky warrior with that two-foot baluster projecting from his bowl-like helmet and those big moccasins with their turned up, pointy toes."

"Those can't be moccasins," I insisted. "The American Indian invented the moccasin, and Korea is located in Asia, some six thousand miles across a deep ocean from America."

"Then what would you call them?" she countered.

After pondering the problem for several seconds, I admitted, "Well, they could be called moccasins, I suppose."

After flashing a triumphant glance toward me, she resumed, "That woven uniform with all of the fancy trimmings and frou-frou, especially those funny wings at the side of each calf: What function could they possibly serve?"

"Maybe they were intended to help the man become airborne," I ventured.

"If you come up with another idiotic suggestion like that one, you won't 'ave an 'air on your 'ead," she retorted with an appropriate gesture.

"Well, *bleeped* if I know what they could be used for," I admitted. "But that jerkin may have been fabricated from woven reeds or bamboo to serve as a form of mail, albeit a very primitive mail. After all, he appears to be a very primitive *male*."

Ignoring the pun, she granted, "That's logical. And the same materials may have been employed in the remainder of the uniform to protect the arms, thighs, and so forth."

Spot Checking

After inspecting exhibits in the adjoining building, we spot checked the buildings of the countries that LC had mentioned. When an entrance was unimpeded by waiting visitors, we entered it; otherwise we assumed that the exhibits were limited to films of the country's industrial potentials and continued on to the next building with physical exhibits. No doubt we missed some very interesting exhibits, such as those of the *Côte d'Ivoire* (Ivory Coast), Cuba, and a few others, but I made a point of seeing the Malaysian exhibits since I had journeyed through a small corner of the country.

On the way back to the Stadium Gate, we checked the waiting period at the Gamble Street Bridge monorail station and found a familiar sign.

"Still a two-hour wait at seven o'clock!" LC exclaimed. "The commission surely missed the boat on that monorail system."

"It can't be called missing the boat," I observed, "but that monorail system is going to dog them through most of nineteen eighty-six."

A Mobile Parking Lot?

At the Stadium Gate we thankfully slumped against the hard, plastic-covered rear seat of a taxicab. "What's the destination, please?" inquired the driver.

Belatedly I removed a small card from a jacket pocket and peered at it with the help of sporadic flashes of dim light from the street lamps that we passed. Finally I replied, "Please take us to the parking lot at eleven twenty-four Alberni Street."

The distance seemed longer than it had during the previous trip, but that may have been due to the fact that the current driver was somberly silent, whereas the previous one had chattered like a happy magpie.

He found Alberni Street easily enough; however, after checking some of the street numbers, he declared, "There's no eleven twenty-four; furthermore, there's no parking lot on Alberni Street."

Through the murky glass of the adjacent window, I suspected that I could see the parking lot, despite the encroaching dusk, but I refused to refute the man's claims. Instead, I requested, "Please drop us off here, and we'll locate the parking lot. I'm sure that it's located somewhere in this area."

"Are you very sure?" he demurred. "This may be a long way from where your car is parked."

"I recognize the area," I rejoined, "and I'm quite sure that we'll find the parking lot right away."

"Well, okay, if that's what you want to do," he muttered reluctantly.

As the cab's lights disappeared into the gloom, LC turned to me and said, "I suspect that the parking lot is located right there." And she pointed downgrade from Alberni Street.

"I suspect that you're right," I responded with a chuckle. "In the States I would have suspected that driver of ulterior motives, but I've found most Canadians to be basically honest. He may be new to the city. After all, Expo Eighty-six has created a lot of local employment, so the city may have been invaded by many out-of-towners."

The parking lot proved to be "right there," and the car was parked just as we had left it. After seating ourselves in it, I gave the parking ticket to LC and said, "Stow this with the rest of our receipts. If nothing more, it'll serve as a souvenir." Then I inserted the key into the ignition switch and turned it; then the motor immediately erupted.

I had not yet maneuvered the car from its space when LC shouted, "Hey! Didn't you see this?" And she thrust the parking ticket before my eyes.

After quickly slamming on the brakes, I thundered, "Don't do that! You almost caused me to smash into a parked car."

"Well, look at it!" she shouted.

So I impatiently turned off the ignition switch, pulled the emergency brake home, and stared at the large red letters: PLACE UP ON THE DASHBOARD. Below the warning, in smaller red letters, were the words *Vehicle not displaying valid ticket on dashboard will be towed away or charged at owner's expense.*

Actually daring to look into her eyes, I mildly mumbled, "So?"

"So that oversight could have cost us dearly," she retorted accusingly.

"I don't see how," I responded loudly. "It plainly states 'at owner's expense,' and we don't even own the *bleeped* car."

Her back stiffened against the seat, as it usually does when she prepares for a prolonged fray. Then she suddenly sagged and wearily whispered, "I'm too tired to try to pound a semblance of sense into your head."

As the car slipped smoothly into the heavy traffic, I relaxed against the back of the seat, smiled guilelessly at her, and said, "According to that statement, the trip to the border should be quiet and peaceful." Then I placed my right hand on her left knee and gently patted it.

"You can bet on it," she whispered, slumping against the locked door and cradling her head on her right elbow. Within ninety seconds there were the sounds of heavy breathing.

32

Vancouver to Ontario

Vancouver to Bellingham

We traveled along Georgia Street to Howe Street, turned right, and soon found that it converged with Seymour at the Granville Street Bridge. After passing over False Creek, we continued along Granville Street across a large part of the city to Marine Drive. It eventually looped around the Arthur Laing Bridge interchange to an on-ramp that provided access to the Oak Street Bridge and Highway 99.

After crossing the North Arm of the Fraser River into Richmond, which encompasses the central part of Lulu Island, Highway 99 resumed as the Fraser Delta Thruway. True to its name, the thruway passed *thru* Richmond and Lulu Island. Then it passed *thru* the George Massey Tunnel, which passes under the Fraser River, and continued *thru* the flat delta to the international boundary line, where it stopped abruptly. Since it did not continue *thru* into the U.S., it obviously was no thruway after all, so that name had to be a misnomer.

Bellingham Apparently the reduced speed, the flickering light rays from street lamps, plus the stop-and-go motions of the car disturbed LC's slumbers, since she stirred uneasily, sat up, and blinked owlishly at the rapidly changing urban scene.

"This must be Bellingham," she murmured.

"Uh-huh," I grunted.

"Are you hungry?" she inquired with a birdlike cock of her dark-brown curls.

"Huh-uh," I grunted.

"Come to think of it," she murmured, "since we snacked all day long at Expo Eighty-six, neither of us should be hungry, so how about skipping dinner?"

My left hand left the steering wheel and experimentally patted my paunch. "Suits me," I said. "So let's look for a motel."

Bellingham to Seattle

Early in the following morning, after a night in the Val-U Inn, we resumed traveling with the intention of breaking our fast en route. When a road sign indicated an upcoming turnoff, I looked across at LC and asked, "Would you like to stop at Mount Vernon for breakfast?"

"I'm not hungry yet," she replied. "But we could stop and get some gas."

After glancing at the fuel gage, I protested, "But the tank's almost a quarter full; besides, we should make one stop accommodate both refueling requirements."

"It's closer to an eighth than a quarter full," she rejoined.

After rechecking the fuel gage, I concentrated on my task until another road sign indicated the upcoming Arlington turnoff. "Are you hungry yet?" I asked.

"No," she answered. "But we could stop for some gas."

When the road sign indicating the Everett turnoff came into view, I casually suggested, "This might be a good place to stop for breakfast."

"I'm not hungry yet," she murmured, "but we really should stop for gas."

After checking the gas gage for the umpteenth time, I irritably growled, "We still have plenty of gas."

"But we shouldn't risk running out," she objected.

"And we shouldn't have to make two stops for breakfast and gas," I retorted.

"Okay, then let's stop here," she urged. "After getting the gas, we can look for a good restaurant."

"Too late," I muttered. "We just passed the turnoff."

"Then let's stop at Edmonds," she pleaded.

"It's too remote," I objected. "Besides, it's next door to Seattle, so why not wait? The chances of finding a good restaurant there should be much better."

"But we might run out of gas before we get there," she protested.

"Meantime I've run out of patience," I fumed. We won't run out of gas and that's guaranteed."

Seattle   Unfortunately, I passed up several turnoffs into the Seattle area, because there appeared to be no suitable restaurants in their immediate vicinities. Meanwhile my companion clamored maddeningly about our obvious fuel problem. In sheer desperation I finally swung the car onto a turnoff that deposited us in a decrepit industrial area.

"Why did you turn off there?" LC exploded. "We won't ever find a service station here, much less a good restaurant."

"I didn't want to run out of gas on the freeway," I admitted meekly.

Strangely enough, my acknowledgment of the existence of the oft-predicted crisis appeared to calm her fears. "Maybe there's a service station somewhere in this mess after all," she murmured. With that, she peered far ahead; then, turning her head, she scanned the farthest reaches of the street behind us and muttered, "Just nothing, absolutely nothing."

"This isn't a major thoroughfare," I observed, "so keep your eyes peeled for a heavily traveled crossroad."

We must have traveled more than a mile without encountering either a major thoroughfare or a service station. Suddenly she shouted, "There's one!"

"One what?" I countered.

"A service station," she retorted.

"Where?" I asked anxiously. "I can't see it."

"Far ahead on the right side of the street," she replied.

Simultaneously the motor coughed, and my heart immediately plunged to the bottom of my grateful stomach. But after my foot automatically eased up on the accelerator, the motor reluctantly responded, so I carefully nursed it along. However, it wasn't the prospect of a five- or six-block walk for a gallon of gas that I feared as much as the ensuing tirade from my partner. Since I had guaranteed that we wouldn't run out of gas, she was entitled to one. Aside from that, I have always treated my guarantees like promises, so I was honor bound to deliver the freight.

Somehow the motor must have sensed the enormity of my problem, because it behaved admirably all of the way to the service station. But the strain must have been too much for it, since it died just before I turned off the ignition switch. Meanwhile my heart had escaped from the carnal clutches of my otherwise empty stomach and resumed its putt-putt-putt-boom beat. And my mood had catapulted from the deepest of dungeons to a pinnacle of almost hysterical relief, because I wouldn't have to renege on my guarantee after all.

Through the grimy office window I saw a long, angular figure precariously suspended between the worn plastic seat of a tilted-back chair and the point where two oil-stained shoes were prominently stacked one atop the other on the edge of a cluttered desktop. Since the sounds of our arrival had generated no reactions from the spare frame, I assumed that the eyes beneath the bill of the greasy, denim cap were closed. Therefore I unlocked my seat belt, opened the door, struggled out from beneath the steering wheel, and deliberately slammed the door closed. As I had expected, the gaunt figure was galvanized into action: The shoes struck the concrete floor simultaneously with the forelegs of the chair, and the office door abruptly burst open in response to a square shoulder as the man ducked his head, but not before the door header tilted the cap to the rear of his head.

Still rubbing the sleep from his eyes, he shouted, "Good morning!" while several long strides were rapidly consuming the distance between the doorway and the car.

"And a good morning to you!" I loudly responded. Then, reacting to LC's imperative gesture, I moved around the car while she lowered the adjacent window.

"This is one of those maverick stations," she whispered. "Shouldn't we get only five gallons and fill up later at a reputable station?"

"Are you kidding?" I countered. "After all of the trouble we've encountered in finding this one, I don't intend to look for another one for three hundred miles. Besides, this gas probably comes from the same barrel as that of the so-called reputable station."

"Shall I fill it up?" called the attendant from the rear of the car.

"Please do," I called back to him.

"We certainly won't find any good restaurants around here," LC predicted with a sweeping gesture toward the factories and warehouses that dominated the area. Then, with an air of overt satisfaction, she added, "So we'll have to make a second stop after all."

"Since you aren't hungry, why don't we skip breakfast?" I inquired maliciously.

It is common knowledge that a man's stomach possesses neither arms nor hands, but I swear that at the very next instant my empty stomach reached up and clutched my heart. In fact, it may have been only my quick thinking that saved me from a most unusual heart attack.

"Why are you dancing up and down like a demented dervish?" LC inquired.

"I'm merely trying to shake some kinks out of my muscles," I lied, while my stomach reluctantly settled down into place.

"Obviously both of us can afford to diet a bit," she resumed. "In fact, we should enjoy brunch all the more."

"Okay," I agreed. "We'll break our fast at noon." And, incredible as it seems, I felt a sharp shudder from the area of my stomach.

As I turned away, she called, "Be sure to get the exact number of gallons, because I want to be able to determine how many miles this car is getting out of each gallon of gas. We might consider buying one sometime."

"Okay," I repeated.

"Shall I check the oil, sir?" inquired the attendant.

"No," I replied. "We added a quart when we last got gas."

"Then that'll amount to fourteen seventy," he said. After returning the nozzle to its cradle, he carefully wiped his oil-stained hands on a wad of oil-stained waste, casually inserted it into an oil-stained right hip pocket, advanced a couple of steps, and extended an oil-stained palm.

"How many gallons did that amount to?" I asked, as I placed a twenty-dollar bill on the oil-stained palm.

"Fourteen and seven-tenths," he replied.

"Sir!" LC interjected. "Do you happen to know how many gallons of gas this tank holds when it's full?"

Despite the oil stains, the man's manner was almost courtly as he bowed his head so that he could look directly into her eyes. "Fourteen and seven-tenths, ma'm," he answered succinctly.

"Then we must have been nearly out of gas!" she exclaimed.

"We were out of gas," I ruefully interposed. Then, to forestall any further comments from her, I opened the door and squeezed beneath the steering wheel.

"Thank you, folks!" called the attendant. "Come again!"

From the right hemisphere of my brain, Pancho remarked, "Thank Allah that you and your oil-stained hands happened to be at this particular spot, mister."

"Amen!" I muttered.

"I beg your pardon," LC said.

"That wasn't meant for your ears," I responded with a guilty expression.

"Then you must have been talking to yourself again," she retorted.

"Not this time," I muttered obscurely, quickly turning the ignition switch. But the motor refused to start, and after two more attempts it still refused to start.

"I warned you about this maverick gas," LC reminded me superciliously.

"The gas is okay," I insisted. "It just takes a bit of pumping to get it from the gas tank into the carburetor. That's why the motor stopped when we rolled into the station; the carburetor was empty." After I turned the ignition switch again, my theory was justified by a loud roar from the motor.

Seattle to Mount Rainier

After studying the freeway high above us, LC murmured, "I wonder which is the best direction for us to go to get onto the freeway."

"The same direction that we are going," I insisted. "We don't want to waste any miles backtracking. What we should do is get on a street that parallels the freeway and follow it to the first cross street that has a ramp leading onto the freeway."

"That would work fine if all of these streets didn't run diagonally to the freeway," she observed caustically. "But the freeway designers must have provided access to it for the local factory workers, so keep driving."

"That's logical," I conceded, "but I'm not fully convinced that either the freeway or these streets were logically planned."

"Just ahead of us is another freeway that must intersect with the one we want to get onto," she murmured, "so why not drive alongside it and take the first ramp onto it? In fact, there's one!" she shouted with an arm outstretched toward it. "Take it!"

There wasn't sufficient time for a second opinion, so I wildly swung the car onto it and immediately regretted the action. "But this ramp takes us in the wrong direction!" I protested.

"Ohhh," she exhaled softly, "we **are** going the wrong direction, aren't we?" With scarcely a pause, she proposed, "Let's take the next turnoff, cross to the other side of the freeway, and take the next ramp onto it. That maneuver will take us back to our freeway."

I carefully refrained from pointing out to her that such a solution required no great amount of ingenuity; instead, I slowly burned throughout the two miles we traveled away from our objective to the next turnoff. And my mood wasn't improved one bit when we arrived on the opposite side of the freeway and found no ramp leading onto it.

"The engineering skills of the Great Northwest's Swedes have been vastly overrated!" I shouted. "They don't know anything about planning freeway systems!"

"I'm sure that they knew what they were doing," she temporized. "If you hadn't passed up so many good turnoffs, we would have found both a good restaurant and a legitimate service station."

"That was a legitimate service station!" I fumed. "It merely lacked some of the finer and more costly niceties."

"Such as a neat attendant and good gas," she retorted. "We may have been the first and last people to patronize that station all morning."

I maintained a sullen silence throughout the trip alongside our last objective to the initial one, where, just by chance, I stumbled onto an on-ramp. In fact, if the car hadn't insisted on entering it, I might have missed it.

As the car cruised up the ramp and onto the freeway, LC exclaimed, "That was a bit of luck!"

"What do you mean by 'luck'?" I demanded with a sharp sense of guilt. "Wye, I saw it the second that we rounded the turn."

"It didn't look that way to me," she retorted. "In fact, if that on-ramp hadn't practically reached out and engulfed the car, I'll bet you would've missed it."

Since I was still fuming from all of the previous mishaps, I literally exploded, "Are you implying that I'm not a good navigator?"

After looking archly at me for a moment, she silently turned toward the window; consequently, I drew the only conclusion that remained to me. "Okay," I blurted. "In that case you can be the navigator between here and Mount Rainier."

I really should have exercised better judgment because LC probably is the world's worst navigator. Wye, one time she plotted a course from our home in Fullerton to a shop in Anaheim—a distance of only seven miles—and if I hadn't intervened, she would have ended up halfway around the world on the island of Bali. Furthermore, with a set of pontoons, a sail, and a strong tail wind, she and the old Chevy might have made it, too, because she has a lot of talents, but navigation definitely isn't one of them.

With that knowledge in mind, I should have ensured that we were on the right road when we left Puyallup, but a road sign indicated that Mount Rainier was ahead, so we continued along U.S. Highway 405 to the point where State Highway 7 intersected with it. There another road sign indicated that Mount Rainier was to our left, so I turned onto Highway 7.

After traveling several miles with no roadside assurance that we were on the right one, LC murmured, "It seems that we're going in the wrong direction."

I glanced uneasily toward her and asked, "What direction do you think we're traveling?"

"West," she replied.

My expression must have reflected my emotions, because she practically cringed before protesting, "But you know very well that I never know what direction we are going."

"Surely you can determine what direction we are going at this hour," I rejoined. "After all, we are traveling directly toward the sun."

"What sun?" she countered with a gesture toward the gray, overcast sky.

"There's a discernible glow through those clouds directly ahead of us," I pointed out with a similar gesture. "If west is the only direction that we have to worry about, then forget it, because we aren't going west."

"But we should be going east," she said.

"We what!" I shouted, slamming on the brakes and allowing the car to skid to a stop along the shoulder of the road. "Let me look at that map for a minute." After a brief inspection of it, I mumbled, "Hmm. Apparently we are still on Highway Seven, because there are no other roads through these woods."

"According to that sign back at the turnoff, this is supposed to be the road to Mount Rainier," she responded defensively.

"And it **is** the road to Mount Rainier," I rejoined. "All we have to do is to stay on it as far as Elbe and turn onto State Highway Seven O Six, which goes through Mount Rainier National Park."

"But we aren't supposed to go through the park," she objected. "We should go through Enumclaw and Parkay."

After another brief study, I agreed, "True, we could have gone that way, but there's no apparent reason why we can't continue on from here. We will still get to the peak, but from the opposite side of the mountain."

In turn, she studied the map. "Why can't we take Highway Seven O Six to Highway Forty, which will take us near the peak?" she inquired hopefully. "Then from Highway Forty we can take Highway Four Ten, which is the same road that we would've taken east from Puyallup."

Since she had repeated most of my suggestions, I pensively studied her for a moment, decided against pointing it out to her, and said, "Okay, so we continue **west**."

With resentful eyes, she murmured, "This road better turn east pretty soon, or we'll end up in Northern California."

"You should have said, 'end down in Northern California,' " I observed, but she ignored both the observation and me.

Soon after we entered the park, a small dam appeared on the right side of our radar screen, so we stopped to put it on film while arbitrarily including the picturesque stream that tumbled through the tortuous canyon below the dam. A short time later we came upon a veritable tunnel created by large, overhanging evergreen trees that justified the same action. Somewhat farther along the road we stopped just beyond the end of a new concrete bridge. From that point I carried the camera to the center of the bridge and managed to trap a striking if not spectacular view of Mount Rainier. In its foreground a stream tumbled picturesquely over huge boulders and ledges into a canyon that was etched into a landscape shrouded by pine trees.

Some distance beyond that point we rounded a sharp curve, beyond which a stretch of straight and relatively low-gradient roadway extended some two thousand feet through a forest of pines and firs. About midway of it I spotted the first evidence of wildlife, so I allowed the car to slow to a stop about two hundred feet from the animal. Meantime LC turned from a preoccupied study of the scenery and looked askance at me.

"Haven't you seen the deer, *dear*?" I inquired with a teasing smile.

"No," she answered. "Where is it?"

"Ahead of the car in the ditch on the left side of the road," I responded with an appropriate gesture. "It's grazing on the new grass."

"Oh!" she exclaimed. "Isn't it darling?"

"No, it is a deer, *dear*," I insisted. "A fawn if you insist on accuracy. Would you like to take a picture of it?"

She nodded; then, as if on second thought, she looked speculatively at me.

"No, you take it," I responded to her silent query. "I'm not about to struggle out from beneath this steering wheel and try to photograph a wild creature that's sure to bolt as soon as it sees me."

"Okay," she agreed reluctantly. "But it'll be a waste of time, because the fawn will spook and scamper off into the forest as soon as we get close enough for a good shot."

"Why don't you get out here and creep up on the critter?" I suggested.

"It's worth a try," she granted, reaching for the camera.

"Don't close the door," I warned her, as she slowly slid through the opening onto the shoulder of the roadway. "The sound of the slam might startle it."

With a nod she cautiously crossed the road and moved stealthily along its shoulder to within about fifty feet of the slender creature. There, slowly raising the camera, she focused the lens on it. Deciding to risk a few more steps, she slowly lowered the camera, crouched low, and crept to within about thirty feet of the animal. Since it appeared to be ignoring her, she cut that distance in half. Even then the creature exhibited no tokens of alarm, so she inched forward to within about seven feet of it, stopped, and looked anxiously at it. As if on cue, the fawn calmly raised its head, looked at her, nonchalantly flicked its stubby tail, and resumed grazing.

In the meantime LC nervously fidgeted with the camera's controls and impatiently waited for the animal to look at her again. Finally it raised its head, nodded it a couple of times as if to speed a mouthful of grass on its way, and turned inquiring, big, brown eyes toward her. But she didn't respond in time. After turning its gaze to a particularly luscious clump of grass that stood between them, the fawn moved a step closer to the camera bug and neatly nipped off the clump of grass.

When LC triumphantly returned to the car, I immediately remarked, "That's no wild animal. In fact, I would bet a bundle that it's a family pet." But that was no *wild* bet, since I had belatedly remembered that just beyond the last turn we had passed an intersecting trail that meandered through the trees to an isolated log cabin.

As the car climbed higher and higher, patches of snow began to appear beneath the fir trees and on the north sides of boulders. Soon the entire mountainside was covered with the cold, white stuff, and it became progressively deeper with every incremental increase in elevation.

Mount Rainier Suddenly the car rounded a high, snow-covered shoulder on our left and entered a spacious parking area. Beyond a high snowbank at the far side of it, a large, circular building crouched beside a slope that rose steeply toward a rugged mountain peak. Just beyond the building the snow-covered background was picturesquely pocked by a few stands of evergreen trees, but only the harsh, sheer surfaces of the multifaceted rock, which constituted the 14,410-foot, snow-clad peak of Mount Rainier, were visible above that level. While I was studying all of that magnificent scenery, the car was careening across the parking lot at unabated speed.

"Don't run into that snowbank," LC warned. "You might not be able to back out of it on this icy pavement."

"I don't intend to run into it," I retorted. "I'll park alongside the last car in that line."

"You'd better slow down," she came again.

"There's no problem," I muttered confidently. "Besides, there's a slight upgrade." Then I applied the brakes, and the car slid smoothly into the snowbank.

"Now, you've done it!" she screamed.

Self-consciously turning off the ignition switch, I unlocked my seat belt, squeezed from beneath the steering wheel, and stepped through the open doorway onto the icy surface. After a cautious inspection of the situation, I returned to the open door. Despite my cautious maneuvering, I slipped on the treacherous glare ice and would have suffered a hurtful fall if, on its own volition, one hand had not successfully grasped the door for support.

Simultaneously LC screamed, "Be careful!"

While cautiously recovering my equilibrium, I came to the soul-warming conclusion that for the first time in almost two decades she had actually exhibited some concern for my welfare.

Then she added, "I would surely hate to have to ride in an ambulance with you all of the way to the closest hospital, especially since there probably isn't a hospital within fifty miles of this place."

Sadly I crawled behind the steering wheel and repeatedly stamped my shoes against the carpeted floorboard.

"The ice is cold, huh?" LC speculated.

After pondering the question briefly, I obscurely answered, "Yes. Along with some other things, I've found it to be anything but *soul* warming."

"What did you find out there?" she inquired.

After fixing my preoccupied eyes on her, I answered, "A car in a snowbank."

"What are you going to do now?" she persisted.

"I'm going to back this car out of that snowbank," I answered with a confidence consisting of solid brass.

"Don't spin the wheels," she warned, "because this car might slide into the car next to it."

Gripping the steering wheel very tightly with both hands, I carefully restrained an overpowering impulse to unload my mind, because I have yet to use such words in the presence of a lady. Not only is the use of such words uncouth in such a situation, but it is illegal in most of the higher cultures. But the present American society must not know it.

When I had finally recovered control of my emotions, she callously commanded, "Close the door!"

Understandably, I pulled the door closed with such a vicious slam that the car shook from stem to stern. Suddenly the adjacent car seemed to move slowly forward into that snowbank, of all things, but a quick glance at it revealed that there was no driver in it.

"We are moving backward!" screamed my partner into my right ear.

"This certainly is the strangest earthquake that we've ever experienced," José silently informed me in a conversational vein.

"We're moving faster!" LC screamed. "Apply the brakes!"

"I have applied the brakes!" I retorted. Then, after looking back and scanning the area behind the car, I risked a quick glance at my partner, whose terrified eyes were riveted on me.

"Well, do something!" she screamed. "Even if it's wrong, do something!"

"Like this?" I countered with a slow turn of the steering wheel.

Her eyes expressed amazement, as the car slowly rotated ninety degrees and came to a stop. "How did you do all of that?" she asked, after recovering her aplomb.

I was surprised by the gleam of respect in her eyes; nevertheless, I reluctantly confessed, "It was much easier than I expected. Of course, the shock of the slamming door shook the car free from the snow, so it began to roll downgrade on that sheet of glare ice until I applied the brakes; then it slid on the ice. Since you've lived in snow country, you know that such ice is produced in several different ways. In this case the sun created snow melt, which slowly seeped from the base of the snowbank and spread across the pavement until the sun ducked out; then the melted snow froze as smooth as glass. That's the nature of such things."

"But why did the car stop sliding when it struck this particular area?" she asked.

"The snowplow and the sun didn't quite clear all of the snow from this area," I answered. "After the sun decamped, the snow and the tire tracks through it froze, and the hard, roughened surface provided sufficient friction to stop the car."

With a nod of approval, she murmured, "Very good."

Ginning up my most enigmatic glare, I asked, "Would you have been able to figure out all of that in time to stop the car from sliding out of the parking lot and across the road into that two-thousand-foot canyon?"

Following some uneasy fidgeting, she coolly replied, "I would never have driven the car into that snowbank in the first place."

Of course, there is no logical rebuttal to such an argument, so I defiantly drove the car back across the parking area, parked it in front of the hole in the snowbank, and for some inexplicable reason it remained there. Usually she would have protested throughout the maneuver, but she may have been too emotionally exhausted to generate reasons for such protests, much less to make them.

After sitting and staring at the big, reinforced concrete building for some time, I said, "It's surprising to see so much glass in that particular building."

"Why so?" she inquired.

"In this area, where low ambient temperatures prevail throughout most of the year, window area should be held to a minimum to preclude high heating costs," I replied.

Following a moment's thought, she countered, "How else could the visitors view the surrounding mountain peaks from every point on the compass? In fact, the views from those huge windows must be magnificent."

"Perhaps so," I conceded. "Since you helped pay for that fancy structure, would you like to go utilize some of those windows?"

"No, it's not worth it," she answered. Then, in response to my critical expression, she added, "It's just too cold out there."

"It can't be that cold," I muttered, reaching for the camera.

My first artistic effort combined a view of the smaller and also circular sun deck of the sprawling structure with the towering peak. The second one was directed across the gaping canyon that separates Mount Rainier from a long line of rugged, snow-capped peaks extending in a southwesterly direction like a file of burly soldiers. During a clear day the smoke and vapors from the cone of Mount Saint Helens may be detected from that high point, provided that she is smoking, of course. And she really shouldn't do that, because it is detrimental to her health; in fact, she lost her head in her last great orgy.

Upon returning to the car, I said, "While out there I saw a sign that identifies this huge building as the Visitor's Center."

"According to that sign," she said, pointing to a sign standing in the snowbank that blocked an ongoing thoroughfare, "the road is closed beyond this point, so we can't get through to the Chinook Pass from here."

"Hmm," I mumbled. "Let's take another look at that map."

She pawed through the items that had collected in the tray of the center console and finally withdrew the map. I accepted it, opened it, and laid it across the console so both of us could study it.

"Obviously we'll have to return past the Seven Ten intersection and continue to State Highway Twelve," she observed. "It'll take us to the lower end of Highway Four Ten, which will have already passed through the Chinook Pass on its way to Yakima."

"And it'll take us through White Pass," I added.

"I'm sorry I missed Highway One Sixty-five out of Puyallup," she responded with penitent eyes. "From it we could have gone by way of Highway Forty through Enumclaw and Parkay to Four Ten. That would've been a much shorter route to Yakima."

"It would've been somewhat shorter," I conceded, "but not enough shorter for anybody to become upset about."

Pressing the palm of her left hand against the top of my right hand, she leaned forward, cocked her head, looked up at me from beneath dark eyelashes, and murmured, "You're a good guy." After a loaded pause she added, "Most men would have exploded over this debacle."

"How do you know that I haven't exploded internally and ruptured some blood vessels?" I responded with a wry smile. "And how do you happen to know so much about the behavior of most men?" There was a sharp splat! And the back of my right hand tingled throughout the time that she folded the map and returned it to the tray.

"Such a sadistic woman!" I exhaled with accusing eyes, but she ignored me. Then I draped my tingling, apparently useless flipper across the lower quadrant of the steering wheel, but she continued to ignore my distress.

Mount Rainier to Yakima

The ensuing journey provided no startling scenery and few indications of a rural population. Meanwhile silence prevailed between us for long intervals of time.

Finally I asked, "Isn't Yakima an Indian name?"

Since no answer was forthcoming, I peered at her and saw that she hadn't fallen asleep in an upright position. Since her eyes were directed ahead, I passed my right hand in front of them. She turned them to me with a questioning expression, so I repeated the question.

"I answered yes," she replied.

I shook my head dolefully, because it was characteristic of her to respond so softly that I often failed to hear the answer.

"In fact," she resumed, "the Yakima Indian Reservation is located just a few miles south of here. It's one of Washington's largest reservations, but I believe the Coleville Indian Reservation is larger. It's located directly northeast of the Chief Joseph Dam."

"According to one of my reading sources, the Northern Pacific Railroad reached Yakima in eighteen eighty-five," I volunteered. "That advance of civilization, along with the development of a large system of irrigation canals, is reported to have turned the Yakima Valley into one of the most productive sources of fruits and vegetables in the state."

"That's true," she chimed in. "The valley does produce big crops of apples, peaches, pears, and cherries."

"What!" I exclaimed. "No bananas and pineapples?"

She responded with a destructive stare, so I hurriedly changed the subject. "According to that map there's a big firing range northeast of the city."

Apparently she had nothing to contribute to the subject, so silence returned to the Europa.

Yakima For a city with a population of about fifty thousand people, Yakima proved to be a relatively good stop. Even though the Thunderbird Motor Inn quoted lodging rates beyond our self-imposed budget, shortly after registering at the Red Lion Motel we returned to its dining room for a belated dinner.

The neatly attired host escorted us to a table, and a waiter immediately appeared to solicit our orders. While we waited for them to be delivered, I carefully studied the design and decor of the large, somewhat elongated dining room.

"There's no doubt that men are chauvinistic pigs," LC interjected into my thoughts with a faint smile. "Nevertheless, I prefer to be served by men."

"You like men, period," I retorted.

"Most normal women do like men," she countered.

"True," I agreed. "But you normal women should try to limit your relations to the man of your choice."

"I always have," she retorted with a long stare.

Once more I decided that it was time to change the subject. With a sweeping gesture toward the room and its decor, I stated, "This is pretty plush for a small city."

"It's nice," she conceded.

Then silence settled about the table. Apparently we were too weary to support an ongoing conversation, even though the hands of the clock had not reached the hour of nine. But when the waiter delivered our meals, I wasn't too weary to notice the significant glances exchanged between him and another waiter who happened to pass at the time. Furthermore, I didn't fail to detect the significant glances exchanged by two other waiters as they passed in an adjacent aisle. Definitely there was something in the wind, despite obvious attempts by the personnel to be urbane, so a cold but burning resentment grew within me. Even the host's effusive farewell failed to curb the resentment. All too apparently Big Brother had struck again in the Great Northwest.

Despite the memory of that ugly shadow in the background, I elected to return to the Thunderbird's coffee shop for breakfast. It was a typical maneuver, intended to verify the observations of the previous evening, but it was wasted since that environment appeared to be perfectly normal. Why the difference? Who knows? Despite all of my research, I don't know. In fact, I've never understood the colossal mystery from its genesis.

Yakima to La Grande

Several miles south of Yakima we veered southeast along the Yakima River through Buena, Sunnyside, and a stretch of semi-agricultural terrain. After crossing the river into Prosser, we resumed our journey in the same direction on a state highway that soon turned south to Paterson; then it veered east along the Columbia River into the state of Oregon. In relatively rapid succession we passed through Hermiston and turned onto an interstate highway, which, according to the road map, continued southeast to Pendleton, a city of about fifteen thousand inhabitants.

While we were approaching the city, I looked at our chauffeur and said, "Since the sun has not yet reached its zenith, let's not tarry long in this urban outpost because it doesn't appear to be very *urbane.*"

"How can you determine when the sun has reached its zenith?" she inquired with an eloquent gesture toward the leaden sky.

"By my watch," I retorted.

"After considering how erratically the Mountain and Pacific time zones have been defined, how can you be sure that twelve o'clock by your watch accurately determines the sun's zenith?" she persisted. "Wouldn't sidereal time be more accurate?"

"How can I see the stars at high noon, especially today?" I countered with a sweeping gesture toward the sky. Glancing down at my wristwatch, I did a quick double take. Then I surreptitiously restored its heart beat, but the circumspection was wasted.

"Nevertheless, that probably would be just as effective as resorting to your watch," she suggested with a knowing leer.

"So it stopped," I admitted ruefully. "Your stomach can't be running on solar time anyway, because you are never hungry at normal times."

"Possibly we should stop here for a light lunch, since this city may be as urbane as any place we'll find between here and Boise," she said. "However, I'm not hungry yet."

I leaned forward, checked the fuel gage, and commanded, "Drive on, fair damsel. If we become too hungry in the upcoming wilderness, we can always live off the land."

"How?" she countered. "We have no gun, and you're too fat to run down a rabbit."

While I studied her with malevolent eyes, she happily marked an imaginary *1* on the windshield. Finally I muttered, "That's pretty rough fare from a lady."

"We aren't called the fair sex for nothing," she cheerfully rejoined, marking another imaginary *1* on the windshield.

"Well," I began pensively, "some of you she-males are called the fair sex for practically nothing."

"Now who's playing rough?" she countered.

"I'm sorry," I muttered.

"Me, too," she murmured; then she marked an imaginary line through the two imaginary marks. After a moment's thought, she raised the heel of her right hand and rotated it about the imaginary marks as if she were scrubbing away the whole imaginary thing.

"Hey!" I shouted. "Watch the road! You almost clipped that big semi. With all of this fooling around you're going to propel us head on into one of those big trucks."

"That would be better than running head on into a Volkswagen," she retorted.

After fixing an incredulous stare on her, I foolishly asked, "Why?"

"Because the truck would leave us with no pain whatsoever," she replied, "but the Volkswagen might leave us still hurting." Understandably that strange philosophy plunged me into a deep, thoughtful silence; in fact, it persisted clear across a wide valley.

Several miles beyond the city the highway followed an upward gradient to a sheltered lookout, from which we were able to scan the far-flung splendor of the practically treeless valley through which we had passed. But it was not entirely treeless, because clusters of imported trees surrounded most of the widely separated groups of ranch buildings. In terms of a thumbnail sketch the lookout consisted of a twenty-foot-square concrete slab whose edges were guarded by heavy wooden rails attached to several six- by six-inch wooden columns that also supported its shingled roof. All of its exposed wooden surfaces were freshly painted, and the surrounding landscape was neatly maintained. Since that was the only structure of its type that we encountered throughout the entire trip, I've often wondered if it might not have been constructed by some generous rancher to provide transient visitors that magnificent view of his beloved valley.

As we mounted the slab and looked out across the rolling prairie in the foreground, LC exclaimed, "Look at that massive green and brown checkerboard!" Obediently my eyes focused on the somewhat evenly distributed rectangles of new crops of grain, hay lands, and cultivated fields that covered the floor of the valley over which we had traveled from still another wide expanse of rolling prairie.

"To some viewers those remote clusters of farm and ranch buildings may create impressions of human isolation and loneliness," I ventured. "What's more, the whistling of the wind as it gusts through the tall, dry spires of last season's stand of prairie grass may reinforce those impressions."

"Both the whistling wind and this view tug at some of my fondest memories," LC murmured. "Since both of us spent our childhoods on the windswept plains of central Canada, this scene should remind you of that area, too."

"It does," I said, "but it also reminds me of my misspent childhood. For example, I vividly remember a similar scene during a much earlier part of one year when the dormant prairie grass and the stubble from the last season's grain crops were literally packed in and covered by snow. In the meantime just outside the kitchen door there was nothing but frigid space in the glass tube of the thermometer, because the mercury had crept into the bulb at the bottom of the tube, and it was desperately reaching its hands through the kitchen wall toward the glowing top of the kitchen range. Believe me, if that globule had turned into Mercury, he was the coldest deity that ever left a warm domain above the Roman Empire."

"Aw, you don't have an ounce of romance in your soul," she protested. "Even with all of that ice and snow, those were beautiful times."

"It was much too cold for romance," I responded with an inadvertent shiver.

"And you were much too young for romance," she responded with a chuckle.

That was a challenge that I had to meet, so I said, "Romantically I was a very precocious brat; fortunately, however, there were no female brats within miles of that lonely farmhouse."

"I wish that I had known you then," she murmured wistfully.

"That would have been impossible," I retorted. "At that time you weren't even a gleam."

After some half-hearted pushing and shoving we returned to the car, and things returned to normal for the day. In other words, they returned to more of the same.

La Grande   Beyond the lookout the car climbed steadily to 3,800-foot Deadman Pass; then it cruised past Meacham and through a range of relatively unimpressive mountains. Finally it turned from the highway onto the main thoroughfare of La Grande, a city of somewhat less than ten thousand inhabitants, so the name wasn't justified. Likewise, the facade of the Smokehouse Restaurant lacked grandeur on a *grand* scale.

As we strolled toward its unimpressive entrance, I muttered, "It surely doesn't look inviting."

"Well, don't blame me for stopping here," LC retorted. "You're the one who trained the car to seek out such offbeat places, so don't blame me. Blame the car, because it deliberately turned into the parking lot and parked itself. In fact, it ignored my efforts when I swung the steering wheel away from this place."

I looked thoughtfully at her while José suggested, "LC's a great copycat, so you can only blame yourself for that ridiculous alibi."

Finally I muttered, "Some car," to which she responded with a very virtuous smile and flounced through the entrance.

A plump and relatively mature, brunette waitress led us to one of the several unoccupied tables, laid two food- and coffee-stained menus on it, and silently departed. Meanwhile from her expression I detected certain tokens, which indicated that she had recognized me. To my knowledge I had never seen her before.

After she left, LC whispered, "I agree that it looks uninviting, and other people must think so, too, because we appear to be the only customers."

"The sun passed its zenith some time ago," I observed with teasing eyes. But my mind refused to accept the lateness of the hour as a legitimate excuse. After glancing at the menu, I suggested, "Why don't you order for me while I go wash my hands."

"Okay," she agreed. "What do you want?"

"I'll gamble on the hamburger," I answered, rising.

"Hmm," she mumbled. "Even though you're a lousy gambler, I'll order two of them."

In the untidy washroom I discovered that the inlet in the tank of the only water closet had been steadily diverting water directly into its outlet for several months. After adjusting the fixture so that it functioned properly, I speculatively addressed the grimy lavatory. Doubtfully shaking my head, I turned the reluctant handle of the hot water faucet, but not even a dyspeptic belch issued from it. An inspection of the turnoff valve beneath the lavatory revealed that whoever had closed it had also removed the handle.

After another shake of my head, I turned on the cold water faucet, thrust my hands beneath it, and scrubbed away the rust and green slime from them without disturbing the sliver of dirty soap that lay conveniently on one corner of the lavatory. Then I looked about for a paper towel dispenser and actually found one, but some disenchanted soul had raised its lid to warn other customers of its emptiness.

Abruptly my frustrations burst their bonds, which induced me to look up imploringly toward all of the foreign dieties in the heavens above. Regretfully shaking my head, I looked down and began to emphatically exhort all of the demons within the earth to lower the boom on such irresponsible parties. The tirade served no good purpose except to release some of the pressure under my wig. Since it gained no paper towel for me, I bitterly shook most of the water from my hands and dried them on my handkerchief.

Meantime Pancho mildly suggested, "This experience proves that Americans shouldn't be criticized for traveling abroad in lieu of traveling across America."

"But you're comparing the dregs of America with the elite of foreign countries," José protested.

En route from the washroom to the table, I happened to glance in the direction of the grill and found the waitress locked in a confidential conversation with the fry cook. The man stood facing me, while the woman lounged across an adjacent counter with her ample back to me. When the fry cook saw me, he murmured something to her that induced her to turn and look at me, but she quickly turned away when she encountered my steady gaze.

While I was seating myself at the table, LC said, "Our hamburgers have arrived, and they actually appear to be edible, so you are a pretty good gambler after all."

"There was a *bleeped* good reason why I was gone so long," I explained. "I had to overhaul the plumbing system before I could use it."

"It was that bad, huh?" she inquired, absently cutting a bite from her hamburger.

"Even worse!" I retorted, viciously slicing a piece from my burger. "Earlier you predicted a very primitive area ahead of us, and we've reached it."

Suddenly a high, off-key whistle emanated from behind the partial wall that hid the relatively remote grill.

"Wow!" exclaimed LC. "What a queer whistle. You're right. This place has to be pretty primitive when its people haven't even learned to whistle on key."

"A queer whistle implies a queer whistler," I said.

"Naw, not in this area," she retorted. "They've all migrated to San Francisco and Hollywood."

"Not necessarily," I mumbled around a bite of burger. "Sadists are queer, and they're found in many remote areas, such as the Arabic states and even in the Irish Republican Army."

"This hamburger isn't bad," she remarked with an equal disregard for etiquette.

Later, while I was standing beside the cashier's counter, I looked across the head of the aloof waitress-cashier and saw that the fry cook was idly lounging against a work counter that stood in a rather shadowy area of the kitchen.

Unexpectedly Pancho injected, "If it weren't for the clawlike fingers that curl so ghoulishly around the far edge of yon countertop, I would totally discount what appears to be a hairy leg with a cloven hoof that projects just beyond the base of yon counter."

"That's no illusion, believe me!" José burst forth. "And neither is the forked tail that just lashed out from behind yon counter. It surely looks like Big Brother is playing this circuit."

After accepting the change from the woman, I turned away from the cashier's counter toward the entrance and mumbled, "You guys have been confused by a bunch of shadows again."

"I beg your pardon," LC murmured, as I held the door for her.

"Huh?" I grunted.

"You've been talking to yourself again," she answered accusingly.

"No," I retorted. "I've been thinking aloud."

"What's the difference?" she demanded.

I paused until she reached my side; then, placing my right arm around her shoulders, I pulled her alongside me and asked, "Why don't you be quiet and give me some time to think?"

"That's too hazardous!" she retorted. "Every time you begin to think, we get into trouble."

La Grande to Boise

The car chose to resume its southeasterly journey along the same interstate highway, which ultimately found its way between several small mountains to the Powder River. After crossing the river, whose bed proved to be as dry and powdery as its name implied, the highway bypassed Baker; then it erupted from out of the rolling prairie and wastelands into an area of gently undulating farmlands irrigated by large, overhead sprinkler systems. As the highway slowly dipped down into the Snake River Valley, the terrain became almost flat with just a slight slope toward the river, so surface irrigation replaced the sprinkler systems.

Shortly after we penetrated that area, LC emerged from a state of lethargy long enough to inquire, "Aren't those potato fields out there?"

"You can bet on it," I replied.

"Then they really do raise potatoes in Idaho after all," she remarked.

"These fields are in Oregon," I muttered. "But the fields on the other side of the river are in Idaho, so I suppose that it's safe for you to say that."

"Then Idaho doesn't have to remove the word *potato* from its license plates and substitute the word *onion* on them," she murmured absently.

Turning a puzzled expression in her direction, I asked, "Why would Idaho do a stupid thing like that?"

"It isn't stupid!" she retorted irritably. "The stretch of the Snake River that we last followed through Idaho was surrounded by onion fields. Remember?"

"Yeah, that's right," I conceded after a brief consideration. "Maybe Idaho should change its license plates to 'The Potato and Onion State.'"

"That **would** be stupid!" she retorted. "How could all of those letters be squeezed onto a license plate?" I silently turned a quizzical smile on her while she huffily crossed her knees, turned both the knees and her head toward the door, and lapsed back into lethargy.

Meanwhile the car followed the highway past Ontario and crossed the river into Idaho. From there it was a relatively short run to another bridge that spanned the Boise River, where the car arbitrarily continued on past Caldwell and Nampa. Actually, we might have missed the Boise turnoff had not the car capriciously elected to turn onto it. Since Boise is a relatively small city of scarcely more than fifty thousand inhabitants, the car found a nice motel with relative ease.

Boise The Shilo Inn was located alongside the Boise River in a pretty, parklike setting. Within minutes we agreed that it had been placed in one of the prettiest settings we had ever shared with any motel. Furthermore, it was strategically located relative to a fine restaurant. However, as we entered the restaurant, I detected a familiar attitude in the manner of the young woman who seated us in one of the rustic cul-de-sacs that are so characteristic of the Stuart Anderson chain of Black Angus restaurants.

A pleasant waitress of about forty appeared beside the table with the greeting, "Good evening. Would you like something from the bar?"

"Yes," I replied. "We would like a couple of vodka martinis straight up, please."

"Would you like to order your dinners now or wait awhile?" she asked.

From LC my questioning eyes elicited, "Let's wait awhile."

"Okay," the woman responded cheerfully. "I'll be right back with your cocktails."

As she departed from the area, José remarked, "She appears to behave normally enough, but we can't ignore the covert glances of the several younger waitresses who have gathered in the area, so Big Brother must have preceded us to this place."

I chose to ignore the opinion, but some seconds later José's partner added, "That conclusion appears to be substantiated by the stream of busboys that's flowing past our table with no apparent objectives except the satisfaction of their small-town curiosities about an oddity that we happen to know doesn't exist at our table."

"Yeah," José agreed, "they would have done better by studying Big Brother and his minions when they showed up. After all, some journalists claim that Big Brother's ranks are infested with them—oddities, that is."

The martinis arrived on schedule and, as usual, I shared half of mine with LC. If an occasional ingestion of one and a half martinis can be called alcohol abuse, she is our only alcoholic.

We had almost finished our prime rib dinners when our slender waitress and three other waitresses gathered beside an adjacent table and sang happy birthday to the youngest member of the family occuping it. Then they cheerfully clapped their hands. Meanwhile we and several other friendly diners within the immediate area collaborated in the action.

After the noise had subsided, I leaned from my chair into the aisle and attracted the attention of our waitress with a raised forefinger. "Myrna, what is the name of this group of songbirds?" I called to her. "I'm a Hollywood scout, and I would like to. . . ."

"Oh, I'll just bet that you're a Hollywood scout," she interjected with a delighted laugh, advancing to our table. Dividing a friendly smile between us, she added, "We always try so hard, but we never seem to get any better."

"But you shouldn't expect to improve on perfection," I protested.

"Don't try to kid me," she rejoined. "I've been around too long for that, but thanks for trying anyway. However, even though we are far from perfect, people seem to enjoy what we do."

"Of course, they do," LC interposed. "They respond to what's in the hearts of the singers, not to how well it's done."

"That seems to be true," agreed the slender woman eagerly.

Then the two women engaged in a discussion of human psychology, during which I was forced to sit in open-mouthed wonder while marveling at some of the sinuous logic behind that girl talk.

After the waitress returned to her other customers, I cleared the dinnerware from my paper place mat and began to scribble on it some of the dialogue that had preceded the clinical discussion. In the meantime the waitress reappeared and paused to observe my efforts.

"I hope that you don't mind my use of this mat," I muttered. "Actually, it's only paper, so it'll have to be destroyed anyway."

"No problem," she insisted. "But let me get a fresh one for you."

"No, this one will serve my purpose quite well," I insisted. "However, thank you for being so thoughtful and cooperative."

"He's an author," LC interjected. "That's why he's making some notes of the things that have been said. He may want to use them in his book."

"Oh!" exclaimed the waitress. "I've never met an author before." After subjecting me to a long study, she asked, "What are the names of some of your books?"

"I'm not that type of author," I admitted with a wry smile. "Heretofore I've been involved in technical writing for large corporations; however, I'm currently in the midst of writing a book covering my experiences during a trip around the world. Some people might call it a travelogue, but I intend to make a lot more of it than that."

"Oh!" she exclaimed. "That should be very interesting."

"I'm trying hard to make it that way," I admitted. "No doubt any success will depend largely on my ability to convert my normally dull, precise words into more colorful and lyrical ones."

"What's the name of your book?" she inquired.

"*Misadventures of an American Abroad*," I replied. Then, after considering the probable impact of the word *misadventures* on the mind of a person who must have been exposed to Big Brother's nefarious influences, I added, "Not that I participated in any liaisons, because I didn't; however, I was subjected to some extremely unusual experiences involving people who had been misinformed."

"Oh, I see," she murmured with a puzzled expression.

Meanwhile I intercepted an equally puzzled expression from LC; consequently, I concluded that neither of them actually "saw," so I added, "You'll have to read the book to fully understand what happened."

"When will it be published?" she asked.

"Assuming that the First Amendment isn't summarily terminated, it should be published sometime in nineteen eighty-eight," I replied.

"If you'll give me your name and the name of the book, I'll look for it on the booksellers' shelves about that time," she said.

Nodding, I selected a free corner of the mat and scribbled the information on it. After tearing off the corner and presenting it to her, I said, "This is not only my nom de plume, but it's my original name. Above it I've written the name of the book, so you can't miss it. In fact, you shouldn't miss it, because I am writing it for people like you."

"Thank you," she murmured, folding the piece of paper and placing it in the coin pocket of her uniform. "I don't intend to miss it."

"It would be particularly nice for us if we could miss the check for this nice meal," I suggested with a wry smile.

"Oh, that can't happen," she insisted. "Like MacArthur, I shall return." Stepping back into the aisle, she almost collided with a busboy who had just rounded a corner with a tray of soiled dishes poised overhead. After deftly avoiding him, she turned toward us and wiped nonexistent perspiration from her brow.

"MacArthur had only war machines to avoid," I said, "so it was easy for him to return; however, after another encounter like that one, you may not be so fortunate."

"I shall return," she insisted. Then, raising her right hand high above her brown locks as if it clasped the handle of a sword, she added, "I have to, or I'll be drawn and quartered by the management."

Our waitress had been a friendly little minx, and we had reciprocated, but I made a point of not making any friendly overtures to the aloof, young hostess as we filed past her toward the doorway; besides, she was *sooo* aloof.

Meanwhile, Pancho suggested, "Very likely she communicated Big Brother's message to one or more of those young waitresses, whose covert glances made them so conspicuous."

"Very likely she did," José concurred. "If so, she might be startled to learn that, by doing so, she became an accomplice in a particularly vicious crime against one of America's finest senior citizens—a man of infinitely high standards."

We awakened early in the following morning with the soft sounds of the Boise River still rippling in our ears. Our first order of the day was a trip along its tree-shrouded bank for a half-dozen snapshots of its mildly turbulent waters. Then we checked out of the motel and moved a short distance to a fast-food restaurant.

Boise to Ogden

Our route from the restaurant took us southeast through Mountain Home, which proved to be considerably less than mountainous, and the interstate highway continued in the same direction through several other small towns. Eventually we deliberately turned off of it onto a somewhat less traveled U.S. highway that ultimately crossed the deep gorge of the Snake River into Twin Falls.

Twin Falls Area Actually we intended to view neither the gorge nor the falls; we intended to see the Balanced Rock. That proved to be a misguided intention, because we must have traveled fifty miles during a fruitless search for the highly publicized rock. Eventually we found a farm road which, according to a roadside sign, provided access to it, but an adjacent sign indicated that the road was closed. So we returned to the Shoshone Falls and the adjoining park, which proved to be worth part of the otherwise wasted detour.

From the Twin Falls area we traveled east through the relatively flat Snake River basin to a point beyond Burley, where the highway turned southeast through rough and apparently uninhabited terrain to Brigham City. From that point we retraced our previous route to the outskirts of Ogden, where we camped for the night in the Big Western High Country Inn.

Ogden From the inn we traveled several circuitous miles in a futile attempt to find a favorable dining establishment, so we settled on the small restaurant that adjoined the inn. The meal may have been acceptable, but I wouldn't know that, because my mind was too occupied by the familiar tokens that I observed in the behavior of the two young waitresses.

Ogden to Salt Lake City and Environs

From necessity we had breakfast at the same establishment with little change in the behavior of the personnel. But I eagerly accepted the weatherman's gift of a day which broke with a blaze of brilliant sunlight that greatly amplified the beauty of the snow-capped Wasatch Mountains on our left as we traveled along the softly shimmering waters of the great lake justifiably named Salt. It was a relatively short distance to Salt Lake City, so the morning was still young, and the ambient temperature was just comfortably warm when we parked the car along one of the curbs that surrounded the square containing Mormon structures, whose towers literally pierced the cloudless, blue sky.

The Mormon Complex As we strolled through the massive, iron gate that had just been opened into the complex, LC murmured, "Isn't it beautifully landscaped?"

After inspecting her mien, I withheld a similar opinion because she was lost in appreciation of the surrounding plants and green lawns. Instead, I suggested, "Let's take some shots of the Assembly Hall. Some of this architecture is not only impressive but downright beautiful."

While studying one side of the structure, she absently handed the camera to me and said, "Those two figures over there are interesting. I wonder what they are pulling."

My eyes turned in the same direction. "Hmm," I mumbled. "It appears to be some sort of a cart. Since we are in no hurry, why don't we stroll that way and take a picture of it?" Then I peered through the viewfinder at the vine-covered Assembly Hall, which reminded me of some of the prettier brick and mortar churches that I had seen.

As we drew closer to the cart, my companion remarked, "Oh, there aren't just two figures; it's a family. That's the head of an infant projecting from the bedding on the floor of the cart, and a small boy is helping to propel the cart forward by pushing on the rear of it while it's being pulled by the father and his eldest son. What a nice symbol of every family member's cooperation."

"Those early settlers must have endured backbreaking hardships to forge homes for themselves in this somewhat desolate land," I muttered. "It's sad that so many of our current crop of Americans sit idly and demand that the government provide all of their needs. That's not the kind of philosophy that built this land into the great nation that it once was."

"True, it's a has-been nation," she agreed. "Wye, many Americans won't even fight to preserve the freedom that people like these struggled and fought so hard to win for them." And she swept a hand toward the figures about the cart.

Pausing before a metal plaque, she said, "According to these words, the Ashcroft Monument commemorates some three thousand settlers who left Iowa City for the Salt Lake Valley during the middle of the last century." Turning her eyes to me, she added, "Two hundred fifty of those people died en route. That seems to indicate that they weren't deterred by the hardships entailed in making a wagon trail through virgin territory to the land of their dreams."

Nodding agreement, I peered upward at the spires of the Mormon Temple and suggested, "If we walk along this big, paved promenade far enough, we should be able to get all of the temple onto one of these frames."

"Perhaps you could include the huge water fountain in it," she suggested.

"What water fountain?" I asked.

"That one," she responded, swinging one hand toward a point midway of the promenade.

"And you claim to be near-sighted," I responded derisively.

"That isn't far," she protested. "In fact, it can't be over a hundred yards from here."

"Then I must be getting near-sighted," I retorted, "because I can't see any water fountain."

"But the water isn't flowing now," she said.

I was about to contend that it wasn't a water fountain until water flowed from it, but I wisely dropped the subject.

Beyond the so-called water fountain we came upon two more statues that proved to be likenesses of Joseph and Emma Smith. While I speculatively studied them, LC paused beside them and read aloud, "All I have to give to the poor, I'll give to this society."

"That's a sound philosophy," I said. "In other words, take care of your own poor and keep the government out of it. That not only eliminates large chunks of government overhead, but it forestalls enormous amounts of political chicanery and corruption."

"That's the Mormon office building," she informed me, while unnecessarily pointing to the huge structure that stood alongside the promenade. "And that relief map of the hemisphere on its wall would make a nice background for a snapshot of the water fountain."

"What water fountain?" I mumbled, peering through the viewfinder toward the Mormon Temple. Fortunately, water suddenly burst forth from the fountain, so I was able to obtain a nice shot of it with the temple in the background.

As I rolled the film ahead, she moved toward me and asked, "What's next on your agenda?"

"What do you mean by referring to the agenda as mine?" I countered. "This is a joint venture, so what's next on our agenda?"

"I would like to see that big open-pit mine that we saw from the aircraft shortly before we arrived here," she replied.

"Okay," I agreed, "let's go see it."

"Wouldn't you like to see it, too?" she inquired with an anxious smile.

"I never intended to miss it, irrespective of whether it was on your agenda or mine," I responded with a smile.

The Bingham Mine We must have traveled about thirty miles from the Mormon center before we found Bingham Canyon beyond the southwestern outskirts of the city. At the entrance of the canyon we passed several small buildings on our right, one of which advertised copper wares of all kinds. Some distance beyond that point we came upon a small security office with a mechanically operated gate at each side. As the car came to a stop at the near corner of the security office, a uniformed man swung through the nearest of the shack's two open doorways and approached the car.

"Good day," he greeted us.

"Yes, it's a fine day," I granted cheerfully, "but this appears to be as far as we can go."

"Presently that's the case," he said.

"Is there some vantage point from which we can view the pit?" I asked.

"Yes," he replied, "there's a point from which visitors have been permitted to overlook it, but we have been having some labor problems, so that area has been closed temporarily."

"So the company and its property are being held hostage to the whims of a few radical labor leaders," I suggested.

The man's eyes met mine squarely. "Yes," he admitted. "Some people have very little respect for either the rights or the property of other people. Consequently, we have to refuse access to that viewpoint not only to protect visitors from injury, but to protect the company from lawsuits by visitors who might be injured by the illegal activities of particularly aggressive union members."

"Okay, we understand your problem," I said. Then, while preparing to reverse our direction of travel, I added, "We hope that you don't encounter any really big problems."

Smiling faintly, he backed away from the vehicle, courteously waved, and called, "Have a nice day."

"What a nice, courteous officer!" LC exclaimed when we were again under way.

"He isn't a policeman," I pointed out to her, "so there's a difference in his behavior. Besides, he's employed by a large corporation that has to maintain good public relations, since most of its products end up in the hands of the public in one form or another."

"Let's stop at that copper shop we passed on the way into the canyon," she requested.

After nodding agreement, I turned the steering wheel left, and the *bleeped* car deliberately selected one of the parking spaces in front of the shop. It must have had a mind of its own—that crazy car.

The establishment was practically a replica of other copper shops that we had visited during our travels. As usual, there was an assortment of copper cookware plus numerous copper gimmicks directed to the tourist trade. Early photographs of the canyon, its first miners, and some of their tools decorated several of the walls. And some of those old tools were stacked along the walls of one room. While we were examining the displays, I didn't fail to note the studied gaze of one of the elderly women who served the customers. But I had expected as much.

As I swung the door open to make our exit, LC asked, "Do you think that we can find our way to the lake from here?"

"Of course, we can," I replied. "We can do anything your little heart desires."

She smiled up at me. Then she linked her right arm with my left arm and gently patted it with her left hand as we squeezed through the opening together.

While holding the car door open for her, I inquired, "What do we have here?" And I followed up the question by pointing a forefinger at the brown-jacketed pamphlet clasped in her right hand.

"It's called *Mining's Living Legacy*," she replied.

"Where did you get it? At the copper shop?" I persisted, assuming command of the vehicle.

"No," she replied. "That nice officer gave it to me while you were studying the rim of the canyon."

"Hmm," I rumbled. "And what did you give him for it while I was studying the rim of the canyon?"

She smiled faintly and then belatedly smacked the top of my wrist.

"I can't trust you for one second," I muttered darkly.

"Be quiet and keep your eyes on the road, or you'll run off of it," she advised, just as I deliberately swung the car onto a shoulder of the road.

"Why did you do that?" she burst forth. "There may be nails or sharp metal in the mining trash that has been dumped alongside this road."

"Naw," I responded confidently. "As usual, there's a purpose in my madness. I want to take a picture of this rusty old conveyor system."

After returning from my mission, she asked, "Did you look at the tires? I saw some pieces of rusty sheet metal piled against the barbed-wire fence. We might have ridden over some more of it on this shoulder."

"Don't be such a worry wart," I admonished her. "There was nothing on the shoulder except tar, some of which I collected on one shoe."

She subsided into a sulk, so I tried one of my infectious grins on her, but she deliberately turned toward the window and glowered at the unprepossessing surroundings.

After we got under way, she opened the pamphlet and said, "According to these words, copper ore was first discovered in Bingham Canyon in eighteen sixty-three."

"Hmm," I murmured. "That was about one hundred twenty years ago."

"One hundred twenty-three years ago," she rejoined superciliously. "Silver and lead ores also were discovered about the same time." Then she exclaimed, "Would you believe that only two percent of the ore is copper?"

"That's enough when it's mined and processed economically," I responded with an air of confidence that was 100 percent bluff.

"Apparently they've done that," she murmured. "They immediately built a concentrating plant near Garfield, since that was the nearest source of sufficient water. Meanwhile, they were being ridiculed by most of the so-called mining authorities of those times for trying to economically process such low-grade ore."

"That's typical of the *bleeped* human race," I muttered. "Every *jassack* is an authority on all aspects of a process once he has made a few points in just one of its fields. But they must have moved into the operation very quickly."

"Not quickly enough to attract much attention," she retorted. "The initial company was not formed until nineteen three, so the action was anything but rapid."

While she became lost in the printed pages, I decided to refrain from any more incorrect assumptions. Abruptly she burst forth: "Would you believe that that hole back there is the largest man-made excavation on this earth?"

I expressed adequate surprise but carefully refrained from a comment.

"Furthermore," she resumed, "it has produced more than eight million tons of copper, which were sold for more than six billion dollars, a sum that exceeds the combined sales from the Comstock Lode, the Klondike, and the California gold rush by a factor of eight."

I was so moved by the revelation that I incautiously exclaimed, "Some gold mine!"

To which she retorted, "No! Some copper mine!"

I bowed my head in defeat and again resolved to stick to my previous resolve.

The two-lane road eventually intersected with a highway. After obeying the stop sign, I urged the car to greater and greater speeds. In the meantime a rhythmic thumping sound began to emanate from the direction of the right, front wheel. Of course, my companion directed accusing eyes at me, but she refrained from expressing her suspicions in words as I silently swung the car onto the shoulder of the highway and brought it to a stop.

When I returned from inspecting the problem, she asked, "Is the tire flat?"

"No," I replied, "but a gob of tar is embedded in the tread of it, and that's what's causing the thumping sound. At still higher speeds, the front end of the car probably will shimmy."

Her steady gaze spoke volumes, but she didn't say, "I told you so."

At forty miles per hour the car did shimmy. After stopping at a service station, I employed a couple of dollar bills to con a reluctant mechanic into removing most of the tar with a screw driver.

Great Salt Lake After leaving the service station, I pointed the car in the general direction of the lake. Meanwhile, LC dug out a road map and offered to guide me, but I courteously declined the offer, because that woman can exchange north and south quicker than the flick of a ground squirrel's tail. Preferring to fly by the seat of my pants, I hit the south end of the lake dead on. In fact, the same wide, four-lane highway conveyed us on into the lake.

Finally LC volunteered, "It seems so strange to be traveling along a highway with water on both sides of it. I wonder if it's safe."

"Any minute now I fully expect the highway to sink into the water," I retorted, "into all four feet of it."

"Oh," she responded in relieved tones, "if it's no deeper than that, I can stand up in it."

"Provided that the buoyancy of your body in that salt water allows your feet to reach the bottom," I rejoined. In response to her startled expression, I added, "But you can't drown in that salt water unless you float on your face. However, this area is covered by flood water, so it may not be as salty as usual."

While she was digesting that bit of news, my attention was attracted to a group of concrete buildings that stood about a hundred yards from the highway. "Look at what happened to the factory that processes our salt," I commanded.

"Oh, how amazing!" she exclaimed. "And it really is the same company. I wonder whom we'll obtain our salt from now."

"The same one," I retorted.

"How can that be?" she countered. "The lower part of that factory is submerged in water."

"That won't hurt the salt," I rejoined. "However, it may make it a bit more salty."

"I don't see how that could be," she began. Then she looked sharply toward me and struck the first of several sharp blows on my poor, innocent right knee.

Finally, deciding that we had ventured as far into the swollen lake as the visual returns warranted, I executed an illegal U-turn, and we returned to the city of the Latter-day Saints.

For the coming night we eventually settled on a somewhat elevated, one-room residence in the Super 8 Motel of Salt Lake City. We suspected that its relatively economical cost might prove to be representative of its caliber, but it turned out to be quite satisfactory.

As usual, LC registered for both of us, since, early on, I had conned her into the task on the grounds that we should keep the charges for the entire trip on one credit card. Actually I wasn't trying to take advantage of her, because we always share equally in the costs of such ventures. And I wasn't trying to avoid being recognized by the various lodges' personnel, but I did gain a certain malicious satisfaction from circumventing some of Big Brother's nationwide traps. Mostly I was trying to avoid an encounter with one of his weirdos in such an establishment, one of the particularly sadistic type who might endeavor to embarrass me without considering its effect on my ultrasensitive companion. In fact, that has been one of my most trying self-imposed responsibilities during the last twenty years, and fortunately I have been rather successful.

The Holiday Inn An example of such a situation occurred in the restaurant of the Holiday Inn, which was located diagonally across the street from our abode. The maître d'hôtel proved to be an extremely nervous man of about thirty-five.

"Good evening," he greeted us with a heavy accent. Absently picking up two menus, he asked, "Is it two for dinner?" and conspicuously continued to avoid eye contact.

"Yes, please," I replied.

He quickly led us to a nearby table, laid a menu beside two of the four plates, and left. Scarcely more than a minute passed before I overheard the distinctive timbre of his voice speaking as if into a telephone, and the tones seemed to be deliberately subdued. That, in itself, was not so strange, but I hadn't heard the sounds of a telephone's buzzer, so he must have placed the call. Furthermore, his tones possessed an imperative quality as if they were urging someone to help him.

Within a few minutes a lone man appeared at the maître d's podium, and a subdued conversation ensued between the two men, who appeared to be about the same age. Then the newcomer was escorted to an adjacent table located behind my right shoulder. From the corner of my right eye I carefully studied the slender, dark-complexioned man; meanwhile he evinced more than normal interest in us.

A slender, dark-complexioned waiter, who also may have been thirty-five, arrived to take our orders, which he did with a minimum of courtesy. Soon I was amazed to hear a low, wheezing whistle from the newcomer's table. Also noticing it, LC directed her eyes from across the table to the man, and the whistling stopped.

Then she leaned toward me and softly inquired, "Isn't that strange behavior for someone in a public place like this?"

After deliberately turning my head and looking back at the man, I redirected my gaze toward her and rather loudly replied, "True, it's strange behavior, but he may be out of place in this environment, since he's probably the house detective or one of the hotel's other menials.

"Shh," she hissed. "He might hear you."

After responding with an enigmatic glance, I raised my cocktail to my lips to hide my fury with the man for having aroused my beloved's curiosity.

Within seconds the man arose and left without exciting more than a questioning glance from the maître d'. Apparently the newcomer had lost his appetite.

We were consuming our desserts when the distant doorway of the kitchen swung open and another dark-complexioned man appeared in the opening. While one hand restrained the door and the other one adjusted his tall, white headgear, he stood there and stared directly past the heads of several other diners in the direction of our table.

Detecting my prolonged gaze, LC turned her head and looked in the same direction. "Hmm," she murmured. "There seem to be an awful lot of dark-complexioned people in this place. Even the chef appears to be French."

"Or Greek," I offered with a chuckle.

After the waiter performed the magic of juggling our payment, we strolled slowly past the maître d' toward the glazed doorway. Meanwhile the man suddenly turned his back to us and became deeply engrossed in some menus that must have required his undivided attention.

"Even he is a funny little man," LC opined.

"Yeah," I rumbled. "That place appears to be loaded with funny little men."

While we silently continued onward toward the motel, José remarked, "If that's an example of Big Brother's Mormon supporters, I've just lost my respect for the church."

"Those guys weren't Mormons," Pancho rejoined, "but they surely fitted our concept of what Big Brother's minions look like: dark-skinned, evil-eyed, and just plain weird."

"I didn't see them in quite the same light," José objected. "The way I saw them. . . ."

"Stop it, you guys," I mumbled.

"I beg your pardon," LC interjected. Then she fixed worried eyes on me while we strolled on in silence toward the motel.

Before returning the car to the rental agency, we stopped at a service station and stuffed its tank with gas to avoid the agency's exorbitant refill charge. To that point we had traveled three thousand miles on the button, and the car stood seven miles from the airport, so we had rambled around over a relatively large part of the continent in just a week. And the air travel to and from the City of the Saints doubled the distance.

Despite LC's signature on the contract, I chose to turn in the keys at the rental agency's depot. When I entered the stuccoed, one-story, wood-frame office building and moved toward the long counter, one of two mature women turned from a task and looked at me; then she abruptly stopped what she was doing and stared at me. Just beyond her a small man in a brown-tweed business suit also looked at me with an expression that quickly changed from one of indifference to one of curiosity.

While the woman and I approached the counter, she inquired, "Can I help you?"

My eyes fixed pensively on hers, but her eyes repeatedly wandered away from them. "I would like to report a minor mechanical problem on this vehicle," I responded, tendering the keys to her.

Meantime the small man began to trudge toward us with an interested air, while the woman stood wordlessly before me with the keys dangling from her lax fingers. When he came to a stop beside her, she turned to him with a relieved expression and murmured, "Maybe you should handle this." Then she darted away.

In part the man's expression changed to one of extreme congeniality as he asked, "What seems to be the problem?"

I continued to study his probing eyes while my mind slowly formulated a reply. "Well," I drawled, "we drove the car onto a shoulder at the Bingham mine and picked up a gob of tar in the tread of the right, front tire. Even though I had a service station mechanic remove most of it with a screw driver, the car still shimmies at speeds above forty miles per hour. Obviously, it'll require more attention before it's delivered to the next customer."

"I'll have the problem looked into," he promised. "Thank you for reporting it to us."

"Since the problem developed while the car was in our possession, it is the least that I could do," I mumbled, uneasily suffering the man's strange stare.

"Did you have a nice trip?" he asked, and his eyes continued to probe my features.

"Yes," I replied. "Indirectly we drove some three thousand miles between here and Expo Eighty-six, and the car behaved beautifully."

"Fine, I'm glad it did," he responded with an air of dismissal. So I turned away with a relieved sigh.

In the meantime both sides of my brain began to analyze the man's strange behavior. "Without doubt," José began, "it was initiated by some of Big Brother's machinations."

"But did you note how much his curiosity faded after he talked to Al for a while?" countered his mate.

"Yeah," José replied. "Maybe flying saucers wouldn't create so much curiosity and excitement if their observers could get close enough to them to discover that they really are not flying saucers."

"Obviously human minds create many more problems than they solve," Pancho opined.

Salt Lake City to Ontario

In general, the return flight was relatively uneventful. We were assigned to a pair of seats located directly behind two deadheading pilots, who occupied the first two seats aft of the entrance on the left side of the aircraft. Even though they were only pilots, one of them seemed to demand a lot of service from the stewardesses. For example, shortly after the craft landed at the Ontario terminal, the pilot in the aisle seat looked back and imperiously signaled to one of the busiest stewardesses, and she hurried to his side.

"Get my topcoat," he commanded imperiously, pointing indiscriminately upward.

The young woman obediently raised the horizontal door located directly above our seats and searched futilely through the storage compartment. Then she stepped forward beside the man's seat and inquired, "Did you mean this one, sir?" duplicating his indiscriminate gesture.

"No!" he retorted irritably. "I pointed directly to it."

"I'm sorry that I misunderstood you," she responded placatingly. Then she stood erect, raised the adjacent horizontal door, and pulled forth the carefully folded garment. Staring pensively down at the back of the man's head, she shook the folds from the dark fabric, neatly folded it, and laid it across his right arm. And he accepted it without a word of thanks.

I silently condemned him for being a chauvinistic boor. His actions reminded me of the many times that I had observed a fat engineering manager as he lolled in his swivel chair and exchanged small talk with an associate while, at his command, his secretary hurried out to get cups of coffee for them. In my opinion such actions are based on the age-old pecking order. Surely human beings should have progressed far beyond that point in the last ten million years. Obviously, however, some of them have not evolved as rapidly as others, and that pilot was about to convince me that he was one of them.

After the door was opened, the two pilots moved forward from their seats into a small alcove to allow the passengers to pass while they waited for associates, possibly the pilots of the craft. Fortunately LC preceded me into the aisle, so she was not in a position to observe the chauvinist as he fixed his eyes on mine.

As usual in such cases, I coldly returned his rude stare until we had passed them. Then, in taunting tones, he called, "Have fun."

"Of course, he wasn't entirely to blame because Al shouldn't have tweaked his beak with his defiant stare," Pancho observed.

"But the *bleeped* pilot should have been smarter than to accept Big Brother's words verbatim," José protested.

"He should have been smarter, period," Pancho rejoined. "But he had already demonstrated the level of his intelligence in his dealings with the stewardess. Obviously she was fully aware of his shortcomings."

Homecoming After we were under way from the airport to our abode, LC relaxed against the back of the seat and sighed deeply.

"You sound tired," I suggested.

"I am," she admitted. "It has been a wonderful trip, but I'm very glad to be home. I don't want to leave again until. . . ."

"Until the next time," I ventured.

"Well," she began with a chuckle, "I suppose that's true, but I don't want it to be right away."

Then she placed an arm against the door and rested her head against it. In the meantime my mind dallied with the many unpleasantnesses that I had been forced to endure so that she could enjoy a brief respite from the tedium of her work. Of course, she didn't know how much I hated such trips, but I refused to penalize her for the products of Big Brother's miscarriages. It was my cross, and I had always been man enough to bear it, but never passively. Some day, and I sensed that it was drawing nigh, I would be in a position to confront that evil entity. My only fear was that fate might intervene before that momentous day.

BOOK 4

THE RETURN OF CHARLIE

33

An Unexpected Visitor

Charlie

I must have been sacked out on the sofa for some time when the door chimes seemed to sound, so things appeared to be a bit hazy as I sat upright, swung my sock-clad feet over its edge, slipped them into my house slippers, and unsteadily arose. Everything still seemed to be somewhat hazy when I arrived at the two carpeted steps leading up to the floor of the entry, so that may have been the reason for the stumble, but I don't remember falling. I fumbled with the door latch for several seconds, and that also seemed to indicated that I wasn't fully awake.

"Charlie!" I exclaimed sharply to the image of the gray-haired man who stood smiling so expectantly at me from beyond the screen door. "I'm sorry, but I must have forgotten that you called to tell me you were coming. Come to think of it, I don't remember that you did call."

"I didn't call because I was sure that I wouldn't be able to get through to you," he replied, "so I decided to surprise you."

"Man, did you ever!" I exclaimed. Then, after a thoughtful pause, I added, "By the way, Charlie, I seem to recall a rumor that the sun had set on you for the last time. In fact, I vaguely remember driving to your home high up on Sunset Crest Drive, where members of your family invited me, along with several other friends and relatives, to celebrate your demise." After another thoughtful pause, I exclaimed, "Man! Are they going to be disappointed!" Then, after studying the man's pallid features, I burst forth: "Or was that entire operation just one big, fat scam to get the Internal Revenue Service off of your tail?"

"No, it wasn't that," he replied. "What you heard is true. Not only do I have an entirely new status but a brand new address."

"Then you came directly up here from . . . ," I began.

"No," he interjected, "I. . . ."

"But how did you get past Saint Peter?" I countered incredulously.

"I didn't," he admitted ruefully.

"Then you are holed up in purgatory," I speculated.

"No," he responded with a hint of irritation, "things on the other side are nowhere near like what some self-proclaimed authorities on the subject claim them to be." Then he stopped, fixed one of his all-too-familiar glares on me, and exploded,

"Al! Don't you have any manners whatsoever? Aren't you going to invite me in?"

"I'm sorry, Charlie," I apologized. Then, hurriedly unlatching the screen door, I pushed it open and added, "Do come in."

While slowly drifting past me, he murmured, "I didn't bring any magazines with me because all of our periodicals are on tapes." Then, favoring his gimpy leg, he cautiously moved down the two steps onto the carpeted floor before adding, "Consequently, we have only to slip a tape into a video recorder and press a button. Then an article or on-site report by one of the world's best news correspondents is displayed on the screen, and his opinions are expressed in a manner similar to those of your TV newscasters."

"That must be very convenient," I suggested.

"And a *bleep* of a lot better, because all of the errors have been corrected," he said. "In fact, you would never recognize an article from one of your news magazines after it has been modified and presented on a video screen in accordance with our high-tech system."

"The articles of our journalists are that bad, huh?" I parried, joining him on the carpet of the living room.

"They are worse than bad!" he retorted. "They are terrible."

"Well, let's go and pour a drink for you," I suggested. "Fortunately most of the Scotch in the last of the two bottles that I got just before you went to the hospital has remained untouched."

"How much is left?" he inquired anxiously.

"It's almost full," I answered.

"Let's see," he murmured thoughtfully. "When the liquid contents of liquor bottles were changed from a fifth of a gallon to equivalent liters, they ended up at some seven hundred fifty milliliters, so that bottle could still have close to seven hundred milliliters in it." After mentally checking his calculations, he mumbled, "Hmm, that may be enough."

Characteristically he followed me into the kitchen, where I opened one of the two cabinet doors above the range, removed a whiskey bottle, and placed it on the tiled deck near the porcelain sink. As I turned toward the refrigerator, my eyes swept across the man's six-foot frame, and, despite his previous illness, they found it unchanged. Not only were his shoulders broad and erect, but the width of his torso still appeared to continue straight down from his armpits. In creating a caricature of him, a cartoonist might begin by placing a close-coupled head on a somewhat paunchy, bricklike body. Then he would add a wild, Hawaiian sport shirt and allow it to hang loosely over the hips of a pair of too long, light-brown, plaid shorts. Of course, a really good cartoonist would stop the shorts just above of a pair of knobby knees and add two pipe-stem legs. He also would add a pair of noisily colorful three-quarter-length socks and a pair of large sport shoes. To properly embellish the head, he would add a substantial amount of conservatively cut gray hair, gray eyebrows, blue-gray eyes, a relatively prominent nose, and a large mouth with thick, sensuous lips surrounded by a white moustache and a small, white goatee.

After removing a tray of ice cubes from the refrigerator, I slipped it out of its plastic storage bag into the sink.

"That was a clever idea, Al," Charlie said. "I'm going to suggest that the association adopt it so our ice cubes don't melt away during the defrost cycles."

"The bag also guards against the absorption of frozen-food odors by the ice cubes," I said. "Consequently, the taste of your Scotch isn't impaired by contaminated ice cubes."

"Unfortunately we don't have any Scotch," he muttered.

"You don't have any Scotch!" I shouted. Then, with a stabbing stare, I asked, "Are you sure that you didn't end up in the bowels of the earth along with that horned critter with the forked tail?"

"I'm sure," he insisted. "Honest, Al, it isn't hell. True, some things could be a lot better. For example, since your surgeon general discovered that cigarettes are bad for people's health, the association has outlawed them, too." Then he stopped short, glared at me as if I were responsible for his problems, and shouted, "Can you top that! The association has outlawed both liquor and cigarettes for people who have no physical organs whatsoever! Wye, that law is almost as as bad as some of those generated by your Congress. Nevertheless, as stupid as some of those laws obviously are, sometimes I regret my decision to voluntarily check out from this earth."

Nodding sagely, I murmured, "I suspected that you had something to do with it."

"What else would any smart man do?" he countered with challenging eyes. "It would have been stupid of me to suffer needlessly through terminal cancer of the liver."

"Very likely that was a product of too many heavy saturations of Scotch," I ventured.

Staring stonily at me, he defiantly claimed, "It can't hurt me now: no liver." Then, frowning deeply, he added, "But no Scotch either."

"Hmm," I mumbled. "That really must be hell."

"It's not hell!" he shouted. "How many times do I have to tell you that?" Then, after a pause, during which his mind must have interpreted my statement in its proper perspective, he resumed, "Nevertheless, it does have some of the aspects of hell. For example, just before the association was about to toss me into the fiery depths, some of its softer hearted members responded to my pleas for clemency. However, before they would sponsor me, they forced me to sign an agreement never to use cigarettes, liquor, or foul language on the premises. Even though I signed it, I'm still on probation, and that bothers me no end." After a thought-filled moment, he added, "In fact, no end bothers me a lot."

"That really must be hell," I muttered.

"It isn't hell!" he retorted. "And I'm going to prove it to you." Pausing until it became apparent to him that I was hooked, he continued: "One time, while all of the members of the association were in the conference room, I unlocked and pushed down the spring-loaded trap door in the floor of our club room and peeked into the glowing pit below. Of course, that was against the rules, but an evil demon made me do it."

With a knowing nod, I said, "Obviously you won't be on probation very much longer. But what did you see?"

He stared pensively at me for an unreasonably long time. Then, sensing that frustration was about to drive me up a wall, he said, "You'll never believe what I saw, Al."

"Well, what in *bleep* did you see?" I shouted.

"Okay, okay," he responded, "I'm coming to it. There's no reason for you to get your *bleeps* in an uproar, and there's certainly no reason for foul language."

"You twenty-four-carat phony," I fumed. "That's a classic example of the kettle calling the pot black. But get on with the story."

After very deliberately pausing, he scratched the back of his neck, paused again, and finally murmured, "As I was about to say, I unlatched and pushed down the spring-loaded trap door in the floor of our club room and peeked into the glowing pit below."

"You've already said that," I interjected bitterly.

"Yeah, but you interrupted my train of thought," he protested virtuously.

"All right, all right," I growled. "But go on and tell me what you saw."

"Apparently that trap door opens into the dressing room of some very exotic chorus girls," he responded with glistening eyes. Then he paused and fixed a preoccupied gaze on the tray of melting ice cubes.

"Go on," I urged him.

"Well," he began. Then, after very deliberately pausing, he scratched the back of his neck, paused again, and added, "Without doubt those were the most beautiful women that I've ever seen."

"Were they nake . . . ," I began; then I hurriedly added, "I mean: How were they dressed?"

"Like chorus girls, of course," he retorted.

"All right!" I shouted. "Go on, go on!"

"They must have heard my gasp of admiration," he resumed, "because they immediately looked up at me, but not one of them appeared to mind my peeking in the least. In fact, one particularly voluptuous brunette seemed to take quite a shine to me, because she began to give me the eye right off. Then some blondes and redheads began to give me that come hither look, too, but I prefer brunettes, so. . . ."

"That's obvious," I interjected. "Your wife is also a voluptuous brunette."

He stopped right on dead center, eyed me coldly, and complained, "Why did you have to bring her up at this particular time? Surely you realized that it would make me feel untrue to her."

"I'm sorry," I apologized. "But go on with the story."

"Well, the brunette was not about to be outbid by those pasty blondes and redheads," he said, "So right there on those glowing coals she began to do a particularly seductive dance with lots of undulations and even some bumps and grinds."

"There's nothing new about that," I muttered. "Minus the glowing coals, that can be seen every night of the week at any of the local discos and on several of the TV channels. It's no wonder that the burlesque theaters have had to resort to pure porn to survive or submit to Chapter Eleven, because the competition from the other so-called entertainment media has become *hor-end-ous*."

For some reason he glared at me, possibly because I had both interrupted his story and denigrated it. "But you should have seen that brunette perform," he resumed dreamily. "In fact, all of those beauties were as hot as Fourth of July firecrackers, so. . . ."

"No wonder," I interjected. "The ambient temperature down there must have been as hot as hell."

After another glare he resumed: "So I suddenly decided that we should become better acquainted; however, when I started to climb down through that opening, one of the other inmates tapped me on the shoulder and whispered to me something that stopped me cold." Turning stark, distraught eyes to me, he forlornly murmured, "Of course, you are too naive to know about such things, Al, but that guy told me that those perfectly gorgeous gals have no. . . ."

"I know, I know," I interjected, "and that's the hell of it."

"How did you know that?" he countered with a startled expression.

"Well, that's not quite the way I heard it," I confessed, "but it corresponds closely to a very old story that a very old traveling salesman told me ages ago." Moving a step closer to him, I placed a consoling right hand on his left shoulder and said, "Don't let that unfortunate experience upset you, Charlie. With time off for good behavior, eventually you may qualify for an assignment in the upper level. Things of that nature may be a lot better up there; however, I greatly doubt it."

"No, I'm better off where I am," he insisted. "Even though we have no vacations or a pension plan, we do have all the benefits of the most advanced technology, and we don't have to stoke any furnaces or preen any feathers." He stopped abruptly, looked intently at me, and said, "For your information, Al, my current address is Space Level Zero. In case my probation is rescinded, the lower one is Space Level Minus. The upper one is Space Level Plus, but don't bother to send a letter to either of those other addresses, especially to Space Level Minus."

"Ahem," I rumbled. "Since paper is flammable, I see your point."

"Unfortunately those names are needlessly long," he observed. "And that also applies to the name *association*. Immediately after arriving at Space Level Zero, I suggested that the name *association* be abbreviated; however, not only did the members unanimously vote down my three-letter version of it, but they threw me into the brig for a month."

After a thought-filled moment, I nodded knowingly and said, "I understand why they turned it down, but I don't understand why you were thrown into the brig for only a month."

Turning startled eyes toward mine, he glared at me and growled, "What the *bleepin' bleep* is holding up my drink? Stop fooling around with all of this trivia and get into high gear with it."

"I'm sorry, Charlie," I apologized, hurriedly opening another cabinet door. From a shelf I quickly removed two nearly hemispherical glasses, on each of which the word *RAMS* was etched midway of one side. After placing the glasses beside the tray of ice cubes and removing a pair of tongs from a drawer, I loosened the cubes with a quick twist and placed three of them into each glass. The same cabinet drawer produced a one– and one-half–ounce jigger, which I set on the deck beside the glasses. Picking up the whiskey bottle, I unscrewed its metal cap and poured enough liquor into the jigger to inundate its top line; then I transferred the liquor into one of the glasses and repeated the operation two times. Another trip to the refrigerator netted a half-gallon plastic container of chilled spring water, from which I removed the red plastic top and poured enough of its contents into the liquor-free glass to float the tops of the three ice cubes to a point just short of its rim.

Picking up the glass containing the liquor, I thrust it into Charlie's hands and commanded, "Say when."

Eagerly clutching the glass in both hands, he rested the bottom of it against the top of his paunch while I suspended the opening of the water bottle over it and slowly tilted the bottle into a horizontal position.

"When!" he shouted urgently.

"But I haven't poured any water yet," I protested.

"I know," he retorted, "but I don't want you to spoil it."

"I won't spoil it," I promised. Then, squeezing the flexible bottle just a smidgen, I allowed a single drop of water to trickle from the opening into the liquor.

"When!" he screamed.

"Okay, okay," I muttered. "I wasn't about to pour any more into it. After all of these years, I should know how much water you want in your drink."

He paused and peered into the libation with the anticipatory expression of an urchin who was about to indulge his favorite sweet tooth. Finally, raising the glass to his lips, he slurped loudly while I literally cringed from the repulsive sound. Then, with a benign smile, he returned the glass to its seat on his paunch with his right hand and wiped several tears from his eyes with the other one.

"Ahhh!" he exclaimed with an ecstatic expression. "It's just right."

Then he coughed so convulsively that a few drops of the liquor splashed from within the glass onto the front of his lurid shirt. After carefully touching his right forefinger to each of the drops, he placed the finger between his lips and sucked noisily on it.

In the meantime I stood by and thought: What a revoltingly gluttonous creature that man is. "Charlie, that poison's going to be the death of you yet," I grimly predicted.

"Yep, it was the liquor that did me in," he granted indifferently.

"Oh, yeah, that's right," I muttered. "I keep forgetting that party up at your home and the reason for it."

After scanning the area, he growled, "Don't you have even one comfortable chair in this *bleepin'* place?"

"Of course, we do," I retorted. "Furthermore, you know exactly where to find it. Actually, you should send LC a check for a new recliner, because you've practically worn out the recliner that she purchased to relax her arthritic joints."

"We don't use checks in Space Level Zero," he responded with an air of smug satisfaction, moving through the dining area toward the living room. "We rely entirely on electronic devices."

"Here, let me clear that ashtray for you," I proposed. Then, hurriedly removing it from the lamp stand that stood beside the recliner, I dumped its accumulation of buttons, needles, pins, and bits of thread into LC's adjacent sewing basket. After moving a coaster into a more convenient position on the lamp table, I went to get my glass of water on the rocks.

When I returned, the man was starting a cigarette. After the flame reluctantly took hold, he slumped against the back of the big chair and inhaled deeply. Recalling the association's edict, the fag surprised me for several reasons, and one of them was the lack of readily available cigarettes, since neither LC nor I smoked.

"Where did you get that cigarette?" I asked.

A sly smile crept across his pallid features. "There's more than one way to skin a cat," he answered.

"That may apply to skinning a cat," I conceded, "but it doesn't explain where you got that cigarette."

"I have a whole pack of them," he crowed. Removing the pack from a shirt pocket, he triumphantly waved it over his head.

"Okay, so you stopped at a market and bought a pack," I speculated.

"How in *bleep* could I ever buy anything at a market?" he asked. "Not only did the undertaker filch all of the change from my pockets, but the association issues scrip to us, so how could I buy anything at a market?"

After briefly pondering the question, I admitted, "I don't know, but I'm in no mood for this question-and-answer game, so you tell me how you got them."

The sly smile returned. "Well," he began, "I've already told you that Space Level Zero possesses the most advanced technology in the whole Space System."

"So?" I said.

"So I've spent a lot of time in our technical library," he responded.

"And you cut up the pages of some technology books into fine flakes and stuffed them into slender cylinders of tissue paper," I suggested.

"Naw, that wouldn't have been any *bleepin'* good," he retorted contemptuously. "I used the books to determine which of our bushes to select; then I added a small amount of the gardener's insecticide to the leaves from one of them. In fact, I've even considered patenting the idea, because my method is much simpler than growing and processing tobacco leaves. Our gardener has missed the boat by being so stingy with the insecticide. If he had increased the strength of the spray to the level that I employed, he could have harvested a fine crop of tobacco directly from those particular bushes."

My incredulous eyes literally clamped onto his. "And what's the principal ingredient of that particular insecticide?" I asked.

"Nicotine, of course," he admitted. "What of it?"

"So most of that insecticide is derived from tobacco plants," I retorted. "Consequently, it's much easier and more economical to grow tobacco plants and make tobacco directly from their leaves."

After briefly focusing his eyes on the ceiling, he exclaimed, "Ohhh! That's right. It is a more direct method."

"Furthermore," I resumed, "not only is the nicotine in that insecticide extremely concentrated, but very likely other potent bug-killing chemicals were incorporated." Stopping abruptly, I carefully studied his pallid features. "Man, throw that thing away right now!" I hurriedly commanded. "It can kill you!"

After fixing his eyes on mine for an instant, he burst into uproarious laughter. "Don't be ridiculous, Al," he said. "How can it kill a dead man?" Then he took a long drag on the fag, inhaled deeply, blew two beautiful smoke rings, and accurately speared each of their centers with a stream of the vile-smelling smoke.

"Oh, yeah, I forgot again," I muttered while coughing deeply and frantically fanning the murderous fumes away from my head with an open hand.

Charlie on Religion

"Meanwhile I'm trying to figure out how to make alcohol out of some of the foodstuffs in Space Level Zero's pantry," Charlie resumed in the arrogant tones that he was so prone to employ. "Obviously I'll need another source of liquor after you join me."

"Who says that I'm going to join you?" I countered.

"Aw, Al, you wouldn't take the high road when I took the middle road, would yuh?" he protested. "Surely you wouldn't choose to spend eternity with that bunch of goodie-two-shoes up there, would yuh? Huh? Who would you play chess with?"

"I had the impression that you were a confirmed atheist," I rejoined. "How come this sudden reference to heaven?"

"I wasn't referring to a heaven," he retorted. "I was referring to Space Level Plus."

"Apparently Space Level Plus has many of the characteristics of heaven," I observed.

"Who knows anything about heaven?" he countered stubbornly. "Has any earthling seen this so-called heaven?"

"Well," I began thoughtfully, "according to the Bible. . . ."

"The Bible, bah!" he interjected sharply. "According to one philosopher, now defunct, the Bible is nothing but a pack of lies created by several different people. For that reason most of the scientific community ignores it. Furthermore, according to physicist Alan Guth, who discovered the theory of the inflationary universe, the laws of physics point away from a designer in the creation of the universe."

"But he admitted that the universe may have been the only free lunch," I countered. "Furthermore, he claimed that it could have been created in someone else's basement. Don't those opinions imply a suspicion that a potential designer may have been involved?"

"Well, Guth may have been a bad choice," he admitted reluctantly.

Having gained a momentary advantage, I said, "According to the beliefs of another physicist and Nobel Prize winner, Steven Weinberg, the more the universe becomes understandable to mankind, the more it seems to lack objectivity. Don't those beliefs imply a certain disenchantment with the current physical knowledge of the universe?"

"Nobody's perfect," he retorted philosophically. "Least of all, any scientist."

"That's so true," I said. "For example, after some recent research a group of scientists have arrived at the conclusion that there may not be any other life out there in space after all."

"That's typical of the scientific community," he rejoined. "About the time that one group of scientists has firmly established certain scientific philosophies, another group proves those philosophies to be mistaken."

"Meanwhile, billions of our tax dollars are being wasted on these mistaken scientific philosophies," I complained.

"I've been doing some pretty deep thinking," he said, "and I've come to the conclusion that everything on this earth has been beautifully engineered. Furthermore, the same fine design techniques appear to have been employed on the solar system; otherwise the sun, the moon, and the other planets wouldn't function so well."

"So you've come to the conclusion that there must have been a master mechanic in the wings," I suggested. "That conclusion requires no great intelligence, since most of the world's least informed people, including the aborigines and several brands of jungle savages, have drawn similar conclusions throughout the last several millenniums."

"That's what bothers me," he muttered. "The fact that so many of the world's dumbest people have some sort of a deity, sometimes several of them."

"But your recent experiences must have changed your point of view somewhat," I suggested.

"True," he admitted, "but I've uncovered no evidence of a deity."

"If there were such a deity," I began thoughtfully, "he would never permit the bad guys of this world to win so consistently over the good guys; consequently, Big Brother would have been clapped in chains long ago."

"So you've come around to admitting that this whole mess started with the 'Big Bang,' " he speculated.

"Not necessarily," I replied, "because no one has been able to tell me who triggered the Big Bang."

"It could have evolved from a repetitive cycle of expansions and collapses of the interstellar mass," he suggested. "And all of that so-called fine engineering may have evolved from billions of years of gradual physical adjustments and alignments. Perhaps the next collapse of the universe and subsequent Big Bang won't come about for billions of years. After that who can predict that there won't be another earthlike planet with some form of life on it? Or several of them for that matter?"

"That touches on Friedman's Big Bang theory," I said. "But how about the Steady State theory . . . and the Plasma Universe theory."

He paused and slurped annoyingly. "Let's not waste any more time on a subject that no two people ever completely agree on," he suggested. "However, before dropping it, I would like to point out that if some deity did create this mess, he had to possess an enormous amount of power. Therefore, he should have sufficient power to control all of the human beings on this relatively small earth, but such has not been the case. In fact, humanity is rapidly destroying everything on this planet."

"Okay, then humanity may be stronger than its creator," I ventured. "Consequently, like billions of maggots, it may eventually destroy the earth and the entire universe."

Charlie turned worried eyes to me and exclaimed, "Hey! That's getting into my territory! Why don't you guys get organized and do something about it? We don't have much in Space Level Zero, but we don't want it to be destroyed by a bunch of dumb earthlings."

"That's the primary problem," I said, "too many dumb earthlings. According to one survey, over ninety percent of them are dumb."

"And some of the remaining eight or nine percent aren't even that smart. Hey, Al?" Charlie probed with a teasing smile.

"Speak for yourself, Charlie," I retorted firmly.

But he chose to generalize: "The intelligence of human beings is the most overrated commodity on earth."

"But their politicians keep telling them otherwise," I observed. "Of course, they have ulterior motives."

Charlie nodded, raised his glass, slurped maddeningly, and said, "There's one thing about Space Level Plus that bothers me though."

"What's that?" I inquired.

After again slurping maddeningly, he answered, "In the ceiling of Space Level Zero's club room I recently discovered a second trap door that's located directly above the trap door in the floor."

Sensing a sudden surge of interest, he paused and blew a couple of smoke rings and surreptitiously studied my reactions. Despite my resolve not to cater to his sadistic nature by clamoring for more information, I suddenly sensed that my eyes were avidly searching the room for some sort of bludgeon.

"You'll never believe this, Al," he insisted.

"Just try me, Charlie," I pleaded distractedly. Meanwhile I firmly clasped the fingers of both hands into fists to keep their nails from clawing my face.

A delighted gleam leaped into his eyes. Leaning forward and peering closely at my features, he inquired, "Are you feeling well, Al? You appear to be extremely tense and overwrought. Maybe you'll be joining me sooner than you expect to."

That was the proverbial last straw. "Charlie!" I shouted furiously. "Never will I join you! I'll go to hell first!"

Realizing that he had gone too far, he quickly stated, "As far as I know, that upper trap door is rarely used. To my knowledge it has been used only once during my residence in Space Level Zero. At that time I happened to be standing beside the lower trap door, planning a course of action for the next conference of the association, when a tremendous uproar erupted from overhead. I first mistook it for thunder, but there's no atmosphere in space, so I realized that it couldn't be thunder."

He paused, ostensibly to drag on the fag, but an evil glint from the corner of one eye indicated otherwise. Eventually he resumed: "I didn't have sufficient time to properly analyze the situation before the upper trap door suddenly burst open, and a figure clad entirely in a white, diaphanous fabric hurtled through the opening, zipped past me like that, slammed against the lower trap door, and flashed through the opening." Then he sharply swept the palms of his hands past each other, indicating the speed of the action.

"Hmm," I mumbled. "Saint Peter must have gotten pretty mad. Huh? But why would he cast an angel directly into hell?"

"How was I to know?" he asked irritably. Then, recognizing his departure from character, he quickly added, "That is, if it was an angel, and if it was Saint Peter who did the casting. However, I happened to notice that the fingers of the figure's right hand clutched the strings of a bra, which trailed it into the pit."

"Oh-oh!" I exclaimed.

"Yeahhh," he murmured pensively, "but I don't see why mild hanky-panky like that should warrant such a severe sentence. Now if that had been an even more intimate garment, say a pair of. . . ."

"Yeah!" I loudly interjected.

After favoring me with a glance that literally dripped irritation, he added, "That action might have been justified."

"But that may not have been the figure of an angel," I said. "You didn't mention any wings."

"Well," he drawled pensively, "that bothered me for a while too. However, I finally concluded that during the uproar the wings were stripped from the figure in somewhat the same manner that the insignia of a court-martialed officer is stripped from his uniform before he's thrown into the brig."

After suspiciously studying the man's eyes, I said, "Regardless of your oft stated views on religion, I'm going to make a salient observation: You obviously suspect that the figure was that of an angel, even though you have no proof of it. Doesn't that constitute faith?"

"I have no proof that the figure had possessed wings," he admitted. "But when it plummeted through that upper opening, a couple of white feathers fluttered through it."

"How do you know that it was a male angel?" I skeptically countered. "For some unknown reason I've always assumed that since angels are usually depicted as feminine creatures, they have to be females. Besides, I've never known any man who could qualify as an angel. In fact, that bra might have belonged to the outcast."

"If so, a male in drag may have slipped through the gate," he suggested.

"That's extremely unlikely," I said. "Especially if it was Saint Peter who made that pitch. I doubt that he would ever allow one of those critters to get within a hundred light years of his pearly gates. Furthermore, I doubt that the figure ever bore anything with feathers on it."

"I suspected that you would doubt me," Charlie muttered wryly, "so I brought along the proof!" Then, thrusting a thumb and forefinger into a shirt pocket, he raised two white feathers aloft and waved them triumphantly overhead.

His gloating eyes so irritated me that I rashly rejoined, "So you found a couple of white wyandotte chicken feathers. All that you need, now, is a beaded headband, and you can join the next Wyandot Indian powwow." But even I realized that the weak rejoinder contributed nothing to the argument.

Charlie on the World's Problems

While I continued to sulk, that man absently reached for the glass, raised it to his lips, slurped irritatingly, returned the glass to the coaster, belched loudly, and leaned back against the recliner. Then he swept the fag to his lips, drew heavily on it, inhaled noisily, and exhaled a smoke-filled sigh of supreme contentment.

Finally he broke what normally would have been silence: "Well, Al, which of the world's problems shall we solve today?"

"The huge Russian bear is still pounding on the poor little Afghanistan mountain goat," I volunteered.

"Yeah," he agreed, "and Iran hasn't subdued Iraq yet. But let's pick one that's closer to home base, such as Panama and its canal."

"Oh, that one infuriates me!" I exclaimed.

"I expected it to," he responded with a self-satisfied smile. "I still remember the comment you made in your letter to President Carter just after he promised to give that hundred-billion-dollar gem to Panama at the end of this century."

"But he earned that comment," I growled. "Nobody in his right mind would ever turn over a valuable canal to a tiny Central American state that's currently controlled by a corrupt warlord. The least that he should have done was to sell it to Panama for an amount equal to its assessed value."

"Don't be ridiculous," he retorted. "Panama doesn't have that kind of money. But the canal really should remain in the hands of the U.S. because of its important military value. Furthermore, in the hands of that despot, Noriega, it could be used to bleed the world's shipping industry. But Carter didn't do that all by himself."

"President Ford agreed with him," I granted, "but he never distinguished himself by any excesses of good judgment either."

"I'm referring to the Congress," he retorted, "not an ex-president."

"But the Congress has been making mistakes like that for the last fifty years," I said.

"The presidents have been contributing their share," he insisted. "For instance, Reagan had his Irangate, Nixon his Watergate, Johnson his extension of hostilities in Vietnam, Kennedy his Bay of Pigs and. . . ."

He paused as if seeking assistance, so I added: "And Eisenhower lied to the American people about the Powers incident."

"Hmm, yeah," he conceded. "But all Truman did was take long walks that harmed no one."

"He made the biggest mistake of the lot," I declared.

"What could that be?" he asked incredulously.

"Well," I began, "after the treaties with Germany and Japan were signed, he should have proclaimed that the United States was to serve as the marshal of world peace from then to eternity."

"Aw, he couldn't have done that," Charlie protested.

"Why not?" I countered.

"Well," he began. Then, after stalling for an instant, he added, "That would have been inconsistent with this country's democratic ideals. Besides, policing the entire world would have been too costly, and the taxpayers would have rebelled."

"But I seem to remember many complaints from the taxpayers regarding the loss of American lives and the expenditures of billions of dollars during the wars with Korea and Vietnam," I said. "Furthermore, media protests are already being voiced regarding our potential involvement in the Middle East conflict."

"But the nations of the world have been at war from time to time throughout history," he rejoined, "and nobody is ever going to stop them."

"A couple of aircraft flights to Japan stopped World War Two," I reminded him. "If, after signing the peace treaties, this nation had warned the world at large that nuclear bombs would be dropped on the advancing forces of any aggressive nation, peace could have been maintained. In fact, that air force probably would have had to demonstrate its technique only once to convince all warlike nations that peace on earth had become permanent. Besides, there was a good reason why we could have tapped the other nations for sufficient funds to maintain that small peacekeeping force. After all, who could defy us? No other nation had an atomic bomb."

"Hmm, you may have a point," he reluctantly admitted, "especially when one considers the current costs of the American and Russian weapons arsenals." Then, after a brief study, he shouted, "In fact, that's one *bleep* of a good idea! Why didn't you broach it to someone?"

"I did," I retorted. "I broached it to some of my colleagues, who, of course, were a very small part of the government of this country, but they claimed we couldn't do that, because it would have been inconsistent with this country's democratic ideals." Then, after short pause, I smiled angelically at him and added, "Consequently, I didn't present the idea to Truman and suggest that he call a special session of the House and Senate to adopt it."

Charlie on the Nation's Problems

Apparently he recognized his words, because he scowled deeply and tacked back to a previous subject. "Actually, Roosevelt was the biggest stinker of the lot," he claimed.

"Why?" I inquired.

"Because he caused Pearl Harbor," he replied. Then, in response to my skeptical expression, he added, "Surely you remember what that admiral reported in the book that I loaned to you."

"As I told you when I returned that book to you, I never found enough time to read all of it," I retorted. "Nevertheless, I agree with you but for a different reason: I hold FDR responsible for initiating our present socialistic government."

"Naw, he wasn't responsible for that," Charlie insisted. "The Democratic party introduced and sponsored all of the socialistic programs."

"The party did help," I conceded, "but Roosevelt was the prime mover. Since his time the Democrats have continued to use socialistic issues to buy votes, and the practice has cost our taxpayers billions of dollars in government giveaways, bungling, and corruption."

"Then the Democratic party really should be reidentified," he suggested with a wry smile, transferring the fire from an all but burned out butt to the end of a fresh cigarette.

"What do you claim it should be called?" I asked.

"The American Socialist party," he retorted with sparkling eyes. Then, in response to the doubt in my eyes, he asked, "Why not? After all, it's the party that has espoused all of the socialistic programs, including Social Security, Medicare, and the other welfare programs."

"Well," I drawled, "basically that's so, but a few dumb Republicans voted for some of those goodies too. But I seem to remember that there already is an American Socialist party."

"But those were the smarter Republicans," he insisted with a chuckle. "They also knew how to buy votes with the taxpayers' money. As for that other American Socialist party, since the two parties seem to have the same political objectives, let them join forces."

"Yeah, that practice of buying votes with the taxpayers' money is one of the primary reasons that the system doesn't work," I growled. "When I'm president, I'm going to outlaw the transfer of wealth from the nation's producers to its nonproducers."

"However, if you do become president, and may Allah forbid it," Charlie murmured with piously rolled eyes, "you couldn't generate such a law. That function is relegated only to the Congress—and indirectly to the Supreme Court, that is, if it chooses to assume that function—and that it chooses to do much too often for the good of the people."

"And that's another thing that's wrong with the system," I fumed. "This country should never claim to be a democracy as long as the will of the voters can be circumvented by a Congress that deliberately drags its legislative feet so that the Supreme Court is forced to render a politically unpalatable and often very biased decision on an unpopular issue. Then both the Congress and the Court blame the decision on the Constitution."

After pondering briefly, he suggested, "With a socialist congress and a similarly inclined Supreme Court, perhaps the name of the nation should be changed."

"And what might the name be?" I inquired with a suspicious stare.

"Well," he began with a half-smile, "since the Russians call their nation the Union of Soviet Socialist Republics, it would be consistent for this socialistic nation to be called the Union of American Socialist States."

I frowned deeply and firmly shook my head. But he cheerfully ignored me. "Back to the law that you proposed," he resumed. "The law to outlaw the government's seizure and transfer of wealth through discrimatory taxation. You could never get the Congress to even consider such a law, because its passage would destroy the strongest lever that the members of Congress possess for being voted into office and for remaining there." Leaning forward in the big chair, locking his eyes on mine, and assuming a very confidential air, he stated, "The only way that the American taxpayer can survive is to vote the *bleep bleeped* Congress clear out of existence."

After looking warily across one shoulder to see if Big Brother was peering across it, my eyes locked back onto his watery orbs. "But, Charlie," I protested in shocked tones, "You are literally advocating the overthrow of our government."

"So have me thrown into prison," he retorted defiantly. "I'm not the first American to criticize the system and suggest vital changes to it."

"Come to think of it," I said thoughtfully, "how can they throw you into prison?"

"Huh?" he grunted. Then the expressions on his features practically mirrored the rapid acceleration of the wheels within the enclosure behind them. Meanwhile his eyes began to gleam brighter and brighter until they were ablaze. "By *bleep*!" he shouted. "Do I ever have those *bleep bleeped bleeps* of *bleeps* by their *bleepin' bleeps*, and the *bleep bleeped bleeps* of *bleeps* can't do a *bleepin'* thing about it."

"Yeah, but how are you going to suggest your vital changes to them?" I inquired.

He paused with the cigarette halfway to his lips; then his eyes assumed that cloudy appearance that usually indicates intense concentration. Finally they cleared. Absently placing the cigarette between his lips, he drew deeply on it and exhaled a swirling cloud of smoke. Then, with a particularly fraternal air, he smiled at me through the smoke. To me that smile meant only one thing.

"No, Charlie!" I responded violently, "I won't be your fall guy!"

"But you already know how I feel about those things," he murmured with pleading overtones. "Besides, you can present my ideas more tactfully and coherently than I ever could."

I realized that for Charlie those words were a supreme sacrifice, because it was against the man's nature to admit that any other man was superior to him in any respect whatsoever. Nevertheless, I firmly shook my head.

"Aw, Al, you aren't going to cross up an old pal, are yuh?" he pleaded. "All you have to do is to put my words in your computer and run them through the printer."

"And for doing that I could end up in the Bastille," I observed. "Furthermore, that task can become extremely complicated, especially after you've had a few drinks, because there may be more *bleeps* than words on some of the pages."

"Naw, you're a pretty clever lad, Al," he said. "You'll know how to meet every exigency that arises." Then, after employing that *bleeped* fraternal smile again, he added, "You should be pleased to collaborate with me, Al, because you are the only earthling I will trust with such an important assignment."

"That's because I'm the only one naive enough to be conned into it by you," I muttered.

Without leaving the chair, he leaped at the slip and clinched my fate with the words: "So it's agreed."

"Those words weren't meant to imply that I've made a commit. . . ." I began.

Shouldering aside the words, he said, "Your first assignment will be to look at the law concerning illegal aliens."

"If we ignore the fact that it won't work, what is there to look at?" I countered. Then I realized that the old fox actually had trapped me.

"Of course, it won't work!" he ranted. "However, first of all, I want to know why Congress went ahead with the amnesty provision when almost three-quarters of the voters were dead set against it. I seem to remember that this nation was founded on the principle of government of the people by the people."

"The congressmen approved it because they weren't smart enough to determine how to find and dispose of the millions of illegal aliens," I said. "Furthermore, at least one member of the Congress has admitted as much."

"The Russians could do it," he insisted. "Then they would build another Berlin wall along the entire Mexican border and man it with soldiers to ensure that the wetbacks didn't return. If we had any leadership, we could do that too."

"But that would be inconsistent with this nation's democratic ideals," I reminded him. "Besides, what about our shorelines? How would we keep smugglers from putting the aliens ashore from launches? How will we keep the 'boat people' of several other countries from coming ashore when overpopulation in the Third World countries becomes an even greater problem?"

"This nation has several large military forces in training," he replied, "and there's no major reason why they can't be deployed along its borders and shorelines. The Russians effectively guard their borders, so there's no reason why we can't do it. If this nation can't defend itself from an invasion of unarmed aliens, how in *bleep* can it defend itself from armed soldiers trained by an enemy to invade the country and subdue its populace?"

"Apparently some of our impractical democratic ideals should be sacrificed in the interest of national security," I suggested with taunting eyes.

Charlie reached for his glass, placed it to his lips, tipped its bottom up, tilted his head back, and gulped loudly. Then he removed it from his lips, stared accusingly into it, thrust it toward me, and growled, "I can use a refill and a *bleep* of a lot less phony philosophy."

"Okay, Charlie," I said, arising to comply with the request. "I'll be right back."

"And don't put so much water in this one," he called after me.

Several minutes later I returned, placed the recharged glass in his hands, and asked, "What's your opinion of the 'Seven Elves'?"

"The what?" he asked.

"The Seven Elves," I repeated. "In other words, the seven Democrats, mostly senators, who are running for the presidency."

"Then why didn't you call them senators or whatever they are?" he growled.

"Because the news media have taken to calling them the Seven Elves because they are such small-timers," I explained.

"All senators are small-timers," he retorted, "and they'll never be anything else. That's why I've always contended that senators should be barred from running for the presidency—that and the fact that too many stupid people will vote for them because they have become well known."

"But the purpose of an election is to allow the voters to exercise their prerogative to vote for whomever they choose," I objected.

"But they never get a chance to exercise that prerogative," he insisted. "Party politicians decide on the candidate for whom they want the people to vote; then they run him for the office. It's no wonder that only forty percent of the potential voting bloc goes to the polls. Political parties never put up candidates whom the voters can respect."

"In my opinion Teddy Kennedy falls into that category," I muttered. "Nevertheless, millions of voters clamored to vote for him during the last presidential race. As far as I'm concerned, the senators should have drummed him out of office immediately after he pulled that trick at Chappaquiddick, but we don't have any statesmen in our Congress, just politicians."

"Teddy's personal life is none of the voters' *bleep bleeped* business!" Charlie shouted. "A congressman should be selected to represent his constituents, and he should be judged by his ability to do that alone."

"I disagree with that philosophy in its entirety," I shouted. "In addition to being a capable representative of his constituents, any member of the Congress should not only be a man of letters but a man of exemplary moral character."

"Oh, so your congressman has to be a gentleman and a scholar," he retorted contemptuously.

"There's nothing wrong with that picture," I insisted. "The members of the British Parliament endeavor to present that type of facade, and when one of them fails to meet those standards he is expected to resign. If he should fail to do so, I'm sure that he would be tossed out of the House of Parliament onto his pinstripes."

"But there have been more recent and even worse cases than Teddy's," he said. "In fact, there has been a case of statutory rape and one of homosexual acts with a minor within the last two years."

"And the Congress did nothing about them," I rumbled.

"With that caliber of character in the Congress, surely you agree with my contention that congressmen should be barred from running for the presidency," he eagerly suggested like a small boy seeking the approval of a peer.

After briefly pondering the sudden turnabout, I conceded, "I agree in part; however, in addition to being a model of social propriety, a candidate for the presidency should also possess a wealth of experience in leadership, and few congressmen possess it. On a much smaller scale, that kind of leadership can be found in the chairs of the state governments; otherwise we have only the heads of large corporations to resort to unless the top generals of our armed services are utilized.

"Carter was a governor before he became president," Charlie pointed out with a sneer.

"Every president should have good judgment," I hurriedly injected. "Unfortunately I can recall no president who has exhibited that quality to a degree of excellence."

We lapsed into a period of semisomnolence, which Charlie finally ruptured. "But what about the people's morals?"

"That's a potent subject," I conceded. "According to something that I recently read, some two weeks ago New York had a Gay-Lesbian Pride Parade."

"Yeah," he responded, "I read about that in the *New Yorker*.

"I distinctly remember you telling me that you don't get any magazines at Space Level Zero," I rejoined.

"We don't," he retorted. "I should have said that I read about it in a corrected version of the *New Yorker*'s article on one of our video systems." Then, in response to my nod, he resumed: "I can't understand how anybody can participate in that type of a demonstration with pride."

"What bothered me most was the tolerance with which the parade was treated in that article," I muttered. "It actually seemed to defend the actions of those weirdos."

"The article may have been written by a gay," he suggested. "Of course, I don't know what may have been in your article, because ours was cleaned up and corrected for our consumption."

"What did your queer inmates have to say about it?" I inquired.

"We don't have any of those things," he responded with a chuckle. "All of that carrion bypasses our facility on its way into the fiery pit."

"But homosexuals have some well-defined legal rights in this country," I stated. "How does it happen that they haven't acquired similar rights in Space Level Zero?"

"Because they aren't entitled to them," he responded angrily. "They've never had any rights in the past, so why should this government suddenly grant them rights?"

"Because some idiot psychologists claim that they have different sexual impulses than the rest of us," I retorted caustically.

"Impulses that they were never born with, by *bleep*," he retorted. "Mother Nature never intended them to behave that way."

"Without doubt you're right about that," I agreed, "but some psychologists claim that those impulses are inherent in some people."

"*Bleep bleep!*" Charlie exploded. "Mother Nature doesn't work that way. Furthermore, those particular psychologists may be gay, and they may be trying to justify their strange behavior by means of those false claims."

"That makes sense to me," I said. "However, if society continues to cater to those creatures, they'll infect more and more of its members. In my opinion homosexuals should be isolated from society to protect the upcoming generations from their insidious perversions."

"Okay, so we make them crawl back into their closets," he suggested.

"That would be a step in the right direction," I admitted. "At least new generations won't gain the impression that such behavior is accepted by society. But I still say that they should be isolated from society and isolated from each other."

"That may even cure them of their stupid compulsions," he suggested.

"I contend that any human being with a sound mind can control his impulses if he wants to," I insisted. "Otherwise we wouldn't have total chastity among the members of certain religious orders. The behavior of those people is a typical example of the ability of the human mind to prevail over human matter."

After a thought-filled silence, Charlie said, "According to some historians, aside from oral contacts, the Greeks considered no sexual act to be against nature."

"Consequently, the Greek and Roman societies became totally undisciplined," I retorted, "and that's why their positions of power in the world faded. But Plato considered all unusual sexual acts to be against the laws of nature, so he wasn't in accord with those beliefs."

"True," Charlie rumbled. "But Plato also considered incest to be more than just a violation of the existing social conventions, so he may not have been a typical Greek."

"The people who wrote the Bible expressed very firm beliefs regarding some of those sexual practices," I began in a new vein. "For example, quoting from Leviticus, 'If a man also lie with mankind, as he lieth with a woman, both of them shall have committed an abomination: they shall surely be put to death; their blood shall be upon them. . . .' "

"Leave the Bible out of it!" Charlie roared. "It consists of only the rantings of some early Jewish bigots."

"But it does express the philosophies of that culture in those times," I protested. "We could do with some of those philosophies in this country."

Apparently Charlie saw no reason to contest my claims, so we returned to woolgathering for a while. Finally, after clearing his throat, he said, "Actually there's no valid reason why people with AIDS shouldn't be isolated too. People with leprosy used to be isolated so that they wouldn't infect other people, and leprosy has never been considered to be a life-threatening disease like AIDS has. Since AIDS is a deadly product of several different and increasingly popular contact sports that many people are extremely reluctant to give up, it would help tremendously if people who have been infected by AIDs were isolated."

"Unfortunately contact isn't the only way that it's transmitted," I said. "I'll never forget the contempt that boiled up in me when, at the start of the epidemic, a well-known doctor appeared on TV and positively stated that people shouldn't be so terrorized by the disease, because it could be transmitted only by sexual contact."

"Yeah," Charlie growled. "Little did he know about it."

"Right!" I retorted. "At the time I turned to LC and said, 'There's no reason why that disease can't be transmitted by transfusions of contaminated blood and by the bites of certain insects, such as fleas and mosquitoes.' Within a few weeks both of those possibilities were verified by teams of medical scientists. One of this country's biggest problems is the number of self-proclaimed authorities who voluntarily appear on TV and confidently mislead an entire population of gullible listeners by expressing their unvalidated opinions."

"We have shared our contempt for the medical profession several times,"

Charlie reminded me, "so don't expect an argument from me. Recently, however, some medical people have been infected by contact with the blood of AIDS patients, so I've begun to temper that contempt with sympathy."

"And another stupid development stems from legal actions currently under way by AIDS patients to recover damages from some doctors who have refused to accept them in their clinics for that very reason," I muttered.

"Right!" Charlie practically shouted. "That state of affairs has evolved from your ambulance-chasing shysters. In my opinion there's no greater threat to the future of this nation than that posed by the legal profession."

"Charlie!" I exclaimed quizzically. "I already know how much you despise lawyers, but why have you made such a far-out claim?"

He took my measure with a level gaze, so I assumed that his answer would be either unpublishable or of tremendous importance, and it turned out to be both. "The reason why I despise those *bleep bleeped* crooked lawyers is because too many of the *bleeps* turn out to be *bleeps* of *bleepin'* congressmen."

"So you really hate them because they are so well trained in the circumvention of justice as well as the law," I translated liberally.

"That's part of it," he granted, "but you missed one important point."

"No, Charlie," I rejoined, "I didn't miss a thing. From that excellent rendition, I've concluded that you are a very fine judge of both lawyers and congressmen."

His glowing smile would have completely wrecked the features of the average man, but Charlie was no average man. And he proceeded to prove it by thrusting his empty glass toward me. But he was slowing down a bit, so he dispensed with the usual authoritative demand for less water.

Upon returning with the drink, I found that he had moved my huge, unabridged dictionary from the bookcase onto the coffee table. Thrusting the glass toward him, I teasingly suggested, "Just ask me for the spellings or definitions of the words that you're seeking and save the time of wading through the endless pages of that big book."

Instead, he inquired, "How old is this *bleeped* thing, anyway?"

"I don't know," I admitted. "But it was first copyrighted in nineteen three."

Glancing sharply up at me, he said, "You really should get a new one."

"Why?" I asked. "The spellings and definitions of words haven't changed that much during the last century."

"But many words have been added to the English language since that time," he replied.

"If you mean four-letter words, forget it," I recommended.

"Naw," he grunted. "They hark clear back to the era of the caveman. I mean modern words, such as those that have crept into the language in conjunction with new scientific developments."

"But nineteen three was the first copyright date. Remember?" I countered. "The most recent copyright date is nineteen sixty-four."

"Aside from the fact that the book is still old, you deliberately misled me," he muttered resentfully.

"What are you looking for?" I inquired in an effort to sidetrack the trend of the discussion.

"The Constitution of the United States," he replied.

"That's in the back of the book," I informed him. "It starts on page one thirty-five."

"It's in the back of this six-inch-thick tome, and it starts on page one thirty-five," he blurted angrily. "Come on, Al, let's stop the *bleepin'* horseplay. There have to be more than two thousand pages in this thing."

"That's the page number of the index," I explained.

"Oh!" he exclaimed with a self-conscious air. Then, seconds later, he growled, "I'm at page one thirty-five, but this isn't what I'm looking for."

"Well, what in *bleep* are you looking for then?" I asked impatiently.

"I want the Bill of Rights," he retorted.

"Why didn't you tell me that in the first place?" I muttered. "It's on page one thirty-eight."

"After turning to the page, he looked up at me and asked, "How in *bleep* did you know that?"

"We earthlings have some of the most advanced technology in the entire Space System," I answered arrogantly.

"Huh!" he grunted. "You just have a good memory."

"Why the sudden interest in the Bill of Rights?" I asked.

"This country will be celebrating the Constitution's bicentennial in nineteen eighty-eight," he replied, "so I want to develop some ammunition for you to throw at the politicians when they glowingly describe how well that inefficient piece of paper has functioned during the last two hundred years."

"It might work if our legal eagles were smart enough to correctly interpret it," I muttered. "But the Constitution still starts on page one thirty-five."

"I know that!" he retorted. "But I intend to limit our review of it to just the Bill of Rights, because many people are claiming rights to which I am pretty *bleeped* sure they're not entitled."

"Such as . . . ," I said.

"Such as Article One," he muttered. "There aren't quite four lines of print, but your legal eagles have written millions of words defining the limits of those four lines, and all that they have succeeded in doing is to restrict the freedom of every man, woman, and child within the boundaries of this great nation."

"Watch it, Charlie," I warned him. "You're in danger of sounding like a political orator."

"But this is a very serious matter," he insisted. "For example, what would happen if you were to speak out against any one of the other races?"

"Very likely I would be thrown in jail," I replied.

"You're not just woofin'," he muttered. "In some parts of this country that's exactly what would happen to you."

"And in other parts of it I might be thrown in jail for opposing someone who was speaking out against one of the other races," I rejoined.

"And that's another thing that's wrong with the system," he said. "There's no uniformity in the administration of the same laws."

"How does that apply to freedom of speech, freedom of the press, and the right to petition?" I asked.

"But it does apply," he protested. "Don't you see that the rights of individuals are being restricted by the whims of legal administrators in certain sectors of this country?"

"But that's human nature, and human nature can't be changed," I replied. "I'm bothered much more by the news media's policies of employing freedom of speech to justify their deliberate use of suppositions and politically biased opinions during their attacks on some of the nation's most responsible public figures. Some of them seem to delight in their self-appointed roles of king makers—or breakers. I suspect that some of them have been particularly chagrined by Reagan's ability to withstand their attacks throughout his two terms. I'm convinced that Sam Donaldson was particularly irked by that. For instance, when the Iran-Contra affair was first uncovered, he charged in at top speed, and his every malicious innuendo indicated that, by the power vested in his newscasts, he was determined to destroy the president all by himself. That kind of irresponsible behavior can destroy not only the man in power but the country itself."

"Are you referring to that preening and posturing Washington news commentator?" Charlie inquired.

"Yeah," I replied, "the news hound who speaks with a snarl and always acts as if he's impatient to consume the bone of contention before his fellow news hounds can get a woof in edgeways."

"But that situation has prevailed since before the turn of the century," Charlie said. "For example, on February six, eighteen sixty-three, while Sherman was camped at Vicksburg, he wrote at length about the news media. According to him, the newspapers declared him to be their inveterate enemy and openly claimed that they would write him down. Of course, in writing him down, they were writing both the cause and the country down. Sherman also claimed that no army detachment moved which was not attended by correspondents of hundreds of newspapers. Consequently, they encumbered the armies' transports, published without stint vital information on the movements of troops, and even included their commanders' names. In conclusion he claimed that never had an enemy a better corps of spies than the army carried; furthermore, it was paid, transported, and fed by the government.

After a minuscule pause, he added, "The situation hasn't changed much, huh?"

"Obviously the system has never worked," I replied.

"Right!" he retorted. "But let's go on to Article Two."

That egotistical character and I actually tore apart and reconstructed every article in the Bill of Rights during our efforts to create order out of chaos. Of the millions of Americans who have inherited the responsibility of governing themselves, we attacked that self-imposed task as if we were the only ones who were actually doing their parts. Unfortunately that may have been the case.

Apparently we ran out of gas simultaneously, since each of us voluntarily settled back against the backs of our respective chair and sofa and allowed silence to reign for several minutes.

Finally Charlie suggested, "Why don't we summarize the summary of our findings for the benefit of posterity?"

"I doubt that any of posterity will bother to read it," I replied. "Besides, according to several sources, much of the current crop is illiterate."

"You do have a point," he admitted, "but let's assume that some members of the upcoming generations are not only literate but also sufficiently interested in the phenomenal growth of Big Brother to read your book. Consequently, they'll be trapped into reading the summary of our summary."

I looked incredulously at him while the implication slowly filtered through the various substrata of my ivory-clad brain. "But my book is a travelogue!" I protested violently.

"*Bleep bleep!*" he retorted. "Your book is about Big Brother and his sins, and it's the logical place for my summary of a summary."

"Why?" I countered.

"Because Big Brother has evolved and flourished under the Constitution of this nation," he answered.

"True," I conceded pensively, "but that wasn't the fault of the Constitution. It was the fault of governmental administrative bodies."

"*Bleep bleep!*" Charlie exploded. "It was the fault of the people for allowing governmental administrative bodies to get so far out of control. After all, the Constitution wasn't designed for government by administrative bodies. It was designed for government of the people by the people. Remember?"

"But the administrative bodies have found ways to circumvent that," I muttered.

"That's because the people are too *bleeped* lazy to exercise their prerogatives," he retorted. "But don't give me any more lip. Get a sheet and a pencil of paper, and I'll dictate the summary to you."

I paused to study the man's flushed features while José and Pancho hurriedly checked his words. Finally Pancho reported, "Yep, that's what he said: 'Get a sheet and a pencil of paper.' "

Warily fixing my eyes on the man, I gently inquired, "Do you really feel up to it at this time, Charlie?"

"If you mean am I drunk," he growled, "what if I am? I can still think straighter than anybody else in this *bleepin'* room."

"Okay, Charlie," I reluctantly agreed. However, since I had been confronted by similar demands from him in the past, I had already resolved to follow my policy of shelving the material as soon as he left.

"And don't plan to shelve this material as soon as I leave," he warned. "If you do, I swear by the horns of old Nick that as soon as you arrive at Space Level Zero, I'll shove you through the trap door into that blazing inferno."

What else could I do but comply with the wishes of a man who was reading my mind? Therefore, the following items are presented exactly as they were dictated to me.

A Summary of Summaries

Item 1. Completely clarify, revise, and adapt the Constitution of the United States and the Bill of Rights to reflect effective government of the people and by the people within the requirements of the current social order.

Item 2. The Congress shall assign to the Navajo Indian tribe the task of recovering the Panama Canal, since Indian givers may succeed where Caucasians might fail.

Item 3. A good con artist, such as ex-president Nixon, shall be assigned the task of conning the U.S. Congress and the Russian Politburo into transferring their nuclear arsenals to the United Nations (UN). The UN shall then employ them to clobber any aggressive army that crosses its borders into another country.

Item 4. The Congress shall not legislate or transfer the funds of any citizen or group of citizens to any other citizen or group of citizens. Meanwhile the Congress shall progressively reduce the budgets of all of the nation's socialistic programs at a prescribed annual rate until they have been eliminated.

Item 5. The Congress shall locate all illegal aliens and extraterrestrials (ETs), including all members of their immediate families, irrespective of place of birth, and extradite them to their native lands or planets. A shuttle may be employed in the transfer of ETs if necessary.

Item 6. The Congress shall require that all of our military forces be withdrawn from foreign soil and relocated along this nation's borders and shorelines to guard them from attacks by any enemy, including drug smugglers and boat people.

Item 7. The Congress shall dissolve big government, that is, the one in Washington, D.C., and reestablish the right of each state government to control the state's destiny. All governmental functions beyond the scope of the states' governments, such as the nation's defense and its foreign relations, shall continue to be the responsibility of the federal government.

Item 8. The Congress shall establish a four-year term for every elected member with half of the seats alternately up for grabs at two-year intervals. No incumbent shall be permitted to campaign for himself or for a party member. Each incumbent shall regain or lose his seat on the basis of his performance record, which shall be submitted to the voters.

Item 9. Since the Congress obviously cannot establish and enforce an appropriate code of ethics for its members, the Supreme Court shall establish such a code, hear the cases of offenders, and delegate punishments through the attorney general's office.

Item 10. The solicitation of taxpayers' funds ($1.00) shall be discontinued. No candidate for public office shall be permitted to withhold excess campaign funds for his personal gain during his tenure or after his retirement. In fact, all such acts shall be deemed breaches of conduct under the rules of the code of ethics.

Item 11. Each citizen of voting age shall retain the right to exercise one vote; however, the vote of each literate voter (assumed to be a high school graduate in this illiterate land) shall carry a double value, that is, the equivalent of two votes.

Item 12. The Congress shall limit its expenditures to the nation's income. No annual budget deficits shall be sanctioned, and the taxpayers shall not be required to insure the safety of either domestic or foreign investments, such as bank loans. Nor shall any part of the nation's wealth be distributed to any foreign nation under any guise.

After pausing momentarily, Charlie muttered, "Al, I'm going to add one that we haven't discussed, but I'm sure that you'll concur with my opinion on it."

"But that'll be Item Thirteen," I protested. "Surely you don't want to invite disaster.

"Why not?" he countered. "After all, this country started with thirteen colonies and look what they turned into."

"I've looked," I muttered, "and I've found that they've turned into a disaster."

"That's not so," he retorted. "Not yet anyway." Then, with a cold glare, he commanded, "Nevertheless, add the following:

Item 13. Upon filing for reelection, each member of the Congress shall submit to his constituents an accounting of all of his major expenditures during his term in office. Furthermore, the salary of each congressman shall be approved by his constituents. There shall be no more voluntary pay increases in open defiance of the voters and no more gratuities or fees for public appearances. All of the congressman's time shall be devoted to the service of the electorate.

"And here's another one," he added in his most domineering manner. "Another one that must be included."

Item 14. The *bleepin'* Congress shall ensure that all citizens enjoy equal rights, including those of public figures, whose rights of protection from indiscriminate attacks and ridicule by the nation's clowns and from similar members of the news media have been blatantly ignored by the courts."

"Maybe we should delete the word *bleepin'*," I suggested.

"Naw, leave it in," he insisted. "It's just punctuation."

After penciling the last word, I said, "There's no logical reason why this stuff should appear in my travelogue."

"Yes, there is," he insisted. "Obviously I can't publish it in Space Level Zero and get it into the hands of the U.S. voters, and that's so obvious that only a dummy would question it. Besides, I'm banking on the book being published in nineteen eighty-eight."

"What bearing does that have on the subject?" I asked.

"Since nineteen eighty-eight is the bicentennial of the Constitution, it will be much in the limelight, so that's the best time to institute reforms to a document that has never really worked, despite the glowing claims of various politicians and journalists. Furthermore, your experiences with Big Brother prove that it doesn't work."

"But the Constitution doesn't specifically cover my problems with Big Brother," I objected.

"Oh, but I strongly suspect that it does," he rejoined with a particularly overbearing air. "It even covers the tendencies of certain governmental agencies, such as the CIA, the IRS, the FBI, and others, to ignore it and ride roughshod over private citizens and small groups of people who have little or no political clout. Actually it's the responsibility of the administration to see that such malfunctions don't occur, but few of its members have done more than campaign for reelection and try to cover up the stupid bunglings of inefficient political appointees. Consequently, the voters may have to create a nonpartisan or multipartite body of responsible private citizens to act as a watchdog over the functions of the administrative branches of the government."

"That could help," I conceded, "but it'll take more than that to dislodge Big Brother, because he has become entrenched throughout the world."

"It would also help if the party moguls presented candidates of higher caliber to the voters," he resumed without commenting on my observation. "But too many of the voters are either illiterate or indifferent to the qualifications of the candidates, and that's anything but conducive to effective government by the people." His eyes turned interrogatively toward me, and I nodded, so he added, "With the advent of women's suffrage, the party moguls have discovered that candidates don't have to know a *bleeped* thing about governing a nation, but they must have both charisma and sex appeal. Consequently, too many of the candidates are popular public figures, such as football players, actors, or astronauts, who have been deliberately selected by the party moguls because they possess not only charisma and sex appeal but wide public exposure."

"I don't have any respect whatsoever for the electorate," I muttered. "If it continues to tolerate the overbearing political posturing of a congressman like a Tip O'Neill, the irresponsible behavior of a Ted Kennedy, and the womanizing, drunkenness, and perverse sexual practices of others, then it deserves the government that it elects, because most of those characters serve only as the tip of an enormous and very corrupt political iceberg."

Break Time

It had been a grueling task, so both of us were content to relax for a while. Eventually Charlie placed his hands on the armrests of the big chair, leaned forward, and slowly pushed himself upright. Then, turning to me, he said, "I would like to borrow your bathroom for a minute."

"It's all yours," I responded with a needless gesture toward the half-bath, which was located off of the small hallway leading from the kitchen to the door that let into the attached garage. Then, as an afterthought, I called, "There are paper hand towels atop the water closet."

Meanwhile I arose, picked up the ashtray, brushed into it several clumps of ashes from the surface of the lamp table, and disposed of the accumulation. Then I washed and dried the tray.

The Gardeners I had just replaced the tray when Charlie sauntered into the room and suggested, "Why don't we take a look at the garden?"

Since the same suggestion had been made dozens of times throughout the years, I could have predicted its timing and his exact words, so it was not by chance that I was meandering toward the far corner of the room. Pausing there, I drew the vertical venetian blinds so that we could push aside the big, sliding, glazed door and step out onto the patio.

"What!" he immediately shouted. "No tomato plants."

"I've told you several times that we don't have sufficient space in this tiny patio garden for them," I rejoined.

"But you had such beautiful tomato plants along that fence at the ranch," he retorted.

"I turned this plot over to LC," I said, "and she chose to plant rosebushes instead of tomato plants."

"Apparently she's a much better gardener than you are," he observed. "Those roses are beautiful."

It was typical of the man to insert a compliment and then try to ruffle my feathers; nevertheless, I mildly pointed out, "As usual, you are comparing apples and oranges."

"Aw, you are just jealous because she's a better gardener than you are," he countered. "Besides, I am comparing roses and tomatoes, not apples and oranges."

That was the man's unique way of making friends and influencing people, but the tactics were so familiar to me that it never occurred to me to be incensed by them. Furthermore, I had finally learned to cope with the problem, so I admitted, "Yes, there's no doubt that LC's a better gardener than I am."

"Aw, *bleep bleep!*" he retorted. "Nobody can grow nicer tomatoes than you can."

I sensed a faint smile, but it wasn't in response to the compliment; it was in response to the man's eagerness to take the opposite side in any debate, regardless of how illogical his claims might have to be.

Losing interest in the garden, he absently mumbled, "Hmm," turned toward the opening, and stepped back into the living room. Pausing beside the lamp table, he frowned down at the empty glass and asked, "Why didn't you get me another drink while I was in the bathroom? You had plenty of time."

"Because I was otherwise occupied," I retorted. Picking up the glass, I turned in the direction of the kitchen.

34

The Book Review

During the preparation of the drink, sounds emanating from the living room seemed to indicate that the television set had been turned to a stock market report. When I delivered the drink, I asked, "Are you still playing the stock market, Charlie?"

After a slurp, he set the glass on its coaster, leaned against the back of the recliner, and belched loudly. Then, in gloating tones, he murmured, "This is sheer luxury, Al. I wonder what the members of the association would say if they could see me now."

"That statement seems to imply that you are AWOL," I suggested. "Are you absent without leave, Charlie?"

The Author

After squirming for a moment, he finally admitted, "Shore. What else? The association would never have approved my application for a pass to visit you." Then he stopped abruptly, pondered briefly, and said, "By the way, Al, when you come to join me, be sure to use an alias, because you'll never get into Space Level Zero under your nom de plume."

"Why not?" I asked.

"Well," he began uneasily, "since you wrote that book, you're sort of persona non grata in Space Level Zero.

"But how can that be?" I inquired. "The book hasn't even been published yet."

"Nevertheless, we have a Xerox copy of it," he replied. "But the association has X-rated it, so we aren't supposed to read it. However, I always read those books first, and that's how I discovered that you had completed it."

"From that statement I'm led to suspect that your association must consist of high-level politicians and bureaucrats," I said.

"No, all of those guys go right past Space Level Zero straight into Space Level Minus," he responded with a derisive chuckle. "Actually the association consists of defrocked priests." Then he laughed outright.

And I joined him, because Charlie doesn't—that is, Charlie didn't—have much of a sense of humor, so I've always encouraged his few humorous overtures.

After the laughter had subsided, I asked, "What did you think of my book?"

"Well, you are one *bleep* of a lot better engineer than author," he answered with a soothing smile.

I had expected such an answer; therefore, since it neither surprised nor miffed me, I mildly claimed, "At least I'm good at something."

"I didn't say that you were a good engineer," he retorted. "I said that you are a better engineer than author."

"According to your words, I'm a *bleep* of a lot better engineer than author," I responded with a glare. "So doesn't that imply that I'm a good engineer?"

"It would if you were any *bleeped* good as an author," he responded with a triumphant expression.

"Hmm," I mumbled while pensively studying the top of the coffee table. "You may have a point; that is, if you are correct in either of those statements."

Accepting the thrust gracefully, he smiled faintly and inquired, "What was the purpose of all of that scribbling anyway?"

"Didn't you get my message?" I countered.

"Yeah," he drawled, "but we've always had a Big Brother, even before George Orwell recognized the beast and predicted the impact of the electronic age on his nefarious activities, so your message has not only been wasted, but it's repetitious."

"Has it been wasted now?" I countered. "How many people know, through the medium of your so-called electronic age, that Big Brother's influence has been spread all over the world? Do they know that people's civil rights are being deliberately ignored in every country that I visited."

Research

"I didn't know that, of course," he reluctantly admitted. "However, after reading that book, I decided to determine why you had been persecuted in every one of those countries, including this one, so I did some research."

"What kind of research?" I inquired, turning hopeful eyes toward him.

"You'll never believe this, Al," he said, "but we have a computer disk with your entire history on it."

"Shades of Big Brother," I muttered. "That's incredible. Nevertheless, under the circumstances I have to believe it. So what kind of earth-shaking history did that disk reveal to you?"

"I couldn't find a *bleep bleep bleepin'* thing against you," he ruefully admitted. "That puzzled me so much that I decided to run the disk on Big Brother to see if I could find some reference to you on it, but I couldn't even find a disk on him."

"Incredible!" I exclaimed. "His political influence must extend all of the way into your association."

"I doubt that," he said wryly. "All of those defrocked priests are nonpartisans. If any of them had been found to possess any political connections whatsoever, he would have been catapulted right through Space Level Zero's trap door into the fiery pit. However, in the library's indexes I did find a listing under Big Brother with a note: 'See CIA, FBI, IRS, KGB, KKK, or any of the several terrorist groups.' "

"I suppose that any one or all of them could be members of Big Brother's massive army," I muttered.

"Under CIA I found nothing," he said. "However, under FBI I immediately struck pay dirt," he added with gleaming eyes. "Back in the thirties, about the time that your problem arose, J. Edgar Hoover was the boss of the FBI, and he rode roughshod over everybody in his organization. If somebody threatened his position, he got rid of him, if. . . ."

"He might have fired the guy or shuffled him onto a back burner," I interjected, "but I doubt that he physically got rid of anybody."

"Maybe," Charlie reluctantly conceded, "but it's alleged that he used his forces to collect dirt on the weirdo politicians in the nation's capital and that he used the dirt to gain his own political ends by applying the tremendous power implicit in such information."

"What did he have to gain?" I asked. "According to what I've read about him, he was an extremely ambitious bachelor with no known vices, and. . . ."

"True, he was a bachelor," Charlie interjected, "but I've read that he often took a specific lieutenant along on his business trips, and. . . ."

"So some evil-minded people assigned a foul purpose to what may have merely been a simple professional relationship," I interjected.

"Defend him if you will," Charlie retorted huffily, "but according to some book reviewers' reactions to a recent book about him, one reviewer who is associated with one of the nation's top newspapers stated that the book is a gripping, nauseating account of an extremely twisted character who manipulated the underside of the American psyche very effectively."

"Those words merely represent one man's reaction to the words in that book," I began, "and. . . ."

"Furthermore," he imperiously interposed, "another reviewer stated that it is astonishing and terrifying that a man like J. Edgar Hoover could have attained so much power in this nation. And he added that the situation hasn't changed, because it could happen again. And a third reviewer claimed that the authors had produced a classic study of how the American democratic system can be corrupted from within on a colossal scale. And he insisted that no one can really understand the facts of raw power in America without reading the book."

"But those were only publicity hypes by well-known literary people to help sell the book," I protested.

"Nevertheless, that man could have been the source of your problem," he insisted. "He was at the helm of the FBI at the right time, and he could have infected his organization with the same sort of disease that appears to drive Big Brother today. Who is to say that the same putrid policies are not still employed by the FBI?"

"I'm sure that J. Edgar Hoover never heard of me," I muttered.

"I'm not so sure of that," Charlie rejoined. "Furthermore, I learned from one disk that you had visited an FBI office in nineteen forty-two. Maybe that was your big mistake."

"But that office was located on the West Coast, three thousand miles from J. Edgar Hoover," I observed. "However, I admit that the visit was a big mistake, since not only did the agent deliberately lie to me, but I suspect that he literally blackballed me for life because I pointed out to him that what he was telling me didn't make any sense. But I finally did collaborate in the stupid program he proposed, and that did prove to be the biggest mistake of my. . . ."

"According to the disk you have no criminal record whatsoever," Charlie injected. "So why should he blackball you unless you antagonized him? Did you antagonize him?"

"Well," I began reluctantly, "I have to admit that he was pretty mad at me for implying that he was lying to me, but that was no justification for the program of character assassination that Big Brother has conducted against me for the last forty-five years."

"How do you know that it began forty-five years ago?" he countered.

"It may have begun before that," I conceded, "but the incident that I'm about to employ as a reference point occurred one evening in nineteen forty-three while a couple of friends, my ex-wife, and I were out bowling. Just as I turned away from making one of my rare strikes, I overheard a young woman say, 'But he doesn't appear to be the type.' "

"But that in itself meant nothing," Charlie protested. "Besides, she could have been referring to someone else."

"But she wasn't referring to someone else," I grimly rejoined. "When I turned away from making the strike, my eyes happened to sweep that area, and I particularly noticed how intently she was staring at me. Furthermore, her young male friend must have been the source of the reference, because he was also staring at me. Consequently, I became so infuriated because my efforts to collaborate with that agent had been turned against me that I solemnly swore an oath to fight fire with fire from that instant on, and I've continued to do so for the last forty-five years."

"So that's the real reason for this book," he ventured.

"One of them," I granted. "But I also intend to complete a very detailed autobiography that will expose many of Big Brother's attacks on me in **this** country. I intend to make that my most telling counterattack. No doubt it will be my swan song, if I last that long."

"But you must not have fought fire with fire," Charlie objected. "According to the disk you've always stayed within the limits of the law. Apparently Big Brother hasn't done so."

"Okay," I responded wearily. "So my fire was merely the glimmer of a candle with which I lighted my way through the impenetrable darkness that has surrounded me during the last forty-five years. Obviously no single individual can successfully fight Big Brother by himself."

"You must have either antagonized or confused someone in a very powerful position," Charlie persisted. "And that opinion is supported by the fact that the attacks were so widely distributed. For example, the incident that occurred late one night in San Diego about thirty years ago."

"But I was living in Los Angeles at that time," I rejoined.

"True," he conceded. "But you made frequent trips back to San Diego, where you had lived for a year prior to that time."

"That must have been the time that I picked up Polly for a night on the town," I suggested.

"I don't remember her name," he said, "but she was a schoolteacher."

"Yes, Polly was a schoolteacher, but I had come to know several pretty schoolteachers in the San Diego school system," I responded with a chuckle.

"Nevertheless, the two of you drove clear out to La Mesa to dine, and. . . ."

"That was because she **was** a schoolteacher," I interjected. "I didn't want to create any problems for her by our happening onto some of her associates, who might have recognized me from one of Big Brother's slanderous distributions, so I deliberately drove out to La Mesa."

"That was thoughtful of you," he murmured. "But the tactic must not have been completely successful, since you acquired an attentive observer."

"Oh, yes," I responded with a chuckle. "You must be referring to the character who was parked across the street from Polly's apartment when I left it at about two o'clock in the morning."

"You really shouldn't have teased that poor guy," Charlie insisted with a laugh.

"But all I did was to shout a message to him," I protested.

"True," he admitted. "But how would you have reacted to the words, 'Okay, you can knock it off now, because I'm going to sack out alone for the remainder of the night'? Especially if you had been staked out for four dark hours in a cold, damp car?"

"It did sort of set him off," I admitted with a reminiscent smile.

"Set him off!" Charlie retorted. "That wasn't the half of it. According to our video's report, he immediately started the car, took off like a rocket, made a tire-screaming U-turn, gunned the motor like he was late for a coffee break with his buddies, and. . . ." Charlie stopped, looked at me with a slow shake of his head, and added, "If you had been standing in the gutter instead of on that curb, the morning papers would have reported that you had been struck by a hit-and-run driver, and I'm not woofin', because that guy had blood in his eyes."

"Maybe," I granted reluctantly. "He was pretty mad, all right."

"But did it ever occur to you that he might have been Polly's steady boyfriend?" he asked.

"No," I replied, "because there was a letter *E* on the car's license plate, which indicated tax exempt, so it must have been a bureau's vehicle. Besides, Polly had claimed that she had no steady boy friend. I've always followed a policy of never knowingly interfering with an established combination of any kind, be it with a gal and her boyfriend or her husband."

After a patronizing glance at me, he archly inquired, "Have you ever considered the possibility that she might have had an occasional boyfriend who was a member of the San Diego police department?"

I studied the question briefly and doubtfully shook my head.

"I still suspect that you've deliberately antagonized too many of the wrong people," he insisted with an admiring smile.

After pondering the smile for a moment, I nodded in response to a recurring suspicion that Charlie had always been extremely anti-establishment. "You used the word *wrong* correctly," I conceded. And he responded with a boisterous laugh.

"I ran across another funny episode on that disk," he resumed. "It covered the time when you picked up a slick chick at that huge U-shaped bar in the Scandia Restaurant. From there the two of you repaired to her apartment, where you stayed an unconscionably long time."

"Oh, yeah," I responded with a reminiscent smile. "I know which one you are referring to, but I don't remember her name."

Turning reproachful eyes to me, he chuckled, shook his head, and added, "But the funniest part developed after the following dinner date with her."

"I don't remember anything particularly funny about it," I muttered.

"Obviously it wasn't funny to you," he said, "but it was hilarious to me." Then he erupted into a series of "ho-ho-hos!" Finally, after wiping the tears of mirth from his eyes, he resumed: "No doubt while the two of you were approaching her apartment the second time, you were expecting another easy conquest. But when you came to a stop before the door, she first glanced apprehensively up and down the dimly lighted street; then she said, 'You may come in for a while, if you like, but you mustn't stay as long as you did last time.' "

"Yeah, that seemed funny to me, too," I agreed. "But it seemed to be a lot more illogical than funny."

"But that wasn't the punch line," Charlie protested. "It came later when she insisted that you leave just minutes after entering the apartment. Remember? And remember when she also insisted, 'Really, I'm not that easy. In fact, I suspect that you hypnotized me last time.' " Then he burst forth with more irritating guffaws. After wiping the tears from his eyes, he burbled, "Al, did you really hypnotize that poor, innocent, little lass?" Then he repeated those *bleeped* irritating guffaws.

"No, of course not!" I retorted with considerable heat. "And she was no poor, innocent, little lass, or she would never have been seated solo at that big bar."

He recovered his usual solemn mien, nodded agreement, and said, "But it struck me as extremely odd that, after accompanying you to the door, she stepped out onto the landing with you and glanced apprehensively up and down the street as if expecting to find someone staked out there."

"That struck me as odd, too," I muttered.

"Maybe she had a boyfriend in the Beverly Hills police department," he suggested with a probing gaze.

"Maybe just a jealous boyfriend," I countered.

Ignoring the possibility, he suggested, "Maybe she used the same alibi on her policeman." Then, in response to my puzzled stare, he added, "Maybe she told him that you had hypnotized her."

"Naw," I retorted. "Nobody would ever believe that, because everybody knows that people can't be hypnotized to do something that is contrary to their scruples."

"Maybe she was unscrupulous," he countered, again with another of those irritating guffaws. Meanwhile, I stared grimly into space.

After a moment of beautiful silence, he resumed: "I'm surely glad that I looked up your history, Al. Now I have the honest to *bleep bleep* on you."

"I'm sure you didn't find anything in it that I should be ashamed of," I muttered. "Plenty that I shouldn't be proud of, but nothing to be ashamed of."

"I found nothing that you should be ashamed of," he admitted, "and much to be proud of, especially the dozens of nubile wenches that you seduced during an interval of some twenty years."

"That's something that no man should be proud of," I murmured. "In fact, it's something that I should be ashamed of."

"If it was against your principles, then why did you do it?" he asked.

After pondering the question for some time, I finally answered, "The primary reason hinged on an incident that occurred at Lockheed's Burbank facility in late nineteen forty-nine. I had been working in the engineering department about three months when I received an offer from a local job shop to work at Boeing's Renton plant for about double my then-current salary."

"But you still had to obtain a release from Lockheed to accept the job," Charlie suggested. In response to my nod, he caustically added, "And they still call this a free country."

Not deigning to respond to the statement, I resumed: "After I put up a big sob story about requiring that much income to pay alimony and still feed myself, Lockheed reluctantly granted my request for a release."

"By *bleep!*" Charlie exclaimed. "The company accidentally did something right for once."

Ignoring the interruption, I continued: "During the morning of my departure from the plant I became locked in a discussion with a tall, acerbic character, named Dave something-or-other, with whom I had been working on a design assignment."

"That must have been the guy who wrecked the chess ladder," he interposed.

"Yes," I replied. "Even though Dave had never played the game, he quickly picked it up during lunch periods by detecting the mistakes of players who were competing for positions on the chess ladder."

"Then he started pointing out those mistakes to the players," Charlie said. "Not only was that against the rules, of course, but it made the players madder than *bleep*."

"Yeah," I responded with a mildly protesting glance. "So one of them finally said, 'Okay, Dave, if you know so *bleeped* much about the game, why aren't you playing it?' And he accepted the challenge. Not only did he beat everybody who would play chess with him, but he started at the bottom of the chess ladder and worked his way to the top." Pausing briefly, I glanced at Charlie and added, "Dave was one *bleep* of a smart cookie."

"I got a big kick out of that particular part of the disk," Charlie murmured. "In fact, the man possessed so many of the characteristics that I admire in a man: intelligence, bluntness, tactlessness, arrogance, and. . . ."

"Come to think of it," I interrupted him with a snide smile, "Dave reminds me so much of another obnoxious character that I happened to meet during a later term at Lockheed."

With a dark glower, Charlie muttered, "Skip the compliments and get on with the contents of that discussion with Dave."

"At one vital point during the aforementioned discussion with Dave," I began, "I was gloating to him about my good fortune, when he suddenly retorted, 'That's all very fine, Al, but there are to be no more girls. No doubt that last one loved it, but there are to be no more girls like her.' " After pausing to study Charlie's intent eyes, I added, "Needless to say, I was struck dumb, because his words didn't make any sense whatsoever."

"He was referring to the redhead," Charlie suggested. "But why should he make such a statement when you never made the grade with her? And why should he say 'there are to be no more girls like her' unless he had been briefed by Big Brother?" He stopped, fixed his eyes on mine, and bluntly asked, "By the way, Al, why didn't you make the grade with that gal?"

Smiling ruefully, I answered, "First off, I was so infatuated with her that my romantic soul refused to lower the relationship to the degrading level of animalistic pleasure."

"Huh!" he grunted. "You and your romanticism. No wonder you lost that little beauty. Very likely she was yearning for some of that animalistic pleasure, so she finally dropped you when you didn't come across."

"But there was another reason," I protested. "Her little, white-haired mother always acted as a chaperon when we were together because she feared that my ex would sue for alienation of affections, and she made sure that there was no justification for it."

"Oh-ho!" he exclaimed loudly. "So it wasn't romanticism after all. It was parental restraint."

"But the chaperon wasn't the primary reason," I protested. "The redhead had occasionally been dating a successful industrialist in the Burbank area before she met me, and one of those dates came up shortly after we were more or less committed."

"Oh-ho!" Charlie crowed. "So jealousy reared its ugly head."

"No, not really," I said. "According to my code of ethics, loyalty is the most important element in the relations of a man and woman. And I looked on that date as evidence of disloyalty. Besides, I suspected that the girl's mother was trying to match her daughter with a successful businessman, and she didn't particularly care who it was as long as he was successful. Even at twenty-five, that girl still accepted her mother's guidance in all matters."

"So Dave had obtained faulty information from Big Brother," Charlie speculated.

"It must have been Big Brother," I replied. "After all, Burbank was much too far from Pasadena for local gossips to have conveyed such suspicions to him; besides, I can think of no logical reason for the local gossips to visit Burbank. It had to be a highly organized gossip-gathering agency, and who is better qualified in that respect than Big Brother?"

"So that's why you seduced all of those nubile wenches," Charlie murmured thoughtfully.

"Don't forget that I had been warned that there were to be no more girls," I reminded him.

"So you reacted defiantly to what you suspected to be a dictate from some high official," he suggested.

"Dave never would have voluntarily selected those words," I insisted. "Besides, they didn't sound like his words, so they had to come from some such source. Consequently, most of the incidents that you've mentioned involved several strokes in the name of freedom, and every one of them was directed at Big Brother, even though the true identity of my nemesis was unknown to me at the time. However, knowing it would have added incentive."

"I can understand why you followed that course," he muttered. "Under the same circumstances I would have reacted similarly. But why did you stop?"

"Eventually I decided that most of those seductions had not evolved from my sex appeal," I answered ruefully. "In fact, I began to suspect that Big Brother's slander was attracting more so-called victims to me than it diverted from me."

"Do you mean that he was cutting his own throat?" Charlie inquired incredulously. "That he actually misinterpreted the psychology of all of those she-males?" Then, without waiting for an answer, he burst into violent laughter.

Meanwhile I solemnly studied the largest of the wall mirrors mounted on the three exposed sides of chimney, which projected up from the fireplace to the vaulted ceiling.

After the laughter subsided, he insisted, "I'm not laughing at you, Al. I'm laughing at Big Brother's stupid psychology."

"There can be no doubt that it was stupid," I agreed. "However, it was anything but funny, because that type of fault-laden psychology has ruined not only my life but the lives of thousands of other innocent people in this loudly claimed land of freedom."

"What I can't understand is why you gave up all of that good stuff," he murmured dreamily. "Why didn't you continue to *bleep* Big Brother by using his mistaken psychology to your advantage?"

"But I had discovered that it wasn't to my advantage," I objected. "In fact, I finally concluded that I had allowed myself to slip into the same cesspool with Big Brother. Besides, by nature I'm strictly a one-woman man, so I resolved that since the circumstances prohibited a normal monogamous relationship, I would cease to have any relations with the opposite sex."

"Or any other sex?" Charlie ventured.

There must have been fire in my eyes, because he hurriedly insisted, "I was only kidding, Al. It was the stupid statement by that blond idiot in the dining room of the Stoller Hotel that induced me to say it."

"Charlie, I've never tried any other sex," I rumbled. "And I've never had any inclination to do so. Furthermore, I've never practiced any other type of perversion."

"I know, I know," he responded in placating tones. "I was only kidding, and I'm sorry that I mentioned it. Okay?"

"Okay," I muttered. "But I never take kindly to any such remarks, even in a kidding vein."

"But how did you happen to break away from abstinence?" he asked. Then, since my eyes countered with a pair of question marks, he added, "LC has been with you how long now?"

"Almost twenty years," I replied. "As for the answer to your first question, that's none of your *bleeped* business."

"Aw, Al," he responded with a soft chuckle. "I already know the answer to that one. I merely wanted to determine if you knew the answer to it. I ran the videotape on that little romance, and you obviously exhibited all of the typical tokens of a deeply infatuated swain. It was during the forepart of it that the particularly romantic scene in the Villa Capri occurred. Remember? But I was unable to determine what brought it about."

After a moment of deep thought, I began, "One day in nineteen sixty-eight, while I was employed as a research specialist by the Rockwell International Space Division on the *Apollo* program, I happened to overhear part of a conversation between two of the engineering group's inveterate female gossips just as one of them said, 'Gene told me that he saw Al in Beverly Hills with a woman last night.'"

After an absent glance at Charlie, I added, "Since my name had been used in vain, I moved my swivel chair somewhat closer to the open doorway of my office so that I wouldn't miss any of the misinformation."

"You eavesdropped on your associates!" exclaimed Charlie with a horrified expression from which falsity literally dripped.

After accurately assessing the true nature of the exclamation, I tolerantly explained, "This was a case of fighting fire with fire."

"That's sufficient justification," he conceded. "But what was so startling about the statement?"

"Nothing," I answered. "But I was deeply shocked when the listener inquired, 'Was he with that little queer?'"

"She must have been referring to the blonde that you had previously dropped for that very reason," Charlie suggested.

After thoughtfully studying him, I restrained an impulse to ask how he happened to know about that episode, since he would only have referred to the book; if not, he would have referred to the disk containing my history. "Yeah," I finally admitted. "That previous experience had introduced a lot of caution into my relations with the opposite sex. Consequently, I resolved to determine whether the woman was referring to my most recent paramour, and that was why the so-called romantic scene evolved."

"According to the video, she must have set the hook deeply," he suggested with a chuckle. "Even though the two of you were seated on opposite sides of that small table, you had planted your elbows in the middle of it so that you could cup her hands in yours while you stared soulfully into her dark-brown eyes." Then he shook his head and murmured, "My oh my, how romantic you were."

"Charlie!" I growled. "Have you no respect whatsoever for a person's privacy."

"*Bleep* no!" he retorted. Then, after smiling maliciously at me, he added, "Just after you revealed that office gossip to her, you explained, 'I have to confess that some time before I met you I unknowingly dated such a woman for a few months, so I've become a bit gun shy. However, I've assumed that the gossip-monger was referring to that woman; nevertheless, I have to know for sure that such is the case, so I'm asking you to assure me that she wasn't referring to you.'"

He paused, bestowed an admiring smile on me, and added, "It must have taken a lot of guts to ask that question, especially since she could have dropped you cold for even considering such a possibility."

"But I had to know," I muttered.

"No doubt you were vastly relieved when she countered with 'What do you think, Al?' "

"Yes," I admitted. "After all, it was the perfect response, because she had already indicated her faith in me in spite of the fact that Big Brother must have tried to destroy me in her eyes; therefore, the least that I could do was to meet her faith on even terms."

"But why no wedding bells?" he asked.

"That proved to be a rather sticky problem," I admitted. "Since she had been reared in an extremely religious environment, she yearned for the usual ceremony. Eventually I was forced to explain, albeit in generalities, that I intended to become involved in a life-and-death struggle with an unknown adversary. Therefore, no one should become directly associated with me, because I was determined that none of my family, friends, or close associates should be exposed to likely recriminations from an obviously ruthless Unknown."

"That was a wise precaution," Charlie muttered. "Without doubt, Big Brother will stop at nothing to protect the false image that he has created for himself. Furthermore, it's unlikely that his morals have improved since the demise of J. Edgar Hoover, because that kind of corruption is not readily erased." Turning his bleary eyes to me, he said, "Apparently you've never discussed Big Brother with her."

"Never," I replied. "However, I've long suspected that she may know more about his operations than I do, because I've detected his influence in the behavior of practically every woman with whom I've ever associated. Seemingly both of us have arbitrarily decided to treat him as something out of this world, so we've ignored him."

"Man!" Charlie exclaimed. "That sounds like the best place for him—out of this world."

After absently nodding agreement, we shared an interval of silence until he inquired, "Would she go with you to another country?"

"At the time that I was about to begin the world tour we discussed the possibility, and she indicated that I had merely to beckon, and she would join me. At that time I was hopefully planning to spend my remaining years in an atmosphere of peace and tranquility in some remote country, such as New Zealand."

"But New Zealand proved to be infected, too," he suggested. In response to my silent nod, he inquired, "Would you have gone through the ceremony there so late in your life?"

"I've considered it," I admitted, "but there is another important problem."

"Oh," he responded with raised eyebrows. "I haven't run across that in my research. What's the nature of it?"

"It made its appearance during our very first date," I answered. "At the time we were seated in one of the booths on the first level of what used to be Robaire's Restaurant, which was located just north of Wilshire Boulevard on La Brea Boulevard." After pausing to briefly confer with José and Pancho, I resumed: "Shortly after the cocktails had been served, I noticed that LC's eyes kept straying upward to a particular area of the mezzanine located just beyond a narrow stairway at the rear of the main dining room. Of course, I assumed that there must be something of considerable interest to attract so much of her attention, so I looked in the same direction and discovered that she was eye-flirting with a couple of relatively young men who were seated at a table near the railing that graced the open side of the mezzanine."

"Oh-oh!" Charlie remarked. "So the devil slipped into the love bower."

"You might say that," I conceded. "My first impulse was to discontinue the association, but I decided that it could have been just an isolated occurrence, so I decided to put her on probation."

"Some women do things like that to build up their egos," he observed. "Very likely few of them would follow up on such a flirtation even if an opportunity presented itself."

"That may be the case," I agreed. "In fact, several women have attempted to engage me in such a game while a date or husband was sitting across a dinner or cocktail table from them, but I've always refused to collaborate with them. In my opinion such behavior indicates not only a psychological flaw but a lack of loyalty. Since I consider loyalty to be the most important element in any human relationship, I placed a hold on the relationship with LC until her behavior eventually proved or disproved the presence of a problem."

"And what has her behavior eventually proved?" he inquired.

"As far as I'm concerned, she is still on hold," I replied. "In fact, that was one reason why we ceased to have physical relations about eight years ago."

"Eight years!" he exploded. "That's incredible. Why didn't you just separate?"

"Even though we have deliberately kept our finances segregated, we have jointly acquired some real property," I answered. "Consequently, that property has served as sort of a bonding agent."

"Nevertheless, it would have been much better if you had separated," he insisted.

"We've had a long-standing agreement that she is to inform me when she wishes to break off the association," I explained.

"Perhaps there's an even greater bond than just the property," he speculated.

"Perhaps," I granted, "but I'll believe that when I perceive some token of total loyalty."

"But that should not be a two-way street," he protested.

"I've never been disloyal to her, even in my thoughts," I retorted.

"Even when some semi-naked beauty appears on the TV screen?" he inquired whimsically.

"I always switch to another channel," I retorted. "Those remote control units serve purposes other than the avoidance of commercials." Then, as an afterthought, I added, "Besides, I refuse to submit to the decadence inherent in such pornography."

"Man!" he exclaimed. "What self-discipline."

"That's what LC implied one time," I murmured. Then, in response to the question in his eyes, I added, "One Saturday morning I happened to wander into the kitchen of our home in Topanga Canyon at a moment when she was standing beside the sink, looking intently through the window above it. She must not have heard me enter the room, because, upon detecting my presence, she started sharply, cast a guilty glance toward me, and hurriedly turned away from the window. Consequently, she revealed the figure of Bruce, a tall, lanky neighbor, whose eyes were riveted on the window. Since he also guiltily averted his eyes, I assumed that she had been eye-flirting with him."

"Maybe it was just a collection of coincidences," Charlie suggested.

"No, it wasn't," I said. "When I turned accusing eyes on her, she burst into tears and confessed, 'I can't help myself. In fact, you and your strict self-discipline have been so good for me, because it keeps me on an even keel.' "

"But it's the nature of women to flirt," he protested. Then, as an afterthought, he added, "And it's the nature of men to respond to flirtation."

"At times I've responded, too," I admitted. "However, after a person has reached middle age, it's my opinion that that person should act his or her age."

Another brief silence encroached on us until Charlie finally grunted, "Aw, I don't think you have any more self-discipline than I have."

I looked at the man's flushed features and the bleary eyes that peered so vacuously toward me through the surrounding cloud of tobacco smoke and smiled tolerantly. It was so characteristic of the man to contradict himself, sometimes within the same sentence.

"Self-discipline is one of my greatest virtues and finest assets," I insisted. "However, while I still pursued my misguided program against Big Brother, very often I would deliberately fake a total lack of self-discipline to excite my so-called victim."

"What do you mean by that?" he asked.

"I deliberately conveyed the impression to the victim that I was consumed with an overwhelming passion for her," I explained.

"Obviously it worked," he responded with shining eyes.

With a reminiscent smile, I absently nodded agreement.

"Man!" he erupted into my reverie. "I sure wish that I had known that when I was free-lancing."

"It's a basic element of human psychology," I insisted. "Everybody has to learn how to employ the basic elements of human psychology, or he doesn't survive in society."

"Hmm," he mumbled. "I didn't survive in it, but that wasn't the reason."

Conclusions

Since both of us were casting about for another subject, a long silence ensued until Charlie resurrected one. "You'll never get away with it!" he erupted.

"Get away with what?" I inquired.

"With attacking Big Brother," he replied. "No individual has ever succeeded against such formidable odds. He is too big and unscrupulous. Besides, I can't visualize you as a Jack-the-Giant-Killer."

"It isn't my intention to try to destroy him," I said. "I merely hope to make people aware of his presence so that they can take the proper steps to subdue him before he becomes uncontrollable."

"You won't get to first base," he insisted. In response to my questioning eyes, he added, "Surely you haven't forgotten how placid and tractable the average citizen is—just as placid and tractable as a red steer in a lush pasture. And that's why he's so placid and tractable—for him, living conditions are acceptable."

After smiling appreciatively at the mental picture, I mildly protested, "But nobody has written in opposition to Big Brother since the Grim Reaper forced George Orwell to lay his pen aside. It's time that the power of the pen over the sword be retested."

"Huh-uh," he grunted. "The nib of your pen will be bent into the shape of a pretzel. Look at what happened to Robert Oppenheimer shortly after the product of his genius so propitiously terminated the war with Japan. Big Brother nailed his hide to the barn door for no good reason whatsoever."

"As I remember it," I began, "no direct charges were ever leveled against him."

"Right!" Charlie shouted angrily. "That's the way the beast works. And what can you do when Big Brother *bleeps* you in a like manner? What can you do when he claims that his files contain certain evidence that must not be revealed to the public because it threatens the nation's security. That's what he did to Bob Oppenheimer."

"Wasn't Oppenheimer speared because of his wife's alleged association with a communist group or because of some similarly innocuous charge?" I asked.

"Nobody really knows," he growled, "but I'll bet my fireman suspenders that it amounted to nothing more than gossip. That's all that that beastly threat to our civil rights ever deals with."

"You'd better not gamble away your fireman suspenders," I warned him. "Your probation may be suddenly revoked. Immediately after you return from being AWOL, for instance.

"But the beast has persecuted many more victims than Oppenheimer," I insisted. "Don't forget the Japanese-Americans, who were so wrongfully imprisoned in concentration camps for the duration of the war with Japan, and don't forget that they've never been properly reimbursed for the loss of their properties and for the time they spent in those concentration camps."

"And the current president of this nation actually had the insufferable gall to claim that too much time had elapsed for those people to recover their losses," Charlie chimed in with a grim expression. "In other words, there's a time limit on an individual's civil rights. With that kind of a person at the helm of this nation, how can you possibly win?"

José and Pancho studied the question for some time. Finally, with their help, I replied, "Against such odds, I can't expect to win. Even if I did, I would never be granted any damages like the Japanese were."

"But those damages were only tokens delivered with a lot of political pap," Charlie protested. "Justice was ignored."

"At my age damages would serve no practical purpose," I rejoined. "All I want is. . . ."

"All you want is Big Brother's scalp," Charlie interjected with an exuberant chuckle.

I paused, considered the proposition, and, with a wide grin, admitted, "Well. . . yes. That seems to be a fair retribution for what he has done to me. But that would deprive thousands of other innocent victims of just retribution. In my opinion, when one of Big Brother's minions fumbles the ball in the future and creates similar problems for other innocent victims, he should not only be discharged from his plush government position, but he should be stripped of every government goodie, including his pension. That would make the other minions of the sect think twice before indiscriminately throwing their bureaucratic weight around."

"That seems to be a bit severe," Charlie protested.

"But not nearly as severe as the travail of the innocent victim," I growled.

"Well, I suppose that the punishment should fit the crime," he granted. "After all, slander's a particularly vicious crime."

"Furthermore, the beast has a habit of spreading it all over the world," I pointed out.

He pondered momentarily and nodded. Then, turning a fraternal grin on me, he shouted, "Okay, Al! Then let's nail the critter's hide to the barn door."

"Thanks, Charlie," I murmured. "During my time of need you have proved to be a friend indeed."

"But I refuse to appear before the Congress on your behalf," he retorted. "Get Ollie North; he's experienced in dealing with those dimwits."

Excepting Charlie's noisy drags on the cigarette and his intermittent slurps, silence prevailed for several minutes. Finally he inquired, "What do you plan to do after the book is published, Al?"

"I have yet to complete my autobiography," I answered. "It must be completed, because I'll probably need it to protect me from Big Brother's counterattacks."

"How can it protect you?" he asked.

"So far I've deliberately written it in sufficient detail to reveal my entire life; consequently, nobody will be able to make any false charges against me."

"*Bleep bleep!*" he shouted. "Anybody can make false charges against you. The problem is to refute them successfully."

"No doubt you're right," I conceded. "But I'm banking on people being capable of reading between the lines and accurately assessing my true character."

"Most of the smart ones will be capable of those functions," he conceded. "However, intelligence tests indicate that only five to seven percent of them are reasonably smart."

"Hmm," I mumbled. "You do have a point."

"Furthermore, people have always believed whatever they choose to believe," he added, "regardless of whether it makes sense or not."

"Hmm," I repeated. "Nevertheless, I shall continue as planned, because I have no better recourse."

"Good luck," he volunteered with a smile. "I guarantee that you'll need it."

I nodded agreement, and we plunged into a long silence. Finally I resumed: "Charlie, I may be voluntarily joining you sometime after the book is published."

"Great!" he exclaimed. "But why voluntarily?"

"If my publicity plan for the book fails to work as well as I expect it to," I answered, "I may resort to the ultimate sacrifice as a means of exciting more publicity to sell the book."

"Do you mean that you might do something really rabid like commit hara-kiri before a joint session of the houses of Congress?" he inquired with an extremely incredulous expression.

"Well," I began, "that never occurred to me, but it's a brilliant idea, Charlie."

"Would you really do it, Al?" he inquired softly with a probing gaze.

After a thoughtful nod, I countered, "Why not? It fits the picture perfectly. The Japanese samurai used to resort to it when they lost face."

"But a samurai warrior committed hara-kiri only when he was responsible for that loss of face," he protested. "When someone else impugned his character, he challenged the slanderer to a duel with sabers that invariably ended in the death of one of them."

"So you are suggesting that I challenge Big Brother to a duel," I responded with a derisive laugh. "I would rather commit hara-kiri in front of the Congress. It would give my book more publicity. Besides, it would be in character for Big Brother to shoot me in the back during a duel."

"Yeah," Charlie muttered thoughtfully, "that's what he has been doing right along. But it takes a lot of *guts* to commit hara-kiri."

"To a man of honor, who has endured even more grueling emotional pain for fifty years, that brief moment of physical pain would be as nothing," I replied.

"You are a man of honor," Charlie admitted, "but high ideals no longer fit into the scheme of things."

"If I should lack the courage for hara-kiri," I resumed, "I could always select the rooftop of a big TV station or an equally big newspaper. With adequate warning to the news media, a jump should get my book plenty of publicity."

"And that was what you had in mind before I mentioned hara-kiri," Charlie muttered with conviction. "And I'll bet you would do it."

"I have nothing to lose," I muttered. "Long ago I learned that once accused, always guilty. Even if Big Brother should recant, no one will believe it. I have good reason to voluntarily join you, Charlie."

"Don't be too hasty about it," he rejoined. "I might get caught peeking through the trap door in the floor of Space Level Zero and not even be there when you arrive."

Parting

Silence prevailed once more; meanwhile Charlie almost dropped off into slumber land, but I deliberately interrupted his fall with a loud, "Charlie! Are you capable of driving home safely?"

"Huh?" he grunted. Then, stirring and independently focusing each of his bleary eyes on mine, he countered, "Sso you wanta know if I'm too drunk to drive."

"I didn't say that," I protested.

"No, yuh didn'," he rumbled in slurred tones, "but that wass what you wass tinkin'."

How does one respond to a party who is reading one's mind? Since I had never encountered such a situation before, I responded as intelligently as I could—by withholding my counsel.

Meanwhile Charlie leaned forward in the big chair and stolidly stared between his spread legs at the carpet. Finally, shaking his head in confusion, he asked, "What in *bleep* happent to the pattern in dis *bleep bleeped* carpet while I've bin sittin' here? Has it faded or sumpin'?"

"It never had a pattern," I answered.

"Humph," he mumbled. "I'da sworn dat id wass a light bronze wid a darker bronze pattern."

Since the color of the carpet was an unobtrusive golden orange and since his words described the carpet on the floors of the last house in which LC and I had lived, I decided that the man was in trouble, so I suggested, "Let me call a taxi for you, Charlie. You're in no shape to drive home."

Apparently the suggestion sobered him up a bit. "What good will a taxi do me?" he shouted in clear-cut words. Then he stared accusingly at my glass of ice cubes and water, which were completely innocent of any guilt.

"Oh, yeah," I murmured. "I'm confused, not drunk. I mistakenly assumed that you had driven the old, brown Oldsmobile."

"Even if I had driven it, it would never have been capable of making the steep climb out of here," he declared.

"What steep climb?" I asked. "We don't have any steep hills around here."

"When I leave here, I'll have to take off straight up," he arrogantly informed me. "Obviously the Olds could never have gotten off the pavement even if I could have driven it here from Space Level Zero."

A Space Taxi   Momentarily the confusion in my mind cleared, or so it seemed. "That's right," I muttered. "You couldn't have driven the Olds. By the way, how in *bleep* did you get here?"

"By taxi," he responded with a wavering gaze that literally accused me of imbecility. "How else?"

"A taxi!" I shouted. "What kind of a taxi can travel all the way from Space Level Zero to this point on earth?"

"A space taxi, of course," he responded smugly.

"Do you mean to tell me that you've had a space taxi waiting all of this time?" I countered. Arising purposefully, I added, "That I have to see!"

"No, its not waiting!" he shouted. "I sent it back to the fleet tank at Space Level Zero."

"Why did you do that?" I asked. "You should've had the driver switch on the clock and wait for you. That would have been a *bleep* of a lot more economical than for him to make the round trip between here and Space Level Zero."

"But I'm the driver," he retorted. "Besides, I didn't want one of the defrocked priests to discover that it was missing, so I set the autopilot on Return and sent it back to the tank. Furthermore, I didn't want to leave it in your parking lot, because somebody might steal it."

"Hmm," I mumbled. "What would you do then?"

"There wouldn't be much that I could do, since it's my only link between here and there," he replied. "About all I could do would be to search for it." Then, looking whimsically at me, he added, "Meanwhile, after nightfall, it's very likely that I would scare the *bleep* out of every superstitious pedestrian that I encountered in the vicinity of a cemetery."

"Hmm," I mumbled thoughtfully. Then, after fixing a piercing gaze on him, I asked, "Are stranded visitors from Space Level Zero the ghosts that some people claim to have seen?"

"They could be," he responded with a leer.

After I conferred with José and Pancho for a few seconds, they nervously suggested that I ask, "How do you know that the space taxi will return?" And I did.

"Because it's programmed to return when I summon it," he answered.

"That's encouraging," José observed silently in relieved tones. "I, for one, certainly hope that Charlie doesn't become a permanent guest."

"A *women*!" Pancho exclaimed.

"That's supposed to be *amen*, Stupid," José responded contemptuously.

"Choose whatever you want," Pancho retorted stubbornly, "but I happen to prefer *women* . . . and you can leave off the *stupid,* Stupid."

Then, to distract them and forestall any potential violence in that constricted space, I hurriedly asked, "Charlie, how far is it from here to Space Level Zero?"

"That's classified information," he replied, "but it must be trillions of miles."

"Then you must have been a long time on the road—in space, that is," I said. "And I certainly don't envy you the return journey."

"Aw, it won't take any time at all," he murmured. "Just a few seconds, in fact."

"You have to be kidding!" I exclaimed.

"No, its a *bleepin'* fact," he insisted. "After all, I'll be traveling at Space Mach one billion."

"How does Space Mach One compare to our Mach One?" I inquired.

"At sea level your Mach One is equal to seven hundred thirty miles per hour," he began thoughtfully. "And Space Mach One is equal to the velocity of light, which is one hundred eighty-six thousand miles per second. Hmm," he mumbled. "That multiplied by thirty-six hundred seconds would make Mach One about six hundred seventy billion, six hundred eighty thousand miles per hour. Therefore, Space Mach One is about nine hundred eighteen thousand, seven hundred forty times faster than your Mach One."

"But the velocity of Space Mach one billion would be one billion times the speed of light," I objected. "According to the physicists, nothing can travel at a greater velocity than the speed of light."

"So you've been listening to those dumb scientists again," he responded with a particularly patronizing air that has always infuriated me. "Have you forgotten the many self-announced authorities on the sound barrier who once claimed that no aircraft could ever exceed it?" I nodded numbly, so he added, "Then bear with me when I tell you that I'm going to return to Space Level Zero at a velocity that's one billion times the speed of light. Besides, as you know, Einstein claimed that time slows down at ultrahigh velocities, so it'll take practically no time for me to return to Space Level Zero."

"Are you trying to tell me that the space taxi is capable of traveling at velocities that can get you back to Space Level Zero before you left there to come here?" I asked incredulously.

"It could be," he allowed. "That is, if it travels enough faster during the return trip than it did during the initial trip to compensate for the time that I've been here."

"Hmm," I mumbled. "I'm wasting time here on earth, so how can I join your gang?"

"Don't forget that you have to pass through an initiation ritual," he warned me. "However, I'll be glad to instruct you on how to go about it."

"Oh, yeah, that's right," I said. "But I should wait until I've completed my autobiography. Besides, I don't want to provide anybody with any justification for claiming that I ran out on a war, like this country did in Vietnam."

"Well, I should get going before the three o'clock traffic becomes so congested that the car will have to crawl all the way home," he murmured. Then he placed his hands on the armrests and very carefully pushed himself up from the cushion.

"But you don't have to leave now for that reason," I said. "You won't be going to your home. Remember? And you won't be going by way of the Santa Ana Freeway."

"Oh, that's right," he murmured. "Somehow I can't get used to the fact that things have changed so much since my last visit."

Then he moved cautiously across the room toward the small foyer; meanwhile I arose and watchfully went to accompany him. At the two steps that led up to the floor of the foyer, he paused, turned his bloodshot eyes to me, and exclaimed, "Oops! I forgot to call my taxi."

"The telephone is on the far end of the breakfast bar," I reminded him. "Remember?"

"Aw, I don't need no *bleep bleeped bleepin'* telephone," he retorted. "They are as obsolete as *bleeps* on a boar." Then he inserted the thumb and forefinger of his right hand into the left pocket of his garish shirt and withdrew a one-inch-long cylindrical object. Inserting the small end between his lips, he blew an ear-piercing blast on it.

"How can a police whistle summon a space taxi?" I inquired skeptically. "In space there's no atmosphere to conduct the sound waves, even if they would carry that far."

"It doesn't operate on that principle," he replied.

"On what principle does it operate?" I asked.

"This is a product of a very advanced technology," he responded evasively. "I would be glad to explain it to you, but you would be unable to understand the explanation since I would have to resort to technical terms that are completely foreign to earthlings."

Readily recognizing the subterfuge, I didn't press him for the answer. In the past I had learned that whenever Charlie didn't know the answer to one of my questions, he invariably employed the excuse that the explanation was beyond the scope of my comprehension.

"How long will we have to wait?" I asked.

"It's probably standing out there now," he answered.

"Aw, that just can't be!" I insisted.

"Oh, but it can be," he responded with a superior smile. Then he returned the whistle to his lips but withdrew it slightly and said, "After I toot on this thing, listen carefully, and you'll hear a similar response from the space taxi." Then he blew two short blasts on the whistle. Almost instantly a similar "beep-beep!" sounded from beyond the front door.

"I have to see that thing," I insisted, placing my left foot on the first of the two carpeted steps.

A Reluctant Adios But Charlie placed a restraining hand on my right arm and murmured, "I want to thank you for attending that gathering at my home. But I'm sorry that my son was so outspoken about my use of foul language. I never realized how much he disliked it."

"You were there!" I exclaimed incredulously. "I didn't see you."

"How could I allow anybody to see me at what corresponded to my wake?" he inquired disgustedly.

"Of course, you couldn't allow anybody to see you, Charlie," I responded in mollifying tones. "As usual, I didn't think before I spoke."

"Furthermore," he resumed, "you didn't have to agree so readily with him when he said, 'I've always told my father that playing the stock market is just like betting on the horse races.' "

"But you've picked out only the negative remarks," I objected. "How about those regarding your virtues?"

"Name one," he demanded.

For an instant I was cornered. Realizing that he was sure to read my mind, I struggled to keep it blank. Fortunately I have been particularly well endowed in that respect.

"Al," he said in condemning tones, "as usual, your mind is a complete blank. I want you to tell me what my family really thinks of me, no matter how gruesome it may be."

Those words provided an avenue of escape for me, and I eagerly accepted it. "Charlie," I murmured, "they love you; they love your memory, that is."

"Aw, you are just saying that to make me feel good," he protested while tears of happiness began to leak from his red-rimmed eyes, stream down his flushed cheeks, and join his delighted smile. In emotion-strained tones, he incredulously inquired, "They still love me despite how obnoxious and mean I've been to them?"

"Yes, Charlie," I muttered. "Under that rude, crude exterior they sensed the beat of a kind and loving heart, so they couldn't help but love you. Furthermore, I sensed it, too, because you befriended me when no one else would make friendly overtures to me. Now, since you are my only friend, I'm going to miss you very much."

He hurriedly raised his left hand and wiped the tears from his eyes. Then, thrusting the other hand toward me, he muttered, "Adios, amigo. It has been great seeing you again. Actually, I tried to call you before I left home for Space Level Zero, but you must have been away from home."

"I was away from home," I replied, returning the firm handclasp. "I sensed that you had called while I was out, so I wasn't really surprised when your son called and informed me that you had checked out."

"I requested that he let you know," he murmured.

"He informed me to that effect," I said.

We stood there and uneasily eyed each other, as two old friends are prone to do during such partings. Finally he repeated, "Adios, amigo," and added a crushing squeeze to the handclasp before withdrawing his hand.

"As usual, I'll see you off," I muttered when he carefully raised his gimpy leg to start the ascent.

"No, I'll see myself off," he responded with typical rudeness.

"I'll see you off," I insisted, endeavoring to follow him up the steps.

"No, I'll see myself off," he repeated stubbornly, placing the palm of his right hand against the top of my head and pushing down—or so it seemed.

Despite my confusion, I continued to employ the leverage of my legs to force the top of my head against that immovable restraint. Eventually I discovered that by relaxing my legs, the pressure against the top of my head ceased. Slowly opening my eyes, I found myself supine on the sofa with my feet planted firmly against one of its armrests while my head rested against the other one. Experimentally extending my legs, I found that the pressure on the top of my head increased.

"Hmm," I mumbled. "I must have dreamed that Charlie was here." While I was sitting up and looking about the room, my eyes detected the two empty glasses. "But I don't remember setting out those glasses and the ashtray," I mused. Then familiar sounds seemed to drift to my ears, the sounds of the motor of an old, brown Oldsmobile as its engine sprung to life. "That has to be Charlie," I muttered, hurriedly stuffing my sock-clad feet into their respective house slippers. Then, jumping to my feet, I charged up the two steps, crossed the foyer to the front door, and quickly swung it open.

A Flying Saucer? The only human being in view was Sharon, who was watering the shrubs alongside the near corner of her home on the opposite side of the street.

Raising one hand in a friendly greeting, she called, "Hi, Al! It surely is a beautiful day, isn't it?"

"Yes, it is," I agreed. "Did you happen to see an elderly gentleman leave here in an old, brown Oldsmobile within the last minute?"

"No," she responded with a shake of her curlers, "but I did see. . . ." Stopping abruptly, she glanced along the street in one direction and repeated the glance in the other direction; then she reached toward the adjacent box hedge and removed a camera from atop it. After placing the end of the hose in an adjacent flower bed, she strode across the street and came to a stop about five feet from me. "No," she repeated, "but I did see something, and I still refuse to believe what I saw."

It seemed that a cold hand suddenly clutched my heart. "What did you see that you refuse to believe?" I inquired breathlessly.

She carefully studied my intent eyes for a moment; then, after shaking her head, she insisted, "Al, you would never believe me if I told you."

"I'll try very hard," I promised. "What did you see?"

After peering speculatively up at me for a few seconds, she tensely whispered, "Al, do you believe in flying saucers?"

I almost shook my head, but Pancho abruptly injected, "If you shake your head, she'll never tell you what she saw."

So I cautiously replied, "An awful lot of people claim to have seen them."

Apparently she interpreted my reply as being in the affirmative sense, because her features relaxed somewhat. "Al," she began tentatively, "I swear that just before you opened your door, a bearded, old man took off from your sidewalk in what looked like a cross between a moped and a *trisha*."

"Which direction did he go?" I asked.

"Straight up!" she retorted.

"Straight up!" I exclaimed incredulously.

"I told you that you'd never believe me," she responded resentfully.

"I believe you, Sharon," I assured her. "Believe me, I do believe you, but it seems a bit incredible that either a moped or a *trisha* would take off straight up all by itself, because they are designed to travel horizontally along reasonably level surfaces."

"Oh, but it didn't take off all by itself," she countered. "It was suspended on a slender pole from the central point of the lower surface of a flying saucer." Then she hid her eyes behind the palm of her left hand and exclaimed, "Oh! I didn't intend to tell you that, because I knew that you'd never believe me."

"But I haven't said that I don't believe you," I pointed out to her.

"You do believe me!" she exclaimed in tones that could have been construed as indicating either incredulity, conviction, or both.

"But you should never tell anyone else about this," I advised her, absently noting the soft sounds of an upstairs window being opened in the house that adjoined Sharon's. "Above all, don't accidentally tip your hand to your husband," I warned, "because I doubt that he would be so tolerant."

Simultaneously I heard a scandalized gasp from that open, upper-story window, and my eyes involuntarily turned toward the figure of the mature woman who crouched in the shadows just beyond it. She quickly withdrew into the shadows, but there was no doubt in my mind that she had overheard my warning.

"On second thought," I muttered, "maybe you should tell him all about it. That may be the lesser of two evils."

"No, it's better that I don't tell him," she responded with a deep frown. "If I do tell him, he might have me placed in a straight jacket and put away for keeps." Then, turning away, she returned to the hose, which too obviously had fulfilled its purpose in the flower bed.

Pensively turning about, I stepped through the open doorway and muttered, "By nightfall Big Brother will have on tape his *bleeped*-up version of what he assumes to be the latest of my affairs, and it'll be ready for shipment to all points of the compass."

"Oh, Al!" Sharon suddenly screamed excitedly from my doorstep.

"Yes, Sharon," I responded wearily from the open doorway.

"I have the proof!" she reported triumphantly. "Here, look!" she commanded, imperatively extending her right hand toward me.

Absently accepting the photo print, I said, "I'd invite you in, but the neighbors might talk."

"But look at the snapshot!" she commanded with shining eyes.

"I intend to," I responded rather irritably. "No doubt it's lovely, because all of the quickie snapshots you've taken of your tiny granddaughter have turned out beautifully."

"But that isn't a snapshot of her!" she shouted. "Look at it!"

So I looked at it, and even I could sense the wide grin that spread across my ancient features.

"I often place the camera on the hedge while I'm watering the plants so that it's at hand in case my granddaughter happens to assume a particularly cute pose," she explained. "Since it was so convenient, I quickly picked it up and snapped a shot of that old man just as he was about to take off."

"Hey!" I exclaimed. "This is great! Now you can tell your husband all about the flying saucer and submit this as proof."

"And that's what I'm going to do right now, because there he comes," she jabbered excitedly. Turning away, she veered across the street toward the middle-aged man with the military bearing, who was striding so rhythmically along the sidewalk toward their home.

"And be sure to show it to your neighbor to the north," I called to her.

"Yeah, and be shuah to expline the whole situation to huh," José silently volunteered, "because she'll cut yoah bloody throat if you leave anything to huh imagineyeshun."

"I didn't realize that you had acquired an Australian dialect, José," I remarked.

"Aye, mitey," he responded in jaunty tones, "Oy acquired it whoile we wuh travelin' across that bloody Nulahbah Pline."

"Naw, that's a lotta *bleep!*" Pancho injected. "He might have been infected by it then, but he just started usin' the *bleep bleeped* dialect just now, so he's just putting on some *bleep bleeped bleepin'* airs."

"At least I wasn't infected by foul language," José retorted sans the dialect. "At the rate Pancho is going, he'll soon be *bleeping* just like Charlie."

"But not soon enough," Pancho insisted, "because this is the end of the *bleepin'* book."

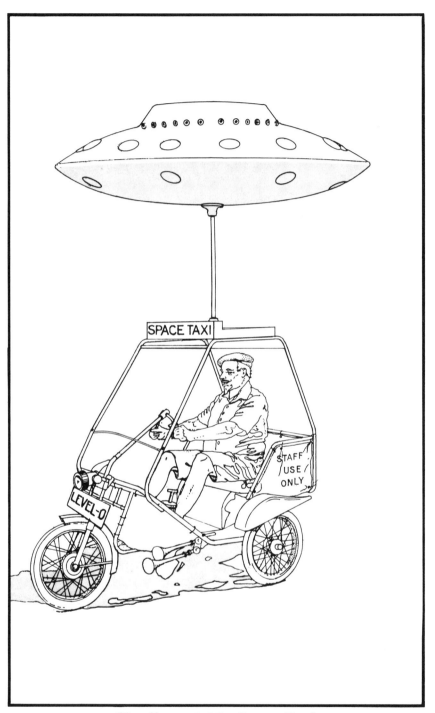

Charlie and His Space Taxi

Index